The Ultimate Moving Average Handbook

Valeriy Zakamulin · Javier Giner

The Ultimate Moving Average Handbook

Bringing Science into the Art of Trend Following

palgrave
macmillan

Valeriy Zakamulin
School of Business and Law
University of Agder, Norway
Kristiansand S, Norway

Javier Giner
Econ Acc & Finance, Fac of Econ
University of La Laguna
San Cristóbal de La Laguna, Spain

ISBN 978-3-031-90906-1 ISBN 978-3-031-90907-8 (eBook)
https://doi.org/10.1007/978-3-031-90907-8

This Palgrave Macmillan imprint is published by the registered company Springer Nature Switzerland AG
The registered company address is: Gewerbestrasse 11, 6330 Cham, Switzerland

This book is dedicated to those who seek clarity in the complex world of moving averages. It was not born out of the need to publish, but from a deeper drive—to bring order to the existing chaos, establish an objective framework for analysis, and challenge the myths surrounding so-called superior moving averages. May it serve as a guide for rigorous inquiry and a step toward deeper understanding.

Preface

Book Motivation

The concept of trend-following has captivated traders and investors for centuries, offering a systematic approach to identifying and capitalizing on market trends. At the heart of this approach lies the use of moving averages, a powerful tool for smoothing price trajectories by filtering out short-term noise to reveal the underlying direction of price movements.

There are numerous types of moving averages employed in trend-following, each distinguished by its mathematical structure and requiring at least one parameter, most commonly the size of the averaging window. These moving averages serve as the foundation for a variety of trend-following rules, which seek to exploit persistent market movements by triggering entry and exit signals based on price and trend dynamics.

Despite the widespread use of moving averages and their importance in trend-following strategies, there is a surprising lack of systematic and comprehensive coverage in existing literature. No single book serves as a definitive reference on the various types of moving averages and the trend-following rules built upon them. This gap highlights the urgent need for a thorough handbook to guide traders, researchers, and practitioners in understanding and applying these essential tools.

While moving averages are effective at smoothing price trajectories, their major drawback is the delayed identification of trend turning points. Traders seek moving averages that are both smooth and responsive. As a result, new types of moving averages are constantly introduced, each claiming to improve upon its predecessors in balancing these two qualities. However, such claims are based solely on anecdotal evidence and visual demonstrations rather than rigorous analysis.

The core issue lies in the absence of quantitative metrics to objectively assess and compare the properties of moving averages. While traders use a metric to evaluate the average lag time of a moving average, this approach is based on an ad hoc measure proposed nearly 60 years ago. Since its introduction, its validity and suitability for accurately measuring lag time have never been questioned.

The problem becomes even more pronounced when evaluating the smoothness of a moving average. To date, no universally accepted or systematically developed metric exists to quantify smoothness. Without such a measure, traders and analysts are left without the essential tools to objectively compare different moving averages based on their effectiveness in smoothing the price trajectory.

In our view, however, quantitatively measuring the properties of individual moving averages offers limited insight. This is because, in trend-following strategies that use moving averages, the trading signal is not driven by the value of a single moving average alone. Instead, the signal typically emerges from the relationship between the current price and the moving average, the interactions between multiple moving averages, or changes in a moving average's value over time. Therefore, it is more important for traders to assess the responsiveness and smoothness of the trading signal generated by the entire trend-following rule, rather than focusing exclusively on the individual moving averages that form part of the rule.

With an abundance of moving averages and trend-following rules at their disposal, traders are overwhelmed by the sheer variety of choices available. The key question, however, is not which moving average is the best, but rather how to identify the ideal combination of the trading rule and moving average that strikes the best balance between such properties as responsiveness and smoothness, ultimately leading to the highest profitability. Additionally, traders must determine the optimal parameters for the moving averages used in the trading rule, as these parameters can vary significantly depending on the unique characteristics of the financial market being traded.

Due to the complete lack of answers to the most pressing questions traders face, contemporary trend-following with moving averages remains more of an art than a science. While traders have long relied on intuition and experience to guide their decisions, there has been little to no systematic exploration of how to objectively evaluate and optimize moving averages and the strategies built upon them. This book emerged from the desire to provide a comprehensive reference on the various types of moving averages and the trend-following rules derived from them. However, it soon became clear that merely cataloging these tools was insufficient. There is an urgent need to introduce scientific rigor into the practice of trend-following. Specifically, a framework for quantitatively assessing the properties of trend-following rules based on moving averages is essential. Such a framework would empower traders and researchers with the tools necessary to objectively evaluate, refine, and optimize their strategies, thereby transforming trend-following from an art into a more data-driven science.

Book Purpose and Structure

The goals of this book are twofold. First, it serves as a comprehensive reference on the various types of moving averages and the trend-following rules derived from them. Second, and more importantly, it bridges the gap between the art and science of trend-following by presenting a scientifically grounded, quantitative framework for evaluating moving averages and the trading rules they support.

Rather than merely focusing on the quantitative properties of moving averages themselves, we identify the core properties that define the effectiveness of trend-following rules based on moving averages. Contrary to common belief, we argue that there are not just two, but three primary properties that underpin these rules. While responsiveness is undeniably essential, we contend that traders often confuse smoothness with accuracy. It is critical to understand that high smoothness does not necessarily equate to high accuracy, and vice versa. Therefore, alongside responsiveness, we propose that the primary properties of trend-following rules are smoothness and accuracy.

We present methods to quantify the accuracy, responsiveness, and smoothness of trading rules. These metrics are grounded in the assumption that financial markets operate within two distinct regimes: bull and bear markets. However, while this model motivates our approach, the metrics themselves are non-parametric and do not rely on specific assumptions about the characteristics of each regime. The accuracy and smoothness metrics assess the correctness and stability of trading signals within a given market regime. In contrast, the responsiveness metric evaluates how quickly the trading rule detects regime shifts.

These metrics allow for a detailed analysis of the properties of trend-following rules that use moving averages. With these quantitative tools, we can assess the validity of claims that some moving averages provide superior responsiveness and smoothness compared to others. Additionally, our approach enables us to explore the concept of the optimal trading rule, addressing the question of which trend-following rule achieves the best balance between accuracy and responsiveness, or between smoothness and responsiveness.

Finally, this book explores key questions related to determining the optimal parameters of trading rules for following trends in specific financial markets, as well as the most effective practical implementation of these rules. We argue that answering these questions requires making specific parametric assumptions about market dynamics and market frictions. We demonstrate that the optimal parameters for the moving averages used in trend-following can vary significantly based on the unique characteristics of the financial market in question. Additionally, we evaluate the accuracy of existing empirical methods for identifying the optimal rules and examine the consequences of using suboptimal rules. Finally, we explore the question of the optimal trading frequency for trend-following strategies.

This book is divided into four parts, along with an introductory chapter and a concluding chapter. Each part contains two to four chapters.

Introduction, Chapter 1: This chapter begins by exploring the origins of trend following and the historical evolution of moving averages. It then examines the academic perspective on trend-following, tracing its shift from initial skepticism about the existence of trends to growing recognition of the momentum effect in financial markets. The chapter concludes by describing the current challenges of trend-following with moving averages and explaining how this book addresses them.

Part I: The first part of the book introduces conventional moving averages and offers a detailed exploration of various trend-following trading rules based on them. The analysis reveals the anatomy of trend-following rules, with insights that can be used to deduce the properties of these trading rules.

Chapter 2: This chapter starts by explaining the rationale for using moving averages, providing the general formula for their calculation, and discussing the three conventional types. It then examines the existing measure of lag time for moving averages, highlighting its misleading nature. Finally, the chapter concludes by exploring the mathematical properties of moving averages in detail.

Chapter 3: This chapter begins by introducing and clarifying various trend-following trading rules, using specific examples for illustration. It then demonstrates that calculating a trading indicator in any rule based on moving averages of prices is equivalent to computing a single moving average of price changes or returns. Our analysis shows that, despite the apparent variety among trading rules and moving averages, their fundamental differences stem from the weighting function used to calculate the moving average of returns. Consequently, the properties of trading rules can be directly determined from the weighting function applied to returns.

Part II: In this part of the book, we start by identifying the key properties of trend-following rules and introduce methods to quantify them. These metrics are derived exclusively from the return weights assigned to each trading rule. Next, we provide analytical solutions for these quantitative measures, focusing on rules based on conventional moving averages, and propose a framework for systematically comparing and contrasting trend-following rules based on their quantitative characteristics. Using a combination of analytical and numerical techniques, we then determine the optimal trading rule. Finally, we explore how negative weights influence the properties of trend-following rules.

Chapter 4: This chapter suggests that a trading rule should possess three key properties: accuracy, responsiveness, and smoothness. To evaluate these properties, three quantitative measures are introduced. These measures are based on the assumption that market returns randomly alternate between bull and bear states. Importantly, the proposed measures do not depend on the parameters of the regime-switching model for returns, but instead rely solely on the return weights within the trading indicator.

Chapter 5: This chapter presents analytical results for the accuracy, responsiveness, and smoothness measures of trend-following rules using conventional moving averages. The results emphasize a key aspect of trading rule design: improving one property, such as accuracy or smoothness, often comes at the expense of another, such as responsiveness. The chapter then uses the quantitative metrics to compare and contrast different trading rules. This analysis reveals that some rules perform exceptionally well in terms of responsiveness and accuracy, while others strike a compelling balance between responsiveness and smoothness.

Chapter 6: The properties of trend-following rules ultimately stem from variations in return weights, enabling the use of analytical and numerical techniques to identify optimal trading rules. This chapter uncovers trading rules that optimize individual properties or combinations of two or three properties.

Chapter 7: Traders have proposed several variants of zero-lag moving averages that are said to respond immediately to market changes. A key characteristic of these moving averages is the assignment of negative weights to distant prices. The previous chapter's results also suggest that incorporating negative weights can reduce lag time while maintaining high smoothness. This chapter examines the impact of negative weights on trading rule properties and assesses whether zero-lag moving averages truly exhibit minimal delay.

Part III: Moving averages can be divided into conventional and exotic types. The latter category is extensive and often poorly understood, with many myths and anecdotal claims surrounding them. This part aims to introduce the most popular exotic moving averages, classified into three types: those with enhanced smoothness, reduced lag time, and those inspired by Digital Signal Processing (DSP). The second objective is to quantitatively evaluate the claims associated with these moving averages.

Chapter 8: The quantitative metrics presented in this book enable the examination of moving averages believed to offer high smoothness. This chapter aims to determine whether using these moving averages, rather than conventional ones, can enhance the efficiency of trend-following rules.

Chapter 9: The creators of zero-lag moving averages claim they are both extremely fast and highly smooth, but these claims lack objective support. With the availability of quantitative measures, we can now comprehensively and objectively analyze the characteristics of zero-lag moving averages. This chapter examines whether these averages truly exhibit zero lag time and high smoothness simultaneously and if they outperform traditional moving averages.

Chapter 10: Many exotic moving averages are inspired by DSP techniques. This chapter begins by exploring the connection between moving averages and digital filters applied to price time series, noting that these filters are often analyzed in the frequency domain rather than the time domain. It then examines the properties of conventional moving averages and the trend-following rules derived from them through the lens of DSP principles. Finally, the chapter introduces several DSP-inspired moving average variants and investigates whether they possess unique characteristics absent in conventional or other exotic moving averages.

Part IV: While quantitative measures enable objective comparison of the properties of trend-following rules based on moving averages, they cannot identify the optimal parameters for following trends in a specific financial market. This part covers advanced topics on determining the optimal parameters for trading rules tailored to particular markets and explores the most effective practical implementation of these rules.

Chapter 11: This chapter begins by arguing that determining the optimal parameters of a trading rule requires specific assumptions about market dynamics and frictions. It then presents a fairly general model of a persistent return process and identifies the optimal technical indicator for trend-following. The chapter also demonstrates how trading costs affect the properties of the optimal trading indicator.

Chapter 12: This chapter uncovers the optimal trading rule in a two-state regime-switching model, with bull and bear market states representing the two regimes. It examines how the parameters of the optimal trading rule depend on the statistical properties of returns in each state, the probability distribution of state changes, and the level of trading costs. The chapter demonstrates that the optimal parameters of the trend-following rule can vary significantly based on the unique characteristics of the financial market in question.

Chapter 13: Traders typically rely on backtesting to identify the best trading rule, a method widely regarded as thorough and effective. However, this chapter examines the precision of backtesting and finds it to be extremely poor, suggesting that traders typically use suboptimal trend-following rules. The chapter then explores the loss in profitability from using a non-optimal rule and whether imperfect trend-following rules still offer a performance advantage over passive investment strategies.

Chapter 14: This chapter explores the decision of determining the optimal trading frequency for a trend-following strategy, specifically examining whether it is best to follow trends on a daily, weekly, or monthly basis. The question is analyzed using two alternative theoretical approaches, both leading to the same conclusion.

Conclusion, Chapter 15: The concluding chapter opens by revisiting the book's overarching purpose, setting the stage for a detailed summary of its key contributions to the field of trend-following with moving averages. These contributions begin with the identification and formulation of the fundamental properties of trend-following rules, along with the development of methods to quantify them. Building on this foundation, the book applies these metrics to conduct an objective analysis of a wide range of moving averages, aiming to identify the most effective ones. Finally, it explores the critical question of how to select the optimal trading rule for tracking trends in specific financial markets, providing practical insights grounded in scientific rigor.

Audience and Prerequisites

This book is not for casual readers who believe trend-following with moving averages offers a simple and effortless path to wealth. Instead, it is designed for serious, mathematically inclined readers who seek an in-depth understanding of the subject.

Our primary audience consists of traders, investment professionals, and researchers seeking a comprehensive understanding of trend-following with moving averages. The book also serves as a valuable resource for students and academics interested in the quantitative analysis of financial markets. By introducing academic rigor, we aim to inspire readers to approach trend-following not just as an art, but as a discipline firmly rooted in science.

Most of the chapters in Parts I through III are accessible, requiring little more than a high school-level understanding of mathematics and statistics. Analytical derivations are provided in the appendices of each chapter and can be skipped without loss of continuity.

Part IV delves into more mathematically intensive material. A full understanding of these chapters assumes familiarity with financial econometrics and time-series models. However, readers less experienced in these areas can still benefit by focusing on the results and conclusions, leaving the mathematical details for further study.

Kristiansand, Norway
La Laguna, Spain
February 2025

Valeriy Zakamulin
Javier Giner

Acknowledgments This book is the culmination of years of research by the authors. Like any academic work, it is not only the product of its authors but also of the support, insights, and contributions of many individuals and institutions. From colleagues and research collaborators to the tools and technologies that facilitated our analyses, numerous factors have shaped this book. While it is impossible to acknowledge everyone who has influenced our work, we would like to extend our sincere gratitude to the following individuals and groups.

We are particularly indebted to Wesley Gray, CEO of Alpha Architect, and Gary Antonacci, founder of Optimal Momentum, for their continuous encouragement and support of our academic efforts in trend-following and active investment strategies. Their engagement and enthusiasm have been both motivating and inspiring. We are also deeply grateful to Henry Stern, whose insightful discussions on moving average trading rules, which began in 2013 and continue to this day, have significantly enriched our understanding of the subject.

Nearly all the quantitative and empirical analyses in this book were conducted using the R programming language. We extend our appreciation to the R Development Core Team for providing such a powerful open-source statistical computing environment, and to the RStudio development team for their excellent integrated development environment, which has been instrumental in our research.

For English editing and text refinement, we acknowledge the invaluable assistance of ChatGPT. Our thanks go to OpenAI for developing this remarkable tool, which has greatly facilitated the writing process for non-native English speakers.

We also express our gratitude to Tula Weis and her colleagues at Palgrave for their support in bringing this book to publication. Their professionalism and guidance throughout the process have been truly appreciated.

Finally, and most importantly, we thank our families for their unwavering love, patience, and support over the years. Their encouragement has been invaluable, and this book would not have been possible without them.

Valeriy Zakamulin
Javier Giner

Competing Interests The authors have no competing interests to declare that are relevant to the content of this manuscript.

Contents

About the Authors

Valeriy Zakamulin is a Professor of Finance at the School of Business and Law at the University of Agder in Norway. With a diverse academic background spanning engineering and finance, he holds an MS in Radio Engineering as well as an MS in Economics and Business Administration. Before transitioning into finance, he worked as a research fellow in computer science, where he developed hardware and software solutions—an experience that laid the foundation for his analytical and quantitative approach to financial research.

After earning his Ph.D. in Finance, Prof. Zakamulin joined the faculty at the University of Agder, where he has been teaching graduate-level courses in finance. His research interests focus on technical trading strategies, moving averages, and asset allocation. He is particularly known for his rigorous investigations into the mathematical properties of moving averages and their effectiveness in trend-following strategies.

A prolific researcher, Prof. Zakamulin has authored numerous academic papers on these topics and has published the book *Market Timing with Moving Averages*, offering both theoretical insights and empirical findings on trading rules. He has established a highly productive collaboration with Prof. Javier Giner from the University of La Laguna in Spain, with whom he has co-authored several influential papers on trend-following strategies and regime-switching models.

Prof. Zakamulin's research is widely cited in both academic and practitioner circles, shaping the understanding of quantitative investment strategies. His contributions help bridge the gap between theoretical finance and real-world applications, providing valuable tools for portfolio management and systematic trading.

Javier Giner is an Associate Professor of Financial Economics at the University of La Laguna in Spain. With a Ph.D. in Physics, his academic journey spans multiple disciplines, reflecting a strong foundation in quantitative and computational methods.

Early in his career, Prof. Giner specialized in room acoustics, applying his expertise in physics to study sound behavior in enclosed spaces. This work honed his analytical skills and deepened his proficiency in mathematical modeling. Over time, his research interests shifted toward financial economics, where he applies advanced statistical and computational techniques to model financial time series, analyze volatility, and develop investment strategies, particularly those based on moving averages.

Prof. Giner has built a highly productive collaboration with Prof. Valeriy Zakamulin from the University of Agder in Norway, with whom he has co-authored several influential papers on trend-following strategies and regime-switching models. Their joint research provides critical insights into the mathematical properties of moving averages and their effectiveness in financial markets.

Beyond his collaborative work, Prof. Giner actively explores new frontiers in financial modeling, leveraging his interdisciplinary background to develop innovative approaches to quantitative investing. His research continues to contribute to the refinement of statistical methods in finance, enhancing risk assessment and strategy optimization in dynamic market environments.

Acronyms

Types of Moving Averages

ALMA	Arnaud Legoux Moving Average
DEMA	Double Exponential Moving Average
EMA	Exponential Moving Average
EPMA	End Point Moving Average
GMA	Gaussian Moving Average
HMA	Hull Moving Average
LMA	Linear Moving Average
MA	Short for Moving Average of any type
SMA	Simple Moving Average
SWMA	Sine Weighted Moving Average
T3	Tillson Moving Average
TEMA	Triple Exponential Moving Average
TMA	Triangular Moving Average
TRIX	Triple-smoothed Exponential Moving Average
WEMA	Weighted Exponential Moving Average
WMA	Wilder Moving Average
ZLEMA	Zero Lag Exponential Moving Average

Trend-Following Trading Rules

MA-D	Moving Average Direction rule. MA denotes a moving average of any type. For example, if the moving average is the EMA, then this rule becomes EMA-D rule

MA-C	Double Moving Average Crossover rule. MA denotes a moving average of any type. For example, if the moving average is the LMA, then this rule becomes LMA-C rule
MACD	Moving Average Convergence/Divergence rule
MOM	Momentum trading rule
P-MA	Price and Moving Average crossover rule. MA denotes a moving average of any type. For example, if the moving average is the SMA, then this rule becomes the P-SMA rule
TR	Short for a Trading Rule of any type

Quantitative Metrics

ALT	Average Lag Time of a trading rule, short for ALT(TR)
ALT(MA)	Average Lag Time of a Moving Average
ALT(TR)	Average Lag Time of a Trading Rule
NSF	Noise Suppression Factor of a trading rule
SMI	Smoothness Index of a trading rule

Digital Filters

BP	Band-Pass filter
FIR	Finite Impulse Response filter
HP	High-Pass filter
IIR	Infinite Impulse Response filter
LP	Low-Pass filter

Other Acronyms

AR	AutoRegressive process
ARMA	AutoRegressive Moving Average process
DFT	Discrete Fourier Transform
DSP	Digital Signal Processing
EMH	Efficient Market Hypothesis
ENW	Expected Number of Whipsaws
HI	Herfindahl Index
HR	Hit Ratio
IDFT	Inverse Discrete Fourier Transform
MR	Miss Ratio
Prob(Reversal)	Probability of a position reversal
SNR	Signal to Noise Ratio
TC	Transaction Costs

List of Figures

List of Tables

1

Introduction

1.1 Origins of Trend-Following

Traders rely heavily on the idea of recurring patterns in stock prices. This belief comes from studying historical price charts and noticing that past price movements often repeat in identifiable patterns, which can offer chances for profit. Early technical analysis focused on finding these repetitive behaviors to guide trading decisions. By recognizing patterns like head and shoulders, triangles, or double tops and bottoms, traders aimed to predict possible future price movements.

Through careful analysis of historical price patterns, traders have observed that prices tend to demonstrate directional movements over time, characterized by periods of upward or downward momentum. This observation led to the development of the trend-following strategy, which revolves around identifying the direction of the trend and capitalizing on it until data suggests a trend reversal.

The roots of trend-following trace back centuries, grounded in the fundamental idea of observing and profiting from price movements. Central to this approach is the timeless principle of "buy low and sell high," which focuses on entering positions when prices are expected to rise and exiting when they are anticipated to fall, allowing traders to capitalize on market trends. Over time, the strategy evolved gradually, transitioning from early conceptual practices to a more structured and systematic trading methodology, incorporating tools like moving averages and momentum indicators.

The origins of trend-following can be traced to early commodity trading. Traders and merchants would observe market behavior, particularly supply and demand dynamics, to make their trading decisions. While these early prac-

V. Zakamulin and J. Giner, *The Ultimate Moving Average Handbook*,
https://doi.org/10.1007/978-3-031-90907-8_1

tices were not as formalized as today's trend-following strategies, they laid the groundwork for recognizing and capitalizing on trends in market movements.

Ancient civilizations such as Mesopotamia, Egypt, India, and China were key players in global trade, particularly in agricultural commodities like wheat, barley, rice, and spices. The supply of these goods often followed seasonal cycles, which led to predictable price fluctuations. Traders noticed that prices typically dropped during harvest periods, when supply was abundant, and rose during off-seasons, when supply was scarce. By purchasing during low-price periods and selling when prices increased, these early traders practiced a basic form of trend-following.

In 17th-century Japan, the Dojima Rice Exchange became the first organized futures market, where rice merchants and samurai could trade rice contracts. These futures contracts allowed traders to lock in prices for future deliveries, reducing the uncertainty of fluctuating market conditions. Traders on the exchange observed long-term trends in rice prices, driven by factors like supply shocks, weather patterns, and government policies. Wealthy merchants and speculators profited by recognizing and riding these price trends.

Though David Ricardo, a renowned economist of the 19th century, did not explicitly discuss trend-following strategies, his work on economic principles laid the foundation for understanding market behavior. Ricardo's theories on supply, demand, and price movements played a key role in shaping the modern understanding of markets, laying the foundation for the development of trend-following practices. One of his most famous quotes, "Cut short your losses and let your profits run on," is often seen as a precursor to trend-following, particularly in the context of trading strategies that capitalize on ongoing market movements. While Ricardo was not directly writing about trend-following, his approach shares core principles with modern trend-following techniques.

By "cutting short one's losses," Ricardo advised that when an investor holds an asset and its price begins to fall, they should sell the asset immediately to limit further losses. On the other hand, by "letting one's profits run on," he suggested that when prices are rising, investors should hold their positions until the trend shows signs of reversal. This approach to managing positions mirrors the essence of trend-following, where traders aim to minimize losses while maximizing the potential of profitable trends.

In the late 19th century, Charles H. Dow, a journalist and co-founder of *The Wall Street Journal*, laid the foundation for trend-following through the development of Dow Theory. Dow proposed that markets move in distinct, identifiable trends—primary, secondary, and minor—which traders could leverage by recognizing and aligning with the prevailing primary trend.

The primary trend represents the most significant and long-term market movement, reflecting the overall direction of the market over months or even years. This dominant trend can either be a bull market (upward trend) or a bear market (downward trend), typically lasting from a year to several years. Economic fundamentals such as GDP growth, interest rate changes, corporate earnings, and macroeconomic factors drive the primary trend. It sets the broad direction of the market and serves as the basis for strategic decisions, such as long-term investments or portfolio adjustments.

Secondary trends are shorter-term movements that counteract the primary trend. These trends represent corrections or recoveries within a broader bull or bear market. In a bull market, secondary trends manifest as downward corrections, while in a bear market, they are upward recoveries. Secondary trends typically last from a few weeks to several months and are driven by temporary market reactions to economic news, earnings reports, or geopolitical events. They present opportunities for traders to capitalize on counter-trend movements or adjust positions while remaining aligned with the primary trend.

Minor trends are the smallest and most fleeting market movements, occurring within secondary trends. These short-term fluctuations typically last a few days to a few weeks and are often driven by market noise, day-to-day news, trader sentiment, and short-term speculation. Minor trends generally last less than three weeks and are not considered significant in Dow Theory, as they do not reflect the broader market direction. While they may be relevant for short-term traders or scalpers, they are largely ignored by long-term investors who focus on the primary and secondary trends.

The three market trends identified in Dow Theory exist simultaneously, functioning as overlapping layers of price movement. Each trend operates on a different time scale and reflects distinct underlying forces. The primary trend represents the dominant, long-term direction of the market, shaping its general trajectory over months or years. The secondary trends occur within the context of the primary trend, representing shorter-term fluctuations that often act as counter-trend movements, such as corrections in a bull market or recoveries in a bear market. These trends provide intermediate direction but do not invalidate the broader primary trend. Finally, minor trends are the smallest and most short-lived movements, driven by day-to-day market noise, sentiment, and immediate reactions to news or events. These short-term fluctuations are typically less relevant to long-term investors but can provide opportunities for more active traders.

In addition to Charles H. Dow, who is often credited with founding the theoretical foundation for identifying market trends, several other influential figures contributed to the development of trend theory and market behavior.

These include Ralph Nelson Elliott, John Magee and Robert Edwards, and Harold M. Gartley.

In the 1930s, Ralph Nelson Elliott developed *Elliott Wave Theory*, one of the most influential models for understanding market trends and price movements. Elliott believed that market prices follow recurring cycles, which he termed "waves." According to his theory, these waves are driven by the collective psychology of market participants and follow a predictable pattern, offering a framework for understanding market behavior.

Harold M. Gartley was a key figure in the field of technical analysis. His influential book, *Profits in the Stock Market* (1935), provided valuable insights into market behavior and price patterns, emphasizing the significance of recognizing trends and predicting market movements. Gartley's work on price swings and patterns has had a lasting impact on trend-following strategies and technical analysis, especially in identifying and acting on reversal signals.

In the mid-20th century, John Magee and Robert Edwards co-authored *Technical Analysis of Stock Trends* (1948), a pivotal work in formalizing and expanding the theory of stock market trends. Their book popularized chart patterns like head and shoulders, double tops, and triangles, which are still used to identify the direction and potential reversals of market trends. Their contributions bridged the gap between Dow's foundational qualitative insights and the more quantitative methods employed by later analysts.

1.2 Rise of Moving Averages: A Key Tool in Trend-Following

Detecting trend direction in the stock market is challenging due to the inherent noise in stock prices. Smoothing the price series is essential to reveal underlying trends, and using moving averages is a simple yet effective approach for this purpose.

We believe that the idea of applying moving averages to smooth price series was "in the air" at the time. The concept of moving averages was well within reach in the early 1900s, ready to be independently discovered by multiple individuals. As a result, pinpointing the first person to apply moving averages is extremely difficult.

One of the earliest documented suggestion to use moving averages for smoothing economic time series can be attributed to Ragnar Frisch, a Norwegian economist and co-recipient of the first Nobel Memorial Prize in Economic Sciences in 1969. In his book *Analysis of Statistical Time Series* (1927), Frisch investigated mathematical methods, including moving averages, to smooth economic data and identify trends. However, his focus was on applying these methods to macroeconomic indicators, such as GDP, to analyze business cycles rather than stock prices.

Harold M. Gartley's book, *Profits in the Stock Market* (1935), is widely regarded as one of the earliest documented applications of moving averages in trading. Gartley introduced these averages as tools for detecting trends and determining optimal entry and exit points, laying the foundation for what would become a cornerstone of technical analysis. The moving average he employed, now commonly known as the Simple Moving Average (SMA), was instrumental in shaping modern trend-following strategies.

One of Gartley's key contributions was the introduction of the price and SMA crossover rule to identify trend direction. He recommended using SMAs with window lengths ranging from 50 to 200 days, intervals still prevalent among traders today. According to this rule, if the price rises above the SMA, it signals the beginning of an uptrend, suggesting a potential buying opportunity. Conversely, if the price falls below the SMA, it indicates a downtrend, prompting consideration of selling or exiting positions.

Recognizing the noise and false signals often generated by the price and SMA crossover rule, Harold M. Gartley also introduced the double SMA crossover rule, an enhancement designed to improve signal reliability. This method replaces the most recent price in the analysis with a shorter SMA, effectively smoothing out short-term fluctuations and reducing the impact of market noise.

In this approach, the shorter SMA is typically calculated using a window of 10 to 20 days, while the longer SMA retains a window of 50 to 200 days, as in the original method. The rule generates a Buy signal when the shorter SMA crosses above the longer SMA, indicating the potential start of an uptrend. Conversely, a Sell signal is triggered when the shorter SMA crosses below the longer one, suggesting the onset of a downtrend.

The double SMA crossover rule not only addresses the limitations of using raw price data but also adds a layer of confirmation to trend signals. This refinement has made it one of the most enduring strategies in technical analysis, frequently used alongside other indicators to develop robust trading systems. Gartley's insight into combining moving averages of different time frames has influenced countless trend-following techniques, underscoring the foundational nature of his work in modern trading.

The invention of exponential smoothing is widely attributed to Robert G. Brown, whose pioneering work in the 1950s and early 1960s laid the groundwork for this powerful time series analysis technique. Brown developed methods such as single exponential smoothing, double exponential smoothing, and multiple exponential smoothing, providing a systematic approach to smoothing economic and other time series data. His influential 1963 book, *Smoothing, Forecasting, and Prediction of Discrete Time Series*, formalized these methods and introduced them to a broader audience, cementing their role in forecasting.

In addition to introducing the Exponential Moving Average (EMA), Brown was among the first to thoroughly examine the inherent lagging behavior of moving averages. He observed that while moving averages are effective in smoothing price trajectories and filtering noise, they inevitably lag behind the actual data. This lag poses a significant limitation, as it delays the ability of moving averages to react promptly to shifts in trends.

Brown proposed a method to quantify the average lag time of the moving average using a measure analogous to the "center of mass" in physics. He defined the lag as the "average age" of the data points contributing to the moving average, effectively capturing the degree to which the moving average trails behind the actual price trajectory. This conceptualization provided deeper insights into the tradeoffs between smoothness and responsiveness in moving average techniques.

Brown demonstrated that the EMA is the optimal forecasting method when the price process can be modeled as a constant value plus noise. For more complex scenarios, such as when the price process represents a linear trend plus noise, he showed that optimal forecasting requires the use of both a single EMA and a double EMA. The double EMA is defined as the recursive application of the EMA to itself, thereby enhancing the method's ability to capture trends with greater accuracy.

Extending this logic, Brown proposed a general framework for forecasting when the underlying process is modeled by an n-th degree polynomial plus noise. He advocated using a sequence of EMAs of orders 1 through n, where each successive EMA accounts for higher-order components of the trend. For example, the second-order EMA is simply the double EMA. This hierarchical approach underscores the versatility and adaptability of exponential smoothing methods in capturing a wide range of data patterns. Brown's groundbreaking work not only addressed the mathematical challenges of smoothing and forecasting but also influenced the broader adoption of exponential smoothing in fields as diverse as finance, economics, and operations research.

Starting in the 1990s, the development of various moving averages experienced explosive growth, driven by several key technological and market shifts. This period marked a transformation in financial analysis and trading, largely fueled by the widespread availability of personal computers, which empowered individual traders and analysts with the tools needed to apply sophisticated algorithms and data analysis techniques. The growth of the Internet, which became increasingly accessible to the general public, played a crucial role by providing a wealth of financial information in real time. This allowed traders to access up-to-date stock market data, news, and analytics from virtually anywhere in the world.

As a result, a broader segment of the population became familiar with technical analysis and the use of moving averages, which are fundamental tools for identifying trends and making trading decisions. The increasing computational power of personal computers enabled traders to explore more sophisticated forms of moving averages. These advanced types of moving averages are often referred to as "exotic" moving averages, distinguishing them from traditional ones like the SMA and EMA.

Some of these exotic moving averages are believed to offer superior smoothing properties, enhancing the ability to filter out market noise more effectively. Others are claimed to have zero average lag time, providing more timely signals while maintaining smoothness. Additionally, many moving averages have been inspired by techniques from Digital Signal Processing (DSP), which aim to improve the accuracy and responsiveness of trend detection in dynamic market conditions. These innovations have expanded the range of moving averages available to traders, offering greater flexibility and the potential for more refined and optimized trading strategies.

1.3 Academic View on Trend-Following

1.3.1 Market Trends: Fact or Fiction?

Modern finance theory, which emerged in the 1950s, rests on the assumption of investor rationality. This rationality is not constrained but rather assumes unbounded rationality. Under this framework, all investors are assumed to make purely rational decisions, have access to complete and perfect information, and possess the capability to solve complex optimization problems without limitations. Consequently, the market prices of financial assets are thought to fully reflect all available information at any given moment.

A critical implication of this theory is that new information—whether it pertains to individual stocks, specific sectors, or the broader economy—arrives randomly and unpredictably. This randomness ensures that no patterns can be systematically exploited to gain an advantage. As soon as new information becomes available, rational investors process it instantaneously, leading to immediate adjustments in asset prices to reflect this new data.

This framework underpins the *Efficient Market Hypothesis* (EMH), which is classified into three forms: weak, semi-strong, and strong efficiency. These levels represent the extent to which different types of information are incorporated into asset prices. Even the weak form of market efficiency asserts that all historical price data and trading volumes are fully reflected in current prices. As a result, there are no predictable patterns in stock prices, rendering technical analysis ineffective for generating consistent excess returns. The implication is that past price movements cannot be used to predict future price movements.

Until the 1990s, nearly all academics, heavily influenced by the assumptions of investor rationality and the EMH, largely dismissed trend-following strategies, a core aspect of technical analysis, as ineffective. They argued that in an efficient market, where prices fully reflect all available information, past price patterns or trends have no predictive power for future price movements. As such, trend-following was deemed a futile endeavor, as price changes were considered random and driven solely by new, unforeseeable information. This perspective reinforced the view that systematic attempts to exploit trends could not consistently yield superior profits.

However, during the late 1980s, the EMH began facing challenges from empirical evidence and behavioral finance theories, which highlighted instances of market inefficiencies. For example, the weak form of market efficiency asserts that stock prices follow a random walk, meaning that each new price change is independent of past price changes. Contrary to this notion, empirical studies by Summers (1986), Fama and French (1988), and Lo and MacKinlay (1988) uncovered patterns in stock prices, including short-term momentum and medium-term mean reversion. Short-term momentum refers to the tendency of prices to persist in their current direction. Mean reversion refers to the tendency for prices to moderate after periods of extreme movement, relative to their recent trend or growth trajectory. For example, after an unusually strong price increase, prices may grow more slowly or even decline temporarily, aligning more closely with their longer-term growth rate or expected trend.

These findings suggest that stock price movements are not entirely random, highlighting opportunities to exploit potential inefficiencies. For instance, short-term momentum in stock prices reflects the presence of trends. If such trends exist, a trend-following strategy designed to capitalize on them should, in theory, outperform a passive buy-and-hold approach in terms of profitability.

The paper by Brock et al. (1992) is a landmark study that significantly shifted the academic perspective on technical analysis, particularly on trend-following strategies. This influential work investigates the profitability of simple technical trading rules, such as moving averages and momentum-based strategies, when applied to stock market data. The study focuses on popular methods like price and SMA crossover rules, as well as double SMA crossover rules.

The findings in the paper reveal that these simple and popular technical rules can generate profitable trading signals. Specifically, returns following Buy signals are consistently positive, while those following Sell signals are negative. An additional key observation is that returns after Buy signals are substantially less volatile compared to those after Sell signals, underscoring the potential risk-reducing benefits of these strategies. Among the examined methods, the most profitable trading signals arise from trend-following rules based on moving averages, highlighting their effectiveness in capturing market trends.

The paper by Brock et al. (1992) is also notable for being published in the most prestigious financial journal. Achieving publication in such a journal requires undergoing a rigorous peer-review process conducted by renowned academics in the field. This ensures that only the most innovative, well-researched, and high-quality studies are accepted for publication. The inclusion of this paper in such a respected journal underscores its significance and impact on the academic and financial communities.

The study by Brock et al. (1992) was groundbreaking in providing the first robust evidence for price persistence and the effectiveness of trend-following rules. It also posed a significant challenge to the EMH, questioning the notion that financial markets are fully efficient. Perhaps most importantly, this study served as a catalyst for extensive subsequent research into the phenomenon of momentum in financial markets, laying the foundation for a deeper understanding of price trends and market behavior.

In academic studies, the term price momentum is more commonly used than price trends. In financial markets, momentum is a short-term phenomenon that refers to the tendency of an asset's price to continue moving in the same direction, either upward or downward, for some time. This concept is based on the observation that assets with strong past performance tend to continue performing well, while those with poor past performance are likely to remain underperformers in the near term.

The term momentum is typically used in the context of momentum trading strategies, which aim to capitalize on price persistence. These strategies often involve buying assets that are trending upward (exhibiting positive momentum) and selling or shorting assets that are trending downward (exhibiting negative momentum). Momentum strategies are broadly divided into two types: cross-sectional momentum and time series momentum. Both rely on the premise that past price movements can predict future trends, but they differ in their focus and implementation.

The paper by Jegadeesh and Titman (1993) is a seminal study that provided the first comprehensive empirical evidence of cross-sectional momentum in stock returns. It demonstrated that a simple strategy of buying past winners (top-performing stocks) and selling past losers (worst-performing stocks) generates significant positive abnormal returns. In this context, past winners are defined as stocks with the highest returns over the past 3 to 12 months, while losers are those with the lowest returns over the same period. Notably, the cross-sectional momentum strategy focuses on an asset's performance relative to other assets in the same group, emphasizing relative ranking rather than absolute performance.

The study by Moskowitz et al. (2012) is another foundational contribution to the momentum in asset prices, formally introducing and analyzing the concept of time series momentum across multiple asset classes. In contrast to cross-sectional momentum, time series momentum evaluates each asset's past performance individually and takes positions based on its historical trend. This strategy bets that an asset's past trend, whether upward or downward, will continue into the future. Specifically, an asset is bought if its past return over a chosen horizon (e.g., 12 months) is positive and sold if its return is negative. Notably, the time series momentum strategy focuses on an asset's absolute performance, emphasizing its individual price movements rather than its relative performance compared to other assets in the same group. The study provided robust evidence that time series momentum is a pervasive phenomenon, applicable across diverse asset classes, including equities, bonds, currencies, and commodities.

The paper by Jegadeesh and Titman (1993) is widely regarded as the landmark study on the cross-sectional momentum strategy, while the paper by Moskowitz et al. (2012) is considered the pivotal work on the time series momentum strategy. Both studies sparked extensive academic research, further reinforcing the substantial evidence for the momentum effect in financial markets.

Similarly, the study by Brock et al. (1992) spurred numerous follow-up studies that explored the profitability of trend-following strategies based on moving averages. These strategies, in essence, also capitalize on the time series momentum effect. However, there is a notable distinction between these trend-following studies and the research initiated by Moskowitz et al. (2012). The trend-following strategies stemming from the work of Brock et al. (1992) are typically implemented using a single risky asset, most often a stock market index. In these strategies, the investment approach involves allocating capital to the index when the trading signal is a Buy and shifting to the risk-free asset when the signal is a Sell.

By now, there are likely more than a thousand published academic papers documenting the existence of momentum in various financial markets and the profitability of momentum and trend-following strategies. The goal of this section is not to provide a comprehensive review of this vast body of literature. Instead, we aim to highlight mainly the landmark studies that have significantly shaped our understanding of momentum and its role in financial markets. These landmark studies, along with the wealth of subsequent research they inspired, have convincingly demonstrated that momentum is a pervasive phenomenon in financial markets. It is observed across a wide range of asset classes, including equities, bonds, currencies, and commodities, over multiple time horizons and in diverse geographic regions.

1.3.2 Why Do Trends Exist?

Momentum has become a cornerstone of both academic research and practical investment strategies, influencing portfolio management, risk assessment, and algorithmic trading. To reinforce the scientific foundation supporting the practical application of these strategies, academics have sought to explain the existence of momentum in financial markets. These explanations can be broadly categorized into behavioral and business-cycle explanations.

Behavioral finance is a field of study that combines insights from psychology and economics to understand how psychological factors and cognitive biases influence financial decision-making, investor behavior, and market outcomes. Unlike traditional finance, which assumes that investors are rational and markets are efficient, behavioral finance acknowledges that people often make decisions based on emotions, biases, and imperfect information, which can lead to market inefficiencies, anomalies, and irrational behavior.

Behavioral finance provides several explanations for the existence of momentum in financial markets, focusing on how cognitive biases and psychological factors influence investor behavior. These explanations suggest that momentum arises from the ways investors process information, make decisions, and interact with each other, often leading to market inefficiencies. Key behavioral factors that contribute to momentum include:

Underreaction to New Information: Investors often fail to immediately incorporate new information into asset prices, leading to gradual price adjustments over time. When new information becomes available, investors may take time to fully adjust their expectations, resulting in a delayed price response and the continuation of trends.

Overconfidence and Herding Behavior: Investors tend to overestimate their own knowledge and abilities, which leads to excessive risk-taking and market trends that become amplified over time. This overconfidence encourages herding behavior, where investors blindly follow the actions of others, even in the absence of new information. As more investors join the trend, prices move further away from their fundamental value, reinforcing momentum and prolonging price movements.

Representativeness Bias: Investors often anchor their expectations on historical prices, using past trends as a reference point to predict future performance. The representativeness bias further amplifies this tendency by leading investors to believe that past trends are representative of future performance. As a result, they may mistakenly extrapolate recent performance into the future, perpetuating momentum in the market. For example, if an asset has been performing well over the last few months, investors may expect this trend to continue, even if market conditions change.

These behavioral factors, often working together, create a feedback loop that reinforces the persistence of momentum in financial markets. Investors' tendency to underreact to new information, coupled with herd behavior and emotional biases, prevents market prices from fully incorporating all available information in a rational and timely manner, as assumed by efficient market theories. Consequently, momentum emerges in ways that would not be anticipated in a perfectly rational, efficient market, leading to predictable trends that can be exploited by astute investors.

While behavioral finance offers several potential explanations for the existence of trends in financial markets, a significant challenge remains: the lack of studies that explicitly test and confirm the hypothesis that a specific behavioral factor directly causes the momentum effect. The paper by Brook et al. (2024) is a notable exception, as it establishes a clear link between investors' underreaction to new information and the existence of price trends. Specifically, this study tests a trend-following strategy that exploits the positive or negative impact of macroeconomic indicators—such as GDP, inflation, exchange rates, bond yields, and credit spreads—on stock prices. The authors demonstrate that economic news has a persistent effect on stock prices, and that a trend-following strategy based on this news is highly profitable.

While behavioral finance offers competing explanations for momentum based on investor limited rationality and cognitive biases, business-cycle explanations for the existence of momentum do not rely on assumptions of investor irrationality. Instead, these explanations provide a more scientifically grounded link between market fundamentals and the momentum effect, offering empirical evidence that momentum arises from cyclical fluctuations in economic conditions. This view suggests that momentum is driven by fundamental economic shifts, rather than by psychological biases or cognitive errors, aligning more closely with rational models of market behavior. Charles H. Dow was among the first to explain the existence of primary trends (bull and bear markets) by attributing them to cyclical variations in economic fundamentals, such as GDP growth, interest rates, corporate earnings, and other macroeconomic factors.

The idea that economic activity in each country experiences recurrent fluctuations, known as business cycles, has been extensively documented in the literature. A business cycle refers to the natural fluctuations in economic activity over time, typically measured by changes in GDP, employment, and industrial production. It consists of two main phases: expansion and contraction (or recession). During the expansion phase, economic activity grows as businesses increase production, hire more workers, and invest in new projects. Consumer demand rises, driving higher sales and profits. In the contraction phase, the economy begins to slow, and business activities decline. Consumer demand falls, leading companies to reduce production. During this phase, businesses may face challenges such as lower sales, higher inventory levels, and rising costs, which can result in bankruptcies or mergers.

While understanding the precise causes of these cycles remains a significant challenge in economic research, with various business-cycle theories offering alternative explanations, the existence of business cycles is widely accepted. From this standpoint, a key conclusion arises: in a rational expectations model, stock market movements should reflect the forward-looking behavior of investors, who base their decisions on expectations about the future state of the economy. This alignment between stock market fluctuations and business cycles is well documented in economic literature.

The paper by Novy-Marx (2015) provides evidence showing that momentum in stock prices is driven by fundamental momentum. Specifically, the study demonstrates that momentum in firm fundamentals, such as earnings momentum, plays a significant role in explaining the performance of price momentum strategies. Similarly, the study by Yu et al. (2023) finds that cyclical movements in valuation ratios, including Dividend-to-Price, Earnings-to-Price, and Book-to-Market, translate into corresponding cyclical movements, or trends, in stock returns. These studies suggest that trends in stock returns are closely linked to underlying economic and fundamental factors, offering a more grounded explanation for momentum in financial markets.

1.4 Challenges of Trend-Following With Moving Averages

1.4.1 Challenges of Moving Averages

Applying the moving average to price data is a long-standing technique in finance, widely used for analyzing market trends. The primary objective of the moving average is to smooth the inherently noisy and fluctuating price data, thereby revealing the underlying trend direction more clearly. This smoothing process makes it easier for traders to identify potential buy or sell signals and understand the market's broader movement.

Traders generally agree that an effective moving average should exhibit strong smoothing capabilities to filter out short-term price fluctuations that can obscure the underlying trend. To address this need, numerous variants of moving averages have been proposed, each designed to enhance smoothness and adapt to different market conditions.

One straightforward approach to achieving greater smoothness is the use of double and triple moving averages. A double moving average applies the moving average calculation to its own output, effectively smoothing the already-smoothed data. Similarly, a triple moving average extends this concept by recursively applying the moving average three times. These recursive methods progressively reduce noise and provide a clearer view of the trend. Another way to enhance the smoothing properties of a moving average is through the careful selection of price weights. By adjusting the weight assigned to recent versus older prices, traders can fine-tune the smoothness of the moving average.

However, traders also recognize a critical tradeoff: the smoothed trajectory of the moving average inherently lags behind the actual price trajectory. This lag occurs because the moving average relies on past price data to calculate its value. Moreover, traders understand that the extent of this lag is directly linked to the level of smoothness. The smoother the moving average, the longer its lag time tends to be. This relationship presents a dilemma: while greater smoothness reduces noise and improves trend clarity, it delays signals, making them less responsive to sudden market changes. Balancing smoothness and responsiveness is a fundamental challenge when selecting or designing a moving average for trading strategies.

The ideal moving average should be both smooth and responsive—a balance that is challenging to achieve. To address this, traders have proposed various types of so-called "zero-lag" moving averages. These are advertised as possessing minimal lag while maintaining strong smoothing capabilities, making them seemingly perfect for trend-following.

In designing new variants of moving averages, some traders draw inspiration from Digital Signal Processing (DSP) techniques. From a DSP perspective, a moving average is essentially a type of digital filter, whose behavior can be analyzed and optimized in the frequency domain rather than the time domain. This approach provides a deeper understanding of how the filter interacts with price data by isolating and evaluating its impact on different frequency components, such as noise and trends.

One of the key advantages of DSP techniques is their ability to design filters with specific desired characteristics, such as reduced lag or enhanced smoothness. Building on this, some traders have proposed replacing conventional moving averages with variants based on known digital filter designs. These alternatives, often adapted from low-pass filters in DSP, are tailored to suppress high-frequency noise while preserving the essential low-frequency trend signals. Proponents of these DSP-inspired moving averages claim that they offer superior performance compared to traditional moving averages, boasting better smoothing properties and reduced lag.

However, claims regarding the superiority of "zero-lag" moving averages and DSP-inspired moving averages lack any scientific backing. These assertions are typically supported by persuasive narratives and anecdotal examples rather than by systematic, evidence-based studies. This highlights the urgent need for critical mathematical validation to objectively assess their purported benefits.

To properly evaluate these claims, it is essential to establish quantitative metrics that enable traders to measure key properties of moving averages, such as their average lag time and smoothness. These metrics would provide a standardized framework for comparing different moving averages, allowing traders to determine whether a given method truly offers a meaningful improvement or simply trades one property for another.

Developing and applying such metrics would not only enhance the transparency of claims made about novel moving averages but also empower traders to make informed decisions based on measurable performance rather than marketing hype or subjective impressions.

Robert G. Brown, in his seminal work *Smoothing, Forecasting, and Prediction of Discrete Time Series* (1963), introduced a metric to measure the average lag time of a moving average. This metric calculates the average "age" of the data contributing to the moving average, inspired by the concept of the center of mass in physics. Remarkably, this measure has persisted in use among traders for over six decades, without significant scrutiny or reevaluation of its validity.

There are, however, two significant issues with Brown's average lag time measure that raise doubts about its accuracy and appropriateness. The first issue is the lack of justification for this measure. Specifically, Brown's average lag time measure is introduced as an ad hoc metric, without a solid theoretical foundation to support its appropriateness. While Brown rigorously proves the optimality of using a single EMA in specific contexts, the average lag time measure lacks a similar justification. It is presented without a thorough derivation or explanation of why it accurately captures the concept of lag. This lack of grounding leaves its relevance and reliability open to question.

The second, more fundamental issue is that the measure fails to consistently represent the lagging behavior of a moving average. The lag time is essentially computed as the average time difference between the current moment and the moment when past price is equal to the current moving average value. While this approach seems intuitive, it leads to contradictory interpretations. Specifically, in an uptrend, the moving average lags behind the price, and the average lag time captures the time delay effectively. In stark contrast, in a downtrend, the moving average leads the price, meaning the average lag time measure evaluates the time difference as a lead time rather than a lag time. As a result, this metric implies that the moving average is a lagging indicator during price increases but becomes a leading indicator during price decreases. This directly contradicts the widely accepted notion among traders that the moving average is always a lagging indicator of price action.

These inconsistencies highlight significant flaws in Brown's average lag time measure. If the metric evaluates lag incorrectly or inconsistently, its usefulness as a tool for understanding or comparing moving averages becomes highly questionable.

This contradiction invites a critical reassessment of the measure. It may be necessary to develop a more rigorous and theoretically sound metric that accurately and consistently captures the lagging nature of moving averages, irrespective of market conditions. Such a metric would not only resolve the inconsistencies in Brown's measure but also improve the precision of quantitative analysis in financial market studies.

In summary, while there exists a metric intended to measure the lag time or responsiveness of a moving average, this metric requires critical reassessment due to its conceptual inconsistencies and lack of rigorous justification.

The situation is even more problematic when it comes to evaluating the smoothness of a moving average. To date, no universally accepted or systematically developed metric exists to quantify smoothness. Without such a measure, traders and analysts are left without the essential tools to objectively compare different moving averages based on their effectiveness in smoothing the price trajectory.

The total absence of a standard measure for smoothness in moving averages may stem from the inability of traders to agree on a precise definition of smoothness. Two competing perspectives dominate the discourse.

The first perspective aligns smoothness with the ability of the moving average to reduce noise in price data. From this viewpoint, a smoother moving average is one that filters out short-term price fluctuations, effectively isolating the underlying trend. According to this interpretation, smoothness is synonymous with the noise reduction capability of the moving average. A smoother moving average is considered more effective in suppressing the "randomness" in price movements, thereby providing a more accurate trading signal.

The second perspective defines smoothness in terms of the stability of trading signals generated from the moving average. Proponents of this view argue that higher smoothness corresponds to fewer period-to-period fluctuations in the moving average's value, resulting in fewer erratic or "whipsaw" trades. In this sense, smoothness is linked to the consistency of the trading signal. A smoother moving average produces signals that are less reactive to minor price changes, reducing the frequency of false signals and enhancing the stability of trading decisions.

These competing definitions highlight the complexity of the concept of smoothness. For some, it is about the technical filtering of noise, while for others, it is about the practical impact on trading outcomes. This divergence in interpretations complicates the task of developing a universally accepted smoothness measure.

A resolution may require creating two distinct metrics that address each perspective individually. For instance, a noise reduction metric could quantify the extent to which the moving average filters out high-frequency price fluctuations. In addition, a signal stability metric could measure the consistency of trading signals or the reduction in false trades over a given period. Such clarity in metrics would allow traders to select the appropriate measure based on their specific needs, bridging the gap between theoretical properties and practical applications.

However, in our view, the quantitative measurement of the properties of individual moving averages holds limited value. This is because the trading signal in trend-following strategies that rely on moving averages is not determined by the value of a single moving average in isolation. Instead, the signal typically arises from the relationship between the current price and the moving average, the relationship between multiple moving averages, or the change in the value of a moving average over time. Thus, logically, it is far more important for traders to be able to measure the responsiveness and smoothness of the trading signal generated by the overall trend-following rule, rather than focusing solely on the individual moving averages used within the rule.

For instance, let us consider a situation where we can measure the average lag time and smoothness of a single moving average. In the case of a double moving average crossover rule, where the trading signal is based on the relationship between the short and long moving averages, the key question becomes: what are the responsiveness and smoothness of the trading signal produced by this rule? For example, does the lag time of the double crossover rule simply equate to the sum or difference of the lag times of the individual moving averages, or does it depend on a more complex function of the two lag times?

The core point here is that even if we could quantify the characteristics of the individual moving averages used within a trading rule, such information is of limited relevance in practical terms. What truly matters is understanding how to quantify the characteristics of the trading rule itself, which is based on the interaction of multiple moving averages and other market conditions.

Therefore, the focus should shift from measuring the properties of individual moving averages to assessing the properties of the trading rules that incorporate them. In other words, we must develop tools to measure the responsiveness, smoothness, and overall performance of the trading signals produced by moving average-based rules, rather than simply analyzing the behavior of the moving averages in isolation. This would allow traders to better understand how their rules are likely to behave in real-world market conditions, facilitating more informed decision-making and strategy optimization.

1.4.2 Challenges of Trend-Following Trading Rules

In contrast to the proliferation of moving average variants since the early 1990s, there has been little progress in developing new trend-following rules based on moving averages. The most popular trend-following rules have remained largely unchanged since their introduction in Harold M. Gartley's seminal book, *Profits in the Stock Market* (1935). These rules include the price and moving average crossover rule and the double moving average crossover rule.

Another straightforward approach is the directional moving average rule, which determines the trend based on the slope of the moving average. If the moving average value increases, the trend is upward; if it decreases, the trend is downward. Similarly, the momentum rule evaluates the difference between the current price and the price a specified number of periods ago. A higher current price indicates an uptrend, while a lower current price signifies a downtrend.

An interesting trend-following method is the moving average envelope rule, which involves plotting two bands around a moving average—one above and one below. These bands are offset by a fixed percentage or specific number of points, forming a "channel" that represents the typical price range around the moving average. When the channel is narrow, a price move above the upper band suggests a buy signal, while a move below the lower band indicates a sell signal. When the channel is wide, a price above the upper band signals overbought conditions, and a price below the lower band suggests oversold conditions.

The origins of the moving average envelope technique are unclear and cannot be attributed to a specific individual or time. It is likely an approach that has evolved organically over a long period. In contrast, the origins of the Moving Average Convergence/Divergence (MACD) rule are well documented. The MACD was developed by Gerald Appel, who mentioned in his book *Technical Analysis: Power Tools for Active Investors* (2005) that he introduced the rule in the late 1970s.

The MACD rule generates trading signals using three EMAs and is considered one of the most controversial trend-following techniques. The controversy stems from its lack of a definitive interpretation. Some traders view the MACD signal as an indicator of trend direction, helping to capture momentum, while others interpret it as a measure of overbought or oversold conditions, leading to divergent strategies. Despite these differing perspectives, the MACD rule remains a widely used tool in technical analysis.

Despite the vast number of scientific papers on the momentum effect in financial markets, academic research predominantly focuses on two main approaches: relative momentum and absolute (or time series) momentum strategies. Both strategies involve analyzing a universe of individual assets, classifying them as winners or losers based on their past cumulative returns, typically over a 12-month period. The momentum strategy is a long-short strategy that seeks to capitalize on these classifications by buying winners and selling (or short-selling) losers, aiming to exploit the persistence of past performance into the future.

The momentum long-short strategy is primarily accessible to institutional investors, such as hedge funds, due to the substantial capital, infrastructure, and resources required for short selling and managing a diversified portfolio of long and short positions. This limitation makes the strategy impractical for small investors, rendering it less relevant to their investment practices.

Small investors often adopt simplified approaches, such as the long-only trend-following strategy, which involves investing in an asset when its price trends upward and switching to a risk-free asset when it trends downward. In this strategy, Buy and Sell signals are typically generated using trend-following rules based on moving averages. As a result, the explosive growth in the development of new moving average techniques is primarily aimed at catering to small investors, providing them with tools to refine their decision-making and enhance the effectiveness of their trend-following strategies.

Small investors aiming to implement a long-only trend-following strategy often face an overwhelming number of decisions. First, they must choose an appropriate trend-following rule from the set of existing options. Second, they need to select a suitable moving average from a large universe of available types. Finally, each moving average requires the selection of an appropriate averaging window size.

Without a clear understanding of the commonalities and differences between various trading rules and specific moving averages, investors face a daunting challenge. They need a structured methodology to analyze and compare the different options. More importantly, to objectively assess the advantages and disadvantages of each choice, investors require a set of quantitative metrics to evaluate the various characteristics of trend-following rules.

What are the relevant quantitative metrics for evaluating trend-following strategies? Since the trading signals generated by these rules typically lag behind the price action, it is crucial for traders to have a metric that measures the responsiveness of the trend-following rule. Responsiveness refers to how quickly the strategy reacts to changes in market conditions, particularly shifts in price trends.

As discussed above, the smoothness property of trend-following rules can be interpreted in two ways. First, smoothness can be seen as the noise reduction property, where less erratic price movements lead to a clearer trend direction. The less noise in the price trajectory, the easier it becomes to identify the prevailing trend and make more accurate trading decisions.

Second, smoothness can refer to the reduction in period-to-period fluctuations in the value of the moving average. The fewer the fluctuations in the moving average, the more stable and reliable the trading signals generated by the trend-following rule. In this interpretation, smoothness helps minimize frequent position reversals, reducing the likelihood of whipsaw trades—situations where the strategy mistakenly enters and exits trades in quick succession, often due to short-term market noise.

Both the noise reduction property and the reduction in the number of position reversals property are equally important. However, in our view, the smoothness property is more closely associated with the reduction in position reversals, which results in more stable and consistent trading signals. This stability helps prevent erratic shifts in positions, leading to lower transaction fees and reducing the potential for conflicting signals that could confuse traders. On the other hand, the noise reduction property is primarily concerned with the accuracy of the trend-following rule in identifying the trend direction. By filtering out market noise, this property ensures that the strategy can effectively capture the true market trend without being misled by short-term fluctuations.

For example, when prices are trending upward or downward, the trend-following rule must accurately identify the trend direction. Accuracy in this context can be measured by the percentage of correct trading signals, indicating how well the rule captures the prevailing trend. However, when prices are moving sideways, there is no clear trend, and the trend-following rule is less effective in generating correct signals. In such situations, it is crucial for the rule to minimize the number of position reversals. To achieve this, the signals generated by the trend-following rule must be stable, meaning they should exhibit smoothness to avoid reacting to short-term fluctuations and reducing unnecessary trades. Smoothness, in this context, can be measured by the expected number of position reversals. Fewer position reversals indicate greater smoothness, as the trend-following rule avoids unnecessary changes in direction during sideways price movements.

All in all, there is an urgent need to measure the responsiveness, accuracy, and smoothness of a trend-following rule. The ability to use quantitative metrics that evaluate these characteristics can significantly simplify the process of selecting the most appropriate trading rule and moving averages to use within that rule. These metrics provide traders with objective measures to assess how well a rule adapts to market conditions, captures trends accurately, and minimizes unnecessary trades, ultimately enabling more informed and efficient decision-making.

With these three metrics in hand, traders can quantify the key properties of trend-following rules and select the one that is most optimal for their needs. However, optimality in this context means that, for example, the double EMA crossover rule may perform better than the price and SMA crossover rule. Specifically, given a particular averaging window size in the price and SMA rule, we can identify a double EMA crossover rule, with appropriate sizes for the shorter and longer EMAs, that exhibits superior properties in terms of responsiveness, accuracy, and smoothness compared to the price and SMA crossover rule.

Given the proven superiority of the double EMA crossover rule, the next challenge is determining how to select the appropriate sizes for the shorter and longer EMAs to achieve the best profitability in a specific financial market. The critical point here is that trend change dynamics and price volatility can vary significantly across different financial markets. As a result, the same window sizes used in the double EMA crossover rule may not be optimal across all markets. Consequently, the best-performing EMA sizes must be tailored to the characteristics of each individual market to maximize profitability.

The current approach to selecting the best trading rule for a specific financial market typically involves backtesting a set of existing rules. Backtesting means testing the profitability of different trend-following rules by applying them to historical data with various window sizes for the moving averages used in these rules. The outcome of the backtest identifies the trading rule and the corresponding moving average parameters that deliver the best performance in the past.

The problem with this approach is overfitting. Overfitting occurs when a model or strategy is excessively tailored to historical data, capturing noise and specific patterns that were present in the past but may not necessarily reflect future market behavior. This results in a strategy that works well on past data but fails to perform as expected in real-world, future scenarios.

In the context of backtesting, overfitting means that the trading rule identified as the "best" in the past may perform poorly in the future, even if the market dynamics remain the same. This happens because the rule is overly complex or too finely tuned to the quirks of historical data, leading it to pick up on short-term fluctuations or non-representative patterns that do not recur in the future. Additionally, future market dynamics may differ from those in the past, further undermining the effectiveness of a backtested strategy.

Therefore, when conducting a backtest, it is essential to use methods that address the potential overfitting problem. Additionally, academics are still unsure about the accuracy of backtesting methods in identifying the optimal trading rule. Lastly, the potential discrepancy between past and future market dynamics highlights the importance of selecting a rule that may not be the best in the backtest but demonstrates robust profitability across various market conditions.

When implementing a trend-following strategy, traders must decide on the optimal trading frequency. Many intuitively believe that daily trading is superior to weekly or monthly trading, reasoning that frequent monitoring allows for quicker reactions to market movements. However, this agility comes with a downside: it increases the risk of being misled by false signals, commonly known as "whipsaws."

Interestingly, few academic studies have explored whether daily trading truly outperforms lower-frequency trading. The existing studies are largely empirical, which poses a limitation—their findings are tied to specific financial markets and historical periods, making them difficult to generalize. This highlights the pressing need for a theoretical framework to determine the optimal trading frequency.

Typically, the trend-following strategy is a "bang-bang" strategy, where 100% of the capital is allocated to either the risky or risk-free asset. There is a strong intuition that the bang-bang strategy may be suboptimal. A more optimal approach could involve a strategy where the percentage allocated to the risky asset adjusts based on the strength of the trend. However, there is a noticeable lack of academic studies exploring alternatives to the bang-bang trend-following strategy. One notable exception is a recent study by Goulding et al. (2023), which proposes a strategy where the allocation to the risky asset is determined by the direction of both short-term and long-term trends.

A trend-following strategy is often designed to capture the primary trend in the stock market. The presence of secondary trends can negatively impact the profitability of such a strategy. Since trend-following strategies typically have a significant lag time, they are not well suited to follow shorter, secondary trends. As a result, these strategies may issue trading signals too late, rendering them ineffective. For example, a Sell signal may be triggered after a market correction has already ended and is replaced by a market rebound.

When a sharp drop in stock prices occurs, it is sometimes not due to deteriorating market fundamentals, but rather because investors panic in anticipation of negative market news. When investors later realize their fears were unfounded, stock prices quickly rebound to their previous levels. This dynamic is often referred to as a V-shaped recovery. A trend-following rule based on moving averages typically struggles to react promptly to such sharp drops followed by rapid recoveries. This is because trend-following strategies are generally designed to follow primary trends and are not equipped to respond quickly to short-term fluctuations like those seen in a V-shaped recovery.

Consequently, secondary trends, along with sharp drops and quick recoveries, can undermine the profitability of trend-following strategies intended to capture primary trends. Therefore, there is a need to develop trend-following strategies that can effectively capitalize on both primary and secondary trends, while also demonstrating robust performance during large, sharp price movements followed by a quick reversion to the original level.

1.5 How We Address the Challenges in This Book

It is impossible to address all the challenges related to moving averages and the trend-following rules based on them in a single book. However, this book strives to tackle most of the key challenges discussed earlier.

In the first part of the book, we introduce conventional moving averages and the trend-following trading rules based on moving averages. This part concludes that, despite the variety of moving averages and their associated trading rules, the computation of the trading indicator for any trend-following rule, whether based on a single or multiple moving averages of prices, can be reformulated as the computation of a single weighted average of returns within the averaging window. In this form, a visual inspection of the return weights enables a straightforward understanding of the trading rule's concept, facilitating the identification of both commonalities and differences among various trading rules. However, this visual inspection falls short of deducing which rule is the most smooth or responsive, highlighting a limitation in discerning such nuances through visual means.

In the second part of the book, first and foremost, we identify the key properties of trend-following rules based on moving averages and propose methods to quantify them. These properties are accuracy, responsiveness, and smoothness. Accuracy reflects the rule's ability to reduce noise in trading signals, while smoothness is related to the stability of these signals over time. Responsiveness, on the other hand, captures the average delay between a trend change and the corresponding adjustment in the trading signal.

To evaluate these properties, we introduce three quantitative measures based solely on the return weights of the moving average used in a trading rule's technical indicator. These metrics provide a transparent and objective framework for comparing different trend-following rules, offering a clearer basis for assessing their performance and characteristics.

Subsequently, we provide analytical solutions for the three key metrics of the trend-following rules based on conventional moving averages. Our analytical results allow the traders to understand how the parameters of the trading rules depend on the choice of the moving average and the size of the averaging window in the selected moving average. Our findings also highlight a crucial aspect of trading rule design. Enhancing one property, such as accuracy or smoothness, inevitably results in a compromise on another property, such as responsiveness. Achieving optimal balance in all quantitative measures simultaneously is a challenging task.

Having obtained the analytical solutions for all quantitative measures, we utilize these metrics to compare and contrast the trading rules in search of one that excels in effectiveness across all measures. Regrettably, our analysis suggests that there is no single rule that outperforms in all three measures simultaneously. Nonetheless, our findings do reveal that certain rules provide a favorable tradeoff between specific metrics. For instance, some rules excel in responsiveness and accuracy, striking a balance that makes them well suited for capturing market trends and generating reliable signals. On the other hand, there are rules that offer a compelling tradeoff between responsiveness and smoothness, resulting in stable and timely trading signals over time.

The availability of key quantitative metrics enables us to uncover the trading rule that is optimal with respect to one or multiple metrics. This is possible because the differences among trading rules fundamentally arise from variations in their return weights. By leveraging these distinctions, analytical and numerical techniques can be employed to determine the shape of return weights that either maximizes a specific property or achieves the most favorable tradeoff among two or more properties.

Our investigation provides invaluable insights into the design of optimal trend-following rules, revealing the precise shapes of return weights that optimize individual properties or achieve superior tradeoffs among multiple properties. For instance, we determine the shape of return weights for the trading rule that maximizes smoothness within a given averaging window size. Similarly, we identify the shape of return weights for the trading rule that achieves maximum responsiveness while maintaining a specified level of smoothness. In essence, we uncover the configuration of the trading rule that excels in both responsiveness and smoothness, striking a balance that aligns with the goals typically sought in "zero-lag" moving averages.

In the third part of this book, we review the wide array of exotic moving averages used for trend-following, including those with enhanced smoothness, the "zero-lag" moving averages, and the DSP-inspired moving averages. The primary focus of this part is to critically examine the claims regarding the superiority of these moving averages.

Our investigation reveals that moving averages with enhanced smoothness tend to lack responsiveness. Among the various "zero-lag" moving averages, only a few offer an optimal tradeoff between responsiveness and smoothness. Additionally, we find that while these "zero-lag" moving averages improve responsiveness, they do so at the expense of accuracy. Finally, we observe that most DSP-inspired moving averages exhibit characteristics similar to those of the "zero-lag" moving averages.

In the final fourth part of the book, we explore several key questions from a theoretical perspective. First, we investigate what type of technical trading rule is optimal in a financial market where the return process randomly shifts between bull and bear regimes. We identify the optimal type of trading rule and analyze how its parameters relate to the parameters of the return process and the level of trading costs.

Second, we examine the precision of backtest methodologies in identifying the optimal trading rule. Our findings reveal that this precision is typically poor, meaning that traders often employ suboptimal rules for trend-following. Nevertheless, we demonstrate that even a suboptimal trend-following strategy tends to outperform a passive buy-and-hold approach.

Finally, we address the question of the optimal trading frequency for trend-following. Our conclusion is that there is no discernible advantage in trading with daily data over using weekly or monthly data, suggesting that less frequent trading may still yield competitive results.

References

Appel, G. (2005). Technical Analysis: Power Tools for Active Investors. *Financial Times.* Prentice Hall.

Brock, W., Lakonishok, J., & LeBaron, B. (1992). Simple Technical Trading Rules and the Stochastic Properties of Stock Returns. *Journal of Finance, 47*(5), 1731–1764.

Brooks, J., Feilbogen, N., Ooi, Y. H., & Akant, A. (2024). *Economic Trend.* White Paper. AQR Capital Management.

Brown, R. G. (1963). *Smoothing, Forecasting and Prediction of Discrete Time Series.* Prentice-Hall.

Edwards, R. D., & Magee, J. (1948). *Technical Analysis of Stock Trends.* CRC Press.

Fama, E. F., & French, K. R. (1988). Permanent and Temporary Components of Stock Prices. *Journal of Political Economy, 96*(2), 246–273.

Frisch, R. (1927). *The Analysis of Statistical Time Series.*

Gartley, H. M. (1935). *Profits in the Stock Market.* Health Research Books.

Goulding, C. L., Harvey, C. R., & Mazzoleni, M. G. (2023). Momentum Turning Points. *Journal of Financial Economics, 149*(3), 378–406.

Jegadeesh, N., & Titman, S. (1993). Returns to Buying Winners and Selling Losers: Implications for Stock Market Efficiency. *Journal of Finance, 48*(1), 65–91.

Lo, A. W., & MacKinlay, A. G. (1988). Stock Market Prices do not Follow Random Walks: Evidence from a Simple Specification Test. *Review of Financial Studies, 1*(1), 41–66.

Moskowitz, T. J., Ooi, Y. H., & Pedersen, L. H. (2012). Time Series Momentum. *Journal of Financial Economics, 104*(2), 228–250.

Novy-Marx, R. (2015). *Fundamentally, Momentum is Fundamental Momentum.* Working Paper, National Bureau of Economic Research.

Summers, L. H. (1986). Does the Stock Market Rationally Reflect Fundamental Values? *Journal of Finance, 41*(3), 591–601.

Yu, D., Huang, D., & Chen, L. (2023). Stock Return Predictability and Cyclical Movements in Valuation Ratios. *Journal of Empirical Finance, 72*, 36–53.

Part I

Moving Averages and Trend-Following Trading Rules

2

Basics of Moving Averages

2.1 Introduction

Traders often operate on the assumption that stock prices exhibit recurring patterns. This idea originates from analyzing historical price movements, where certain formations seem to repeat, potentially signaling profitable opportunities. Early technical analysis was dedicated to recognizing these repetitive structures to aid trading decisions, with patterns like head and shoulders, triangles, and double tops or bottoms used to forecast future price behavior.

By closely studying historical price trends, traders observed that prices often move directionally over time, displaying periods of sustained upward or downward momentum. This insight led to the development of trend-following strategies, which seek to identify and follow trends until there are clear signs of reversal.

One challenge traders face is the inherent noise in price data, which complicates identifying trend directions. To mitigate this challenge, traders utilize moving averages as a tool for trend detection. Moving averages offer a smoothed representation of price movements over a specified time frame, facilitating the identification of trend directions. Essentially, moving averages calculate the average price of an asset over a specified number of periods, effectively filtering out short-term fluctuations and noise in the data.

Scientific research shows that humans have an innate tendency to seek patterns, driven by the brain's preference for order and predictability. Recognizing familiar patterns helps individuals make sense of their environment and anticipate future events, whether identifying faces, navigating social interactions, or making decisions. In the uncertain realm of financial markets, spotting recurring patterns offers a sense of structure and predictability. By identifying

V. Zakamulin and J. Giner, *The Ultimate Moving Average Handbook*,
https://doi.org/10.1007/978-3-031-90907-8_2

patterns in stock prices or market behavior, traders aim to extract valuable insights that inform their decisions and, potentially, predict future outcomes. This pattern-seeking behavior underscores a fundamental aspect of human cognition: the drive to understand and manage complex environments.

But are repeating patterns truly present in stock prices? While patterns like head and shoulders, triangles, or double tops and bottoms remain a subject of scientific skepticism, the existence of price trends is widely acknowledged. Extensive research provides compelling evidence for trends and the effectiveness of trend-following strategies in achieving long-term profitability.[1]

This brings us to a crucial question: which moving average is best for trend-following investments? Over the years, traders have introduced various types of moving averages, with each new type often claimed to be superior to existing ones. However, claims of superiority are typically based on anecdotal evidence and visual demonstrations rather than rigorous scientific analysis.

The confusion surrounding moving averages stems from the absence of scientifically grounded quantitative metrics for comparing their characteristics. If such metrics existed, they could help traders objectively evaluate and refine existing moving averages and trend-following strategies while also inspiring the creation of new ones with enhanced properties.

When discussing the key characteristics of moving averages, traders frequently emphasize responsiveness and smoothness. They often describe a moving average as a "smoothing tool with a time lag." While responsiveness is commonly quantified using a metric known as average lag time, there is no widely accepted measure of smoothness for moving averages. Later in this book, we argue that trend detection accuracy is another essential characteristic. Although smoothness is often equated with accuracy, we will illustrate that a smooth moving average can exhibit poor accuracy, while a less smooth one may achieve superior accuracy.

In this chapter, we introduce the fundamental concept of a moving average, which involves calculating a weighted sum of historical prices within a specified window length. We then proceed to discuss conventional types of moving averages. We postpone the presentation of numerous exotic moving averages to prevent overwhelming the reader with excessive information.

Next, we examine the commonly used metric for evaluating the average lag time of a moving average. We explain its shortcomings, including its failure to accurately measure lag time and its misleading suggestion that average lag time can be reduced to zero. This misconception has led to the development

---

[1] A critical distinction must be made regarding the performance of trend-following strategies. While they often outperform passive buy-and-hold strategies over the long term, their short-term performance can be inconsistent, sometimes underperforming relative to buy-and-hold approaches.

of numerous "zero-lag" moving averages. We demonstrate how to correctly measure the average lag time and show that so-called "zero-lag" moving averages still exhibit non-zero lag times.

Finally, this chapter presents a comprehensive exploration of the key mathematical properties of moving averages. Among the properties discussed are homogeneity, additivity, associativity, and commutativity, which are fundamental to understanding the behavior and applications of moving averages. Homogeneity and additivity highlight the ability of moving averages to scale and combine inputs in predictable ways, while associativity and commutativity emphasize the invariance of results regardless of the order in which operations are performed. These properties lay the foundation for more advanced concepts in time series analysis, enabling a deeper understanding of how moving averages function and their role in smoothing and forecasting data.

2.2 Moving Averages and Their Alignments

The word "average" has multiple meanings. In this book, "average" refers to a single value that represents the central tendency or typical value of a set of prices. It simplifies a set of prices into one number that is generally representative of the middle of the data. In everyday language, "average" usually refers to what is formally called the "mean," or more specifically, the "arithmetic mean" in mathematics.

Suppose we have a time series of price observations $\{P_1, P_2, \ldots, P_T\}$, where T is the sample length. The average price in the sample, or arithmetic mean, is calculated as:

$$A = \frac{1}{T} \sum_{i=1}^{T} P_i.$$

In words, the average price is found by summing all the prices and then dividing this sum by the total number of price observations.

A moving average is a statistical technique used to smooth out data by creating a series of averages from different subsets of a full dataset. The moving average helps to highlight trends and patterns over time by reducing the impact of short-term fluctuations.

A moving average is calculated using a fixed-size window, which we denote by n. The first moving average value is computed using the data from the first observation to the n-th observation:

$$MA_1(n) = \frac{1}{n}\sum_{i=1}^{n} P_i.$$

The second moving average value is obtained by shifting the window one observation forward, calculating the arithmetic mean of the prices from the 2nd observation to the $(n + 1)$-th observation:

$$MA_2(n) = \frac{1}{n}\sum_{i=2}^{n+1} P_i.$$

The last moving average value is computed using the observations from $T - n + 1$ to T:

$$MA_{T-n+1}(n) = \frac{1}{n}\sum_{i=T-n+1}^{T} P_i.$$

It is important to note that the number of moving average values we can calculate is fewer than the total number of observations. For a sample of size T, we can compute only $T - n + 1$ moving average values.

After calculating all the values of the moving average, we have two time series. The first time series consists of the historical prices, while the second is the moving average of those prices. How do we align these two time series? By aligning the two time series, we mean the process of adjusting or synchronizing them so they can be compared meaningfully over time. In time series analysis, alignment ensures that the data points from both series correspond to the same time periods or points of interest.

There are essentially two methods of alignment: centering the moving average and right-aligning the moving average.

If the current time is t, the centered moving average is calculated using k observations both before and after this time. In this case, the size of the averaging window is $n = 2k + 1$, and the centered moving average at time t is computed as:

$$MA_t(n) = \frac{1}{n}\sum_{i=-k}^{k} P_{t+i}.$$

This means that the moving average for a given time point takes into account data points from both sides of that point.

In contrast, the right-aligned moving average is calculated by averaging the prices in the window from time $t - n + 1$ to time t:

$$MA_t(n) = \frac{1}{n} \sum_{i=0}^{n-1} P_{t-i}.$$

In this case, the moving average for a given time point considers only the data points from the left side.

Figure 2.1 displays the monthly closing values of the S&P 500 index from January 2004 to April 2010. This figure also includes the centered moving average and the right-aligned moving average calculated over an 11-month window.

The moving average should not only smooth out price fluctuations and highlight the trend direction but also help traders identify turning points in the trend in a timely manner. In this context, the curves in the figure seem to suggest that the centered moving average is superior to the right-aligned moving average. This is because the peaks and troughs in the centered moving average align closely with the peaks and troughs in the S&P 500 index values. In contrast, the peaks and troughs in the right-aligned moving average lag behind the corresponding peaks and troughs in the S&P 500 index values.

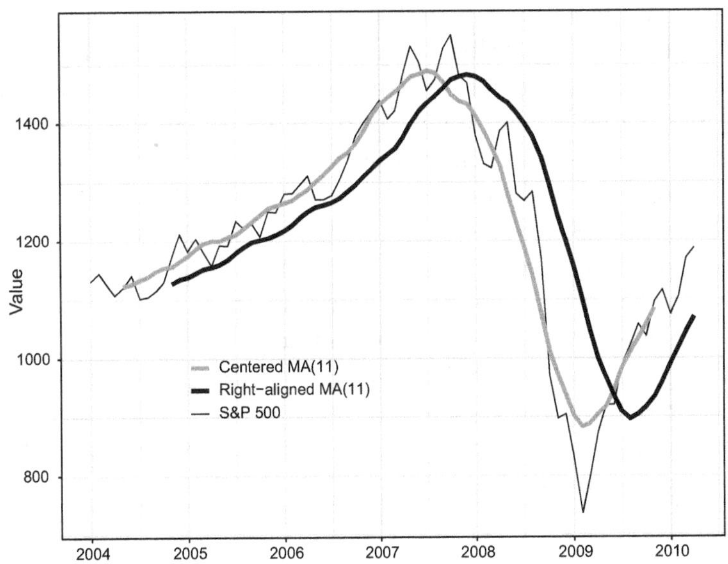

Fig. 2.1 Centered moving average and the right-aligned moving average calculated over an 11-month window computed using the monthly closing prices of the S&P 500 index

While the right-aligned moving average is clearly a lagging indicator of price action, the centered moving average may give the impression of having no lag. However, this perception is misleading. Both moving averages are actually lagging indicators because they are calculated using previous data, that is, data available at the time of computing the moving average value.

While it is relatively easy to identify turning points in trends using past data, doing so in real time is extremely challenging. For example, when we analyze the historical price dataset used to create Fig. 2.1, we can accurately determine that the S&P 500 index reached its bottom in February 2009. It is important to note that the centered moving average value for February 2009 is calculated using index values from September 2008 to June 2009.

If the current time is February 2009, we do not have knowledge of the future index values starting from March 2009. This means we cannot compute the centered moving average for the current time. More critically, to assert that the index hit its bottom in February 2009, we need to know that the centered moving average increases afterward. Therefore, we must have access to future index values beyond June 2009. Consequently, the February 2009 bottom in the index values can only be identified after June 2009, at the earliest in July 2009.

In contrast to the time-t value of the centered moving average, the time-t value of the right-aligned moving average is calculated using only the available data at time t. Additionally, the window size for the centered moving average must be an odd integer, while the window size for the right-aligned moving average can be any integer value. Lastly, the curve representing the right-aligned moving average does not give the wrong impression that this moving average can identify the peaks and troughs in the prices in real time without delay. Therefore, the right-aligned moving average makes more sense than the centered moving average when the goal is to predict the future direction of the trend.

When traders calculate the moving average, they often use the "weighted arithmetic mean" rather than the "arithmetic mean." The weighted arithmetic mean is similar to the ordinary arithmetic mean, but it assigns different weights to the data points, meaning that some points have a greater influence on the final average than others. For instance, to enhance the responsiveness of the moving average, more recent prices are given greater weight, enabling the average to react more quickly to recent price changes.

2.3 General Weighted Moving Average

To compute a general weighted moving average at time t, one uses the last closing price P_t and $n-1$ lagged prices P_{t-i}, where i ranges from 1 to $n-1$. Each price contributes to the average with its own weight. Formally, a general weighted moving average of a price series P at time t is given by:

$$MA_t(n, P) = \frac{w_0 P_t + w_1 P_{t-1} + w_2 P_{t-2} + \ldots + w_{n-1} P_{t-n+1}}{w_0 + w_1 + w_2 + \ldots + w_{n-1}} = \frac{\sum_{i=0}^{n-1} w_i P_{t-i}}{\sum_{i=0}^{n-1} w_i}, \tag{2.1}$$

where w_i represents the weight assigned to price P_{t-i} in the computation. It is important to note that at least two prices are needed to compute a moving average. That is, one should have $n \geq 2$. When only one price is used, the moving average equals the last closing price, expressed as $MA_t(1, P) = P_t$.

When the price weights are normalized, meaning that the sum of weights equals one, $\sum_{i=0}^{n-1} w_i = 1$, the moving average is calculated as follows:

$$MA_t(n, P) = \sum_{i=0}^{n-1} w_i P_{t-i}. \tag{2.2}$$

In this case, each price is multiplied by its corresponding weight, and then these weighted prices are summed together to obtain the moving average.

At the next time step, $t+1$, a new moving average is calculated using the closing prices from $t-n+2$ to $t+1$. It is crucial to note that a moving average always employs a rolling data window with a constant length of n. This means that the size of the averaging window remains constant, as do the price weights. The price data is the only change occurring with each new moving average computation.

It is important to note that a moving average is typically calculated using closing prices, not adjusted for dividends. There are a couple of reasons for this practice. First, these unadjusted prices are directly observable in financial markets, unlike prices adjusted for dividends. Second, adjusting for dividends can introduce inaccuracies in identifying trends and generating trading signals. Dividends can distort price movements, making it more challenging to identify underlying trends.

Traders still rely heavily on moving averages of prices to spot potential buying or selling opportunities. The main reason is that historical prices are readily available in financial markets. Traders can visually analyze price charts and easily overlay one or more moving average lines onto them. However, as we are going to emphasize several times in this book, focusing solely on prices can often be misleading. Let us illustrate this problem with a simple example.

Suppose we observe two consecutive prices P_{t-1} and P_t and want to determine whether prices are in an uptrend or downtrend. When using moving averages of prices, the typical methodology is as follows: traders calculate the moving average of prices, with one of the simplest being $MA_t(2, P) = (P_t + P_{t-1})/2$. Then, they compare the last price with the value of the moving average. If $P_t > MA_t(2, P)$, prices are considered to be in an uptrend. Otherwise, they are regarded as being in a downtrend. What is the rationale behind this decision rule? We will explain it in detail later in this section, but at first glance, the reasoning is not immediately clear.

A simple alternative method for detecting the trend direction is to examine the price difference $\Delta P_t = P_t - P_{t-1}$ to see if it is positive or negative, indicating whether the price has increased or decreased. This approach can be extended to consider n consecutive price changes. Specifically, the general rule can be as follows: if the weighted average of these price changes is positive, it suggests an upward trend; if negative, it indicates a downward trend.

Focusing on price changes is preferred because consecutive prices are closely related. For example, P_t and P_{t-1} differ only by ΔP_t. To illustrate, consider $P_{t-1} = 200$ and $P_t = 201$. The price difference is just 0.5%, indicating 99.5% similarity between the two prices. In contrast, consecutive price changes tend to show low similarity, even if they have the same sign.

While we acknowledge the usefulness of using moving averages of prices to analyze price trends visually, we believe that another approach, focusing on price changes instead of actual prices, is better suited for formal mathematical analysis of moving averages and trading rules based on them. Our reasoning stems from the observation that consecutive prices largely overlap, leading to the concealment of the incremental information provided by each new price. By looking at price changes, which exhibit only a weak dependence, we can better understand the importance of each new piece of information from consecutive prices.

Now, we will introduce an alternative representation for the moving average of prices, which expresses it in terms of a moving average of price changes. This alternative representation offers valuable insights into the relationship between the last price and the moving average of prices. Understanding this relationship is key to comprehending the rationale behind various trend-following rules used by traders.

The motivation behind the alternative representation of a moving average stems from viewing a series of stock prices as a dynamic process evolving over time. To introduce this representation, we define the notation for a price change between times $t - i - 1$ and $t - i$:

$$\Delta P_{t-i} = P_{t-i} - P_{t-i-1}.$$

With this notation, we can express a relationship between the last closing price and the price i periods before as follows:

$$P_{t-i} = P_t - \Delta P_t - \Delta P_{t-1} - \ldots - \Delta P_{t-i+1} = P_t - \sum_{j=0}^{i-1} \Delta P_{t-j}, \quad i \geq 1.$$

We substitute the expression for P_{t-i} into Eq. (2.1) and obtain (note that the expression is not valid for $i = 0$):

$$\begin{aligned} MA_t(n, P) &= \frac{w_0 P_t + \sum_{i=1}^{n-1} w_i \left(P_t - \sum_{j=0}^{i-1} \Delta P_{t-j}\right)}{\sum_{i=0}^{n-1} w_i} \\ &= P_t - \frac{\sum_{i=1}^{n-1} w_i \sum_{j=0}^{i-1} \Delta P_{t-j}}{\sum_{i=0}^{n-1} w_i}. \end{aligned}$$

Interchanging the order of summation in the double sum above yields:

$$MA_t(n, P) = P_t - \frac{\sum_{j=0}^{n-2} \left(\sum_{i=j+1}^{n-1} w_i\right) \Delta P_{t-j}}{\sum_{i=0}^{n-1} w_i} = P_t - \sum_{j=0}^{n-2} \theta_j \Delta P_{t-j}, \tag{2.3}$$

where the weight θ_j is given by:

$$\theta_j = \frac{\sum_{i=j+1}^{n-1} w_i}{\sum_{i=0}^{n-1} w_i}, \quad j \in [0, 1, \ldots, n-2]. \tag{2.4}$$

Consequently, any moving average can be expressed as the last closing price minus the weighted sum of the previous price changes. In conventional moving averages, which we will discuss further in this chapter, the weights are positive, meaning $w_i > 0$ for all i. As a result, in such cases, the sequence of weights θ_j generally decreases with increasing j:

$$\theta_0 \geq \theta_1 \geq \ldots \geq \theta_{n-2}.$$

Therefore, regardless of the specific shape of the weighting function for prices w_i, the weighting function for price changes θ_j generally assigns higher weights to more recent price changes and lower weights to older ones.

Equation (2.3) yields valuable insight into the relationship between the last price P_t and the value of the moving average $MA_t(n, P)$:

$$P_t - MA_t(n, P) = \sum_{j=0}^{n-2} \theta_j \Delta P_{t-j}.$$

This equation indicates that the last closing price is not equal to the value of the moving average of prices unless $\sum_{j=0}^{n-2} \theta_j \Delta P_{t-j} = 0$. For instance, this equality holds true when the price remains constant throughout the averaging window. In such cases, $\Delta P_{t-j} = 0$ for all j, resulting in the last closing price being equal to the moving average value.

Furthermore, this equation suggests that when prices increase on average, the last closing price exceeds the moving average of prices, $P_t - MA_t(n, P) > 0$. In other words, in such scenarios, the moving average is below the last closing price. Conversely, when prices decrease on average, the moving average is above the last closing price, $P_t - MA_t(n, P) < 0$.

2.4 Average Lag Time of a Moving Average

Every trader is familiar with the concept of a moving average being referred to as a "lagging indicator." Essentially, this term implies that there is a delay between the occurrence of price actions and the subsequent response of the moving average to these actions. However, to truly understand this delay, we need to delve deeper into the specifics.

When we talk about "price action" in relation to a moving average, we refer to the fluctuations and changes in the price of a financial asset over time. These movements can range from minor fluctuations to significant trends, and the moving average aims to capture and smooth out these variations.

The challenge arises when we attempt to quantify the delay between price action and the moving average's response to this action. Without a precise definition of relevant price action, accurately measuring this delay becomes inherently tricky. As the saying goes, "The devil is in the details."

Despite the inherent challenges, traders often resort to a measure known as the average lag time of a moving average. In this section, we aim to introduce and elucidate this measure, shedding light on what it truly signifies—specifically, the type of delay it represents.

Traders continue to use the measure introduced by Robert G. Brown in his seminal 1963 book, *Smoothing, Forecasting, and Prediction of Discrete Time Series*, to determine the average lag time of moving averages. Brown's approach draws inspiration from the concept of the center of mass in physics. In mechanics, calculating the center of mass involves finding the weighted average position of all the parts of an object, where each part's position is weighted by its mass. Analogously, Brown proposed calculating the average lag time of a moving average by determining the weighted average age of the data points contributing to it.

In particular, the price observation at time $t - i$ has weight w_i in the moving average calculation, where it lags behind the most recent observation at time t by i periods. Consequently, the incremental delay from each observation at $t - i$ is proportional to $w_i \times i$. The average lag time represents the time at which all weights can be considered concentrated.

Expressed mathematically, the average lag time of a moving average, denoted as ALT(MA), can be estimated using the formula:

$$\underbrace{(w_0 + w_1 + \ldots + w_{n-1})}_{\text{Sum of all weights}} \times \text{ALT(MA)} = \underbrace{w_0 \times 0 + w_1 \times 1 + \ldots + w_{n-1} \times (n-1)}_{\text{Weighted sum of delays of individual observations}}.$$

Thus, the average lag time of a moving average is given by:

$$\text{ALT(MA)} = \frac{\sum_{i=1}^{n-1} w_i \times i}{\sum_{i=0}^{n-1} w_i}. \tag{2.5}$$

Notably, since the most recent observation has a lag time of 0, the weight w_0 does not contribute to the computation of the weighted sum of delays of individual observations.

The formula for the average lag time can be rearranged as follows. First, we express $\sum_{i=1}^{n-1} w_i \times i$ as a double sum:

$$\sum_{i=1}^{n-1} w_i \times i = \sum_{i=1}^{n-1} w_i \sum_{j=1}^{i} 1.$$

Second, by interchanging the order of summation in the double sum above, we get:

$$\sum_{i=1}^{n-1} w_i \sum_{j=1}^{i} 1 = \sum_{j=1}^{n-1} \sum_{i=j}^{n-1} w_i.$$

Now, let us start indexing j from 0 instead of 1. The reason for doing this becomes apparent shortly. With this change, we have:

$$\sum_{j=1}^{n-1} \sum_{i=j}^{n-1} w_i = \sum_{j=0}^{n-2} \sum_{i=j+1}^{n-1} w_i.$$

Finally, the formula for the average lag time is expressed as:

$$\text{ALT(MA)} = \frac{\sum_{j=0}^{n-2} \sum_{i=j+1}^{n-1} w_i}{\sum_{i=0}^{n-1} w_i} = \sum_{j=0}^{n-2} \theta_j, \tag{2.6}$$

where the weight θ_j represents the weight given by (2.4). This formulation demonstrates that the average lag time is computed using the same weights as the alternative representation for the moving average formula.

To grasp the nature of the delay measured by ALT(MA), let us consider a scenario where the price change remains constant over time. This assumption implies that $\Delta P_{t-j} = \Delta P$ for all t and j. Under this assumption, the difference between the latest price and the moving average value can be expressed as:

$$P_t - MA_t(n) = \sum_{j=0}^{n-2} \theta_j \Delta P = \text{ALT}(MA) \times \Delta P. \tag{2.7}$$

In simpler terms, the difference between the latest price and the moving average value equals ALT(MA) multiplied by the price change over one period. Consequently, the larger the ALT(MA), the larger this difference.

It is worth observing that Eq. (2.7) indicates that the gap between the most recent price and the moving average value widens as ΔP increases. The magnitude of ΔP correlates with the trend's strength, meaning that stronger trends correspond to larger values of ΔP. Thus, an increase in the difference between the last price and the moving average value indicates an increase in trend strength.

Another valuable observation derived from Eq. (2.7) is as follows. Theoretically, two distinct moving averages can utilize different weighting methods while still sharing identical lag times. In such situations, during periods of sustained price increases or decreases, all moving averages with corresponding lag times typically move together, resulting in significant overlap among their lines.

It is instructive to visually demonstrate the relationship between the time series of stock prices, the moving average of prices, and the average lag time. However, understanding this relationship requires some mathematical groundwork. Again, for clarity in illustration, we assume that the stock price steadily increases between times 0 and t. Specifically, we suppose that the stock price dynamic is given by:

$$P_t = P_0 + \Delta P \times t, \tag{2.8}$$

where $\Delta P > 0$ is an arbitrary constant.

At first glance, it might seem improbable that stock prices would consistently rise due to the inherent volatility in real stock markets. However, it is important to clarify that we do not refer to the lag time of a moving average but rather the "average" lag time. In essence, this suggests that, on average, the fluctuations in stock prices can be overlooked.

According to our assumption, the value of the moving average at time t is determined by:

$$\begin{aligned} MA_t(n) &= P_t - \sum_{j=0}^{n-2} \theta_j \Delta P = P_0 + \Delta P \times t - \Delta P \sum_{j=0}^{n-2} \theta_j \\ &= P_0 + \Delta P \times \left(t - \sum_{j=0}^{n-2} \theta_j \right). \end{aligned} \tag{2.9}$$

We can define the average lag time of the moving average, ALT(MA), between the time series of prices and the moving average of prices with the relationship:

$$MA_t(n) = P_{t-\text{ALT(MA)}}. \tag{2.10}$$

This equation indicates that the value of the moving average at time t equals the value of the price lagged by ALT(MA) periods.

Since the price at t is given by Eq. (2.8), the price ALT(MA) periods before this price equals:

$$\begin{aligned} P_{t-\text{ALT(MA)}} &= P_0 + \Delta P \times t - \Delta P \times \text{ALT(MA)} \\ &= P_0 + \Delta P \times (t - \text{ALT(MA)}). \end{aligned} \tag{2.11}$$

Substituting the expressions for $MA_t(n)$ and $P_{t-\text{ALT(MA)}}$ into Eq. (2.10), we get:

$$P_0 + \Delta P \times \left(t - \sum_{j=0}^{n-2} \theta_j \right) = P_0 + \Delta P \times (t - \text{ALT(MA)}).$$

Consequently, we arrive at the following result for the ALT(MA):

$$\text{ALT(MA)} = \sum_{j=0}^{n-2} \theta_j.$$

It is important to note that we have arrived at the same formula for the average lag time as that obtained from computing the center of mass of the price weights in a moving average. Graphically, the relationship between the stock price, the value of the moving average, and the average lag time is depicted in Fig. 2.2.

Now, we can fully understand what is measured by the metric known as the average lag time of a moving average. Specifically, the ALT(MA) equals the time difference between the time-t value of the moving average and the previous time at which the price equals the same value. This relationship is expressed in Eq. (2.10).

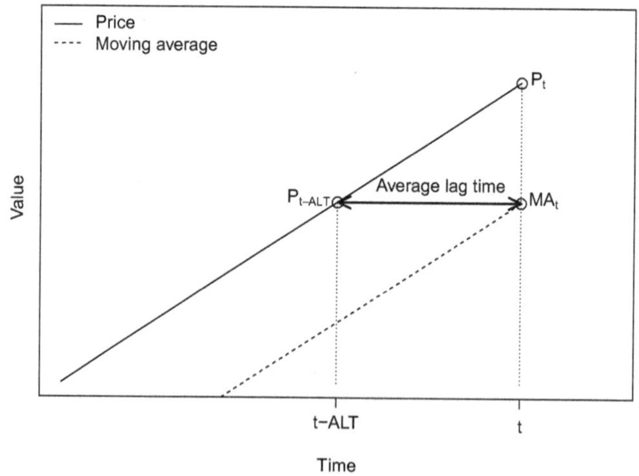

Fig. 2.2 Illustration of the average lag time between the time series of stock prices and the moving average of prices

It is important to highlight that the "delay" occurs exclusively during price increases. In this situation, the moving average trails behind the price. Conversely, when the price decreases, the moving average precedes the price. In this instance, the ALT(MA) does not signify a delay but rather a lead time.

Therefore, given the mathematical concept behind the average lag time of the moving average, it seems counterintuitive to label the moving average as a lagging indicator in all scenarios. It behaves as a lagging indicator only when prices increase.

In concluding this section, it is worth noting that John F. Ehlers, a renowned expert in technical analysis, offers similar illustrations to those depicted in Fig. 2.2 to clarify the concept measured by the ALT(MA). To verify the alignment of our illustration with his, we can refer to his works, such as Ehlers (2002) and Ehlers (2004), among others.

2.5 Conventional Moving Averages

2.5.1 Simple Moving Average

The Simple Moving Average (SMA) calculates the arithmetic mean of n prices:

$$SMA_t(n, P) = \frac{P_t + P_{t-1} + P_{t-2} + \ldots + P_{t-n+1}}{n} = \frac{1}{n}\sum_{i=0}^{n-1} P_{t-i}. \tag{2.12}$$

It is important to note that in this moving average, each price observation carries the same weight $w_i = 1$.

An alternative representation for the SMA is:

$$SMA_t(n, P) = P_t - \sum_{j=0}^{n-2} \frac{n-j-1}{n} \Delta P_{t-j}. \tag{2.13}$$

In this representation, the sequence of weights for the price changes is:

$$\theta_0 = \frac{n-1}{n}, \theta_1 = \frac{n-2}{n}, \ldots, \theta_{n-2} = \frac{1}{n}.$$

These weights linearly decrease from $\frac{n-1}{n}$ down to $\frac{1}{n}$.

The average lag time of SMA is given by:

$$\text{ALT}(SMA) = \frac{n-1}{2}. \tag{2.14}$$

This formula can be found in Zakamulin (2017), Chap. 3.

2.5.2 Linear Moving Average

A Linear (or linearly-weighted) Moving Average (LMA) is calculated as:

$$\begin{aligned} LMA_t(n, P) &= \frac{nP_t + (n-1)P_{t-1} + (n-2)P_{t-2} \ldots + P_{t-n+1}}{n + (n-1) + (n-2) + \ldots + 1} \\ &= \frac{\sum_{i=0}^{n-1}(n-i)P_{t-i}}{\sum_{i=0}^{n-1}(n-i)}. \end{aligned} \tag{2.15}$$

In a linear moving average, the weights decrease in an arithmetic progression. Specifically, in the LMA(n), the latest observation has weight n, the second latest $n-1$, and so forth, down to one.

Often, a linear moving average is referred to as a Weighted Moving Average (WMA) in the literature. However, calling the linear moving average a weighted moving average is inaccurate. Any moving average is inherently a weighted moving average, as each price observation generally carries a unique weight. The term linear moving average is more fitting as it reflects the type of weighting function employed in this average.

An alternative representation for the LMA is:

$$LMA_t(n, P) = P_t - \sum_{j=0}^{n-2} \frac{(n-j-1)(n-j)}{2} \Delta P_{t-j}. \tag{2.16}$$

In this representation, the sequence of weights for the price changes is:

$$\theta_0 = \frac{(n-1)n}{2}, \theta_1 = \frac{(n-2)(n-1)}{2}, \ldots, \theta_{n-2} = 1.$$

These weights decrease from $\frac{(n-1)n}{2}$ down to 1 in a nonlinear fashion.

The average lag time of LMA is given by (see Zakamulin, 2017, Chap. 3):

$$\text{ALT}(LMA) = \frac{n-1}{3}. \tag{2.17}$$

It is important to observe that the ALT of the LMA is shorter than that of the SMA when both moving averages are calculated using the same window size n. This reduction in ALT(MA) is achieved by assigning larger weights to the most recent prices.

2.5.3 Exponential Moving Average

Exponential smoothing is primarily attributed to Robert G. Brown, whose work in the 1950s and early 1960s laid the foundation for this technique. He developed methods for smoothing economic time series, which later became known as single exponential smoothing, double exponential smoothing, and multiple exponential smoothing. Brown's 1963 book, *Smoothing, Forecasting, and Prediction of Discrete Time Series,* formalized these methods and played a key role in popularizing their use in forecasting.

Robert G. Brown proposed the Exponential Moving Average (EMA) as a solution to the shortcomings of the SMA. His primary motivation for replacing the SMA with the EMA was to enhance computational efficiency of the moving average. The SMA, at each step, is computed as the average of the n most recent prices, as shown in Eq. (2.12). However, the computation can be made faster using the following recursive formula:

$$SMA_t(n, P) = SMA_{t-1}(n, P) + \frac{P_t - P_{t-n}}{n}, \qquad (2.18)$$

where $SMA_{t-1}(n, P)$ is the SMA value at the previous time step $t-1$ and P_{t-n} is the price from n periods ago.

While the recursive formula (2.18) is significantly more efficient than the direct calculation in Eq. (2.12), it still requires knowledge of the price P_{t-n} from n steps prior. This dependency can complicate real-time computations, particularly when managing large datasets or streaming data.

In contrast, the EMA addresses this limitation by relying only on the most recent price and the previous EMA value. The recursive formula for the EMA is:

$$EMA_t(\lambda, P) = (1-\lambda)P_t + \lambda\, EMA_{t-1}(\lambda, P), \qquad (2.19)$$

where $EMA_t(\lambda, P)$ and $EMA_{t-1}(\lambda, P)$ are the EMA values at times t and $t-1$, respectively, and $0 < \lambda < 1$ is the smoothing constant (also called the decay factor). The parameter λ controls the weighting of the previous EMA value in computing the current EMA, with smaller values of λ giving more weight to recent prices. This recursive computation of the EMA eliminates the need for historical prices beyond the most recent price, making it more efficient for real-time applications and simpler to implement in practice.

An alternative representation of the EMA is given by:

$$
\begin{aligned}
EMA_t(\lambda, P) &= \frac{P_t + \lambda P_{t-1} + \lambda^2 P_{t-2} + \ldots}{1 + \lambda + \lambda^2 + \ldots} \\
&= \frac{\sum_{i=0}^{\infty} \lambda^i P_{t-i}}{\sum_{i=0}^{\infty} \lambda^i} = (1 - \lambda) \sum_{i=0}^{\infty} \lambda^i P_{t-i}. \qquad (2.20)
\end{aligned}
$$

Note that since $\lambda < 1$, the EMA assigns greater weights to the most recent prices. By adjusting the value of λ, we can control the weights given to recent prices and, therefore, the responsiveness of this moving average.

Note that, unlike the SMA and LMA, the EMA is computed with an averaging window of infinite size. However, because the weights assigned to prices decrease rapidly, prices at longer lags have very small weights in the EMA computation. Essentially, distant prices are disregarded. For instance, if $\lambda = 0.8$, then the weight of a price at lag 20 is approximately $0.8^{20} \approx 0.01$. This means that the weight of this price is only about 1% of the weight of the most recent price.

It is important to note that the SMA, like most moving averages, is defined by the size of its averaging window, n. In contrast, the EMA is characterized by its decay constant, λ. Brown recognized that this difference in parameterization could make it difficult to directly compare the responsiveness of the SMA and EMA. To address this, he proposed a unification approach that relates the EMA to the window size n. Specifically, Brown suggested that the EMA with a window size n should exhibit the same lag time as the SMA with the same window size.

This approach enables a direct comparison between the SMA and EMA, as the window size n becomes a common reference. By adjusting the decay constant λ to match the lag time of the SMA with window size n, the EMA can be calibrated to offer similar responsiveness as the SMA. This unification makes it easier to select the appropriate moving average for a given application, ensuring consistency in how different types of moving averages respond to changes in the data.

The lag time of the EMA is determined by the equation (see Zakamulin, 2017, Chap. 3):

$$
\text{ALT}(EMA) = \frac{\lambda}{1 - \lambda}.
$$

Equating the lag time of the SMA(n) with that of the EMA(λ) yields the condition:

$$\frac{n-1}{2} = \frac{\lambda}{1-\lambda}.$$

This condition leads to the formula for computing λ in the EMA(n):

$$\lambda = \frac{n-1}{n+1}. \tag{2.21}$$

As a result, the formula for the EMA can be expressed as:

$$EMA_t(n, P) = (1-\lambda)\sum_{i=0}^{\infty} \lambda^i P_{t-i}, \quad \lambda = \frac{n-1}{n+1}. \tag{2.22}$$

In this formulation, it may appear that the EMA(n) is computed using n price observations. However, n is solely utilized to determine the decay constant λ, while the EMA(n) is computed using an infinite number of price observations.

It is worth noting that according to its definition, the average lag time of the EMA(n) equals that of the SMA(n):

$$\text{ALT}(EMA) = \frac{n-1}{2}. \tag{2.23}$$

This implies that, according to the ALT(MA) measure introduced by Robert G. Brown, the EMA(n) and SMA(n) exhibit the same level of responsiveness.

An alternative representation for the EMA(n) is:

$$EMA_t(n, P) = P_t - \sum_{j=0}^{\infty} \lambda^{j+1} \Delta P_{t-j}. \tag{2.24}$$

In this representation, the sequence of weights for the price changes is:

$$\theta_0 = \lambda, \theta_1 = \lambda^2, \theta_3 = \lambda^3, \ldots.$$

2.5.4 Multiple Exponential Moving Average

In principle, a multiple EMA may not be considered a conventional moving average. However, since this method dates back to Robert G. Brown's work in 1963, we find it relevant to discuss multiple EMAs in this chapter.

The use of multiple EMAs is grounded in the following concept. Brown advocated that if the data sequence P_t is modeled by the following process:

$$P_t = a_0 + \varepsilon_t, \tag{2.25}$$

where a_0 is a value that occasionally changes and ε_t is a zero-mean random variable, then the single EMA provides the optimal forecast of the value of P_{t+1}, which equals to the value of a_0.

The process given by Eq. (2.25) represents a constant value plus noise. In contrast, if the process follows a linear trend plus noise, modeled as:

$$P_t = a_0 + a_1 t + \varepsilon_t, \tag{2.26}$$

where a_1 is a constant and t is time, then the optimal forecast for the future value P_{t+1} can be achieved using both the single EMA and the double EMA. The double EMA is defined as applying the EMA to the EMA itself:

$$\begin{aligned} &EMA_t(n, EMA(n, P)) \\ &\quad = (1 - \lambda) EMA_t(n, P) + \lambda\, EMA_{t-1}(n, EMA(n, P)). \end{aligned} \tag{2.27}$$

In this case, the optimal estimate of, for example, the value of a_0 is given by:

$$a_0 = 2\, EMA_t(n, P) - EMA_t(n, EMA(n, P)). \tag{2.28}$$

In other words, the value of a_0 is estimated as twice the single EMA minus the double EMA.

In the same book, Brown developed the optimal exponential forecast for a process modeled by an m-th degree polynomial plus noise:

$$P_t = a_0 + a_1 t + \frac{a_2}{2} t^2 + \ldots + \frac{a_m}{m!} t^m + \varepsilon_t, \tag{2.29}$$

where $a_0, a_1, \ldots, a_m$ are constants, t is time, and ε_t is a random error term. In this case, the optimal forecast for the future value of the process can be obtained using multiple EMAs of orders from 1 to m. For example, the second-order EMA is simply the double EMA, as it represents the application of the EMA to the EMA itself.

2.5.5 Wilder Moving Average

The Wilder Moving Average (WMA) was introduced by Wilder (1978). Although it is not a conventional moving average and is rarely utilized, it is worth mentioning briefly in this chapter because it shares similarities with the EMA. Specifically, the WMA is calculated using the following formula:

$$WMA_t(n, P) = (1 - \lambda) \sum_{i=0}^{\infty} \lambda^i P_{t-i}. \tag{2.30}$$

Apparently, the formula for the WMA is identical to that of the EMA. However, the distinction between the two lies in how the decay parameter λ is determined. For the WMA, the decay constant is calculated as:

$$\lambda = \frac{n-1}{n}. \tag{2.31}$$

Essentially, the WMA closely mirrors the EMA. Furthermore, when n is relatively large, the decay constant in the WMA becomes almost indistinguishable from that in the EMA.

2.5.6 Illustrations and Discussions

Traders commonly believe that recent prices hold more useful information about where a stock's price might go next compared to older prices. That is why they prefer using moving averages and trend-following rules that give extra weight to the most recent price data. For instance, both the LMA and EMA focus more on recent prices, leading traders to think they are superior to the SMA. To support this idea, traders often rely on visual aids. In the upper panel of Fig. 2.3, there is an example of such an aid. This plot shows the values of the SMA(16) and LMA(16) calculated using monthly closing prices of the S&P 500 index from January 1998 to December 2007. The curves in the plot indicate that the LMA(16) closely trails behind the S&P 500 index with less delay than the SMA(16).

Indeed, the ALT of the LMA is shorter than that of the SMA when both moving averages are calculated using the same window size for averaging. Specifically, the ALT of LMA(n) amounts to 2/3 of the ALT of SMA(n). Does this imply that the LMA is superior to the SMA? While many traders might answer yes to this question, we challenge this belief.

If traders seek a moving average with a shorter lag time, they can achieve this by reducing the window size in the SMA instead of using the LMA. Therefore, a fair comparison of the characteristics of the two moving averages necessitates using the LMA and SMA with identical lag times. The lower panel in Fig. 2.3 displays the values of SMA(11) and LMA(16) computed using the same stock

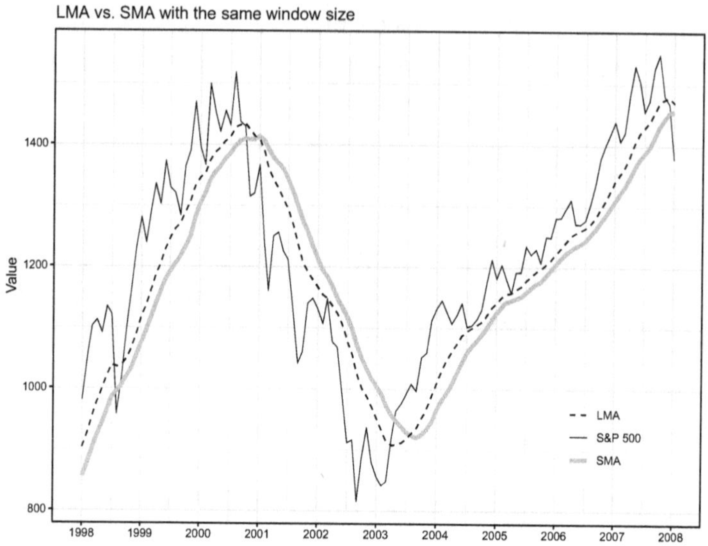

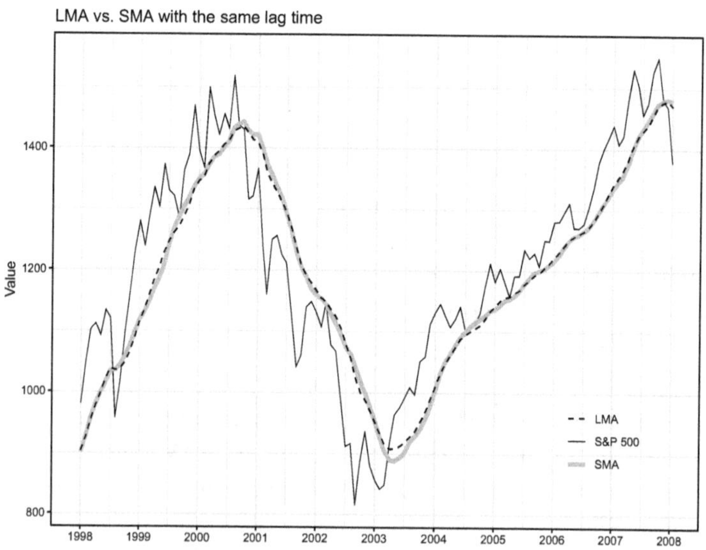

Fig. 2.3 LMA and SMA applied to the monthly closing prices of the S&P 500 index

index values. Both moving averages have a lag time of 5 months. Surprisingly, contrary to the widespread belief that these two types of moving averages are fundamentally distinct, they exhibit close alignment.

To further explain our approach and rationale, suppose we agree that a moving average should be smooth and responsive. To compare the characteristics of two different moving averages, it is logical to ensure that both have the same level of responsiveness and then assess which one is smoother. However, when using a visual aid like the illustration in the lower panel of Fig. 2.3, it is challenging to definitively determine which moving average is superior in terms of smoothness. This highlights the pressing need for a universally accepted metric that can quantify the smoothness of a moving average.

To clarify the root of confusion and elucidate why the SMA and LMA with identical lag times appear highly similar, the left panel of Fig. 2.4 portrays the price weighting functions of SMA(11) and LMA(16). Evidently, these two functions are inherently distinct because each price lag seems to contribute differently to the moving average's value. This discrepancy fuels the belief that the values of these two moving averages differ significantly.

In contrast, the right panel of the same figure depicts the price-change weighting functions of SMA(11) and LMA(16), where both functions appear remarkably similar. Specifically, the disparities between the two price-change weighting functions are negligible. This similarity helps elucidate why the two moving averages closely track each other. As a price-change weighting function indicates the contribution of each price-change lag to the moving average's value, one could argue that it represents the dynamic characteristics of a moving average. Consequently, it could be further argued that a price-change weighting function offers much more pertinent information regarding the properties of a moving average than its corresponding price weighting function.

Traders similarly believe that the EMA is superior to the SMA because the EMA assigns more weight to recent prices. However, confirming this belief is not straightforward. By definition, the lag time of EMA(n) is identical to that of SMA(n), making both moving averages equally responsive.

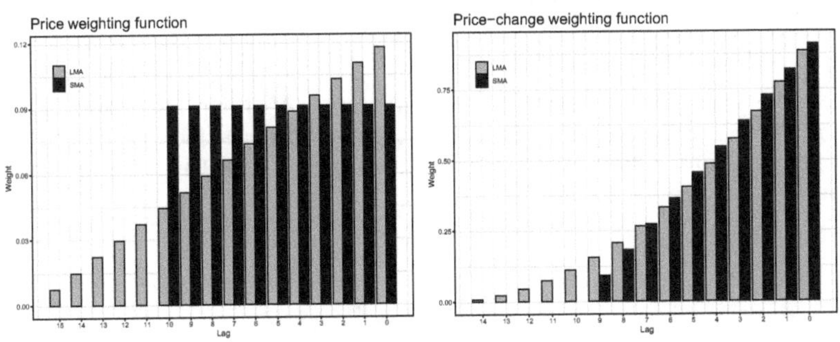

Fig. 2.4 Weighting functions of LMA(16) and SMA(11) with the same lag time of 5 periods. In the price weighting functions, Lag i denotes the lag of P_{t-i}. In the price-change weighting functions, Lag j denotes the lag of ΔP_{t-j}

Is the EMA better than the LMA? Once more, a fair comparison necessitates evaluating the moving averages with the same average lag time. The left panel of Fig. 2.5 displays the price weighting functions of LMA(16) and EMA(11), sharing the same lag time of 5 months. Meanwhile, the right panel in the same figure showcases the price-change weighting functions of LMA(16) and EMA(11). These plots suggest only minimal disparities between the two moving averages. Consequently, the properties of these ostensibly distinct moving averages are largely indistinguishable.

In summary, upon closer examination, it becomes apparent that all conventional moving averages share numerous similarities despite initial perceptions of significant differences. The average lag time of any moving average increases with a larger averaging window size. Consequently, enhancing the responsiveness of a moving average can be achieved through two distinct methods. First, a trader can opt for the LMA(n) with a shorter lag time instead of either the SMA(n) or EMA(n). Alternatively, one can reduce the size of the averaging window in either the SMA(n) or EMA(n). When two different conventional moving averages have the same lag time, the discrepancies between them are minimal.

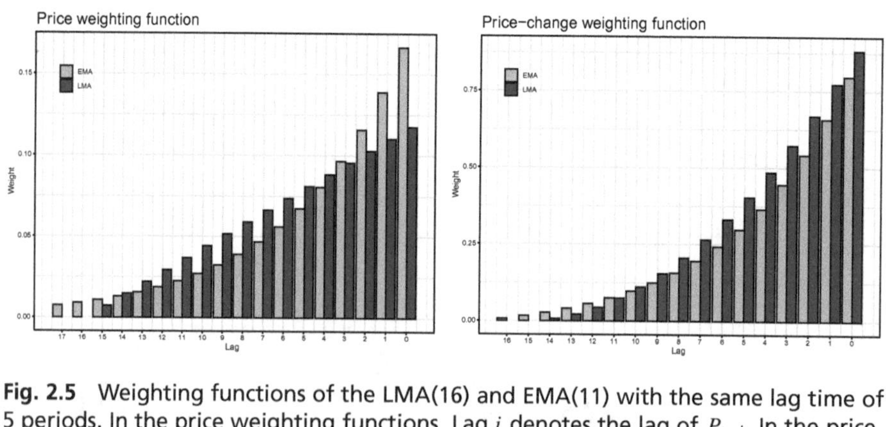

Fig. 2.5 Weighting functions of the LMA(16) and EMA(11) with the same lag time of 5 periods. In the price weighting functions, Lag i denotes the lag of P_{t-i}. In the price-change weighting functions, Lag j denotes the lag of ΔP_{t-j}. The weights of the EMA are cut off at lag 17

2.6 How to Measure Average Lag Time Correctly

At the beginning of this section, let us look into what is measured by the metrics known as the average lag time of a moving average. As suggested by the curves in Fig. 2.2, the average lag is a measure that makes sense only when the price is trending upward. In this case, the average lag time quantifies the time difference between the value of a moving average and the previous price whose value equals the moving average. Formally, at time t, the value of the moving average equals $MA_t(n, P)$, where P denotes the past prices used to compute its value. We identify the first previous price for which the following equality holds: $P_{t-\text{ALT(MA)}} = MA_t(n, P)$. The ALT(MA) represents the delay time.

It is crucial to note that the moving average tends to lag behind the price when prices steadily increase, whereas it leads the price when prices steadily decrease. Consequently, the moving average acts as a lagging indicator only when prices are in an uptrend. When the prices are in a downtrend, the moving average becomes a leading indicator. So, the question arises: why do traders consistently view a moving average as a lagging indicator?

The existence of a lag time suggests there is a delay between price actions occurring and the subsequent response of the moving average. Thus, for a moving average to consistently be a lagging indicator, it is crucial to specify precisely what we mean by "price actions." What exactly are the relevant price actions that correctly determine the lag time of a moving average?

Figure 2.6 motivates how the true average lag time of a moving average should be assessed. This figure depicts the hypothetical price dynamics: prices initially rise, then fall, and subsequently rise again. It is essential to note three distinct periods where prices exhibit trends and two distinct turning points between these trends.

In chronological order, the price actions consist of an uptrend, a turning point, a downtrend, another turning point, and finally, an uptrend again. When considering the price trends, a moving average acts as a lagging indicator during price increases and as a leading indicator during price decreases. However, when focusing on the turning points between these trends, a moving average consistently acts as a lagging indicator. This means that a turning point in a moving average always lags behind a turning point in the price trends.

Consequently, Fig. 2.6 implies that the true lag time of a moving average is the delay between a turning point in the price trend and the corresponding turning point in the moving average. It is important to note that the equality $P_{t-\text{ALT(MA)}} = MA_t(n, P)$ is no longer applicable for computing the true lag

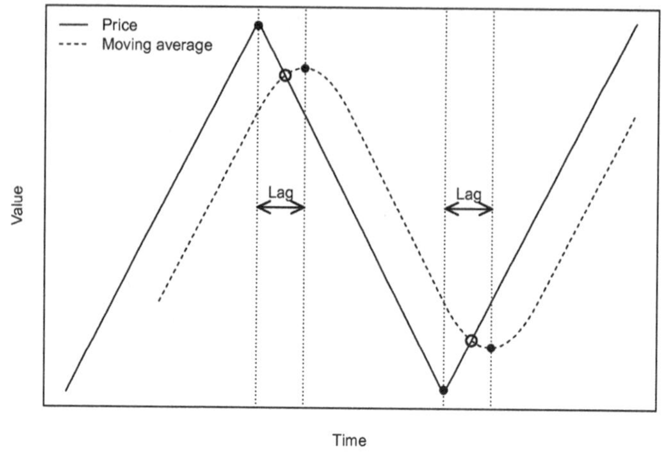

Fig. 2.6 Figure illustrates the correct method for measuring the true average lag time of a moving average. Black circles indicate the peaks and troughs of both the price and its moving average, while hollow circles mark the points where the price crosses the moving average line. The **Lag** represents the true average lag time, defined as the time delay between a turning point in the underlying trend and the corresponding turning point in the moving average

time of a moving average. Instead, we require a completely different condition to measure the average lag time correctly.

To elaborate on the condition for correctly measuring the lag time of a moving average, let us suppose that the one-period change in the stock price is ΔP when prices increase and $-\Delta P$ when prices decrease. It is important to note that we ignore the noise in the prices, as our objective is to compute the average lag time. Additionally, we assume that, on average, the increase in price during an uptrend matches the decrease during a downtrend. This assumption aligns well with observed real-world data.

The simplest method to determine the trend direction is by observing whether the value of the moving average increases or decreases. Specifically, if the value of the moving average rises over a period, the price trend is upward; otherwise, it is downward. Formally, we examine whether the one-period change in the value of the moving average is positive or negative:

$$\Delta MA_t(n) = MA_t(n) - MA_{t-1}(n) = \sum_{i=0}^{n-1} w_i \Delta P_{t-i},$$

where, for simplicity, we assume that the price weights are normalized meaning that $\sum_{i=0}^{n-1} w_i = 1$.

For concreteness, let us assume that the price trend is upward until time t_0. At time t_0, there's a turning point in the trend, indicating that the price trend becomes downward after this time. Under our assumptions, up to and including time t_0, the change in the value of the moving average is given by:

$$\Delta MA_{t_0} = \sum_{i=0}^{n-1} w_i \Delta P = \Delta P > 0.$$

This indicates that the change is positive and equals ΔP.

At time $t = t_0 + 1$, following the change in the price trend direction, the change in the moving average's value becomes:

$$\Delta MA_{t_0+1} = -w_0 \Delta P + \sum_{i=1}^{n-1} w_i \Delta P = \left(\sum_{i=1}^{n-1} w_i - w_0 \right) \Delta P > 0.$$

We assume that at this time, the change in the value of the moving average is positive. Moving forward to time $t = t_0 + 2$, the change in the moving average's value is determined as:

$$\Delta MA_{t_0+2} = \left(\sum_{i=2}^{n-1} w_i - \sum_{i=0}^{1} w_i \right) \Delta P > 0.$$

Again, we assume the change is positive. However, eventually, at time $t = t_0 + k$, the change in the value of the moving average becomes negative:

$$\Delta MA_{t_0+k} = \left(\sum_{i=k}^{n-1} w_i - \sum_{i=0}^{k-1} w_i \right) \Delta P < 0.$$

Consequently, it takes k periods for the moving average to recognize the change in the trend direction.

Based on this explanation, the correct average lag time of a moving average can be computed as:

$$\arg \min_{k \in [1, n-1]} \sum_{i=0}^{k-1} w_i \geq \sum_{i=k}^{n-1} w_i. \tag{2.32}$$

In simpler terms, the true average lag time k represents the minimum number of lags that satisfy the condition where the sum of price weights from lag 0 to lag $k-1$ is greater than or equal to the sum of price weights from lag k to lag $n-1$. Intuitively, the average lag time corresponds to the lag that divides the price weights into two parts, ensuring that the sum of weights in each part is equal. Formally, this can be expressed as:

$$\sum_{i=0}^{k-1} w_i = \sum_{i=k}^{n-1} w_i. \tag{2.33}$$

It is crucial to note that both Eqs. (2.32) and (2.33) are valid regardless of whether the price weights w_i are normalized or not. This is because, without normalization, we must divide both sides of the equations by the sum of all weights. Still, computing the correct average lag time requires finding the lag number that divides the price weights into two equal parts.

Equation (2.33), which determines the correct average lag time of a moving average, appears to be different from the average lag time specified by Eq. (2.5). However, in certain specific cases, both equations yield the same value. For instance, as inferred from Eq. (2.33), when the price weights in the moving average are symmetrical around the middle, the true average lag time of a moving average equals $n/2$. This scenario aligns with the case of the SMA(n), for which the ALT(MA) metric provides essentially the same value.

Generally, the true average lag time of a moving average specified by Eq. (2.33) differs from the ALT(MA) computed using Eq. (2.5). For instance, the ALT(MA) of the LMA(n) is $(n-1)/3 \approx 0.333n$. However, the true average lag time of the LMA(n) is approximately $0.293n$, which is slightly smaller. Similarly, for the EMA(n), the ALT(MA) is $(n-1)/2 \approx 0.5n$, whereas the true average lag time is approximately $0.347n$, significantly smaller in comparison.[2]

Nevertheless, despite demonstrating how to determine correctly the average lag time of a moving average, we will refrain from further elaborating on and utilizing this measure. Our focus in this book is not on measuring the characteristics of individual moving averages but rather on the characteristics of trend-following rules. We argue that the characteristics of individual moving averages are largely irrelevant because traders never rely on a single moving average to determine the trading signal.

The trading signal in a trend-following rule is often determined by the relationship between the last closing price and the value of the moving average. When the last closing price is above the moving average, the trading signal is

[2] We do not show the analytical derivations for the true average lag times of the conventional moving averages because this book primarily aims to quantify the characteristics of trend-following rules, rather than focusing on individual moving averages.

Buy; otherwise, the trading signal is Sell. Therefore, the relevant lag time is the delay between the turning point in the trend and the change in the trading signal. For example, as depicted in Fig. 2.6, the relevant lag time is the time between either the peak or trough in the price trend and the intersection of the price with the value of the moving average. These intersections are depicted by the hollow circles in the figure. Conversely, the true lag time of a moving average is the time between the peak or trough in the price trend and the subsequent peak or trough in the moving average. These points are illustrated by black circles in the figure. Obviously, the average lag time of the considered trading rule is shorter than the true lag time of a moving average.

We argue that not just the average lag time, but all characteristics of individual moving averages are largely irrelevant. This is because trading signals in a trend-following strategy typically arise from the interaction between the most recent closing price and the moving average, or from the relationship between multiple moving averages. Therefore, the focus should be on evaluating the characteristics of trend-following rules, rather than just the characteristics of individual moving averages.

2.7 Fooled by Average Lag Time Measure

In the previous section, we showed that the metric used to calculate the average lag time of a moving average is generally incorrect. However, besides being incorrect, there is another serious problem with this measure. Specifically, this measure creates an impression that the average lag time of a moving average can easily be reduced to zero. Over years, traders have proposed many so-called "zero-lag" moving averages. Examples of these moving averages are the Hull Moving Average (HMA), the End-Point Moving Average (EPMA), and the Zero-Lag Exponential Moving Average (ZLEMA).[3]

To understand how easily the average lag time of a moving average can be manipulated, let us revisit its calculation:

$$\text{ALT}(MA) = \frac{\sum_{i=1}^{n-1} w_i \times i}{\sum_{i=0}^{n-1} w_i} = \sum_{j=0}^{n-2} \theta_j,$$

where w_i represents the price weight and θ_j represents the price-change weight. If we insist that all weights are positive, then the only way to decrease the lag time is by reducing the weights of the most distant price observations.

[3] These moving averages are called "exotic" moving averages and will be discussed later in this book.

However, in doing so, the shortest possible lag time is achieved when all weights focus solely on the most recent price observation. In this scenario, the shortest possible lag time is just one period.

Allowing negative price weights in a moving average can reduce the lag time to zero or even a negative number. In such cases, what was originally a lagged indicator of price action can transform into a coincident or even a leading indicator.

It is puzzling that traders typically aim to construct zero-lag moving averages instead of exploring negative-lag alternatives. If feasible, a negative-lag moving average could offer advantages. Here is why: when small investors employ a trend-following strategy, they typically deal with passive mutual funds tracking indices like the S&P 500. Orders for buying or selling are executed sometimes over several days, not instantly. Hence, having insight into price action ahead of time is preferable.

Traders probably avoid creating negative-lag moving averages because, in this case, they anticipate skepticism. After all, how could a leading indicator be created solely from past prices? This obstacle is less apparent for the potential existence of zero-lag moving averages.

When traders introduce a zero-lag moving average, they typically provide a rule for computation but do not disclose that the lag time reduction is achieved through negative price weights. Not all purported zero-lag moving averages achieve precisely zero lag time. The EPMA is an example of a moving average with exactly zero lag time. The EPMA(n) calculates the average price by fitting a least squares straight line through the most recent n price observations.

The left panel in Fig. 2.7 illustrates the price weighting function of the EPMA(12), while the right panel depicts the price-change weighting function of the EPMA(12). Notably, in this moving average, the distant price weights are negative. Examining the plot of the price-change weighting function reveals that most weights assigned to price changes are negative. Furthermore, given that this moving average achieves zero lag time, the sum of all price-change weights equals zero.

To showcase that the EPMA identifies turning points in price trends with a delay, Fig. 2.8 illustrates its behavior as prices first increase and then decrease. Visual inspection of the curves in the figure confirms that when prices rise or fall, the EPMA shows zero average lag time. For example, during the upward price trend, the moving average line aligns perfectly with the price line. This alignment might create the illusion that the EPMA is a coincident indicator of price action. However, a different perspective emerges when we examine the delay between a price peak and the subsequent peak in the moving average. In this case, it becomes apparent that the delay is not zero at all. For example, the

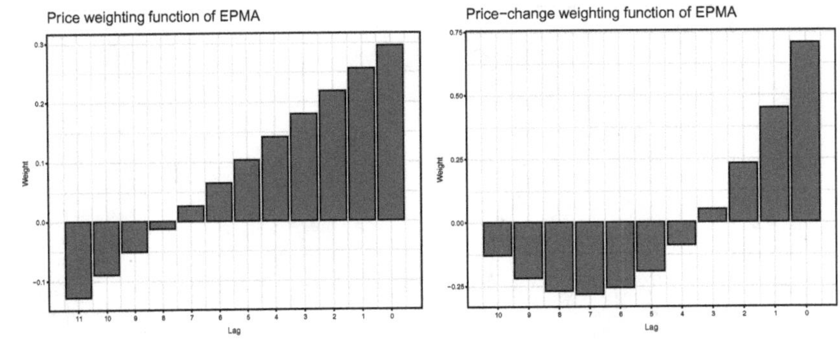

Fig. 2.7 Price weighting function and the price-change weighting function of the EPMA(12)

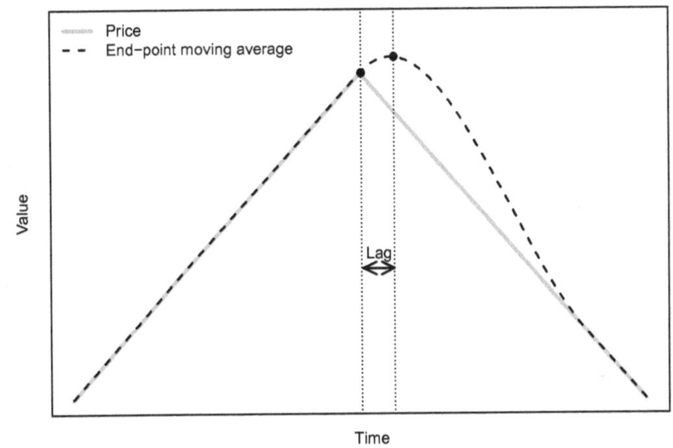

Fig. 2.8 Illustration of average lag time and the true lag time of the EPMA

true average lag time of the EPMA(12) equals two periods. That is, the true average lag time of the EPMA(12) equals that of the SMA(4).

The behavior of the EPMA around a trend reversal mirrors the typical behavior of any zero-lag moving average. Before a trend reversal, the moving average aligns closely with the price line. Following the reversal, the moving average maintains its trajectory, surpassing the price before eventually changing direction. This phenomenon is known as "overshooting." Subsequently, it takes considerable time for the moving average to converge back toward the price.

For illustrative purposes, Fig. 2.9 presents the values of the EPMA(12) and SMA(4) computed using monthly closing prices of the S&P 500 index from January 1998 to December 2007. Despite having the same true lag time, these two distinct moving averages often exhibit non-coinciding values. However,

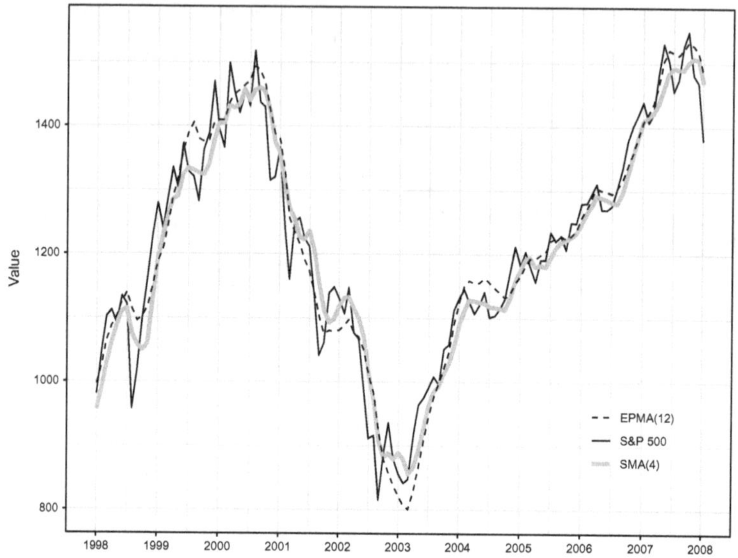

Fig. 2.9 EPMA(12) and SMA(4) applied to the monthly closing prices of the S&P 500 index

our primary observation is that there are no clear indications that definitively establish which of these two moving averages is superior.

2.8 Properties of Moving Averages

For simplicity, we assume that the weights in the moving average are normalized, meaning $\sum_{i=0}^{n-1} w_i = 1$. Under this assumption, the moving average is computed as:

$$MA_t(n, P) = \sum_{i=0}^{n-1} w_i P_{t-i}. \tag{2.34}$$

When the weights are normalized, the moving average represents a weighted mean of the prices. This normalization ensures that the value of the moving average remains in the same range as the input data. Moreover, if the price is constant, the moving average equals this constant value.

If the sum of weights does not equal one, the result of the computation in Eq. (2.34) is not a moving average but a weighted sum. To compute the moving average in such cases, normalization must be applied. The formula becomes:

$$MA_t(n, P) = \frac{\sum_{i=0}^{n-1} w_i P_{t-i}}{\sum_{i=0}^{n-1} w_i},$$

where the denominator, $\sum_{i=0}^{n-1} w_i$, is referred to as the normalization factor. This normalization ensures that the computed value represents the weighted mean of the prices, regardless of the initial sum of the weights. The normalized weight is calculated as:

$$w_i' = \frac{w_i}{\sum_{i=0}^{n-1} w_i},$$

where w_i' is the normalized version of the original weight w_i.

The moving average is computed as the sum of the element-by-element multiplication of the weight vector w and the price vector P. In mathematical terms, this operation is known as *convolution*. Specifically, the convolution of the weight vector $w[t]$ and the price vector $P[t]$ yields the moving average $MA[t]$. This can be expressed as:

$$MA[t] = w[t] * P[t],$$

where the symbol $*$ represents the convolution operation.

To describe the computation more precisely, we use the standard definition of convolution. For the moving average, this results in the following formula:

$$MA[t] = \sum_{i=0}^{n-1} w[i]P[t-i],$$

where the sum represents the weighted sum of the n most recent prices, with the weights given by the vector w. The index $t-i$ shifts the price vector P relative to the weight vector w.

Having established that the moving average computation is a convolution operation, most of the properties of moving averages can be derived from the properties of convolution. The properties of convolution are well known and can be found in many books, for example, in Smith (1997).

First and foremost, convolution is a *linear operation*, meaning that it satisfies both the *additivity* and *homogeneity* properties.

Additivity Property

The additivity property states that the convolution of the sum of two time series $X[t]$ and $Y[t]$ is equal to the sum of their individual convolutions with the same weight vector $w[t]$. In mathematical terms:

$$w[t] * (X[t] + Y[t]) = w[t] * X[t] + w[t] * Y[t].$$

For moving averages, this translates to:

$$MA_t(n, X + Y) = MA_t(n, X) + MA_t(n, Y).$$

This property essentially means that the moving average of the sum of two time series is equal to the sum of their individual moving averages.

Homogeneity Property

The homogeneity property indicates that if a is a scalar, the convolution of the scalar multiplied by a time series is equal to the scalar multiplied by the convolution of the time series. Mathematically, this is expressed as:

$$w[t] * (aP[t]) = a \cdot w[t] * P[t].$$

In terms of moving averages, this becomes:

$$MA_t(n, aP) = a \cdot MA_t(n, P).$$

This property means that scaling the time series by a constant a scales the resulting moving average by the same factor.

Combined Linearity

Combining both the additivity and homogeneity properties gives the following expression for the convolution of a linear combination of two time series:

$$MA_t(n, a \cdot X + b \cdot Y) = a \cdot MA_t(n, X) + b \cdot MA_t(n, Y),$$

where a and b are scalars. This shows that convolution distributes over scalar multiplication and addition, highlighting its linearity.

In addition to linearity, two other fundamental properties of convolution are the *associative* and *commutative* properties.

Associative Property

Let $w_1[t]$ and $w_2[t]$ be two vectors of price weights, each specifying the weights in a particular moving average, denoted as MA_1 and MA_2. Furthermore, assume that the first moving average uses a window of n observations, while the second uses a window of m observations.

The associative property of convolution states that when performing multiple convolutions, the grouping of the functions (or time series) does not affect the result. Mathematically, the associative property can be expressed as:

$$w_2[t] * (w_1[t] * P[t]) = (w_2[t] * w_1[t]) * P[t].$$

In the context of moving averages, this property means that the moving average of another moving average is again a moving average. Specifically, we have:

$$MA_{2,t}(m, MA_1(n, P)) = MA_{3,t}(q, P),$$

where $q = n + m - 1$, and MA_3 is the resulting moving average with price weights w_3, which are computed as:

$$w_3[t] = \sum_{k=0}^{n-1} w_1[k]w_2[t-k], \quad \text{for } t = 0, 1, \ldots, n+m-1. \tag{2.35}$$

Here, we assume that $w_2[i] = 0$ for $i < 0$ or $i > m - 1$, meaning that any indices outside the range of the weight vectors are treated as zero.

For instance, if $n = m = 3$, then the vector w_3 has 5 elements given by the following formulas:

$$\begin{aligned}
w_3[0] &= w_1[0]w_2[0], \\
w_3[1] &= w_1[0]w_2[1] + w_1[1]w_2[0], \\
w_3[2] &= w_1[0]w_2[2] + w_1[1]w_2[1] + w_1[2]w_2[0], \\
w_3[3] &= w_1[1]w_2[2] + w_1[2]w_2[1], \\
w_3[4] &= w_1[2]w_2[2].
\end{aligned}$$

This example illustrates how the weights of the composite moving average MA_3 are computed by convolving the two weight vectors w_1 and w_2. The resulting vector w_3 has a length of $n + m - 1$, which corresponds to the combined window size of the two moving averages.

Using linear algebra, the weight vector $\mathbf{w}_3$ can be computed as a matrix multiplication. Specifically, the vector $\mathbf{w}_3 = [w_3[0], w_3[1], w_3[2], w_3[3], w_3[4]]$ is the result of multiplying the weight vector $\mathbf{w}_1 = [w_1[0], w_1[1], w_1[2]]$ with a matrix constructed from the vector $\mathbf{w}_2 = [w_2[0], w_2[1], w_2[2]]$. The matrix is defined as follows:

$$\mathbf{W}_2 = \begin{bmatrix} w_2[0] & w_2[1] & w_2[2] & 0 & 0 \\ 0 & w_2[0] & w_2[1] & w_2[2] & 0 \\ 0 & 0 & w_2[0] & w_2[1] & w_2[2] \end{bmatrix}.$$

This matrix represents a shifted version of the vector $\mathbf{w}_2$, where each row corresponds to a shift in the weight vector.

This multiplication can be written as:

$$\mathbf{w}_3 = \mathbf{w}_1 \cdot \mathbf{W}_2.$$

The associative property of convolution allows us to group convolutions in any order, meaning that the convolution of a time series with the result of another convolution is equivalent to convolving the weight vectors first and then applying the result to the time series. This property ensures that the moving average of a moving average yields another moving average, maintaining consistency in the analysis.

Commutative Property

The commutative property of convolution states that the order in which the operands are convolved does not affect the result. In other words, for two vectors $w_1[t]$ and $w_2[t]$, their convolution satisfies the following equation:

$$w_1[t] * w_2[t] = w_2[t] * w_1[t].$$

In the context of moving averages, this property means that the order of applying two moving averages does not impact the final result. Specifically, if we compute a moving average of a moving average, the order of operations can be reversed without changing the outcome. Mathematically, this can be expressed as:

$$MA_{2,t}(m, MA_1(n, P)) = MA_{1,t}(n, MA_2(m, P)).$$

This means that when calculating a moving average of a moving average, we can either first compute the moving average MA_1 of the price data P, and then apply the second moving average MA_2 to the result, or first compute MA_2 of the price data P and then apply MA_1 to the result. Both methods will yield the same final moving average.

The commutative property reflects the fact that the process of applying weights to data, whether it is price data $P[t]$ or a previous moving average, does not depend on the order in which the operations are performed. This is especially useful in time series analysis, where the results of weighted averaging (moving averages) remain consistent, regardless of how we sequence the individual steps. In practice, this allows flexibility in choosing the order of operations when combining multiple moving averages, providing more options for data preprocessing or smoothing without altering the overall outcome.

The commutative property also implies that the weight vector w_3, rather than being computed using Eq. (2.35), can alternatively be calculated as follows:

$$w_3[t] = \sum_{k=0}^{m-1} w_2[k]w_1[t-k], \quad \text{for } t = 0, 1, \ldots, n+m-1. \tag{2.36}$$

This form of the weight vector computation reflects the interchangeability of the two weight vectors w_1 and w_2 in the convolution, consistent with the commutative property of the operation.

Convolution Power and Central Limit Theorem

Consider a vector of price weights w of length n. Suppose we perform the convolution of this vector with itself k times. This operation is known as the convolution power, and is denoted by w^{*k}, which can be formally expressed as:

$$w^{*k}[t] = \underbrace{w[t] * w[t] * \ldots * w[t]}_{k \text{ times}}.$$

In the context of moving averages, a twofold convolution corresponds to a double-smoothed moving average, a threefold convolution represents a triple-smoothed moving average, and so on. More generally, the convolution power represents a multi-step smoothed moving average, where the number of steps is indicated by the power k.

A crucial question is: what is the distribution of weights in a k-smoothed moving average as k becomes large? The Central Limit Theorem (CLT) provides the answer. As the convolution power k increases, the distribution of the weights in the resulting moving average approaches the Gaussian (Normal) distribution.

This result holds true regardless of the original distribution of weights in a single moving average. In other words, no matter the form of the weight vector w (whether it is uniform, exponential, or any other distribution), as k becomes large, the weight distribution in a multiple-smoothed moving average tends to resemble the Gaussian distribution. The CLT suggests that the repeated application of convolution effectively "smooths out" the weight distribution, causing it to converge to a normal distribution with increasing k.

Thus, the convolution power serves as a natural mechanism for smoothing data. As the number of smoothing operations increases, the distribution of weights in a multiple-smoothed moving average gradually becomes more symmetric and bell-shaped, ultimately approximating the well-known Gaussian distribution.

Indeed, when the price weights are normalized, they can be interpreted as the probability distribution function (PDF) of a discrete random variable. Convolution of two PDFs results in a new PDF, which represents the probability distribution of the sum of two independent random variables. Extending this idea, the k-th convolution power represents the PDF of the sum of k independent random variables, all with identical distributions.

According to the CLT, as the number of independent random variables increases, the distribution of their sum (or average) converges to the Gaussian distribution, regardless of the original distribution of the individual variables. Therefore, the CLT provides a solid theoretical foundation for the convergence of the weights in a multiple-smoothed moving average to a normal distribution as the number of convolutions increases.

This result underscores that the repeated application of convolution not only smooths the data but also results in a distribution that is increasingly concentrated around the mean, with decreasing skewness and kurtosis. This behavior is characteristic of Gaussian distributions, reinforcing the link between convolution and the CLT. As a consequence, the moving average process, when performed iteratively (through repeated convolution), naturally leads to a smoothing mechanism that asymptotically behaves like a normal distribution, even if the initial weights deviate from it.

Thus, the convolution power does not just smooth the data but also brings it closer to a Gaussian form, which is particularly useful in statistical analysis, signal processing, and various fields that rely on the properties of normal distributions for making predictions and decisions.

2.9 Properties of the Average Lag Time Measure

Average Lag Time of Multiple-Smoothed Moving Averages

When the weights of a moving average are normalized so that $\sum_{i=0}^{n-1} w_i = 1$, the average lag time of a moving average, denoted by $\mathrm{ALT}(MA)$, is given by:

$$\mathrm{ALT}(MA) = \sum_{i=0}^{n-1} w_i \cdot i. \tag{2.37}$$

Now, consider the vector of normalized price weights, $w = [w_0, w_1, \ldots, w_{n-1}]$, where n represents the length of the vector. We can interpret these weights as a probability distribution by defining a discrete random variable x that takes values from the set $\{0, 1, \ldots, n-1\}$, with probabilities:

$$P(x = i) = w_i, \quad \text{for} \quad i = 0, 1, \ldots, n-1.$$

The expected value (mean) of this random variable, denoted $\bar{x}$, is given by:

$$\bar{x} = E[x] = \sum_{i=0}^{n-1} i \cdot w_i. \tag{2.38}$$

By comparing Eqs. (2.37) and (2.38), we see that the average lag time of a moving average is equivalent to the expected value of the corresponding probability distribution. This interpretation provides a probabilistic perspective on the ALT(MA) measure, reinforcing its role as a weighted average of time indices.

As the k-th convolution power corresponds to the PDF of the sum of k independent and identically distributed (i.i.d.) random variables, the expected value of this convolution power is the sum of the expected values of the individual random variables. Thus, for k independent random variables x_i with identical distributions, the expected value of the sum is:

$$E\left[\sum_{i=1}^{k} x_i\right] = \sum_{i=1}^{k} E[x_i] = k \cdot \bar{x}.$$

In the context of moving averages, when the moving average is applied iteratively (i.e., multiple convolutions of the moving average), the average lag time of the multiple-smoothed moving average is simply the sum of the average lag times of the individual moving averages. This relationship is expressed as:

$$\mathrm{ALT}(MA^{*k}) = k \cdot \mathrm{ALT}(MA),$$

where MA^{*k} denotes the application of the moving average to itself k times. Thus, the average lag time of a multiple-smoothed moving average grows linearly with the number of iterations, k, reflecting the cumulative effect of smoothing over successive iterations.[4]

Additionally, the ALT of the moving average of a moving average is the sum of the ALT values of each individual moving average. Specifically, for two moving averages MA_1 and MA_2, we have the following relationship:

$$ALT(MA_2(MA_1)) = ALT(MA_1) + ALT(MA_2).$$

In other words, when applying a moving average (such as MA_2) to a time series that has already been smoothed by another moving average (such as MA_1), the total delay (or lag time) is the sum of the lag times of each individual moving average. Each additional application of a moving average adds its own ALT to the total delay of the smoothed series.

Linearity of the Average Lag Time Measure

Consider a moving average with normalized weights, i.e., $\sum_{i=0}^{n-1} w_i = 1$. In this setting, the moving average of prices and its average lag time, denoted by $\mathrm{ALT}(MA)$, are defined as:

$$MA_t(n, P) = \sum_{i=0}^{n-1} w_i \, P_{t-i}, \quad \mathrm{ALT}(MA) = \sum_{i=0}^{n-1} w_i \cdot i.$$

Now, consider a moving average that is a linear combination of k moving averages. Without loss of generality—and for simplicity—assume that each of these moving averages has the same window size n. Then, we can express the combined moving average as:

[4] Note also that the window size of a multiple-smoothed moving average grows approximately linearly with the number of iterations. Specifically, if the window size of a single moving average is n, then the window size of a k-smoothed moving average is given by $k(n-1)+1$.

$$MA_t(n, P) = \sum_{j=1}^{k} a_j MA_{j,t}(n, P) = \sum_{j=1}^{k} a_j \sum_{i=0}^{n-1} w_{j,i} \, P_{t-i}, \qquad (2.39)$$

where $\{a_1, a_2, \ldots, a_k\}$ is a set of real coefficients and $\{w_{j,0}, w_{j,1}, \ldots, w_{j,n-1}\}$ are the normalized weights of the moving average MA_j. Note that Eq. (2.39) suggests that the weight w_i in the moving average $MA_t(n, P)$ is given by:

$$w_i = \sum_{j=1}^{k} a_j w_{j,i}, \quad i \in [0, 1, \ldots, n-1].$$

Proposition 2.1 *The average lag time of a moving average formed as a linear combination of moving averages equals the corresponding linear combination of the individual average lag times:*

$$ALT(MA) = \sum_{j=1}^{k} a_j \, ALT(MA_j).$$

Proof By definition, the average lag time of MA is:

$$\mathrm{ALT}(MA) = \sum_{i=0}^{n-1} w_i \cdot i.$$

Substituting the expression for the combined weights yields:

$$\mathrm{ALT}(MA) = \sum_{i=0}^{n-1} \left(\sum_{j=1}^{k} a_j w_{j,i} \right) \cdot i. = \sum_{j=1}^{k} a_j \sum_{i=0}^{n-1} w_{j,i} \cdot i$$
$$= \sum_{j=1}^{k} a_j \, \mathrm{ALT}(MA_j),$$

since, by definition, $\mathrm{ALT}(MA_j) = \sum_{i=0}^{n-1} w_{j,i} \cdot i$. *This completes the proof.*

A key requirement is that the normalized weights of a moving average must sum to one. In the case of a combined moving average, we have:

$$\sum_{i=0}^{n-1} w_i = \sum_{j=1}^{k} a_j \sum_{i=0}^{n-1} w_{j,i} = 1.$$

Since each individual moving average is normalized (i.e., $\sum_{i=0}^{n-1} w_{j,i} = 1$ for every j), it follows that the coefficients of the linear combination must satisfy:

$$\sum_{j=1}^{k} a_j = 1.$$

For example, consider the case with $k = 2$. The normalization condition becomes:

$$a_1 + a_2 = 1.$$

This means that once a_1 is chosen, a_2 must be $a_2 = 1 - a_1$.

When the coefficients a_j are strictly positive, one might construct a moving average as:

$$MA_t(n, P) = 0.5 \cdot MA_{1,t} + 0.5 \cdot MA_{2,t}.$$

However, the coefficients a_j are not required to be strictly positive. For instance, one could also define:

$$MA_t(n, P) = 1.5 \cdot MA_{1,t} - 0.5 \cdot MA_{2,t}.$$

As an illustration of how the average lag time behaves under linear combinations, consider the moving average:

$$0.5 \cdot SMA(n) + 0.5 \cdot LMA(n),$$

where $SMA(n)$ and $LMA(n)$ denote two different moving averages. Its average lag time is given by:

$$ALT\Big(0.5 \cdot SMA(n) + 0.5 \cdot LMA(n)\Big) \\ = 0.5 \cdot ALT\big(SMA(n)\big) + 0.5 \cdot ALT\big(LMA(n)\big).$$

Another interesting example involves a double moving average. Let MA be any moving average and let $MA(MA)$ denote its double moving average.

Then, by linearity:

$$ALT\big(2 \cdot MA - MA(MA)\big) = 2 \cdot ALT(MA) - ALT\big(MA(MA)\big).$$

Since it holds that $ALT\big(MA(MA)\big) = 2 \cdot ALT(MA)$, we obtain:

$$ALT\big(2 \cdot MA - MA(MA)\big) = 2 \cdot ALT(MA) - 2 \cdot ALT(MA) = 0.$$

Remarkably, this construction yields a moving average $2 \cdot MA - MA(MA)$ with an average lag time of zero!

2.10 Summary

In this chapter, we began by defining the general weighted moving average of past prices. Essentially, the concept of a weighted moving average is quite straightforward. It entails calculating a weighted sum of historical prices over a specified window length. It is important to note that every moving average adheres to this definition. Nevertheless, there is an ongoing debate among traders about the most effective weighting scheme for a moving average.

Conventional types of moving averages start with the Simple Moving Average (SMA), where each price carries equal weight in the calculation. Despite being the oldest and perhaps the most widely used moving average in practice, many traders find the SMA suboptimal. This is because distant price observations hold the same weight as recent ones in the SMA computation. Traders typically believe that recent prices contain more relevant information about future price direction compared to older prices. Hence, they argue that a moving average should assign larger weights to the most recent price data.

Moving averages that give more weight to recent prices include the Linear Moving Average (LMA) and the Exponential Moving Average (EMA). In the LMA, the weights assigned to prices decrease linearly, whereas in the EMA, they decrease exponentially. One distinct feature of the EMA is that it is calculated based on the concept of an averaging window of theoretically infinite size. However, because the price weights decrease rapidly, prices from the distant past have practically no influence on the EMA value.

Usually, traders define the EMA based on the averaging window size, as is customary for all moving averages. However, this window size is employed to calculate the decay constant, which governs the rate of decrease for the price weights in the EMA. Once the decay constant is determined, the EMA is computed using an averaging window of infinite size.

We also introduced an alternative way to represent moving averages, which involves the last closing price and the weighted moving average of the price changes within the averaging window. We argued that this alternative presentation, focusing on price changes, is superior to the standard representation in terms of prices. Our rationale stems from the observation that consecutive prices largely overlap, leading to the concealment of the incremental information provided by each new price. By considering price changes, which exhibit only a weak dependence, one can better discern the role and significance of each new piece of incremental information from consecutive prices.

A moving average serves to smooth prices in order to highlight the direction of the trend. However, since it relies on past prices, there is a delay between price actions and the moving average's response to them. Hence, traders look for a moving average that is smooth and responsive. Over time, traders have introduced different types of moving averages, often asserting each new type's superiority over existing ones. However, these claims of superiority lack scientific support and are mostly based on anecdotal evidence and visual demonstrations.

Determining the superiority of different types of moving averages requires establishing a set of desirable properties they should possess. In order to compare and contrast the properties of different moving averages, these properties must be assessed using quantitative metrics. Currently, the average lag time of a moving average is the only commonly accepted metric traders use to measure its responsiveness.

We provided a detailed explanation of the measure used to evaluate the average lag time of a moving average. Subsequently, we presented analytical solutions for the average lag times of conventional moving averages. These solutions indicate that the lag time of the LMA is shorter than that of the SMA. However, by definition, the EMA and SMA lag times are the same when computed using the same averaging window. Furthermore, these solutions suggest that the delay time increases as the size of the averaging window increases. Consequently, we conclude that the lag time of a moving average can be reduced in two ways: first, by using a moving average that places greater emphasis on the most recent prices, and second, by decreasing the size of the averaging window in a moving average.

Traders commonly view the LMA as superior to the SMA due to its greater responsiveness. However, we argued that this perception holds true only when both moving averages are computed using the same averaging window. To accurately compare the properties of two different moving averages, it is crucial to ensure that they have the same lag time. We then demonstrated, using visual aids, that all conventional moving averages exhibit similar behavior when they share the same lag time.

Following this, we contended that the average lag time measure generally inaccurately evaluates the average lag time of a moving average. We demonstrated the correct method for measuring the average lag time of a moving average. Furthermore, we illustrated that a commonly used metric for assessing the average lag time of a moving average measures the delay time accurately only when a moving average employs a weighting scheme that is symmetrical around the center.

Afterward, we contended that the commonly used metric for assessing the average lag time has another significant issue besides its inaccuracy. Specifically, it creates the impression that one can reduce the average lag time of a moving average to zero. As a result of this impression, over the years, traders have put forward numerous so-called "zero-lag" moving averages. However, we illustrated that zero-lag moving averages, in reality, still have non-zero lag times.

Finally, this chapter examined the mathematical properties of moving averages, highlighting their linearity, associativity, commutativity, and convolution. It was demonstrated that moving averages are linear, satisfying both additivity and homogeneity, and can be understood as a convolution of weight and price vectors. The order in which moving averages are applied does not affect the outcome, illustrating their associativity and commutativity. When applied repeatedly, moving averages produce a weight distribution that increasingly resembles a Gaussian distribution, as explained by the Central Limit Theorem. The chapter also addressed the property of average lag time, noting that it increases with each application of the moving average, and explained that the total lag time for multiple applications is simply the sum of individual lags.

References

Brown, R. G. (1963). *Smoothing, Forecasting and Prediction of Discrete Time Series.* Prentice-Hall.

Ehlers, J. F. (2002). Zero-Lag Data Smoothers. *Technical Analysis of Stocks & Commodities, Volue, 20*(7), 26–31.

Ehlers, J. F. (2004). *Cybernetic Analysis for Stocks and Futures: Cutting-Edge DSP Technology to Improve Your Trading.* Wiley.

Smith, S. W. (1997). *The Scientist and Engineer's Guide to Digital Signal Processing.* California Technical Pub.

Wilder, J. W. (1978). New Concepts in Technical Trading Systems. *Trend Research.*

Zakamulin, V. (2017). *Market Timing with Moving Averages: The Anatomy and Performance of Trading Rules.* Palgrave.

3

Trend-Following Trading Rules and Their Anatomy

3.1 Introduction

Trend-following strategies are popular among both individual traders and institutional investors. They can be applied to various asset classes, including stocks, bonds, currencies, and commodities. Trend-following strategies are rooted in the concept that once a trend is established in the market, it is more likely to continue than reverse in the near future. Therefore, the core idea is to identify and follow the direction of prevailing trends, whether upward or downward, and to position oneself accordingly to profit from those trends.

Traders and investors use various trading rules to identify the direction of trends in asset prices. Once a trend is identified, the strategy involves entering positions in the direction of the trend. This could mean buying an asset that is trending upward or selling an asset that is trending downward. In the context of this book, entry and exit points are determined by signals produced by trading rules based on moving averages of historical prices.

A "trading rule" outlines how a trading signal is determined. For instance, consider this example: "If the current stock price exceeds its 200-day moving average, buy the stock. Conversely, sell the stock if the current price falls below the 200-day moving average." In this scenario, the trend direction hinges on the relationship between the current price and the 200-day moving average. When the current price of the stock is above the moving average, it suggests an uptrend, indicating a buying opportunity. Conversely, when the price is below the moving average, it signals a downtrend, prompting a sell decision.

A "technical indicator" within a trading rule refers to a specific mathematical calculation employed by traders to analyze historical price data and predict

V. Zakamulin and J. Giner, *The Ultimate Moving Average Handbook*,
https://doi.org/10.1007/978-3-031-90907-8_3

future price movements in financial markets. In the example provided earlier, the technical indicator is determined as follows:

$$I_t^{\mathrm{TR}} = P_t - MA_t(200, P),$$

where I_t^{TR} represents the value of the technical indicator within the trading rule denoted by TR, P_t denotes the current closing price, while $MA_t(200, P)$ represents the 200-day moving average of prices.

Subsequently, the value of the technical indicator translates into the trading signal according to the following rule:

$$\text{Signal}_{t+1} = \begin{cases} \text{Buy} & \text{if } I_t^{TR} > 0, \\ \text{Sell} & \text{if } I_t^{TR} \leq 0. \end{cases} \tag{3.1}$$

In other words, the trading signal is to Buy when the value of the technical indicator is positive and Sell otherwise. It is important to note that the trading signal, denoted as Signal_{t+1}, is generated at the end of period t and applies to period $t + 1$. For instance, if the trading signal indicates Buy, a trader purchases the stock at the end of period t and retains it until at least the end of the subsequent period, $t + 1$. If the trader already possesses the stock during period t, they maintain ownership throughout the following period.

In this chapter, our objective is to introduce the standard trend-following rules that rely on moving averages of prices and explain their anatomy. These rules include the price and moving average crossover rule, the double moving average crossover rule, the momentum rule, and the moving average direction rule. Depending on the rule, the technical indicator is calculated using either the change in a single moving average, the relationship between the latest price and the moving average of past prices, or the relationship between two moving averages calculated using different numbers of past prices.

It is noteworthy that in any trend-following rule, the technical indicator is consistently computed using historical prices, including the current price:

$$I_t^{TR} = f(P_t, P_{t-1}, P_{t-2}, \ldots),$$

where $f(\cdot)$ represents the mathematical function dictating how the value of the technical trading indicator is calculated, and P_{t-i} is the price at time $t - i$. Subsequently, the generation of the trading signal in any rule is determined by the sign of the computed value, as depicted in Eq. (3.1).

After describing the trend-following rules, we demonstrate that the technical indicator in any of these rules, which utilizes the latest price and either a single moving average or multiple moving averages of prices, can be represented by a single weighted sum of prices:

$$I_t^{TR} = \sum_{i=0}^{n} \upsilon_i P_{t-i},$$

where υ_i represents the weight of price P_{t-i}, and the sum of all weights equals zero.

Furthermore, we demonstrate that the technical indicator in any trend-following rule utilizing the latest price and either a single moving average or multiple moving averages of prices can be expressed by a single moving average of price changes or returns:

$$I_t^{TR} = \sum_{i=0}^{n-1} \theta_i \Delta P_{t-i} = \sum_{i=0}^{n-1} \theta_i r_{t-i},$$

where θ_i is the weight of $\Delta P_{t-i} = P_{t-i} - P_{t-i-1}$, which represents the change in price from time $t - i - 1$ to time $t - i$, and $r_{t-i} = \Delta P_{t-i}/P_{t-i-1}$ denotes the return over the same time interval. The sum of all weights θ_i is positive and can be normalized to one. We argue that this representation offers the most insightful information regarding the economic intuition behind the trading rule and its characteristics, including smoothness and responsiveness.

In concluding this chapter, we convincingly demonstrate that assessing the properties of a single particular moving average of prices is largely irrelevant in practical applications because trading signals in trend-following rules are rarely generated solely based on the value of a single moving average. Therefore, the focus must be shifted toward evaluating the properties of a trading rule. Furthermore, we illustrate that there is a direct link between the shape of the weighting function for returns and key properties of the trading rule, such as smoothness and responsiveness.

3.2 Trading Rules

3.2.1 Price and Moving Average Crossover Rule

On any trading platform, traders can view the historical price line of a stock. To smooth out price fluctuations and emphasize the direction of the trend, traders can request that a trading platform displays a moving average line alongside the price line. How can one determine the current trend direction by examining the price and moving average lines?

In the previous chapter, we illustrated that when prices trend upward, resulting in a positive average price change, the moving average tends to fall below the current price. Conversely, when prices trend downward, leading to a negative average price change, the moving average typically rises above the current price. Moreover, the trend's strength correlates with the distance between the current price and the moving average of past prices, with a stronger trend characterized by a greater separation between the two.

As a result, the relationship between the last price and the moving average of past prices suggests the following trading rule: buy the financial asset when the price surpasses the moving average and sell the asset when the price falls below the moving average. The alteration in the trading signal occurs when the price intersects the moving average. In particular, when the price crosses the moving average from below, a Sell signal transitions into a Buy signal. Conversely, when the price crosses the moving average from above, a Buy signal transforms into a Sell signal.

Therefore, the trend direction can be determined using the following rule:

$$\text{Trend direction} = \begin{cases} \text{Upward} & \text{if } P_t - MA_t(n, P) > 0, \\ \text{Downward} & \text{if } P_t - MA_t(n, P) \leq 0, \end{cases}$$

where P_t is the last observed price and $MA_t(n, P)$ denotes the moving average computed using n last historical prices.

This rule is commonly known as the price and moving average crossover rule. The calculation of the technical indicator in this rule involves subtracting the moving average value from the last closing price:

$$I_t^{\text{P-MA}}(n) = P_t - MA_t(n, P).$$

In this equation, $I_t^{\text{P-MA}}(n)$ represents the technical indicator for the price and moving average crossover rule at time t.

We denote this rule as the P-MA rule. This notation underscores how the trading signal in this rule is derived. Here, "MA" denotes a general weighted moving average. Conventional types of moving averages include the Simple Moving Average (SMA), Linear Moving Average (LMA), and Exponential Moving Average (EMA). Consequently, the P-SMA rule signifies the price and simple moving average crossover. Similarly, the P-LMA and P-EMA rules represent the price and linear and exponential moving average crossovers, respectively.

For illustrative purposes, the upper panel in Fig. 3.1 plots the daily prices of the S&P 500 index from January 1998 to December 2007, along with the values of the 200-day SMA. The shaded areas in this plot represent the periods during which this rule generates a Sell signal. The lower panel in the same figure displays the values of the technical trading indicator for the P-SMA(200) rule.

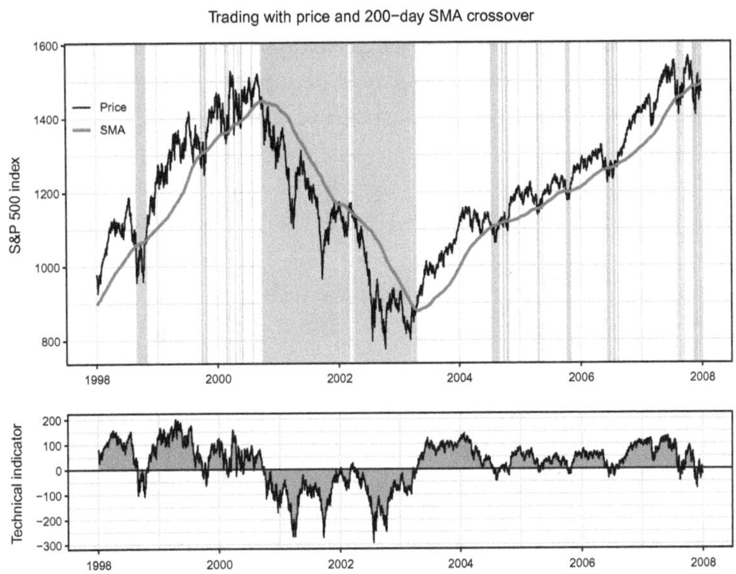

Fig. 3.1 Trading with the price and 200-day SMA crossover. The upper panel plots the daily prices of the S&P 500 index from January 1998 to December 2007, along with the values of the 200-day SMA. The shaded areas in this plot represent the periods during which this rule generates a Sell signal. The lower panel displays the values of the technical trading indicator for the P-SMA(200) rule

3.2.2 Double Moving Average Crossover Rule

Due to the inherent fluctuations in prices, the trading signal produced by the P-MA rule tends to be noisy, lacking consistency and smoothness. Consequently, it is common to encounter situations where the technical indicator initially suggests one direction, only to swiftly change to the opposite signal unexpectedly. This issue arises not from the frequency of trading signals but rather from the majority of these signals being false, as they go against the prevailing trend. Such false trading signals are commonly referred to as "whipsaws."

When traders are said to be whipsawed, it means they experience losses or setbacks due to these false signals, especially when they must pay trading costs.

This phenomenon can be frustrating and challenging for traders, undermining their attempts to accurately predict market movements and make profitable trades. To mitigate the impact of whipsaws, traders often employ the double moving average crossover rule.

As the name suggests, the double moving average crossover strategy utilizes two moving averages: one fast (short) and responsive, and the other slow (long) and smooth. Specifically, the fast moving average employs an averaging window of size s, while the slow moving average uses an averaging window of size l, where $l > s$. Typically, both moving averages are of the same type.

The technical trading indicator of the double moving average crossover rule is calculated as follows:

$$I_t^{\text{MA-C}}(s, l) = MA_t(s, P) - MA_t(l, P). \tag{3.2}$$

In this equation, $I_t^{\text{MA-C}}(s, l)$ represents the technical indicator for the double moving average crossover rule at time t, $MA_t(s, P)$ denotes the fast moving average computed using s last historical prices, and $MA_t(l, P)$ represents the slow moving average computed using l last prices.

We denote this rule as the MA-C rule. When specifying that the double moving average crossover employs a particular type of conventional moving average, we utilize the notation SMA-C, LMA-C, or EMA-C. For instance, the notation SMA-C indicates that the crossover rule utilizes the simple moving average.

When prices trend upward, the slow moving average typically falls below the fast moving average. In contrast, when prices trend downward, the slow moving average tends to rise above the fast moving average. Furthermore, the stronger the trend, the larger the distance between the fast and slow moving averages.

A crossover occurs when the fast moving average crosses the slow moving average either from below or from above. The former crossover is commonly referred to as a bullish crossover or a "golden cross." Conversely, the latter crossover is often termed a bearish crossover or a "death cross." The most typical combination in trading involves utilizing two simple moving averages with window sizes of 50 and 200 days.

It is worth noting the evident relationship:

$$I_t^{\text{MA-C}}(1, n) = I_t^{\text{P-MA}}(n).$$

In simpler terms, the double moving average crossover rule simplifies to the price and moving average crossover rule when the size of the shorter averaging window reduces to one.

For illustrative purposes, the upper panel in Fig. 3.2 plots the daily prices of the S&P 500 index from January 1998 to December 2007, along with the values of the 50- and 200-day SMAs. The shaded areas in this plot represent the periods during which this rule generates a Sell signal. The lower panel in the same figure displays the values of the technical trading indicator for the SMA-C(50,200) rule.

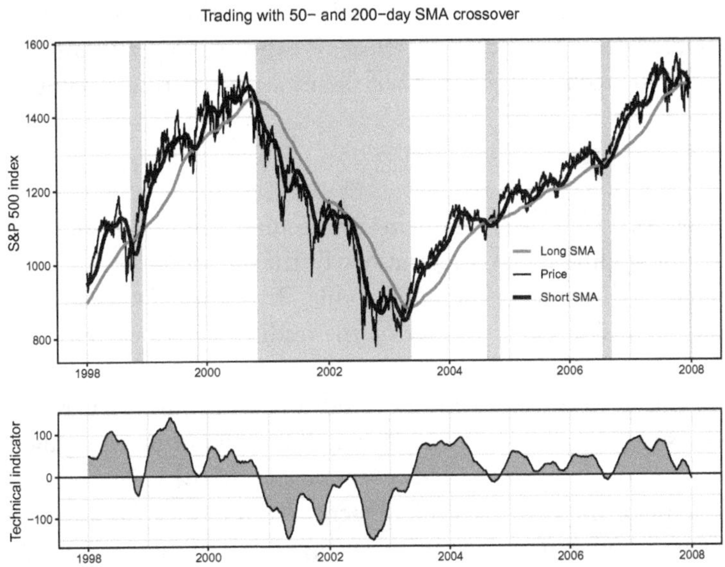

Fig. 3.2 Trading with the 50- and 200-day SMA crossover. The upper panel plots the daily values of the S&P 500 index over the period from January 1998 to December 2007, as well as the values of the 50- and 200-day SMAs. The shaded areas in this plot represent the periods during which this rule generates a Sell signal. The lower panel displays the values of the technical trading indicator for the SMA-C(50,200) rule

Comparing the number of Sell signals between the P-SMA(200) rule (depicted in Fig. 3.1) and the SMA-C(50,200) rule (shown in Fig. 3.2) provides valuable insights. From 1998 to 2008, the P-SMA(200) rule generated 49 Sell signals, roughly equivalent to 5 signals per year. In contrast, the SMA-C(50,200) rule only produced 6 Sell signals, approximately once every 2 years. This means that switching from the P-SMA(200) rule to the SMA-C(50,200) rule leads to a significant eightfold decrease in the number of trading signals. Excessive trading, especially when transaction costs are substantial, can erode the benefits of trend-following investing due to frequent whipsaws. Even in scenarios with minimal transaction costs, opting for less trading is preferred because it helps traders avoid emotional decision-making and adhere to a well-considered long-term investment strategy.

3.2.3 Momentum Rule

The momentum rule is perhaps the simplest and most fundamental trend-following rule. In this rule, the last closing price P_t is compared with the closing price $n - 1$ periods ago, P_{t-n+1}. A Buy signal is triggered when the current closing price exceeds the closing price from $n - 1$ periods ago. Essentially, this rule assumes that if prices have been rising (falling) over the last $n - 1$ periods, they will likely continue to rise (fall) in the next period. In simpler terms, the trend observed over the past $n - 1$ periods is expected to persist into the future.

Formally, the technical indicator of the momentum rule is computed as:

$$I_t^{\text{MOM}}(n) = P_t - P_{t-n+1}. \tag{3.3}$$

In this equation, $I_t^{\text{MOM}}(n)$ represents the technical indicator for the momentum rule. The trading signal is determined by the sign of this technical indicator.

We refer to this rule as the MOM rule. To indicate the number of past observations considered in computing the trading signal, we use the notation MOM(n).

In this book, we focus solely on trend-following rules that rely on moving averages of past prices. At first glance, the momentum rule might appear unrelated to moving averages. However, the MOM(n) rule can be viewed as a specific type of the P-MA(n) rule. Essentially, the price P_{t-n+1} from $n - 1$ periods ago can be seen as the moving average value of the past n prices, where the weight assigned to the oldest price is one, and the weights of all other prices are zero.

Visualizing the trading signals in crossover rules is straightforward through plotting historical prices alongside moving average lines. Additionally, the gap between the price and moving average lines indicates the trend's strength. Thus, crossover rules serve as valuable visual tools for making financial decisions in trading. On the other hand, visualizing the trading signal in the momentum rule proves challenging since trading platforms rarely exhibit a lagged price line.

For illustrative purposes, the upper panel of Fig. 3.3 displays the daily values of the S&P 500 index from January 1998 to December 2007, along with the index values lagged by 200 days. The shaded areas in this plot highlight the periods when the rule generates a Sell signal. The lower panel depicts the values of the technical trading indicator for the MOM(200) rule.

The momentum rule is less popular than crossover rules because traders find its signals less smooth, as it does not rely on moving averages. Traders also believe this rule lacks responsiveness since both the most recent price and past price are given equal weight in generating the trading signal. As a result, it is

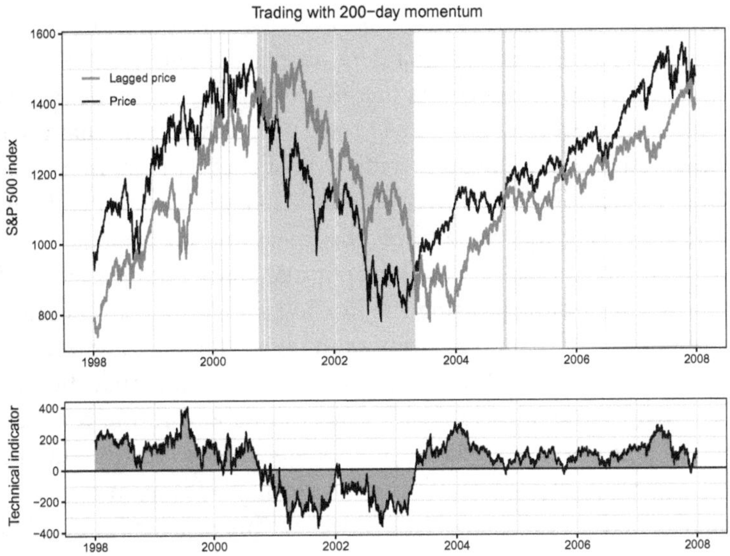

Fig. 3.3 Trading with the 200-day momentum. The upper panel plots the daily values of the S&P 500 index over the period from January 1998 to December 2007, as well as the index values lagged by 200 days. The shaded areas in this plot indicate the periods where this rule generates a Sell signal. The lower panel plots the values of the technical trading indicator for the MOM(200) rule

commonly agreed that the momentum rule poorly filters out short-term noise and is slow to capture trend reversals. Another drawback is the difficulty in visualizing the momentum rule's trading signals.

3.2.4 Moving Average Direction Rule

Concluding our review of trend-following rules, we discuss the moving average direction rule. This rule operates on a simple principle: when prices trend upwards, the moving average of prices typically rises, and conversely, in downtrends, the moving average tends to decline. Accordingly, a Buy signal is generated when the moving average value has increased over the last period, while a Sell signal is triggered otherwise.

Formally, the technical indicator for the moving average direction rule is computed as follows:

$$I_t^{\text{MA-D}}(n) = MA_t(n) - MA_{t-1}(n). \tag{3.4}$$

In this equation, $I_t^{\text{MA-D}}(n)$ represents the technical indicator for the moving average direction rule, $MA_t(n)$ denotes the current value of the moving average, and $MA_{t-1}(n)$ represents the previous value of the moving average.

This rule is referred to as the MA-D rule. When indicating that the moving average direction rule employs a specific type of conventional moving average, we use the notation SMA-D, LMA-D, or EMA-D. For example, the notation LMA-D signifies that this rule utilizes the linear moving average.

This trading rule probably is the least popular among those reviewed for two main reasons. First, while plotting the moving average line is straightforward, visually identifying entry and exit points can be challenging, especially during sideways price movements. Second, traders tend to believe that the latest closing price provides the most crucial information about future price direction compared to past prices. As a result, they prefer rules where the trading signal explicitly involves comparing with the last closing price or, at the very least, a short moving average of past prices. However, this belief is unfounded. Later in this chapter, we will demonstrate that the SMA-D rule corresponds to the MOM rule. Besides, an MA-D rule often corresponds to a specific P-MA rule. Consequently, in principle, this rule is as effective at predicting future price direction as other trading rules.

For illustrative purposes, the upper panel of Fig. 3.4 shows the daily values of the S&P 500 index from January 1998 to December 2007, alongside the values of the 200-day SMA. The shaded areas in this plot highlight the periods when the SMA-D(200) rule generates a Sell signal. The lower panel depicts the values of the technical trading indicator for the SMA-D(200) rule.

3.3 Technical Indicator as a Weighted Sum of Prices

In this section, we aim to demonstrate that the technical indicator in any trend-following rule that uses the last price and either a single moving average or multiple moving averages of prices can be represented by a weighted sum of prices where the sum of all price weights equals zero. To keep things simple, we assume that the weights assigned to prices in a moving average are normalized, meaning that the sum of all weights equals one, expressed as $\sum_{i=0}^{n-1} w_i = 1$.

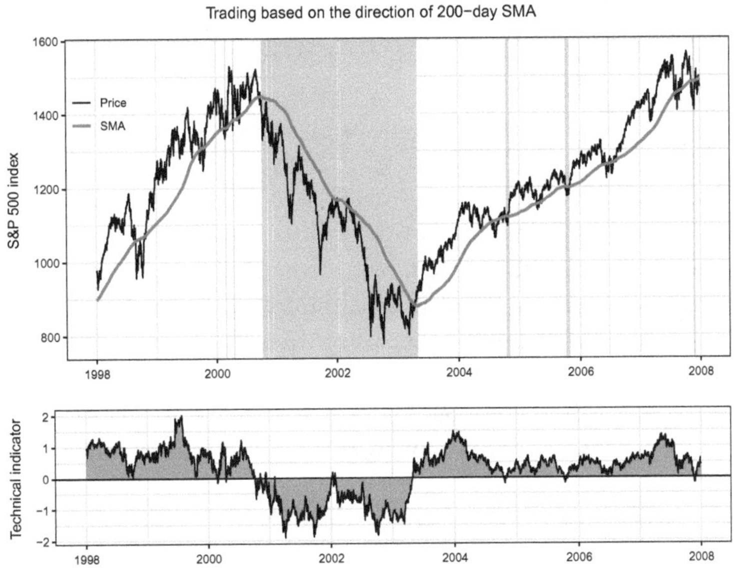

Fig. 3.4 Trading based on the direction of the 200-day SMA. The upper panel plots the daily values of the S&P 500 index over the period from January 1998 to December 2007, as well as the values of the 200-day SMA. The shaded areas in this plot indicate the periods where this rule generates a Sell signal. The lower panel plots the values of the technical trading indicator for the SMA-D(200) rule

First, let us examine the P-MA(n) trading rule, where the technical indicator is calculated as:

$$I_t^{\text{P-MA}}(n) = P_t - MA_t(n, P) = P_t - \sum_{i=0}^{n-1} w_i P_{t-i}$$
$$= (1 - w_0)P_t - \sum_{i=1}^{n-1} w_i P_{t-i}.$$

It is important to note that each price contributes to calculating the technical indicator. In this indicator, the weight of the last, most recent price is $1 - w_0$, while the weights of all other prices are $-w_i$, where $1 \leq i \leq n - 1$. It is worth mentioning that the total sum of weights equals zero.

Second, consider the MA-C(s, n) rule, where the shorter and longer window sizes are denoted by s and n, respectively. The technical indicator in this rule is calculated as follows:

$$I_t^{\text{MA-C}}(s,n) = MA_t(s,P) - MA_t(n,P)$$
$$= \sum_{i=0}^{s-1}(w_i^s - w_i^n)P_{t-i} - \sum_{i=s}^{n-1} w_i^n P_{t-i},$$

where w_i^s represents the weights of the shorter moving average, and w_i^n represents the weights of the longer moving average. Once again, the technical indicator reflects a moving average of all prices within the window spanning n price observations. Each price generally carries a unique weight in this moving average. To clarify, the weights assigned to the first s prices are $w_i^s - w_i^n$, where $0 \leq i < s$, while the weights of the remaining prices are $-w_i^n$, where $s \leq i \leq n-1$. It is also important to note that the sum of all these weights equals zero.

Third, consider the MOM(n) rule, where the technical indicator is calculated as:

$$I_t^{\text{MOM}(n)} = P_t - P_{t-n+1}.$$

Here, it is important to highlight that the weight of the most recent price is one, while the weight of the oldest price is minus one. Prices between the most recent and oldest prices in the window have zero weights. Once more, the sum of all these weights is zero.

Fourth and finally, consider the MA-D(n) rule, where the technical indicator is computed as:

$$I_t^{\text{MA-D}}(n) = MA_t(n,P) - MA_{t-1}(n,P)$$
$$= w_0 P_t + \sum_{i=1}^{n-1}(w_i - w_{i-1})P_{t-i} - w_{n-1}P_{t-n}.$$

Here, it is worth noting that the weight of the most recent price is w_0, the weight of the most distant price is $-w_{n-1}$, and the weights of the other prices are $w_i - w_{i-1}$ for $1 \leq i \leq n-1$. And just like before, the sum of all these weights amounts to zero.

Consequently, the computation of the technical trading indicator in each rule can be expressed in the following general form:

$$I_t^{TR}(n) = \sum_{i=0}^{m} v_i P_{t-i}, \tag{3.5}$$

where $m = n$ in the MA-D rule and $m = n - 1$ in all other rules, υ_i represents the weight of price P_{t-i}, and the sum of all price weights equals zero:

$$\sum_{i=0}^{m} \upsilon_i = 0.$$

For illustration purposes, Fig. 3.5 displays the price weights utilized to calculate the value of the technical trading indicator in the MOM(12), P-SMA(12), SMA-C(3,12), SMA-D(11), and LMA-D(11) rules. All these technical indicators utilize past prices within a window spanning 12 observations.

The representation of the technical indicator as a weighted sum of prices with zero-sum weights sometimes allows traders to discern the commonalities among various trading rules by visually observing the price weights. For instance, as depicted in Fig. 3.5, it is evident that the SMA-D(n) rule is equivalent to the MOM($n + 1$) rule. This equivalence can be formally demonstrated through the following calculation:

$$\begin{aligned} \text{SMA-D}_t(n) &= \text{SMA}_t(n, P) - \text{SMA}_{t-1}(n, P) \\ &= \frac{1}{n}(P_t + P_{t-1} + \ldots + P_{t-n+1}) \\ &\quad - \frac{1}{n}(P_{t-1} + \ldots + P_{t-n+1} + P_{t-n}) \\ &= \frac{1}{n}(P_t - P_{t-n}) = \frac{1}{n}\text{MOM}_t(n+1). \end{aligned}$$

Consequently, the value of the technical indicator of the SMA-D(n) rule equals the value of the technical indicator of the MOM($n + 1$) rule divided by n. Since the sign of the computed value determines the trading signal, these two rules generate the same trading signals.

Likewise, one can formally establish the equivalence of the P-SMA($n + 1$) rule and the LMA-D(n) rule. Hence, contrary to the common belief among traders, the P-MA generally is not superior to the MA-D rule. For example, the P-SMA(n) rule demonstrates better responsiveness compared to the SMA-D(n) rule, yet the P-SMA($n + 1$) rule is entirely equivalent to the LMA-D(n) rule.

The P-MA rule offers a clearer visual representation than the MA-D rule, making it easier to identify entry and exit points when analyzing price and moving average lines. However, visual clarity becomes irrelevant when technical indicators are computed and trading signals are executed by a computer. In

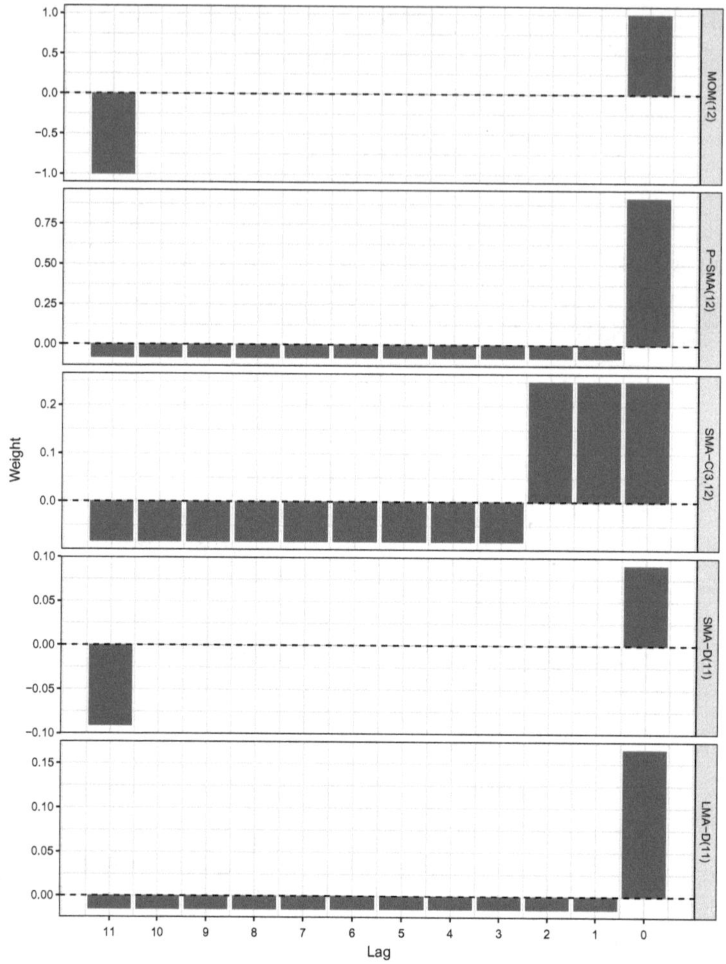

Fig. 3.5 Illustrations of the price weights utilized to calculate the value of the technical trading indicator in the MOM(12), P-SMA(12), SMA-C(3,12), SMA-D(11), and LMA-D(11) rules

this case, a trading rule's effectiveness depends entirely on its responsiveness in detecting trend changes and its accuracy in determining trend direction.

While representing the technical indicator as a weighted sum of prices may sometimes help traders identify commonalities among different trading rules, this approach has limited utility. Visual examination of price weights within a technical indicator does not provide insight into the underlying rationale of a trading rule. For instance, in the P-MA rule, the weight of the most recent price is positive, while the weights of all other prices are negative. What does this imply? How do these weights signal the trend direction?

Moreover, how can these price weights be utilized to calculate, for instance, the average lag time of a trading rule? As demonstrated in the previous chapter, assessing average lag times demands a step-by-step examination of when the trading signal shifts following a trend reversal. In this context, it is essential to concentrate on the weights associated with price changes rather than the price weights.

3.4 Technical Indicator as a Moving Average of Price Changes

This section aims to demonstrate that the technical indicator in any trend-following rule that uses the last price and either a single moving average or multiple moving averages of prices can be represented by a single moving average of price changes. We remind the reader the notation for a price change between times $t-i-1$ and $t-i$:

$$\Delta P_{t-i} = P_{t-i} - P_{t-i-1}.$$

First, let us consider the MOM(n) rule where the technical indicator equals the difference between the last closing price P_t and the price $n-1$ periods ago, P_{t-n+1}. We can compute P_{t-n+1} as the difference between the last closing price and the cumulative sum of all previous price changes:

$$P_{t-n+1} = P_t - \Delta P_t - \Delta P_{t-1} - \ldots - \Delta P_{t-n+2} = P_t - \sum_{i=0}^{n-2} \Delta P_{t-i}.$$

As a result, the technical indicator in the MOM(n) rule can alternatively be calculated as:

$$I_t^{\text{MOM}}(n) = P_t - P_{t-n+1} = P_t - \left(P_t - \sum_{i=0}^{n-2} \Delta P_{t-i}\right) = \sum_{i=0}^{n-2} \Delta P_{t-i}.$$

Therefore, this technical indicator computes the simple moving average[1] of all price changes between times $t-n+1$ and t. It is worth noting that the time

[1] Strictly speaking, this technical indicator calculates an equally weighted sum of price changes. In a simple moving average, this sum is further divided by the number of terms. However, since the trading signal depends only on the sign of the sum, it can be freely rescaled—for instance, normalized to one. Therefore, we can interpret this indicator as computing the simple moving average of price changes.

interval $[t - n + 1, t]$ encompasses n prices but only $n - 1$ price changes. In other words, the number of price changes equals the number of prices minus one.

Second, consider the P-MA(n) rule where the technical indicator equals the difference between the last closing price P_t and the weighted moving average of the last n price observations, $MA_t(n, P)$. In the preceding chapter, we derived an alternative representation for the general weighted moving average:

$$MA_t(n, P) = P_t - \sum_{i=0}^{n-2} \theta_i \Delta P_{t-i},$$

where θ_i represents the weight of the price change ΔP_{t-i}. The weight θ_i is computed using the following formula:

$$\theta_i = \frac{\sum_{j=i+1}^{n-1} w_j}{\sum_{j=0}^{n-1} w_j},$$

where w_j denotes the weight of price P_{t-j}.

Consequently, the technical indicator in the P-MA(n) rule can be calculated as:

$$\begin{aligned} I_t^{\text{P-MA}}(n) &= P_t - MA_t(n, P) = P_t - \left(P_t - \sum_{i=0}^{n-2} \theta_i \Delta P_{t-i} \right) \\ &= \sum_{i=0}^{n-2} \theta_i \Delta P_{t-i}. \end{aligned}$$

Thus, this technical indicator computes the weighted moving average of all price changes between times $t - n + 1$ and t.

Third, consider the MA-D($n - 1$) rule, where the technical indicator is calculated as follows:

$$\begin{aligned} I_t^{\text{MA-D}}(n-1) &= MA_t(n-1, P) - MA_{t-1}(n-1, P) \\ &= \frac{\sum_{i=0}^{n-2} w_i P_{t-i}}{\sum_{i=0}^{n-2} w_i} - \frac{\sum_{i=0}^{n-2} w_i P_{t-i-1}}{\sum_{i=0}^{n-2} w_i} \\ &= \frac{\sum_{i=0}^{n-2} w_i \left(P_{t-i} - P_{t-i-1}\right)}{\sum_{i=0}^{n-2} w_i} = \frac{\sum_{i=0}^{n-2} w_i \Delta P_{t-i}}{\sum_{i=0}^{n-2} w_i}. \end{aligned} \quad (3.6)$$

Apparently, the technical indicator computes the weighted moving average of $n-1$ price changes. It is crucial to highlight that in this rule, the weights of price changes are identical to the weights of prices. Additionally, in contrast to the previously considered rules, in this rule, we use not n but $n-1$ price observations to compute the moving averages of prices. This choice ensures that the technical indicator consistently computes the moving average of the last $n-1$ price changes in all rules.

Fourth and finally, consider the MA-C(s, l) rule, where the shorter and longer window sizes are denoted by $s > 1$ and $l > s$, respectively. The technical indicator in this rule is calculated as follows:

$$
\begin{aligned}
I_t^{\text{MA-C}}(s, l) = MA_t(s, P) - MA_t(l, P) &= \left(P_t - \sum_{i=0}^{s-2} \theta_i^s \Delta P_{t-i}\right) \\
&\quad - \left(P_t - \sum_{i=0}^{l-2} \theta_i^l \Delta P_{t-i}\right) \\
&= \sum_{i=0}^{l-2} \theta_i^l \Delta P_{t-i} - \sum_{i=0}^{s-2} \theta_i^s \Delta P_{t-i} \\
&= \sum_{i=0}^{s-2} (\theta_i^l - \theta_i^s) \Delta P_{t-i} + \sum_{i=s-1}^{l-2} \theta_i^l \Delta P_{t-i},
\end{aligned}
$$

where θ_i^l denotes the weights of the price changes in the longer moving average and θ_i^s represents the weights of the price changes in the shorter moving average. Like before, the technical indicator in this rule calculates a single moving average of price changes. The first $s-1$ weights are $\theta_i^l - \theta_i^s$, and the subsequent weights are θ_i^l.

Therefore, across all rules, the technical trading indicator computes a single moving average of price changes. To simplify the notation, from now on, we designate n as the number of price changes in a technical indicator. Hence, the general formula for the technical indicator in all rules becomes:

$$
I_t^{TR}(n) = \sum_{i=0}^{n-1} \theta_i \Delta P_{t-i}, \tag{3.7}
$$

where θ_i represents the weight of price change ΔP_{t-i}. With this notation, the number of price observations is $n + 1$ in the MOM, P-MA, and MA-C rules. In contrast, the number of price observations is also n in the MA-D rule.

With the updated definition of n, the weights of price changes in the P-MA and MA-C rules should be calculated using the following formula:

$$\theta_i = \frac{\sum_{j=i+1}^{n} w_j}{\sum_{j=0}^{n} w_j}, \quad i \in [0, n-1],$$

where w_j denotes the weight of price P_{t-j}, and the number of price observations used to compute the moving average of prices equals $n + 1$.

It is worth emphasizing that the trading signal is determined based on the technical indicator's sign. As a result, the weights of price changes can be freely adjusted without altering the trading signals. Therefore, the following technical indicator:

$$I_t^{TR}(n) = \sum_{i=0}^{n-1} c \times \theta_i \Delta P_{t-i}, \tag{3.8}$$

which uses the weights $c \times \theta_i$, is entirely equivalent to the technical indicator in Eq. (3.7) for any $c > 0$. This property allows us to freely rescale the weights in a technical indicator to create a convenient weighting scheme.

It is also important to note that in a moving average, the sum of the weights is typically normalized to 1 to ensure the result reflects a true "average" of the data points. Generally, however, the sum of the weights θ_i differs from 1. Nevertheless, since these weights can be freely rescaled, they can always be normalized to 1 if their sum is positive. This is why we refer to a technical indicator as being computed using a moving average of price changes, even if the sum of the weights assigned to those price changes is not exactly 1.

Now, let us examine the weights of price changes in all trading rules. We begin with the MOM rule, which computes the simple moving average of price changes. Here, all price changes are given the same weights:

$$\text{Weights in the MOM rule:} \quad \theta_0 = 1, \quad \theta_1 = 1, \ldots, \theta_{n-1} = 1.$$

Moving on, we consider the weights of price changes in the P-MA rule. Since these weights can be freely rescaled, we can compute them using the following formula:

$$\theta_i = \sum_{j=i+1}^{n} w_j.$$

For instance, in the P-SMA rule where all price weights are equal to one, the weight of price change θ_i is given by:

$$\theta_i = \sum_{j=i+1}^{n} 1 = n - i, \quad i \in [0, n-1].$$

Specifically, in the P-SMA(n) rule, the weights θ_i decrease linearly from n down to one:

$$\text{Weights in the P-SMA rule:} \quad \theta_0 = n, \quad \theta_1 = n - 1, \ldots, \theta_{n-1} = 1.$$

In the P-LMA rule, where the price weights linearly decrease from $n + 1$ to one, the weight of price change θ_i is given by:

$$\theta_i = \sum_{j=i+1}^{n} (n - j + 1) = \frac{1}{2}(n - i + 1)(n - i), \quad i \in [0, n-1].$$

Specifically, the analytical solution for the weight θ_i is obtained using the formula for the sum of an arithmetic sequence. As the formula suggests, in the P-LMA(n) rule, the weights θ_i decrease nonlinearly from $n(n + 1)/2$ down to one:

$$\text{Weights in the P-LMA rule:} \quad \theta_0 = n(n+1)/2, \\ \theta_1 = (n-1)n/2, \ldots, \theta_{n-1} = 1.$$

In the P-EMA rule, where the price weights decrease exponentially from one to zero, the weight of price change θ_i is given by:

$$\theta_i = \sum_{j=i+1}^{\infty} \lambda^j = \frac{\lambda^{i+1}}{1+\lambda}, \quad i \in [0, \infty), \quad \lambda = \frac{n-1}{n+1}.$$

Here, the analytical solution for the weight θ_i is obtained using the formula for the sum of a geometric sequence. Since the weights can be freely rescaled, a convenient rescaling constant is $c = (1 + \lambda)/\lambda$. As a result, in the P-EMA(n) rule, the weights θ_i decrease exponentially from one to zero:

$$\text{Weights in the P-EMA rule:} \quad \theta_0 = 1, \quad \theta_1 = \lambda, \quad \theta_2 = \lambda^2, \ldots.$$

For illustrative purposes, Fig. 3.6 depicts the shapes of the price-change weighting functions in the MOM(20), P-SMA(20), P-LMA(20), and P-EMA(20) rules. It is worth noting that while in the momentum rule, all price changes have equal weights, in all other rules, the weight of the price change decreases as the lag number increases. In other words, in all rules except the momentum rule, the weighting function gives more weight to the most recent price changes.

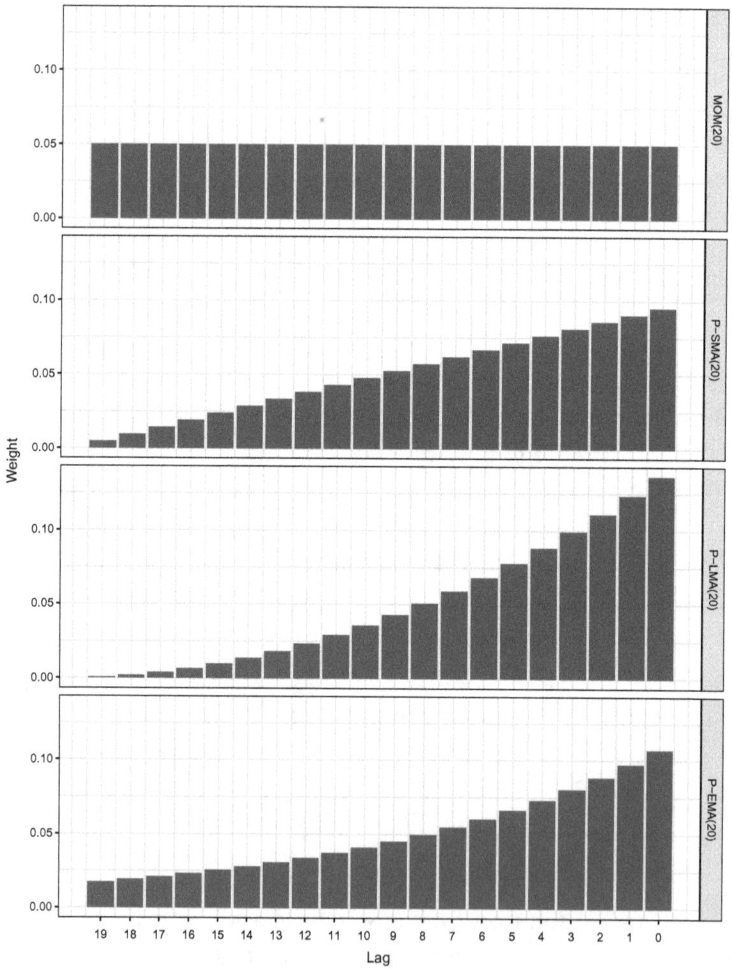

Fig. 3.6 Illustrations of the weights of price changes utilized to calculate the value of the technical trading indicator in the MOM(20), P-SMA(20), P-LMA(20), and P-EMA(20) rules. The weight at lag i corresponds to the weight of ΔP_{t-i}. The weights of the price changes in the P-EMA(20) rule are cut off at lag 19

We remind the reader that now $n = 20$ represents the number of price changes in the computation of the moving average, not the number of prices. It is also crucial to note that the rule's name reflects the type of moving average that uses prices. However, the type of moving average that uses price changes is generally different. For instance, the P-SMA rule utilizes the simple moving average of prices. On the other hand, the technical indicator of this rule employs a linear moving average of price changes. Only in the P-EMA rule are both moving averages of the same type.

In the MA-D rule, the weights of price changes mirror the weights of prices. For instance, the SMA-D rule utilizes the simple moving average of prices, and similarly, its technical indicator employs the simple moving average of price changes. Notably, the technical indicator of the MOM rule also utilizes the simple moving average of price changes. Therefore, the SMA-D rule is equivalent to the MOM rule.

Moving forward, the LMA-D rule utilizes the linear moving average of prices, which is also utilized in its technical indicator. Similarly, the linear moving average is employed in the technical indicator of the P-SMA rule. Hence, the LMA-D rule is equivalent to the P-SMA rule.

Finally, the EMA-D rule employs the same exponential moving average for both prices and price changes. Likewise, the P-EMA rule utilizes the exponential moving average for both prices and price changes. Therefore, the EMA-D rule is equivalent to the P-EMA rule.

For illustrative purposes, Fig. 3.7 depicts the shapes of the price-change weighting functions in the SMA-D(20), LMA-D(20), and EMA-D(20) rules.

To correctly compute the weights of price changes in the MA-C(s, l) technical indicator, initially, both θ_i^l and θ_i^s must be calculated as:

$$\theta_i^s = \frac{\sum_{j=i+1}^{s} w_j^s}{\sum_{j=0}^{s} w_j^s}, \quad \theta_i^l = \frac{\sum_{j=i+1}^{l} w_j^l}{\sum_{j=0}^{l} w_j^l},$$

where w_j^s represents the price weights used in the shorter moving average and w_j^l signifies the price weights used in the longer moving average within the MA-C(s, l) rule.

Subsequently, the weights of price changes for this technical indicator can be obtained as follows:

$$\theta_i = \begin{cases} \theta_i^l - \theta_i^s & \text{when } 0 \le i < s, \\ \theta_i^l & \text{when } s \le i \le l - 1. \end{cases}$$

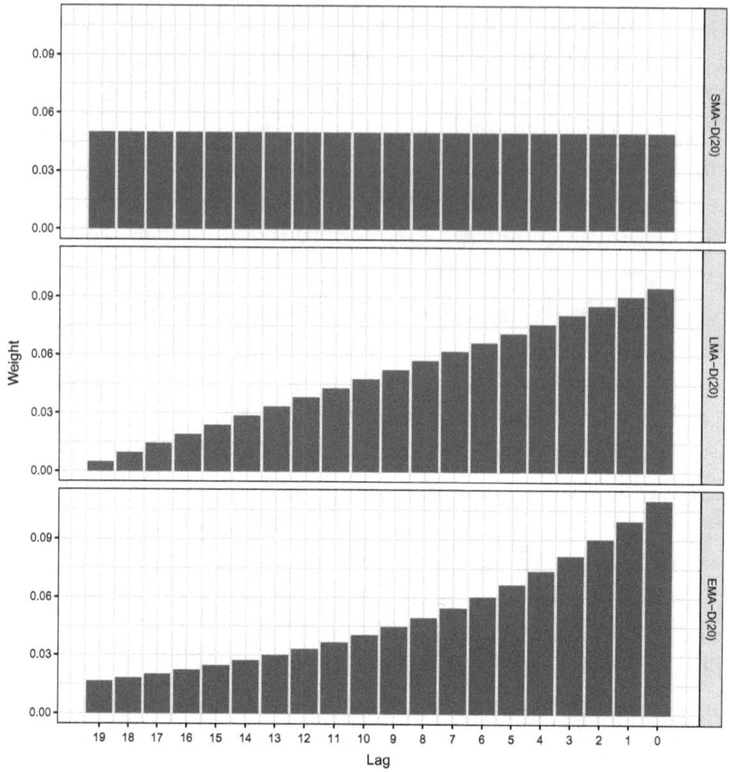

Fig. 3.7 Illustrations of the weights of price changes utilized to calculate the value of the technical trading indicator in the SMA-D(20), LMA-D(20), and EMA-D(20) rules. The weight at lag i corresponds to the weight of ΔP_{t-i}. The weights of the price changes in the EMA-D(20) rule are cut off at lag 19

Another useful representation for the technical trading indicator for the MA-C(s, l) rule, where s and l denote the number of price changes, is given by:

$$I_t^{\text{MA-C}}(s,l) = \sum_{i=0}^{s-1}(\theta_i^l - \theta_i^s)\Delta P_{t-i} + \sum_{i=s}^{l-1}\theta_i^l \Delta P_{t-i}. \tag{3.9}$$

The MA-C rule reduces to the P-MA rule when the size of the shorter moving average reduces to 1. In this case, the last price is used instead of the shorter moving average. To understand the effect of using the shorter moving average instead of the last price, let us present the computation of the trading signal in the P-MA rule in the following form:

$$I_t^{\text{P-MA}}(l) = \sum_{i=0}^{s-1} \theta_i^l \Delta P_{t-i} + \sum_{i=s}^{l-1} \theta_i^l \Delta P_{t-i}. \tag{3.10}$$

Comparing Eqs. (3.9) and (3.10) reveals that the price-change weighting functions for both rules, MA-C(s, l) and P-MA(l), are identical beginning from lag s and beyond. In contrast, compared to the price-change weighting function of the P-MA(l) rule, the price-change weighting function of MA-C(s, l) rule assigns smaller weights to the most recent price changes (from lag 0 to lag $s - 1$). Typically, the price-change weighting function in the P-MA(l) rule overweights the most recent price changes. Hence, the reduction of weights of the most recent price changes in the MA-C(s, l) rule makes its weighting function for price changes underweight both the most recent and the most distant price changes.

For example, in the P-SMA(s, l) rule, the weights of price changes are given by:

$$\theta_i^s = \frac{s-i}{s+1}, \quad \theta_i^l = \frac{l-i}{l+1}.$$

Consequently, the technical indicator in this rule is computed as:

$$I_t^{\text{SMA-C}}(s, l) = \sum_{i=0}^{s-1} \left(\frac{l-i}{l+1} - \frac{s-i}{s+1} \right) \Delta P_{t-i} + \sum_{i=s}^{l-1} \frac{l-i}{l+1} \Delta P_{t-i}.$$

As another example, the weights of price changes in the P-EMA(s, l) rule are given by:

$$\theta_i^s = \lambda_s^{i+1}, \quad \theta_i^l = \lambda_l^{i+1},$$

where

$$\lambda_s = \frac{s-1}{s+1}, \quad \lambda_l = \frac{l-1}{l+1}.$$

As a result, the technical indicator in this rule is computed as:

$$I_t^{\text{EMA-C}}(s, l) = \sum_{i=0}^{\infty} \left(\lambda_l^{i+1} - \lambda_s^{i+1} \right) \Delta P_{t-i}.$$

For illustrative purposes, Fig. 3.8 depicts the shapes of the price-change weighting functions in the SMA-C(5,20), LMA-C(5,20), and EMA-C(5,20) rules. The plots in this figure demonstrate that in all MA-C rules, the price-change weighting function has a hump-shaped form where the peak is located closer to the right end of the shape where the lag zero is situated. Specifically, starting at lag zero, the weights first increase, reach a maximum, and then decrease. In the P-SMA(s, l) rule, the peak is positioned precisely at lag s. In the other rules, the peak is located close to lag s.

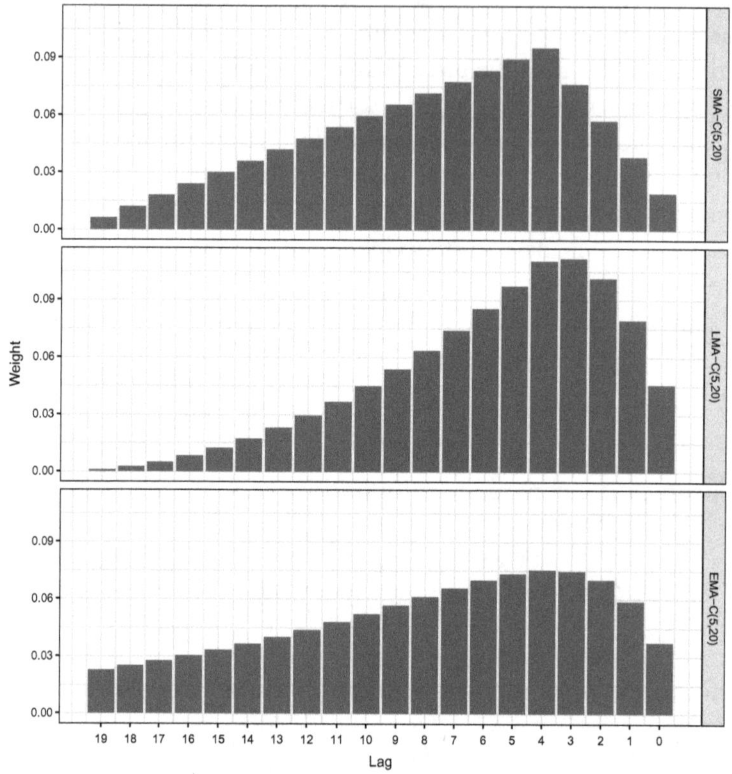

Fig. 3.8 Illustrations of the weights of price changes utilized to calculate the value of the technical trading indicator in the SMA-C(5,20), LMA-C(5,20), and EMA-C(5,20) rules. The weight at lag i corresponds to the weight of ΔP_{t-i}. The weights of the price changes in the EMA-C(5,20) rule are cut off at lag 19

3.5 Average Lag Time and Smoothness of Trading Rules

The previous section showed that a technical indicator in any trend-following rule, which relies on the last price and one or more moving averages of prices, can be simplified to a single moving average of price changes. This representation offers valuable insights into the economic reasoning behind a technical indicator and the characteristics of trend-following strategies.

To begin with, we have discovered that in any technical indicator using traditional moving averages, the weights assigned to price changes are always positive. This property indicates that when prices increase on average within a specific time window, the value of the technical indicator is positive, triggering a Buy signal.

Therefore, a commonality exists in various technical indicators: the weights assigned to price changes are positive. However, when technical indicators rely on conventional moving averages, the weighting function for price changes can take three distinct forms. The first form equally weighs all price changes. The second form gives greater weight to recent price changes. In the third form, the weights adopt a hump shape, diminishing the impact of both recent and distant price changes.

We can logically infer that the characteristics of trading rules are influenced by the shape of the weighting function for price changes. Rules with similar shapes are likely to have comparable properties. For instance, all P-MA rules, irrespective of the type of conventional moving average used, should demonstrate similar properties. This is because these rules give greater weight to the most recent price changes. Conversely, the MOM and MA-C rules are expected to display distinct properties both among themselves and in comparison with the P-MA rules.

This section aims to provide an initial qualitative exploration of trading rules' characteristics and their relationship with the shape of the weighting function for price changes. The next chapter will present a detailed discussion of the key properties of trend-following rules. At this point, our focus is on examining trading rules' smoothness and responsiveness.

Why do we concentrate on smoothness and responsiveness in this section? The rationale behind this choice is that traders typically emphasize the importance of a moving average being both smooth and responsive. Currently, among traders, there is only one widely accepted measure for evaluating the responsiveness of a moving average, known as the average lag time of a moving average. However, there is no universally accepted measure for assessing the smoothness of a moving average.

We start by discussing the responsiveness of trend-following rules. Throughout this discussion, we reiterate that the metric known as the average lag time of a moving average is largely irrelevant in practical applications, primarily for two reasons.

First, it measures the lag time of a moving average inaccurately. This measure is only applicable in cases where prices consistently trend either upwards or downwards. However, the correct and pertinent measure of the lag time of a moving average should reflect the delay between a turning point in the trend and the subsequent turning point in the moving average.

Second, and more importantly, most trading rules identify the turning point in the trend earlier than a turning point in the moving average becomes apparent.

To demonstrate the average lag time of various trading rules, let us consider a scenario where prices steadily rise and then fall. It is important to note that we can safely disregard any price noise, as our main focus is on the average price behavior. This price behavior is illustrated in Fig. 3.9. Additionally, this figure displays the values of both short (fast) and long (slow) simple moving averages.

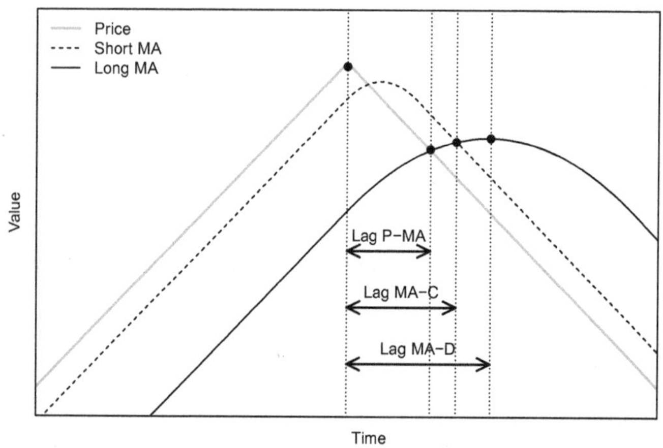

Fig. 3.9 Illustration of the average lag times of different trading rules

The average lag time of the MA-D rule corresponds to the delay between the turning point in the price trend and the subsequent turning point in the moving average. Understanding how to accurately measure the average lag time of a moving average enables us to determine the average lag time of this rule. It is essential to note that the metric used to measure the average lag time of a moving average yields a correct delay time only when the price weights are symmetrical around the middle. Among traditional moving averages, only the SMA meets this condition. Hence, only the average lag time of the SMA measure reflects its true lag time.

The P-MA rule generates a new trading signal when the price crosses the long moving average. It is important to note that the delay time of the P-MA rule is significantly shorter than the delay time of the MA-D rule. This means that even if we accurately determine the average lag time of a moving average, the average lag time of the P-MA rule is shorter than this value.

The MA-C rule triggers a new trading signal when the short moving average crosses the long moving average. As depicted in Fig. 3.9, the average lag time of this rule falls somewhere between the average lag times of the P-MA and MA-D rules. Even if we accurately determine the average lag times of the short and long moving averages, these times offer no insight into how to measure the average lag time of the MA-C rule.

Two important conclusions emerge from this illustration and discussion. First, we need to shift our focus from the average lag time of a moving average to the average lag time of a trading rule. The average lag time of a trading rule denotes the delay between a turning point in the trend and the subsequent change in the trading signal. Second, although we currently lack precise knowledge of the average lag time of the trading rules, we have learned that the ranking of the rules, from the most responsive to the least responsive, is as follows: the P-MA rule, the MA-C rule, and the MA-D rule. This implies that different rules exhibit varying average lag times, which are also influenced by the type of moving average used.

In our illustration, all moving averages are simple moving averages. Consequently, in this scenario, the MA-D rule is identical to the MOM rule, where all price changes are equally weighted. For the P-MA rule, the weights of price changes decrease with the lag number. Lastly, in the MA-C rule, the weights assigned to distant price changes are the same as in the P-MA rule. However, compared to the P-MA rule, the weights of the most recent price changes are reduced in the MA-C rule.

Hence, we can conclude that enhancing the responsiveness of the trading rule can be achieved by assigning greater weights to the most recent price changes. Put simply, overweighting recent price changes enhances responsiveness. Conversely, responsiveness diminishes when the weights of recent price changes are reduced. However, the least responsive scenario occurs when all price changes are weighted equally.[2]

We proceed with discussing the smoothness of trading rules. In the next chapter, where we introduce a quantitative measure for smoothness, we argue that smoothness is logically associated with the frequency of position changes. In other words, the smoother the trading rule, the less frequent the changes in the trading signal. Although we currently lack a measure to directly evaluate

---

[2] As we will see in the next chapter, the average lag time of a trading rule equals $n/2$ when the weighting function for price changes is symmetrical around the middle. In theory, the weights of price changes in a trading rule could increase with the lag number. As a result, the average lag time of a trading rule can exceed $n/2$. However, this situation is highly improbable because it would involve using moving averages that give excessive importance to distant prices.

the number of position reversals over a specific time frame, this number can be estimated using historical data.

Specifically, Sect. 3.2 of this chapter demonstrates the generation of the trading signal in all rules utilizing historical data on the S&P 500 index over ten years. All moving averages depicted in the illustrations are simple moving averages. Hence, we can compare not only the responsiveness of the rules based on simple moving averages but also their smoothness.

In the MOM rule, which is equivalent to the SMA-D rule, the trading signal changes 18 times over ten years. In contrast, the P-SMA rule experiences 49 signal changes, while the SMA-C rule changes its signal only 6 times.

To properly compare the properties of trading rules based on smoothness and responsiveness, it is essential to ensure that all rules exhibit the same level of responsiveness. Then, we can evaluate the rules' smoothness. The best rule would be the one that achieves the highest level of smoothness for the same level of responsiveness.

The rules we compare demonstrate varying levels of responsiveness and smoothness. However, certain conclusions emerge clearly. First, the P-MA rule, which gives more weight to recent price changes, emerges as the most responsive but least smooth trading rule. Second, the MA-C rule, characterized by a hump-shaped weighting function for price changes, exhibits the highest level of smoothness and the second-best responsiveness. Third, the MOM and SMA-D rules, where all weights are equal, rank as the least responsive but second-best regarding smoothness.

Overall, the key takeaway from this section's discussion is that the shape of the weighting function for price changes plays a crucial role in determining the properties of trend-following rules.

3.6 Returns Instead of Price Changes

Our analysis shows that calculating the technical indicator in all trend-following rules based on moving averages of prices can be represented as the computation of a single moving average of price changes:

$$I_t^{TR} = \sum_{i=0}^{n-1} \theta_i \Delta P_{t-i},$$

where θ_i is the weight of ΔP_{t-i}, which represents the change in price from time $t - i - 1$ to time $t - i$:

$$\Delta P_{t-i} = P_{t-i} - P_{t-i-1}.$$

Let us denote by r_{t-i} the capital gain return from time $t - i - 1$ to time $t - i$. Using this notation, we can express the price P_{t-i} as the previous time's price P_{t-i-1} multiplied by the gross return between these two times:

$$P_{t-i} = P_{t-i-1}(1 + r_{t-i}).$$

Consequently, the price change ΔP_{t-i} is given by:

$$\Delta P_{t-i} = r_{t-i} P_{t-i-1},$$

and the formula for computing the technical indicator can be rewritten as:

$$I_t^{TR} = \sum_{i=0}^{n-1} \theta_i r_{t-i} P_{t-i-1}.$$

Since the sign of the technical indicator determines the trading signal, multiplying all terms in the technical indicator by a positive constant does not change the generated trading signals. In other words, rescaling each term in a technical indicator creates an equivalent technical indicator. Let us use $1/P_t$ as a rescaling constant. The equivalent technical indicator is then:

$$\begin{aligned} I_t^{TR} &= \sum_{i=0}^{n-1} \theta_i r_{t-i} \frac{P_{t-i-1}}{P_t} \\ &= \theta_0 r_t \frac{P_{t-1}}{P_t} + \theta_1 r_{t-1} \frac{P_{t-2}}{P_t} + \ldots + \theta_{n-1} r_{t-n+1} \frac{P_{t-n}}{P_t}. \end{aligned}$$

Each term in the sum above can be seen as the product of $\theta_i r_{t-i}$ multiplied by the fraction P_{t-i-1}/P_t. We aim to justify that $P_{t-i-1}/P_t \approx 1$ for all reasonable values of i.

This approximation holds true, assuming that the price changes moderately between consecutive time intervals. Therefore, if the value of i is not substantial, the ratio P_{t-i-1}/P_t remains close to 1. This assumption is often valid in financial markets where price changes are typically gradual over short periods, resulting in negligible differences in the ratio of consecutive prices.

Expanding on this argument, let us delve into the practical implications. A moving average typically utilizes an averaging window of no more than a year. With daily data, this implies that the maximum value for n is 250, reflecting the average number of trading days in a year.

In the United States, the average annual capital gain return for a portfolio of large stocks is about 8%. Translated to a daily basis, this averages out to approximately 0.032%. Consequently, for i values ranging from 0 to 249, each fraction $\frac{P_{t-i-1}}{P_t}$ approximately equals:

$$\frac{P_{t-1}}{P_t} = 0.99968 \approx 1, \quad \frac{P_{t-2}}{P_t} = 0.99936 \approx 1, \quad \frac{P_{t-250}}{P_t} = 0.92 \approx 1.$$

Even in the worst-case scenario, where the approximation deviates to 0.92, this slight variation is inconsequential for most trading rules. Moreover, the weights θ_i diminish in most trading rules as the lag number increases. Consequently, the distant lags where the approximation is less accurate have minimal impact on the value of the technical indicator. This reinforces the reliability of the approximation for practical purposes.

To summarize, we have demonstrated that the technical indicator can be calculated using returns instead of prices:

$$I_t^{TR} = \sum_{i=0}^{n-1} \theta_i r_{t-i},$$

where θ_i represents the weight of r_{t-i}. In essence, this means that the technical indicator in all trend-following rules based on moving averages of prices can be computed as a single moving average of returns.

Acar (1998) was the first to propose the concept of approximating the computation of a technical indicator for a trading rule based on the moving average of prices by calculating a moving average of returns instead. Acar conducted a Monte Carlo simulation to validate this approximation, demonstrating that two alternative technical indicators produced identical trading signals in at least 97% of cases.

Throughout the rest of this book, we will exclusively examine the properties of the technical indicator that calculates the moving average of past returns rather than past price changes. This choice offers several advantages from both econometric and modeling perspectives. In theoretical finance and financial econometrics, models predominantly focus on returns rather than price changes or raw prices. This preference stems from theoretical models' assumption: stationary processes with constant parameters over time. For instance, these models require the process's mean value and standard deviation to remain constant over time. Such stability characterizes returns but not price changes. With prices increasing exponentially over time, both the mean price change and the standard deviation of the price change also tend to increase.

Hence, by adopting the return-based approach, we gain access to a diverse array of financial models explicitly tailored for analyzing returns, along with numerous established techniques in financial econometrics. This enables us to delve into the profitability and optimality of different trading rules with greater depth and precision. Moreover, we can explore the intriguing question of identifying the most optimal trading rule under specific return processes. This exploration opens up avenues for devising more effective trading strategies.

3.7 Summary

While the core idea of trend-following seems straightforward—simply "jump on a trend and ride it"—its application poses significant challenges for traders. These challenges stem from two main factors. First, the inherent volatility in prices creates ambiguity when identifying the direction of a trend. To mitigate this, traders often rely on moving averages to smooth out these fluctuations and reveal the underlying trend. Second, the multitude of trend-following rules based on moving averages adds another layer of complexity. Traders must navigate through various alternatives, a task made daunting by the lack of a clear understanding of the similarities and differences among these rules.

In this chapter, we first introduced the standard trend-following rules based on moving averages of prices and elucidated the economic logic underpinning the formulation of these rules. These rules include the price and moving average crossover (P-MA) rule, the double moving average crossover (MA-C) rule, the momentum (MOM) rule, and the moving average direction (MA-D) rule. Depending on the specific rule, the technical indicator is computed using either the change in a single moving average, the comparison between the latest price and the moving average of previous prices, or the comparison between two moving averages calculated with different historical price data.

The MA-D rule is based on a simple concept: when the moving average rises (falls), it indicates an upward (downward) trend. However, relying solely on a single moving average can make pinpointing entry and exit points challenging. This difficulty is addressed by comparing the latest closing price with the moving average value: if the last price surpasses (falls below) the moving average, it suggests an upward (downward) trend. This forms the rationale behind the P-MA rule.

One significant drawback of the P-MA rule, particularly when applied to daily data in trend-following strategies, is its lack of smoothness in trading signals. Consequently, trading profits often suffer from frequent whipsaws. The MA-C rule overcomes this issue by utilizing a short moving average instead of the last closing price. Lastly, the MOM rule operates on the straightforward principle that an upward (downward) trend is indicated when the last closing price exceeds (falls below) the price from a few periods ago.

After detailing the trend-following rules, we showed that the technical indicator in all these rules can be simplified to a weighted sum of prices where the sum of all price weights equals zero. However, this simplified representation has limited practical value because visually inspecting price weights within a technical indicator does not offer useful insights into the underlying economic intuition behind a trading rule.

Moving forward, we illustrated that the technical indicator in any trend-following rule, which incorporates the latest price alongside either a single moving average or multiple moving averages of prices, can be simplified to a single moving average of price changes or returns. This simplification provides the most valuable and insightful information regarding the economic rationale behind the trading rule.

The challenge lies in the fact that while moving averages of prices are crucial for visualizing how trading signals are produced, the sheer variety of trading rules and types of moving averages makes it impossible to discern the commonalities and differences between them. Conversely, representing each rule as a single moving average of returns provides a comprehensive and lucid perspective on the relationships between different rules. For instance, we showcased that many of the MA-D rules are equivalent to either the P-MA or MOM rules. This equivalence is not discernible through visual inspection of the moving averages alone.

Our analysis uncovered that despite the apparent diversity among various trading rules and moving averages, the fundamental distinction between these technical indicators lies in the weighting function employed to calculate the moving average of returns. Furthermore, in cases where technical indicators rely on conventional moving averages, the weighting function for returns can be categorized into three distinct forms. The first form evenly distributes weight across all returns. The second form assigns greater weight to recent returns. Finally, the third form adopts a hump-shaped weighting, reducing the influence of both recent and distant returns.

In conclusion, we emphasized the clear connection between the shape of the weighting function for returns and key characteristics of the trading rule, such as smoothness and responsiveness. For instance, overweighting the most recent returns, as seen in the P-MA rule, enhances the trading rule's responsiveness. Conversely, when traders prioritize a smooth trading experience, they opt for a rule that diminishes the influence of both recent and distant returns, as exemplified by the MA-C rule.

Overall, our analysis led us to the conclusion that the properties of trading rules can be deduced from the weighting function for returns. Consequently, it appears theoretically feasible to quantify the properties of a trading rule solely by examining its weighting function for returns. This is precisely what we aim to demonstrate in the following chapter.

References

Acar, E. (1998). Expected Returns of Directional Forecasters. In E. Acar & S. Satchell (Eds.), *Advanced Trading Rules* (pp. 51–76). Butterworth-Heinemann.

Zakamulin, V. (2017). *Market Timing with Moving Averages: The Anatomy and Performance of Trading Rules*. Palgrave.

Part II

Quantitative Assessment of Trading Rules

4

Quantifying Key Properties of Trend-Following Rules

4.1 Introduction

Traditionally, traders have placed significant emphasis on analyzing the properties of individual moving averages. They typically seek moving averages that are both smooth and responsive, and these two essential qualities are often assessed by visually comparing the moving average curve with the price curve. However, comparisons made through visual inspection are inherently subjective and prone to biases. What is more important, this narrow approach fails to consider a critical aspect: in trend-following rules, trading signals are practically never based on a single moving average. Hence, it is essential to shift our focus to evaluating the properties of trend-following rules themselves, rather than merely scrutinizing the characteristics of the moving averages employed within these rules.

Undoubtedly, the identification of the most critical properties of trend-following rules is a topic of debate. In our perspective, to effectively "trade with the trend," a trend-following rule should exhibit the following three fundamental properties:

1. Provide high accuracy in trend identification: In order to achieve profitability, it is vital for the trend-following rule to generate trading signals that align with the prevailing price trend. In an upward-trending market, where prices are rising, the rule should generate a bullish signal. Conversely, in a downward-trending market characterized by price declines, the rule should generate a bearish signal.
2. React quickly to trend changes: In addition to producing trading signal that aligns with the price trend, a trend-following rule should also possess the

V. Zakamulin and J. Giner, *The Ultimate Moving Average Handbook*,
https://doi.org/10.1007/978-3-031-90907-8_4

ability to promptly respond to changes in the trend. The effectiveness of the rule in trend identification relies on its agility in adapting to shifting price trends. By swiftly adjusting its trading signal based on new price data, the responsive rule can accurately capture the evolving dynamics of the trend.

3. Possess good smoothing properties: Lastly, it is crucial for a trend-following rule to minimize the occurrence of position reversals. Position reversals happen when the rule generates signals that frequently change the direction of a trading position. These frequent reversals typically result in higher trading costs, reduced profitability, and increased uncertainty for traders. To mitigate position reversals, the rule should utilize an appropriate smoothing technique to provide more stable signals.

For the first time ever, we advocate that traders, who are regularly exposed to the notion of smoothness, confuse the smoothness with the accuracy. This confusion stems from the lack of a clear and precise definition for "smoothness." Traditionally, traders associate smoothness with the moving average's capability to minimize or eradicate the influence of noise, volatility, or short-term fluctuations in the underlying data. Consequently, evaluating the smoothness of a moving average is commonly perceived as quantifying its ability to reduce noise.

In reality, what traders label as "smoothness" is, in fact, the accuracy of the moving average. We strongly emphasize the importance of distinguishing between accuracy and smoothness concerning a moving average. While accuracy does involve the reduction of noise, smoothness refers to the absence of jagged or erratic changes in the moving average's value. Thus, we assert that a moving average must possess not two but three essential properties.

It is essential to emphasize that the calculation of the trading signal within a trend-following rule can be understood as the computation of a weighted moving average of returns. Consequently, the properties of a trend-following rule are intrinsically tied to the properties of the associated moving average of returns. Notably, this moving average of returns should possess the following three key properties: accuracy, smoothness, and responsiveness.

In this chapter, we propose how to quantify these properties. The quantitative measures we suggest are derived exclusively from the return weights attributed to each trading rule. By employing these quantitative metrics, we facilitate clear and objective comparisons between different trend-following rules, allowing for a more informed evaluation of their characteristics.

4.2 Theoretical Framework

The previous chapter reveals a fundamental insight: calculating any technical trading indicator, whether based on one or multiple moving averages, can essentially be understood as computing a single moving average of returns over a specific averaging window. Consequently, while various trend-following rules and moving averages used in these rules may appear distinct at first glance, their true dissimilarity lies solely in the choice of weighting function utilized for computing the moving average of returns. This insight represents a significant advancement in understanding the shared characteristics and distinctions among different trend-following rules relying on moving averages. However, these commonalities and differences can currently be evaluated only through visual examinations of return-weighting functions in various rules. For traders to make informed decisions, it is essential to objectively assess the properties of these rules using quantitative measures. Ultimately, the goal is to identify a rule with the most favorable attributes, necessitating a quantitative evaluation approach.

Formally, the value of the technical indicator at time t is computed using n return lags:

$$I_t(n) = \sum_{i=0}^{n-1} \theta_i r_{t-i}, \tag{4.1}$$

where r_{t-i} is the return lag i and $\{\theta_0, \theta_1, \ldots \theta_{n-1}\}$ are the weights of each return lag. Among the multitude of technical indicators available, their differences primarily arise from the variations in the return weights employed in each unique rule. Our objective is to evaluate the fundamental properties of a trading rule by utilizing these return weights.

In order to successfully accomplish our objective, it is crucial to employ an appropriate and easily comprehensible model for returns that justifies the practice of trend-following. Additionally, this model should accurately replicate the well-known stylized facts observed in financial asset returns. These key facts encompass fat tails, negative skewness, and volatility clustering (Cont, 2001). Our approach to quantifying the numerical characteristics of trend-following rules is based on a widely accepted two-state regime-switching model. This model has been proven to effectively replicate the aforementioned stylized facts (Timmermann, 2000; Frühwirth-Schnatter, 2006). In this model, returns follow a stochastic process that randomly switches between bull and bear states. Notably, the market states are identifiable and exhibit persistence. As a result, this model provides a solid justification for the adoption of trend-following investing strategies.

Specifically, we assume that the return r_t is a discrete-time stochastic process that randomly switches between two states (regimes): bull and bear. The return distribution depends on the state in the following manner:

$$r_t = \begin{cases} \mu_0 + \sigma_0 z_t & \text{in the bear state,} \\ \mu_1 + \sigma_1 z_t & \text{in the bull state,} \end{cases} \tag{4.2}$$

where μ_0 and σ_0 are the mean and standard deviation of returns in the bear state, μ_1 and σ_1 are the mean and standard deviation of returns in the bull state, and z_t is an identically and independently distributed over time random variable with zero mean and unit variance. It is important to note that we assume independence of returns within each state, implying that all covariances $Cov(z_i, z_j)$ are equal to zero when $i \neq j$.

To learn the parameters of the bull and bear states, we conduct an empirical study. This study uses the monthly capital gain returns on the Standard and Poor's (S&P) Composite index, covering the period from January 1870 to December 2020. The data are collected from two sources: Professor William Schwert (https://www.billschwert.com/gws_data.htm) provides the index returns from January 1870 to December 1927, while the index returns from January 1928 to December 2020 are computed using the index values downloaded from Yahoo Finance (https://finance.yahoo.com/).

To identify the turning points of bull and bear markets, we employ a widely accepted method proposed by Pagan and Sossounov (2003). Essentially, this method adapts the dating algorithm developed by Bry and Boschan (1971) for identifying US business cycle turning points using GDP data, with minor modifications. The algorithm serves as a pattern recognition tool, employing a set of rules. It begins by detecting peaks and troughs in the data series. Subsequently, the algorithm applies several censoring operations to ensure that a complete stock cycle spans at least 16 months and that a market state persists for a minimum of 5 months, unless there is a stock price rise or fall exceeding 20%. Table 4.1 presents the summary statistics of the bull and bear market states. The table includes information on the number of states, mean durations of the states, as well as mean returns and standard deviations of returns.

Between 1870 and 2020, a total of 42 bull markets and 41 bear markets were observed. The estimated parameters for bull and bear markets exhibit close agreement with the findings reported in studies by Pagan and Sossounov (2003) and Gonzalez et al. (2005). On average, a bull market spans approximately 28 months, while a bear market lasts around 15 months. Notably, the average duration of a bull market is roughly twice as long as that of a bear market. In terms of absolute mean returns, both bull and bear markets exhibit

Table 4.1 Summary statistics of the estimated parameters of bull and bear market states. Duration is measured in months, while mean returns and standard deviations are annualized and reported as percentages

	Bull states	Bear states
Number of states	42	41
Mean duration	28.3	15.2
Mean return	26.7	−28.5
Standard deviation	14.2	14.8

similar values, averaging around 27%. The standard deviation of returns in bear markets is slightly higher at 14.8% compared to 14.2% in bull markets. It is important to highlight that the primary distinguishing factors between bull and bear markets are their mean returns and durations, while the standard deviation of returns shows marginal variation between the two.

The two-state stochastic process for returns, as defined by Eq. (4.2), is a commonly used model in finance. However, it is important to acknowledge that this model assumes the same mean return and standard deviation within each individual bull (bear) market. Nevertheless, this assumption may deviate from reality, as it is more reasonable to expect that each distinct bull (bear) market possesses its unique values for mean return and standard deviation of returns. To highlight this aspect, Fig. 4.1 illustrates the estimated densities of mean returns and standard deviations for both bull and bear markets. The plots in this figure are constructed based on the estimated mean returns and standard deviations of returns for each specific bull and bear market state.

The density plots for the standard deviation of returns in bull and bear markets show considerable volatility differences within each market type. Each category includes both low-volatility and high-volatility bull and bear markets. However, these plots suggest that the overall volatility differences between bull and bear markets are relatively small, as reflected by the similarity in their density plots.

Likewise, market states can exhibit absolute mean returns that are nearly zero, as well as high absolute mean returns. The density plot illustrating the mean returns during bear markets essentially mirrors the density plot of the mean returns during bull markets when viewed across the vertical axis. This characteristic further strengthens the understanding that the disparity in mean returns between bull and bear markets solely resides in the sign of the mean return.

In summary, Fig. 4.1 illustrates that the key differentiation between bull and bear market returns is the sign of their mean returns. Bull markets demonstrate

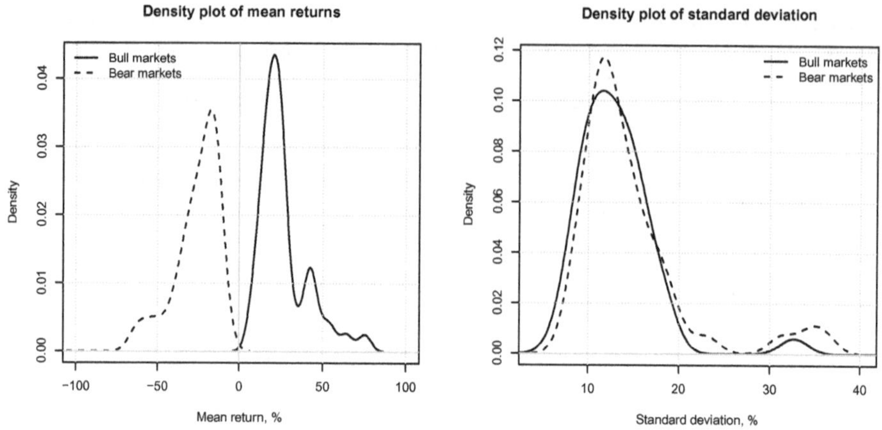

Fig. 4.1 Estimated densities of mean returns and standard deviations in bull and bear markets. The left panel shows the density of mean returns, while the right panel displays the density of return standard deviations

positive mean returns, whereas bear markets display negative mean returns. Moreover, the distributions of absolute mean returns and standard deviation of returns remain remarkably similar across both market states.

Our empirical study suggests that it is reasonable to assume that the standard deviation of returns in both states is equal, denoted as $\sigma_0 = \sigma_1 = \sigma$. On the other hand, the mean state returns only differ in their sign: $\mu_0 = -\mu$, $\mu_1 = \mu$, where μ represents a positive value. To facilitate analytical tractability, we further assume that the returns in each state follow a normal distribution. Specifically, the return r_t behaves according to:

$$r_t \sim \begin{cases} \mathcal{N}(-\mu, \sigma^2) & \text{in the bear state,} \\ \mathcal{N}(\mu, \sigma^2) & \text{in the bull state,} \end{cases}$$

where, for example, the notation $r_t \sim \mathcal{N}(\mu, \sigma^2)$ indicates that r_t is normally distributed with mean μ and variance σ^2. Alternatively, the model for returns can be written in the following manner:

$$r_t = \mu_s + \sigma z_t, \tag{4.3}$$

where z_t is a standard normal random variable, $z_t \sim \mathcal{N}(0, 1)$, and $\mu_s \in \{-\mu, \mu\}$ is the mean return in state s.

Before proceeding further, it is crucial to highlight the following point. We utilize the model defined by Eq. (4.3) to support the calculation of our numerical measures. This model relies on several assumptions, such as the constant mean return and standard deviation of returns in each bull (bear) state. However, as we delve into this chapter, we will discover that most of these assumptions are not vital for the computation of these measures. For instance, our measure of accuracy in trend identification is independent of specific values for σ and μ, as long as $\mu \neq 0$.

Next, we will derive a useful result that we will employ several times throughout the remainder of this chapter. This result is derived under the assumption of a continuation of the market trend in the same direction, meaning that we assume the market state remains unchanged. Given this scenario, what can we infer about the value of the technical trading indicator?

A normal distribution is a member of the family of distributions known as "stable distributions." A distribution is considered stable if a linear combination of random variables with that distribution also follows the same distribution. In our specific context, this implies that the value of the technical indicator, which is calculated as a weighted average of normally distributed returns, adheres to a normal distribution. Therefore, we can express it as $I_t(n) \sim N(\mu_I, \sigma_I^2)$, where μ_I and σ_I represent the mean value and standard deviation of the technical indicator, respectively. Furthermore, we can represent the technical indicator as:

$$I_t(n) = \mu_I + \sigma_I z_t, \tag{4.4}$$

where, as before, z_t denotes a standard normal random variable.

Let us compute μ_I and σ_I. Inserting expression (4.3) into the expression for the value of the technical indicator (4.1), we obtain:

$$I_t(n) = \sum_{i=0}^{n-1} \theta_i r_{t-i} = \sum_{i=0}^{n-1} \theta_i (\mu_s + \sigma z_{t-i}) = \mu_s \sum_{i=0}^{n-1} \theta_i + \sigma \sum_{i=0}^{n-1} \theta_i z_{t-i}.$$

The computation of the mean and the variance of $I_t(n)$ yields:

$$\mu_I = E[I_t(n)] = \mu_s \sum_{i=0}^{n-1} \theta_i, \tag{4.5}$$

$$\begin{aligned} \sigma_I^2 &= Var(I_t(n)) = Var\left(\sigma \sum_{i=0}^{n-1} \theta_i z_{t-i}\right) \\ &= \sigma^2 \sum_{i=0}^{n-1} \sum_{j=0}^{n-1} \theta_i \theta_j Cov(z_i, z_j) = \sigma^2 \sum_{i=0}^{n-1} \theta_i^2. \end{aligned} \tag{4.6}$$

The last equality follows from the fact that $Cov(z_i, z_j) = 0$ when $i \neq j$ and $Cov(z_i, z_i) = 1$. Consequently, the standard deviation of the technical indicator is given by:

$$\sigma_I = \sigma \sqrt{\sum_{i=0}^{n-1} \theta_i^2}. \tag{4.7}$$

4.3 Accuracy in Detecting Trend Direction

To successfully "trade with the trend," it is crucial to determine the direction of the trend. This involves examining the value of the technical trading indicator based on a trend-following rule. There are numerous trend-following rules available, including those that utilize a single moving average and crossover rules that employ two moving averages. In this section, our objective is to introduce a sensible measure that enables us to compare the accuracies of different technical indicators in detecting trend direction.

The measure of accuracy we propose addresses the following question: assuming the trend continues in its current direction, which rule from the set of alternative rules generates the most accurate trading signal? This question is pertinent because, due to data noise, a trading rule may produce a Sell signal when the trend is bullish or a Buy signal when the trend is bearish. By evaluating the accuracy of trading signals, we can identify the rule that generates the fewest false signals.

Let us consider two alternative methods for generating a trading signal. The first method relies on observing the value of the last return, denoted as r_t. The second method involves observing the value of the technical indicator, denoted as $I_t(n)$. In both cases, if the observed value is positive, the trading signal is classified as Buy. Conversely, if the observed value is negative, the trading signal is classified as Sell. Now, how can we compare the accuracy of these two alternative methods?

Due to the presence of noise in the data, achieving perfect accuracy in detecting trend direction is not possible. There will be instances where we correctly identify the trend direction, while other times we make errors. To measure the accuracy of trend direction detection, we can employ a widely used metric called the "Hit ratio." The Hit ratio is a measure commonly utilized in science and engineering fields.

Definition 4.1 Hit ratio (HR) is the fraction of times a correct identification of trend direction is made.

Another relevant ratio is the "Miss ratio" (MR), which quantifies the proportion of times an incorrect identification of the trend direction is made. These two ratios, the Hit ratio and the Miss ratio, can be computed using the number of Hits and Misses as:

$$\text{HR} = \frac{\text{Hits}}{\text{Hits+Misses}}, \quad \text{MR} = \frac{\text{Misses}}{\text{Hits+Misses}}.$$

Hits are the number of times the trend direction is determined correctly, whereas Misses represents the number of times the trend direction is determined incorrectly. The total number of times the trend direction was identified is the sum of Hits and Misses.

Note the following identity:

$$\text{HR} + \text{MR} = 1.$$

Hence, these two ratios naturally lend themselves to interpretation as probabilities. For instance, the Hit ratio (HR) can be understood as the probability of correctly identifying the trend direction. Therefore, we compute the HR as follows[1]:

$$HR(v) = \begin{cases} \text{Prob}(v > 0) & \text{if } \mu_s > 0, \\ \text{Prob}(v < 0) & \text{if } \mu_s < 0, \end{cases}$$

where v represents the observed value (r_t or $I_t(n)$), and Prob(·) denotes the probability. In other words, assuming a bullish market trend, the HR of observation v is the probability of correctly identifying an upward price trend. Conversely, assuming a bearish market trend, the HR of observation v is the probability of correctly identifying a downward price trend. It is important to highlight that both probabilities are equal based on our return model. That is, the HR is the same in both bull and bear markets. Therefore, in the subsequent presentation, we will restrict our attention to the case where $\mu_s = \mu > 0$.

The computation of the HR of returns yields:

$$Prob(r > 0) = Prob(\mu + \sigma z > 0) = Prob\left(z > -\frac{\mu}{\sigma}\right) = \Phi\left(\frac{\mu}{\sigma}\right), \tag{4.8}$$

[1] Note that we assume the continuation of the current trend direction. For example, if prices have been trending upward until now, we expect this upward trend to persist in the next period.

where $\Phi(.)$ denotes the cumulative distribution function of a standard normal random variable.

Similarly, the computation of the HR of the technical indicator gives us:

$$Prob(I(n) > 0) = Prob(\mu_I + \sigma_I z > 0) = Prob\left(z > -\frac{\mu_I}{\sigma_I}\right) = \Phi\left(\frac{\mu_I}{\sigma_I}\right). \tag{4.9}$$

Remark 4.1 Recall that $0 \leq \Phi(x) \leq 1$, $\Phi(0) = 0.5$, and both $\frac{\mu}{\sigma} > 0$ and $\frac{\mu_I}{\sigma_I} > 0$. Hence, assuming that the trend continues in the same direction, we can infer that $HR > 0.5$. In other words, the percentage of accurate trend identifications exceeds 50%. It is worth noting that the highest attainable HR value is 100%.

To determine which method of generating trading signals is more accurate, we can compare the ratios $\frac{\mu}{\sigma}$ and $\frac{\mu_I}{\sigma_I}$. Because function $\Phi(x)$ is increasing in x, a higher ratio of the mean return to the standard deviation of returns corresponds to a higher HR. Consequently, when evaluating multiple alternative technical indicators, the indicator with the highest $\frac{\mu_I}{\sigma_I}$ ratio is considered the most accurate. Our current objective is to thoroughly examine and analyze this ratio.

A technical trading indicator plays a crucial role in extracting trading signals from noisy data. In our case, the data represents return observations, where each observation consists of two components: the signal and the noise. We can express this relationship as:

$$r_t = \underbrace{\mu}_{\text{signal}} + \underbrace{\sigma z_t}_{\text{noise}}.$$

where the signal is represented by the mean return μ, and the random noise is captured by the product σz_t.

The concept of "signal-to-noise ratio" is a fundamental measure used to evaluate the quality and reliability of a signal in the presence of noise. It quantifies the ratio of the strength or magnitude of the desired signal to the level of unwanted background noise or interference. In various fields, including science, engineering, and finance, signals are often contaminated by random noise or unwanted disturbances.

Definition 4.2 Signal-to-noise ratio (SNR) compares the level of signal to the level of noise. Typically, SNR is defined as the ratio of signal power to noise power.

The signal-to-noise ratio provides a way to assess how well the desired signal stands out from the background noise. A higher SNR indicates a stronger, more distinguishable signal relative to the noise, resulting in better signal quality and more accurate detection or estimation.

In the context of trend-following in trading, the SNR helps determine the accuracy of identifying the underlying trend direction amid the noise present in return observations. By comparing the signal-to-noise ratio of different technical indicators or methods, it becomes possible to assess their effectiveness in extracting reliable signals from noisy data. A higher SNR suggests a more accurate and robust trend-following indicator.

In our specific context, we employ the following approach to compute the SNR:

$$SNR(v) = \frac{E[v]}{Std(v)},$$

where v represents the observed value, which can be either r_t (return observation) or $I_t(n)$ (technical indicator). $E[v]$ refers to the expected value of v, while $Std(v)$ represents the standard deviation of v. It is worth emphasizing that the noise power is measured by $Std(v)$, whereas the signal power is measured by the value of $E[v]$.

The signal-to-noise ratio (SNR) of the return r_t is determined by the following equation:

$$SNR(r) = \frac{E[r_t]}{Std(r_t)} = \frac{\mu}{\sigma}. \tag{4.10}$$

It is important to note that the SNR increases as the mean return μ strengthens, indicating a more pronounced signal. Conversely, the SNR decreases when the standard deviation of returns σ increases, suggesting a greater presence of noise.

When the signal power significantly outweighs the noise power, the SNR becomes large, making it relatively easy to identify the trend direction simply by observing the return value. This occurs when the return observation predominantly contains the signal component. However, in financial markets, the noise power is typically substantially greater than the signal power. Consequently, in order to extract the signal from the noise, it becomes necessary to reduce the noise power through appropriate techniques or methods.

Consider now the SNR of the technical indicator $I_t(n)$. Using formulas (4.5) and (4.7) we obtain:

$$SNR(I(n)) = \frac{\mu_I}{\sigma_I} = \frac{\mu \sum_{i=0}^{n-1} \theta_i}{\sigma \sqrt{\sum_{i=0}^{n-1} \theta_i^2}} = \frac{\sum_{i=0}^{n-1} \theta_i}{\sqrt{\sum_{i=0}^{n-1} \theta_i^2}} SNR(r). \tag{4.11}$$

This result suggests that the SNR of the technical indicator is equal to the SNR of the returns multiplied by the following factor:

$$NSF(\theta_0, \ldots, \theta_{n-1}) = \frac{\sum_{i=0}^{n-1} \theta_i}{\sqrt{\sum_{i=0}^{n-1} \theta_i^2}},$$

where the notation $NSF(\theta_0, \ldots, \theta_{n-1})$ means that this factor is computed using the return weights $\theta_0, \ldots, \theta_{n-1}$. Consequently, we can express this relationship as:

$$SNR(I(n)) = NSF(\theta_0, \ldots, \theta_{n-1}) \times SNR(r). \tag{4.12}$$

Note that the factor $NSF(\theta_0, \ldots, \theta_{n-1})$ satisfies the following two useful properties.

Property 4.1 The factor $NSF(\theta_0, \ldots, \theta_{n-1})$ remains unchanged when the return weights are scaled by a positive constant. In other words, it can be demonstrated that:

$$NSF(c \times \theta_0, \ldots, c \times \theta_{n-1}) = NSF(\theta_0, \ldots, \theta_{n-1}),$$

where c represents any positive real number. This property implies that one can freely adjust the scaling of the return weights for the technical indicator without affecting its accuracy in detecting trend direction.

Property 4.2 The order of weights in a technical indicator has no impact on the value of the NSF. This is because changing the order of weights does not alter the value of the factor. Therefore, one can freely rearrange the order of return weights in the technical indicator without affecting its accuracy in detecting trend direction.

Suppose that in a technical indicator, the sum of return weights is strictly positive, $\sum_{i=0}^{n-1} \theta_i > 0$. In such a scenario, it is possible to normalize the weights[2] so that they satisfy the following condition:

$$\sum_{i=0}^{n-1} \theta_i = 1.$$

[2] More precisely, the normalization factor c in this case can be obtained as $\frac{1}{\sum_{i=0}^{n-1} \theta_i}$.

When the weights are normalized, the NSF can be calculated as follows:

$$NSF(\theta_0, \ldots, \theta_{n-1}) = \frac{1}{\sqrt{\sum_{i=0}^{n-1} \theta_i^2}} = \frac{1}{\sqrt{HI(\theta_0, \ldots, \theta_{n-1})}},$$

Here, $HI(\theta_0, \ldots, \theta_{n-1})$ refers to the Herfindahl index, also known as the Herfindahl-Hirschman index. The Herfindahl index is a widely accepted measure of market concentration and competition among market participants. It is defined as:

$$HI(\theta_0, \ldots, \theta_{n-1}) = \sum_{i=0}^{n-1} \theta_i^2, \text{ subject to } \sum_{i=0}^{n-1} \theta_i = 1.$$

This index is also utilized to assess the concentration of investment portfolios.

Proposition 4.1 *The lower bound of the Herfindahl index is given by:*

$$HI(\theta_0, \ldots, \theta_{n-1}) \geq \frac{1}{n}.$$

Assuming all return weights are nonnegative, $\theta_i \geq 0$ for all i, the upper bound of the Herfindahl index is given by:

$$HI(\theta_0, \ldots, \theta_{n-1}) \leq 1.$$

The lower bound is achieved when $\theta_i = \frac{1}{n}$ for all i. In other words, the Herfindahl index reaches its minimum value when the returns are equally weighted. The upper bound is achieved when one of the θ_i values is 1, while all other θ_j values are 0 for $j \neq i$. Thus, the Herfindahl index reaches its maximum when all the weight is concentrated on a single return observation.

The proof is given in the Appendix to this chapter.

Remark 4.2 Based on Proposition 4.1, it follows that:

$$1 \leq NSF(\theta_0, \ldots, \theta_{n-1}) \leq \sqrt{n}.$$

In simpler terms, the value of $NSF(\theta_0, \ldots, \theta_{n-1})$ is bounded between 1 and $\sqrt{n}$, representing the lower and upper limits, respectively. It is important to highlight that the lower bound of 1 is established assuming nonnegative weights. However, if negative weights are permitted, this lower bound can potentially decrease, possibly even reaching a negative value.

Remark 4.3 The preceding remark leads us to the following conclusion:

$$SNR(r) \le SNR(I(n)) \le \sqrt{n}\, SNR(r).$$

In other words, the SNR of a technical indicator is constrained within a certain range. The lower limit is determined by the SNR of the returns themselves, while the upper limit is the SNR of returns multiplied by the square root of the number of return lags n.

Remark 4.4 It is generally anticipated that:

$$SNR(I(n)) > SNR(r).$$

In other words, the SNR of the technical indicator is typically higher than the SNR of the returns themselves.

Remark 4.5 It is worth noting that when the weights are normalized, the signal power of the technical indicator is equivalent to that of the return observation. This can be seen from the following equality:

$$E[I_t(n)] = \mu \sum_{i=0}^{n-1} \theta_i = \mu = E[r_t].$$

Simultaneously, the noise power of the technical indicator is either less than or equal to that of the return observation, as expressed by:

$$Std(I_t(n)) = \sigma \sqrt{HI(\theta_0, \ldots, \theta_{n-1})} \le \sigma = Std(r_t).$$

This inequality is a consequence of Proposition 4.1, which establishes that $\sqrt{HI(\theta_0, \ldots, \theta_{n-1})} \le 1$. Typically, the noise power of a technical indicator is lower than the noise power of a return observation:

$$Std(I_t(n)) < Std(r_t).$$

For example, in the case of equally weighted returns, the noise power of the technical indicator is $\frac{\sigma}{\sqrt{n}}$, which is smaller than the noise power σ of the returns. These observations collectively suggest the following conclusion: a technical indicator reduces noise power while maintaining signal power.

The aforementioned conclusion provides the rationale behind the name given to this factor.

Definition 4.3 The factor $NSF(\theta_0, \ldots, \theta_{n-1})$ is defined as the **Noise Suppression Factor**:

$$NSF(I(n)) = \frac{\sum_{i=0}^{n-1} \theta_i}{\sqrt{\sum_{i=0}^{n-1} \theta_i^2}}.$$

Remark 4.6 Due to the higher SNR of a technical indicator compared to that of returns, the ability to accurately detect trend direction is significantly enhanced when using the technical indicator. Consequently, the HR of the technical indicator exceeds that of returns. In essence, utilizing a technical indicator enables extracting the signal from the noise with superior accuracy.

Remark 4.7 It is essential to emphasize the following key point. To compare the accuracies of different technical indicators, one can examine their respective NSFs. A higher NSF indicates superior accuracy in detecting trend direction, irrespective of the specific values of the mean return μ and the standard deviation of returns σ, as long as $\mu \neq 0$. This is due to the fact that the NSF quantifies the enhancement of the SNR in the return observation. In particular, regardless of the SNR of the return, the SNR of the technical indicator is equal to the SNR of the return multiplied by the NSF.

Remark 4.8 Remarkably, the MOM(n) technical indicator, which calculates the difference between the last price and the price $n + 1$ periods ago, stands out as the most accurate technical indicator. Despite its simplicity, the MOM(n) technical indicator demonstrates exceptional noise reduction capabilities compared to other technical indicators computed with an averaging window of size n. This is primarily due to the fact that the MOM(n) technical indicator utilizes equal weights for the last n returns, resulting in the maximum achievable NSF.

In conclusion of this section, we present a visual representation of the accuracies associated with two different methods of generating a trading signal. The first method involves observing the value of the last return r_t, while the second method involves observing the value of the technical indicator $MOM_t(12)$. The market returns are assumed to be observed on a monthly basis. We vary the signal-to-noise ratio of returns within the range $SNR(r) \in [0, 1]$. In real markets, at the monthly frequency, the signal-to-noise ratio of returns is typically around 0.5 in both the bull and bear states of the market. This value falls within the middle of the selected range for $SNR(r)$.

Figure 4.2 illustrates the hit ratios of the return and the MOM(12) technical indicator as a function of $SNR(r)$. These hit ratios are computed using the following formulas:

$$\text{HR}(r) = \Phi(SNR(r)), \quad \text{HR}(MOM(12)) = \Phi\left(\sqrt{12} \times SNR(r)\right),$$

where $\sqrt{12}$ represents the NSF of the MOM(12) technical indicator.

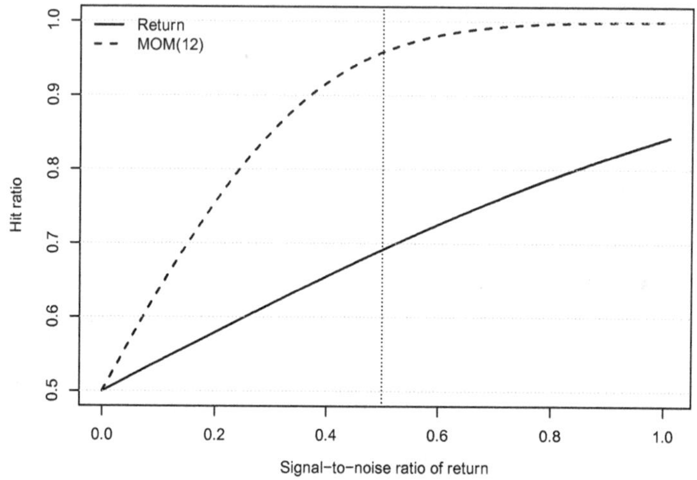

Fig. 4.2 Comparison of hit ratios between the MOM(12) technical indicator and the return, plotted against the signal-to-noise ratio of returns. The dotted vertical line represents the typical signal-to-noise ratio observed in a market state

The curves depicted in Fig. 4.2 clearly demonstrate the substantial improvement in accuracy achieved by employing the MOM(12) rule for detecting trend direction. For instance, when the signal-to-noise ratio of returns matches its typical value, the method solely based on observing the value of the last return achieves an accuracy of approximately 70%. In other words, the correct trend direction is identified about 70 times out of 100 observations. In contrast, utilizing the technical indicator of the MOM(12) rule allows for an impressive accuracy of correctly identifying the trend direction around 95 times out of 100 observations.

4.4 Average Delay in Identifying Trend Turning Points

Traders often quote the saying, "The trend is your friend, until it bends," to highlight the temporary nature of trends. This implies that in order to trade successfully with the trend, it is crucial not only to determine its direction accurately but also to identify turning points as early as possible. Technical indicators of trend-following rules try to accomplish these two tasks. When prices are in an upward trend, a reliable technical indicator should generate a Buy signal. However, when the upward trend ends and a downward trend begins, the indicator must promptly recognize this change and generate a Sell signal.

Different trend-following rules exist, including those that utilize a single moving average and crossover rules that involve two moving averages. Regardless of the type of trading rule, a well-known issue with all trend-following rules is the delayed identification of trend turning points. In this section, our objective is to present a sensible measure for comparing the average lag times of various technical indicators in detecting these turning points.

Here, we assume that there is a change in the market state at a specific time, denoted as t_0. Before t_0, the prices have been consistently trending upward for a sufficiently long time. However, at t_0, the trend reverses, indicating a turning point in the trend. Subsequently, starting from t_0, the prices exhibit a downward trend for a sufficiently long time.

It is important to note that when we refer to "a sufficiently long time," we consider the time period during which the accuracy of trend direction detection reaches its maximum. Typically, this duration corresponds to the number of return lags in the technical indicator.

In this analysis, our goal is to compute the average lag time between the reversal of the trend and the point when a Buy signal is replaced by a Sell signal. It is important to note that we could alternatively assume that before t_0, prices were in a downward trend, and from t_0 onward, they began trending upward. However, in our model defined by Eq. (4.3), the average delay time in detecting trend turning points remains constant. Specifically, the average lag time in identifying a turning point is the same whether it occurs between bullish and bearish markets or vice versa.

Due to the inherent randomness in financial asset returns, the lag time of a technical indicator is also subject to randomness. As a result, there is uncertainty surrounding the duration it takes for a technical indicator to identify a change in the trend direction. However, it is possible to estimate the average lag time, which provides a measure of the typical delay. Additionally, if needed, we can assess the level of uncertainty associated with the lag time.

Definition 4.4 The concept of **Average Lag Time** of a trading rule, denoted as ALT(TR), refers to the average duration it takes for a technical indicator to identify a shift in the trend direction. ALT(TR) serves as a metric to gauge the typical time delay a technical indicator exhibits in recognizing trend changes.

The term "average" is synonymous with "mean," which represents a measure obtained by disregarding uncertainties. In the context of technical indicators, the ALT(TR) can be assessed under the assumption of no noise in the return data. In this scenario, the value of a technical indicator corresponds to the mean value of the underlying process

Previously, we explored the concept of the "average lag time of a moving average," ALT(MA). However, it is important to clarify a common misconception regarding this measure. Contrary to popular belief among traders, the average lag time of a moving average does not directly represent the average delay in identifying trend turning points. In order to address this misconception, Fig. 4.3 provides a graphical illustration comparing the average lag time of the SMA of prices and the average lag time of the price and SMA crossover (P-SMA) rule. The solid line in the figure represents the price trend, while the dashed line depicts the value of the SMA of prices.

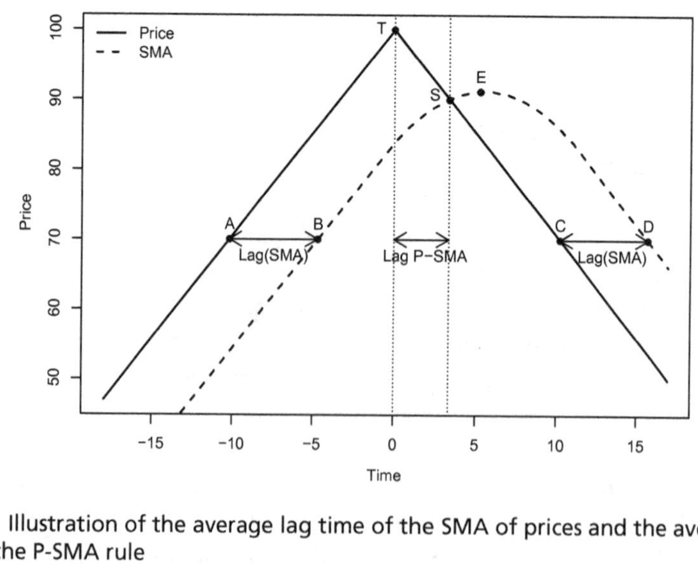

Fig. 4.3 Illustration of the average lag time of the SMA of prices and the average lag time of the P-SMA rule

Until time $t_0 = 0$, the mean return is μ, therefore, the average change in price between two consecutive observations is given by $\Delta P_t = \mu P_t$. Subsequently, starting from time t_0, the mean return becomes $-\mu$, resulting in an average price change given by $\Delta P_t = -\mu P_t$. Under a first-order approximation, the average price exhibits a linear increase until t_0, followed by a linear decrease. The peak in the price is marked as point T.

It is important to recall that in the P-SMA rule, the trading signal depends on the relationship between the price and the SMA of prices. Specifically, if the price is above the SMA, then the trading signal is Buy; otherwise, the trading signal is Sell. Notably, the change in the trading signal occurs at point S. The average lag time between the change in trend direction and the change in the trading signal equals the time difference between points S and T.

The average lag time of the SMA provides a measure of the time delay between the price and the SMA of prices. However, it is crucial to emphasize that the average lag time of a moving average accurately characterizes the time lag only when both the price and the moving average exhibit steady increases or decreases. In Fig. 4.3, the average lag time of the SMA corresponds to the time difference between points B and A, as well as between points D and C. These points represent the "lagged versions" of each other, with point B (D) belonging to the SMA of prices and point A (C) belonging to the price trend.

However, when the price trend changes its direction and the SMA of prices bends, the average lag time of a moving average cannot be determined in the same manner. For instance, in Fig. 4.3, it is unclear where the lagged version of point T in the price trend lies. The curves in the figure indicate that the SMA never reaches the level of T in the price, suggesting that point T has no corresponding lagged version in the SMA. One might assume that the lagged version of the price peak T is represented by the peak in the SMA denoted by point E. However, the time lag between points E and T does not reflect the time delay in the change of the trading signal of the P-SMA rule.

It is worth noting that the time lag between points E and T aligns with the average lag time of the SMA. However, while this identity holds for the SMA, it generally does not apply to other types of moving averages. In summary, the clear conclusion drawn from the illustration in Fig. 4.3 is that the average lag time of the P-SMA rule does not equate to the average lag time of the SMA.

The concept of the "average lag time of a moving average" becomes further complicated when a trading rule involves the use of multiple moving averages of prices. For instance, in a double moving average crossover rule, the trading signal is generated based on the relationship between a shorter moving average and a longer moving average. In such cases, how do we determine the average time delay in detecting trend turning points? Does it equal the sum or the difference of the average lag times of the two moving averages?

The complexity intensifies when a trading rule incorporates three moving averages. In contrast, when formulated in a return-based framework, any technical indicator is computed using a single moving average of returns. Therefore, once we understand how to compute the average lag time of a technical indicator, the number of moving averages of prices utilized to generate the trading signal in a trend-following rule becomes irrelevant.

From now on, whenever we refer to the average lag time, it will always be in the context of the average lag time of a trading rule, denoted as ALT(TR). To simplify our notation, we will use "ALT" to represent the average lag time of a trading rule. Since a trading signal in any rule is generated based on the value of its corresponding technical indicator, the ALT of a trading rule is essentially the same as the ALT of its technical indicator.

Let us now delve into our approach for computing the ALT of a technical indicator. In our model, the price trend remains upward until time t_0. Therefore, up to and including time t_0, the average value of the technical indicator can be expressed as:

$$E[I_t(n)] = \sum_{i=0}^{n-1} \mu\theta_i > 0.$$

The inequality holds true since $\mu > 0$ and $\sum_{i=0}^{n-1} \theta_i > 0$. It is crucial for this inequality to hold in order for the technical indicator to generate a Buy signal when the trend is bullish.

At time $t = t_0 + 1$, following the change in the price trend direction, the technical indicator's average value becomes:

$$E[I_t(n)] = -\mu\theta_0 + \sum_{i=1}^{n-1} \mu\theta_i = \mu\left(-\sum_{i=0}^{0} \theta_i + \sum_{i=1}^{n-1} \theta_i\right) > 0.$$

We assume that, at this time, the technical indicator value is positive. Moving forward to time $t = t_0 + 2$, the mean value of the technical indicator can be determined as:

$$E[I_t(n)] = -\mu(\theta_0 + \theta_1) + \sum_{i=2}^{n-1} \mu\theta_i = \mu\left(-\sum_{i=0}^{1} \theta_i + \sum_{i=2}^{n-1} \theta_i\right) > 0.$$

Again, we assume the technical indicator value to be positive at this time. However, eventually, at time $t = t_0 + k$, the technical indicator value changes its sign:

$$E[I_t(n)] = \mu \left(-\sum_{i=0}^{k-1} \theta_i + \sum_{i=k}^{n-1} \theta_i \right) < 0.$$

Consequently, it takes an average of k periods for the technical indicator to recognize the change in the trend direction.

Based on this explanation, the ALT of a technical indicator can be computed as:

$$\arg \min_{k \in [1,n-1]} \sum_{i=0}^{k-1} \theta_i \geq \sum_{i=k}^{n-1} \theta_i. \tag{4.13}$$

In simpler terms, the ALT represents the minimum number of lags, k, that satisfy the condition where the sum of return weights from lag 0 to lag $k - 1$ is greater than or equal to the sum of return weights from lag k to lag $n - 1$. Intuitively, the average lag time corresponds to the lag that divides the return weights into two parts, ensuring the sums of weights in each part are equal. Formally, this can be expressed as:

$$\sum_{i=0}^{\text{ALT}-1} \theta_i = \sum_{i=\text{ALT}}^{n-1} \theta_i. \tag{4.14}$$

Another valuable relationship arises from the fact that the sums of weights in each part are equal and each sum is equivalent to half of the total sum of weights. This relationship can be expressed as follows:

$$\sum_{i=0}^{\text{ALT}-1} \theta_i = \frac{1}{2} \sum_{i=0}^{n-1} \theta_i = \frac{1}{2} A, \tag{4.15}$$

where A represents the total sum of return weights in a technical indicator.

In order to derive analytical results for the average lag times of different technical indicators, equality (4.15) is more convenient to use than equality (4.14) or inequality (4.13).

Property 4.3 The scaling of return weights by a positive constant does not affect the average lag time of a technical indicator. Specifically, it can be shown that if:

$$\sum_{i=0}^{\mathrm{ALT}-1} \theta_i \geq \sum_{i=\mathrm{ALT}}^{n-1} \theta_i,$$

then necessarily

$$\sum_{i=0}^{\mathrm{ALT}-1} c \times \theta_i \geq \sum_{i=\mathrm{ALT}}^{n-1} c \times \theta_i,$$

where c is any positive real number. This property indicates that one can freely re-scale the return weights of the technical indicator without altering its average lag time.

Property 4.4 If the return-weighting function is symmetrical about the center $\frac{n}{2}$, then the average lag time is at the center point, ALT$= \frac{n}{2}$. This is because in this case, the center point divides all return weights into two parts, ensuring that the sum of weights in each part is equal.

Remark 4.9 It is important to note that the average lag time of a technical indicator does not depend on the return volatility σ.

Remark 4.10 Similarly, the average lag time of a technical indicator does not depend on the mean return μ_s, as long as the absolute values of the mean returns are the same in both market states.

If there are variations in the absolute mean returns between the two market states, the calculation of the average lag time can be adjusted to accommodate these mean return values. However, it is important to note that in such scenarios, there will be two average lag times: one for detecting a turning point between a bull and bear market state, and another for detecting a turning point between a bear and bull market state. In this particular case, our proposed ALT measure does not accurately represent the average delay time in identifying trend turning points. Nevertheless, the ALT can still be employed to compare the responsiveness of different trading rules. This is because if a rule is most responsive when the absolute values of the mean returns are equal, it typically remains the most responsive even when the mean returns differ.

In conclusion, this section offers two insightful illustrations. The first illustration demonstrates the average reaction of a technical indicator to a trend's turning point, providing valuable insights. The second illustration showcases the dynamic changes in the hit ratio of a technical indicator during and after a trend's turning point, providing further meaningful observations.

Figure 4.4 illustrates the mean returns and the reaction of the technical indicator of the P-SMA rule to the change in the mean return values. The scenario assumes that the mean return until time $t_0 = 0$ is $\mu = 0.2$. From time t_0 onward, the mean return changes its sign to $\mu = -0.2$. The dashed line in the figure represents the mean return values, with t_0 corresponding to the peak in the price trend. The solid line depicts the response of the P-SMA technical indicator to the price trend change. It is important to note that while the mean returns switch instantaneously from μ to $-\mu$, the value of the P-SMA technical indicator gradually decreases from μ to $-\mu$. Please note that this illustration assumes that the return weights are normalized such that $\sum_{i=0}^{n-1} \theta_i = 1$. At point S, the technical indicator changes its sign from positive to negative. Consequently, the average lag time of the P-SMA technical indicator corresponds to the time difference between points S and T.

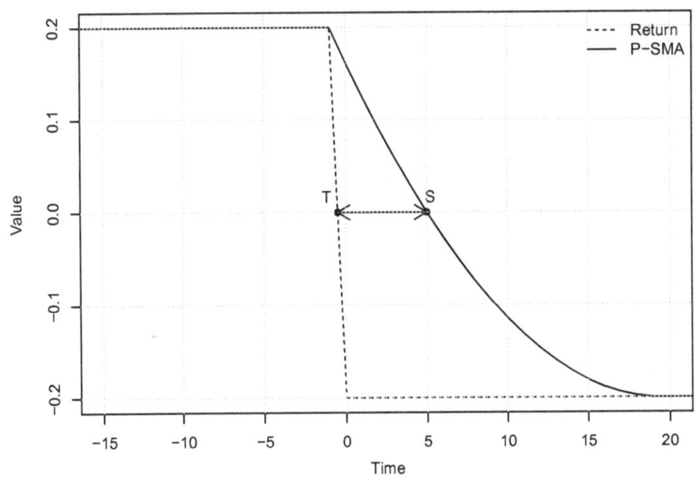

Fig. 4.4 Change in the mean returns and the value of the P-SMA technical indicator

Figure 4.5 visually depicts the change in the hit ratio of the P-SMA technical indicator during and after a turning point in the trend. Until time t_0, the hit ratio reaches its maximum value, indicating that the trend direction is identified with the highest accuracy possible for this technical indicator. However, when the trend abruptly changes its direction, the hit ratio of the technical indicator drops to its minimum. This means that immediately after t_0, the trend direction is identified with the lowest possible accuracy. This occurs because the technical indicator produces a strong Buy signal while the prices are decreasing.

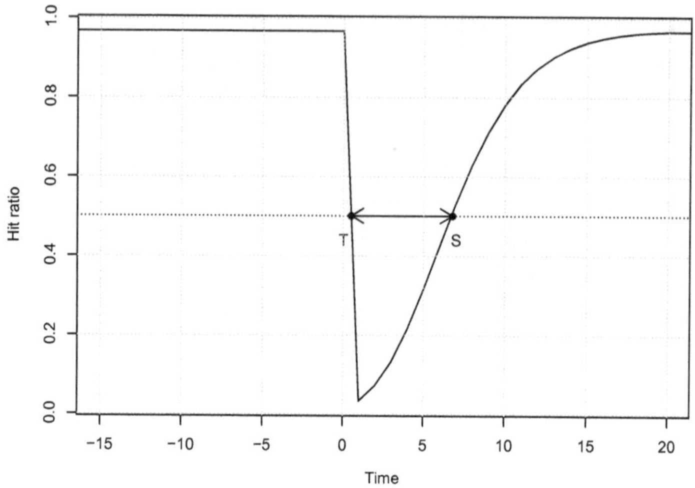

Fig. 4.5 Hit ratio of the P-SMA technical indicator over the turning point in the trend

As time progresses, the hit ratio gradually increases toward its maximum value. In Fig. 4.5, the average lag time of the P-SMA technical indicator corresponds to the time difference between points S and T. Point T represents the time when the price trend reaches its peak value. Point S, on the other hand, lags behind point S by k periods. The mean value of the technical indicator at point S can be expressed as:

$$E[I_t(n)] = \mu_I = \mu\left(-\sum_{i=0}^{k-1}\theta_i + \sum_{i=k}^{n-1}\theta_i\right) = 0,$$

where $t = t_0 + k$. By definition, k represents the average lag time of the technical indicator. Consequently, at point S, $HR(I(n)) = \Phi(0) = 0.5$. This implies that point S represents the intersection of the hit ratio with the 0.5 (50%) level. Therefore, the ALT of a technical indicator is also the average time it takes for the hit ratio to reach a 50% accuracy level after a change in the trend.

4.5 Understanding and Quantitative Assessment of Smoothness

Traders place great importance on the smoothness and responsiveness of moving averages. While responsiveness is easily understood as the time it takes to identify trend reversals, the concept of smoothness seems to lack a precise definition in the trading community. It is evident that traders may not have a clear understanding of what they mean when they refer to smoothness. The issue lies in the absence of a concise and well-defined definition for this term. In essence, smoothness is defined as the opposite of roughness, where roughness implies an uneven and irregular surface.

In the realm of moving averages, smoothness typically pertains to the ability of the average to mitigate or eliminate the impact of noise, volatility, or short-term fluctuations present in the underlying data. Following this logic, assessing the smoothness of a moving average involves quantifying the extent to which it reduces noise. One way to measure the smoothness of a moving average is by calculating the standard deviation of the price data around the moving average line. A lower standard deviation suggests that the moving average effectively filters out price fluctuations, resulting in a smoother line. Conversely, a higher standard deviation indicates that the moving average is less proficient at reducing price noise, resulting in a less smooth line.

The example presented in Fig. 4.6 highlights the limitation of using the standard deviation of noise as a reliable measure of smoothness. In this scenario, we consider two distinct moving averages employed for trend detection. Both moving averages exhibit errors in identifying the trend direction. In our hypothetical example, the sets of error values for both moving averages are the same, but their temporal structures differ. More specifically, the time series of errors for the first moving average follows a sine wave pattern, indicating a certain regularity in the spatial distribution of errors. On the other hand, the time series of errors for the second moving average is generated by arranging the errors of the first moving average in a completely random sequence.

It is important to note that the error distributions for the two moving averages in question are identical. Specifically, the mean errors are zero (as per construction), and the standard deviations of the errors are equal. While these similarities may initially suggest that the moving averages possess an equivalent level of accuracy in identifying trends, it does not necessarily imply that they exhibit the same level of smoothness. In fact, upon visual examination, it becomes apparent that the second moving average is less smooth compared to the first. This observation is substantiated by the fact that the error associated

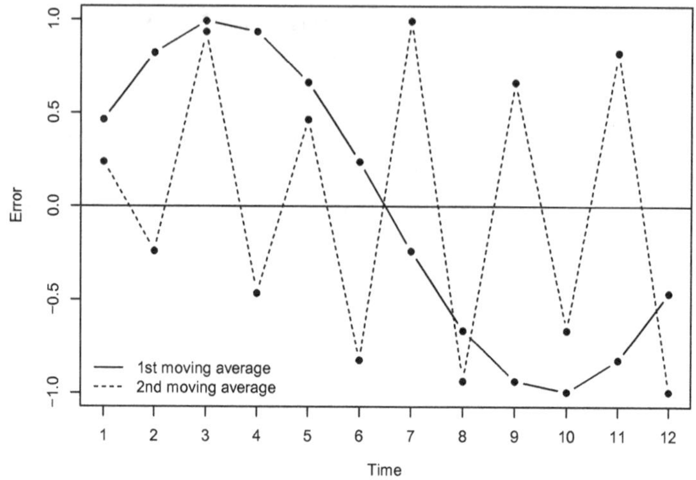

Fig. 4.6 Distributions of errors over time when using two different moving averages to identify the trend direction

with the second moving average displays more jagged or erratic movements, indicating a less effective smoothing process.

The example provided above effectively demonstrates that the smoothness of a moving average is not determined by the standard deviation of the errors, but rather by the variability between consecutive pairs of errors. In scientific terminology, smoothness is closely linked to the level of spatial dependence exhibited by the errors. Put simply, the greater the degree of spatial dependence, the smoother the moving average is considered to be.

Our previous discussion highlights an important distinction that traders often overlook when discussing the smoothness of a moving average. In reality, what they are referring to as smoothness is actually the accuracy of the moving average. However, we recognize the need to differentiate between accuracy and smoothness in relation to a moving average. It is crucial to note that a high level of accuracy does not necessarily guarantee a high degree of smoothness and vice versa. There are scenarios where a moving average may excel at accurately identifying trends but falls short in terms of its effectiveness in smoothing out fluctuations.

Our objective is not merely to assess the smoothness of a moving average, but rather to evaluate the smoothness of a technical indicator derived from a trend-following rule based on moving averages. To achieve this, we propose utilizing the lag one autocorrelation of the technical indicator as a metric to measure the serial dependence present in the trading signal. We argue that this measure of autocorrelation provides a reasonable assessment of the smoothness of a technical indicator.

We begin our argument with an important observation shared by many traders, which revolves around a common challenge in trend-following known as whipsaw trades. Whipsaw trades represent unnecessary and detrimental trades that undermine the profitability of a trading strategy. These trades are particularly problematic as they incur transaction costs with each execution, ultimately impacting the overall profitability.

Whipsaw trades occur when the trading rule generates signals that frequently reverse the direction of a trading position. They become most pronounced during periods when price movements lack a clear and sustained direction, often referred to as sideways or ranging markets. Consequently, it becomes imperative for a trend-following rule to minimize the frequency of position reversals in order to address the issue of whipsaw trades effectively.

Fortunately, the problem of the optimal trend-following with transaction costs has recently been addressed in the paper by Zakamulin and Giner (2023). Among other things, this paper establishes a formula for expected transaction costs and determines the analytical solution for the return-weighting function of a technical indicator that minimizes these costs. The primary discovery in this study is the direct proportionality between expected transaction costs and the probability of a position reversal. This probability decreases as the lag one autocorrelation of the technical indicator increases. The presentation in the rest of this section follows along the lines of the presentation in the paper by Zakamulin and Giner (2023), offering a more detailed exploration of the presented concepts.

Let us consider a scenario where we have prior knowledge of the probability of a position reversal between times t and $t+1$. A position reversal occurs when a Buy signal generated at time t changes to a Sell signal at time $t+1$ or vice versa. To calculate this probability, we use the following formula:

$$\begin{aligned} Prob(\text{Reversal}) = \; & Prob(I_{t+1}(n) > 0, I_t(n) < 0) \\ & + Prob(I_{t+1}(n) < 0, I_t(n) > 0), \end{aligned}$$

where $Prob(\text{Reversal})$ represents the probability of a position reversal. $Prob(I_{t+1}(n) > 0, I_t(n) < 0)$ denotes the probability of a Sell signal at time t and a Buy signal at time $t+1$, while $Prob(I_{t+1}(n) < 0, I_t(n) > 0)$ represents the probability of a Buy signal at time t and a Sell signal at time $t+1$. The probability of a position reversal is the sum of these two probabilities.

Given our knowledge of the reversal probability over one period, we can determine the expected number of trades, denoted as $E[N]$, over a time interval of length T periods using the following formula:

$$E[N] = T \times Prob(\text{Reversal}),$$

where T denotes the duration of the time interval.

The aforementioned formula provides us with an estimate of the expected number of trades within a given time frame based on the probability of position reversal over one period. Once we have this estimate, we can proceed to approximate the average transaction costs associated with these trades. Transaction costs in capital markets typically encompass three primary components: the bid-ask spread (half of its size), brokerage fees (commissions), and market impact costs. Additionally, specific equity markets may involve various taxes, delay costs, opportunity costs, short borrowing costs, and other factors. Determining the precise amount of transaction costs can be challenging due to several factors, including the investor type, liquidity of the financial asset, trade volume, and the prevailing market conditions. As a result, effectively incorporating realistic transaction costs into theoretical models poses inherent complexities.

In order to simplify the treatment of transaction costs, researchers often make the assumption that these costs are proportional to the amount traded, as discussed in Davis and Norman (1990), Dai et al. (2010), and Olivares-Nadal and DeMiguel (2018). Under this assumption, when a trader enters or exits a position in stocks, the transaction costs can be represented as a fixed percentage, denoted as κ, which is subtracted from the returns generated by the trend-following strategy. Consequently, we can calculate the expected amount of transaction costs, denoted as $E[TC]$, using the following formula:

$$E[TC] = \kappa E[N] = \kappa T \times Prob(\text{Reversal}),$$

where TC represents the amount of transaction costs. Please note that in our definition, transaction costs are considered as a reduction in returns. For the purpose of illustration, let us assume that the probability of a position reversal is 5%, and if a reversal occurs, the trader incurs a loss of 0.2% of the realized returns on a trade. Over a span of 100 periods, the expected return loss would amount to $0.002 \times 100 \times 0.05 = 0.01$, which is equivalent to 1%.

The main challenge lies in computing the probability of a trade reversal analytically. A closed-form solution for the probability of reversal is available under the following condition:

$$Prob(\text{Reversal}) = Prob(I_{t+1}(n) > \mu_I, I_t(n) < \mu_I) + Prob(I_{t+1}(n) < \mu_I, I_t(n) > \mu_I),$$

where μ_I represents the mean value of the technical indicator $I(n)$. Since the process for $I(n)$ is symmetrical around the mean under our assumption of normally distributed returns, we conclude that

$$Prob(I_{t+1}(n) > \mu_I, I_t(n) < \mu_I) = Prob(I_{t+1}(n) < \mu_I, I_t(n) > \mu_I),$$

and the probability of reversal can be computed, for example, as:

$$Prob(\text{Reversal}) = 2 \times Prob(I_{t+1}(n) > \mu_I, I_t(n) < \mu_I). \tag{4.16}$$

It is important to note that it is analytically feasible to compute the probability that the value of the technical indicator $I(n)$ reverses around its mean value. For example, we can compute $Prob(I_{t+1}(n) > \mu_I, I_t(n) < \mu_I)$, which corresponds to the probability that at time t, the value of $I(n)$ is less than the mean, and at the subsequent time $t+1$, the value of $I(n)$ is greater than the mean. This solution is known as Sheppard's formula (refer to Sheppard, 1899). The application of Sheppard's formula in financial contexts, specifically to determine correlations between trading rules and evaluate the expected number of position reversals in a trading rule, was first introduced by Acar and Lequeux (1996) and Lequeux and Acar (1998).

To justify our simplifying assumption that we are going to make, it is important to highlight the prevalence of whipsaw trades in sideways or ranging markets, where price movements lack a clear and sustained direction. With this in mind, let us consider a scenario where the market prices indeed exhibit a sideways pattern, implying a mean return of zero, $\mu = 0$. In such sideways markets, we can assume that the value of a technical indicator follows a normal distribution centered around zero mean, $\mu_I = 0$, with a variance of σ_I^2:

$$I(n) \sim \mathcal{N}(0, \sigma_I^2).$$

In other words, the technical indicator generates white noise that fluctuates randomly around zero. Consequently, the technical indicator generates random Buy and Sell signals within sideways markets. Importantly, each signal has an equal unconditional probability: $\Phi(I(n) > 0) = \Phi(I(n) < 0) = 0.5$. Specifically, the technical indicator generates a Buy or Sell signal with a 50% probability. Notably, this probability remains constant regardless of the standard deviation value, σ_I. Therefore, irrespective of the standard deviation, Buy and Sell signals are always generated with equal probabilities.

At a cursory glance, it may appear that both the technical indicator and the return act as mere noise generators in sideways markets, as they generate random Buy and Sell signals with equal probabilities. Consequently, one might be inclined to conclude that trading based on trend-following rules offers no advantage over trading based solely on returns in such market conditions, as no clear signal is present. However, this conclusion is erroneous. While it is true that the unconditional probability of the technical indicator generating a Buy (Sell) signal, in the absence of a trend, is 50%, it is important to recognize that the conditional probability does not remain at 50%.

The conditional probability of generating a Buy or Sell signal in a technical indicator is not solely dependent on the current market conditions but is typically influenced by the trading signals generated in previous time periods. This persistence in trading signals is a key feature of the indicator. For instance, if a Buy signal is generated at time t, the probability of generating another Buy signal at time $t+1$ tends to be higher than the probability of generating a Sell signal. This persistence effect contributes to a reduction in the number of whipsaw trades experienced. This reduction depends on the weighting function for returns $\{\theta_0, \theta_1, \ldots \theta_{n-1}\}$.

The trading signal generated by a trend-following indicator demonstrates persistence due to its calculation involving the averaging of returns over a defined window. When the averaging window is moved forward by one observation, the most recent return observation is included in the computation, while the most distant return observation is dropped. Importantly, it should be noted that both the old and new trading signals are derived from a substantial number of similar return observations.

By incorporating multiple return observations in the calculation, the trend-following indicator maintains a degree of continuity and persistence in its signals. This persistence is achieved by blending the contributions of past and present return observations, resulting in a gradual and consistent adjustment to the trading signal as new data is incorporated. The similarity in the return observations utilized in the computation of the old and new trading signals contributes to the persistence observed in the indicator's output.

Now, let us proceed to derive analytically the expected number of position reversals and the expected amount of transaction costs under the simplifying assumption that the market prices exhibit a sideways pattern. In this scenario, both $\mu = 0$ and $\mu_I = 0$, and we can analytically compute the probability of a position reversal using Eq. (4.16). By applying Sheppard's formula, we obtain:

$$Prob(\text{Reversal}) = \frac{1}{2} - \frac{1}{\pi} \arcsin(AC1(I(n))), \tag{4.17}$$

where $\arcsin(\cdot)$ represents the inverse trigonometric sine function, and $AC1(I(n))$ corresponds to the first-order autocorrelation function of the technical indicator $I(n)$. Specifically, it measures the correlation between $I_{t+1}(n)$ and $I_t(n)$. The computation of this correlation is given by:

$$AC1(I(n)) = \frac{Cov(I_{t+1}(n), I_t(n))}{\sqrt{Var(I_{t+1}(n))Var(I_t(n))}}, \tag{4.18}$$

where $Cov(I_{t+1}(n), I_t(n))$ represents the covariance between $I_{t+1}(n)$ and $I_t(n)$, while $Var(I_{t+1}(n))$ and $Var(I_t(n))$ denote the variance of $I_{t+1}(n)$ and $I_t(n)$, respectively. Consequently, in sideways markets, we can compute the expected number of position reversals and the expected amount of transaction costs as follows:

$$E[N] = T\left(\frac{1}{2} - \frac{1}{\pi} \arcsin(AC1(I(n)))\right), \quad E[TC] = \kappa E[N].$$

Remark 4.11 It is important to note that neither the expected number of position reversals nor the expected amount of transaction costs depend on the return volatility σ. Surprisingly, in both turbulent and calm market times, the expected number of whipsaw trades is the same.

If all return weights in a technical indicator are positive, $\theta_i > 0$ for all i, then the first-order autocorrelation is also positive. In this case, $0 \leq AC1 < 1$ (it is important to remember that 1 is the maximum limit for autocorrelation). Consequently, $0 \leq \arcsin(AC1) < \frac{\pi}{2}$. The function $\arcsin(x)$ is increasing in x. Therefore, the probability of a position reversal decreases as the value of the first-order autocorrelation increases. To illustrate this relationship, Fig. 4.7 plots the probability of a position reversal against the first-order autocorrelation of a technical indicator. Notably, when the first-order autocorrelation is zero, the probability of a position reversal is 50%. However, as the first-order autocorrelation approaches unity, the probability of a position reversal approaches zero.

The preceding discussion advocates that the smoothness of a technical indicator can be quantified by its first-order autocorrelation. A higher first-order autocorrelation indicates greater persistence in the generated trading signals, resulting in fewer position reversals and lower transaction costs.

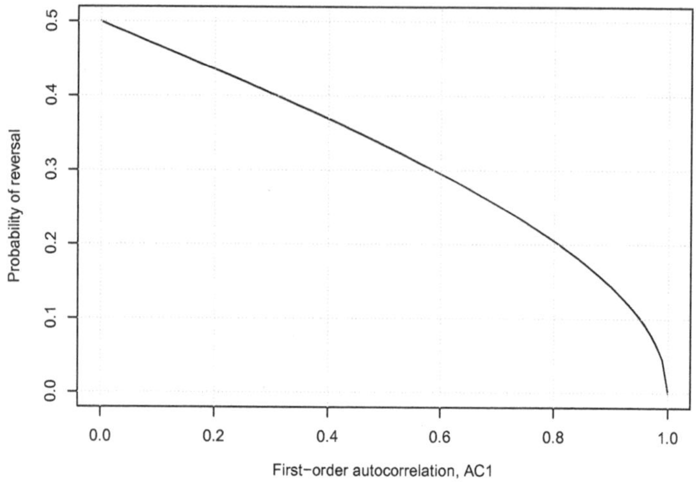

Fig. 4.7 Probability of a position reversal versus the first-order autocorrelation function of a technical indicator

Definition 4.5 To better reflect the property measured by the first-order autocorrelation, we introduce the term **Smoothness Index** (SMI) as an alternative name for the first-order autocorrelation AC1.

Now, let us derive the analytical expression for $SMI(I(n))$. The definition of the first-order autocorrelation is provided by Eq. (4.18). The variances $Var(I_{t+1}(n))$ and $Var(I_t(n))$ share a similar structure and can be expressed as shown in Eq. (4.6). The covariance between $I_{t+1}(n)$ and $I_t(n)$ can be calculated as follows:

$$Cov(I_{t+1}(n), I_t(n)) = \sigma^2 \sum_{i=0}^{n-2} \theta_i \theta_{i+1}.$$

Therefore, the smoothness of the technical indicator $I(n)$ can be determined by the following expression:

$$SMI(I(n)) = \frac{\sum_{i=0}^{n-2} \theta_i \theta_{i+1}}{\sum_{i=0}^{n-1} \theta_i^2} = \frac{\theta_0\theta_1 + \theta_1\theta_2 + \ldots + \theta_{n-3}\theta_{n-2} + \theta_{n-2}\theta_{n-1}}{\theta_0^2 + \theta_1^2 + \ldots + \theta_{n-2}^2 + \theta_{n-1}^2}. \quad (4.19)$$

It is important to observe that the smoothness of a technical indicator is solely dependent on the return weights. In other words, $SMI(I(n)) = SMI(\theta_0, \theta_1, \ldots, \theta_{n-1})$. The smoothness index possesses a useful property, as stated below:

Property 4.5 The smoothness of a technical indicator remains unchanged when the return weights are scaled by a positive constant. In particular, it can be demonstrated that

$$SMI(c \times \theta_0, c \times \theta_1, \ldots, c \times \theta_{n-1}) = SMI(\theta_0, \theta_1, \ldots, \theta_{n-1}),$$

where c represents any positive real number. This implies that the return weights of the technical indicator can be freely re-scaled without affecting its smoothing property.

In matrix notation, we can express the smoothness index as follows:

$$SMI(I(n)) = \frac{\boldsymbol{\theta}' \boldsymbol{Q} \boldsymbol{\theta}}{\boldsymbol{\theta}' \boldsymbol{I} \boldsymbol{\theta}}, \tag{4.20}$$

where $\mathbf{a}'$ denotes the transpose of $\mathbf{a}$, $\boldsymbol{\theta} = [\theta_0, \theta_1, \ldots, \theta_{n-1}]'$ represents the $n \times 1$ vector of return weights, $\boldsymbol{I}$ corresponds to the $n \times n$ identity matrix, and $\boldsymbol{Q}$ is the $n \times n$ matrix given by:

$$\boldsymbol{Q} = \begin{bmatrix} 0 & 0 & 0 & \ldots & 0 \\ 1 & 0 & 0 & \ldots & 0 \\ 0 & 1 & 0 & \ldots & 0 \\ \vdots & \vdots & \vdots & \ddots & \vdots \\ 0 & 0 & 0 & \ldots & 0 \end{bmatrix}. \tag{4.21}$$

It is worth noting that the identity matrix $\boldsymbol{I}$ is a square diagonal matrix, with all entries on the main diagonal equal to 1, while the rest of the entries are 0. On the other hand, matrix $\boldsymbol{Q}$ is also a square matrix, with all entries below the main diagonal equal to 1, and the remaining entries set to 0.

Now we seek to address a fundamental question: which weighting function maximizes the smoothness for a given number of return lags, denoted as n? To answer this question, we must solve the following optimization problem:

$$\max_{\boldsymbol{\theta}} SMI(I(n)) = \max_{\boldsymbol{\theta}} \frac{\boldsymbol{\theta}' \boldsymbol{Q} \boldsymbol{\theta}}{\boldsymbol{\theta}' \boldsymbol{I} \boldsymbol{\theta}}. \tag{4.22}$$

While this problem can be efficiently solved numerically using standard non-linear optimization techniques, our objective is to find an analytical solution.

The optimality condition for $\boldsymbol{\theta}$ can be derived by setting the partial derivative of $SMI(I(n))$ with respect to $\boldsymbol{\theta}$ equal to zero. Taking the derivatives, we can utilize some useful results from matrix calculus. For a non-symmetric matrix $\mathbf{A}$ and vector $\mathbf{x}$, $\frac{\partial \mathbf{x}'\mathbf{A}\mathbf{x}}{\partial \mathbf{x}} = (\mathbf{A} + \mathbf{A}')\mathbf{x}$. When $\mathbf{A}$ is symmetric, $\frac{\partial \mathbf{x}'\mathbf{A}\mathbf{x}}{\partial \mathbf{x}} = 2\mathbf{A}\mathbf{x}$.

After having taken the derivative of $SMI(I(n))$ with respect to $\boldsymbol{\theta}$, we obtain:

$$\frac{\partial SMI(I(n))}{\partial \theta} = \frac{(\boldsymbol{Q} + \boldsymbol{Q}')\boldsymbol{\theta}(\boldsymbol{\theta}'\boldsymbol{I}\boldsymbol{\theta}) - 2\boldsymbol{I}\boldsymbol{\theta}(\boldsymbol{\theta}'\boldsymbol{Q}\boldsymbol{\theta})}{(\boldsymbol{\theta}'\boldsymbol{I}\boldsymbol{\theta})^2}.$$

By setting this expression equal to zero, the first-order condition simplifies to:

$$\mathbf{B}\boldsymbol{\theta} = \lambda \boldsymbol{I}\boldsymbol{\theta}, \tag{4.23}$$

where $\lambda = 2\,SMI(I(n))$ and matrix $\mathbf{B} = \boldsymbol{Q} + \boldsymbol{Q}'$.

The matrix $\mathbf{B}$ represents a specific variant of a tridiagonal Toeplitz matrix, where the main diagonal consists of zeros, and both the lower and upper diagonals consist of ones:

$$\boldsymbol{B} = \begin{bmatrix} 0 & 1 & 0 & \ldots & 0 \\ 1 & 0 & 1 & \ldots & 0 \\ 0 & 1 & 0 & \ldots & 0 \\ \vdots & \vdots & \vdots & \ddots & 1 \\ 0 & 0 & \ldots & 1 & 0 \end{bmatrix}. \tag{4.24}$$

Note that the first-order condition of optimality can be stated as:

$$(\boldsymbol{B} - \lambda \boldsymbol{I})\boldsymbol{\theta} = 0. \tag{4.25}$$

The solution to Eq. (4.25) is a well-explored problem in linear algebra, involving the determination of eigenvectors and eigenvalues of a matrix. Specifically, for our case, we consider the matrix $\boldsymbol{B}$, which corresponds to a tridiagonal Toeplitz matrix. Analytical solutions exist for finding the eigenvalues and eigenvectors of such matrices (see Noschese et al., 2013). In our specific case, matrix $\boldsymbol{B}$ has n eigenvalues given by:

$$\lambda_k = 2\cos\left(\frac{k\pi}{n+1}\right), \quad k \in [1, n]. \tag{4.26}$$

Furthermore, the components of the eigenvector $\boldsymbol{\theta}_k$ associated with the eigenvalue λ_k are given by:

$$\theta_{i,k} = \sin\left(\frac{(i+1)k\pi}{n+1}\right), \quad i \in [0, n-1], \quad k \in [1, n]. \tag{4.27}$$

It is worth noting that the eigenvalues λ_k exhibit a monotonically decreasing pattern as k increases from 1 to n. As $SMI(I(n))$ is defined as $\lambda/2$, and our objective is to maximize $SMI(I(n))$, the analytical solution for the maximum smoothness index corresponds to half of the largest eigenvalue of the matrix $\boldsymbol{B}$. Given that the largest eigenvalue is λ_1, we can conclude that $\lambda = \lambda_1$. Therefore, the maximum value of $SMI(I(n))$ is given by:

$$SMI(I(n))^* = \cos\left(\frac{\pi}{n+1}\right). \tag{4.28}$$

Evidently, the maximum smoothness of the technical indicator increases as the number of return lags, denoted as n, increases. In the limit, as n approaches infinity, the maximum smoothness approaches unity:

$$\lim_{n\to\infty} SMI(I(n))^* \to 1.$$

The components of the eigenvector associated with the largest eigenvalue can be determined as follows:

$$\theta_{i,1} = \sin\left(\frac{(i+1)\pi}{n+1}\right), \quad i \in [0, n-1]. \tag{4.29}$$

It is important to note that eigenvectors possess uniqueness up to a scaling factor. This property aligns with the observation that the smoothness index remains unaffected by positive scaling of the return weights. Consequently, the return weights corresponding to the technical indicator with maximum smoothness can also be expressed as:

$$\theta_{i,1} = c \times \sin\left(\frac{(i+1)\pi}{n+1}\right), \quad i \in [0, n-1],$$

where c represents any positive real value.

Figure 4.8 displays the return weights (eigenvectors) associated with the three largest eigenvalues, λ_1, λ_2, and λ_3, for an averaging window of size $n = 30$. In the top panel of the figure, the return weights corresponding to the first largest eigenvalue λ_1 are presented. Notably, the technical indicator that uses these return weights demonstrates the highest level of smoothness compared to all other indicators. This particular technical indicator utilizes the sine-weighted moving average (SWMA) of returns. The SWMA derives its weighting from the first half of a sine wave cycle, resulting in a higher emphasis on return observations in the middle of the averaging window; the return weights gradually decrease toward the borders of the window.

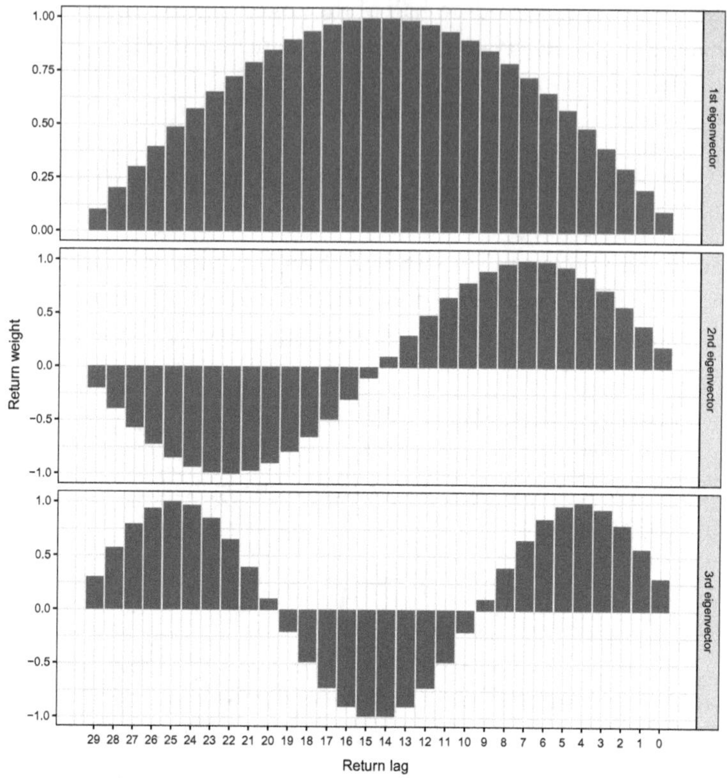

Fig. 4.8 Return weights (eigenvectors) associated with the three largest eigenvalues for an averaging window of size $n = 30$. Notably, the eigenvector linked to the 1st eigenvalue reveals the weighting function of the technical indicator that exhibits the highest smoothness among all indicators

The middle and bottom panels of Fig. 4.8 plot the return weights associated with the 2nd and 3rd largest eigenvalues, λ_2 and λ_3, respectively. Both weighting functions exhibit sine waves with increasing frequencies. These visualizations lead to an insightful observation. The frequency of the sine wave corresponding to the 1st eigenvalue, λ_1, represents the fundamental frequency, denoted as $f = \frac{1}{2(n+1)}$, or the 1st harmonic. Similarly, the sine wave linked to the kth eigenvalue, λ_k, represents the kth harmonic of the fundamental frequency. The frequency of the kth harmonic is given by $k \times f$. The collection of n harmonic functions forms a basic set of smooth functions.

The basic set of smooth functions provides a foundation for constructing various complex waveforms that exhibit high smoothness. For instance, the SMIs of the return weights associated with the 1st and 2nd eigenvalues are 0.995 and 0.980, respectively. By superimposing these return weights, a new smooth function of return weights can be created, resulting in a waveform with a shape depicted in Fig. 4.9. Notably, the SMI of this composite shape equals 0.987, which falls between the SMIs of the 1st and 2nd harmonics. This approach of combining basic harmonic functions allows for the generation of more complex and versatile waveforms while still maintaining a considerable level of smoothness.

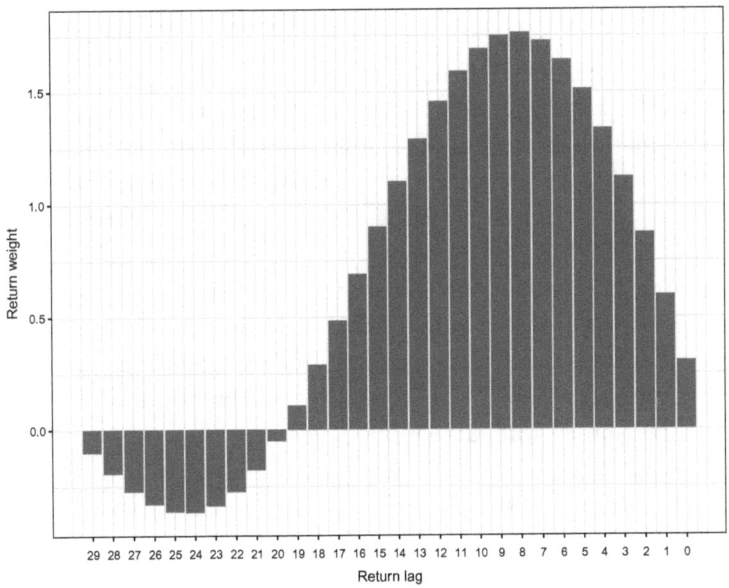

Fig. 4.9 Return weights created by superimposing the return weights of the 1st and 2nd harmonics

Our analytical expression for the probability of a position reversal is established under the assumption of a sideways market, where the mean return is zero, resulting in a signal-to-noise ratio of return also being zero. However, an intriguing question arises: how does the probability of a position reversal change as the (absolute value of the) mean return increases? This question is precisely addressed by the following proposition.

Proposition 4.2 *As the signal-to-noise ratio of returns approaches infinity, the probability of a position reversal decreases to zero. In mathematical terms:*

$$\lim_{SNR(r)\to\infty} Prob(Reversal) \to 0.$$

The proof for this proposition can be found in the Appendix. It is worth noting that we express the proposition in terms of the signal-to-noise ratio of returns, denoted as $SNR(r)$, as it provides a more natural framework than using the price drift alone. This is because the probability of a position reversal not only decreases with an increase in mean return but also when the standard deviation of returns decreases.

Remark 4.12 Proposition 4.2 holds true for all trading rules, independent of the value of the first-order autocorrelation function. This is due to the fact that as the signal-to-noise ratio of returns approaches infinity, all trading rules achieve 100% accuracy in detecting trend direction. Consequently, the trading signal remains constant as long as there is no change in the trend direction.

To summarize, in sideways markets, the probability of a position reversal shows an inverse relationship with the first-order autocorrelation of a technical indicator. Specifically, a higher first-order autocorrelation leads to a lower probability of a position reversal. Consequently, the technical indicator exhibiting the highest first-order autocorrelation experiences the lowest expected number of whipsaw trades. Can this result be extended to cover the bull and bear markets? Our thorough and extensive numerical simulations unequivocally support an affirmative answer to the question.

For illustrative purposes, Fig. 4.10 showcases the probability of a position reversal plotted against the signal-to-noise ratio of returns for two technical indicators: MOM(10) and SWMA(10). Notably, the MOM(10) indicator exhibits superior accuracy in detecting trend direction over a window of 10 observations. In contrast, the SWMA(10) indicator displays the lowest number of position reversals within the same window size.

When the signal-to-noise ratio of returns is zero, the MOM(10) indicator shows a higher probability of a position reversal compared to the SWMA(10) technical indicator. Importantly, this relationship persists even as the signal-to-noise ratio of returns gradually increases from zero. Hence, the MOM(10) indicator consistently maintains a higher probability of reversal relative to the SWMA(10) indicator under varying signal-to-noise conditions.

When the mean return deviates from zero, it is important to acknowledge that our analytical expression for the expected number of position reversals

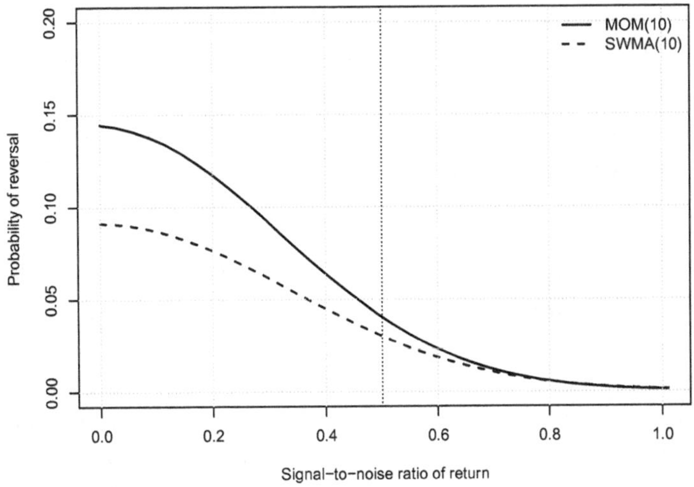

Fig. 4.10 Probability of a position reversal versus the signal-to-noise ratio of returns for the MOM(10) and SWMA(10) technical indicators. The dashed vertical line represents the typical signal-to-noise ratio observed in a market state

serves as an approximation rather than an exact calculation. Nevertheless, this approximation does not preclude us from utilizing the SMI measure effectively to compare the smoothing properties of different technical indicators. By comparing the SMI values of various technical indicators, we can still gain valuable insights into their respective abilities to handle potential whipsaw trades when the mean return is non-zero. In summary, while the analytical expression may be approximate when the mean return is non-zero, the SMI remains a valuable tool for assessing and comparing the smoothing effectiveness of different technical indicators, aiding traders in making informed decisions in dynamic market conditions.

4.6 Summary

To begin the summary, it is worth repeating that the calculation of the trading signal within a trend-following rule can be understood as the computation of a weighted moving average of returns. In particular, the value of the technical indicator at time t is computed using n return lags:

$$I_t(n) = \sum_{i=0}^{n-1} \theta_i r_{t-i},$$

where r_{t-i} is the return at lag i and $\{\theta_0, \theta_1, \dots \theta_{n-1}\}$ are the weights of each return lag. Logically, the properties of a trend-following rule should be intrinsically tied to the associated moving average of returns.

In this chapter, we propose that the technical indicator should exhibit three fundamental properties: accuracy, responsiveness, and smoothness. To assess these properties, we introduce the following three measures:

- Noise Suppression Factor (NSF): This metric gauges the ability of the technical indicator to filter out noise and provide an accurate signal for making trading decisions.
- Average Lag Time (ALT): The ALT measure helps us understand how quickly the technical indicator responds to trend changes, indicating its timeliness in generating trading signals.
- Smoothness Index (SMI): The SMI quantifies the level of smoothness in the technical indicator, indicating the stability and consistency of the trading signal over time.

The motivation for how to compute the proposed measures stems from a well-established regime-switching model for returns. According to this model, returns adhere to a stochastic process that alternates between bull and bear states in a random manner. Importantly, these market states are identifiable and display persistence. Consequently, this model offers a solid rationale for embracing trend-following investing strategies.

In our pursuit of a well-informed selection of model parameters for the regime-switching model, we undertake an empirical study. While we do make certain parametric assumptions, it is noteworthy that our quantitative measures are not contingent on these parameters. Instead, they solely rely on the return weights within the technical indicator. In essence, our measures are inspired by the model but exhibit a high degree of independence from specific parameter values. This characteristic ensures the robustness and applicability of our approach, as it enables us to derive meaningful insights about the numerical characteristics of trend-following rules, while avoiding undue sensitivity to parameter variations.

The accuracy measure for detecting trend direction is calculated using the following formula:

$$NSF = \frac{\sum_{i=0}^{n-1} \theta_i}{\sqrt{\sum_{i=0}^{n-1} \theta_i^2}}.$$

The NSF serves as a metric to gauge the improvement in the signal-to-noise ratio of return observations. Specifically, the NSF measures how effectively a technical indicator reduces the impact of noise while preserving the strength of the underlying signal. Notably, when prices exhibit a clear upward or downward trend, the technical indicator with the highest NSF value emerges as the most accurate one, regardless of the specific mean return and standard deviation of returns.

The ALT is determined by solving the equation:

$$\sum_{i=0}^{ALT-1} \theta_i = \frac{1}{2}\sum_{i=0}^{n-1} \theta_i.$$

It is essential to interpret the ALT literally, as the technical indicator with the shortest ALT exhibits the highest responsiveness "on average." Remarkably, the ALT is independent of the standard deviation of returns. However, it implicitly provides an accurate measure of the average delay time in identifying trend turning points when the absolute value of the mean return in bear markets equals the mean return in bull markets. If this condition is not met, the ALT measure does not accurately represent the average delay time in identifying trend turning points. Nevertheless, the ALT can still be employed to compare the responsiveness of different trading rules. This is because if a rule is most responsive when the absolute values of the mean returns are equal, it typically remains the most responsive even when the mean returns differ.

The smoothness of a technical indicator is calculated using the following formula:

$$SMI = \frac{\sum_{i=0}^{n-2} \theta_i \theta_{i+1}}{\sum_{i=0}^{n-1} \theta_i^2}.$$

While the NSF measure assesses the noise reduction properties or the accuracy of the technical indicator, the SMI is a metric associated with the persistence of the trading signal. Essentially, the SMI quantifies the autocorrelation of the signal generated by the technical indicator. Autocorrelation, also known as serial correlation, is a statistical concept that measures the degree of similarity between a time series and a lagged version of itself. In simpler terms, it examines how a variable is correlated with its past values over time.

Under the assumption of sideways price movements, we derive an analytical relationship that demonstrates a direct link between the SMI and both the expected number of position reversals and the expected transaction costs. As the SMI increases, these expected values decrease. This indicates that technical indicators with higher SMI values exhibit superior smoothing characteristics, resulting in fewer position reversals and lower transaction costs.

One remarkable aspect of the SMI is that it remains independent of the standard deviation of returns. When the prices are trending upward or downward, our analytical relationships between the SMI and the expected number of position reversals and transaction costs are no longer valid. Nevertheless, we demonstrate that this fact does not diminish the effectiveness of using the SMI as a valuable measure to compare the smoothing properties of different technical indicators also in trending markets.

We conclude this summary by presenting Fig. 4.11, which showcases the three fundamental weighting functions used in our analysis. Starting with the top panel, we have the weighting function of the technical indicator with the highest accuracy. This is the weighting function employed in the MOM(n) technical indicator, where all returns are equally weighted. The NSF of this technical indicator is $\sqrt{n}$, which is the maximum possible value for a window of size n observations. Moving to the bottom panel, we observe the weighting function of the technical indicator with the largest SMI. This weighting function is known as the sine-weighted moving average (SWMA), representing the first half of a sine wave cycle. The SMI of this technical indicator is given by $\cos\left(\frac{\pi}{n+1}\right)$.

In the middle panel of Fig. 4.11, we can see the weighting function of the technical indicator with the smallest ALT. This particular weighting function assigns zero weight to all return lags except the most recent one. Consequently, the ALT of this technical indicator is equal to 1. It is worth noting that while this technical indicator is the most responsive, it comes at the cost of being less accurate and smooth. It is interesting to observe that the weighting functions of the most accurate and smooth technical indicators are symmetrical around the center. As a result, the ALTs of these technical indicators are equal to $n/2$.

What constitutes the "ideal technical indicator?" In theory, the ideal technical indicator should maximize both the NSF and the SMI while minimizing the ALT. However, creating a truly ideal technical indicator is not feasible, as demonstrated by the weighting functions depicted in Fig. 4.11. Each quantitative measure is maximized by a specific weighting function for returns, making it challenging to achieve an all-encompassing ideal solution. Instead, the goal could be to find a technical indicator that strikes the best possible tradeoff between NSF, ALT, and SMI.

An educated approach to approximating the ideal technical indicator involves utilizing a weighting function that represents a superposition of the three fundamental weighting functions displayed in Fig. 4.11. By combining the strengths of these individual weighting functions, it becomes possible to approach an optimal solution that balances accuracy, responsiveness, and smoothness in the technical indicator. In summary, while a truly perfect tech-

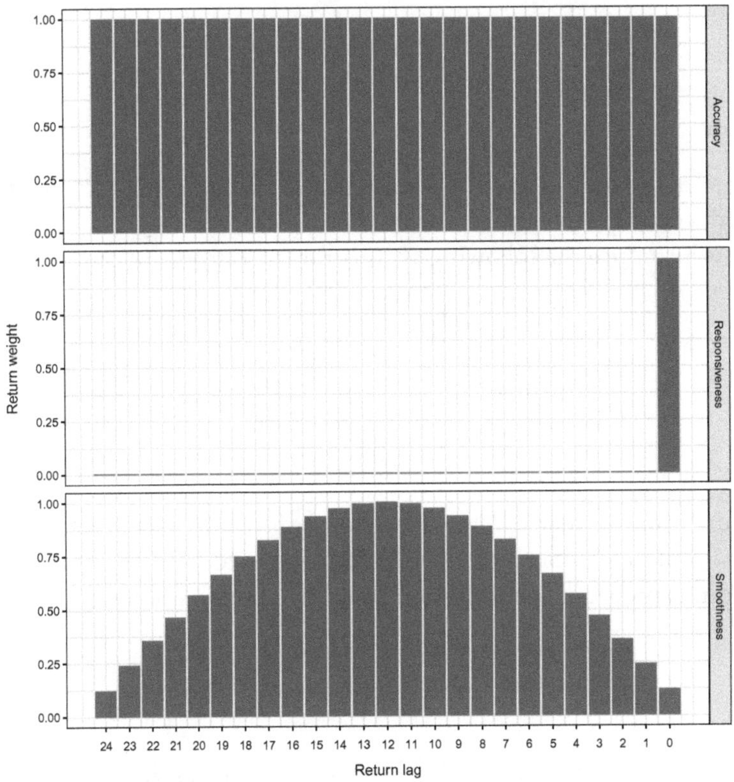

Fig. 4.11 Weighting functions of the technical indicators that maximize (1) accuracy, (2) responsiveness, and (3) smoothness for the averaging window of size $n = 25$ return observations

nical indicator is unattainable due to the conflicting nature of the quantitative measures, the quest for an optimal solution involves leveraging a weighting function that incorporates elements from the fundamental weighting functions to achieve the best possible tradeoff between NSF, ALT, and SMI.

Appendix 4.A Proof of Proposition 4.1

Our primary objective is to address the problem of minimizing the Herfindahl index, represented by the expression $\sum_{i=1}^{n} \theta_i^2$. This optimization task is subject to the condition that the return weights are normalized, as denoted by the constraint $\sum_{i=1}^{n} \theta_i = 1$. To formalize this problem, we express it in the following manner:

$$\min_{\theta_i} \frac{1}{2} \sum_{i=1}^{n} \theta_i^2 \quad \text{subject to} \quad \sum_{i=1}^{n} \theta_i = 1.$$

It is important to note that the coefficient $\frac{1}{2}$ preceding the Herfindahl index is introduced for convenience.

Let us introduce the following vectors for the purpose of our analysis:

$$\boldsymbol{\theta} = \begin{bmatrix} \theta_0 \\ \theta_1 \\ \vdots \\ \theta_{n-1} \end{bmatrix}, \quad \mathbf{1} = \begin{bmatrix} 1 \\ 1 \\ \vdots \\ 1 \end{bmatrix}.$$

It is worth noting that $\boldsymbol{\theta}$ represents an $n \times 1$ vector containing the return weights, while $\mathbf{1}$ signifies an $n \times 1$ vector composed entirely of ones.

We can express our minimization problem in matrix notation as follows:

$$\min_{\boldsymbol{\theta}} \frac{1}{2} \boldsymbol{\theta}' \boldsymbol{\theta} \quad \text{subject to} \quad \boldsymbol{\theta}' \mathbf{1} = 1,$$

where the notation $\boldsymbol{\theta}'$ represents the transpose of vector $\boldsymbol{\theta}$.

The given problem can be classified as a quadratic optimization problem with equality constraints. Specifically, it falls under the category of convex optimization problems, where the local minimum coincides with the global minimum. To address such problems, the method of Lagrange multipliers is commonly employed. By introducing the Lagrangian, we can formulate the solution for $\boldsymbol{\theta}$ as a quadratic program:

$$\min_{\boldsymbol{\theta}, \lambda} \quad L = \frac{1}{2} \boldsymbol{\theta}' \boldsymbol{\theta} + \lambda (1 - \boldsymbol{\theta}' \mathbf{1}).$$

In this expression, λ represents the Lagrange multiplier associated with the equality constraint.

The first-order optimality conditions are expressed as:

$$\frac{\partial L}{\partial \boldsymbol{\theta}} = \boldsymbol{\theta} - \lambda \mathbf{1} = 0, \tag{4.30}$$

$$\frac{\partial L}{\partial \lambda} = 1 - \boldsymbol{\theta}' \mathbf{1} = 0. \tag{4.31}$$

We can further simplify condition (4.30) to:

$$\boldsymbol{\theta} = \lambda \mathbf{1}. \tag{4.32}$$

This equation implies that all weight values are identical and equal to λ. Therefore, the weights can be represented as:

$$\boldsymbol{\theta} = \begin{bmatrix} \lambda \\ \lambda \\ \vdots \\ \lambda \end{bmatrix}$$

To determine the value of λ, we can employ the following technique: premultiplying both sides of Eq. (4.32) by $\mathbf{1}'$, we obtain:

$$\mathbf{1}'\boldsymbol{\theta} = \lambda \mathbf{1}'\mathbf{1}.$$

Since $\mathbf{1}'\boldsymbol{\theta} = 1$, this simplifies to:

$$1 = n\lambda.$$

By solving for λ, we find:

$$\lambda = \frac{1}{n}.$$

This means that in order to minimize the Herfindahl index, each return weight must be set to $\frac{1}{n}$. Consequently, the minimum possible value of the Herfindahl index is:

$$\sum_{i=1}^{n} \frac{1}{n^2} = \frac{n}{n^2} = \frac{1}{n}.$$

Next, let us consider the maximum possible value of the Herfindahl index. Note that, as an assumption, return weights cannot be negative, i.e., $\theta_i \geq 0$. Furthermore, since the sum of weights must equal one, a return weight cannot exceed one, i.e., $\theta_i \leq 1$. Since the first-order conditions of optimality aim to find the minimum, the maximum value represents a "corner solution." In other words, the solution lies on the boundary of the region where return weights satisfy $0 \leq \theta_i \leq 1$. It can be verified that the maximum value is attained when one $\theta_i = 1$ and all other $\theta_j = 0$ for $j \neq i$. In this case, the Herfindahl index reaches its maximum when all the weight is concentrated on a single return observation. Therefore, the maximum possible value of the Herfindahl index is 1.

Appendix 4.B Proof of Proposition 4.2

The probability of reversal is given by:

$$\begin{aligned} Prob(\text{Reversal}) &= Prob(I_{t+1}(n) > 0, I_t(n) < 0) + Prob(I_{t+1}(n) < 0, I_t(n) > 0) \\ &= P_1 + P_2. \end{aligned}$$

The last equality highlights that the probability of reversal is the sum of two probabilities, P_1 and P_2. To shorten the notation, define the following events:

$$A = I_{t+1}(n) > 0, \quad \bar{A} = I_{t+1}(n) < 0, \quad B = I_t(n) > 0, \quad \bar{B} = I_t(n) < 0.$$

Consider probability P_1:

$$P_1 = Prob(I_{t+1}(n) > 0, I_t(n) < 0) = P(A \cap \bar{B}),$$

where $P(A \cap \bar{B})$ emphasizes that probability P_1 is the probability of the intersection of events A and $\bar{B}$.

Note that event $\bar{A}$ ($\bar{B}$) represents the complement of event A (B). The event A and its complement $\bar{A}$ are mutually exclusive and exhaustive. Therefore:

$$P(A) + P(\bar{A}) = 1 \text{ and } P(B) + P(\bar{B}) = 1.$$

We use the following well-known results:

$$\rho_{A,\bar{B}} = \frac{Cov(A, \bar{B})}{\sqrt{Var(A)Var(\bar{B})}}, \qquad Cov(A, \bar{B}) = P(A \cap \bar{B}) - P(A)P(\bar{B}),$$

$$Var(A) = P(A)(1 - P(A)), \quad Var(\bar{B}) = P(\bar{B})(1 - P(\bar{B})),$$

where $Cov(\cdot)$ and $Var(\cdot)$ denote the covariance and variance, respectively, and $\rho_{A,\bar{B}}$ is the correlation coefficient between events A and $\bar{B}$. Thus:

$$P(A \cap \bar{B}) = P(A)P(\bar{B}) + \rho_{A,\bar{B}}\sqrt{P(A)(1 - P(A))P(\bar{B})(1 - P(\bar{B}))}. \tag{4.33}$$

Since under our assumption the returns are independent and normally distributed, we can arrive to the following expressions for the probability distributions of $I_{t+1}(n)$ and $I_t(n)$:

$$I_{t+1}(n) \sim N\left(\mu \sum_{i=0}^{n-1} \theta_i, \sigma^2 \sum_{i=0}^{n-1} \theta_i^2\right), \quad I_t(n) \sim N\left(\mu \sum_{i=0}^{n-1} \theta_i, \sigma^2 \sum_{i=0}^{n-1} \theta_i^2\right),$$

where, for brevity, we suppress the dependence of the price drift on the market state. That is, we use μ instead of μ_s and assume, without the loss of generality, that $\mu > 0$. Consequently, both $I_t(n)$ and $I_{t+1}(n)$ have the same normal probability distribution $N(\mu_I, \sigma_I^2)$. The expressions for the probability of events are:

$$\begin{aligned} P(A) &= Prob(I_{t+1}(n) > 0) = 1 - \Phi\left(-\frac{\mu_I}{\sigma_I}\right) \\ &= 1 - \Phi\left(-\frac{\mu}{\sigma} NSF(I(n))\right), \\ 1 - P(A) &= \Phi\left(-\frac{\mu}{\sigma} NSF(I(n))\right), \\ P(\bar{B}) &= Prob(I_t(n) < 0) = \Phi\left(-\frac{\mu}{\sigma} NSF(I(n))\right), \\ 1 - P(\bar{B}) &= 1 - \Phi\left(-\frac{\mu}{\sigma} NSF(I(n))\right), \end{aligned}$$

where $\Phi(.)$ denotes the cumulative distribution function of a standard normal random variable and $NSF(I(n)) \geq 1$ is the noise suppression factor of the technical indicator $I(n)$.

We can easily note that:

$$P(A) = 1 - P(\bar{B}).$$

Thus, Eq. (4.33) can be rewritten as:

$$\begin{aligned} P(A \cap \bar{B}) &= P(A)(1 - P(A)) + \rho_{A,\bar{B}} P(A)(1 - P(A)) \\ &= P(A)(1 - P(A))(1 + \rho_{A,\bar{B}}). \end{aligned}$$

Now, the final steps in the proof.

$$\lim_{\mu/\sigma \to \infty} 1 - P(A) = \lim_{\mu/\sigma \to \infty} \Phi\left(-\frac{\mu}{\sigma} NSF(I(n))\right) = \Phi(-\infty) = 0.$$

Similarly,

$$\lim_{\mu/\sigma \to \infty} P(A) = 1.$$

Therefore, we conclude that:

$$\lim_{\mu/\sigma \to \infty} P_1 = \lim_{\mu/\sigma \to \infty} P(A \cap \bar{B}) = 0.$$

This results holds regardless of the value of the correlation $\rho_{A,\bar{B}}$. Similarly, we can prove that:

$$\lim_{\mu/\sigma \to \infty} P_2 = \lim_{\mu/\sigma \to \infty} P(\bar{A} \cap B) = 0.$$

Therefore:

$$\lim_{\mu/\sigma \to \infty} Prob(\text{Reversal}) = \lim_{\mu/\sigma \to \infty} (P_1 + P_2) = 0.$$

This completes the proof.

References

Acar, E., & Lequeux, P. (1996). Dynamic Strategies: A Correlation Study. In C. Dunis (Ed.), *Forecasting Financial Markets, Financial Economics and Quantitative Analysis* (pp. 93–124). Wiley.

Bry, G.,& Boschan, C. (1971). Cyclical Analysis of Time Series: Selected Procedures and Computer Programs. *NBER.*

Cont, R. (2001). Empirical Properties of Asset Returns: Stylized Facts and Statistical Issues. *Quantitative Finance, 1*(2), 223–236.

Dai, M., Zhang, Q., & Zhu, Q. J. (2010). Trend Following Trading under a Regime Switching Model. *SIAM Journal on Financial Mathematics, 1*(1), 780–810.

Davis, M., & Norman, A. R. (1990). Portfolio Selection with Transaction Costs. *Mathematics of Operations Research, 15*(4), 676–713.

Frühwirth-Schnatter, S. (2006). *Finite Mixture and Markov Switching Models.* Springer.

Gonzalez, L., Powell, J. G., Shi, J., & Wilson, A. (2005). Two Centuries of Bull and Bear Market Cycles. *International Review of Economics and Finance, 14*(4), 469–486.

Lequeux, P., & Acar, E. (1998). A Dynamic Index for Managed Currencies Funds Using CME Currency Contracts. *European Journal of Finance, 4*(4), 311–330.

Noschese, S., Pasquini, L., & Reichel, L. (2013). Tridiagonal Toeplitz Matrices: Properties and Novel Applications. *Numerical Linear Algebra with Applications, 20*(2), 302–326.

Olivares-Nadal, A. V., & DeMiguel, V. (2018). Technical Note: A Robust Perspective on Transaction Costs in Portfolio Optimization. *Operations Research, 66*(3), 733–739.

Pagan, A. R., & Sossounov, K. A. (2003). A Simple Framework for Analysing Bull and Bear Markets. *Journal of Applied Econometrics, 18*(1), 23–46.

Sheppard, W. F. (1899). On the Application of the Theory of Error to Cases of Normal Distribution and Normal Correlation. *Philosophical Transactions of the Royal Society of London, Series A, 192*, 101–167.

Timmermann, A. (2000). Moments of Markov Switching Models. *Journal of Econometrics, 96*(1), 75–111.

Zakamulin, V., & Giner, J. (2023). Optimal Trend-Following With Transaction Costs. *International Review of Financial Analysis, 90*, Article 102928.

5

Exploring Properties of Rules Based on Conventional Moving Averages

5.1 Preliminaries

In this chapter, our goal is twofold. First, we want to present the analytical results for the Noise Suppression Factor (NSF), Average Lag Time (ALT), and Smoothness Index (SMI) for the trading rules that employ the conventional moving averages: Simple Moving Average (SMA), Linear Moving Average (LMA), and Exponential Moving Average (EMA). These rules are the momentum (MOM) rule, price and moving average crossover (P-MA) rule, double moving average crossover (MA-C) rule, and moving average direction (MA-D) rule. Second, by utilizing these three quantitative measures, we will compare and contrast the trading rules to determine if there exists a rule that excels in effectiveness across all measures.

The value of a moving average of prices at time t is obtained through a weighted average of $n > 1$ past prices, determined as follows:

$$MA_t(n, P) = \frac{\sum_{i=0}^{n-1} w_i P_{t-i}}{\sum_{i=0}^{n} w_i},$$

where P_{t-i} represents the price at time $t - i$, and w_i is the weight assigned to the price P_{t-i} in the computation of the moving average. The key distinction between the SMA, LMA, and EMA lies in the weighting function used for calculating the moving average. Additionally, while the SMA and LMA are computed using an averaging window of a finite size, the EMA is, in principle, calculated using an averaging window of infinite size.

V. Zakamulin and J. Giner, *The Ultimate Moving Average Handbook*,
https://doi.org/10.1007/978-3-031-90907-8_5

The technical indicator in each rule is computed as:

$$\begin{aligned} I_t^{\text{MOM}}(n) &= P_t - P_{t-n+1}, \\ I_t^{\text{P-MA}}(n) &= P_t - MA_t(n), \\ I_t^{\text{MA-C}}(s,l) &= MA_t(s,P) - MA_t(l,P), \\ I_t^{\text{MA-D}}(n) &= MA_t(n,P) - MA_{t-1}(n,P), \end{aligned}$$

where n, s, and l denote the number of price observations used to compute a moving average of prices. The technical indicator's value determines the corresponding trading signal. When the value of the technical indicator is positive, the signal generated is Buy. Conversely, if the value is negative or zero, the signal produced is Sell.

Given the existence of three standard types of moving averages, each trading rule has three distinct variants, with the exception of the MOM rule. Let us consider the P-MA rule as an illustrative example. It branches out into three variants, namely the P-SMA, P-LMA, and P-EMA rules. Correspondingly, we find three variants of the MA-C rule (SMA-C, LMA-C, and EMA-C) and three variants of the MA-D rule (SMA-D, LMA-D, and EMA-D).

In all trading rules, the computation of the trading signal can alternatively be interpreted as the computation of a single moving average of returns. Specifically, the value of the technical indicator in each rule can be calculated using returns as follows:

$$I_t(n) = \sum_{i=0}^{n-1} \theta_i r_{t-i},$$

where r_{t-i} is the return lag i, $\{\theta_0, \theta_1, \ldots \theta_{n-1}\}$ are the weights of each return lag, and n is the number of return lags.[1] Among the diverse range of technical indicators available, their distinctions primarily stem from the variations in the return weights employed in each unique rule.

It is essential to clarify the following convention: when we refer to a trading rule's abbreviation, such as P-SMA(n), we are describing the rule where the trading signal is computed based on the relationship between the most recent price and the SMA of the last $n+1$ prices. Alternatively, the technical indicator for this rule can be calculated as a weighted moving average of n returns.

[1] Strictly speaking, when calculating the moving average of returns using n observations, it is important to note that the corresponding moving average of prices incorporates $n+1$ observations. However, the MA-D rule deviates from this relationship as it aligns the number of price observations in a moving average with the number of return observations. In other words, the MA-D rule maintains an equal number of observations for both prices and returns in the moving average calculation.

However, it is crucial to note that the weighting function for returns typically differs from the weighting function used for prices, except for two specific cases. The first exception applies to rules based on the EMA. In this instance, both the price weights and return weights are the same. The second exception pertains to the return weights in the MA-D rule. Here again, the price weights and return weights align regardless of the MA type.

Additionally, there are a number of equivalent trading rules. Specifically, the SMA-D rule is equivalent to the MOM rule. The LMA-D rule is equivalent to the P-SMA rule. Finally, the EMA-D rule is equivalent to the P-EMA rule. This equivalence implies that these technical indicators employ the same return weighting function during the computation of their respective trading signals.

For every trading rule, the values of the three quantitative measures of interest can be easily computed using numerical methods. However, our primary objective is to derive analytical solutions. Notably, the return weighting function of each technical indicator is inherently discrete. In certain cases, however, obtaining analytical solutions for specific trading rules or quantitative measures can be challenging. A potential approach to address this issue is to assume, for simplicity, that the weighting function of a technical indicator is continuous. Table 5.1 presents a list of P-MA(n) and MA-D(n) trading rules alongside their corresponding weighting functions for returns in both discrete and continuous scenarios.

In the MA-C(s, l) rule, the weighting function for returns is defined as follows:

$$\theta_i = \theta_i^l - \theta_i^s, \tag{5.1}$$

where θ_i^l, with $i \in [0, l-1]$, represents the weighting function in the longer moving average, and θ_i^s, with $i \in [0, s-1]$, represents the weighting function

Table 5.1 List of various trading rules and their corresponding weighting functions for returns. For the EMA, the parameters are defined as follows: $i \in [0, \infty)$ and $x \in [0, \infty)$, with λ represented by $\frac{n-1}{n+1}$. For all other rules, the parameters are constrained as follows: $i \in [0, n-1]$ and $x \in [0, n]$, where i represents an integer number, and x denotes a real number. It is essential to note that the return weights presented in the table are not normalized

Trading rule	Discrete weights	Continuous weights
MOM(n) and SMA-D(n)	$\theta_i = 1$	$\theta_x = 1$
P-SMA(n) and LMA-D(n)	$\theta_i = n - i$	$\theta_x = 1 - \frac{x}{n}$
P-LMA(n)	$\theta_i = \frac{1}{2}(n-i+1)(n-i)$	$\theta_x = \frac{(n-x)^2}{n^2}$
P-EMA(n) and EMA-D(n)	$\theta_i = \lambda^i$	$\theta_x = \lambda^x$

in the shorter moving average. It is important to note that the condition $s < l$ holds, resulting in θ_i^s being assumed to be zero when $i > s$. For clarity, it is crucial to recall that the computation of the technical indicator based on the EMA relies on an infinite number of return lags. Consequently, both return weights, θ_i^l and θ_i^s, are defined for $i \in [0, \infty)$.

Finally observe that, to correctly compute the discrete return weights in an MA-C(s, l) technical indicator, it is crucial to follow these steps. Initially, both θ_i^l and θ_i^s must be calculated as:

$$\theta_i^s = \frac{\sum_{j=i+1}^{s} w_j^s}{\sum_{j=0}^{s} w_j^s}, \quad \theta_i^l = \frac{\sum_{j=i+1}^{l} w_j^l}{\sum_{j=0}^{l} w_j^l},$$

where w_j^s represents the price weights used in the shorter moving average and w_j^l signifies the price weights used in the longer moving average within the MA-C(s, l) rule. Subsequently, the return weights for this technical indicator can be obtained as the difference between the return weights in the longer and shorter moving averages, as given by Eq. (5.1). On the other hand, computing the continuous return weights in an MA-C(s, l) rule can be accomplished using the continuous weights expressions from Table 5.1, while following the rule $\theta_x = \theta_x^l - \theta_x^s$.

5.2 Analytical Results for Accuracy Measure

In a trending market, technical indicators from various trend-following rules generate Buy or Sell signals based on the identified trend direction. However, it is essential to acknowledge that accurately detecting the trend direction is challenging and often falls short of perfection. To assess and compare the accuracies of these trend-following rules, we propose utilizing the NSF measure. The NSF serves as a metric for quantifying the noise reduction capability of a technical indicator within a trend-following rule. In essence, it measures the indicator's effectiveness in identifying the trend direction, regardless of the signal-to-noise ratio of the underlying data. A higher NSF value indicates a more accurate trend direction identification, implying that the technical indicator is better at filtering out noise and capturing the true trend trajectory.

The NSF of the technical indicator $I(n)$ is calculated using the following formula:

$$NSF(I(n)) = \frac{\sum_{i=0}^{n-1} \theta_i}{\sqrt{\sum_{i=0}^{n-1} \theta_i^2}}.$$

It is important to note that the return weights hold a useful property: they can be freely re-scaled without impacting the NSF value. In practice, return weights are commonly left unnormalized. Let N represent the normalization factor. The normalized return weights, denoted by $\frac{\theta_i}{N}$, can be obtained by dividing each individual return weight by this normalization factor. The normalization factor is computed as the sum of non-normalized return weights:

$$N = \sum_{i=0}^{n-1} \theta_i.$$

When the return weights are normalized, the expression for the NSF can be rewritten as follows:

$$NSF(I(n)) = \frac{1}{\sqrt{\frac{1}{N^2}\sum_{i=0}^{n-1}\theta_i^2}} = \frac{1}{\sqrt{VRR(I(n))}}, \tag{5.2}$$

where $VRR(I(n))$ represents the Variance Reduction Ratio of the technical indicator $I(n)$:

$$VRR(I(n)) = \frac{1}{N^2}\sum_{i=0}^{n-1}\theta_i^2.$$

The term "variance reduction ratio" stems from the fact that the variance of the technical indicator, with normalized return weights, is given by $Var(I(n)) = VRR(I(n))\sigma^2$, where σ^2 represents the return variance. It is worth noting that typically $VRR(I(n)) < 1$, indicating a reduction in variance compared to the original returns.

During the derivation of the NSF for different technical indicators, we obtain analytical solutions for their variance reduction ratios. These variance reduction ratios can be readily converted to NSFs using Eq. (5.2). Table 5.2 lists the trading rules and the analytical solutions to the exact and asymptotic NSFs. For all trading rules but the MA-C rules, the exact solution is obtained for the discrete case. In contrast, for all MA-C rules the exact solution is obtained for the continuous case. The derivations of the analytical solutions are given in the Appendix to this chapter.

For convenience, Table 5.2 also presents the asymptotic solutions to the NSFs. These solutions are derived under the assumption of a relatively long averaging window size. By making this assumption, we can simplify the solutions by focusing on the dominant terms and neglecting the less significant ones.

Table 5.2 Trading rules along with their corresponding NSFs. In all rules, except those utilizing the EMA, n denotes the size of the averaging window, whereas s and l denote the size of the shorter and longer windows, respectively. In the P-EMA(n) and EMA-D(n) rules, we define λ as $\frac{n-1}{n+1}$. On the other hand, for the EMA-C(s, l) rule, we set λ as $\frac{l-1}{l+1}$, and β as $\frac{s-1}{s+1}$

Trading rule	Noise suppression factor	
	Exact	Asymptotic
MOM(n) and SMA-D(n)	$\sqrt{n}$	$\sqrt{n}$
P-SMA(n) and LMA-D(n)	$\sqrt{\frac{3n(n+1)}{2(2n+1)}}$	$\frac{\sqrt{3}}{2}\sqrt{n} \approx 0.87\sqrt{n}$
P-LMA(n)	$\sqrt{\frac{5(n^3+3n^2+2n)}{3(3n^2+6n+1)}}$	$\frac{\sqrt{5}}{3}\sqrt{n} \approx 0.75\sqrt{n}$
P-EMA(n) and EMA-D(n)	$\sqrt{n}$	$\sqrt{n}$
SMA-C(s, l)	$\frac{\sqrt{3}}{2}\sqrt{l}$	$\frac{\sqrt{3}}{2}\sqrt{l} \approx 0.87\sqrt{l}$
LMA-C(s, l)	$\sqrt{\frac{5l^2}{3(3l-s)}}$	$0.75\sqrt{l} \leq \frac{\sqrt{5}l}{3\sqrt{l-\frac{s}{3}}} \leq 0.91\sqrt{l}$
EMA-C(s, l)	$\sqrt{-\frac{2\ln(\lambda\beta)}{\ln\lambda \ln\beta}}$	$\sqrt{l} \leq \sqrt{l+s} \leq \sqrt{2l}$

Based on the results presented in Table 5.2, the following noteworthy observations should be highlighted.

Remark 5.1 In every technical indicator, the number of returns lags (n, s, or l) directly influences the NSF and, consequently, accuracy. By increasing the number of return lags, one can improve the rule's precision in detecting the trend direction.

Remark 5.2 As discussed in the previous chapter, among all technical indicators computed using a finite number of lags n, the MOM(n) rule exhibits the highest accuracy with an NSF of $\sqrt{n}$. It is worth noting that this technical indicator utilizes a simple (equally-weighted) moving average of returns.

Remark 5.3 The P-EMA(n) and EMA-D(n) rules exhibit comparable accuracy to that of the MOM(n) rule. However, it is important to note that these technical indicators are computed using an infinite number of return lags. Thus, we interpret the results presented in Table 5.2 as follows: when the technical indicators of these rules are computed using $\lambda = \frac{n-1}{n+1}$, the NSF of these rules equals $\sqrt{n}$.

Remark 5.4 When considering rules that utilize a single SMA or LMA, the asymptotic solution arises when we allow the number of return lags n to approach infinity. Through these asymptotic solutions, we observe that the NSF of these rules is approximately 13%-25% lower than that of the MOM(n) rule.

Remark 5.5 A notable observation is that the NSF of the SMA-C(s, l) rule remains independent of the number of return lags s in the shorter moving average. In other words, regardless of the chosen value for s, the NSF of the SMA-C(s, l) rule remains constant and equals the NSF of the corresponding P-SMA(l) rule.

Remark 5.6 The NSF of the LMA-C(s, l) rule exhibits dependency on the number of return lags in the shorter moving average. Specifically, the lowest NSF of $0.75\sqrt{l}$ is attained as s approaches zero, while the highest NSF of $0.91\sqrt{l}$ is reached when s approaches l. Therefore, it becomes evident that increasing the value of s corresponds to an increase in the NSF of this rule.

Remark 5.7 It is important to observe that, for all rules except the EMA-C(s, l) rule, the maximum NSF does not exceed $\sqrt{l}$ (or $\sqrt{n}$). In contrast, the NSF of the EMA-C(s, l) rule generally surpasses $\sqrt{l}$. Specifically, the lowest NSF of $\sqrt{l}$ is attained when s approaches zero, while the highest NSF of $\sqrt{2l}$ is reached when s approaches l.

Remark 5.8 It is crucial to recognize that the EMA-C(s, l) rule's superior accuracy should be approached with great caution due to its reliance on an infinite number of past return lags. The key factor contributing to this superiority is our assumption that a trend has been present in the recent past and is expected to persist in the near future. This "recent past" duration aligns with the return lags' length in a trading rule. Essentially, when applying rules with a finite number of lags n, our assumption implies that the trend has spanned the last n periods and is anticipated to continue for at least one more period. In reality, trends have limited durations. Typically, as the parameter s approaches 1 in the EMA-C(s, l) rule, the return weights decline rapidly with increasing return lag. Consequently, returns at long lags have only a marginal impact on the trading signal. The situation undergoes a significant shift when s approaches l. At this point, returns at long lags can noticeably influence the trading signal. Importantly, at these extended lags, the trend direction may differ from the trend observed in the recent past.

In concluding this section, we provide graphical illustrations that offer further insights into the accuracies of different technical indicators. We first compare the accuracies of the MOM(12) and various P-MA(12) technical indicators. Figure 5.1 displays the hit ratios of the MOM(12), P-SMA(12), P-LMA(12), and P-EMA(12) technical indicators plotted against the signal-to-noise ratio of returns.

We remind the reader that the hit ratio quantifies the proportion of times a correct identification of the trend direction is made. When the returns follow a normal distribution, the hit ratio of a technical indicator $I(n)$ is computed as follows:

$$HR(I(n)) = \Phi(NSF(I(n)) \times SNR(r)),$$

where $NSF(I(n))$ denotes the NSF of the technical indicator, $SNR(r)$ is the signal-to-noise ratio of returns, and $\Phi(\cdot)$ represents the cumulative distribution function of the standard normal random variable. It is worth noting that the hit ratio is an increasing function of the NSF.

In accordance with the analytical expressions, the MOM(12) and P-EMA(12) rules exhibit the highest hit ratios, followed by the P-SMA(12) rule and the P-LMA(12) rule. Notably, despite the P-LMA(12) rule having an NSF approximately 25% lower than that of the MOM(12) rule, its hit ratio is no more than 7% lower. This is attributed to the hit ratio's nonlinear dependence on the NSF.

Moreover, when the signal-to-noise ratio of returns is extremely low or high, the hit ratios of various trading rules show only marginal differences. These observations lead to the following remark.

Remark 5.9 When the market trend is exceptionally strong, all technical indicators perform equally well in detecting trend direction. Conversely, when the market trend is exceedingly weak, all technical indicators are equally poor. However, in situations where the market trend is neither extremely weak nor extremely strong, the accuracies of various technical indicators may differ significantly.

We now proceed with the illustration of the NSF for various MA-C(s, 12) rules. Specifically, Fig. 5.2 showcases the NSFs of the SMA-C(s, 12), LMA-C(s, 12), and EMA-C(s, 12) rules plotted against the number of lags in the shorter MA, denoted by s. For the sake of comparison, this figure also includes the NSF of the MOM(12) rule, which represents the highest possible value among all trading rules computed using 12 return lags.

To ensure accuracy and validate the asymptotic expressions for the NSFs of various MA-C rules, each rule's NSF in this illustration is computed using a numerical method. This approach demonstrates the reliability and consistency of the asymptotic expressions when determining the NSFs for different MA-C rules.

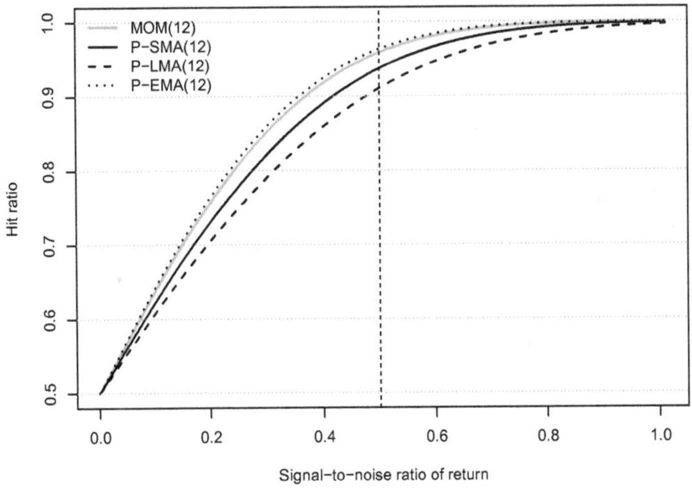

Fig. 5.1 Hit ratios of the MOM(12), P-SMA(12), P-LMA(12), and P-EMA(12) technical indicators plotted against the signal-to-noise ratio of returns. The dashed vertical line represents the typical signal-to-noise ratio observed in a market state

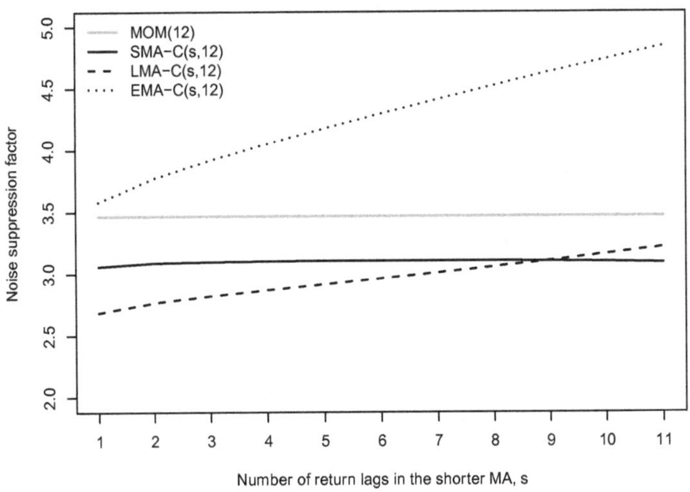

Fig. 5.2 NSFs of various MA-C(s, 12) rules versus the number of return lags s in the shorter MA. To provide a benchmark for comparison, the NSF of the MOM(12) rule is also shown on the graph

The curves depicted in this figure serve as validation for our analytical solutions. For instance, our analytical result for the NSF of the SMA-C(s, 12) rule is based on the simplified assumption of continuous return weights. According to the analytical solution, the NSF of the SMA-C(s, l) rule remains independent of the number of return lags in the shorter MA. The exact computations using a numerical method closely align with the asymptotic analytical solution, providing substantial agreement.

Another example involves the NSF of the LMA-C(s, 12) rule, which exhibits an increase as the number of return lags in the shorter MA grows. This observed behavior concurs very well with our analytical solution.

As predicted by the analytical solution, the NSF of the EMA-C(s, 12) rule surpasses that of the MOM(12) rule and rises with an increasing value of s. At first glance, this behavior may appear puzzling because we know that the MOM(12) rules exhibit the highest NSF when the number of return lags equals 12. The resolution of this puzzle lies in the fact that the technical indicator of the EMA-C(s, 12) rule is computed using an infinite number of return lags.

5.3 Analytical Results for Responsiveness Measure

A technical indicator that utilizes moving averages of past prices is inherently a lagged indicator. To assess and compare the responsiveness of these indicators, we propose utilizing the ALT measure. The ALT serves as a metric for quantifying the average time delay from when the trend changes its direction to when the technical indicator changes its trading signal. For example, if the trend has been bullish and the trading signal has been Buy, at some point, the trend changes to a bearish one. With some delay, the trading signal changes from Buy to Sell. Our goal is to measure the average time delay between the turning point and the generation of the Sell signal.

The ALT of the technical indicator $I(n)$ represents the lag number k that satisfies the following equation:

$$\sum_{i=0}^{k-1} \theta_i = \sum_{i=k}^{n-1} \theta_i .$$

In simpler terms, the ALT is the lag number that divides the return weights into two parts, ensuring that the sums of weights in each part are equal.

Let A denote the total sum of weights:

$$A = \sum_{i=0}^{n-1} \theta_i.$$

Then the ALT represents the solution to the following equation:

$$\sum_{i=0}^{k-1} \theta_i = \frac{1}{2} A.$$

In cases where the return weighting function is continuous, we can find the solution by applying the following condition:

$$\int_0^k \theta(x) dx = \frac{1}{2} A,$$

where A is given by the following integral:

$$A = \int_0^n \theta(x) dx,$$

Whether the return weights are discrete or continuous, each computation is interpreted in a similar manner: the average lag time is the return lag that divides all return weights into two parts, ensuring that the sum of weights in each part is equal.

Table 5.3 presents the trading rules along with their corresponding analytical solutions for their ALTs. The detailed derivations of these analytical solutions can be found in the Appendix section of this chapter.

Based on the results presented in this table, several noteworthy observations come to light.

Remark 5.10 Within each technical indicator, the greater the number of returns lags (n or l), the larger the ALT and the longer the delay in identifying trend turning points. Therefore, the delay can be shortened by decreasing the number of return lags.

Remark 5.11 An effective technical indicator must strike a balance between high accuracy in detecting trend direction and a short delay in identifying trend turning points. It is important to note that both accuracy and delay time

Table 5.3 Trading rules along with their corresponding ALTs. In all rules, except those utilizing the EMA, the parameter n represents the size of the averaging window, while s and l denote the sizes of the shorter and longer windows, respectively. For the rules based on the EMA, the values of n, s, and l determine the decay factor λ. In all MA-C(s, l) rules, k_s and k_l refer to the average lag times of the P-MA(s) and the P-MA(l) rules, respectively. For instance, in the SMA-C(s, l) rule, we have $k_s = \left(1 - 1/\sqrt{2}\right) s$ and $k_l = \left(1 - 1/\sqrt{2}\right) l$. As another example, in the EMA-C(s, l) rule, the values are $k_s = \ln(2)s/2$ and $k_l = \ln(2)l/2$

Trading rule	Average lag time
MOM(n) and SMA-D(n)	$0.5n$
P-SMA(n) and LMA-D(n)	$\left(1 - 1/\sqrt{2}\right) n \approx 0.293n$
P-LMA(n)	$\left(1 - 1/\sqrt[3]{2}\right) n \approx 0.206n$
P-EMA(n) and EMA-D(n)	$\ln(2)/2\,n \approx 0.347n$
SMA-C(s, l)	$k_l + \sqrt{2}\,k_s \approx k_l + 1.414k_s$
LMA-C(s, l)	$k_l + \sqrt[3]{3}\,k_s \approx k_l + 1.442k_s$
EMA-C(s, l)	$k_l + 1/\ln 2\,k_s \approx k_l + 1.443k_s$

are directly influenced by the number of return lags in a technical indicator. Specifically, increasing the number of return lags enhances both accuracy and delay time simultaneously. Therefore, it is essential to recognize that it is not possible to increase accuracy while simultaneously decreasing the delay time. Instead, the goal should be to find the optimal tradeoff between accuracy and delay time for a technical indicator.

Remark 5.12 For all rules except the double crossover rules, the time delay is a linear function of the form $k = bn$, where b is a positive constant and n represents the number of return lags. Arranging the rules in ascending order of their delay time, from shortest to longest, we have: P-LMA(n), P-SMA(n), P-EMA(n), and MOM(n).

Remark 5.13 In the previous section, it was evident that among all rules, excluding the double crossover rules, the MOM(n) rule exhibits the highest accuracy in detecting trend direction, whereas the P-LMA(n) rule shows the lowest accuracy. However, the scenario is reversed concerning the delay in identifying trend turning points. In this case, the P-LMA(n) rule boasts the shortest delay, while the MOM(n) rule experiences the longest delay.

Remark 5.14 The reader should be aware that while the MOM(n) technical indicator employs equal weighting of returns, any P-MA(n) technical indicator tends to place greater emphasis on the most recent returns. As a logical consequence, it becomes feasible to reduce the lag time by giving more weight to the most recent returns, resulting in a shorter delay time. In theory, the shortest conceivable delay time is achieved when all the weight is concentrated on the single most recent return observation. In this context, the MOM(1) technical indicator exhibits the shortest possible lag time. However, it is important to note that this technical indicator concurrently demonstrates the poorest accuracy in detecting trend direction. Hence, there exists a tradeoff between delay time and accuracy, where shorter delay times may lead to a compromise in the ability to accurately identify trend directions.

Remark 5.15 All MA-C(s, l) technical indicators exhibit an average lag time that can be approximated by a linear function of the form $k = k_l + bk_s$, where b represents a positive constant, and k_s and k_l denote the average lag times of the P-MA(s) and P-MA(l) technical indicators, respectively. Remarkably, across all MA-C rules, the value of b remains relatively consistent.

Remark 5.16 As shown in the preceding section, the accuracy of a MA-C(s, l) technical indicator tends to improve when the value of s increases, enabling better trend direction detection. Conversely, the delay in identifying trend turning points of a MA-C(s, l) technical indicator consistently worsens with higher values of s. However, it is noteworthy that the SMA-C(s, l) technical indicator exhibits a unique behavior wherein the number of lags in the shorter MA, denoted by s, does not influence accuracy. Consequently, in the SMA-C(s, l) technical indicator, one can adjust the delay time effectively by varying the value of s without affecting the accuracy.

To conclude this section, we present graphical illustrations that provide further insights into the average lag times of alternative technical indicators. We begin with Fig. 5.3, which demonstrates the responsiveness of the MOM and various P-MA technical indicators. We assume that the mean return till time $t_0 = 0$ equals $\mu = 0.2$. From time t_0, the mean return changes its sign and becomes $\mu = -0.2$. The dashed line in the figure represents the value of the mean returns, with time t_0 corresponding to the peak in the price trend.

The lines in the figure showcase how the value of the MOM(20) and various P-MA(20) technical indicators reacts to the change in the price trend. It is essential to recall that the average lag time refers to the delay between the change in the sign of the mean returns and the time when a technical indicator's value also changes its sign. In other words, it signifies the time difference between t_0 and the moment when a technical indicator intersects the zero line. Notably, the graphical results align precisely with the analytical findings, confirming

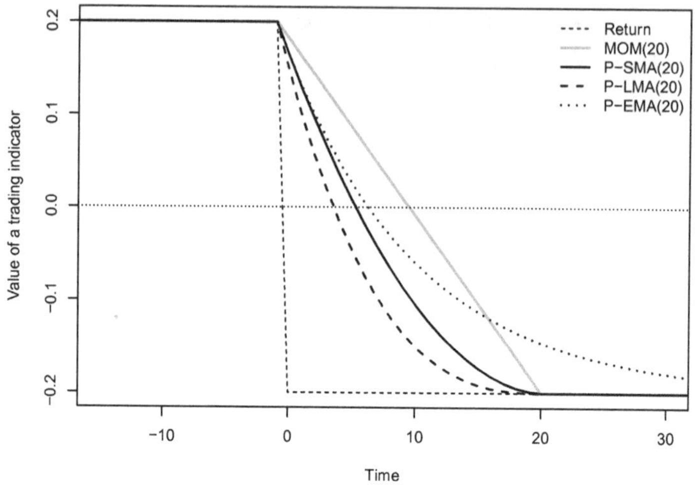

Fig. 5.3 Change in the mean returns and the value of the MOM(20) and various P-MA(20) technical indicators

that the ranking of rules based on their delay time, from shortest to longest, is as follows: P-LMA, P-SMA, P-EMA, and MOM.

Continuing with the illustration of the ALTs of various MA-C(s, 12) technical indicators, we present Fig. 5.4, depicting the ALTs of the S-MAC(s, 12), LMA-C(s, 12), and EMA-C(s, 12) technical indicators in relation to the number of lags s in the shorter moving average. For comparative purposes, this figure also includes the ALT of the MOM(12) rule. The calculation of each technical indicator's ALT employs a numerical method to demonstrate the validity of our approximate expressions for ALTs of different MA-C rules, as reported in Table 5.3.

As observed, the ALT of any MA-C(s, 12) technical indicator increases linearly with the parameter s. Notably, when $s = 1$, the ALT of any MA-C(1,12) technical indicator equals that of the P-MA(12) technical indicator, resulting in an ALT of the MA-C(s, 12) rule that is lower than that of the MOM(12) rule. As s increases, the ALT of the MA-C(s, 12) rule also increases. Eventually, the ALTs of the SMA-C(s, 12) and E-MAC(s, 12) rules surpass that of the MOM(12) rule. However, the ALT of the LMA-C(s, 12) rule consistently remains lower than that of the MOM(12) rule.

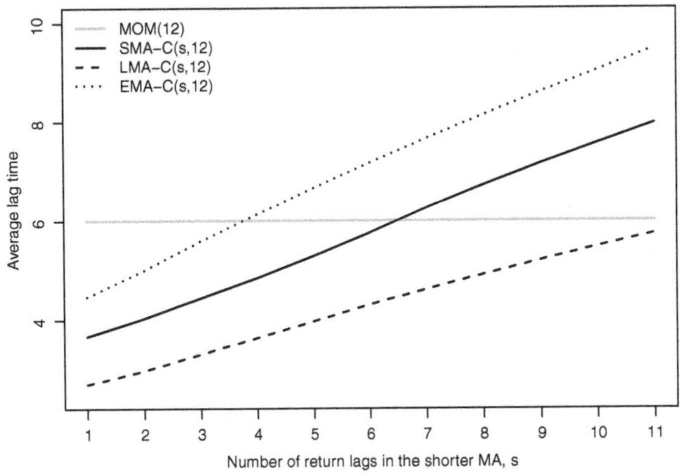

Fig. 5.4 Average lag times of various MA-C(s, 12) rules versus the value of s. For the sake of comparison, this figure also plots the average lag time of the MOM(12) rule

5.4 Analytical Results for Smoothness Measure

An effective technical indicator must not only accurately detect trend directions and timely react to trend changes but also generate a persistent trading signal. When a trading signal lacks persistence, it becomes vulnerable to whipsaw trades, a perilous phenomenon where the indicator's signals frequently prompt reversions of trading positions. This issue is particularly significant in sideways trending markets, where traders may find themselves caught in a frustrating cycle of erroneous trades, potentially leading to losses. To address this problem, traders should seek indicators with improved signal persistence.

The generation of a trading signal depends on the technical indicator's value, which is subsequently converted into a binary outcome. Signal persistence is achieved when the time series of the technical indicator's value displays smoothness, characterized by a high degree of similarity between the time series and a lagged version of itself. Consequently, the smoothness of a technical indicator can be measured by the autocorrelation of the signal generated by the technical indicator.

We suggest quantifying the trading signal's persistence using the SMI measure. The SMI of the technical indicator $I(n)$ is calculated using the following formula:

$$SMI = \frac{\sum_{i=0}^{n-2} \theta_i \theta_{i+1}}{\sum_{i=0}^{n-1} \theta_i^2}.$$

Table 5.4 Trading rules along with their corresponding SMIs. In all rules, except those utilizing the EMA, n denotes the size of the averaging window, whereas s and l denote the size of the shorter and longer windows, respectively. In the P-EMA(n) and EMA-D(n) rules, we define λ as $\frac{n-1}{n+1}$. On the other hand, for the EMA-C(s, l) rule, we set λ as $\frac{l-1}{l+1}$, and β as $\frac{s-1}{s+1}$

Trading rule	Smoothness index
MOM(n) and SMA-D(n)	$\frac{n-1}{n}$
P-SMA(n) and LMA-D(n)	$\frac{n-1}{n+0.5}$
P-LMA(n)	$\frac{(n-1)^5/20+3/8(n-1)^4+(n-1)^3+9/8(n-1)^2+7/15(n-1)}{n(n+1)(n+2)(3n^2+6n+1)/60}$
P-EMA(n) and EMA-D(n)	$\lambda = \frac{n-1}{n+1}$
SMA-C(s, l)	$2\frac{s(s+2)(l-s)+(l-s-1)(l-s+1)(s+1)}{s(2s+1)(l-s)+(l-s+1)(2l-2s+1)(s+1)}$
LMA-C(s, l)	$\frac{6l^3s^4-2l^2s^5-20l^2s^3+20l^2s^2-l^2-2ls-s^2}{2l^2s^4(3l-s)}$
EMA-C(s, l)	$\frac{\lambda+\beta}{1-\lambda\beta} = \frac{ls-1}{ls+1}$

In essence, the SMI represents the first-order autocorrelation of the technical indicator, particularly in sideways markets. Moreover, it proves useful in comparing the persistence of trading signals within trending markets as well.

Table 5.4 presents the trading rules along with their corresponding analytical solutions to the SMI. The derivations of these analytical solutions can be found in the Appendix of this chapter. It is worth noting that while some rules have simple analytical solutions, others are quite complex and do not permit simplification.

After examining the expressions presented in Table 5.4, several noteworthy observations come to light.

Remark 5.17 It is important to note that in all cases, as the number of return lags approaches 1, the SMI tends to zero, and consequently, the probability of a position reversal approaches 50%. Conversely, when the number of return lags significantly increases, the SMI tends to 1, leading to a near 0% probability of a position reversal. This observation highlights the negative relationship between the SMI and the likelihood of position reversals.

Remark 5.18 Previously, we established that the accuracy of trend identification improves as the number of return lags increases in all rules. In addition to this, we have discovered that the smoothness of a technical indicator also shows enhancement with a higher number of return lags. However, it is essential to note that the technical indicator with the highest accuracy for a specific number of return lags does not exhibit the highest level of smoothness and vice versa.

Remark 5.19 For any number of return lags n, the MOM(n) rule demonstrates greater smoothness than the P-SMA(n) rule. This is supported by the inequality:

$$\frac{n-1}{n} > \frac{n-1}{n+0.5} \text{ for all } n.$$

This inequality indicates that the MOM(n) rule consistently exhibits higher smoothness across all possible values of n compared to the P-SMA(n) rule.

Remark 5.20 For any number of return lags n, the P-SMA(n) rule demonstrates greater smoothness compared to the P-EMA(n) rule. This is evident from the inequality:

$$\frac{n-1}{n+0.5} > \frac{n-1}{n+1} \text{ for all } n.$$

This inequality consistently holds true for all possible values of n, indicating that the P-SMA(n) rule consistently outperforms the P-EMA(n) rule in terms of smoothness.

Based on our analysis, we can draw the following conclusions regarding the smoothness of the MOM and P-MA rules. For any number of lags n, the MOM(n) technical indicator outperforms the P-SMA(n) technical indicator, which, in turn, shows better results than the P-EMA(n) technical indicator. As for the P-LMA(n) technical indicator, its analytical expression for smoothness is quite intricate, making it challenging to directly compare with the other rules based on their respective SMIs. Nonetheless, through numerical computations, we find that among the indicators with the same number of lags n, the P-LMA(n) technical indicator exhibits the lowest smoothness. To illustrate this comparison, Fig. 5.5 presents a graphical representation of the SMIs of the MOM and P-MA rules concerning the number of return lags n.

Remark 5.21 Previously, we established that the MOM(n) rule outperforms the P-MA rules with the same number of lags n in terms of accuracy for trend detection. Now, intriguingly, we discover that the MOM(n) rule also achieves the highest level of smoothness. These findings come as a surprise, especially considering that the technical indicator for this rule, in its price-based form, is calculated using only two price observations.

Remark 5.22 For the majority of MA-C(s, l) rules, the analytical expression for the SMI is quite complex. However, we can easily analyze the limiting

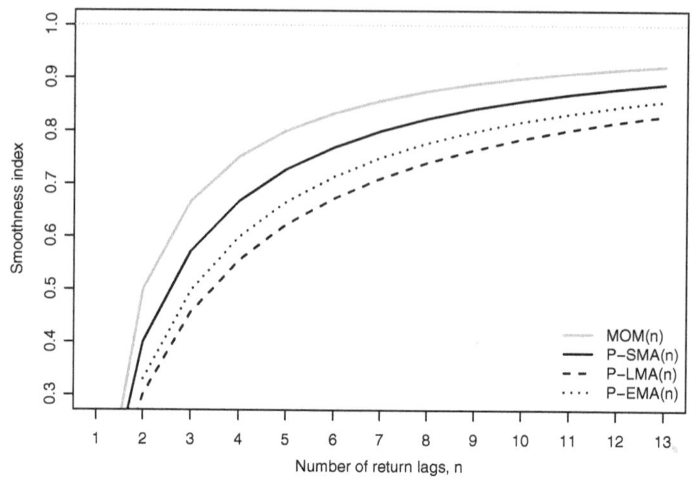

Fig. 5.5 Smoothness of the MOM and P-MA rules versus the number of return lags n

behavior of the SMI when both s and l increase significantly. Specifically, we find that for any MA-C(s, l) rule:

$$\lim_{s\to\infty, l\to\infty} SMI \to 1.$$

In other words, as the number of return lags in both the shorter and longer moving averages increases substantially, the smoothness index approaches unity.

The analytical solutions for the SMI of various $MAC(s, l)$ rules can be quite intricate, making it challenging to conduct simple comparisons in terms of smoothness. To address this, we employ graphical illustrations to depict the smoothness of different MA-C(s, l) rules. Figure 5.6 showcases the SMI plots of the SMA-C$(s, 12)$, LMA-C$(s, 12)$, and EMA-C$(s, 12)$ rules, along with the SMI of the MOM(12) rule for comparison. Upon analyzing the curves in the figure, we can make the following observations. The SMI of the LMA-C$(s, 12)$ and EMA-C$(s, 12)$ technical indicators consistently increases as the value of s (number of lags in the shorter moving average) increases. In contrast, the SMI of the SMA-C$(s, 12)$ technical indicator initially increases, reaching a maximum when s is approximately equal to $l/2$ (half the number of lags in the longer moving average), and then decreases as s continues to rise.

Through our analysis, we have observed that the SMI of the MOM(n) rule surpasses the SMI of any P-MA(n) rule. Nevertheless, we find that by adjusting the number of lags in the shorter moving average s, the SMI of an MA-C(s, n)

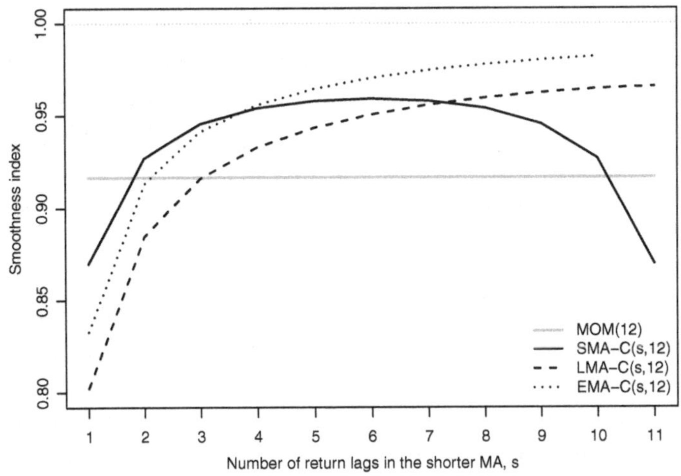

Fig. 5.6 SMIs of various MA-C(s, 12) rules versus the number of return lags s in the shorter moving average. The SMI of the MOM(12) rule serves as a benchmark for comparison

technical indicator can exceed that of the MOM(n) technical indicator. The underlying reasoning behind this result can be explained as follows.

The weighting function associated with the highest SMI takes on a semicircle-like shape. It is essential to note that, in any P-MA(n) trading rule, the weighting function gives more weight to recent return observations while reducing the weight for more distant ones. This shape is noticeably different from a true semicircle. In contrast, although MOM(n) has equal return weights, its weighting function is closer to a semicircle than the one in any P-MA(n) rule. However, appropriately selecting the shorter moving average size in the MA-C(s, n) rule makes it possible to create a weighting function shape that closely approximates a semicircle. For instance, the return function of the LMA-C(11, 12) rule bears a striking resemblance to a semicircle, outperforming the return function of the MOM(12) rule in this aspect.

5.5 Comparing Rules Using Quantitative Measures

Before delving into the methodology of comparing various trading rules using three quantitative measures, let us set the context. In the world of trading, there are several well-known trading rules, including the MOM, P-MA, MA-C, and MA-D rules. Each of these rules has its unique characteristics and applications in the financial markets. The P-MA, MA-C, and MA-D rules offer versatility as they can be implemented with different types of moving averages, such as SMA, LMA, or EMA, resulting in multiple variants for each trading rule. Our primary objective is to identify the most efficient trading rule among these options. Throughout the following presentation, we will primarily focus on examining the MOM, P-MA, and MA-C rules. This choice is deliberate since, typically, each MA-D rule is either equivalent to the MOM rule or a P-MA rule.

Up until now, traders have traditionally assessed the characteristics of different trend-following rules through subjective visual inspections. They typically selected a random historical price sequence, calculated moving averages, and represented the price sequence along with the moving averages in a plot. The properties of trading rules based on these moving averages are then judged visually. However, this approach is highly subjective and prone to biases.

In contrast, we propose a rigorous and scientific approach to evaluate the properties of various trading rules and identify the most efficient one. Our method relies on quantitative measures, providing an objective and unbiased analysis. By employing this systematic approach, we aim to enhance the reliability and validity of the evaluation process for trend-following rules, enabling traders to make well-informed decisions based on solid evidence.

We assess the trading rules using three quantitative measures: NSF, ALT, and SMI. The NSF serves as a gauge to compare the accuracies of various trend-following indicators in detecting the trend direction. A higher NSF indicates better accuracy in trend detection. The ALT helps in comparing the delay times of different technical indicators in detecting trend turning points. A smaller ALT implies a shorter delay time in trend detection. Lastly, the SMI is used to assess the smoothness of various technical indicators. Its value is related to the expected number of whipsaw trades associated with each indicator. A larger SMI indicates a smaller expected number of whipsaw trades.

Formally, the technical indicator $I(n)$ is uniquely specified by n return weights $\{\theta_0, \theta_1, \ldots, \theta_{n-1}\}$. The three measures are computed based on the return weights within a technical indicator:

$$
\begin{aligned}
NSF(I(n)) &= NSF(\theta_0, \theta_1, \ldots, \theta_{n-1}),\\
ALT(I(n)) &= ALT(\theta_0, \theta_1, \ldots, \theta_{n-1}),\\
SMI(I(n)) &= SMI(\theta_0, \theta_1, \ldots, \theta_{n-1}).
\end{aligned}
$$

Through the application of these three measures, our objective is to identify the most efficient technical indicator. To demonstrate our methodology, we will consider two alternative technical indicators labeled as $I_1(n)$ and $I_2(m)$.

Generally, these indicators not only vary in their weighting functions for returns but also in the number of return lags they incorporate. More specifically, the first technical indicator, $I_1(n)$, is calculated using n return lags, whereas the second one, $I_2(m)$, is calculated using m return lags.

For the technical indicator $I_2(m)$ to exhibit greater efficiency than the technical indicator $I_1(n)$, the following conditions must be satisfied:

$$\begin{aligned} NSF(I_2(m)) &\geq NSF(I_1(n)), \\ ALT(I_2(m)) &\leq ALT(I_1(n)), \\ SMI(I_2(m)) &\geq SMI(I_1(n)). \end{aligned}$$

Furthermore, it is essential that at least one of these conditions is strictly met. In other words, $I_2(m)$ is considered more efficient than $I_1(n)$ if it either exhibits better or equivalent accuracy, better or equivalent responsiveness, and better or equivalent smoothness compared to $I_1(n)$. Additionally, $I_2(m)$ must outperform $I_1(n)$ in at least one of these aspects.

Undoubtedly, an efficient trading rule must demonstrate accuracy and responsiveness. However, the significance of smoothness properties is less clear-cut. Smoothness is closely linked to the expected amount of trading costs. A trading rule with higher smoothness incurs lower transaction costs compared to one with lower smoothness. Over time, transaction costs in financial markets have consistently decreased. What were once considerable costs several decades ago have now reduced significantly in many financial markets, making trading costs extremely low nowadays.

In financial markets with negligible trading costs, the effectiveness of various trading rules can be assessed using only two measures: NSF and ALT. The primary focus is on accuracy and responsiveness of the trading rules. Conversely, in markets with significant trading costs, the evaluation can be based on SMI and ALT measures. Here, the emphasis shifts to smoothness and responsiveness of the trading rules.

In the former case, $I_2(m)$ is considered more efficient than $I_1(n)$ if the following conditions hold:

$$\begin{aligned} NSF(I_2(m)) &\geq NSF(I_1(n)), \\ ALT(I_2(m)) &\leq ALT(I_1(n)), \end{aligned}$$

and at least one inequality is strictly satisfied.

In the latter case, $I_2(m)$ is considered more efficient than $I_1(n)$ if the following conditions hold:

$$SMI(I_2(m)) \geq SMI(I_1(n)),$$
$$ALT(I_2(m)) \leq ALT(I_1(n)),$$

and at least one inequality is strictly satisfied.

These two cases offer a simpler and more straightforward quantitative comparison of trading rules since they are evaluated using only two criteria instead of three. This approach enables a more efficient and effective assessment of trading rule performance under different market conditions.

We begin by comparing the effectiveness of two technical indicators, MOM and various P-MA rules (P-SMA, P-LMA, and P-EMA), to identify the most efficient one. Figure 5.7 illustrates the return weights in these indicators, where the MOM rule employs equal return weights, while all P-MA rules overweight the most recent returns.

Visual inspection reveals that the weighting functions in the P-MA rules have similar shapes, whereas the return weights in the MOM rule show a different pattern. This suggests that the properties of the P-MA rules are generally similar to one another but distinct from those of the MOM rule. For instance, the P-MA rules' overweighting of the most recent returns enhances their responsiveness compared to the MOM rule (given the same number of return lags n).

Despite the valuable insights gained from understanding the return weights in these trading rules, it is challenging to determine definitively which rule is the most effective. Our quantitative measures can help greatly in comparing the effectiveness of various trading rules. The simplest comparison can be done by considering only two measures at a time. For example, we can consider either the ALT and NSF measures, or the ALT and SMI measures. The motivation for these two choices is based on the whether the issue of trading costs is severe or not. If trading costs are negligibly small, we can focus exclusively on the ALT and NSF measures. On the other hand, when trading costs are substantial, it is more appropriate to switch to the ALT and SMI measures.

Let us consider the ALT and NSF measures. Already from the previous chapter, we know that the MOM(n) rule is the most accurate rule among all rules where the technical indicator is computed using n return weights. In this chapter, we have also learned that the P-EMA(n) technical indicator has the same accuracy at the MOM(n) technical indicator. Besides, the P-EMA(n) is a more responsive technical indicator than the MOM(n) one. So we conclude that, for any number of lags n, P-EMA(n) rule is more efficient than the MOM(n) rule.

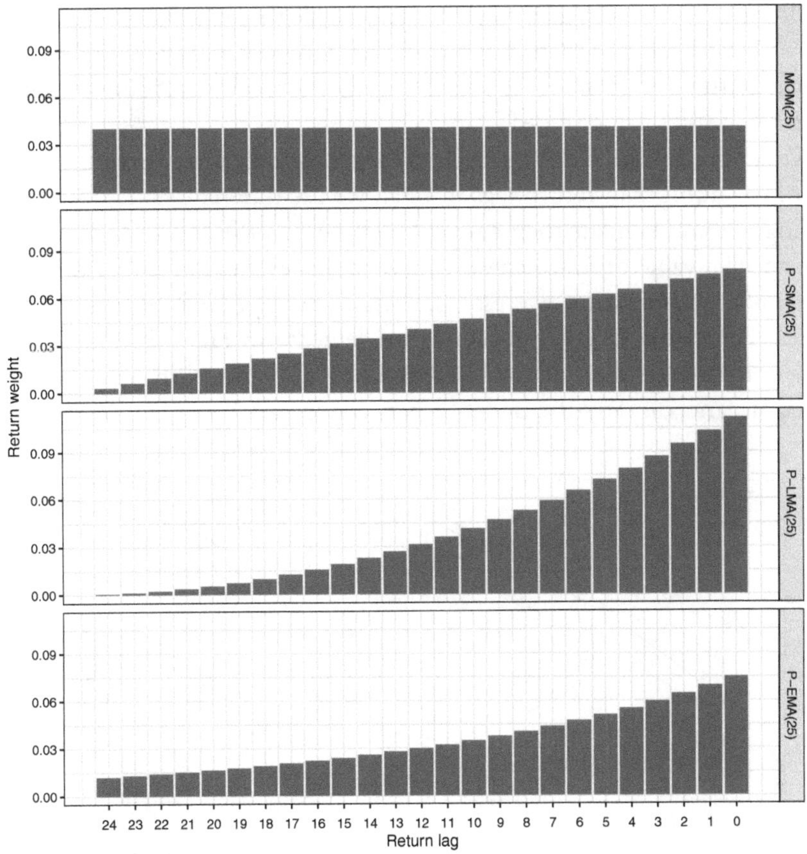

Fig. 5.7 Return weighting functions in the MOM(25), P-SMA(25), P-LMA(25), and P-EMA(25) technical indicators. The weights in the P-EMA(25) indicator are cut off at lag 25

The comparison between the MOM(n) rule and other rules, such as the P-SMA(n) rule, is less straightforward. The MOM(n) rule exhibits higher accuracy, while the P-SMA(n) rule is more responsive. To determine which rule is more efficient, we employ the following procedure. First, we identify the P-SMA(m) rule that matches the responsiveness of the MOM(n) rule. Next, we compare the accuracy of the P-SMA(m) rule to that of the MOM(n) rule. If the accuracy of the P-SMA(m) rule is higher, we can conclude that it is more efficient than the MOM(n) rule. The core idea is that by switching from the MOM(n) rule to the P-SMA(m) rule, which has the same average lag time, we can enhance trading efficiency as it outperforms the MOM(n) rule in terms of accuracy.

Alternatively, we can find the P-SMA(m) rule that matches the accuracy of the MOM(n) rule and then compare the responsiveness of the P-SMA(m) rule to that of the MOM(n) rule. We can apply the same procedure to compare the trading rules using the ALT and SMI measures.

We adopt the following approach to ensure an unbiased comparison regardless of the number of return lags n. First, we use different values of n in each trading rule and evaluate their corresponding ALT, NSF, and SMI measures for each specific value of n. Once we complete this evaluation for all the trading rules under examination, we plot the results in the ALT-NSF and ALT-SMI spaces. The results of this procedure are depicted in Fig. 5.8. The left panel visually represents the tradeoffs between the ALT and NSF measures, while the right panel displays the tradeoffs between the ALT and SMI measures.

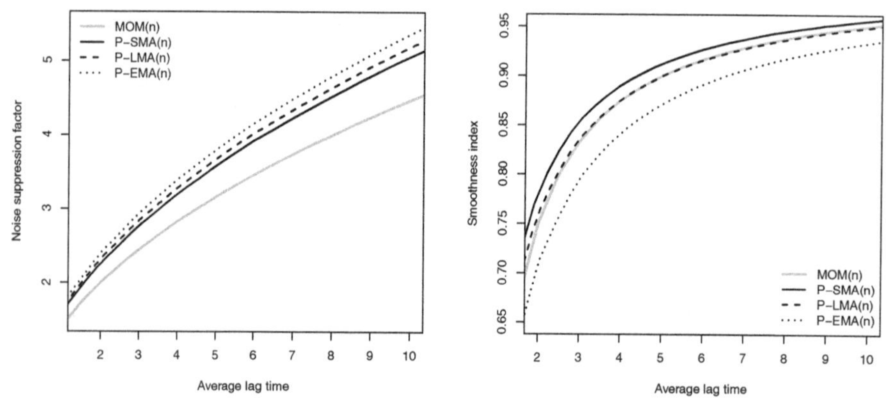

Fig. 5.8 Left panel in this figure illustrates a visual representation of the tradeoffs between the ALT and NSF measures for the MOM and P-MA rules. The right panel displays the tradeoffs between the ALT and SMI measures

To elaborate on our approach, we start by considering an arbitrary technical indicator denoted as $I(n)$. The parameter n varies within the set $\{n_1, n_2, \ldots, n_{\max}\}$. For each specific value of n, we calculate two essential measures: ALT and NSF. The computations yield two sequences: the first sequence represents the values of $ALT(n)$ and is denoted as $\{ALT(n_1), ALT(n_2), \ldots, ALT(n_{\max})\}$, while the second sequence represents the values of $NSF(n)$ and is denoted as $\{NSF(n_1), NSF(n_2), \ldots, NSF(n_{\max})\}$. Having obtained these two sequences, we then create a plot that visualizes the relationship between $NSF(n)$ and $ALT(n)$. This plot effectively generates a curve within the ALT-NSF space.

In the ALT-NSF space, two distinct technical indicators, $I_1(n)$ and $I_2(n)$, generate individual curves. These curves represent the tradeoff between the ALT and NSF measures offered by each technical indicator. A key observation is that the technical indicator $I_2(n)$ is more efficient than the technical indicator $I_1(n)$ if the curve associated with $I_2(n)$ consistently lies above the curve associated with $I_1(n)$ for all values of the ALT measure. In this case, for any given ALT measure, the corresponding NSF measure of $I_2(n)$ surpasses that of $I_1(n)$. That is, for the same average lag time, the technical indicator $I_2(n)$ is more accurate than the technical indicator $I_1(n)$.

The curves in the left panel of Fig. 5.8 clearly indicate that the MOM rule provides the least favorable tradeoff between the ALT and NSF measures. On the other hand, the P-SMA, P-LMA, and P-EMA rules exhibit quite similar tradeoffs, with only marginal differences. Specifically, the P-EMA rule demonstrates a slightly superior tradeoff compared to the P-LMA rule, which, in turn, offers a slightly better tradeoff than the P-SMA rule. Thus, based on the tradeoff between the ALT and NSF measures, the ranking of rules, from best to worst, is as follows: P-EMA, P-LMA, P-SMA, and MOM.

Next, we proceed to compare the rules based on their tradeoffs between the ALT and SMI measures. The curves in the right panel of Fig. 5.8 clearly demonstrate that the P-SMA rule exhibits the most favorable tradeoff between the ALT and SMI, while the P-EMA rule provides the least favorable one. Meanwhile, the P-LMA and MOM rules show nearly identical tradeoffs between the ALT and SMI. Upon closer examination, it becomes evident that the P-LMA rule offers a slightly better tradeoff than the MOM rule. Consequently, based on these two measures (ALT and SMI), the ranking of rules, from best to worst, is as follows: P-SMA, P-LMA, MOM, and P-EMA.

The analysis presented above indicates that, among the MOM and various P-MA rules, there is no single rule that excels in all three quantitative measures. For instance, while the P-EMA rule offers the most favorable tradeoff between accuracy and responsiveness, it simultaneously provides the least favorable tradeoff between smoothness and responsiveness. On the other hand, the P-SMA rule demonstrates the best tradeoff between smoothness and responsiveness, but it ranks second worst in terms of the tradeoff between accuracy and responsiveness. As for the P-LMA rule, it consistently exhibits the second-best tradeoff among the rules.

For clarity, Table 5.5 presents the MOM and various P-MA rules, all having an average lag time of $ALT = 10$. Ideally, the most efficient rule should possess the highest accuracy and smoothness, given the same average lag time. However, no single rule achieves both the highest accuracy and smoothness

Table 5.5 This table lists the MOM and P-MA rules, all having the same average lag times. In each specific rule, except for the P-EMA rule, n represents the number of return lags. However, for the P-EMA rule, n is utilized to compute the decay constant

Trading rule	n	ALT	NSF	SMI
MOM(n)	20	10	4.47	0.950
P-SMA(n)	34	10	5.06	0.957
P-LMA(n)	49	10	5.19	0.950
P-EMA(n)	29	10	5.37	0.933

simultaneously. Therefore, selecting the "best" trading rule can be approached in two distinct ways.

One option is to consider the trading costs involved. For scenarios with substantial trading costs, the optimal rule is the P-SMA, as it provides the best tradeoff between smoothness and responsiveness. Conversely, when trading costs are negligible, the P-EMA rule becomes the preferred choice due to its superior tradeoff between accuracy and responsiveness.

Alternatively, a more balanced approach is to select the best rule "on average," which in this case is the P-LMA rule. It is worth noting that the P-SMA rule is also a sensible option in this scenario. First, the P-SMA rule offers the best tradeoff between smoothness and responsiveness. Second, it exhibits nearly the same tradeoff between accuracy and responsiveness as the P-LMA rule. Last, the SMA-based trading rules are widely familiar among traders and are commonly found in virtually any trading platform, making the P-SMA rule a practical and popular choice.

We continue this section by comparing the effectiveness of the various MA-C(s, l) rules (SMA-C, LMA-C, and EMA-C). Figure 5.9 illustrates the weighting functions in the SMA-C(6,25), LMA-C(6,25), and EMA-C(6,25) technical indicators. The selection of $s \approx l/4$ is widely favored when utilizing a double moving average crossover rule in trading.

It is worth noting that any P-MA(n) rule can be viewed as a limiting case of the corresponding MA-C(s, n) rule when the size of the shorter window approaches 0, i.e., $s \to 0$. What happens when we use a shorter window of length greater than 0? To understand these effects, we can either qualitatively compare the shapes of the return weighting functions in the P-MA and MA-C rules or quantitatively compare their NSF, ALT, and SMI measures.

In the P-MA(n) rule, the return weights monotonically decrease with the lag number. In contrast, the MA-C(s, n) rule exhibits weights that first increase, reach a maximum, and then decrease. The peak of the weighting function typically occurs at a return lag close to s. This shape indicates that the return

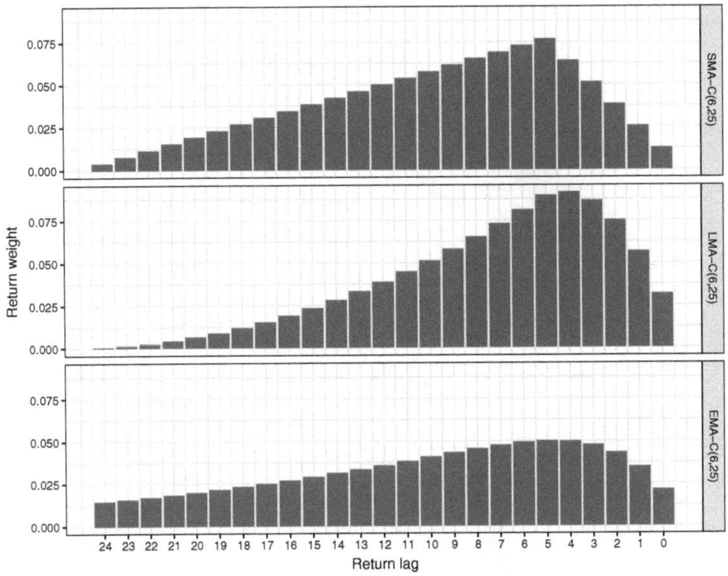

Fig. 5.9 Return weighting functions in the SMA-C(6,25), LMA-C(6,25), and EMA-C(6,25) technical indicators. The weights in the EMA-C(6,25) indicator are cut off at lag 25

weighting function in the MA-C(s, n) rule represents a "smoothed" version of the corresponding P-MA(n) rule. Even a visual comparison reveals that the MA-C(s, n) rule possesses better smoothing properties than the P-MA(n) rule.

However, this enhanced smoothness comes at the expense of responsiveness. The average lag time of the MA-C(s, n) rule is greater than that of the corresponding P-MA(n) rule because the former underweights the most recent returns.

Our analytical solutions for the NSF, ALT, and SMI measures of both the P-MA(n) and MA-C(s, n) rules corroborate the qualitative comparison based on the shapes of the return weighting functions. In general, increasing the size s of the shorter window leads to improved accuracy and smoothness while decreasing the responsiveness of the technical indicator.

However, it remains uncertain whether the tradeoffs between the quantitative measures of the MA-C(s, n) rules lead to improvements or deteriorations in comparison with the tradeoffs observed in the corresponding P-MA(n) rules. To shed light on this, Fig. 5.10 provides an illustration of the tradeoffs. The left panel visually represents the tradeoffs between the ALT and NSF measures for both the P-SMA(n) and SMA-C($n/4, n$) rules. On the other hand, the right panel displays the tradeoffs between the ALT and SMI measures.

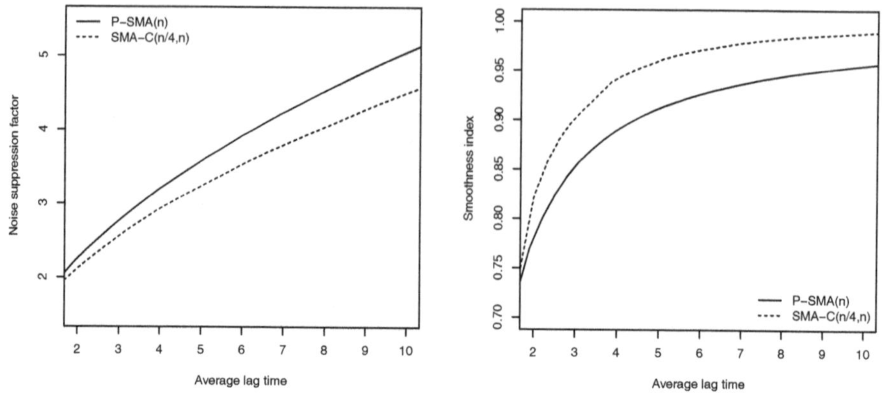

Fig. 5.10 Left panel in this figure illustrates a visual representation of the tradeoffs between the ALT and NSF measures for the P-SMA(n) and SMA-C($n/4, n$) rules. The right panel displays the tradeoffs between the ALT and SMI measures

The curves depicted in these panels indicate that the SMA-C($n/4, n$) rule results in a worse tradeoff between the ALT and NSF measures compared to the P-SMA(n) rule. However, it simultaneously exhibits a better tradeoff between the ALT and SMI measures. In other words, using a shorter moving average of prices instead of the last price enhances the tradeoff between smoothness and responsiveness while deteriorating the tradeoff between accuracy and responsiveness. Notably, these effects are consistent across all the other MA-C rules as well.

In Fig. 5.11, the left panel provides a visual representation of the tradeoffs between the ALT and NSF measures for different MA-C($n/4, n$) rules, while the right panel displays the tradeoffs between the ALT and SMI measures. Additionally, both panels include the tradeoff offered by the MOM(n) rule to facilitate a meaningful comparison.

In principle, the ranking of the MA-C rules aligns with that of the corresponding P-MA rules. To be specific, within the ALT-NSF space, the rules are ranked from best to worst as follows: EMA-C, LMA-C, and SMA-C. In the ALT-SMI space, the SMA-C rule is equally effective as the LMA-C rule, while the EMA-C performs less favorably. Additionally, it is worth noting that the MOM(n) rule consistently exhibits inferior effectiveness when compared to any MA-C rule.

Once again, our analysis leads to the conclusion that no single rule stands out as excelling in effectiveness across all three quantitative measures. However, an important finding emerges from our research: employing a MA-C rule becomes highly advantageous when trading costs pose a significant obstacle that undermines the profitability of trend-following investments.

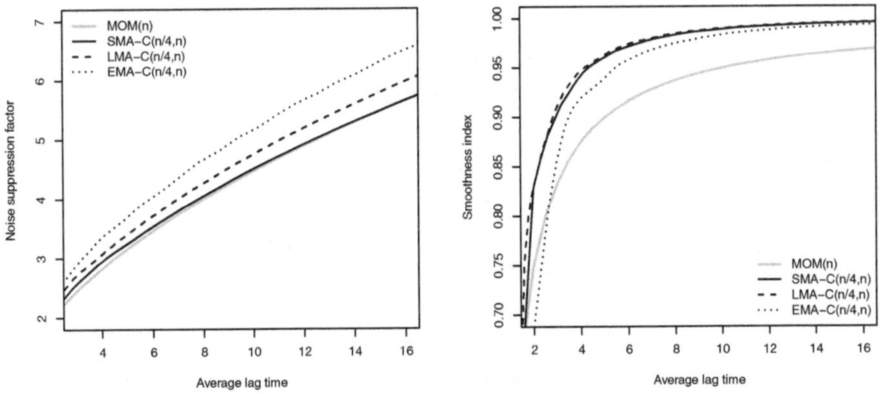

Fig. 5.11 Left panel in this figure illustrates a visual representation of the tradeoffs between the ALT and NSF measures for the MOM(n) and MA-C($n/4, n$) rules. The right panel displays the tradeoffs between the ALT and SMI measures

A key characteristic of any MA-C rule is its ability to significantly improve smoothness effectiveness by increasing the size of the shorter window. Consequently, this feature allows MA-C rules to generate considerably fewer whipsaw trades compared to their corresponding P-MA rules. This reduction in whipsaw trades can be crucial in achieving more consistent and profitable trading outcomes.

5.6 Summary

In the preceding chapter, we introduced three essential quantitative measures for evaluating trend-following trading rules utilizing moving averages. These measures include the Noise Suppression Factor (NSF), Average Lag Time (ALT), and Smoothness Index (SMI). Each of these metrics plays a crucial role in assessing the effectiveness of a trading rule.

The NSF gauges the accuracy of a trading rule, providing insights into its ability to filter out market noise and deliver reliable signals. On the other hand, the ALT measures the responsiveness of the trading rule, giving us an understanding of how quickly it adapts to changing market conditions. Additionally, the SMI quantifies the level of smoothness in the trading signals generated by the rule. This metric is valuable in identifying the stability and consistency of the rule's trading signal over time.

It is important to note that all these measures are exclusively computed using the return weights of the technical indicator, ensuring a comprehensive and objective evaluation of the rule's properties. By utilizing these metrics, traders and investors can make more informed decisions about the effectiveness and suitability of trend-following trading rules in various market scenarios.

In this chapter, first of all, we present the analytical results for the NSF, ALT, and SMI of three fundamental technical indicators that utilize standard moving averages: SMA, LMA, and EMA. These technical indicators consist of the MOM rule, P-MA rule, and MA-C rule. Our analytical results also encompass the properties of the MA-D rule. It is worth noting that in most cases, each MA-D rule is equivalent to either the MOM rule or a P-MA rule.

Our comprehensive analysis reveals intriguing patterns across different technical indicators. For both the MOM(n) and all P-MA(n) technical indicators, we observe a consistent trend: as the value of n increases, the NSF, ALT, and SMI measures also increase. This indicates that with higher values of n, these rules become more accurate and smoother in their performance. However, there is a tradeoff, as the responsiveness of the rules decreases with increasing n. In other words, they become less agile in adapting to rapidly changing market conditions.

Similarly, for all MA-C(s, l) rules, we find a similar relationship. As either s or l increases, the NSF, ALT, and SMI measures also increase. This means that higher values of s (shorter moving average) or l (longer moving average) lead to improved accuracy and smoothness in the trading rules. Yet, once again, this improvement comes at the cost of reduced responsiveness to market fluctuations.

These findings highlight a crucial aspect of trading rule design. Enhancing one aspect, such as accuracy or smoothness, inevitably results in a compromise on another aspect, such as responsiveness. Achieving optimal performance in all quantitative measures simultaneously is a challenging task, and there exists a delicate balance in selecting appropriate values for n, s, and l based on the specific objectives and market conditions.

Having obtained the analytical solutions for all quantitative measures, we utilize these metrics to compare and contrast the trading rules in search of one that excels in effectiveness across all measures. Regrettably, our analysis suggests that there is no single rule that outperforms in all three measures simultaneously.

Nonetheless, our findings do reveal that certain rules provide a favorable tradeoff between specific metrics. For instance, some rules excel in responsiveness and accuracy, striking a balance that makes them well suited for capturing market trends and generating reliable signals. On the other hand, there are rules that offer a compelling tradeoff between responsiveness and smoothness, resulting in stable and timely trading signals over time.

Among the various rules considered, the P-MA rules stand out as they offer an excellent tradeoff between accuracy and responsiveness. Notably, the P-MA rules excel in responsiveness while maintaining a commendable level of accuracy. The ranking of these rules, from best to worst, is as follows: P-EMA, P-LMA, and P-SMA. However, it is worth noting that the differences in effectiveness among these rules are relatively minor when assessed against these two criteria.

The smoothness property holds significant importance in markets where trading costs are substantial. However, even in scenarios where trading costs are relatively small, smoothness still carries advantages, especially when implementing a trading rule on a daily basis. Despite the daily trading costs being negligible, the cumulative effect over an extended period, such as a year, can lead to substantial expected trading costs. Therefore, maintaining smoothness in trading strategies remains beneficial even in situations with seemingly insignificant daily costs.

Among the rules under consideration, the MA-C rules demonstrate the most favorable tradeoff between smoothness and responsiveness when the size of the shorter window is appropriately selected. Notably, all MA-C rules may exhibit exceptional smoothness while still maintaining a satisfactory level of responsiveness. However, it is important to note that achieving this enhanced tradeoff between smoothness and responsiveness comes at a cost: it worsens the tradeoff between accuracy and responsiveness. Therefore, a careful balance must be struck while adjusting the parameters to ensure that the chosen MA-C rule aligns with the desired level of accuracy, smoothness, and responsiveness.

Our main finding suggests that attaining the perfect blend of all quantitative measures remains challenging. Nonetheless, comprehending these tradeoffs holds significant importance, as it empowers traders and investors to align their strategies with their specific objectives and risk tolerance. By carefully selecting a rule that best matches their desired balance of responsiveness, accuracy, and smoothness, market participants can optimize their trading approaches to adapt to different market conditions and achieve their financial goals. This knowledge provides a valuable tool to navigate the complexities of the financial landscape and make informed decisions in pursuit of success.

Appendix 5.A Useful Formulas

Consider the following finite sequence $\{1, 2, 3, \ldots, n\}$ of integer numbers from 1 to n. This is an example of an arithmetic series. The sum of all terms in this sequence is given by:

$$S = \sum_{k=1}^{n} k = \frac{n(n+1)}{2}. \tag{5.3}$$

The sums of powers of this sequence are given by:

$$\sum_{k=1}^{n} k^2 = \frac{n(n+1)(2n+1)}{6} = \frac{2n+1}{3} S, \tag{5.4}$$

$$\sum_{k=1}^{n} k^3 = \frac{n^2(n+1)^2}{4} = S^2, \tag{5.5}$$

$$\sum_{k=1}^{n} k^4 = \frac{n(n+1)(2n+1)(3n^2+3n-1)}{30} = \frac{(2n+1)(3n^2+3n-1)}{15} S. \tag{5.6}$$

Consider the infinite sequence $1, \lambda, \lambda^2, \lambda^3, \ldots$ where $\lambda < 1$. This sequence is an example of a geometric series. The sum of the first s terms in this sequence can be expressed as follows:

$$\sum_{i=0}^{s} \lambda^i = \frac{1-\lambda^{s+1}}{1-\lambda}. \tag{5.7}$$

Furthermore, it is noteworthy that the sum of all terms in this infinite sequence is finite and can be computed as:

$$\sum_{i=0}^{\infty} \lambda^i = \frac{1}{1-\lambda}. \tag{5.8}$$

If the infinite sequence is given by $\{\lambda, \lambda^2, \lambda^3, \ldots\}$, then the formula for the sum of all terms becomes

$$\sum_{i=1}^{\infty} \lambda^i = \frac{\lambda}{1-\lambda}. \tag{5.9}$$

Appendix 5.B Derivation of Analytical Solutions to NSFs

5.B.1 MOM and SMA-D Technical Indicators

The non-normalized discrete return weights are $\{1, 1, \dots, 1\}$. The normalization factor is:

$$N = \sum_{i=0}^{n-1} 1 = n.$$

The variance reduction ratio

$$VRR = \frac{1}{n^2}\sum_{i=0}^{n-1} 1 = \frac{1}{n^2}n = \frac{1}{n}.$$

5.B.2 P-SMA and LMA-D Technical Indicators

The non-normalized discrete return weights are given by $n, n-1, \dots, 2, 1$. To find the normalization factor, we use formula (5.3):

$$N = \sum_{i=0}^{n-1}(n-i) = \sum_{k=1}^{n} k = \frac{(n+1)n}{2}.$$

Next, we compute the variance reduction ratio using formula (5.4):

$$\begin{aligned} VRR &= \frac{1}{N^2}\sum_{i=0}^{n-1}(n-i)^2 = \frac{2^2}{n^2(n+1)^2}\sum_{k=1}^{n} k^2 \\ &= \frac{4}{n^2(n+1)^2}\frac{n(n+1)(2n+1)}{6} = \frac{2(2n+1)}{3n(n+1)}. \end{aligned}$$

As n grows, the asymptotic behavior of the variance reduction ratio is given by:

$$VRR \to \frac{4}{3n}.$$

5.B.3 P-LMA Technical Indicator

The non-normalized discrete return weights are $\{\frac{n(n+1)}{2}, \frac{(n-1)n}{2}, \ldots, 3, 1\}$. The normalization factor is given by:

$$N = \sum_{i=0}^{n-1} \frac{1}{2}(n-i+1)(n-i) = \frac{1}{2}\left(\sum_{i=0}^{n-1}(n-i)^2 + \sum_{i=0}^{n-1}(n-i)\right)$$
$$= \frac{1}{2}\left(\sum_{k=1}^{n} k^2 + \sum_{k=1}^{n} k\right).$$

Apparently, it can be computed using formulas (5.4) and (5.3):

$$N = \frac{1}{2}\left(\frac{n(n+1)(2n+1)}{6} + \frac{n(n+1)}{2}\right) = \frac{n(n+1)(n+2)}{6}.$$

Once the normalization factor is calculated, the variance reduction ratio is given by:

$$VRR = \frac{1}{N^2}\sum_{i=0}^{n-1}\theta_i^2 = \frac{1}{N^2}\sum_{k=1}^{n}\frac{k^2(k+1)^2}{4}$$
$$= \frac{1}{4N^2}\left(\sum_{k=1}^{n} k^4 + 2\sum_{k=1}^{n} k^3 + \sum_{k=1}^{n} k^2\right).$$

In this case, the normalization factor can be computed using formulas (5.4), (5.5), and: (5.6)

$$VRR = \frac{n(n+1)}{8N^2}\left[\frac{(2n+1)(3n^2+3n-1)}{15} + n(n+1) + \frac{2n+1}{3}\right]$$
$$= \frac{n(n+1)}{8N^2}\left[\frac{6n^3+24n^2+26n+4}{15}\right].$$

Factorizing $6n^3 + 24n^2 + 26n + 4 = 2(n+2)(3n^3 + 6n + 1)$ and substituting N, the expression for the variance reduction ratio becomes:

$$VRR = \frac{1}{8}\frac{n(n+1)36}{n^2(n+1)^2(n+2)^2}\frac{2(n+2)(3n^2+6n+1)}{15} = \frac{3(3n^2+6n+1)}{5(n^3+3n^2+2n)}.$$

As n grows, the asymptotic behavior of the variance reduction ratio is given by:

$$VRR \to \frac{9}{5n}.$$

5.B.4 P-EMA and EMA-D Technical Indicators

The technical indicator is computed using an infinite number of return lags. The non-normalized discrete return weights are $1, \lambda, \lambda^2, \ldots$, where $\lambda = \frac{n-1}{n+1}$. To obtain the normalization factor, we use formula (5.8), which gives us $N = \frac{1}{1-\lambda}$.

The variance reduction ratio is expressed as:

$$VRR = \frac{1}{N^2}(1^2 + \lambda^2 + \lambda^4 + \lambda^6 + \ldots).$$

We can evaluate the infinite sum in the round brackets using formula (5.8) for the sum of an infinite geometric sequence, yielding the following result:

$$VRR = \frac{(1-\lambda)^2}{1}\frac{1}{1-\lambda^2} = \frac{1-\lambda}{1+\lambda} = \frac{1}{n}.$$

5.B.5 SMA-C Technical Indicator

The return weights in this crossover indicator are computed as:

$$\theta_x = \theta_x^l - \theta_x^s, \tag{5.10}$$

where θ_x^l represents the weights in the longer moving average, and θ_x^s represents the weights in the shorter moving average. It is assumed that each weighting function is continuous and decreases to zero. Specifically, in this indicator, the return weights are continuous for x in the range $[0, n]$ and linearly decrease from 1 to 0. In other words, $\theta(0) = 1$ and $\theta(n) = 0$.

Consequently, the return weights in the longer moving average are given by $\theta_l(x) = 1 - \frac{x}{l}$, and the return weights in the shorter moving average are given by $\theta_s(x) = 1 - \frac{x}{s}$. The weighting function for this technical indicator is defined as follows:

$$\theta(x) = \begin{cases} \frac{x}{s} - \frac{x}{l} = \frac{l-s}{ls}x & \text{if } 0 < x < s, \\ 1 - \frac{x}{l} & \text{if } s < x < l. \end{cases}$$

From a geometric perspective, the weighting function represents two adjacent right triangles with a common height $h = \frac{l-s}{l}$ at the point $x = s$.

The initial step involves computing the normalization factor. To do this, we need to find the continuous sum of coefficients, represented by $N = \int_0^l \theta(x)dx$. After performing the integration, we obtain the value $N = \frac{l-s}{2}$. Remarkably, this same result can be derived through a geometric argument, taking into account that a definite integral $\int_a^b f(x)dx$ corresponds to the area under the curve of $f(x)$ between a and b.

In the geometric interpretation, the area of two adjacent right triangles can be calculated as $N = \frac{sh}{2} + \frac{(l-s)h}{2} = \frac{lh}{2} = \frac{l-s}{2}$. This geometric approach aligns perfectly with the integration method, confirming the value of the normalization factor.

The variance reduction ratio is given by:

$$VRR = \frac{1}{N^2} \int_0^l \theta^2(x)dx = A + B,$$

where A represents the integral from 0 to s, and B is the integral from s to l.

Now, we proceed to find the expressions for A and B:

$$A = \frac{1}{N^2} \int_0^s \frac{(l-s)^2}{l^2 s^2} x^2 dx = \frac{4}{(l-s)^2} \frac{(l-s)^2}{l^2 s^2} \frac{s^3}{3} = \frac{4s}{3l^2},$$

$$B = \frac{1}{N^2} \int_s^l \left(1 - \frac{x}{l}\right)^2 dx = \frac{4}{(l-s)^2} \frac{(l-s)^3}{3l^2} = \frac{4(l-s)}{3l^2}.$$

Finally, combining these results, we get:

$$VRR = A + B = \frac{4s}{3l^2} + \frac{4(l-s)}{3l^2} = \frac{4}{3l}.$$

5.B.6 LMA-C Technical Indicator

The return weights in this crossover indicator are determined by Eq. (5.10). It is assumed that the weighting function of this rule is continuous over the range $x \in [0, n]$ and decreases from 1 to 0. To find the functional form of $\theta(x)$, we simplify the expression by considering $y = n - x$ for clarity.

In rules based on the SMA, the weight $\theta(y)$ grows linearly from 0 to 1. Conversely, in rules based on the LMA, the weight $\theta(y)$ increases quadratically as $\int_0^y t dt = \frac{y^2}{2}$.

To ensure that the weight $\theta(y)$ equals 1 at $y = n$, we obtain the functional form of the weighting function as $\theta(y) = \frac{y^2}{n^2}$. Consequently, as a function of x, the weighting function becomes:

$$\theta(x) = \frac{(n-x)^2}{n^2} = 1 - \frac{2x}{n} + \frac{x^2}{n^2}.$$

It is worth noting that managing function $\theta(y)$ is more straightforward compared to function $\theta(x)$. As a result, we will focus on integrating function $\theta(y)$ while keeping in mind the necessary domain accommodation. The weighting function for this crossover technical indicator is defined as follows:

$$\theta(y) = \begin{cases} \frac{y^2}{l^2} & \text{if } 0 < y < l - s, \\ \frac{y^2}{l^2} - \frac{(y-(l-s))^2}{s^2} & \text{if } l - s < y < l. \end{cases}$$

The initial step involves computing the normalization factor, represented by N. The continuous sum of coefficients is given by $N = \int_0^l \theta(y)dy$, and after performing the integration, we obtain $N = \frac{l-s}{3}$.

Alternatively, we can arrive at the same result through a geometric argument. The normalization constant N corresponds to the area under the LMA(l) coefficients, which is $\int_0^l \frac{y^2}{l^2}dy = \frac{l}{3}$, minus the area under the LMA(s) coefficients, which is $\int_0^s \frac{y^2}{s^2}dy = \frac{s}{3}$. The resulting value is $\frac{l-s}{3}$. Both methods yield the same value for the normalization factor N, confirming the correctness of the computation.

The variance reduction ratio is given by the expression:

$$VRR = \frac{1}{N^2}\int_0^l \theta^2(y)dy = \frac{1}{N^2}(A + B + C),$$

where these three summands are as follows:

$$A = \int_0^l \frac{y^4}{l^4}dy = \frac{l^5}{5l^4} = \frac{l}{5},$$

$$B = -2\int_{l-s}^l \frac{y^2}{l^2}\frac{(y-(l-s))^2}{s^2}dy = -\frac{s(10l^2 - 5ls + s^2)}{15l^2},$$

$$C = \int_{l-s}^l \frac{(y-(l-s))^4}{s^4}dy = \int_0^s \frac{x^4}{s^4}dx = \frac{s^5}{5s^4} = \frac{s}{5}.$$

Finally, combining these results, we arrive at:

$$VRR = \frac{3(3l - s)}{5l^2}.$$

5.B.7 EMA-C Technical Indicator

We assume that the weighting function of this rule is continuous on $[0, \infty)$ and is determined by Eq. (5.10). Specifically, the weighting function of the long EMA is $\theta_l(x) = \lambda^x$ with $\lambda = \frac{l-1}{l+1}$, whereas the weighting function of the short EMA is $\theta_s(x) = \beta^x$ with $\beta = \frac{s-1}{s+1}$. Consequently, the weighting function of the crossover indicator is given by $\theta(x) = \lambda^x - \beta^x$.

The normalization factor is given by:

$$N = \int_0^\infty (\lambda^x - \beta^x)\, dx = \frac{1}{\ln \beta} - \frac{1}{\ln \lambda}.$$

The variance reduction ratio is given by:

$$\begin{aligned} VRR &= \frac{1}{N^2} \int_0^\infty (\lambda^x - \beta^x)^2\, dx = \frac{1}{N^2} \int_0^\infty \left(\lambda^{2x} + \beta^{2x} - 2(\lambda\beta)^x\right) dx \\ &= \frac{1}{N^2} \left(-\frac{1}{\ln \lambda} - \frac{1}{\ln \beta} + \frac{2}{\ln(\lambda\beta)} \right) = -\frac{\ln \lambda \ln \beta}{2 \ln (\lambda\beta)}. \end{aligned}$$

To analyze the asymptotic behavior of the variance reduction ratio, we can employ the useful approximation $\ln(1 + x) \approx x$ when $x \ll 1$. Applying this approximation, we get $\frac{1}{\ln \lambda} \approx -\frac{l}{2}$ and $\frac{1}{\ln \beta} \approx -\frac{s}{2}$. Consequently, the normalization constant N can be approximated as $N \approx \frac{l-s}{2}$. Combining these approximations together, we arrive at the following asymptotic expression for the variance reduction ratio of this crossover rule:

$$VRR \approx \frac{1}{l + s}.$$

Appendix 5.C Derivation of Analytical Solutions to ALTs

5.C.1 MOM and SMA-D Technical Indicators

The discrete return weights in these rules are represented as $1, 1, \ldots, 1$. To calculate the ALT for these rules, we consider the following condition:

$$\sum_{i=0}^{k-1} 1 = k = \frac{1}{2}n,$$

where n represents the total sum of all the return weights. Consequently, the average lag time can be determined by the formula:

$$ALT = \frac{n}{2}.$$

It is important to note that this result is also a consequence of the symmetrical nature of the return weighting function of these rules, which is centered around the center.

5.C.2 P-SMA and LMA-D Technical Indicators

These rules are characterized by discrete return weights given as $n, n-1, \ldots, 2, 1$. To streamline the derivation process, we introduce a new variable $q = n - k$. Both k and q represent the same return lag, which effectively divides the weighting function into two parts with an equal sum of return weights. However, the distinction lies in their counting methods. While the value of k is obtained through normal counting, starting from the first lag 0, the value of q is derived through reverse counting, starting from the last lag n. In essence, both k and q serve to identify the same lag, but they are expressed differently based on their counting direction.

We are looking for the value of q that solves the following equation:

$$1 + 2 + \ldots + q = \frac{1}{2}\frac{(n+1)n}{2}.$$

Note that the quantity $\frac{(n+1)n}{2}$ represents the sum of all return weights, as indicated by formula (5.3). By utilizing the same formula, the sum of return weights from 1 to q on the left-hand side of the equation can also be computed.

This leads us to the following equation:

$$\frac{(q+1)q}{2} = \frac{(n+1)n}{4},$$

which can be further simplified to:

$$2q^2 + 2q - (n+1)n = 0.$$

Solving this quadratic equation, we obtain the value of q as:

$$q = \frac{\sqrt{n^2 + (n+1)^2} - 1}{2}.$$

The average lag time of these rules can then be expressed as:

$$ALT = n - q = \frac{2n - \sqrt{n^2 + (n+1)^2} + 1}{2}.$$

As n increases, the asymptotic behavior is approximated by:

$$ALT \to \left(1 - \frac{1}{\sqrt{2}}\right) n \approx 0.293n.$$

5.C.3 P-LMA Technical Indicator

To simplify the derivation of the analytical result and the final formula for the average lag time of the P-LMA rule, we assume that the weighting function of this rule is continuous over the range $x \in [0, n]$ and decreases from 1 to 0. To find the functional form of $\theta(x)$, we simplify the expression by considering $y = n - x$ for clarity.

In rules based on the SMA, the weight $\theta(y)$ grows linearly from 0 to 1. Conversely, in rules based on the LMA, the weight $\theta(y)$ increases quadratically as $\int_0^y t\,dt = \frac{y^2}{2}$.

To ensure that the weight $\theta(y)$ equals 1 at $y = n$, we obtain the functional form of the weighting function as $\theta(y) = \frac{y^2}{n^2}$. Consequently, as a function of x, the weighting function becomes:

$$\theta(x) = \frac{(n-x)^2}{n^2} = 1 - \frac{2x}{n} + \frac{x^2}{n^2}.$$

Notably, managing the function $\theta(y)$ is more convenient than handling $\theta(x)$. Therefore, we will perform the integration of $\theta(y)$ while being mindful of the necessary correction at the end. The total continuous sum of all coefficients is given by:

$$A = \int_0^n \theta(y)dy = \int_0^n \frac{y^2}{n^2}dy = \frac{y^3}{3n^2}\Big|_0^n = \frac{n}{3}.$$

Now, we seek to integrate up to $q = n - k$, which satisfies the condition:

$$\int_0^q \frac{y^2}{n^2}dy = \frac{1}{2}\frac{n}{3}.$$

After performing the integration, we arrive at the following equation:

$$\frac{q^3}{3n^2} = \frac{n}{6}.$$

Solving for q, we find $q = \frac{n}{\sqrt[3]{2}}$. As q is counted in reverse order, the solution for the average lag time is expressed as:

$$ALT = n - q = \left(1 - \frac{1}{\sqrt[3]{2}}\right)n \approx 0.206n.$$

5.C.4 P-EMA and EMA-D Technical Indicators

Recall that the EMA is computed using an infinite number of return lags. In these rules, the discrete return weights are represented as $1, \lambda, \lambda^2, \ldots$, with $\lambda = \frac{n-1}{n+1}$.

We aim to find the value of k that satisfies the following condition:

$$1 + \lambda + \lambda^2 + \ldots + \lambda^{k-1} = \frac{1}{2}\frac{1}{1-\lambda}.$$

Here, $\frac{1}{1-\lambda}$ represents the sum of all return weights, as shown in formula (5.8). The sum of the first k return weights (from $i = 0$ to $i = k - 1$) on the left-hand side of the equation can be computed using formula (5.7). Consequently, the resulting equation is:

$$\frac{1-\lambda^k}{1-\lambda} = \frac{1}{2(1-\lambda)}.$$

Solving for k gives us the average lag time for these EMA rules:

$$ALT = \frac{\ln 0.5}{\ln \lambda}.$$

To analyze the limiting behavior of the average lag time, we make use of the approximation $\ln(1+x) \approx x$ when $x \ll 1$. Therefore, $\frac{1}{\ln \lambda} \approx -\frac{n}{2}$. Additionally, $\ln 0.5 = -\ln 2$. Combining these approximations, we arrive at the following approximate expression for the ALT of these rules:

$$ALT \to \frac{\ln 2}{2} n \approx 0.347n.$$

5.C.5 SMA-C Technical Indicator

The return weights in this crossover indicator are computed in accordance with Eq. (5.10), where θ_x^l represents the weights in the longer moving average, and θ_x^s represents the weights in the shorter moving average. It is assumed that each weighting function is continuous and decreases to zero. Specifically, in this indicator, the return weights are continuous for x in the range $[0, n]$ and linearly decrease from 1 to 0. In other words, $\theta(0) = 1$ and $\theta(n) = 0$.

Consequently, the return weights in the longer moving average are given by $\theta_l(x) = 1 - \frac{x}{l}$, and the return weights in the shorter moving average are given by $\theta_s(x) = 1 - \frac{x}{s}$. The weighting function for this technical indicator is defined as follows:

$$\theta(x) = \begin{cases} \theta_1(x) = \frac{x}{s} - \frac{x}{l} = \frac{l-s}{ls}x & \text{if } 0 < x < s, \\ \theta_2(x) = 1 - \frac{x}{l} & \text{if } s < x < l. \end{cases}$$

From a geometric perspective, the weighting function represents two adjacent right triangles with a common height $h = \frac{l-s}{l}$ at the point $x = s$. This piecewise function has to be integrated in order to find the point k that splits the total area in two equal halves.

The total continuous sum of coefficients is represented by the integral $A = \int_0^l \theta(x)dx$, which can be interpreted as the area under the curve of $\theta(x)$. Upon integration, we obtain the value $A = \frac{l-s}{2}$. Alternatively, we can arrive at the same result using a geometric argument: considering the area of two right triangles, $A = A_1 + A_2 = \frac{sh}{2} + \frac{(l-s)h}{2} = \frac{lh}{2} = \frac{l-s}{2}$, where A_1 represents the area under the curve $\theta_1(x)$ and A_2 represents the area under the curve $\theta_2(x)$.

The average lag time, denoted by k, is the point that divides the total area A into two equal parts. In other words, we are seeking the value of k that satisfies the equation $\int_0^k \theta(x)dx = \frac{A}{2}$.

An important observation is that when $s = \frac{l}{2}$, the weighting function $\theta(x)$ becomes symmetrical about the center and represents two equal adjacent right triangles. As a result, both triangles have identical areas, denoted as A_1 and A_2, and each area is equal to $\frac{A}{2}$. Consequently, in this particular case, the average lag time coincides with the center point $k = s = \frac{l}{2}$.

The observation presented in the preceding paragraph indicates that when $s < \frac{l}{2}$, the area A_1 is less than $\frac{A}{2}$. Consequently, to determine the average lag time in this scenario, we need to integrate to a point $k > s$, as the average lag time is greater than s. Conversely, when $s > \frac{l}{2}$, the area A_1 is greater than $\frac{A}{2}$. In this case, to find the average lag time, we need to integrate to a point $k < s$, as the average lag time is less than s.

Therefore, when $s < \frac{l}{2}$, the value of k can be found by solving the equation:

$$A_1 + \int_s^k \left(1 - \frac{x}{l}\right) dx = \frac{A}{2}.$$

This simplifies to:

$$\frac{(l-s)s}{2l} + \left[x - \frac{x^2}{2}\right]_s^k = \frac{l-s}{4},$$

that is:

$$\frac{(l-s)s}{2l} + \left(k - \frac{k^2}{2}\right) - \left(s - \frac{s^2}{2}\right) = \frac{l-s}{4}.$$

Solving this equation, we obtain:

$$k_1 = l - \frac{1}{\sqrt{2}}\sqrt{l(l-s)}. \tag{5.11}$$

On the other hand, when $s > \frac{l}{2}$, the value of k satisfies the equation:

$$\int_0^k \left(\frac{l-s}{ls}x\right) dx = \frac{A}{2}.$$

This simplifies to:

$$\left(\frac{l-s}{ls}\right)\frac{k^2}{2} = \frac{l-s}{4},$$

which leads to $k^2 = \frac{ls}{2}$. Consequently, the solution for k is:

$$k_2 = \frac{1}{\sqrt{2}}\sqrt{ls}. \tag{5.12}$$

It is worth noting that when $s = \frac{l}{2}$, both k_1 and k_2 result in $\frac{l}{2}$, as can be easily verified.

The solutions for the average lag time k can be expressed in the following form:

$$k = \begin{cases} k_1 = \left(1 - \frac{1}{\sqrt{2}}\right) l \sqrt{1 - \frac{s}{l}} & \text{if } s < \frac{l}{2}, \\ k_2 = \frac{1}{\sqrt{2}} l \sqrt{\frac{s}{l}} & \text{if } s > \frac{l}{2}. \end{cases}$$

This formulation makes it evident that the average lag time is proportional to l and depends on the ratio $\frac{s}{l}$. Additionally, as s approaches zero, we have:

$$\lim_{s \to 0} k_1 = \left(1 - \frac{1}{\sqrt{2}}\right) l = k_l,$$

where k_l denotes the average lag time of the P-SMA(l) rule.

The solid line in Fig. 5.12 illustrates the relationship between the fraction k/l and the fraction s/l, where k represents the average lag time of the SMA-C(s, l) technical indicator. A visual examination of this line suggests that the fraction k/l exhibits nearly linear behavior concerning the fraction $\frac{s}{l}$. Furthermore, a similar visual analysis indicates that the average lag time of the SMA-C(s, l) technical indicator also demonstrates an almost linear relationship with the average lag time of the P-SMA(s) technical indicator, denoted as k_s. Since $k = k_l$ when $s = 0$, a sensible linear approximation to the average lag time of the SMA-C rule can be provided as follows:

$$k = k_l + bk_s,$$

where b is a constant and k_l is the average lag time of the P-SMA(l) technical indicator.

Further investigation suggests that selecting $b = \sqrt{2}$ yields a highly accurate fit to the exact theoretical solution at three points $s \in 0, l/2, l$. In the regions

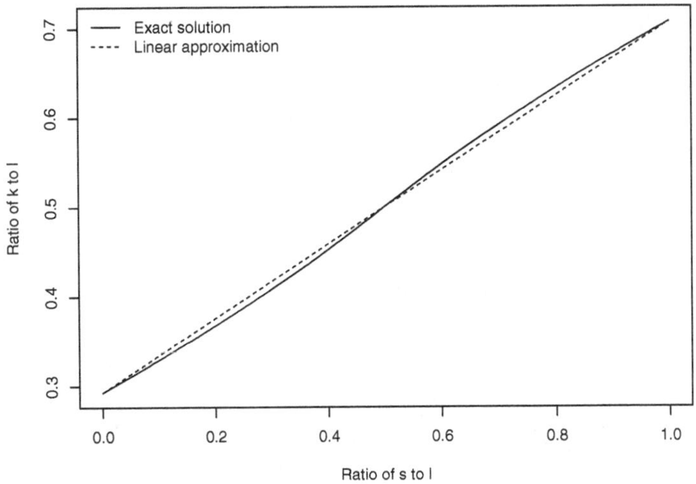

Fig. 5.12 Plot illustrates the relationship between the ratio k/l and the ratio s/l, where k represents the average lag time of the SMA-C(s, l) technical indicator. The solid line represents the exact solution, while the dashed line represents the linear approximation $k = k_l + \sqrt{2}k_s$ to the exact solution. Here, k_l and k_s correspond to the average lag times of the P-SMA(l) and P-SMA(s) technical indicators, respectively

between these points, the approximated solution deviates only slightly from the exact theoretical solution. The dashed line in Fig. 5.12 corresponds to the plotted function:

$$k = k_l + \sqrt{2}k_s.$$

Evidently, this function provides an excellent approximation to the average lag time of the SMA-C rule.

5.C.6 LMA-C Technical Indicator

The crossover indicator's return weights are computed using Eq. (5.10), where θ_x^l represents the weights in the longer moving average, and θ_x^s represents the weights in the shorter moving average. In Section 5.C.3, we derive the weighting function of the P-LMA(n) technical indicator in the continuous case. As a result, we obtain the weighting function of the P-LMA(l) technical indicator as $\theta_l(x) = (1 - x/l)^2 = 1 - 2x/l + x^2/l^2$, and the weighting function of the P-LMA(s) technical indicator as $\theta_s(x) = (1 - x/s)^2 = 1 - 2x/s + x^2/s^2$.

The weighting function in the crossover technical indicator is defined as follows:

$$\theta(x) = \begin{cases} \theta_1(x) = \frac{x^2}{l^2} - \frac{x^2}{s^2} + 2\frac{x}{s} - 2\frac{x}{l} = 2\frac{l-s}{ls}x - \frac{l^2-s^2}{l^2s^2}x^2 & \text{if } 0 < x < s, \\ \theta_2(x) = 1 - 2\frac{x}{l} + \frac{x^2}{l^2} & \text{if } s < x < l. \end{cases}$$

The total continuous sum of coefficients is given by $A = \int_0^l \theta(x)dx$, which can be interpreted as the area under the curve of $\theta(x)$. Upon integration, the resulting value is $A = \frac{l-s}{3}$. Another way to obtain the same result is through a geometric argument: the total area is the difference between the area under $\theta_l(x)$ coefficients, denoted as $A_l = \frac{l}{3}$, and the area under $\theta_s(x)$ coefficients, denoted as $A_s = \frac{s}{3}$, which can be expressed as $A = A_l - A_s$.

To find the average lag time k, we seek the point k where the integral of $\theta(x)$ from 0 to k is equal to half of the total area A, i.e., $\int_0^k \theta(x)dx = \frac{A}{2}$.

We define the area under $\theta_1(x)$ as A_1. It is important to note that when s is sufficiently large, A_1 becomes greater than $A/2$. As a result, to find the average lag time k in this case, we only need to integrate under $\theta_1(x)$. However, if s is relatively small, then A_1 becomes smaller than $A/2$, and to find the average lag time k, we must integrate not only under $\theta_1(x)$ but also under $\theta_2(x)$. Therefore, it becomes crucial to determine the value of s at which A_1 is equal to $A/2$ to ensure the correct integration procedure.

Area A_1 is found as follows:

$$A_1 = \int_0^s \theta_1(x)dx = \int_0^s \left(2\frac{l-s}{ls}x - \frac{l^2-s^2}{l^2s^2}x^2\right)dx.$$

Evaluating this integral, we find:

$$A_1 = \frac{(l-s)s}{l} - \frac{(l^2-s^2)s}{3l^2}.$$

The condition to determine the value of s is given by:

$$\frac{(l-s)s}{l} - \frac{(l^2-s^2)s}{3l^2} = \frac{1}{2}\frac{(l-s)}{3}.$$

After simplification, we arrive at a quadratic equation in s/l:

$$2\left(\frac{s}{l}\right)^2 - 4\frac{s}{l} + 1 = 0.$$

Solving this equation gives us the value of s at which A_1 equals $A/2$:

$$s = \left(1 - \frac{1}{\sqrt{2}}\right) l.$$

Therefore, for $s < (1 - 1/\sqrt{2})l$, the value k satisfies the equation:

$$A_1 + \int_s^k \left(1 - 2\frac{x}{l} + \frac{x^2}{l^2}\right) dx = \frac{1}{2}\frac{(l-s)}{3}.$$

This equation can also be expressed as:

$$\int_0^k \left(1 - 2\frac{x}{l} + \frac{x^2}{l^2}\right) dx - \frac{s}{3} = \frac{l-s}{6},$$

where $s/3$ represents the area under $\theta_s(x)$. Computing the integral leads us to the following equation:

$$\frac{l}{3} - \frac{l\left(1-\frac{k}{l}\right)^3}{3} - \frac{s}{3} = \frac{l-s}{6}$$

which, after simplification, becomes:

$$\left(1 - \frac{k}{l}\right)^3 = \frac{l-s}{2l}.$$

The solution for k is then given by:

$$k_1 = l - \sqrt[3]{\frac{l^2(l-s)}{2}} \tag{5.13}$$

where the subscript 1 indicates the solution for the average lag time in the region where $s < (1 - 1/\sqrt{2})l$.

Now, let us consider the case where $s > (1 - 1/\sqrt{2})l$. In this scenario, we only need to integrate under $\theta_1(x)$ to find the value of k. The equation that k satisfies is given by:

$$\int_0^k \left(2\frac{l-s}{ls}x - \frac{l^2-s^2}{l^2s^2}x^2\right) dx = \frac{1}{2}\frac{(l-s)}{3}.$$

Upon computing this integral, we arrive at the expression:

$$\frac{l}{3} - \frac{l\left(1-\frac{k}{l}\right)^3}{3} - \frac{s}{3} + \frac{l\left(1-\frac{k}{s}\right)^3}{3} = \frac{l-s}{6}.$$

After simplification, we obtain a cubic equation in terms of k:

$$(l+s)k^3 - 3slk^2 + \frac{(sl)^2}{2} = 0. \tag{5.14}$$

In principle, a cubic equation has an analytic solution. However, the algebraic expression for the solution is rather complicated and almost impossible to analyze directly.

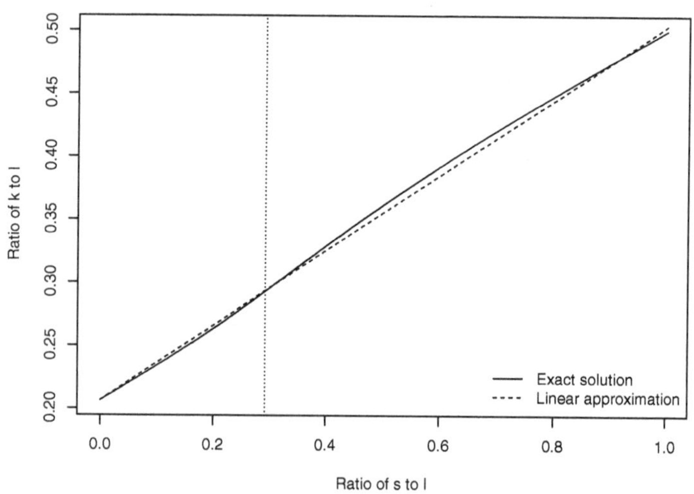

Fig. 5.13 Plot illustrates the relationship between the ratio k/l and the ratio s/l, where k represents the average lag time of the LMA-C(s, l) technical indicator. The solid line represents the exact solution, while the dashed line represents the linear approximation $k = k_l + \sqrt[3]{3}k_s$ to the exact solution. Here, k_l and k_s correspond to the average lag times of the P-SMA(l) and P-SMA(s) technical indicators, respectively. The dotted vertical line shows the location of $s/l = 1 - 1/\sqrt{2}$. To the left of this location, the exact solution is obtained using Eq. (5.13); to the right of this location, the exact solution is obtained by solving cubic equation (5.14)

The plot in Fig. 5.13 depicts the relationship between the ratio k/l and the ratio s/l, where k represents the average lag time of the LMA-C(s, l) technical indicator. The dotted vertical line marks the position of $s/l = 1 - 1/\sqrt{2}$. To the left of this location, the exact solution is obtained using Eq. (5.13); to the right of this location, the exact solution is determined by solving the cubic equation (5.14).

Upon visual observation, the exact solution indicates that the average lag time of the LMA-C(s, l) technical indicator exhibits almost linear behavior concerning the ratio $\frac{s}{l}$. Additionally, a similar visual analysis reveals that the average lag time of the LMA-C(s, l) technical indicator also demonstrates an almost linear relationship with the average lag time of the P-LMA(s) technical indicator, denoted as k_s. Notably, when $s = 0$, we have $k = k_l$, which motivates a practical linear approximation to the average lag time of the LMA-C rule:

$$k = k_l + bk_s,$$

where b is a constant and k_l is the average lag time of the P-LMA(l) technical indicator.

Further analysis suggests that the choice $b = \sqrt[3]{3}$ provides a close fit to the exact theoretical solution. The dashed line in Fig. 5.13 corresponds to the plotted function:

$$k = k_l + \sqrt[3]{3}k_s.$$

Evidently, this function serves as a highly effective approximation to the average lag time of the LMA-C rule.

5.C.7 EMA-C Technical Indicator

We assume that the weighting function of this rule is continuous on $[0, \infty)$ and is determined by Eq. (5.10). Specifically, the weighting function of the long EMA is $\theta_l(x) = \lambda^x$ with $\lambda = \frac{l-1}{l+1}$, whereas the weighting function of the short EMA is $\theta_s(x) = \beta^x$ with $\beta = \frac{s-1}{s+1}$. Consequently, the weighting function of the crossover indicator is given by $\theta(x) = \lambda^x - \beta^x$.

The total continuous sum of coefficients is given by:

$$A = \int_0^\infty (\lambda^x - \beta^x)\, dx = \frac{1}{\ln \beta} - \frac{1}{\ln \lambda}.$$

To find the average lag time k, we look for the point where $\int_0^k \theta(x)dx = \frac{A}{2}$. Therefore, the condition for k is expressed as:

$$\int_0^k (\lambda^x - \beta^x)\, dx = \frac{1}{2}\left(\frac{1}{\ln \beta} - \frac{1}{\ln \lambda}\right).$$

Upon computing this integral and simplifying, we arrive at the following equation:

$$\lambda^k \ln \beta - \beta^k \ln \lambda = \frac{1}{2}(\ln \beta - \ln \lambda). \tag{5.15}$$

Unfortunately, Eq. (5.15) does not admit an analytical solution for k.

To obtain an approximate solution for k, we make the simplifying assumption that $s \ll l$. In this case, $\beta^k \ll \lambda^k$, and consequently, Eq. (5.15) can be simplified to:

$$\lambda^k \ln \beta = \frac{1}{2}(\ln \beta - \ln \lambda).$$

This can be further rewritten as:

$$\lambda^k = \frac{1}{2}\left(1 - \frac{\ln \lambda}{\ln \beta}\right)$$

and the solution with respect to k yields:

$$k = \frac{1}{\ln \lambda} \ln\left(\frac{1}{2}\left(1 - \frac{\ln \lambda}{\ln \beta}\right)\right) = \frac{\ln 0.5}{\ln \lambda} + \frac{1}{\ln \lambda} \ln\left(1 - \frac{\ln \lambda}{\ln \beta}\right).$$

Recognizing that $k_l = \frac{\ln 0.5}{\ln \lambda}$, we can rewrite the equation above as:

$$k = k_l + \frac{1}{\ln \lambda} \ln\left(1 - \frac{\ln \lambda}{\ln \beta}\right), \tag{5.16}$$

where k_l represents the average lag time of the P-EMA(l) technical indicator.

Considering our assumption $s \ll l$, we can use the approximation $\ln(1 - x) \approx -x$ when $x \ll 1$ to further simplify Eq. (5.16) as follows:

$$k \approx k_l - \frac{1}{\ln \beta} = k_l + \frac{1}{\ln 2} k_s, \tag{5.17}$$

where $k_s = \frac{\ln 0.5}{\ln \beta}$ represents the average lag time of the P-EMA(s) technical indicator.

Thus, in a similar manner to the other MA-C rules, the average lag time of the EMA-C(s, l) technical indicator can be approximated by a linear function of the form $k = k_l + b k_s$.

The plot in Fig. 5.14 illustrates the relationship between the ratio k/l and the ratio s/l, where k represents the average lag time of the EMA-C(s, l) technical

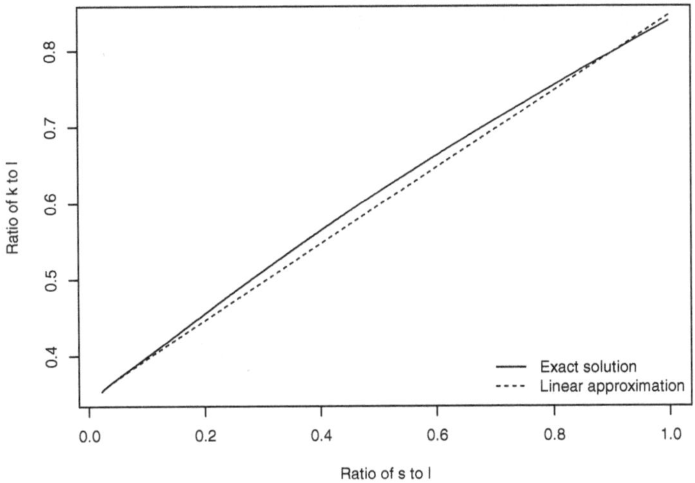

Fig. 5.14 Plot illustrates the relationship between the ratio k/l and the ratio s/l, where k represents the average lag time of the EMA-C(s, l) technical indicator. The exact solution is obtained by solving numerically Eq. (5.15). The dashed line shows the linear approximation $k = k_l + k_s/\ln 2$ to the exact solution, where k_l and k_s are the average lag times of P-EMA(l) and P-EMA(s) technical indicators, respectively

indicator. The dashed line shows the linear approximation $k = k_l + k_s/\ln 2$ to the exact solution. Notably, the linear approximation provides a close fit to the exact theoretical solution. It is interesting to observe that this linear approximation is derived based on the assumption that $s \ll l$.

Remarkably, the curves in Fig. 5.14 clearly demonstrate that the linear approximation is valid and provides a good fit to the exact analytical solution across the entire range of $s/l \in (0, 1)$. This finding highlights the effectiveness of the linear approximation, even when the ratio s/l varies over a wide interval.

Appendix 5.D Derivation of Analytical Solutions to SMIs

5.D.1 MOM and SMA-D Technical Indicators

The return weights for these technical indicators are uniform, given by $1, 1, \ldots, 1$. The analytical solution for the SMI of these indicators is derived as follows:

$$SMI = \frac{\sum_{k=1}^{n-1} 1 \times 1}{\sum_{k=1}^{n} 1^2} = \frac{n-1}{n}.$$

5.D.2 P-SMA and LMA-D Technical Indicators

The return weights of these technical indicators follow a specific pattern: $n, n-1, \ldots, 2, 1$. To compute the smoothness index (SMI) for these indicators, we use the following expression:

$$SMI = \frac{\sum_{k=1}^{n-1} k(k+1)}{\sum_{k=1}^{n} k^2}.$$

The denominator in the fraction above is computed using formula (5.4). The numerator can be rewritten as:

$$\sum_{k=1}^{n-1} k(k+1) = \sum_{k=1}^{n-1} (k^2 + k) = \sum_{i=1}^{n-1} k^2 + \sum_{i=1}^{n-1} k.$$

Using formulas (5.4) and (5.3), the numerator is computed as:

$$\sum_{k=1}^{n-1} k(k+1) = \frac{(n-1)n(2n-1)}{6} + \frac{(n-1)n}{2}$$
$$= \frac{(n-1)n(n+1)}{3}.$$

Finally, combining all the results, we arrive at the expression for the smoothness index:

$$SMI = \frac{\frac{(n-1)n(n+1)}{3}}{\frac{n(n+1)(2n+1)}{6}} = \frac{2n-2}{2n+1} = \frac{n-1}{n+0.5}.$$

5.D.3 P-LMA Technical Indicator

The return weights for these technical indicators follow a specific pattern: $\frac{n(n+1)}{2}, \frac{(n-1)n}{2}, \ldots, 3, 1$. The smoothness index can be computed using the following expression:

$$SMI = \frac{\sum_{k=1}^{n-1} \frac{k(k+1)}{2} \times \frac{(k+1)(k+2)}{2}}{\sum_{k=1}^{n} \frac{k^2(k+1)^2}{4}}.$$

To calculate the denominator, we rewrite it as:

$$\sum_{k=1}^{n} \frac{k^2(k+1)^2}{4} = \frac{1}{4}\left(\sum_{k=1}^{n} k^4 + 2\sum_{k=1}^{n} k^3 + \sum_{k=1}^{n} k^2\right).$$

Using formulas (5.4), (5.5), and (5.6), we compute the denominator as:

$$\sum_{k=1}^{n} \frac{k^2(k+1)^2}{4} = \frac{n(n+1)(n+2)(3n^2+6n+1)}{60}.$$

Next, we rewrite the numerator as:

$$\sum_{k=1}^{n-1} \frac{k(k+1)}{2} \times \frac{(k+1)(k+2)}{2} = \sum_{k=1}^{n-1} \frac{k(k+1)^2(k+2)}{4}$$
$$= \frac{1}{4}\left(\sum_{k=1}^{n-1} k^4 + 4\sum_{k=1}^{n-1} k^3 + 5\sum_{k=1}^{n-1} k^2 + 2\sum_{k=1}^{n-1} k\right).$$

Using formulas (5.3), (5.4), (5.5), and (5.6), after meticulous but straightforward calculations, we get:

$$\sum_{k=1}^{n-1} \frac{k(k+1)}{2} \times \frac{(k+1)(k+2)}{2} = (n-1)^5/20 + 3/8(n-1)^4 + (n-1)^3 + 9/8(n-1)^2 + 7/15(n-1).$$

Finally, combining all the results, we obtain the expression for the smoothness index:

$$SMI = \frac{(n-1)^5/20 + 3/8(n-1)^4 + (n-1)^3 + 9/8(n-1)^2 + 7/15(n-1)}{n(n+1)(n+2)(3n^2+6n+1)/60}.$$

5.D.4 P-EMA and EMA-D Technical Indicators

Recall that these technical indicators are computed using an infinite number of return lags. The return weights of the EMA(n) are $\{1, \lambda, \lambda^2, \ldots\}$ where $\lambda = \frac{n-1}{n+1}$. The smoothness index can be computed as:

$$
\begin{aligned}
SMI &= \frac{1 \times \lambda + \lambda \times \lambda^2 + \lambda^2 \times \lambda^3 + \ldots}{1^2 + \lambda^2 + \lambda^4 + \lambda^6 + \ldots} \\
&= \frac{\lambda(1 + \lambda^2 + \lambda^4 + \lambda^6 + \ldots)}{1 + \lambda^2 + \lambda^4 + \lambda^6 + \ldots} = \lambda.
\end{aligned}
$$

Consequently,

$$SMI = \frac{n-1}{n+1}.$$

5.D.5 SMA-C Technical Indicator

The SMA-C(s, l) technical indicator employs discrete return weights represented as:

$$\theta_k = \begin{cases} \frac{(l-s)k}{(l+1)(s+1)} & \text{if } 1 \le k \le s+1, \\ \frac{l+1-k}{l+1} & \text{if } s+1 \le k \le l. \end{cases}$$

The return weighting function consists of two distinct parts. From lag 1 to lag s, the weighting function increases as k increases due to $l - s > 0$, and it is given by $\frac{(l-s)k}{(l+1)(s+1)}$. From lag $s + 1$ to lag l, the weighting function decreases as k increases and is given by $\frac{l+1-k}{l+1}$. The first part has a constant step size $c = \theta_1 = \frac{l-s}{(l+1)(k+1)}$ until $k = s$. At $k = s + 1$, the return weight reaches its maximum value $\theta_{s+1} = \frac{l-s}{l+1}$. Then, starting from $k = s + 2$, the return weights decrease with a constant step size $e = \theta_l = \frac{1}{l+1}$. Therefore, the return weights of the SMA-C(s, l) technical indicator can be written as:

$$
\begin{aligned}
&\{\theta_1, \theta_2, \theta_3, \ldots, \theta_s, \theta_{s+1}, \ldots, \theta_{l-2}, \theta_{l-1}, \theta_l\} \\
&\quad = \{c, 2c, 3c, \ldots, sc, (l-s)e, \ldots, 3e, 2e, e\}.
\end{aligned}
$$

An important observation is that weight θ_{s+1} can be computed either as $(s + 1)c$ or as $(l - s - 1)e$. Consequently, the smoothness index (SMI) can be computed as:

$$SMI = \frac{\sum_{k=1}^{s} k(k+1)c^2 + \sum_{k=1}^{l-s-1} k(k+1)e^2}{\sum_{k=1}^{s} k^2c^2 + \sum_{k=1}^{l-s} k^2e^2}.$$

The denominator in the expression for the SMI can be computed using formula (5.4):

$$\sum_{k=1}^{s} k^2c^2 + \sum_{k=1}^{l-s} k^2e^2 = c^2\frac{s(s+1)(2s+1)}{6} + e^2\frac{(l-s)(l-s+1)(2(l-s)+1)}{6}.$$

The numerator in the expression for the SMI can be computed using formulas (5.3) and (5.4):

$$\sum_{k=1}^{s} k(k+1)c^2 + \sum_{k=1}^{l-s-1} k(k+1)e^2 = c^2\frac{s(s+1)(s+2)}{3} + e^2\frac{(l-s-1)(l-s)(l-s+1)}{3}.$$

Finally, combining all the results yields the expression for the smoothness index:

$$SMI = 2\frac{s(s+2)(l-s) + (l-s-1)(l-s+1)(s+1)}{s(2s+1)(l-s) + (l-s+1)(2l-2s+1)(s+1)}.$$

5.D.6 LMA-C Technical Indicator

The crossover indicator's return weights are computed using Eq. (5.10), where θ_x^l represents the weights in the longer moving average, and θ_x^s represents the weights in the shorter moving average. The weighting function of this technical indicator in the continuous case is derived in Section 5.C.6. Specifically, the weighting function is defined as follows:

$$\theta(x) = \theta^l(x) - \theta^s(x) = \begin{cases} \left(1-\frac{x}{l}\right)^2 - \left(1-\frac{x}{s}\right)^2 & \text{if } 0 \le x \le s, \\ \left(1-\frac{x}{l}\right)^2 & \text{if } s < x \le l. \end{cases}$$

We are going to compute the smoothness index of this technical indicator as:

$$SMI = \frac{\int_0^{l-1} \theta(x)\theta(x+1)dx}{\int_0^l \theta^2(x)dx}.$$

The integral in the denominator of the fraction above can be computed as:

$$\int_0^l \theta^2(x)dx = \int_0^l \theta^l(x)\theta^l(x)dx - 2\int_0^s \theta^l(x)\theta^s(x)dx + \int_0^s \theta^s(x)\theta^s(x)dx = A + B + C,$$

where the values of the three summands are:

$$A = \frac{l}{5}, \quad B = -\frac{s(10l^2 - 5ls + s^2)}{15l^2}, \quad C = \frac{s}{5}.$$

Consequently, the integral in the denominator is given by:

$$\int_0^l \theta^2(x)dx = \frac{l}{5} - \frac{s(10l^2 - 5ls + s^2)}{15l^2} + \frac{s}{5} = \frac{(3l - s)(l - s)^2}{15l^2}.$$

Next, the integral in the numerator of the smoothness index can be computed as:

$$\begin{aligned}\int_0^{l-1} \theta(x)\theta(x+1)dx &= \int_0^{l-1} \left(\theta^l(x) - \theta^s(x)\right)\left(\theta^l(x+1) - \theta^s(x+1)\right)dx \\ &= \int_0^{l-1} \Big(\theta^l(x)\theta^l(x+1) + \theta^s(x)\theta^s(x+1) \\ &\quad -\theta^l(x)\theta^s(x+1) - \theta^s(x)\theta^l(x+1)\Big)dx.\end{aligned}$$

Accommodating the integral limits, we obtain:

$$\begin{aligned}\int_0^{l-1} \theta^l(x)\theta^l(x+1)dx &= \frac{(l-1)^5}{5l^4} + \frac{(l-1)^4}{2l^4} + \frac{(l-1)^3}{3l^4}, \\ \int_0^{l-1} \theta^s(x)\theta^s(x+1)dx &= \frac{(s-1)^5}{5s^4} + \frac{(s-1)^4}{2s^4} + \frac{(s-1)^3}{3s^4}, \\ \int_0^{s-1} \theta^l(x)\theta^s(x+1)dx &= \frac{(s-1)^3(10l^2 - 5l(s-1) + (s-1)^2)}{30l^2s^2}, \\ \int_0^{s-1} \theta^s(x)\theta^l(x+1)dx &= \frac{10l^2(s^3-1) - 5l(s^4 + 4s^3 - 4s - 1)}{30l^2s^2} \\ &\quad + \frac{(s-1)(s^4 + 6s^3 + 16s^2 + 6s + 1)}{30l^2s^2}.\end{aligned}$$

The sum of all these four summands is given by:

$$\int_0^{l-1} \theta(x)\theta(x+1)dx$$
$$= \frac{(l-s)^2(6l^3s^4 - 2l^2s^5 - 20l^2s^3 + 20l^2s^2 - l^2 - 2ls - s^2)}{30l^2s^4}.$$

Finally, putting everything together yields:

$$SMI = \frac{6l^3s^4 - 2l^2s^5 - 20l^2s^3 + 20l^2s^2 - l^2 - 2ls - s^2}{2l^2s^4(3l-s)}.$$

5.D.7 EMA-C Technical Indicator

The return weights of the EMA-C(s, l) technical indicator are given by $\theta_k = \lambda^k - \beta^k$, for $k \in [1, 2, 3, \ldots]$, where $\lambda = \frac{l-1}{l+1}$ and $\beta = \frac{s-1}{s+1}$. The smoothness index of this technical indicator is computed as:

$$SMI = \frac{\sum_{k=1}^{\infty} \left(\lambda^k - \beta^k\right)\left(\lambda^{k+1} - \beta^{k+1}\right)}{\sum_{k=1}^{\infty} \left(\lambda^k - \beta^k\right)^2}.$$

The denominator in the expression for the smoothness index can be rewritten as:

$$\sum_{k=1}^{\infty} \left(\lambda^k - \beta^k\right)^2 = \sum_{k=1}^{\infty} \left(\lambda^2\right)^k - 2\sum_{k=1}^{\infty} (\lambda\beta)^k + \sum_{k=1}^{\infty} \left(\beta^2\right)^k.$$

Consequently, all infinite sums in the expression above can be computed using formula (5.9). The computations give:

$$\sum_{k=1}^{\infty} \left(\lambda^k - \beta^k\right)^2 = \lambda^2/(1-\lambda^2) + \beta^2/(1-\beta^2) - 2\lambda\beta/(1-\lambda\beta).$$

The numerator in the expression for the smoothness index can be rewritten as:

$$\sum_{k=1}^{\infty}\left(\lambda^k-\beta^k\right)\left(\lambda^{k+1}-\beta^{k+1}\right)$$
$$=\lambda\sum_{k=1}^{\infty}\left(\lambda^2\right)^k-(\lambda+\beta)\sum_{k=1}^{\infty}(\lambda\beta)^k+\beta\sum_{k=1}^{\infty}\left(\beta^2\right)^k.$$

Again, all infinite sums in the expression above can be computed using formula (5.9). These computations give:

$$\sum_{k=1}^{\infty}\left(\lambda^k-\beta^k\right)\left(\lambda^{k+1}-\beta^{k+1}\right)$$
$$=\lambda^3/(1-\lambda^2)+\beta^3/(1-\beta^2)-(\lambda+\beta)\lambda\beta/(1-\lambda\beta).$$

Combining all the results yields the expression for the smoothness index:

$$SMI=\frac{\lambda^3/(1-\lambda^2)+\beta^3/(1-\beta^2)-(\lambda+\beta)\lambda\beta/(1-\lambda\beta)}{\lambda^2/(1-\lambda^2)+\beta^2/(1-\beta^2)-2\lambda\beta/(1-\lambda\beta)}.$$

Even though the resulting expression for the SMI is rather complex, it can be simplified to:

$$SMI=\frac{\lambda+\beta}{1-\lambda\beta}.$$

Finally, substituting the expressions for λ and β yields:

$$SMI=\frac{ls-1}{ls+1}.$$

6

Uncovering the Optimal Trading Rule

6.1 Introduction

Let us begin this chapter by revisiting our progress so far. Initially, we established that the technical indicator of any trading rule, even those based on multiple moving averages of prices, can be calculated as a single moving average of past returns. This computation is represented by the following equation:

$$I_t^{TR}(n) = \sum_{i=0}^{n-1} \theta_i r_{t-i},$$

where $I_t^{\mathrm{TR}}(n)$ represents the time t value of the technical indicator within the trading rule denoted by TR, n signifies the number of return lags in the technical indicator, r_{t-i} denotes the time $t-i$ return, and θ_i is the weight assigned to r_{t-i} in the computation of the moving average of returns. The weight θ_i is computed using the price weights in the moving averages of prices. The set of all return weights constitutes the vector $\boldsymbol{\theta}' = [\theta_0, \theta_1, \ldots, \theta_{n-1}]$. An important point to take away from this finding is that the characteristics of a trading rule are uniquely determined by the properties of the technical indicator associated with that rule.

Subsequently, we introduced a method for objectively evaluating a technical indicator's accuracy, responsiveness, and smoothness. This evaluation is achieved without relying on historical data and empirical simulations. The three key metrics we introduced for this assessment are the Noise Suppression Factor (NSF), Average Lag Time (ALT), and Smoothness Index (SMI). These metrics are calculated utilizing only the return weights in a technical indicator.

V. Zakamulin and J. Giner, *The Ultimate Moving Average Handbook*,
https://doi.org/10.1007/978-3-031-90907-8_6

Therefore, the properties of a trading rule are fully determined by the return weighting function or the shape of return weights in its technical indicator.

Consider a technical indicator $I(n)$ that utilizes return weights specified by the vector $\boldsymbol{\theta}$. The accuracy of the indicator is determined by the function $NSF(\boldsymbol{\theta})$, while its responsiveness and smoothness are calculated using $ALT(\boldsymbol{\theta})$ and $SMI(\boldsymbol{\theta})$, respectively. As the return weights are specific to the technical indicator, alternative notation for computing its characteristics includes $NSF(I(n))$, $ALT(I(n))$, and $SMI(I(n))$.

In the preceding chapter, we performed analytical computations of these metrics for standard trading rules that employ traditional moving averages, namely the Simple Moving Average (SMA), Linear Moving Average (LMA), and Exponential Moving Average (EMA). To conclude, we presented a methodology for comparing and contrasting these trading rules. This methodology helps determine whether there is a rule within the set of standard rules that stands out in terms of effectiveness across all the mentioned metrics.

As the properties of a trading rule are dependent on the shape of return weights in its technical indicator, the task of finding the optimal trading rule is equivalent to finding the optimal shape of return weights. The issue lies in the fact that any trading rule, determined by one or more moving averages of prices, generates a specific shape of return weights. In a trading rule determined by a single moving average of prices, the shape of return weights is rather rigid. Even in a double crossover rule defined by two moving averages of prices, the flexibility of the return weight shapes falls short of encompassing all potentially relevant shapes. Consequently, the best trading rule within the standard set, relying on conventional moving averages, might be significantly distant from the optimal trading rule.

By optimal trading rule, we mean a rule with the most favorable combination of three numerical metrics. Even when exploring non-standard rules and diverse exotic moving averages to identify the best trading rule, there is no assurance that this rule aligns with the optimal one. Therefore, we approach the challenge of determining the optimal trading rule from a distinctly different perspective. Specifically, our focus is solely on the shape of the return weights. We rely mainly on numerical methods to pinpoint the shape that yields the supreme combination of all numerical characteristics.

This chapter aims to determine the optimal trading rule, which is a formidable job due to the following considerations. As previously established, particularly for any standard rule relying on conventional moving averages, enhancing either accuracy or smoothness comes at the expense of responsiveness. Likewise, holding the number of return lags in a trading rule constant, improving accuracy is only feasible with compromising smoothness and vice versa. In essence, enhancing one parameter of a trading rule without negatively impacting other parameters is impossible. The only viable approach is identifying a rule that strikes the optimal balance between accuracy, responsiveness, and smoothness.

The information presented in the previous paragraph conveys both challenges and opportunities. The challenge lies in the difficulty, or perhaps impossibility, of finding a trading rule that is optimal for any market. On the brighter side, there is an avenue to identify the efficient rule concerning either the tradeoff between responsiveness and accuracy or between responsiveness and smoothness. The optimal rule, excelling across all numerical measures, can be envisioned as a kind of "superposition" that integrates the efficiency derived from the optimal rule concerning responsiveness and accuracy and the optimal rule concerning responsiveness and smoothness.

6.2 Methodology

This section introduces and outlines the methodology for identifying the optimal trading rule.

To better illustrate the challenges involved, let us consider an "ideal" trading rule. When we refer to the ideal trading rule, which technical indicator is denoted as $I^*(n)$, we mean a rule that excels in all numerical characteristics. The concept of the ideal trading rule can be formalized as follows:

$$NSF(I^*(n)) \geq NSF(I(m)),$$
$$ALT(I^*(n)) \leq ALT(I(m)),$$
$$SMI(I^*(n)) \geq SMI(I(m)),$$

where $I(m)$ represents any other viable rule. In simpler terms, the ideal trading rule $I^*(n)$ should exhibit better or equal accuracy, better or equal responsiveness, and better or equal smoothness compared to any other conceivable rule $I(m)$. Moreover, $I^*(n)$ must surpass $I(m)$ in at least one of these aspects. Essentially, the ideal trading rule should have the highest accuracy and smoothness and the lowest average lag time among all feasible trading rules.

Regrettably, the ideal trading rule is nonexistent. This conclusion becomes evident through the following illustration: the trading rule $I(n)$ with the highest achievable accuracy is the MOM(n) rule. Any other MOM(m) rule with $m > n$ outperforms the MOM(n) rule in terms of accuracy. Simultaneously, any MOM(m) rule with $m < n$ exhibits superior responsiveness than the

MOM(n) rule. In essence, by adjusting the number of return lags in a trading rule, one can easily enhance either the rule's accuracy or responsiveness.

In principle, we can redefine the concept of the ideal trading rule as follows: the ideal trading rule $I^*(n)$ must outperform any other viable rule $I(n)$ in at least one aspect. It is important to note that, in this definition, all rules under examination employ the same number of return lags n. Under this modified definition, further improvement in the accuracy of the MOM(n) indicator is no longer feasible. However, it remains possible to enhance responsiveness by employing the MOM(m) rule with $m < n$. This is because the MOM(m) rule can still be regarded as the $I(n)$ rule, where the first m return lags are equally weighted, and the remaining $n - m$ lags have zero weight.

The clear takeaway from the discussion above is that constructing the ideal trading rule is not feasible. Instead, the attainable goal is to identify a trading rule that achieves the optimal combination, or the optimal tradeoff, among the three quantitative measures.

The general methodology to find the most efficient combination involves a decision-making approach known as Multi-Criteria Decision Analysis (MCDA). In essence, this methodology revolves around identifying a set of desirable properties, assigning weights to each property, and subsequently computing the weighted sum of properties for each trading rule. The resulting score for each trading rule determines its efficiency based on the specified properties, with the rule attaining the highest score considered the most efficient.

Mathematically, finding the trading rule $I(n)$ with the most efficient combination of quantitative measures can be formulated as:

$$\max_j \quad w_A NSF(I_j(n)) + w_S SMI(I_j(n)) - w_R ALT(I_j(n)), \tag{6.1}$$

where $I_j(n)$ represents the jth trading rule in the set of examined rules, and w_A, w_S, and w_R denote positive weights assigned to the accuracy, smoothness, and responsiveness measures, respectively. It is important to note that both $NSF(I_j(n))$ and $SMI(I_j(n))$ carry positive weights, while $ALT(I_j(n))$ bears an effectively negative weight in the score computation. The negative weight for $ALT(I_j(n))$ is applied because the objective is to praise the trading rule for high accuracy and smoothness while penalizing it for a prolonged average lag time.

Solving problem (6.1) necessitates testing all potential trading rules. As the number of possible rules is, in principle, infinite, directly resolving this problem is not feasible. However, employing numerical methods allows us to address the following task:

$$\max_{\boldsymbol{\theta}} \quad w_A NSF(\boldsymbol{\theta}) + w_S SMI(\boldsymbol{\theta}) - w_R ALT(\boldsymbol{\theta}), \tag{6.2}$$

where $\boldsymbol{\theta}$ is the $n \times 1$ vector of return weights and, for example, the notation $NSF(\boldsymbol{\theta})$ specifies the NSF computed using the return weights $\boldsymbol{\theta}$. In words, instead of testing all conceivable trading rules, we can determine the return weights that maximize the score. These optimized return weights establish the optimal trading rule.

Current numerical optimization methods enable us to solve problem (6.2). However, before resolving this problem, assigning weights to each quantitative measure poses a challenge. The approach to accomplishing this task is not straightforward. For instance, the significance of the smoothness property diminishes when trading costs are negligible. Conversely, in situations where trading costs play a vital role, achieving high smoothness becomes crucial. Nevertheless, even in scenarios with significant trading costs, ensuring high smoothness should not compromise responsiveness. In essence, a trading rule should maintain sufficient responsiveness, even in the face of substantial trading costs.

In summary, determining appropriate weights for each property proves challenging due to significant uncertainty surrounding the accurate identification of their importance. It is crucial to customize these weights based on specific market dynamics and features, including average trend duration, trend strength, and anticipated transaction costs, among others. However, the preceding discussion indicates that considering all three properties becomes essential only when trading costs fall outside the realm of negligible or substantially large. When trading costs can be disregarded, our focus shifts solely to accuracy and responsiveness. Conversely, in situations where trading costs pose a substantial hurdle to the profitability of trend-following investing, attention should be directed toward smoothness and responsiveness. Maximizing the score based on only two properties is a simpler task than maximizing the score incorporating all three properties.

Consider, for instance, the maximization of the score based on accuracy and responsiveness. In this scenario, problem (6.2) simplifies to:

$$\max_{\boldsymbol{\theta}} \quad w_A NSF(\boldsymbol{\theta}) - w_R ALT(\boldsymbol{\theta}). \tag{6.3}$$

In fact, this problem necessitates defining only one weight. Thus, the above problem can be reframed as:

$$\max_{\boldsymbol{\theta}} \quad NSF(\boldsymbol{\theta}) - w\, ALT(\boldsymbol{\theta}), \tag{6.4}$$

where $w = w_R / w_A$. Nonetheless, the challenge lies in selecting the appropriate weight w to strike the right balance between the accuracy and responsiveness of the trading rule.

Fortunately, determining the optimal tradeoff between two numerical measures, as presented in this problem, is a well-known challenge in various scientific fields. A comparable issue arises in the widely recognized optimal portfolio choice problem, where the goal is to find the optimal balance between the portfolio's expected return and its associated risk. This balance is not unique to all investors because it hinges on individual risk preferences, which are often unknown. The standard approach to addressing this challenge involves identifying all efficient combinations of the portfolio's expected return and risk. Subsequently, investors can decide which combination best aligns with their preferences. A portfolio is efficient when it is impossible to enhance the expected return without simultaneously increasing the portfolio's risk. In the risk-expected return space, the collection of all efficient portfolio combinations forms a curve widely referred to as the efficient frontier.

Hence, although determining the appropriate weight w to balance the trading rule's accuracy and responsiveness poses a challenge, identifying all efficient combinations of accuracy and responsiveness is a more straightforward task. To find these efficient combinations, one can fix a specific value for responsiveness and then seek the return weights in a trading rule that maximize accuracy under this fixed responsiveness. This process can be expressed mathematically as follows:

$$\max_{\boldsymbol{\theta}} \quad NSF(\boldsymbol{\theta}) \text{ subject to } ALT(\boldsymbol{\theta}) = k, \tag{6.5}$$

where $k \geq 1$ represents an arbitrary value for the responsiveness measure. By varying the responsiveness value and determining the highest attainable accuracy for each fixed responsiveness, we can identify all efficient combinations of accuracy and responsiveness. Once again, a combination is considered efficient when improving the trading rule's accuracy becomes impossible without simultaneously increasing the average lag time.

Likewise, we can identify all efficient combinations of the trading rule's smoothness and responsiveness. With a solid understanding of which rules are efficient in terms of accuracy and responsiveness, as well as smoothness and responsiveness, exploring and comprehending the properties of trading rules efficient in all three measures becomes more accessible. This is facilitated by the informed assumption that a trading rule excelling across all numerical measures can be conceptualized as a "superposition" of two types of rules. This superposition integrates the efficiency derived from the optimal rule concerning accuracy and responsiveness with that of the optimal rule concerning smoothness and responsiveness.

6.3 Optimization with Respect to One Property

While optimization concerning a single numerical measure has been previously addressed in this book, revisiting these problems is valuable for the sake of completeness and a deeper understanding of trading rules that excel in specific properties. Examining these problems once again provides a more thorough exploration of the issues involved and their outcomes.

In this section, we fix the number of return lags n and determine the return weights $\boldsymbol{\theta}$ for technical indicators that optimize either accuracy, smoothness, or responsiveness measure. It is important to note that each numerical measure remains unaffected by a positive scaling of return weights. This property implies that, in principle, an infinite number of technical indicators exist that, for instance, can achieve the maximum possible accuracy for a specified number of return lags. To arrive at a unique solution, we introduce the following equality constraint:

$$\sum_{i=0}^{n-1} \theta_i = 1.$$

This constraint specifies that the sum of all return weights should equal one. Expressed in matrix notation, this constraint can be represented as:

$$\boldsymbol{\theta}'\mathbf{1} = 1,$$

where $\mathbf{1}$ denotes the $n \times 1$ vector comprising ones.

It is important to note that certain return weights may be negative. However, the requirement for the sum of return weights to be positive is crucial. This sum must be positive to ensure that the technical indicator generates a Buy signal when the trend direction is upward. In such instances, the mean return is positive, and the expected value of the technical indicator can be expressed as:

$$E[I(n)] = \mu \sum_{i=0}^{n-1} \theta_i > 0,$$

which implies that the trading signal is a Buy. Thus, correctly identifying the trend direction necessitates a positive sum of return weights.

The following two problems have unique analytical solutions:

$$\max_{\boldsymbol{\theta}} \quad NSF(\boldsymbol{\theta}) \text{ subject to } \boldsymbol{\theta}'\mathbf{1} = 1, \tag{6.6}$$

$$\max_{\boldsymbol{\theta}} \quad SMI(\boldsymbol{\theta}) \text{ subject to } \boldsymbol{\theta}'\mathbf{1} = 1. \tag{6.7}$$

Specifically, the MOM(n) technical indicator, employing equally weighted returns, achieves the maximum accuracy. The technical indicator, denoted as the SWMA(n) rule, utilizes sine-weighted return weights for maximum smoothness. It is crucial to emphasize that despite permitting negative weights in optimization problems (6.6) and (6.7), both optimal technical indicators exclusively feature positive return weights.

However, achieving the minimization of the ALT does not yield a unique solution when negative weights are permitted. Uniqueness is established only when non-negative weights are mandated, and this is expressed in the following formulation of the problem:

$$\min_{\boldsymbol{\theta}} \quad ALT(\boldsymbol{\theta}) \text{ subject to } \boldsymbol{\theta}'\mathbf{1} = 1 \text{ and } \boldsymbol{\theta} \geq \mathbf{0}, \tag{6.8}$$

where $\mathbf{0}$ represents the $n \times 1$ vector comprising zeros.

Before delving into the reasoning behind the absence of a unique solution when negative weights are allowed, let us first establish that the minimum achievable ALT is 1. The illustration in Fig. 6.1 provides a visual representation of our motivation. We consider the scenario where the current time is labeled as 0. Until this point, the price has been on an upward trend, prompting our technical indicator to generate a Buy signal. In the subsequent time interval, the price may either increase or decrease. If it decreases, time 0 signifies a turning point in the trend; if it continues to rise, time 0 is not a turning point.

Recognizing time 0 as a turning point is only feasible at the subsequent time point, denoted as 1, when a decrease in the stock price is observed. Consequently, the minimum lag time required for turning point detection is 1. At the current time 0, the trading rule lacks the capability to predict future stock prices since it relies solely on prices observed before and including time 0. Up to this point, prices have consistently increased, offering no indications of an impending price drop.[1]

[1] It is important to remind the reader that we assume that the market return follows a model that switches between two states: bull and bear. The transitions between these states are entirely random, making any predictions of trend turning points unfeasible. Recognition of a state change can only occur post factum, after a turning point. We strongly advocate for this theoretical model as the most reasonable

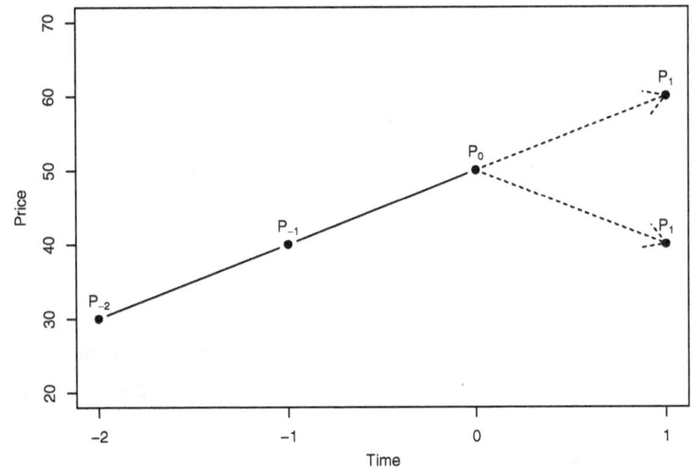

Fig. 6.1 Price trajectory until time 0 and two possible price trajectories after time 0

Therefore, if the lag time of a trading rule were 0, it would signify perfect foresight at time 0 regarding the direction of the stock price in the next period. Similarly, a negative lag time implies the ability to foresee the future trend direction over several periods.

Now that we have established the minimum lag time as 1, the question arises: which trading rules can achieve this level of responsiveness? The most obvious contender is the MOM(1) rule, which utilizes the last return observation to discern the direction of the price trend. However, it is noteworthy that any $I(n)$ rule with the most recent weight set to 1 and all other $n-1$ weights set to 0 also attains an ALT of 1. These technical indicators are equivalent because they effectively rely on a single price weight. Consequently, all these rules correspond to the same solution in the ALT minimization problem.

Allowing negative weights significantly expands the range of technical indicators with the same average lag time. To illustrate the variety of solutions for a trading rule with an ALT of 1, consider the return weights of the following technical indicators:

representation of market dynamics. Although some models may suggest that predicting turning points is possible, we maintain a skeptical stance. For instance, one might posit that the mean market return follows a deterministic function of time, such as a cyclical pattern with a constant duration. This model would enable the anticipation of turning points in the cycle. Nonetheless, we firmly contend that such models are inherently unrealistic.

$$
\begin{aligned}
\boldsymbol{\theta}'_1 &= [1, 0, 0, 0, 0, 0, \dots, 0],\\
\boldsymbol{\theta}'_2 &= [1, a, -a, 0, 0, 0, \dots, 0],\\
\boldsymbol{\theta}'_3 &= [1, a, -a, a, -a, 0, \dots, 0],\\
\boldsymbol{\theta}'_4 &= [1, a, a, -a, -a, 0, \dots, 0],
\end{aligned}
$$

where $a > 0$ is a real number. It is straightforward to verify that each technical indicator within this set satisfies the condition $\sum_{i=0}^{n-1} \theta_i = 1$ and achieves an ALT of 1. As a result, permitting negative weights leads to numerous trading rules with an ALT of 1. Conversely, if negative weights are disallowed, the ALT minimization problem for a given number of return lags n yields a unique solution.

To conclude this section, Fig. 6.2 displays the weighting functions of technical indicators maximizing accuracy, responsiveness, and smoothness. In the top panel, we present the weighting function of the technical indicator achieving the highest accuracy, used in the MOM(n) technical indicator with equal weights on all returns. The middle panel of Fig. 6.2 illustrates the weighting function of the technical indicator minimizing ALT, assigning zero weight to all return lags except the most recent one. Finally, the bottom panel depicts the weighting function of the technical indicator optimizing smoothness, employed in the SWMA(n) technical indicator. The shape of this weighting function corresponds to the first half of a sine wave.

6.4 Optimization with Respect to Two Properties

6.4.1 Maximizing Accuracy for Fixed Responsiveness

The NSF of the technical indicator $I(n)$ is determined using the formula:

$$
NSF(I(n)) = \frac{\sum_{i=0}^{n-1} \theta_i}{\sqrt{\sum_{i=0}^{n-1} \theta_i^2}}. \tag{6.9}
$$

Assuming that the total return weights add up to 1, the NSF expression simplifies to:

$$
\text{NSF}(\boldsymbol{\theta}) = \frac{1}{\sqrt{\sum_{i=0}^{n-1} \theta_i^2}}.
$$

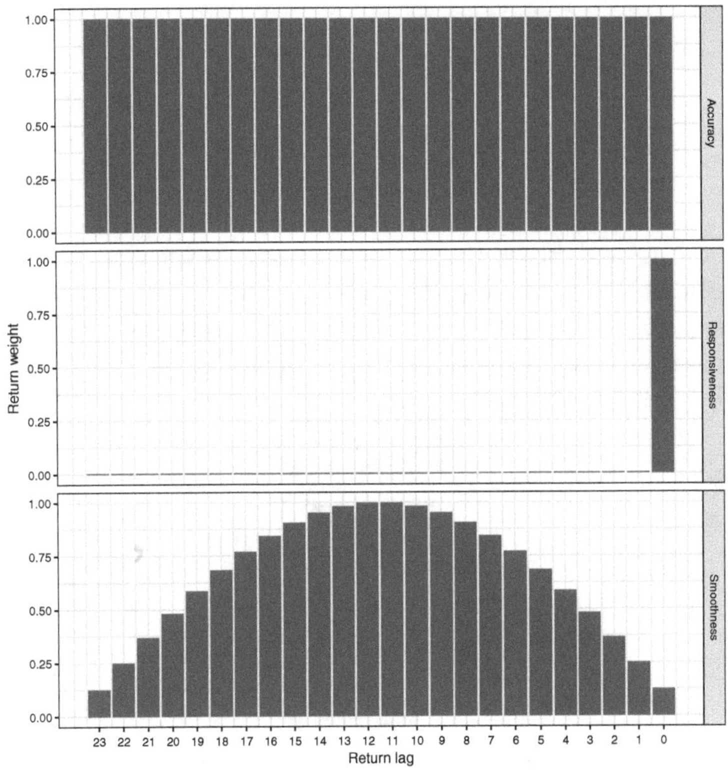

Fig. 6.2 Weighting functions of the technical indicators that maximize accuracy, responsiveness, and smoothness for the averaging window of size $n = 24$ return observations

In matrix notation, the NSF formula can be represented as:

$$\text{NSF}(\boldsymbol{\theta}) = \frac{1}{\sqrt{\boldsymbol{\theta}'\mathbf{I}\boldsymbol{\theta}}},$$

where $\mathbf{I}$ is the $n \times n$ identity matrix.

It is important to note that the expression $\boldsymbol{\theta}'\mathbf{I}\boldsymbol{\theta}$ corresponds to the sum of squared return weights. Additionally, maximizing the NSF is equivalent to minimizing $\boldsymbol{\theta}'\mathbf{I}\boldsymbol{\theta}$. Specifically, as the NSF is inversely proportional to the square root of the sum of squared weights, minimizing this sum results in maximizing the NSF.

The ALT of the technical indicator $I(n)$ identifies the first lag number $k \in [1, n-1]$ satisfying the following inequality:

$$\sum_{i=0}^{k-1} \theta_i \geq \sum_{i=k}^{n-1} \theta_i.$$

It is crucial to understand that when dealing with equality constraints, an optimization problem may theoretically have an analytical solution. However, the presence of an inequality constraint typically precludes the identification of an analytical solution. To facilitate an analytical solution, we assume that ALT is determined by:

$$\sum_{i=0}^{k-1} \theta_i = \sum_{i=k}^{n-1} \theta_i.$$

In matrix notation, the computation of ALT can be expressed as:

$$\boldsymbol{\theta}'\mathbf{k} = 0,$$

where $\mathbf{k}$ is a $n \times 1$ vector defined as follows:

$$\mathbf{k}' = [\underbrace{1, \ldots, 1}_{k \text{ elements}}, \underbrace{-1, \ldots, -1}_{n-k \text{ elements}}].$$

That is, the first k elements of this vector are set to 1, while the remaining $n-k$ elements are set to –1.

To maximize the NSF for a fixed value of ALT, the problem is formulated as follows:

$$\min_{\boldsymbol{\theta}} \frac{1}{2}\boldsymbol{\theta}'\mathbf{I}\boldsymbol{\theta}, \text{ subject to } \boldsymbol{\theta}'\mathbf{1} = 1 \text{ and } \boldsymbol{\theta}'\mathbf{k} = 0. \tag{6.10}$$

Note that the coefficient $1/2$ in front of the sum of squared return weights is introduced for convenience.

Problem (6.10) is a quadratic optimization problem with two equality constraints. It is a convex optimization problem, meaning that the local minimum is also the global minimum. While numerical methods can be used for straightforward computation, a closed-form solution is also obtainable in this case.

Proposition 6.1 *The solution for the optimal weights is given by:*

$$\boldsymbol{\theta}' = [\underbrace{\lambda + \gamma, \ldots, \lambda + \gamma}_{k \text{ elements}}, \underbrace{\lambda - \gamma, \ldots, \lambda - \gamma}_{n-k \text{ elements}}].$$

That is, the first k *weights are set to* $\lambda + \gamma$*, while the remaining* $n - k$ *weights are set to* $\lambda - \gamma$*. The values for* λ *and* γ *are determined by:*

$$\lambda = \frac{n}{4k(n-k)}, \qquad \gamma = \frac{n-2k}{4k(n-k)}. \tag{6.11}$$

The detailed proof of this proposition is provided in the Appendix.

Remark 6.1 It is crucial to highlight that when solving problem (6.10), we do not restrict the weights to be non-negative. Nevertheless, the obtained solution provides strictly positive weights for any k within the range $[1, n-1]$.

Remark 6.2 The meaningful values for the ALT lie within the set $k \in [1, n/2]$. The solution suggests that in this scenario, the initial k weights surpass the remaining $n - k$ weights, except when $k = n/2$. In the latter situation, where ALT equals half the size of the averaging window, the formulas yield $\lambda = \frac{1}{n}$ and $\gamma = 0$. In this case, all weights are identical, effectively restoring the MOM(n) weighting scheme.

Figure 6.3 illustrates the weighting functions of the technical indicator with $n = 24$, where ALT is fixed at $k \in \{3, 5, 8\}$ and NSF is maximized. Notably, with increasing ALT, the values of the initial k weights decrease, whereas the values of the remaining $n - k$ weights increase. As k gradually converges to $n/2$, all weights eventually equalize. Conversely, in the scenario where k approaches 1, Eq. (6.11) indicates that the first weight reaches its maximum value of 0.5, while the sum of all remaining weights equals this initial weight.[2]

Our next step involves determining the optimal combinations of the NSF and ALT. To achieve this, we vary the value of ALT and, for each specific value, compute the maximum possible NSF. Subsequently, we create a plot illustrating the relationship between NSF and ALT, depicting the efficient frontier. This visual representation highlights the best possible tradeoff between NSF and ALT. To show that improving one tradeoff usually results in worsening the other, we also calculate the SMI measures for the optimal rules with the best tradeoff between NSF and ALT. For comparative analysis, we calculate the NSF, ALT, and SMI values for the MOM(24), P-SMA(24), P-LMA(24), and P-EMA(24) rules. It is important to note that the P-MA rules are specifically chosen for their ability to strike a good balance between accuracy and responsiveness among the standard trading rules based on common moving averages.

[2] However, note that the weights can be freely rescaled.

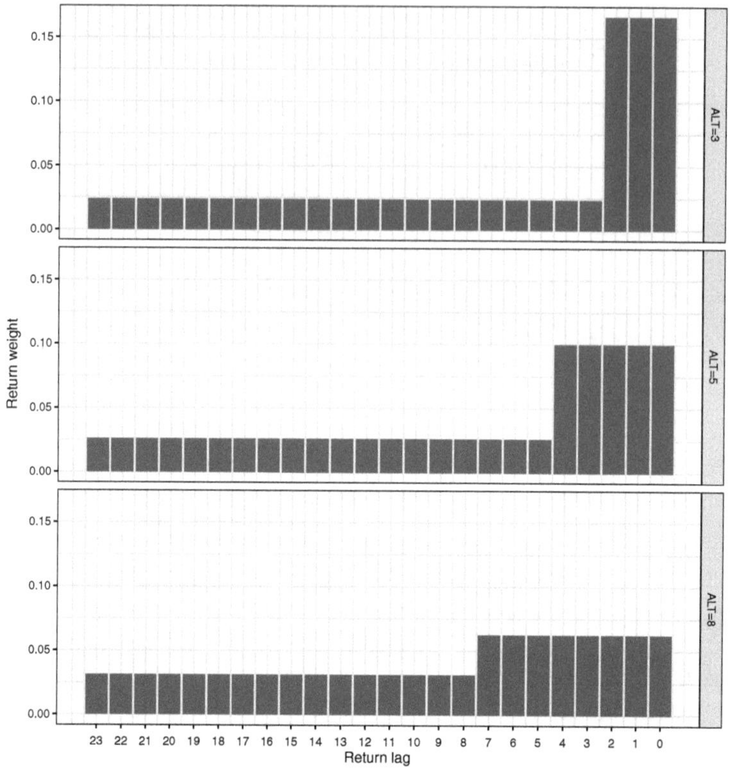

Fig. 6.3 Weighting functions of the technical indicator with $n = 24$ that has the maximum NSF when the ALT takes values in $\{3, 5, 8\}$

The upper panel of Fig. 6.4 depicts the efficient combinations of NSF and ALT. The lower panel of this figure displays how these efficient combinations appear in the ALT-SMI space. The circles indicate the parameter locations for the MOM(24), P-SMA(24), P-LMA(24), and P-EMA(24) rules. The observations from the plot in the upper panel lead to the following conclusions. The optimal trading rule exhibits a superior tradeoff between accuracy and responsiveness compared to the P-SMA and P-LMA rules. However, the advantage of the optimal rule is not substantial. For instance, replacing either the P-SMA or P-LMA rule with the optimal rule reduces the average lag time by 1 while maintaining the same level of accuracy. Meanwhile, as follows from the plot in the lower panel, the P-SMA and P-LMA rules offer a more favorable balance between smoothness and responsiveness than the optimal rule concerning the tradeoff between accuracy and responsiveness. In other words, improving the tradeoff between NSF and ALT comes at the cost of deteriorating the tradeoff between SMI and ALT.

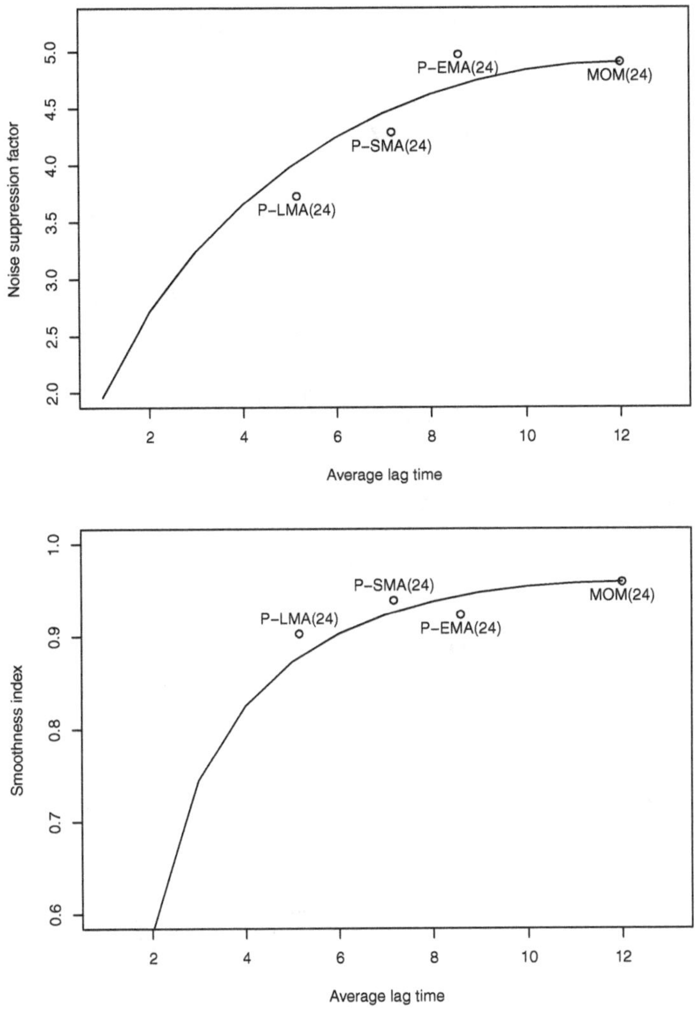

Fig. 6.4 Set of efficient combinations of the NSF and ALT in the ALT-NSF and ALT-SMI spaces. For the sake of comparison, the circles show the location of the parameters of the MOM(24), P-SMA(24), P-LMA(24), and P-EMA(24) rules

The MOM rule is optimal when ALT $= n/2$, a fact known in advance. Surprisingly, the P-EMA rule achieves a better tradeoff between accuracy and responsiveness than the optimal rule. This result may seem counterintuitive initially but is clarified by the fact that the P-EMA(n) rule utilizes infinite return lags, not n lags. The value of n is employed to compute the decay constant in this rule. Thus, it is not entirely fair to compare the parameters of a rule using n return lags with those of the P-EMA(n) rule that employs infinite number of lags.

6.4.2 Maximizing Smoothness for Fixed Responsiveness

The SMI of the technical indicator $I(n)$ is computed using the formula:

$$SMI(\boldsymbol{\theta}) = \frac{\sum_{i=0}^{n-2} \theta_i \theta_{i+1}}{\sum_{i=0}^{n-1} \theta_i^2}. \tag{6.12}$$

Expressed in matrix notation, the SMI formula can be written as:

$$SMI(\boldsymbol{\theta}) = \frac{\boldsymbol{\theta}'\mathbf{Q}\boldsymbol{\theta}}{\boldsymbol{\theta}'\mathbf{I}\boldsymbol{\theta}},$$

where $\mathbf{I}$ is the $n \times n$ identity matrix, and $\boldsymbol{Q}$ is the $n \times n$ matrix defined as:

$$\boldsymbol{Q} = \begin{bmatrix} 0\,0\,0 \dots 0 \\ 1\,0\,0 \dots 0 \\ 0\,1\,0 \dots 0 \\ \vdots\;\vdots\;\vdots\;\ddots\;\vdots \\ 0\,0\,0 \dots 0 \end{bmatrix}.$$

Note that the matrix $\boldsymbol{Q}$ is a square matrix where all entries below the main diagonal are equal to 1, and the remaining entries are set to 0.

Our objective is to fix the number of return lags, n, and the ALT value, k, and then determine the return weights $\boldsymbol{\theta}$ that maximize the SMI measure. We aim to solve this problem under two scenarios: with and without the constraint on non-negative return weights.

If negative weights are allowed, the optimization problem is formulated as:

$$\max_{\boldsymbol{\theta}} SMI(\boldsymbol{\theta}) \text{ subject to } \boldsymbol{\theta}'\mathbf{1} = 1 \text{ and } ALT(\boldsymbol{\theta}) = k.$$

This represents an optimization problem with two equality constraints.

If negative weights are not allowed, the optimization problem includes an additional inequality constraint:

$$\max_{\boldsymbol{\theta}} SMI(\boldsymbol{\theta}) \text{ subject to } \boldsymbol{\theta}'\mathbf{1} = 1,\ ALT(\boldsymbol{\theta}) = k, \text{ and } \boldsymbol{\theta} \geq \mathbf{0}.$$

Since both problems lack analytical solutions, we solve them through numerical optimization. The results are presented in Fig. 6.5. Specifically, the figure depicts the weighting functions of the technical indicator with $n = 24$ that achieves maximum smoothness when ALT takes values in 3, 5, 8. In the left column, return weights are allowed to be negative. In the right column, however, negative weights are not permitted.

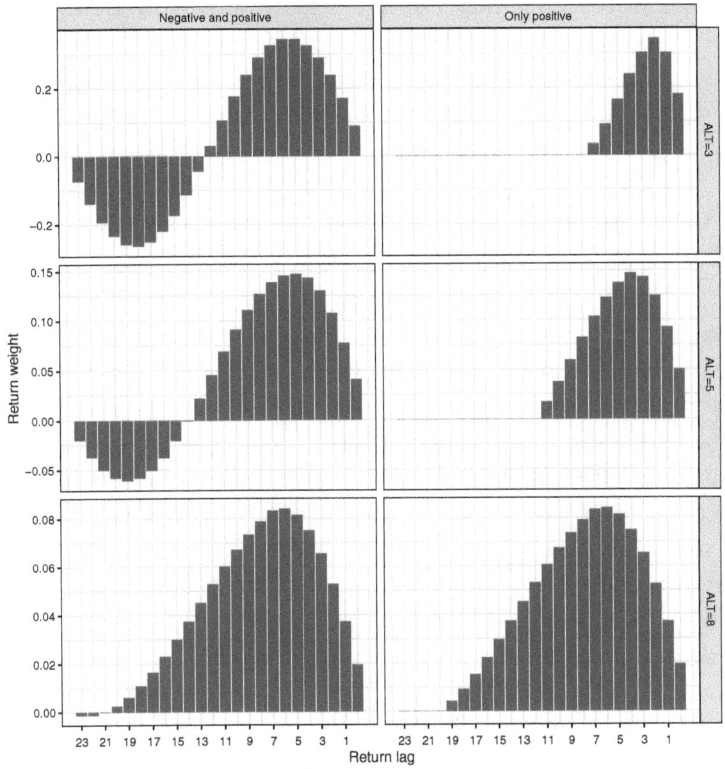

Fig. 6.5 Weighting functions of the technical indicator with $n = 24$ that has the maximum smoothness when the ALT takes values in $\{3, 5, 8\}$. In the left column, return weights are permitted to be negative. In the right column, negative weights are not allowed

Upon visual examination of the weighting functions in Fig. 6.5, several observations emerge. First, when negative weights are prohibited, the optimal weighting function of the technical indicator, striking the best balance between smoothness and responsiveness, takes the form of a smooth hump leaning to the right, directed toward the most recent return lags. This shape is essentially a combination of the shape that optimizes smoothness and the shape that optimizes responsiveness. To see this, note that to maximize smoothness, the return weights must create a symmetrical hump, which shape is derived from the first half of a sine wave. In contrast, to maximize responsiveness, all return weights must concentrate on the most recent return observation. The superposition of these two shapes results in a smooth hump leaning to the right.

Second, when negative weights are not allowed and the ALT is relatively small, the return weights of the optimal technical indicator maintain a qualitatively similar shape, but numerous distant weights become zero. The smaller the ALT, the greater the number of zero distant weights. Evidently, there is no necessity for positive weights at distant lags when aiming for a short ALT.

Third, when negative weights are permitted and the ALT is relatively small, numerous distant return weights turn negative. In such instances, the shape of the weighting function is constructed using harmonics of the sine wave. To better comprehend how this shape is created, it is helpful to revisit the set of smooth shapes. The shape with the highest smoothness is derived from the first half of a sine wave cycle, representing the fundamental frequency denoted as $f = \frac{1}{2(n+1)}$ or the 1st harmonic. The subsequent shape with the next highest smoothness corresponds to the sine wave with a frequency of $2f$ or the 2nd harmonic. The frequency of the kth harmonic is given by $k \times f$. Together, all these harmonic functions form a fundamental set of smooth functions.

The key point is that the shape of the return weights of the optimal technical indicator with a short ALT can be expressed as a linear combination of harmonic functions with the same fundamental frequency. All these functions are inherently smooth, and therefore, their linear combination also results in a smooth function.

As the ALT approaches 1 and weights cannot take negative values, the weighting function becomes concentrated in a single return lag. This shape lacks smoothness, with an SMI of 0 indicating zero autocorrelation between two subsequent trading signals. Achieving high smoothness requires return weights to exhibit a smooth shape across the entire averaging window spanning n return observations. If negative weights are allowed and the ALT approaches 1, the shape of the return weights closely resembles the 2nd harmonic of the fundamental frequency. This shape represents a full sine wave consisting of both positive and negative segments.

Fourth and finally, it is crucial to highlight that when the ALT is relatively large, the return weights are positive, even when negative weights are allowed. In such instances, starting from an ALT of 8, the optimal return weights are almost identical, irrespective of whether negative weights are permitted or not in our specific example. The shape of the optimal return weights manifests as a smooth hump leaning to the right. This shape can be perceived as a smoothed version of the return weights in the SMA-C(s, n) technical indicator, where $s < n/2$. In this indicator, the return weights represent a triangle with a base of n and the peak located at s. Smoothing this shape results in a configuration closely resembling the shape in the optimal trading rule, which achieves the best tradeoff between smoothness and responsiveness when the ALT is relatively large.

Next, we identify the optimal combinations of SMI and ALT and illustrate their relationship by creating a plot depicting the efficient frontier. Specifically, we construct two efficient frontiers: one allowing negative weights and the other prohibiting them. Alongside SMI and ALT, we compute the NSF value for each optimal combination. For comparative analysis, similar to our previous approach, we calculate NSF, ALT, and SMI values for MOM(24), P-SMA(24), P-LMA(24), and P-EMA(24) rules. Additionally, we compute the same measures for the SMA-C(6,24) rule in our analysis. The choice of the latter rule is deliberate, as it is known for maintaining a well-balanced relationship between smoothness and responsiveness.

The upper panel of Fig. 6.6 depicts the efficient combinations of SMI and ALT with and without the restriction on negative weights. The lower panel of this figure displays how these efficient combinations appear in the ALT-NSF space. The circles indicate the parameter locations for the MOM(24), P-SMA(24), P-LMA(24), P-EMA(24), and SMA-C(6,24) rules.

Insights drawn from the upper panel of the plot yield the following conclusions. First, the optimal trading rule showcases a superior balance between smoothness and responsiveness compared to all P-MA rules. For instance, substituting the P-SMA(24) rule with the optimal rule significantly enhances smoothness while maintaining the same level of responsiveness. However, the SMA-C(6,24) rule is nearly optimal with respect to the tradeoff between smoothness and responsiveness. Second, as ALT decreases toward 1 and negative weights are prohibited, the SMI of the optimal trading rule quickly diminishes to 0. Conversely, when ALT is less than 6, allowing negative weights significantly enhances the smoothness of the optimal trading rule compared to employing only positive weights. In this scenario, as ALT approaches 1, the SMI consistently maintains a relatively high level, comparable to the SMI of the optimal trading rule with an ALT of 5. This outcome suggests that allowing negative weights is beneficial.

Simultaneously, the curves in the lower panel of Fig. 6.6 affirm the central idea regarding the interplay between trading rule properties. Specifically, enhancing one property invariably comes at the cost of compromising other properties. Moreover, the greater the improvement in one property, the more pronounced the deterioration in other aspects. In our context, first, the MOM(24), P-SMA(24), P-LMA(24), and P-EMA(24) rules exhibit a better tradeoff between NSF and ALT compared to the optimal trading rule concerning SMI and ALT. Second, although permitting negative weights enhances

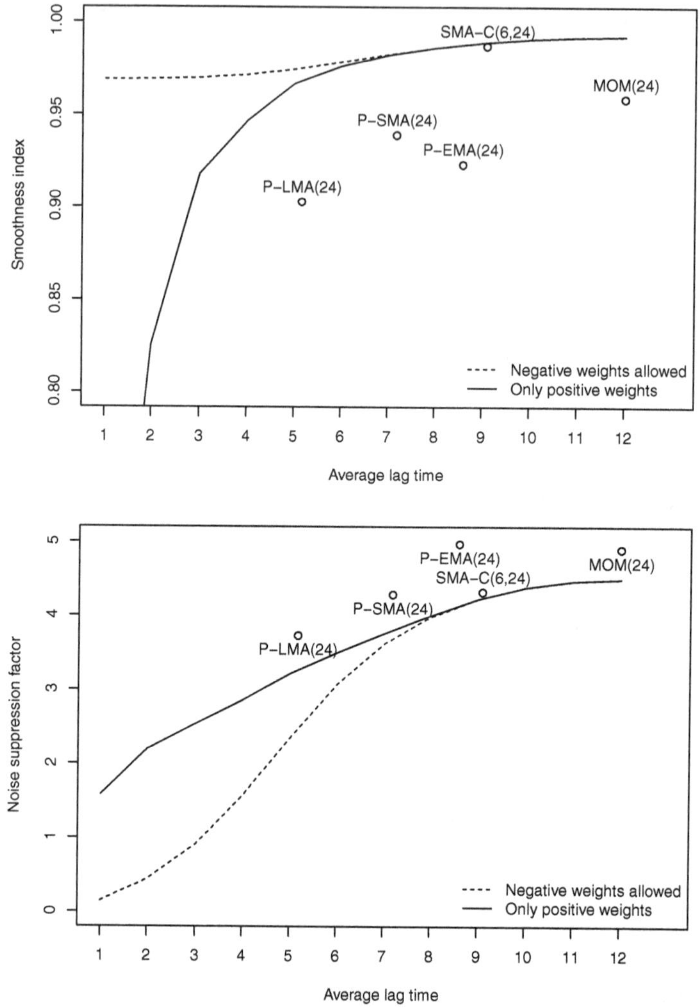

Fig. 6.6 Set of efficient combinations of the SMI and ALT in the ALT-SMI and ALT-NSF spaces. For the sake of comparison, the circles show the location of the parameters of the MOM(24), P-SMA(24), P-LMA(24), P-EMA(24), and SMA-C(6,24) rules

SMI when ALT is relatively small, this enhancement substantially degrades the accuracy of the optimal trading rule. For instance, when ALT is 3 and negative weights are allowed, the NSF of the optimal trading rule is approximately 1. In simpler terms, while being relatively smooth, the accuracy of this trading rule, utilizing n return weights, is comparable to the MOM(1) rule that relies on only one return observation. A further reduction of ALT to 1 still results in a smooth trading rule, but its accuracy approaches zero!

6.4.3 Maximizing Smoothness for Fixed Accuracy

This section explores the problem of maximizing the smoothness of a trading rule while maintaining a fixed level of accuracy. Although this problem may seem less intriguing due to the neglect of responsiveness, it is worthwhile to examine it briefly.

As previously outlined, our approach involves fixing the number of return lags, n, selecting the value of $NSF = k$, and determining the return weights $\boldsymbol{\theta}$ that maximize the SMI measure. Notably, the weighting function of the trading rule, whether maximizing SMI or NSF, is symmetrical around the middle. Consequently, both trading rules possess an ALT of $n/2$. Therefore, it is reasonable to hypothesize that the optimal rule for this problem will also feature a symmetrical weighting function and an ALT of $n/2$.

Furthermore, it is important to recognize that the range for possible NSF values in this problem is quite limited. Specifically, the NSF is constrained from above by the NSF of the MOM(n) trading rule, which is $\sqrt{n}$, and from below by the NSF of the SWMA(n) trading rule. For instance, with $n = 24$, the NSF can vary from 4.496 to 4.899. Starting at an NSF of 4.496, the optimal trading rule corresponds to the SWMA(24) rule. As the NSF approaches 4.899, the optimal rule converges to the MOM(24) rule. Somewhere between these extremes, the shape of the return weights represents a combination of the return weights in the SWMA rule and the MOM rule.

The reason behind the fact that the trading rule that optimizes smoothness also demonstrates a high level of accuracy can be clarified as follows. It is essential to recognize that maximizing the accuracy aligns closely with minimizing the sum of squared return weights, as illustrated in Eq. (6.9). When we aim to maximize smoothness, we are searching for return weights that showcase a substantial sum of products between two consecutive weights while simultaneously maintaining a minimal sum of squared weights, see Eq. (6.12). In essence, the pursuit of smoothness maximization also entails minimizing the sum of squared weights.

Formally, we consider the following optimization problem:

$$\max_{\boldsymbol{\theta}} SMI(\boldsymbol{\theta}) \text{ subject to } NSF(\boldsymbol{\theta}) = m,$$

where m is a given value of accuracy for the trading rule.

Figure 6.7 shows the results of the optimization. Specifically, the top panel in this figure shows the weighting function of the SWMA(24) rule. The bottom panel displays the weighting function of the MOM(24). The middle panel depicts the weighting function of the optimal trading rule that maximizes the smoothness for a fixed accuracy value.

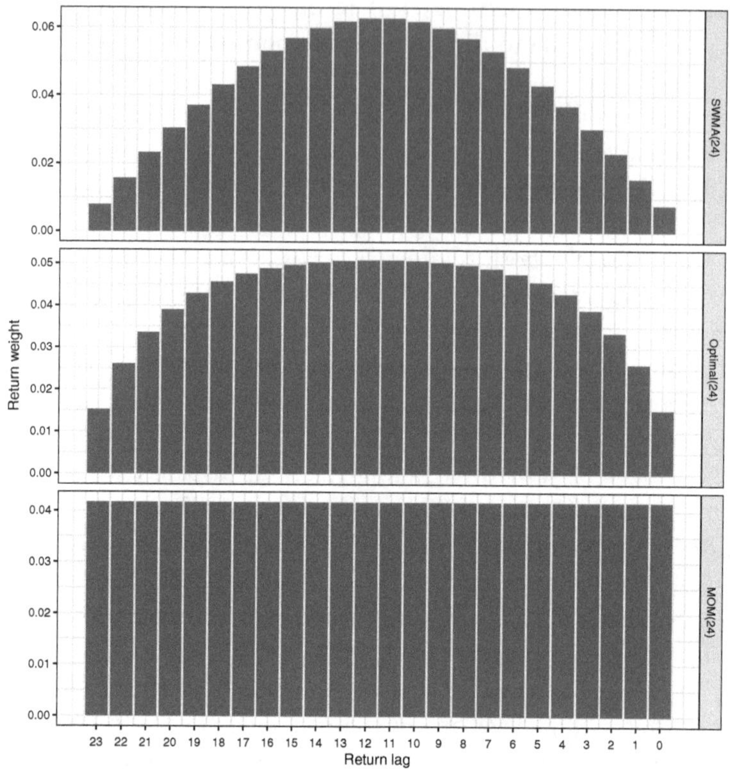

Fig. 6.7 Middle panel illustrates the weighting function of the optimal trading rule that maximizes smoothness for a given accuracy level. The upper panel presents the weighting function of the SWMA(24) rule, which achieves the highest smoothness. The lower panel shows the weighting function of the MOM(24) rule, which attains the highest accuracy

In essence, the optimization results align with our initial expectations. Notably, the return weights in the optimal trading rule exhibit a combination of the return weights in the SWMA rule and those in the MOM rule. The returns are equally weighted in the MOM(n) rule, ensuring the maximum attainable accuracy for a trading rule. As we aim to enhance the smoothness of the trading rule while maintaining a high level of accuracy, a gradual reduction in the weights of both the most recent and distant return observations is necessary. As the shape of the return weights converges toward the SWMA rule pattern, further smoothness improvement becomes unattainable.

6.5 Optimization with Respect to Three Properties

Given our lack of knowledge on how to determine the correct weights for the properties in the maximization problem described by Eq. (6.2), our approach to identifying the optimal trading rule that balances all three properties involves maximizing one property while holding the other two constant. For example, the problem can be formulated as follows:

$$\max_{\boldsymbol{\theta}} SMI(\boldsymbol{\theta}) \text{ subject to } \boldsymbol{\theta}'\mathbf{1} = 1,\ ALT(\boldsymbol{\theta}) = k, \text{ and } NSF(\boldsymbol{\theta}) = m, \tag{6.13}$$

where k represents the chosen level of responsiveness, and m represents the chosen level of accuracy for the trading rule. In simpler terms, the objective is to maximize the SMI while accommodating three equality constraints. The first constraint ensures that the sum of weights equals 1, while the second and third constraints set the values of ALT and NSF. It is important to note that we do not impose restrictions on the weights being non-negative.

It is crucial to emphasize that the results of the optimization problem (6.13) represent the return weights of an efficient trading rule. This is because enhancing the smoothness of the trading rule beyond this point would require compromising accuracy, responsiveness, or both. Similarly, with this efficient trading rule, there's no way to enhance accuracy or responsiveness without negatively impacting the other properties.

With the knowledge at our disposal, we can make an informed guess about the likely appearance of the optimal weighting function in problem (6.13). Suppose that $n = 24$ and the value of ALT is fixed at 7. We are already familiar with the weighting function for the optimal trading rule that maximizes the NSF under a fixed ALT. We denote this maximum value as NSF_{max}. Simultaneously, we know the weighting function for the optimal trading rule that maximizes the SMI under the same ALT, and it yields a lower value of NSF, denoted as NSF_{min}.

Now, consider the trading rule with the maximum NSF that obviously lacks sufficient smoothness. While keeping ALT constant, we can enhance the smoothness of this rule. However, it is essential to remember that improving smoothness comes at the expense of accuracy. The crucial insight lies in recognizing that, with a constant value of $ALT = 7$, the accuracy of the optimal trading rule can only fall within the range $NSF \in [NSF_{min}, NSF_{max}]$. Therefore, as we vary NSF from its minimum to maximum within this range, the resulting shape of the optimal trading rule transitions from the shape that maximizes SMI for a fixed ALT to the shape that maximizes NSF for the same

ALT. Somewhere between these two extremes, the shape of the optimal trading rule can be envisioned as a combination or overlay of these two shapes.

To be specific, when $n = 24$ and $ALT = 7$, the NSF values range between 3.61 and 4.45. Let us consider an arbitrary value within this range, such as 4.2. We then identify the return weights that optimize the SMI for $ALT = 7$ and $NSF = 4.2$. The optimization results are illustrated in Fig. 6.8. The upper panel of this figure displays the return weights maximizing the NSF for $ALT = 7$ while the lower panel exhibits the return weights maximizing the SMI for the same ALT. The middle panel visualizes the return weights maximizing the SMI with fixed values for both ALT and NSF. The shape of the optimal return weights aligns with our prior expectations, as depicted in the middle panel, which portrays a composite form derived from both the upper and lower panel shapes.

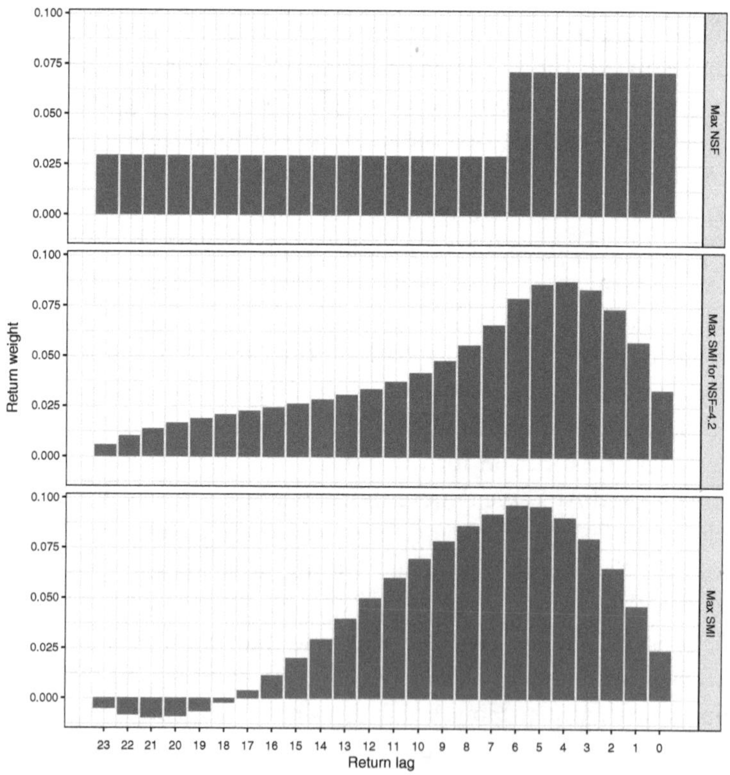

Fig. 6.8 Middle panel depicts the weighting function of the optimal trading rule that maximizes the SMI for a fixed value of the NSF. The upper panel shows the weighting function that maximizes the NSF. The lower panel displays the weighting function that maximizes the SMI. All these weighting functions maintain a constant ALT of 7

In Fig. 6.9, additional illustrations are presented for the weighting function that maximizes the SMI with an ALT of 7, considering three distinct values of the NSF. The curves in this figure distinctly demonstrate the transition of optimal weights, shifting from the form with maximum accuracy to the form with maximum smoothness as the NSF value decreases.

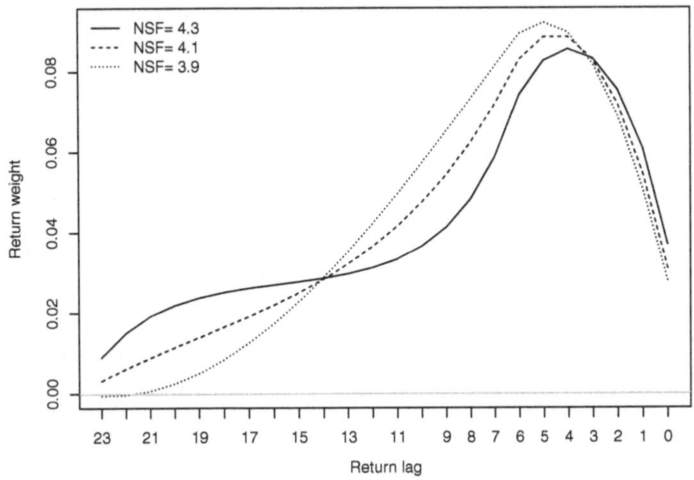

Fig. 6.9 Weighting functions of the optimal trading rule $I(n)$ that maximizes the SMI for a fixed value of the NSF and $ALT = 7$

It is crucial to emphasize that, in this example where ALT is 7, for NSF values less than or equal to 4.2, the weighting function of the optimal technical indicator can be regarded as a smoothed version of the SMA-C(s, n) trading rule. The findings from Section 6.4.2 in this chapter further support that the SMA-C(s, n) trading rule is nearly optimal concerning the tradeoff between smoothness and responsiveness, particularly when the ALT value is not quite small. Collectively, these results suggest that the SMA-C(s, n) trading rule closely approximates the trading rule with the optimal balance between all three numerical properties: accuracy, responsiveness, and smoothness.

Given the proximity of the SMA-C(s, n) trading rule to optimality, a natural question arises: can its properties be enhanced? To explore this, we conduct two numerical experiments, both focusing on the SMA-C(10, 40) trading rule, which we selected as an example for analysis and potential improvement. The choice of the longer moving average length, $n = 40$, is arbitrary. In contrast, the shorter moving average length, $s = 10$, is deliberate, as in real trading, the shorter average typically represents one-quarter of the length of the longer average.

In the first numerical experiment, we aim to construct an optimized trading rule with the same NSF and ALT as the SMA-C(10,40) rule but a higher SMI. We achieve this by solving the problem presented in Eq. (6.13), where k and m represent the ALT and NSF, respectively, of the SMA-C(10,40) rule. In the second experiment, our goal is to construct an optimized trading rule that maintains the same NSF and SMI as the SMA-C(10,40) rule but with a smaller ALT. This is achieved by solving the following problem:

$$\min_{\boldsymbol{\theta}} ALT(\boldsymbol{\theta}) \text{ subject to } \boldsymbol{\theta}'\mathbf{1} = 1, \ NSF(\boldsymbol{\theta}) = m, \ \text{and } SMI(\boldsymbol{\theta}) = q, \tag{6.14}$$

where m and q are the selected values for the NSF and SMI, respectively, of the SMA-C(10,40) rule.

The results of our numerical experiments are depicted in Fig. 6.10. Specifically, this figure shows the weighting function of the SMA-C(10,40) rule along with two optimized weighting functions. The first optimized weighting function maintains the same NSF and ALT as the SMA-C(10,40) rule but achieves a higher SMI. On the other hand, the second optimized weighting function preserves the same NSF and SMI as the SMA-C(10,40) rule but with a reduced ALT.

Our findings indicate that it is feasible to enhance the properties of the SMA-C trading rule, albeit only to a negligible extent. For instance, refining the smoothness of the SMA-C(10,40) rule allows us to decrease the probability of position reversal from 3% to 2.8% only. Similarly, by improving the responsiveness of the SMA-C(10,40) rule, we can only reduce the average lag time from 15.7 to 14.7. In summary, our results underscore why the SMA crossover remains the most widely adopted trend-following rule among traders. This crossover relies on the most widely used and intuitive moving average, making it easy to visualize and interpret. Additionally, it strikes a well-balanced tradeoff across all numerical properties, with only limited potential for further improvement.

6.6 Summary

Trend-following investing is widely embraced for its reliance on a relatively simple and clear investment strategy that has demonstrated historical profitability over the long term. However, the key question for investment professionals employing trend-following strategies is: which trading rule proves most effective in tracking financial market trends? Many studies have addressed

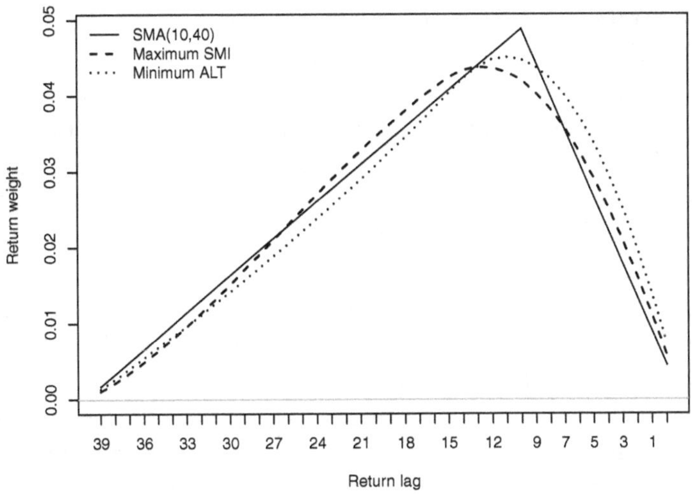

Fig. 6.10 Weighting function of the SMA-C(10,40) rule along with two optimized weighting functions. The first optimized weighting function maintains the same NSF and ALT as the SMA-C(10,40) rule but achieves a higher SMI. The second optimized weighting function preserves the same NSF and SMI as the SMA-C(10,40) but with a reduced ALT

this question by assessing various trend-following rules using historical data, aiming to pinpoint the rule that exhibits superior profitability.

Rather than evaluating the profitability of the trading rules, a few studies have taken a different approach by examining the smoothness and responsiveness of the moving averages incorporated in these rules (examples are Raudys et al. (2013) and Raudys and Pabarškaitė (2018)). The objective was to identify the moving average that strikes the optimal balance between these two properties. Once again, these studies analyzed the parameters of moving averages through historical data.

Previous studies attempting to identify the optimal trading rule and/or the most effective moving average of prices suffer from several drawbacks. First, their outcomes are heavily reliant on the historical data employed in the research. Second, the trading rules (moving averages) under scrutiny often lack the flexibility to encompass the full spectrum of potential trading rules (moving averages). Third, even if a study succeeds in pinpointing the most effective moving average of prices, the trading signal in trend-following rules typically stems from either a price and moving average crossover rule or a double moving average crossover rule. Consequently, there is no assurance that utilizing the best moving average in these rules guarantees the utmost profitability.

In this chapter, we approach the task of uncovering the best trading rule from a distinctly different perspective. More precisely, we aim to determine the optimal trading rule based solely on theoretical considerations. This is feasible because the distinctions among different trading rules ultimately stem from the variations in the return weights. We suggested how to assess quantitatively the accuracy, responsiveness, and smoothness of a trading rule solely based on these return weights. As a result, analytical and numerical techniques can be employed to identify the shape that provides the best combination of all numerical characteristics. It is crucial to emphasize that our approach overcomes all drawbacks of the previous studies on this subject.

Regrettably, to identify the return weights with the optimal combination of all three properties, we must assign appropriate weights to each property in the total score for each combination. This task poses a considerable challenge, given the substantial uncertainty surrounding the precise determination of the importance of each property. Consequently, we address the challenge of determining the optimal trading rule through a step-by-step approach.

First of all, in this chapter, we remind the reader of the shapes of the return weights that optimize individual properties. In the trading rule that maximizes accuracy, the return weights are equal. For the trading rule that maximizes responsiveness, all return weights are concentrated on the most recent return lag. Lastly, the return weights in the trading rule with the highest smoothness derive their form from the first half of a sine wave.

Second, we determine the shapes of return weights in trading rules that provide the best tradeoff between two properties: accuracy and responsiveness, smoothness and responsiveness, and accuracy and smoothness. Intuition proves effective in explaining these shapes. In particular, intuition suggests that the shape of the return weights in the trading rule that offers an efficient tradeoff between smoothness and responsiveness embodies a composite form. This form can be perceived as a blend of the shape maximizing smoothness and the shape maximizing responsiveness. Indeed, in this scenario, the optimal shape represents a smoothed hump inclined toward the most recent return lags.

Likewise, the shape of return weights in the trading rule that achieves a balanced tradeoff between accuracy and responsiveness is primarily concentrated in the most recent return lags. In this instance, the return weights display a pattern where the weights for the most recent lags are equal and large, while the weights for all other lags are also equal but comparatively smaller. Finally, the return weights' shape in the trading rule providing an efficient tradeoff between accuracy and smoothness is a blend of two distinct shapes: the one maximizing accuracy and the one maximizing smoothness.

Third and finally, the shape of the return weights for the efficient trading rule, striking an optimal balance among three properties, can be understood as a blend of two shapes: the shape of the efficient trading rule concerning accuracy and responsiveness and the shape of the efficient trading rule concerning smoothness and responsiveness. An illustrative example of this combined shape is presented in Fig. 6.11, upper panel. Such a shape can be created using diverse trading rules and moving averages. For example, it closely resembles the return weight pattern observed in the double LMA crossover rule, as shown in the lower panel of Fig. 6.11.

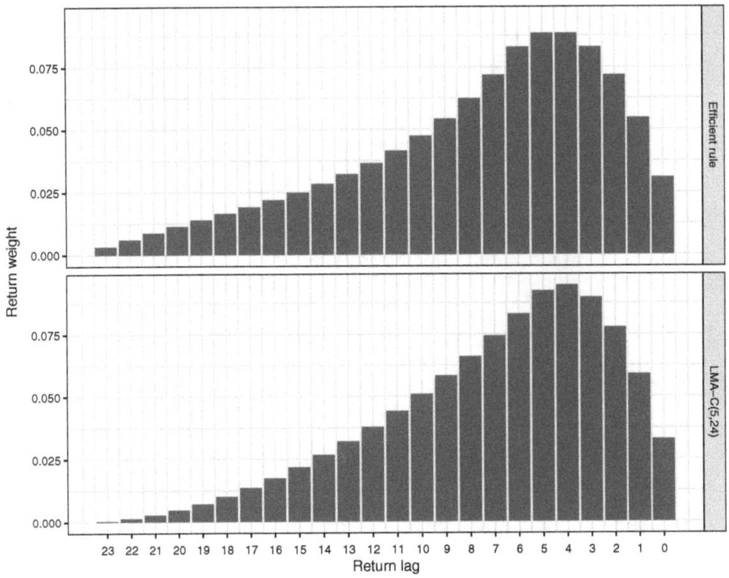

Fig. 6.11 Weighting function of the efficient trading rule with $n = 24$ that strikes the optimal balance between three properties and the weighting function of the LMA-C(5,24) rule

However, even the double SMA crossover rule, widely recognized as the most popular trend-following rule among traders, displays a return weight pattern closely resembling the efficient shape. Notably, our numerical experiments indicate that enhancing the efficiency of this rule is possible, but only to a minimal extent.

Appendix 6.A Proof of Proposition 6.1

A common approach for identifying local maxima and minima of a function subject to equality constraints is the method of Lagrange multipliers. By forming the Lagrangian, we establish that $\boldsymbol{\theta}$ is the solution to the following quadratic program:

$$\min_{\boldsymbol{\theta},\lambda,\gamma} \quad L = \frac{1}{2}\boldsymbol{\theta}'\mathbf{I}\boldsymbol{\theta} + \lambda(1 - \boldsymbol{\theta}'\mathbf{1}) + \gamma\boldsymbol{\theta}'\mathbf{k}.$$

The first-order conditions for optimality are expressed as follows:

$$\frac{\partial L}{\partial \boldsymbol{\theta}} = \mathbf{I}\boldsymbol{\theta} - \lambda\mathbf{1} - \gamma\mathbf{k} = 0, \tag{6.15}$$

$$\frac{\partial L}{\partial \lambda} = 1 - \boldsymbol{\theta}'\mathbf{1} = 0, \tag{6.16}$$

$$\frac{\partial L}{\partial \gamma} = \boldsymbol{\theta}'\mathbf{k} = 0. \tag{6.17}$$

To solve the resulting system of equations, we proceed as follows. Initially, we rewrite condition (6.15) as:

$$\mathbf{I}\boldsymbol{\theta} = \lambda\mathbf{1} + \gamma\mathbf{k}. \tag{6.18}$$

Given that $\mathbf{I}\boldsymbol{\theta} = \boldsymbol{\theta}$, Eq. (6.18) simplifies to:

$$\boldsymbol{\theta} = \lambda\mathbf{1} + \gamma\mathbf{k}. \tag{6.19}$$

It is worth noting that this equation implies that the weights can be expressed as:

$$\boldsymbol{\theta}' = [\underbrace{\lambda + \gamma, \ldots, \lambda + \gamma}_{k \text{ elements}}, \underbrace{\lambda - \gamma, \ldots, \lambda - \gamma}_{n-k \text{ elements}}].$$

To determine the values of λ and γ, we do the following. First, we pre-multiply both sides of Eq. (6.19) by the row vector $\mathbf{1}'$ and get:

$$\mathbf{1}'\boldsymbol{\theta} = \lambda\mathbf{1}'\mathbf{1} + \gamma\mathbf{1}'\mathbf{k}. \tag{6.20}$$

Given that $\mathbf{1}'\boldsymbol{\theta} = 1$, $\mathbf{1}'\mathbf{1} = n$, and $\mathbf{1}'\mathbf{k} = 2k - n$, we can express the resulting equation as:

$$n\lambda + (2k - n)\gamma = 1. \tag{6.21}$$

Second, we pre-multiply both sides of Eq. (6.19) by the row vector $\mathbf{k}'$:

$$\mathbf{k}'\boldsymbol{\theta} = \lambda\mathbf{k}'\mathbf{1} + \gamma\mathbf{k}'\mathbf{k}. \tag{6.22}$$

Given that $\mathbf{k}'\boldsymbol{\theta} = 0$, $\mathbf{1}'\mathbf{k} = 2k - n$, and $\mathbf{k}'\mathbf{k} = n$, the resulting equation becomes:

$$(2k - n)\lambda + n\gamma = 0. \tag{6.23}$$

Finally, to find the values of λ and γ, we must solve a system of two equations with two unknown variables. In matrix notation, this system is represented as:

$$\begin{bmatrix} n & 2k - n \\ 2k - n & n \end{bmatrix} \begin{bmatrix} \lambda \\ \gamma \end{bmatrix} = \begin{bmatrix} 1 \\ 0 \end{bmatrix}.$$

The solutions for λ and γ can be expressed as:

$$\begin{bmatrix} \lambda \\ \gamma \end{bmatrix} = \begin{bmatrix} n & 2k - n \\ 2k - n & n \end{bmatrix}^{-1} \begin{bmatrix} 1 \\ 0 \end{bmatrix},$$

where $\mathbf{A}^{-1}$ denotes the inverse of the matrix $\mathbf{A}$. For a 2×2 matrix, the inverse has a straightforward solution. Utilizing this solution, we find:

$$\begin{bmatrix} \lambda \\ \gamma \end{bmatrix} = \frac{1}{4k(n - k)} \begin{bmatrix} n & n - 2k \\ n - 2k & n \end{bmatrix} \begin{bmatrix} 1 \\ 0 \end{bmatrix}.$$

The final solutions for λ and γ are:

$$\lambda = \frac{n}{4k(n - k)}, \qquad \gamma = \frac{n - 2k}{4k(n - k)}.$$

References

Raudys, A., Lenčiauskas, V., & Malčius, E. (2013). Moving Averages for Financial Data Smoothing. In T. Skersys, R. Butleris, & R. Butkiene (Eds.), *Information and Software Technologies* (pp. 34–45). Springer.

Raudys, A., & Pabarškaitė, Ž. (2018). Optimising the Smoothness and Accuracy of Moving Average for Stock Price Data. *Technological and Economic Development of Economy, 24*(3), 984–1003.

7

Exploring How Negative Weights Impact Trading Rule Properties

7.1 Introduction

Traditional moving averages like Simple Moving Averages (SMA), Linear Moving Averages (LMA), and Exponential Moving Averages (EMA) inherently lag behind price movements. To mitigate or eliminate this lag, traders have proposed various "zero-lag" moving averages.[1] Proponents of these moving averages assert that they can closely follow actual price changes without notable delays, simultaneously offering enhanced smoothness. However, these assertions lack objective support, relying solely on anecdotal evidence and visual examples. No objective evidence has been presented to substantiate these assertions.

The primary reason traditional moving averages are lagging indicators is their reliance on past prices for computation. Interestingly, "zero-lag" moving averages also use past prices, making it seemingly improbable that a moving average can closely track price movements without delay. Despite this, a key distinction lies in the weighting of prices. Traditional moving averages assign positive weights to all prices, while "zero-lag" moving averages incorporate negative weights for many distant prices. As a result, negative price weights are translated into negative return weights within technical indicators for trading rules.

In the previous chapter dedicated to exploring efficient trading rules through optimization techniques, we observed that it is possible to decrease lag time and maintain high smoothness by incorporating negative return weights at

[1] Note that the term "zero-lag" moving average is always written in quotation marks because the trading rules based on these moving averages in reality do not have zero lag times.

V. Zakamulin and J. Giner, *The Ultimate Moving Average Handbook*,
https://doi.org/10.1007/978-3-031-90907-8_7

distant lags. However, it is crucial to recognize that achieving a short delay time and high smoothness comes at the expense of worsening the accuracy of a trading rule. The earlier chapter touched on this subject briefly, and the objective of this chapter is to provide a comprehensive and in-depth discussion of this tradeoff.

In this chapter, we focus on investigating the following questions: what impact do negative return weights at distant lags have on the properties of trading rules? Do "zero-lag" moving averages genuinely exhibit nearly zero delay time? Are these "zero-lag" moving averages genuinely characterized by high smoothness? Lastly, how accurate are "zero-lag" moving averages in practice?

Additionally, there are trend-following rules that go beyond utilizing negative weights at distant lags; they ensure that the sum of all weights equals zero. A notable example of such a rule is the Moving Average Convergence/Divergence (MACD) rule. This chapter also aims to evaluate the properties of these types of rules, including their lag time, smoothness, and accuracy.

7.2 Motivation

To begin the motivation, we want to remind the reader that calculating the trading signal within a trend-following rule can be understood as the computation of a weighted moving average of returns. In particular, the value of the technical trading indicator at time t is computed using n return lags:

$$I_t(n) = \sum_{i=0}^{n-1} \theta_i r_{t-i},$$

where r_{t-i} is the return at lag $i \in [0, n-1]$ and $\{\theta_0, \theta_1, \ldots \theta_{n-1}\}$ are the weights of each return lag. Effectively, the difference between various trading rules arises from utilizing dissimilar return weights.

In this book, we propose that a trading rule should exhibit three essential properties: accuracy, responsiveness, and smoothness. These properties are inherently linked to the weighted moving average of returns, which is precisely defined by the weights assigned to each return lag.

The accuracy of a trading rule is quantified through the Noise Suppression Factor (NSF). This metric assesses the technical indicator's capability to eliminate noise and offer a precise signal for informed trading decisions. The following formula determines the NSF:

$$NSF(I(n)) = \frac{\sum_{i=0}^{n-1} \theta_i}{\sqrt{\sum_{i=0}^{n-1} \theta_i^2}}. \tag{7.1}$$

A higher NSF value indicates a more effective moving average in distinguishing the signal from the noise.

The responsiveness of a trading rule is assessed using the Average Lag Time (ALT). The ALT provides insights into how swiftly the moving average responds to changes in trends, indicating its ability to generate timely trading signals. The following expression determines the ALT for a technical indicator $I(n)$:

$$\arg \min_{k \in [0, n-1]} \sum_{i=0}^{k-1} \theta_i \geq \sum_{i=k}^{n-1} \theta_i. \tag{7.2}$$

In simpler terms, the ALT corresponds to the lag number, denoted as k, where the sum of return weights from lag 0 to lag $k-1$ is greater than or equal to the sum of return weights from lag k to lag $n-1$. Essentially, it is the lag that divides the return weights into two parts, ensuring that the sum of weights in each part is equal. A smaller ALT signifies a more efficient moving average in identifying turning points in trends.

Lastly, the smoothness of a trading rule is evaluated through the Smoothness Index (SMI). The SMI quantifies the degree of smoothness in the moving average, reflecting the stability and consistency of the trading signal over time. The SMI is calculated using the following formula:

$$SMI(I(n)) = \frac{\sum_{i=0}^{n-2} \theta_i \theta_{i+1}}{\sum_{i=0}^{n-1} \theta_i^2}. \tag{7.3}$$

A higher SMI indicates a smoother moving average that produces a more stable signal with fewer trade position reversals.

In conventional trading rules employing standard moving averages like SMA, LMA, and EMA, all return weights are positive. The inherent issue in these trading rules is that it is not possible to decrease the lag time without simultaneously decreasing both accuracy and smoothness. However, numerous exotic moving averages claim to achieve nearly zero lag time while preserving a high level of smoothness.

The common characteristic of these "zero-lag" moving averages is the inclusion of negative values for many distant return weights. Indeed, allowing distant return weights to be negative reduces the ALT of a trading rule. Nevertheless, as highlighted multiple times in this book, enhancing one property of a trading rule invariably comes at the expense of degrading other properties. This motivation aims to illustrate the consequences of improving the responsiveness of a trading rule by incorporating negative weights.

Our motivation employs the MOM(8) trading rule as the initial benchmark for comparison. This trading rule involves $n = 8$ return weights, where all weights are set to 1:

$$\boldsymbol{\theta}_0 = [1, 1, 1, 1, 1, 1, 1, 1].$$

We compute the values of the NSF, ALT, and SMI of this rule and arrive at the following estimates:

$$NSF(\boldsymbol{\theta}_0) = \frac{8}{\sqrt{8}}, \quad ALT(\boldsymbol{\theta}_0) = 4, \quad SMI(\boldsymbol{\theta}_0) = 0.875.$$

It is essential to highlight that this rule attains the highest achievable accuracy for $n = 8$; all other $I(8)$ rules exhibit a lower NSF value than the MOM(8) rule. However, the responsiveness of the MOM(8) rule is quite poor. Specifically, the ALT of the MOM(n) rule equals $n/2$. In our specific case, the ALT is 4.

Now, we alter the weight of the last return lag from 1 to -1. Thus, the return weights for the new trading rule become:

$$\boldsymbol{\theta}_1 = [1, 1, 1, 1, 1, 1, 1, -1].$$

The computed values for the NSF, ALT, and SMI for this rule are as follows:

$$NSF(\boldsymbol{\theta}_1) = \frac{6}{\sqrt{8}}, \quad ALT(\boldsymbol{\theta}_1) = 3, \quad SMI(\boldsymbol{\theta}_1) = 0.625.$$

First, it is crucial to emphasize that the presence of negative weights does not influence the computation of the NSF, ALT, and SMI measures. The formulas in Eqs. (7.1)–(7.3) remain valid even when negative weights are present. Second, compared to the MOM(8) rule, the ALT of the new rule decreases from 4 to 3. This implies that we create a more responsive trading rule by changing the last return weight from positive to negative. However, the NSF of this rule also decreases from $8/\sqrt{8}$ to $6/\sqrt{8}$. In more detail, the NSF equals the sum of weights divided by the square root of the sum of squared weights. Note that now the sum of weights is 6, but the sum of squared weights remains the same as before, equaling 8. The SMI measure of this new rule also decreases from 0.875 to 0.625. Consequently, enhancing responsiveness worsens both accuracy and smoothness.

Continuing in a similar fashion, we replace the last 2 return weights in the MOM(8) rule with -1. Thus, the return weights for the new trading rule are:

$$\boldsymbol{\theta}_2 = [1, 1, 1, 1, 1, 1, -1, -1].$$

The values of the NSF, ATL, and SMI for this rule are:

$$NSF(\boldsymbol{\theta}_2) = \frac{4}{\sqrt{8}}, \quad ALT(\boldsymbol{\theta}_2) = 2, \quad SMI(\boldsymbol{\theta}_2) = 0.625.$$

The ALT of this rule decreases even further from 4 to 2. Simultaneously, the NSF reduces from $8/\sqrt{8}$ to $4/\sqrt{8}$. However, the SMI remains at the same level as that of the rule with only one negative return weight.

Continuing this progression, we replace the last 3 return weights in the MOM(8) rule with -1. The return weights for the resulting rule are:

$$\boldsymbol{\theta}_3 = [1, 1, 1, 1, 1, -1, -1, -1].$$

The values of the NSF, ATL, and SMI for this rule are:

$$NSF(\boldsymbol{\theta}_3) = \frac{2}{\sqrt{8}}, \quad ALT(\boldsymbol{\theta}_3) = 1, \quad SMI(\boldsymbol{\theta}_3) = 0.625.$$

The ALT decreases even further, reaching 1. The NSF also decreases to $2/\sqrt{8}$, but the SMI remains the same as before. Notably, the NSF is now less than 1 because $2/\sqrt{8} \approx 0.71$. The values of the ALT and NSF imply that the responsiveness of this trading rule is comparable to that of the MOM(1) rule, which is based on 1 return observation, but the accuracy is worse. However, while the smoothness of the MOM(1) rule is 0, the smoothness of this rule remains relatively high.

To summarize, we can create an $I(8)$ trading rule that retains the responsiveness of the MOM(1) rule while demonstrating a relatively high level of smoothness. However, the accuracy of this new rule is inferior to that of the MOM(1) rule. Essentially, by incorporating negative weights, we can design a trading rule that matches the responsiveness of the MOM(1) rule while achieving significantly greater smoothness. However, this improvement in smoothness comes at the expense of reduced accuracy.

It is also crucial to highlight that the $I(8)$ rule incorporates 8 return lags, whereas the MOM(1) rule utilizes only one return lag. This implies that for the $I(8)$ rule to function effectively, the duration of the trend must surpass 8 return lags. If the trend duration is shorter than 8 lags, the $I(8)$ rule loses its edge over the MOM(1) rule. In other words, achieving greater smoothness is impossible without increasing the number of return lags in a trading rule. Simultaneously, a greater number of return lags in a trading rule implies that the rule may not operate effectively when the trend duration is short.

In the final step of our progression, we replace the last 4 return weights in the MOM(8) rule with -1. This trading rule is defined by the following weights:

$$\boldsymbol{\theta}_4 = [1, 1, 1, 1, -1, -1, -1, -1].$$

The computation of the NSF, ATL, and SMI for this rule yields the following values:

$$NSF(\boldsymbol{\theta}_4) = 0, \quad ALT(\boldsymbol{\theta}_4) = ?, \quad SMI(\boldsymbol{\theta}_4) = 0.625.$$

Specifically, the NSF of this rule equals 0, indicating zero accuracy. This implies that the Hit ratio of this rule is exactly 50%, and consequently, this trading rule generates random Buy and Sell signals when the trend continues in the same direction. However, the SMI of this rule remains constant at a relatively high level of 0.625. Therefore, although the unconditional probability that this rule generates either a Buy or a Sell signal is 50%, the trading signal shows persistence. For instance, if the last trading signal was Buy, the new trading signal also tends to be Buy. Finally, it is important to note that the ALT for this rule cannot be computed.

The issues with this rule arise from its property that $\sum_{i=0}^{n-1} \theta_i = 0$. In essence, this trading rule does not align with our framework, which is motivated by the two-state regime-switching model for stock market returns. Within our framework, a crucial condition for a meaningful trading rule is that the sum of return weights must be positive. This is imperative to ensure that the trading rule generates a Buy signal during upward trends and a Sell signal during downward trends. Consequently, all trading rules discussed earlier in this section adhere to this requirement, except for the final $I(\boldsymbol{\theta}_4)$ trading rule.

While our definition of the ALT cannot be applied to rules where the sum of return weights is zero, it does not imply that these rules are incapable of generating correct trading signals, at least for a limited period. To elucidate this, let us closely examine the average trading signal of the $I(\boldsymbol{\theta}_4)$ rule when the trend shifts from positive to negative. Before proceeding further, we wish to remind the reader that, in our model, the average market return in a bull market is $\mu > 0$, whereas in a bear market, the mean market return is $-\mu$.

Assume that the price trend remains upward until time t_0. Up to and including time t_0, the average value of the technical indicator can be expressed as:

$$E[I_t(\boldsymbol{\theta}_4)] = \sum_{i=0}^{7} \mu\theta_i = 0.$$

This implies that, on average, the trading signal is neither Buy nor Sell. More precisely, the unconditional probability for both a Buy and a Sell signal is 50%.

At time $t = t_0 + 1$, following the change in the price trend direction, the average value of the technical indicator becomes:

$$E[I_t(\boldsymbol{\theta}_4)] = -\mu \times 1 + \sum_{i=1}^{7} \mu\theta_i = -2\mu < 0.$$

At the subsequent time $t = t_0 + 2$, the average value of the technical indicator is:

$$E[I_t(\boldsymbol{\theta}_4)] = -\mu(1+1) + \sum_{i=2}^{7} \mu\theta_i = -4\mu < 0.$$

Continuing this pattern, the average trading signal from time t_0 to $t_0 + 8$ is as follows:

$$0, -2\mu, -4\mu, -6\mu, -8\mu, -6\mu, -4\mu, -2\mu, 0.$$

In principle, the ALT of this trading rule is 1. However, this trading rule generates on average correct trading signals only over a relatively short time interval of length $n - 1$. Additionally, note the uneven average value of the technical indicator. Initially, it commences at zero at time t_0 and decreases until time $t_0 + 4$, reaching its bottom, before increasing back to zero at time $t_0 + 8$. This pattern implies that the Hit ratio of the technical indicator commences at 50%, attains its peak at time $t_0 + 4$, and ultimately diminishes back to 50%.

It is instructive to compare the average value of the $I(\boldsymbol{\theta}_4)$ indicator with the average value of the $I(\boldsymbol{\theta}_0)$ indicator. The average value of the $I(\boldsymbol{\theta}_0)$ indicator from time t_0 to $t_0 + 8$ is as follows:

$$8\mu, 6\mu, 4\mu, 2\mu, 0, -2\mu, -4\mu, -6\mu, -8\mu.$$

Figure 7.1 illustrates the average reaction to the change in the trend of the technical indicators $I(\boldsymbol{\theta}_0)$ and $I(\boldsymbol{\theta}_4)$. By visually examining the curves in this figure, it becomes evident that the $I(\boldsymbol{\theta}_0)$ indicator, although slow, tends to produce correct trading signals when the trend persists in its direction. On the other hand, the $I(\boldsymbol{\theta}_4)$ indicator, being fast, tends to yield correct trading signals only for a brief period following the turning point in the trend. Hence, within our framework, the technical indicator $I(\boldsymbol{\theta}_4)$ does not identify the direction of the price trend but only detects the times of trend changes.

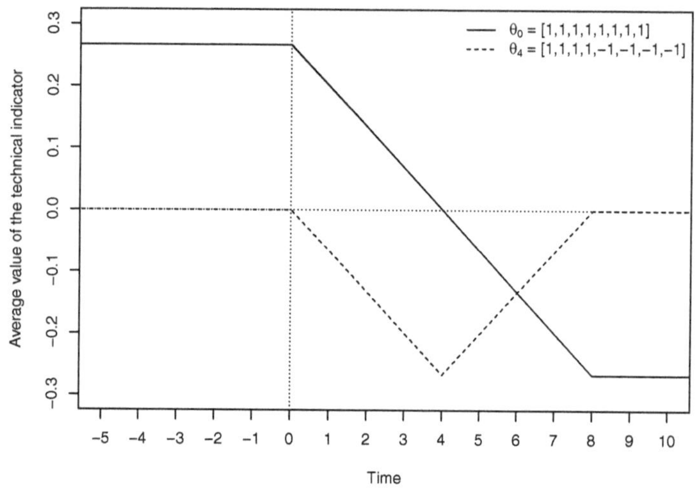

Fig. 7.1 Average reaction to the change in the trend of the trading rule, characterized by the weights $\boldsymbol{\theta}_0 = [1, 1, 1, 1, 1, 1, 1, 1]$ and the trading rule with the weights $\boldsymbol{\theta}_4 = [1, 1, 1, 1, -1, -1, -1, -1]$

Motivated by the high responsiveness of the $I(\boldsymbol{\theta}_4)$ indicator, a trader might be tempted to adopt a trading strategy based on this indicator. Nonetheless, in practical scenarios, the trading signal is contaminated by the noise in data, making it exceptionally challenging to discern whether the $I(\boldsymbol{\theta}_4)$ indicator reflects a genuine trading signal or simply represents random fluctuations caused by noise.

To summarize the implications of incorporating negative weights at distant return lags, it is essential to consider their effects. First, the negative weights effectively reduce the average lag time of the trading rule, potentially bringing it down to 1. However, this reduction in lag time comes at the expense of deteriorating the accuracy of the trading rule in discerning the trend direction. When the average lag time of the trading rule is 1, its accuracy tends to be notably inferior compared to the accuracy achieved by trend detection based on using only one return lag. Nevertheless, this serious drawback is accompanied by a distinct advantage. Specifically, the trading rule with negative weights exhibits considerable smoothness. In other words, negative return weights enable the technical indicator to remain relatively smooth while maintaining high responsiveness. However, it is crucial to note that this heightened responsiveness comes at the cost of notably reduced accuracy.

7.3 Hull Moving Average

In the preceding section, our examination of the impact of negative weights starts with an exploration of the MOM(8) trading rule, where all weights begin as positive. Subsequently, in a step-by-step fashion, we replace the distant return weights with negative values. In this section, we examine a specific example of a "zero-lag" moving average known as the Hull Moving Average (HMA), which Alan Hull introduced in 2005.

To minimize lag time, Hull (2005) proposed a combination of three Linear Moving Averages (LMAs) with different window sizes. The HMA is computed as follows:

$$HMA(n, P) = LMA\left(\sqrt{n}, 2 \times LMA(n/2, P) - LMA(n, P)\right). \quad (7.4)$$

To break it down, the process involves initially computing 2 times the LMA with a window size of $n/2$ and subtracting from it the LMA with a window size of n. Finally, the resulting difference is smoothed using the LMA with a window size of $\sqrt{n}$.

Alan Hull claims that the HMA "almost eliminates lag altogether and manages to improve smoothing simultaneously." Despite making these strong assertions, he does not provide objective evidence to support his statements. Instead, he offers visual representations through graphs, illustrating the values of HMA(n) alongside those of various competing moving averages. While these graphical comparisons offer a qualitative perspective, a more comprehensive approach with quantitative analysis would be beneficial to strengthen the credibility of these claims.

Given the distinct properties of the HMA compared to standard moving averages, it becomes crucial to inquire: how should the HMA be employed in trend-following strategies? Hull provides the answer to this question: "A simple application for the HMA, given its superior smoothing, would be to employ the turning points as entry/exit signals. However, it shouldn't be used to generate crossover signals as this technique relies on lag."

To further clarify Hull's answer and provide a clearer understanding, let us delve into the price and moving average crossover rule, referred to as the P-MA rule in this book. This rule is founded on the concept that a moving average trails behind price movements. Moreover, when the price is on an upward (downward) trend, the moving average is positioned below (above) the price. This relationship is utilized to generate trading signals. However, when a moving average has zero lag time, the conventional P-MA rule becomes ineffective. In this scenario, the only option is to generate trading signals based solely on the direction of the moving average.

Therefore, according to Hull, the HMA is best utilized in the Moving Average Direction rule, or the MA-D rule for short. Specifically, in the HMA-D(n) rule, the trading signal is Buy if the value of HMA(n) increases. Otherwise, the trading signal is Sell.

Hull operates with the concept we refer to as Average Lag Time of a Moving Average (ALT(MA)), which tries to quantify the time lag between the price and its moving average. To provide context, a general moving average is computed as follows:

$$MA_t(n, P) = \frac{\sum_{i=0}^{n-1} w_i \times P_{t-i}}{\sum_{i=0}^{n-1} w_i}, \tag{7.5}$$

where w_i represents the weight of price P_{t-i} in the calculation of the moving average.

The ALT(MA) is determined by the formula:

$$\text{ALT}(MA(n)) = \frac{\sum_{i=1}^{n-1} w_i \times i}{\sum_{i=0}^{n-1} w_i}. \tag{7.6}$$

The ALT(MA) formula implies that it is possible to reduce the lag time of a moving average by incorporating negative price weights.

It is important to note that the MA-D rule possesses a noteworthy property: the return weights in the MA-D(n) rule mirror the same pattern as the price weights in the corresponding MA(n). In essence, the return weights in the MA-D rule represent a rescaled version of the price weights in the corresponding MA.

The formula for the HMA, as given in Eq. (7.4), does not explicitly indicate the presence of negative price weights. The existence of negative weights becomes apparent only after the computation of the price weights in the HMA. To illustrate, Fig. 7.2 showcases the return weights in the HMA-D(40) rule. The weight pattern resembles a damped sine wave. This pattern, familiar from earlier discussions in this book, suggests that the smoothness of the HMA is likely to be quite effective.

The issue lies in the fact that the ALT(MA) provides limited insights into the average lag time for turning point identification. Particularly, in the presence of negative weights, the ALT(MA) may present a significantly inaccurate repre-

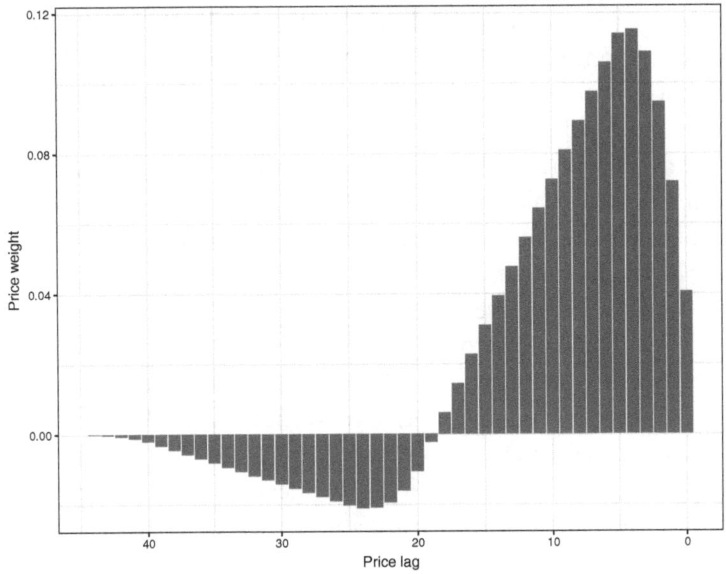

Fig. 7.2 Return weights of the HMA-D(40) rule. This return weights mirror the price weights in the HMA(40)

sentation of the responsiveness of a moving average. Our alternative measure, that can be denoted as the Average Lag Time of a Trading Rule, ALT(TR), offers a correct numerical characterization of the average delay time from the change in trend to the change in the trading signal. To illustrate these points, we compare the parameters of the HMA-D(40) and the P-SMA(19) rules. It is worth noting that the former rule is based on the direction of the 40-period HMA, while the latter rule is the price and 19-period SMA crossover rule.

Table 7.1 outlines the relevant parameters, which include the ALT(MA)s of the HMA-D(40) and P-SMA(19) trading rules, as well as their ALT(TR)s. The HMA-D(40) has a significantly lower ALT(MA) than the P-SMA(19) (1.33 periods versus 9.00 periods). However, the HMA-D(40) and P-SMA(19) rules show very similar ALT(TR) values (5.61 periods and 5.71 periods, respectively).

Table 7.1 ALT(MA)s and ALT(TR)s of the HMA-D(40) and P-SMA(19) trading rules

Parameter	HMA-D(40)	P-SMA(19)
ALT(MA)	1.33	9.00
ALT(TR)	5.61	5.71

In summary, based on their ALT(MA)s, the HMA-D(40) rule appears to be much more responsive than the P-SMA(19) rule. Why are the HMA-D(40) and P-SMA(19) trading rules equally responsive to the changes in the trend? The answer is provided by the illustration in Fig. 7.3. Specifically, this figure depicts the average price dynamics over a turning point between an increasing and a decreasing trend, along with the HMA(40) and SMA(19) of prices. When prices display a well-established trend, the HMA(40) indeed exhibits minimal lag time. However, immediately after a turning point, the HMA(40) continues to rise for a period before eventually reversing. This behavior, known as "overshooting," is a characteristic of all "zero-lag" moving averages. Consequently, due to overshooting, detecting a trend turning point takes a substantially longer time lag compared to the ALT(MA). The vertical dashed line in the plot indicates the time when the HMA-D(40) rule starts generating a Sell trading signal. Notably, the P-SMA(19) rule, which generates a Sell trading signal when the price crosses the SMA of prices from above, also exhibits virtually the same ALT(TR).

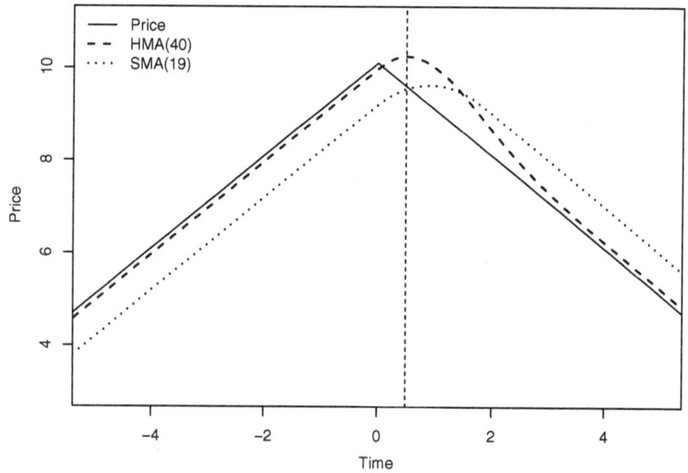

Fig. 7.3 This figure depicts the average price dynamics over a turning point between an increasing and a decreasing trend, along with the HMA(40) and SMA(19) of prices. The vertical dashed line in the plot marks the moment when the HMA-D(40) rule switches the trading signal

The notion of the ALT(MA) is extremely confusing because it creates an illusion that it is possible to construct moving averages with zero lag times. However, ALT(MA) is applicable only in situations where the price trend is firmly established and remains unchanged. When the trend undergoes a reversal, the ALT(MA) measure loses its relevance until the new trend becomes distinctly apparent. For instance, in our case study involving the HMA(40), the actual delay time in turning point identification is much higher than the calculated ALT(MA) of this moving average.

Before we continue, it is important to clarify that the length of the HMA(n) is not solely n lags but rather $n + \sqrt{n} - 1$ lags. This adjustment is necessary because the HMA is a moving average derived from $\sqrt{n}$ lags of another moving average based on n observations. Therefore, in the case of the HMA-D(40), the number of return lags is 45, not 40, accounting for the additional lag due to the square root term.

It is worth mentioning that the HMA-D trading rule exhibits proximity to an efficient trading rule. To elaborate, if we maintain a fixed number of return lags in the trading rule and employ numerical optimization methods to identify a trading rule with equivalent ALT and SMI values as the HMA-D rule but with a higher NSF value, the observed increase in the NSF measure is minimal. Similarly, if we find a trading rule with ALT and NSF values equivalent to the HMA-D rule but with a higher SMI value, the observed increase in the SMI measure is marginal.

Since our goal in this chapter is to explore the effects of negative weights, we want to compare the HMA-D(40) rule with a trading rule where all return weights are positive and this trading rule must possess properties as close as possible to the properties of the HMA-D(40). The results of the previous chapter suggest that a double LMA crossover (LMA-C) rule is a rule with a good combination of the accuracy, responsiveness, and smoothness. We find that LMA-C(4,20) rule is probably the rule closest to the HMA-D(40) rule according to our criteria.

Table 7.2 presents the parameters for both competing rules. This table not only includes the NSF and SMI values but also incorporates the Hit ratio and the Probability of position reversal. These additional quantities are particularly significant as they are the primary parameters of interest, demonstrating a highly non-linear dependence on NSF and SMI. Notably, the HMA-D(40) and LMA-C(4,20) rules exhibit nearly identical ALT values. Despite this similarity, the HMA-D(40) rule is characterized by greater smoothness, while the LMA-C(4,20) rule is noted for higher accuracy. However, it is essential to acknowledge that the differences in smoothness and accuracy measures are relatively small.

Table 7.2 Parameters of the HMA-D(40) and the LMA-C(4,20) rules

Parameter	HMA-D(40)	LMA-C(4,20)
Number of lags	45	20
NSF	3.00	3.59
Hit ratio, %	80.67	85.00
ALT	5.61	5.53
SMI	0.98	0.97
Probability of reversion, %	6.41	7.93

In Fig. 7.4, the upper panel showcases the return weights in the HMA-D(40) rule, while the lower panel illustrates the return weights in the LMA-C(4,20) rule. Loosely speaking, the return weights in the LMA-C(4,20) rule replicate the pattern observed in the positive weights of the HMA-D(40) rule. One significant implication of this coincidence is that the number of return lags in the LMA-C(4,20) rule is considerably smaller than that of the HMA-D(40) rule.

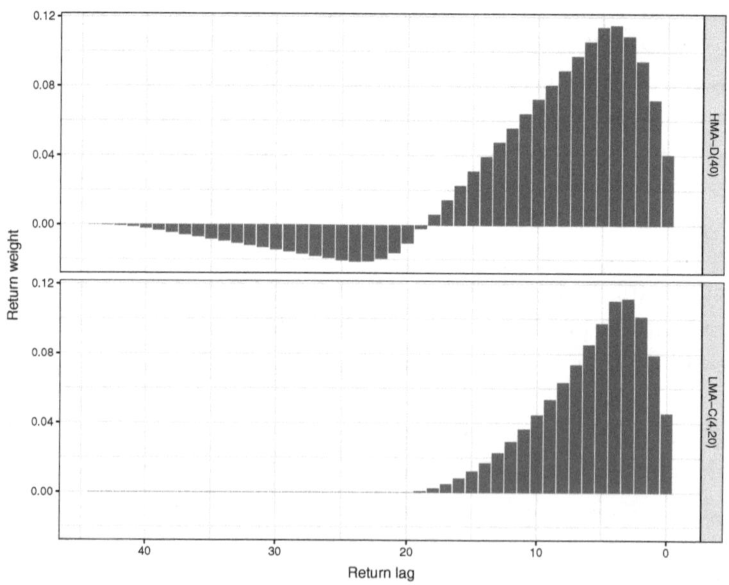

Fig. 7.4 Return weights of the HMA-D(40) and the LMA-C(4,20) rules

The primary distinction between the return weights in the HMA-D(40) and LMA-C(4,20) rules lies in the presence of additional negative weights in the HMA-D(40) rule, specifically from lag 20 to lag 44. These negative weights result in decreased accuracy for the HMA-D(40) rule compared to the LMA-C(4,20) rule, but they contribute to increased smoothness. These outcomes are directly evident from the numerical values provided in Table 7.2.

While Table 7.2 offers valuable insights into the comparative advantages of the two competing rules, it presents a static perspective. Examining these rules in dynamic settings adds another layer of interest. Figure 7.5 illustrates the mean returns and the reactions of the HMA-D(40) and LMA-C(4,20) technical indicators to changes in mean return values. In this scenario, return weights in both rules are normalized, ensuring $\sum_{i=0}^{n-1} \theta_i = 1$. Assuming a mean return of $\mu = 0.2$ until time $t_0 = 0$, the mean return subsequently shifts to $\mu = -0.2$ from time t_0 onward. The dotted line in the figure represents mean return values, with t_0 corresponding to the peak in the price trend. The other lines depict the responses of the HMA-D(40) and LMA-C(4,20) technical indicators to the change in the price trend.

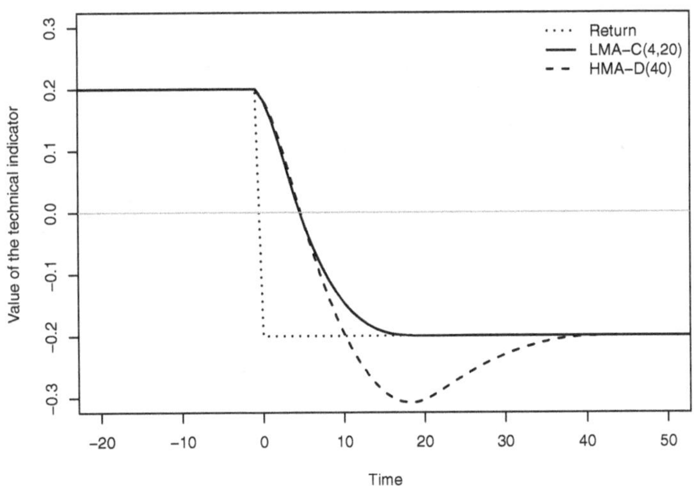

Fig. 7.5 Change in the mean returns and the values of the HMA-D(40) and LMA-C(4,20) technical indicators

It is crucial to highlight that, although the mean returns instantaneously transition from μ to $-\mu$, the LMA-C(4,20) technical indicator exhibits a gradual and monotonic decrease from μ to $-\mu$. Following a trend change, the HMA-D(40) technical indicator also initiates a gradual decrease; however, this decline is non-monotonic. Specifically, the HMA-D(40) indicator first decreases below $-\mu$ and then rebounds to settle at $-\mu$. This phenomenon can also be called "overshooting" and is observed in all "zero-lag" moving averages. The underlying cause of this effect is attributed solely to the presence of negative weights associated with distant return values.

The upper panel in Fig. 7.6 depicts the dynamic response of the HMA-D(40) and LMA-C(4,20) technical indicators to the trend change at time $t_0 = 0$. In contrast to the previous discussion, this panel illustrates the Hit ratios of the two competing indicators. Before time 0, the Hit ratio of the LMA-C(4,20) technical indicator surpasses that of the HMA-D(40) indicator. Following a trend change, both Hit ratios decline to a very low level before gradually rebounding. While the Hit ratio of the LMA-C(4,20) indicator increases gradually and monotonically, the Hit ratio of the HMA-D(40) indicator follows a non-monotonic trajectory and, for a certain duration, exceeds the Hit ratio of the LMA-C(4,20) indicator. In essence, over a relatively short period after a trend change, the HMA-D(40) indicator provides more accurate trading signals than the LMA-C(4,20) indicator.

The fundamental question at hand pertains to determining the superior trading rule. Regrettably, providing a definitive answer proves challenging. The LMA-C(4,20) trading rule demonstrates greater efficiency in terms of accuracy and responsiveness compared to the HMA-D(40) rule. Conversely, the HMA-D(40) trading rule showcases superior efficiency concerning smoothness and responsiveness compared to the LMA-C(4,20) rule. In scenarios where transaction costs carry significant weight, the HMA-D(40) rule may be advantageous over the LMA-C(4,20) rule. Conversely, when transaction costs are present but not as substantial, the LMA-C(4,20) rule could emerge as the more favorable choice.

In concluding this section, it is crucial to highlight another significant advantage of the LMA-C(4,20) rule over the HMA-D(40) rule. This advantage becomes apparent not from the comparison of numerical properties, but from the comparison of the number of return lags in each rule. Specifically, the former rule calculates the trading signal using 20 return lags, while the latter relies on 45 return lags for its trading signal computation. This substantial difference in the number of return lags positions the LMA-C(4,20) rule as superior to the HMA-D(40) rule, especially in scenarios where the trend changes direction frequently. The lower panel of Fig. 7.6 illustrates this point. In this particular scenario, the trend shifts direction at both time 0 and time 10. Notably, the Hit ratios of the two rules remain practically identical between times 1 and 11. However, beyond this period, the Hit ratio of the LMA-C(4,20) rule increases much faster than that of the HMA-D(40) rule. Consequently, the LMA-C(4,20) rule exhibits a significantly swifter response to the second change in the trend compared to the HMA-D(40) rule.

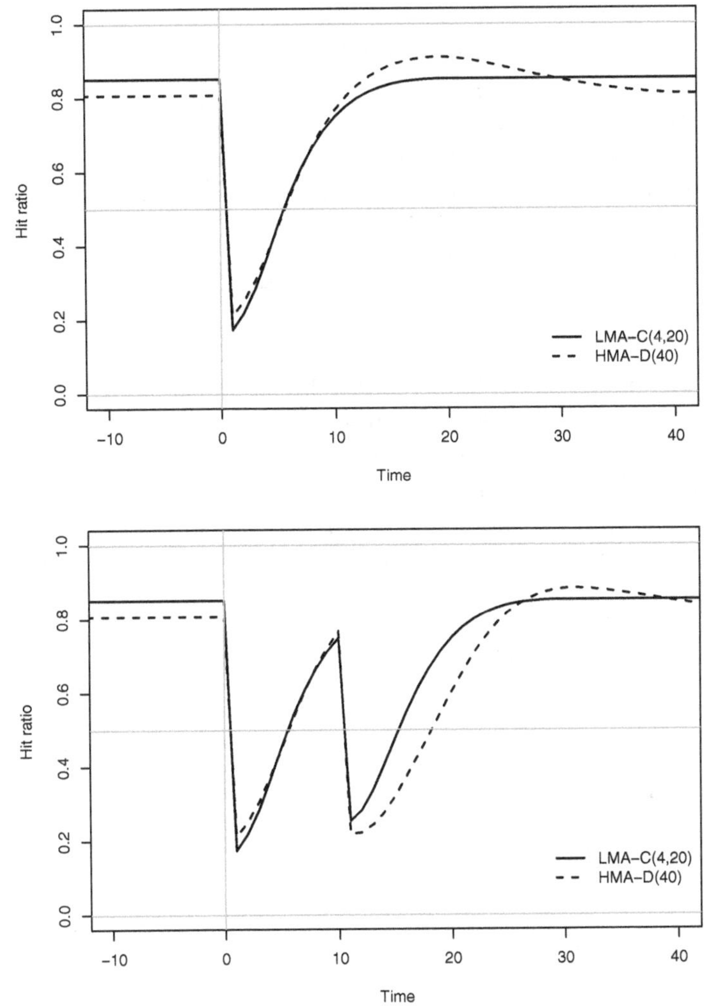

Fig. 7.6 Dynamics of the Hit ratios for the HMA-D(40) and LMA-C(4,20) technical indicators. The upper panel illustrates the dynamics of the Hit ratios when the trend changes direction at time 0. Meanwhile, the lower panel presents the dynamics of the Hit ratios in a scenario where the trend changes its direction at both time 0 and time 10

7.4 Moving Average Convergence/Divergence Rule

The MACD trading rule, proposed by Gerald Appel (2005), involves the computation of a technical trading indicator using three Exponential Moving Averages (EMAs). In the initial step, the double EMA crossover of prices is calculated as follows:

$$\text{EMA-C}_t(s, l) = EMA_t(s, P) - EMA_t(l, P),$$

where s and l represent the sizes of the shorter and longer averaging windows. In the subsequent step, the trading signal is determined as the difference between the double EMA crossover and the smoothed version of this crossover:

$$MACD(s, l, n) = \underbrace{\text{EMA-C}_t(s, l)}_{\text{MACD line}} - \underbrace{EMA_t(n, \text{EMA-C}(s, l))}_{\text{signal line}},$$

where n denotes the size of the smoothing window. It is important to note that in practice, the EMA employs an infinite averaging window size, and the values of s, l, and n are utilized to compute the decay constants.

The EMA-C(s, l) is commonly referred to as the "MACD line," and its smoothed counterpart, the EMA$(n$, EMA-C$(s, l))$, is known as the "signal line." A "MACD crossover" happens when there is a crossing of the MACD and signal lines.

In the return-based formulation, the technical indicator of the MACD rule is computed according to the formula given by Zakamulin (2017), Chap. 5:

$$I_t^{\text{MACD}}(s, l, n) = \sum_{j=0}^{\infty} \left[\left(\lambda_l^j - \lambda_s^j\right) - (1 - \lambda_n) \left(\frac{\lambda_l^j - \lambda_n^j}{1 - \frac{\lambda_n}{\lambda_l}} - \frac{\lambda_s^j - \lambda_n^j}{1 - \frac{\lambda_n}{\lambda_s}} \right) \right] r_{t-j}, \tag{7.7}$$

where r_{t-j} is the return at lag j, and the decay constants are defined as:

$$\lambda_l = \frac{l-1}{l+1}, \quad \lambda_s = \frac{s-1}{s+1}, \quad \lambda_n = \frac{n-1}{n+1}.$$

The window sizes s, l, and n in this context are typically measured in days. Commonly adopted values for these windows are 12, 26, and 9 days. Thus, the prevailing and widely employed MACD trading rule is often referred to as the MACD(12,26,9) rule. Figure 7.7 illustrates the return weights associated with the MACD(12,26,9) rule.

The MACD indicator stands out as one of the least comprehended and most debated among all trend-following indicators. Various recommendations exist regarding how to trade using the MACD line and the signal line. First, the MACD indicator can function as a conventional trend-following indicator. In this scenario, the crossover of the two lines produces trading signals akin to a double moving average system. More precisely, a Buy signal is generated when the MACD line crosses above the signal line, while a Sell signal is indicated when the MACD line crosses below the signal line.

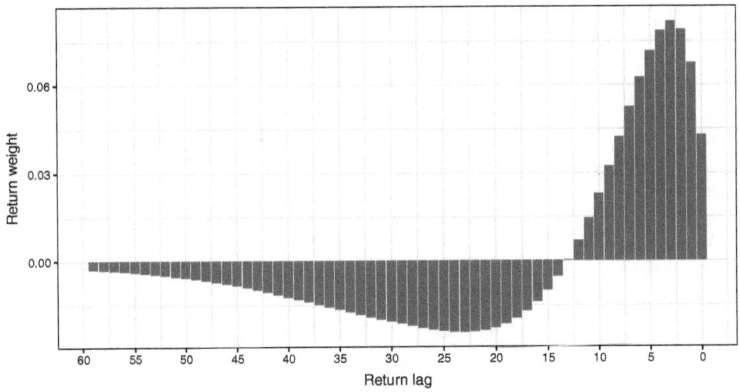

Fig. 7.7 Return weights in the MACD(12,26,9) rule. The return weights are cut off at lag 60

The second strategy takes a contrarian stance compared to the first. In this approach, traders view the MACD indicator not as a trend-following tool but as an indicator revealing overbought and oversold conditions. Overbought conditions arise when the MACD line is notably above the signal line, while oversold conditions occur when the MACD line is considerably below the signal line. Traders can leverage these signals for entering or exiting positions.

Third and finally, some traders employ the MACD to pinpoint shifts in the direction or strength of a price trend. In this perspective, the MACD aids in recognizing instances where the recent momentum in a price suggests a potential alteration in its fundamental trend. This information assists traders in making decisions on when to enter, augment, or exit a position.

Our framework aligns with the perspective that the MACD identifies instances of shifts in the price trend. To elaborate, the sum of all return weights in the MACD indicator equals zero, as demonstrated in Zakamulin (2017), Chap. 5. In other words, in this indicator, $\sum_{j=0}^{\infty} \theta_j = 0$. Hence, within our framework, the MACD is not classified as a trend-following indicator, given its zero accuracy in determining the trend direction when the trend continues.

Simultaneously, the MACD indicator is distinguished by its high smoothness, a deduction drawn from the damped sine-wave form of its return weights. The ALT of the MACD indicator equals 1, a common characteristic among all technical indicators where the sum of all return weights adds up to zero. However, it is worth noting that the MACD tends to provide accurate trading signals only for a relatively brief period following a shift in the trend. Figure 7.8 visually illustrates this aspect, depicting the average response of the MACD(12,26,9) indicator to a shift in the trend from bullish to bearish.

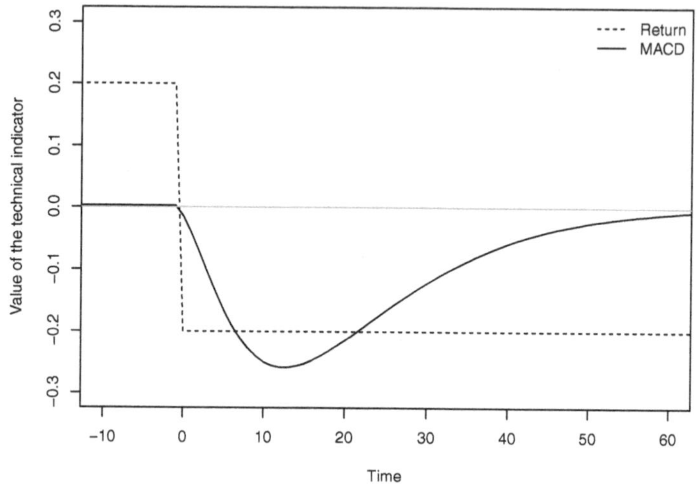

Fig. 7.8 Average reaction of the MACD(12,26,9) indicator to the change in the trend from bullish to bearish

In conclusion, this section aims to demonstrate trading with the MACD(12,26,9) indicator. To enhance clarity, we have used artificially generated stock prices throughout the illustration. These prices simulate both bull and bear market states, which alternate every 60 days. It is important to note that the stock price volatility in our simulation is intentionally set lower than real-world volatility, allowing for a clearer visualization of stock price trends.

Figure 7.9 presents an example of trading using the MACD indicator as a conventional trend-following tool. In this case, the buy and sell signals are generated when the MACD line crosses above or below the signal line. In the upper panel, the stock prices, as well as the 12- and 26-day EMAs, are displayed. The middle panel exhibits the MACD and signal lines, while the bottom panel represents the technical indicator's value, which is the difference between the MACD and signal lines. The shaded areas in the upper panel highlight the periods when a Sell signal is produced using this rule.

The simulated stock prices in our illustration contain a total of four periods with a downward trend. These include three complete bear states and one bear state that begins near the end of the simulated prices. Surprisingly, the MACD(12,26,9) indicator generates a Sell signal during ten periods when used as a conventional trend-following indicator. Not only does the MACD indicator generate more Sell signals than the number of downward trends, but it also produces sell signals during relatively extended periods in the first and second upward trends of the prices.

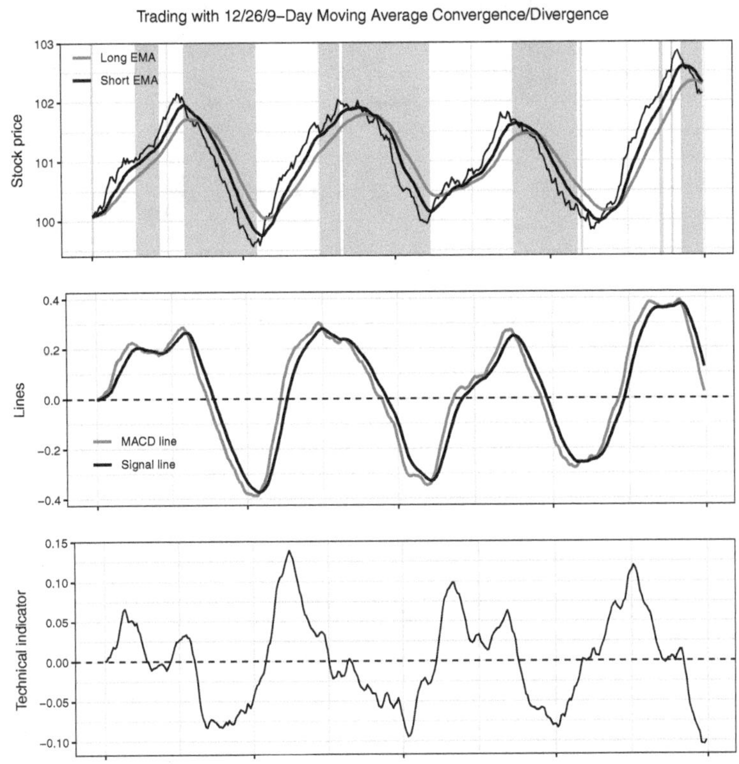

Fig. 7.9 Trading using the MACD(12,26,9) indicator as a conventional trend-following tool. The Sell signal is generated when the Signal line is above the MACD line; in this case the value of the technical indicator is negative. The shaded areas in the upper panel represent the periods during which this rule generates a Sell signal

Figure 7.10 presents an example of using the MACD indicator to detect shifts in the direction of price trends. As illustrated in Fig. 7.8, the MACD technical indicator's value is largest (in absolute value) immediately following a trend shift. The central idea in this type of trading is to observe instances of trend changes based on abnormally high or low values of the technical indicator. In this strategy, a Buy signal is generated when the technical indicator's value crosses the upper threshold from below. A subsequent Sell signal is triggered when the value crosses the lower threshold from above, as demonstrated in the bottom panel of Fig. 7.10. To determine the threshold values, this approach should be backtested using past data to select the values that optimize the accuracy and performance of the MACD indicator.

Observing the upper panel of Fig. 7.10, we can see that the MACD(12,26,9) indicator generates a Sell signal during four periods when used to identify trend shifts. This number aligns with the four downward trends observed in the stock

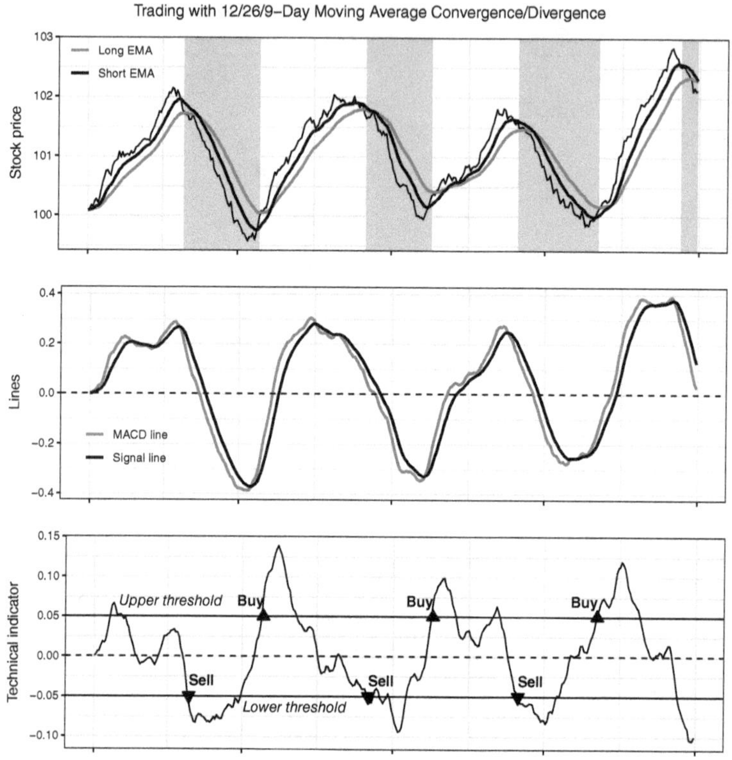

Fig. 7.10 Trading using the MACD(12,26,9) indicator to detect shifts in the direction of price trends. The Sell signal is generated when the value of the technical indicator crosses the lower threshold from above. The subsequent Buy signal is generated when the value of the technical indicator crosses the upper threshold from below. The shaded areas in the upper panel represent the periods during which this rule generates a Sell signal

prices. Consequently, the strategy that utilizes the MACD indicator to detect shifts in price trends is potentially more profitable than the approach that uses the MACD indicator as a conventional trend-following tool.

7.5 Conclusions

In traditional moving averages, both lag time and smoothness increase as the number of lags rises. Essentially, employing a smaller number of lags in a moving average can reduce its lag time. For instance, a 5-day Simple Moving Average (SMA) is more responsive than its 25-day counterpart. However, this improved responsiveness comes at the cost of a less smooth trajectory when compared to the 25-day SMA. At first glance, achieving high responsiveness and good smoothing simultaneously in a moving average seems impossible. This is because, for a smooth result, a higher number of lags is necessary, while responsiveness requires a smaller number of lags.

Nevertheless, there is an ingenious approach to constructing a moving average that excels in both responsiveness and smoothness. In this method, maintaining a relatively high number of lags ensures smoothness in the moving average. To enhance responsiveness while keeping a high number of lags, negative weights are assigned to distant lags. Essentially, recent lags in a moving average carry positive weights, whereas distant lags receive negative weights. This technique is employed in the creation of all "zero-lag" moving averages. Implicitly, these moving averages incorporate a relatively high number of lags along with negative weights assigned to distant lags.

In this chapter, we explored the Hull Moving Average (HMA), a widely recognized example of a "zero-lag" moving average. Despite the asserted instant responsiveness, our analysis uncovers that the average lag time of the trading rule using HMA falls significantly short of being zero. Nevertheless, we affirm that the trading rule based on HMA approaches efficiency in terms of responsiveness and smoothness. Regrettably, this efficiency does not extend to responsiveness and accuracy, as the pursuit of high responsiveness and smoothness comes at the expense of accuracy.

In principle, certain market conditions may justify enhancing the smoothness properties of a trading rule at the expense of its accuracy. This scenario could be relevant when trading costs pose a substantial challenge, significantly impacting the profitability of the trading rule. In such cases, high responsiveness and smoothness advantages may outweigh the drawbacks. It is essential for traders to consider, however, that "zero-lag" moving averages rely on a relatively high number of lags to achieve smoothness. Consequently, these moving averages may struggle to respond accurately to frequent changes in market trends.

Increasing the proportion of negative weights in a moving average enhances smoothness but diminishes accuracy. However, a critical requirement for a sensible trend-following rule is that the sum of return weights must be positive. This condition ensures that the trading signal is Buy during bullish trends and Sell during bearish trends. Interestingly, some trading rules, like the Moving Average Convergence/Divergence (MACD) rule, have a sum of weights equal to zero. While our analysis indicates that the MACD rule is highly responsive and smooth, its accuracy is zero. Nevertheless, the MACD rule still manages to generate correct trading signals, particularly in the short period following a change in trend. Consequently, within our framework, the MACD rule is not strictly a trend-following rule but rather a rule that identifies shifts in the direction of a price trend.

References

Appel, G. (2005). Technical Analysis Power Tools for Active Investors. *Financial Times.* Prentice Hall.

Hull, A. (2005). How to Reduce Lag in a Moving Average. http://www.alanhull.com/hull-moving-average, [Online; Retrieved 27 January, 2024]

Zakamulin, V. (2017). *Market Timing with Moving Averages: The Anatomy and Performance of Trading Rules.* Springer.

Part III

Exotic Moving Averages and Digital Filters

8

Moving Averages with Enhanced Smoothness

8.1 Introduction

The primary purpose of using a moving average of prices is to smooth out price fluctuations and highlight the trend direction. With this in mind, the key requirement for a moving average is high smoothness. The rationale behind this is straightforward: the smoother the moving average, the clearer the market's overall direction. A highly smooth moving average enables traders to more easily identify whether the market is in an uptrend or a downtrend.

The conventional moving averages include the Simple Moving Average (SMA), Linear Moving Average (LMA), and Exponential Moving Average (EMA). They are termed conventional because traders have used them for a long time. However, many traders feel that these conventional moving averages lack sufficient smoothness. Over the years, traders have developed various types of moving averages that are believed to provide better smoothing properties compared to standard options like the SMA, LMA, and EMA.

A simple approach to enhance smoothness involves smoothing a moving average with another moving average, resulting in what is commonly referred to as a "double-smoothed moving average." This newly derived moving average can undergo further smoothing by yet another moving average, creating a "triple-smoothed moving average." This iterative smoothing process can be repeated as needed. Traders argue that these moving averages exhibit superior properties, but their assertion is primarily based on anecdotal evidence.

The creation of moving averages with improved smoothness has, until now, relied primarily on ad hoc ideas and intuition. While traders agree that a moving average should be both smooth and responsive, they have only had a quantitative measure for responsiveness, known as the average lag time of the

V. Zakamulin and J. Giner, *The Ultimate Moving Average Handbook*,
https://doi.org/10.1007/978-3-031-90907-8_8

moving average. As a result, while measuring the responsiveness of a moving average was possible, assessing its smoothness was not feasible.

The development of moving averages with enhanced smoothness has been perplexing for several reasons. First, traders have discussed smoothness and proposed moving averages with improved smoothness without having a method to measure it. Second, they have often equated high smoothness with high accuracy in trend identification, assuming the two are the same. Third, when traders suggest moving averages with better smoothing properties, they frequently overlook the importance of responsiveness. In other words, achieving better smoothness does not automatically ensure better responsiveness. Focusing solely on smoothness while ignoring responsiveness is a mistake.

This book was inspired by the strong need for quantitative measures that can objectively evaluate the properties of trend-following rules based on moving averages. It is important to emphasize that measuring the properties of individual moving averages is of limited interest because trend-following signals typically arise from the relationship between the price and the moving average or the interaction between multiple moving averages. Therefore, the focus should shift to assessing the properties of trend-following rules rather than the characteristics of individual moving averages used in these rules.

In this book, we introduce three novel quantitative measures to evaluate the accuracy and responsiveness of trend-following rules based on moving averages, as well as the smoothness of the trading signals generated by these rules. The availability of these quantitative metrics allows us, for the first time, to examine various moving averages that are believed to have high smoothness. The ultimate goal of our analysis is to determine whether using these moving averages instead of traditional ones can actually improve the efficiency of trend-following rules.

8.2 Evaluating the Effectiveness of Moving Averages with Enhanced Smoothness

There are three main ways to enhance the smoothness of a moving average. The first and most straightforward method is to increase the averaging window size in traditional moving averages, such as SMA, LMA, or EMA. A larger window averages more data points, which helps to reduce short-term fluctuations and random noise. However, many traders believe that the price weighting methods used in the conventional moving averages do not achieve effective smoothing, highlighting the need for more advanced techniques.

The second and the most theoretically sound method focuses on finding the optimal price weights in a moving average that offers the best smoothing for a given window size. However, this approach requires a conceptually justified quantitative measure to assess the smoothness of a moving average. Until now, no such measure existed. This book introduces such a measure for the first time.

The third method to improve the smoothness of a moving average is to apply the moving average two or more times. By applying smoothing multiple times, each successive layer averages out fluctuations that existed in the previous iteration. This layered approach helps to reduce noise further and refine the trend.

Each method of enhancing smoothness has its drawbacks. One apparent drawback can be explained using the well-known measure of average lag time of the moving average. For instance, in a conventional moving average, the average lag time is calculated as $k \times n$, where n is the averaging window size and k is a positive constant, typically less than one half. As a result, increasing the averaging window size in a conventional moving average improves smoothing but also increases the delay time.

Each repeated application of the moving average increases the number of data points used in the calculation. As we will demonstrate later in this chapter, applying the moving average multiple times is equivalent to using a single moving average with modified price weights and a longer averaging window. Thus, the improved smoothness from several applications of the moving average is partly due to the larger window size. Generally, increasing the window size also increases the average lag time in any moving average.

However, as we repeatedly emphasize in this book, the key mistake traders make when assessing moving averages is focusing solely on the properties of individual moving averages. In practice, trading signals in trend-following strategies based on moving averages are almost never triggered by the value of a single moving average alone. Instead, these signals are typically generated by the relation between the price and the moving average or between two or more moving averages. Therefore, the traders should shift focus to studying the properties of trading rules based on moving averages.

In this book, we argue that a trend-following rule should demonstrate three key properties: accuracy, responsiveness, and smoothness. While smoothness is important, it is only one of several key characteristics. Substituting a conventional moving average with one that offers better smoothness could risk reducing the rule's accuracy and responsiveness. The goal of this chapter is not only to review various types of moving averages with improved smoothness but also to evaluate which type is the most effective. More importantly, we want to examine whether incorporating these moving averages into trend-following rules can enhance their overall efficiency.

The generation of trading signals in each trend-following rule based on moving averages can be formalized using mathematical expressions that involve past prices and their corresponding weights. Such an expression defines the technical indicator of a trend-following rule. Instead of using past prices, the technical indicator can also be calculated based on past returns. Specifically, the value of the return-based technical indicator at time t is computed using n return lags as follows:

$$I_t(n) = \sum_{i=0}^{n-1} \theta_i r_{t-i},$$

where r_{t-i} represents the return at lag i, and $\{\theta_0, \theta_1, \ldots, \theta_{n-1}\}$ are the weights assigned to each return lag. These return weights are derived from the price weights.

Our comparison methodology can be illustrated using two rules defined by the technical indicators $I_1(n)$ and $I_2(m)$. Each technical indicator utilizes a different set of return weights and a dissimilar number of return lags. Both rules can use different types of moving averages with enhanced smoothness. Alternatively, one rule may use conventional moving averages, while the other uses moving averages with improved smoothness.

The question we want to answer is which of the two competing rules is the most effective. We compare the properties of the rules using novel quantitative measures that evaluate trading rule characteristics. The first measure is the Noise Suppression Factor (NSF), which assesses the accuracy of a trading rule in identifying the trend direction. The second measure is the Average Lag Time (ALT), which evaluates the average delay between a trend turning point and a change in the trading signal. The third measure is the Smoothness Index (SMI), which assesses the persistence of the trading signal. These measures are based solely on the return weights in a technical indicator, meaning that the performance of a trading rule is determined entirely by the shape of the return weights or the return weighting function.

When evaluating different trading rules, it is crucial to consider multiple metrics at once rather than relying on just one. It is also impossible to use all three quantitative measures simultaneously for comparisons. Previous analysis in this book indicates that no single trading rule excels in all three measures. Therefore, it is better to use a two-metric comparison approach. We recommend evaluating trading rules using the ALT and SMI measures, as well as the ALT and NSF measures, as this approach is both simple and logical.

Our comparison aims to identify a trading rule that effectively balances responsiveness and smoothness, as well as responsiveness and accuracy. For instance, when using the ALT and SMI measures, we aim to find a rule that delivers the greatest smoothness at a given level of responsiveness or the best responsiveness at a specified level of smoothness.

To ensure that the parameters n and m do not affect the selection of the optimal trading rule, we standardize the comparison process. We begin by varying n and m and calculating the ALT and SMI measures for each rule. We then plot a curve in the ALT-SMI space for each trading rule. These curves illustrate the tradeoff between responsiveness and smoothness for each rule. If one curve consistently lies above another, the corresponding trading rule is deemed more efficient. We use a similar approach to compare the rules in the ALT-NSF space.

8.3 Sine Weighted Moving Average

Traders have observed that after several rounds of iterative smoothing, the price weights of a multiple-smoothed moving average tend to form a smooth hump shape. This suggests that, in a moving average with effective smoothing, the price weights likely follow a hump-shaped pattern. The next step is to choose a simple mathematical function that has this smooth, inverse U-shape. The list of such functions is relatively short and includes the Gaussian function (normal distribution), the negative quadratic function, and the sine function. Since the negative quadratic function can produce negative values, the most suitable choices are the Gaussian or sine function.

The Sine Weighted Moving Average (SWMA) was introduced by Patrick Lafferty in (1999). He examined several types of moving averages, including the SWMA, alongside traditional ones such as the SMA, LMA, EMA, and others. Using historical data from the S&P 500 stock market index between 1970 and 1998, Lafferty measured the number of reversals for each moving average. The SWMA had the fewest reversals among the competing moving averages.

It is important to note that Patrick Lafferty defined the smoothness of a moving average in a way similar to how it is defined in this book. Specifically, smoothness refers to the stability and consistency of the trading signal over time. A moving average with higher smoothness reduces the frequency of whipsaw trades, which are rapid position reversals. Recently, Zakamulin and Giner (2023) provided analytical proof that the SWMA has the fewest position reversals among moving averages with the same window size.

The SWMA is calculated using the following formula:

$$SWMA_t(n, P) = \frac{\sum_{i=0}^{n-1} \sin\left(\frac{(i+1)\pi}{n+1}\right) P_{t-i}}{\sum_{i=0}^{n-1} \sin\left(\frac{(i+1)\pi}{n+1}\right)},$$

where $\sin(\cdot)$ is the sine function and $\sin\left(\frac{(i+1)\pi}{n+1}\right)$ represents the weight assigned to the price P_{t-i}.

Figure 8.1 shows the price weights of the SWMA(30). The shape of the price weights follows the first half of a sine wave. For comparison, this figure also displays the price weights of the SMA(30), where all prices are equally weighted.

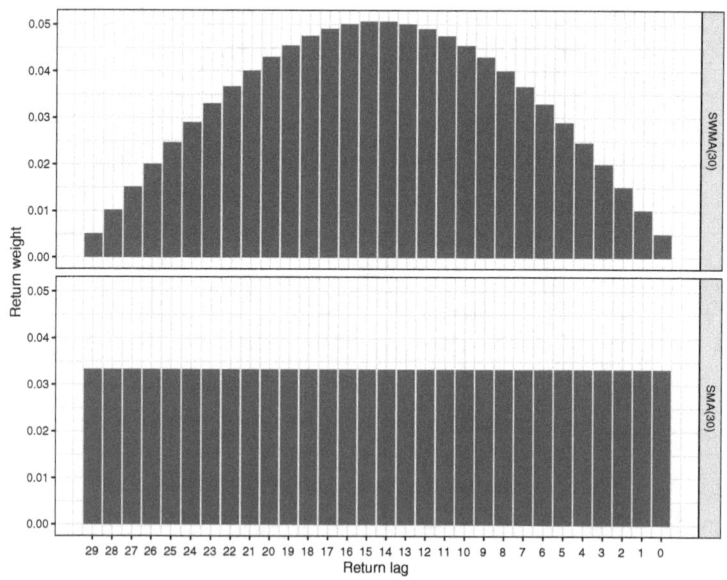

Fig. 8.1 Price weights of the SMA(30) and SWMA(30)

The key question is how to use a moving average with enhanced smoothness for trend-following. There are essentially three traditional trading rules based on moving averages of prices. The first rule is the price and moving average crossover (P-MA). The second rule is the double moving average crossover (MA-C). The third rule is the moving average direction (MA-D) rule.

In the moving average direction rule, a Buy signal is triggered when the moving average value increases, while a Sell signal is triggered when it decreases. In the technical indicator of this rule, the return weights have the same shape as the price weights. For example, the return weights in the SWMA-D(n) rule are given by:

$$\theta_i = c \times \sin\left(\frac{(i+1)\pi}{n+1}\right), \quad i \in [0, n-1],$$

where c represents any positive real value.

Consequently, the return weights in the technical indicators of the SWMA-D(30) and SMA-D(30) rules follow the same pattern as the price weights shown in Fig. 8.1. Note that the return weights in these two rules differ significantly. In the SWMA-D(30) rule, the return weights are much smoother. They gradually rise from zero to a peak and then slowly decline back to zero. In contrast, the return weights in the SMA-D(30) rule rise sharply from zero to a constant level before eventually dropping back to zero. It is worth noting that the SWMA-D(30) rule achieves the highest level of smoothness among all trading rules with a 30-period averaging window.

We argue that the MA-D rule is the most logical choice for trend-following with a moving average that has enhanced smoothness. In the P-MA rule, the return weights decrease as the return lag increases. This means the P-MA rule consistently places more emphasis on the most recent returns, regardless of the weighting function used in the moving average. Consequently, the return weights in both the P-SWMA(30) and P-SMA(30) rules are nearly identical and lack the desired smoothness, as shown in Fig. 8.2.

In the MA-C(s, l) rule, where s and l represent the sizes of the shorter and longer moving averages, the return weights always follow a hump-shaped pattern, regardless of the weighting function used in the moving average. Specifically, the return weights first increase, reach a peak, and then decrease. For illustration, Fig. 8.3 shows the return weights for the SWMA-C(8,30) and SMA-C(8,30) rules. Visual inspection of the return weights in these two seemingly different rules suggests that they are nearly identical.

Therefore, substituting the SMA with the SWMA in either the P-MA or MA-C rule results in little to no change in the quantitative characteristics of these trading rules. In contrast, the SMA-D and SWMA-D rules have notably different smoothness and accuracy properties. It is important to note that the responsiveness of both the SMA-D(n) and SWMA-D(n) rules is the same. Specifically, for all technical indicators calculated with an averaging window of size n, the average lag time is $n/2$ if the return weighting function is symmetrical around the middle. This characteristic is common to both the SMA-D and SWMA-D rules.

Over time, traders have proposed various types of moving averages that are believed to offer better smoothing properties compared to standard ones like

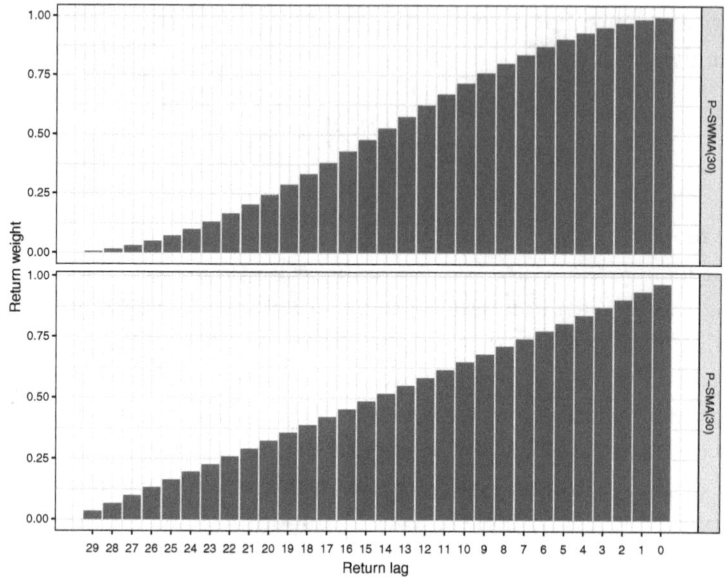

Fig. 8.2 Return weights of the technical indicator of the P-SWMA(30) and P-SMA(30) rules

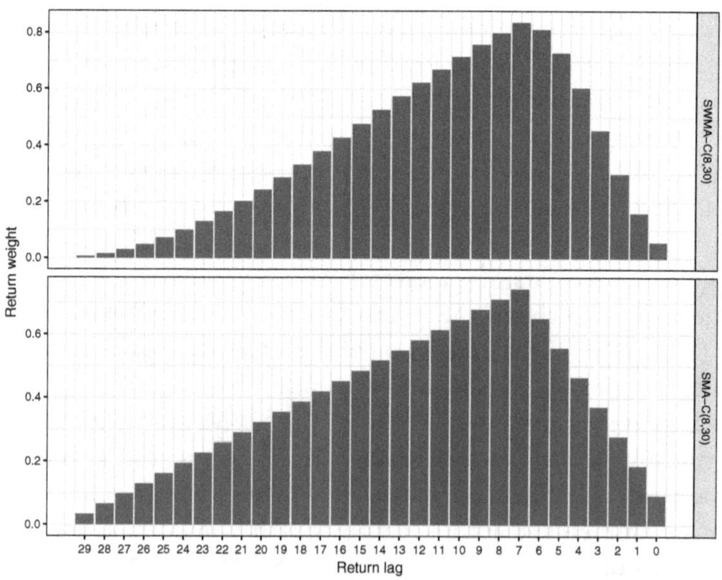

Fig. 8.3 Return weights of the technical indicator of the SWMA-C(8,30) and SMA-C(8,30) rules

the SMA, LMA, and EMA. The SWMA is one such type. Proponents of these moving averages assert that trading based on them is more beneficial than using conventional moving averages. Unfortunately, there is currently no objective evidence to support these claims. The support for these assertions is based only on anecdotal evidence and visual illustrations.

Indeed, the SWMA-D(n) rule has the highest smoothness among all technical indicators with a window size of n. However, the critical question is whether trading with the SWMA-D rule provides advantages over trading with conventional moving averages. It is worth repeating that smoothness is just one of the key properties of trend-following rules. Other crucial properties include accuracy and responsiveness.

For example, the SMA-D(n) rule provides the highest accuracy among all technical indicators with a window size of n return observations. Both the SMA-D(n) and SWMA-D(n) rules have the same responsiveness because their return weights are symmetrical around the middle. Therefore, the SWMA-D rule offers a better tradeoff between responsiveness and smoothness compared to the SMA-D rule. Conversely, the SMA-D rule provides a better tradeoff between responsiveness and accuracy than the SWMA-D rule. As a result, the SWMA-D rule does not offer clear advantages over the SMA-D rule.

To improve responsiveness while maintaining high smoothness, the shape of the return weights in the technical indicator should retain the hump-shaped form but with the peak shifted toward the more recent return lags. This shape is typical in all MA-C rules where the shorter window size is smaller than half the size of the longer window. With this insight, we aim to compare the properties of the SWMA-D(n) rule with the SMA-C($n/4, n$) rule, where the shorter window size is one-fourth of the longer window size.

We compare the properties of the SWMA-D(n) and SMA-C($n/4, n$) rules using the methodology outlined in the previous section. In summary, we first vary n and calculate the ALT, NSF, and SMI metrics for each rule. We then plot curves in the ALT-SMI and ALT-NSF spaces for both trading rules. These curves show the tradeoffs between responsiveness and smoothness, as well as responsiveness and accuracy. If one curve consistently lies above the other, the corresponding trading rule is considered more efficient.

The left panel in Fig. 8.4 shows the combinations of ALT and SMI for the SWMA-D(n) and SMA-C($n/4, n$) rules. The right panel displays the combinations of ALT and NSF for the same rules. From a visual inspection of the curves in each panel, we can draw the following conclusions.

First, the curves in the left panel are nearly identical, indicating that the SWMA-D(n) and SMA-C($n/4, n$) rules provide a similar tradeoff between responsiveness and smoothness. However, in the right panel, the curve for the

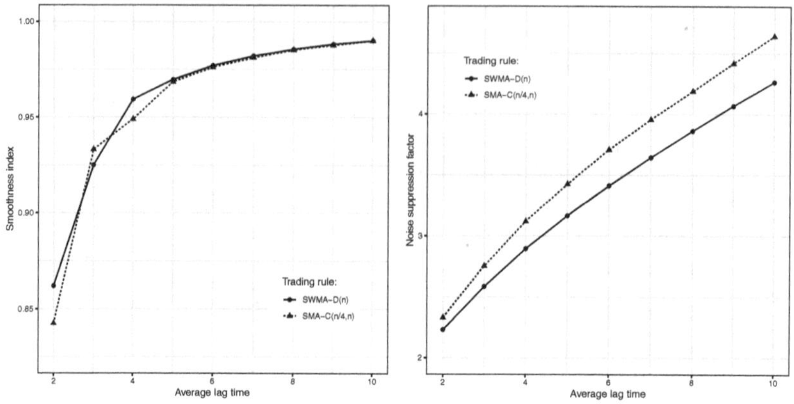

Fig. 8.4 Comparison of the effectiveness of the SWMA-D and SMA-C rules. The left panel plots the set of combinations of the ALT and SMI for the SWMA-D and SMA-C rules. The right panel plots the set of combinations of the ALT and NSF for the same rules

SMA-C($n/4$, n) rule consistently lies above the curve for the SWMA-D(n) rule. This suggests that, for the same level of responsiveness, the SMA-C rule offers greater accuracy than the SWMA-D rule. Overall, we conclude that the SMA-C($n/4$, n) rule is superior to the SWMA-D(n) rule.

8.4 Multiple-Smoothed Moving Averages

Smoothing a moving average with another moving average creates a double-smoothed moving average. For example, suppose we first smooth the prices using a moving average with an averaging window of size n. Next, we apply a second moving average to the results of the first. The second moving average is of the same type and uses the same window size. This double smoothing results in a new moving average of the prices:

$$DSMA_t(k, P) = MA_t(n, MA(n, P)),$$

where the total window size is $k = 2n - 1$.

The double-smoothed moving average provides better smoothness for two reasons. First, its window size is larger than that of the original moving average, and generally, a longer window improves smoothness. Second, the weight distribution of the double-smoothed moving average is a smoothed version of the original weights, leading to improved smoothness in the overall shape.

However, the average lag time of the moving average also increases. By average lag time, we refer to its conventional definition, where, for example, the average lag time of $MA(n)$ is calculated as:

$$\mathrm{ALT}(MA) = \frac{\sum_{i=0}^{n-1} w_i \times i}{\sum_{i=0}^{n-1} w_i},$$

where w_i is the weight of price P_{t-i}.

The average lag time of the double-smoothed moving average is double the average lag time of each individual moving average:

$$\mathrm{ALT}(DSMA) = 2 \times \mathrm{ALT}(MA).$$

While the average lag time does not directly measure the delay between a price trend change and when the trend-following rule adjusts the trading signal, this property indicates that the double-smoothed moving average is twice as slow as a single moving average.

The triple-smoothed moving average provides even greater smoothness than the double-smoothed moving average. However, the drawback is that it reacts even more slowly. As a result, the advantages of multiple smoothing are not obvious. In this section, we will analyze the weighting functions of multiple-smoothed moving averages and explore whether they offer any improvements over traditional moving averages.

8.4.1 Multiple-Smoothed Simple Moving Average

In a Simple Moving Average (SMA), all data points are equally weighted, meaning each price is given the same influence, with a weight of one. When this process is applied twice in sequence, it becomes a double-smoothed SMA. This effectively turns the uniform weighting into one where central data points gain more importance, producing a smoothing effect that resembles a triangular shape on a graph. Hence, this double-smoothed SMA is called the Triangular Moving Average (TMA).

To compute a TMA for a time series, an SMA with a window size of n is first applied to the price data, followed by applying another SMA with the same window size to the result. A triple-smoothed SMA and a quadruple-smoothed SMA are produced by applying the SMA three and four times in sequence, respectively.

Figure 8.5 shows the price weights for the SMA(n), double-smoothed SMA(n), triple-smoothed SMA(n), and quadruple-smoothed SMA(n), with

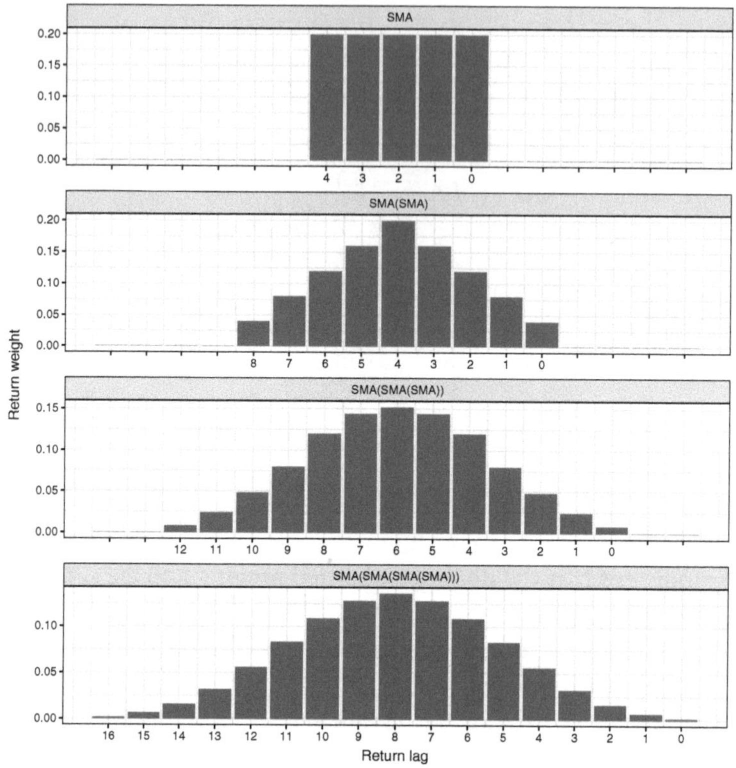

Fig. 8.5 Price weights of the SMA(5), double-smoothed SMA(5), triple-smoothed SMA(5), and quadruple-smoothed SMA(5)

$n = 5$. The first key observation is that each additional smoothing step effectively increases the window size by $n - 1$. As a result, while the simple SMA uses a window size of 5, the double-smoothed SMA uses a window size of 9, and the triple- and quadruple-smoothed SMAs use window sizes of 13 and 17, respectively. In general, the window size of the k-smoothed moving average is approximately $k \times n$, meaning that it increases linearly with each additional smoothing step.

The second key observation is that with each additional iteration of smoothing, the weighting function of the multiple-smoothed SMA gradually takes on a bell-shaped curve, similar to the Gaussian distribution. This is not by chance. The moving average is essentially a convolution operation, which involves combining two functions to create a new function that represents how one modifies the other. When the same function is convolved with itself repeatedly (self-convolution), the result becomes progressively smoother and more symmetric.

This process is analogous to summing random variables, which relates to the Central Limit Theorem.

In processes like moving averages or iterated self-convolution, repeated smoothing makes the data points increasingly resemble a Gaussian distribution. As more convolutions are applied, the result gets closer to a Normal distribution, even if the original data was not normally distributed. This is why, with enough iterations, iterated self-convolution converges to the Normal distribution.

In the limit, as the number of smoothing operations approaches infinity, the weights of the infinitely-smoothed moving average follow a Gaussian distribution. At this point, the averaging window becomes infinitely large, but most of the weights remain concentrated near the center of the window.

Although multiple smoothing of the SMA results in a smooth weight distribution, this distribution is not optimal. We know that the moving average with the highest smoothness is the SWMA. Additionally, the weighting function is symmetric around the center, which leads to poor responsiveness in the moving average. These points raise concerns about the effectiveness of the multiple-smoothed SMA for trend-following purposes.

To validate our concerns, we compare the properties of the MA-D trading rules based on the multiple-smoothed SMA with those of the double SMA crossover rule, where the shorter window size is one-fourth of the longer window size. Our comparison follows the same methodology as before. Specifically, we vary the size of the averaging window n and then calculate the NSF, ALT, and SMI for all the competing rules. Finally, we assess the effectiveness of the rules within the ALT-SMI and ALT-NSF spaces.

The top panel of Fig. 8.6 shows the combinations of ALT and SMI for a selected set of trading rules. These rules include the SMA-D(n) rule, the SMA(SMA)-D(n) rule, the SMA(SMA(SMA))-D(n) rule, the SMA(SMA(SMA(SMA)))-D(n) rule, and the SMA-C($n/4, n$) rule. The bottom panel plots the combinations of ALT and NSF for the same set of rules.

Our conclusions confirm our initial concerns about the efficiency of trend-following rules based on multiple-smoothed SMA. Specifically, the double SMA crossover rule offers a better balance between responsiveness and smoothness compared to any of the multiple-smoothed SMA rules. Additionally, the double SMA crossover rule is at least as effective as the best of the SMA and multiple-smoothed SMA rules in terms of responsiveness and accuracy.

It is also noteworthy that the double-smoothed SMA outperforms both the triple- and quadruple-smoothed SMAs. This is because the trend-following rule based on the double-smoothed SMA shows better performance across all three quantitative measures. Specifically, for the same level of responsive-

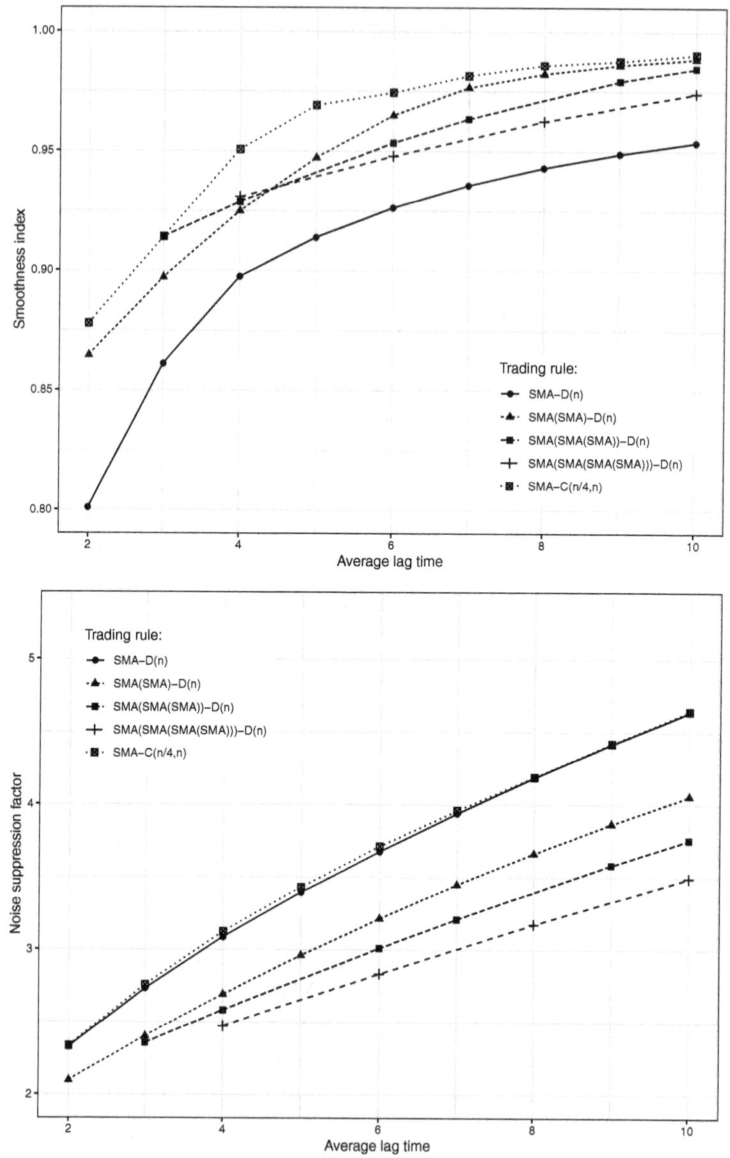

Fig. 8.6 Comparison of the effectiveness of trading rules based on multiple-smoothed SMA. The top panel plots the set of combinations of the ALT and SMI for the selected set of rules. The bottom panel plots the set of combinations of the ALT and NSF for the same rules

ness, the double-smoothed SMA rule offers superior smoothness and accuracy compared to the rules based on the triple- and quadruple-smoothed SMA.

8.4.2 Multiple-Smoothed Linear Moving Average

In a Linear Moving Average (LMA), the weights assigned to prices decrease as the price lag increases. Specifically, when the averaging window has a size of n, the most recent price gets a weight of n, the next price gets a weight of $n - 1$, and so on, until the oldest price has a weight of one. This creates a triangular pattern for the price weights. Unlike the TMA, where the highest weight is at the center of the window, in the LMA, the highest weight is at the beginning of the window.

Figure 8.7 illustrates the price weights for the LMA(n), double-smoothed LMA(n), triple-smoothed LMA(n), and quadruple-smoothed LMA(n), with $n = 5$. Similar to the multiple-smoothed SMA, each additional smoothing step increases the effective window size by $n - 1$. With each iteration, the price weights become progressively smoother.

As the number of iterative smoothing operations increases toward infinity, the shape of the weights in a multiple-smoothed LMA approaches that of a Gaussian distribution. However, with only a few iterations, the weight distribution retains its non-symmetrical form. Notably, the price weights in a double-smoothed LMA resemble the return weights in the double LMA crossover rule. In both cases, the weighting function forms a hump shape, with the peak located near the most recent price (or return) lags.

We assess the effectiveness of the multiple-smoothed LMA using the same methodology as in previous analyses. As before, the benchmark for comparison is the traditional double SMA crossover rule, where the size of the shorter window is one-fourth of the size of the longer window.

The top panel of Fig. 8.8 shows the combinations of ALT and SMI for a selected set of trading rules. These rules include the LMA-D(n) rule, the LMA(LMA)-D(n) rule, the LMA(LMA(LMA))-D(n) rule, the LMA(LMA(LMA(LMA)))-D(n) rule, and the LMA-C($n/4$, n) rule. The bottom panel plots the combinations of ALT and NSF for the same set of rules.

The first notable observation is that the double-smoothed LMA outperforms the triple-smoothed LMA, which in turn is more effective than the quadruple-smoothed LMA. For instance, at the same level of responsiveness, the trading rule based on the double-smoothed LMA provides better smoothness and accuracy compared to the rule based on the triple-smoothed LMA.

The second observation is that the trading rule using the double-smoothed LMA is only slightly better than the double SMA crossover rule when con-

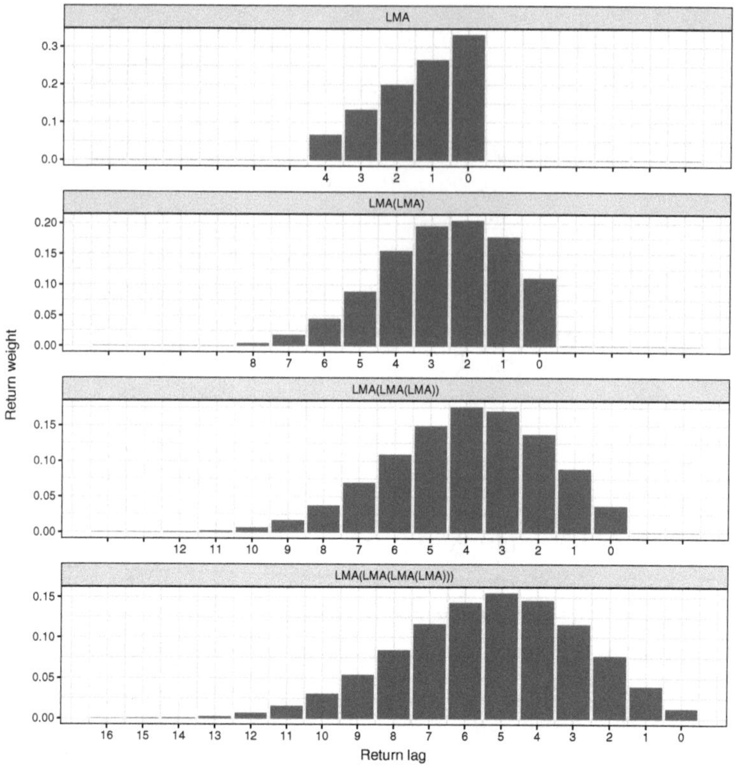

Fig. 8.7 Price weights of the LMA(5), double-smoothed LMA(5), triple-smoothed LMA(5), and quadruple-smoothed LMA(5)

sidering the tradeoff between responsiveness and smoothness. Conversely, the double SMA crossover rule is only slightly better than the double-smoothed LMA-based trading rule in terms of the tradeoff between responsiveness and accuracy. Overall, trading with the double-smoothed LMA is about as effective as trading with the double SMA crossover rule.

The third and final observation is that the trading rule based on the LMA offers the best tradeoff between responsiveness and accuracy compared to any trading rule that uses multiple-smoothed LMA. For instance, while replacing the LMA with the double-smoothed LMA improves the tradeoff between responsiveness and smoothness, it does so at the expense of worsening the tradeoff between responsiveness and accuracy.

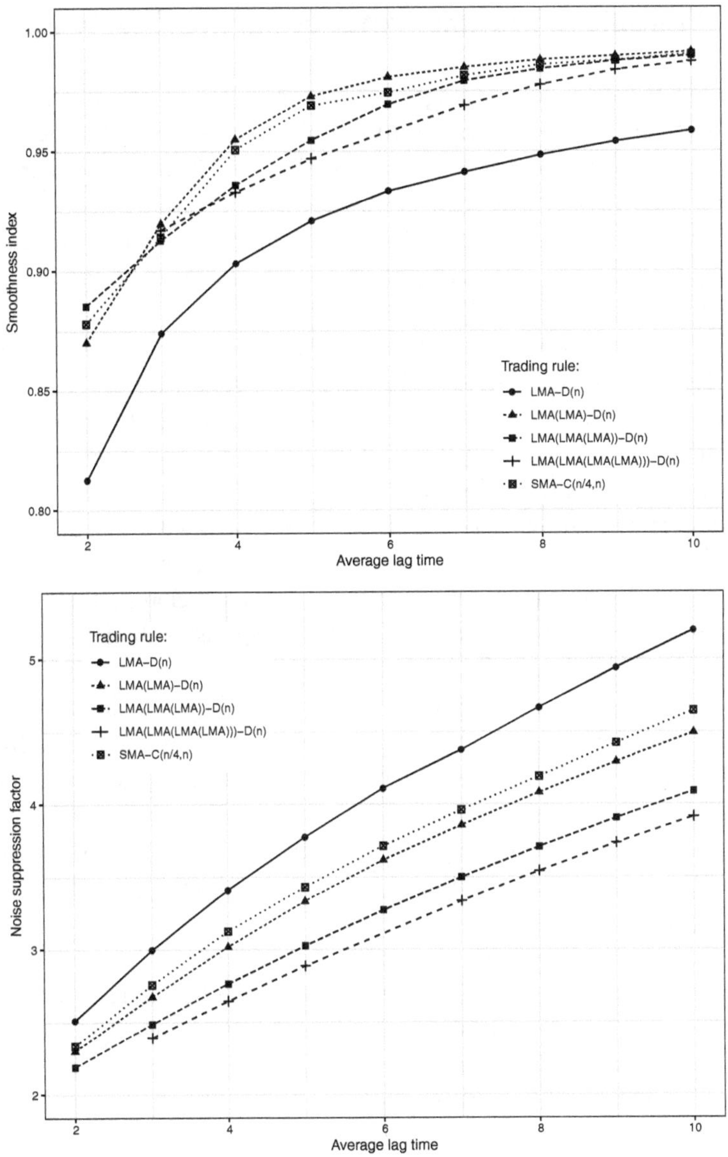

Fig. 8.8 Comparison of the effectiveness of trading rules based on multiple-smoothed LMA. The top panel plots the set of combinations of the ALT and SMI for the selected set of rules. The bottom panel plots the set of combinations of the ALT and NSF for the same rules

8.4.3 Multiple-Smoothed Exponential Moving Average

In an Exponential Moving Average (EMA), the averaging window theoretically extends indefinitely. The price weights follow a decreasing geometric sequence, where the most recent price has a weight of $\lambda^0 = 1$. The next price has a weight of $\lambda^1 = \lambda$, and the price at lag k has a weight of λ^k, where $0 < \lambda < 1$ is the decay constant. Although the EMA is defined using a parameter n, which resembles the window size, this parameter is actually used to calculate the decay constant as $\lambda = (n-1)/(n+1)$.

It is important to note that both the EMA(n) and SMA(n) have the same average lag time, which equals $(n-1)/2$. As a result, during a price trend, these two moving averages tend to move as one, creating the impression that trend-following rules based on the EMA and SMA with the same window size are equally responsive. However, as emphasized throughout this book, the average lag time of a moving average is not directly related to the delay between a trend change and the corresponding shift in the trading signal. In reality, the EMA-D(n) rule responds more quickly to the trend change than the SMA-D(n) rule, while the P-SMA(n) rule is more responsive than the P-EMA(n) rule.

Figure 8.9 shows the price weights for the EMA(n), double-smoothed EMA(n), triple-smoothed EMA(n), and quadruple-smoothed EMA(n), with $n = 10$. In the EMA, the price weights decrease in a geometric pattern, but in any multiple-smoothed EMA, the weights form a hump shape. With each additional smoothing step, the hump shifts further into the past and becomes wider. This increases the smoothness of the moving average, but also lengthens the average lag time.

In the MA-D trading rule, the return weights follow the same pattern as the price weights in the moving average. As a result, the return weights in all MA-D rules based on multiple-smoothed moving averages also form a hump-shaped pattern. This hump-shaped pattern is typical in all MA-C rules as well. Given this, it is worth exploring whether the return weights in the double EMA crossover rule can replicate the shape of the price weights in a multiple-smoothed EMA.

Figure 8.10 shows the weights of the double-smoothed EMA(10) alongside the return weights of the EMA-C(9,10) rule. The plots in this figure suggest that these weights are nearly identical. Therefore, we can conclude that the MA-D rule based on the double-smoothed EMA(n) is equivalent to the EMA-C($n-1, n$) rule.

It is worth noting that in the double SMA crossover rule, the location of the hump can be anywhere inside the averaging window. For example, in the

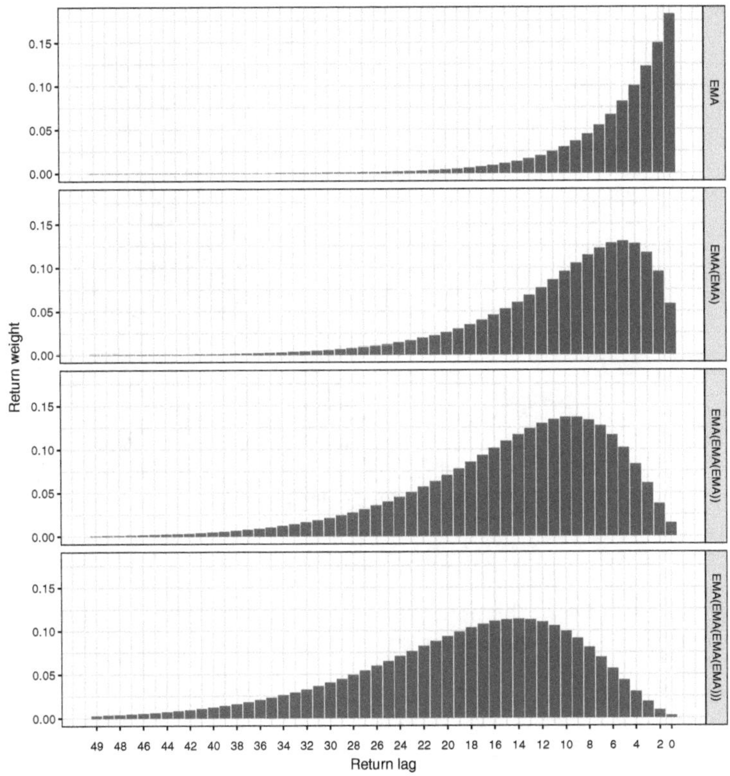

Fig. 8.9 Price weights of the EMA(10), double-smoothed EMA(10), triple-smoothed EMA(10), and quadruple-smoothed EMA(10). The weights are cut off at lag 49

SMA-C($n/2, n$) rule, the hump is located in the middle of the window. In the SMA-C($1, n$) and SMA-C($n-1, n$) rule, the hump is located at the left and right border of the window, respectively. However, even in the EMA-C($n-1, n$) rule, the hump is always located close to the most recent return lags.

Figure 8.11 displays the weights of the triple-smoothed EMA(10) compared to the return weights of the EMA-C(9,10) rule. The plots suggest that the double EMA crossover rule cannot replicate the weights of the triple-smoothed EMA. Likewise, we can conclude that the double EMA crossover rule is also unable to replicate the weights of the quadruple-smoothed EMA.

The triple-smoothed EMA is known as the TRIX moving average:

$$TRIX(n) = EMA(n, EMA(n, EMA(n))).$$

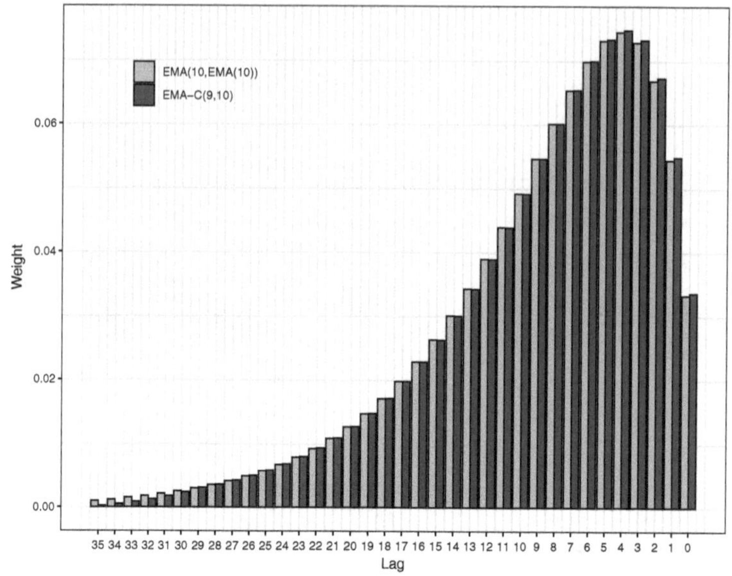

Fig. 8.10 Price weights of the double-smoothed EMA(10) and the return weights of the EMA-C(9,10) rule. The weights are cut off at lag 35

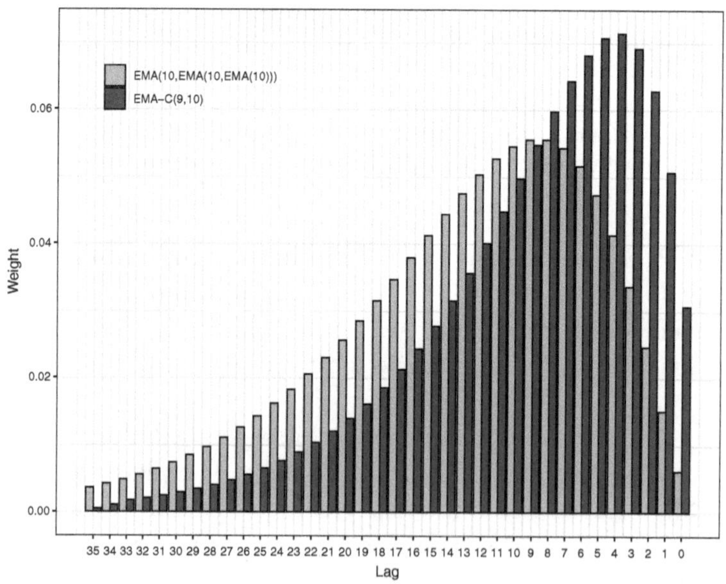

Fig. 8.11 Price weights of the triple-smoothed EMA(10) and the return weights of the EMA-C(9,10) rule. The weights are cut off at lag 35

This moving average was introduced and popularized by Jack K. Hutson in (1984).

The technical trading indicator based on the TRIX is calculated as the percentage change between the current and previous values of the TRIX:

$$I_t^{\text{TRIX}}(n) = \frac{TRIX_t(n) - TRIX_{t-1}(n)}{TRIX_{t-1}(n)}.$$

A Buy signal is generated when the indicator is positive, and a Sell signal is triggered when it is negative. This trading rule is equivalent to the MA-D rule since the indicator's sign is based on the difference between the current and previous values of the TRIX.

In concluding this section, we compare the properties of the MA-D trading rules based on the multiple-smoothed EMA with those of the double EMA crossover rule, where the shorter window size is one half of the longer window size. The top panel of Fig. 8.12 shows the combinations of ALT and SMI for a selected set of trading rules. These rules include the EMA-D(n) rule, the EMA(EMA)-D(n) rule, the EMA(EMA(EMA))-D(n) rule, the EMA(EMA(EMA(EMA)))-D(n) rule, and the EMA-C($n/2, n$) rule. The bottom panel plots the combinations of ALT and NSF for the same set of rules.

The key observation is that all trading rules based on multiple-smoothed EMAs and the double EMA crossover rule have a similar balance between responsiveness and smoothness. Furthermore, the double EMA crossover rule offers nearly the same tradeoff between responsiveness and accuracy as the double-smoothed EMA, and a better tradeoff compared to the triple- and quadruple-smoothed EMAs. However, the most efficient rule in terms of responsiveness and accuracy is the EMA-D rule. Yet, this rule provides the worst tradeoff when it comes to balancing responsiveness and smoothness.

It is important to note that with each iterative smoothing, the minimum possible average lag time (ALT) of the trading rule increases. For example, with double smoothing, the minimum ALT is three. For triple and quadruple smoothing, the minimum ALT rises to five and seven, respectively. This means that each additional smoothing step not only increases the average lag time but also raises the minimum possible lag time.

The conclusions drawn from comparing the properties of the multiple-smoothed EMA are similar to those from the multiple-smoothed LMA. Specifically, trading with the double-smoothed EMA is roughly as effective as trading with the double EMA crossover rule. In contrast, the triple- and quadruple-smoothed EMAs are less effective than the double-smoothed EMA. However, trading with the double-smoothed EMA is less effective than trading with the price and EMA crossover when considering the tradeoff between respon-

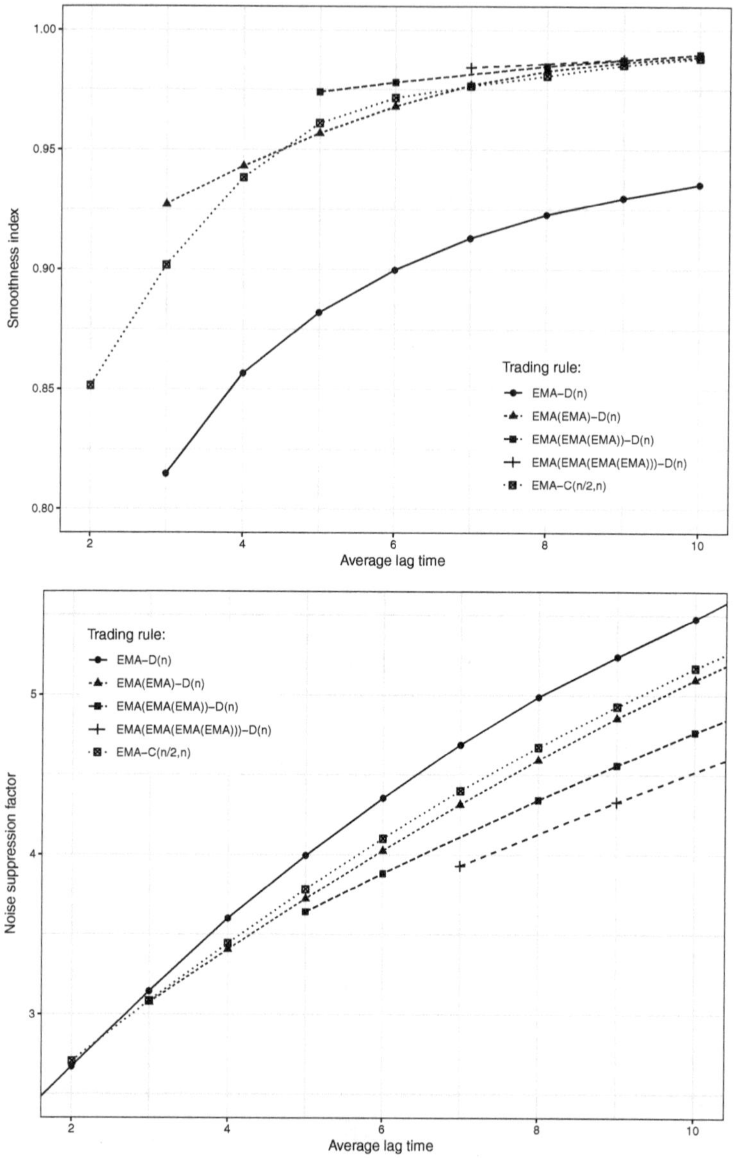

Fig. 8.12 Comparison of the effectiveness of trading rules based on multiple-smoothed EMA. The top panel plots the set of combinations of the ALT and SMI for the selected set of rules. The bottom panel plots the set of combinations of the ALT and NSF for the same rules

siveness and accuracy. As is often the case, improving the tradeoff between responsiveness and smoothness typically comes at the cost of worsening the tradeoff between responsiveness and accuracy.

8.5 Gaussian Moving Average

Applying a moving average repeatedly over many iterations is equivalent to applying a single moving average with weights that follow a Gaussian distribution.

The Gaussian distribution, or normal distribution, has a bell-shaped curve that is symmetric around its mean. The highest point on the curve is at the mean, where most data is concentrated. As you move further from the mean, the curve gradually decreases, with the tails getting closer to the horizontal axis but never touching it. The spread of the curve depends on the standard deviation: a larger standard deviation results in a broader, flatter curve, while a smaller one leads to a narrower, steeper curve.

Since applying a moving average iteratively increases the smoothness of the resulting curve, it is reasonable to assume that a moving average using Gaussian-distributed weights would offer superior smoothing properties. However, the challenge with the Gaussian distribution is that it is defined over the entire real axis, from negative infinity to positive infinity. In contrast, a moving average uses a limited number of weights. However, because the Gaussian distribution is primarily concentrated around its mean, a practical solution is to center the mean in the middle of the averaging window. By defining the standard deviation, we can then calculate the corresponding weights for each price lag within the window.

Formally, let n represent the size of the averaging window. The weight of the price P_{t-i} in the Gaussian Moving Average (GMA) is computed as:

$$w_i = e^{-\frac{(i-m)^2}{2\sigma^2}}, \quad i \in [0, n-1], \tag{8.1}$$

where m is the mean of the Gaussian distribution and σ is its standard deviation. The mean value m is defined as:

$$m = \frac{n-1}{2}.$$

This choice of m places the maximum weight in the middle of the averaging window, ensuring that the moving average achieves optimal smoothing properties.

However, there is an alternative definition for the parameter m:

$$m = 0.$$

In this case, the GMA places more weight on data points closer to the current time. The weights still follow a Gaussian curve, but the peak occurs at the most recent data point, and older data points receive exponentially less influence. The downside of this approach is that it leads to a less smooth moving average. The weighting function, which overemphasizes recent data, becomes similar to those used in the LMA and EMA, reducing the smoothing effect typically desired in the GMA.

Note that the GMA is determined by two parameters: n and σ. The notation GMA(n, σ) means that the GMA uses the window size of n observation, and the standard deviation of the Gaussian distribution is σ. Figure 8.13 illustrates the price weights for GMA(20,5).

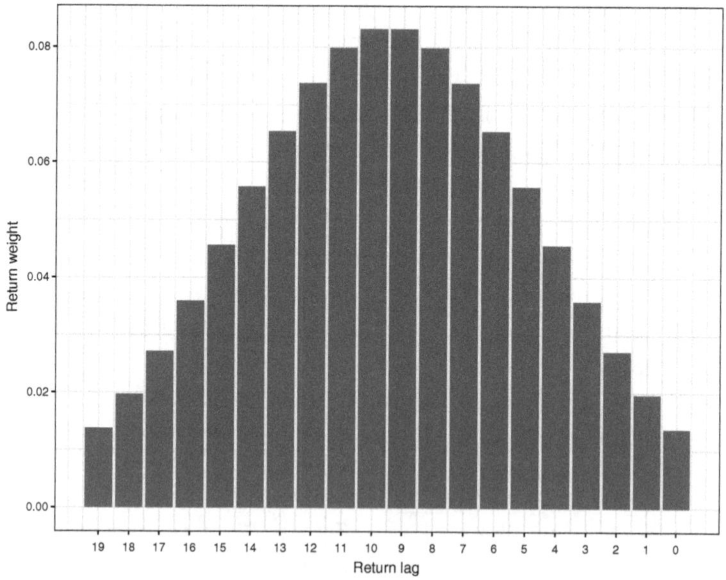

Fig. 8.13 Price weights of the GMA(20,5)

The selection of the optimal standard deviation for the GMA is not immediately apparent. Theoretically, the best choice should enhance the smoothness of the moving average. Therefore, a reasonable approach is to optimize the Smoothness Index (SMI) of the technical indicator for the GMA-D(n, σ) rule. This can be done using standard numerical optimization techniques.

Table 8.1 Optimal fraction k is used to calculate the standard deviation in the GMA(n, σ). The standard deviation is defined as $\sigma = k \times n$, and this value of σ maximizes the smoothness of the GMA-D trend-following rule

Window size n	Optimal fraction k
5	0.400
10	0.300
20	0.250
30	0.233
40	0.225
50	0.220
60	0.217
70	0.214
80	0.212
90	0.211
100	0.210

We carry out the numerical optimization of the SMI for the GMA-D(n, σ) rule, where $\sigma = k \times n$, meaning the standard deviation is set as a fraction of the window size n. In summary, we vary the value of n and, for each n, determine the optimal fraction k that maximizes smoothness. The results are presented in Table 8.1.

The results in the table indicate that the optimal fraction is not fixed but varies with the averaging window size. However, the optimal fraction stabilizes around 0.2 as the window size increases. In other words, when the window size becomes large, the optimal standard deviation approaches one-fifth of the window size.

With the optimal sigma, the GMA behaves similarly to the SWMA. In short, while the GMA possesses high smoothness, it falls short in terms of responsiveness and accuracy. The SMA-C rule, where the shorter window is one-fourth the size of the longer window, outperforms the GMA-D rule.

8.6 Arnaud Legoux Moving Average

The Arnaud Legoux Moving Average (ALMA) was introduced by Arnaud Legoux and Dimitris Kouzis-Loukas in (2009). It was inspired by the GMA. As mentioned earlier, the GMA provides good smoothness but poor responsiveness. To address this issue, Legoux and Kouzis-Loukas proposed shifting the mean of the Gaussian distribution closer to the beginning of the averaging window instead of placing it in the middle. This adjustment gives more weight to recent prices. As a result, the ALMA maintains the smoothness of the Gaussian distribution but improves responsiveness compared to the GMA.

The price weights in the ALMA are calculated using the same formula as in the GMA. Specifically, the weights follow Eq. (8.1). The key difference lies in how the value of m is determined. In the ALMA, m is defined as:

$$m = \alpha(n - 1),$$

where α is known as the "offset."

Consequently, the ALMA is specified by three parameters: n, α, and σ. The notation ALMA(n, α, σ) means that the ALMA uses the window size of n observation, the offset is α, and the standard deviation of the Gaussian distribution is σ. The default values recommended by the creators of the ALMA are $n = 9$, $\alpha = 0.15$,[1] and $\sigma = 6$.

The question is whether the recommended parameters for the ALMA are truly optimal. Put another way: can the efficiency of the ALMA be improved by adjusting the default parameters? The recommended parameters refer to $\alpha = 0.15$ and a standard deviation set to $2/3$ of the averaging window size.

Previously, it was impossible to answer this question due to the lack of quantitative metrics that could objectively assess the characteristics of the technical indicators based on moving averages. However, with the three quantitative measures introduced in this book, we can now answer this question.

Our approach to optimizing the characteristics of the ALMA($n, \alpha, \sigma = k \times n$) focuses on improving the tradeoff between smoothness and responsiveness, while preserving its original balance between accuracy and responsiveness. We achieve this by selecting optimal values for α and k, where k determines the fraction of the averaging window used to calculate the standard deviation.

Our numerical optimizations indicate that the optimal offset is $\alpha = 0.25$,[2] and the optimal standard deviation is $\sigma = n/4$, meaning that it is one-fourth of the averaging window size. Figure 8.14 displays the weights for the ALMA(30, 0.15, 20), where the offset and standard deviation are set to the recommended values. It also shows the weights for the ALMA(30, 0.25, 7.5), where the offset and standard deviation provide the best balance between smoothness and responsiveness. While the difference in offsets is relatively small (0.25 versus 0.15), the difference in standard deviations is significant (one-fourth versus two-thirds of the averaging window size).

---

[1] The literature suggests a recommended value of 0.85 for this parameter. However, substituting this value into Eq. (8.1) results in a reversed sequence of price weights. Under our convention, the weight at lag 0 corresponds to the most recent price. Therefore, to correctly compute the price weights in ALMA using Eq. (8.1), the offset should be set to 0.15.

[2] For a reversed sequence of price weights, the optimal offset is 0.75.

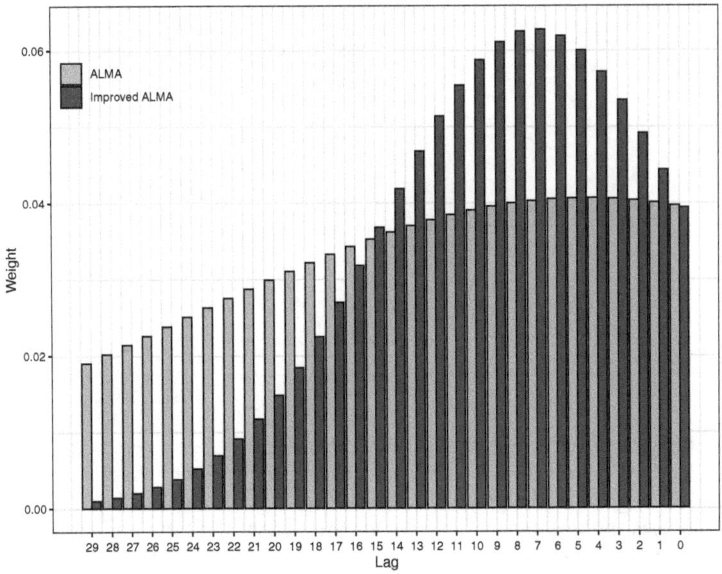

Fig. 8.14 Price weights of the ALMA(30,0.15,20) and the ALMA(30,0.25,7.5). The latter ALMA presents an improved version of the former ALTA

The left panel in Fig. 8.15 shows the combinations of the ALT and SMI for the ALMA-D($n, 0.15, 2n/3$) trading rule and the ALMA-D($n, 0.25, n/4$) rule. The former uses the default parameters for the ALMA, while the latter uses the optimized parameters. The right panel displays the combinations of the ALT and NSF for the same trading rules. The two curves in the right panel nearly overlap, indicating that both rules offer the same balance between accuracy and responsiveness. In contrast, the left panel shows that the curve for the improved ALMA is significantly higher than that for the default ALMA. This means that the improved ALMA provides a much better tradeoff between smoothness and responsiveness. For instance, when the SMI value is 0.95, switching from the default ALMA to the improved ALMA reduces the average lag time from 6.5 periods to 4 periods.

Finally, in this section, we address an important question: does trading with the ALMA offer any advantage over trading based on conventional moving averages? Our answer is absolutely no. The reason is that the shape of the return weights in the ALMA-D rule, even when using optimal parameters, resembles the typical shape found in all double crossover rules. Specifically, the return weights exhibit a smooth, hump-shaped form, with the hump positioned closer to the most recent data point rather than in the middle of the averaging window. This shape can be easily replicated using the double LMA crossover rule, as illustrated in Fig. 8.16.

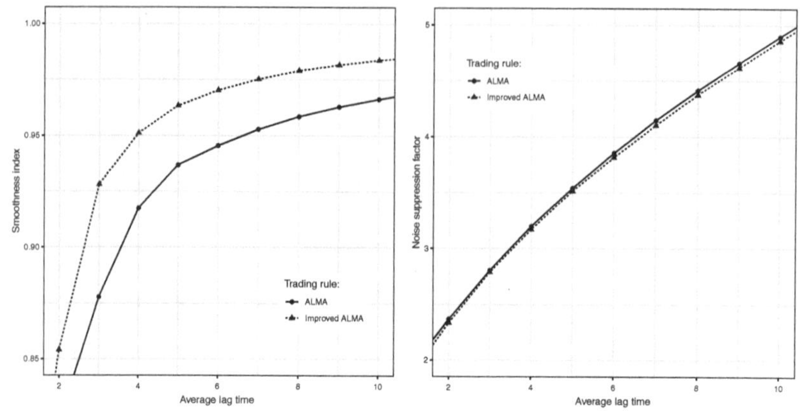

Fig. 8.15 Comparison of the effectiveness of the trading rules based on ALMA and the improved ALMA. The left panel plots the set of combinations of the ALT and SMI for the ALMA-D$(n, 0.15, 2n/3)$ trading rule and the ALMA-D$(n, 0.25, n/4)$ rule. While the former trading rule uses the default parameters for the ALMA, the latter rule uses the optimal parameters. The right panel plots the set of combinations of the ALT and NSF for the same trading rules

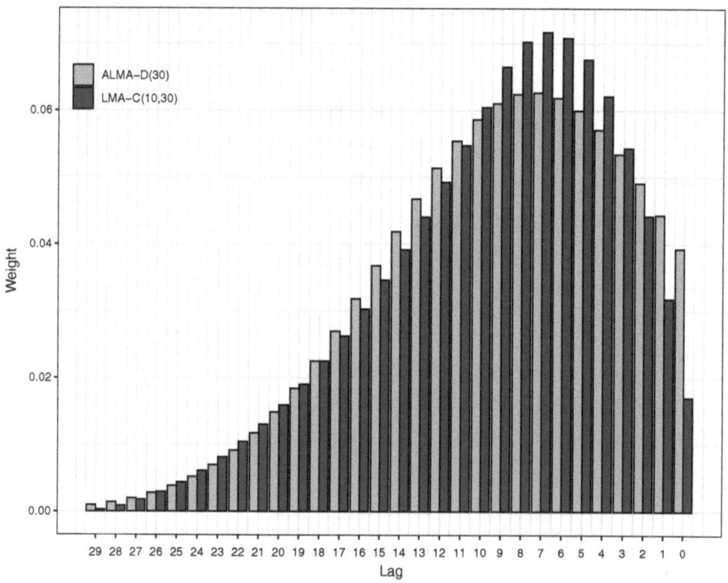

Fig. 8.16 Return weights of the ALMA-D(30,0.25,7.5) rule and the LMA-C(10,30) rule

Specifically, Fig. 8.16 shows the return weights for the ALMA-D(30, 0.25, 7.5) rule and the return weights for the LMA-C(10, 30) rule. It is clear that the return weights in both rules are nearly identical. This observation leads us to conclude that both rules have similar efficiency.

8.7 Compound Smoothing

In the literature, there are examples where one moving average is applied to the result of another moving average. When both moving averages are of the same type and have the same window size, the result is referred to as a double-smoothed moving average. However, if each moving average is of a different type and has a different window size, the process of applying one moving average to the result of another is called "compound smoothing."

Since the result comes from combining two different moving averages, many believe that compound smoothing benefits from both types. They also argue that compound smoothing improves overall smoothness while still being responsive to trends in the data. In this section, we will look at two examples of compound smoothing to see if the moving average produced by this combination creates a new or unusual distribution of weights. We will also discuss whether trading based on compounded moving averages performs more efficiently than traditional trading rules that use standard moving averages.

The first example of compound smoothing is the Weighted Exponential Moving Average (WEMA), proposed by Seng Hansun in (2013). To calculate the WEMA, the Linear Moving Average (LMA) is first applied to the data. Then, the result is further smoothed using the Exponential Moving Average (EMA). Thus, the WEMA is defined as:

$$WEMA_t(m, n, P) = EMA_t(m, LMA(n, P)),$$

where n represents the window size for the LMA, and m is the parameter used to determine the decay constant in the EMA.

In this chapter, we have already discussed the double-smoothed LMA. In the LMA, the weights decrease linearly as the lag increases, meaning that the LMA is not considered a smooth moving average. However, when the LMA is smoothed by another LMA, the weight distribution forms a smooth, hump-shaped curve, which is typical in double moving average crossover rules. In the WEMA, the LMA is smoothed using the EMA, resulting again in a smoothed version of the LMA. Therefore, it can be deduced that the weight distribution in the WEMA is not unique or original.

To illustrate this, Fig. 8.17 shows the return weights of the WEMA-D(10,10) rule alongside the EMA-C(9,10) rule. This figure demonstrates that when the LMA is smoothed by the EMA, the resulting weights form a hump-shaped pattern, similar to the weight distribution found in the double EMA crossover rule. As a result, the performance of the WEMA-D rule is very similar to that of the EMA-C rule.

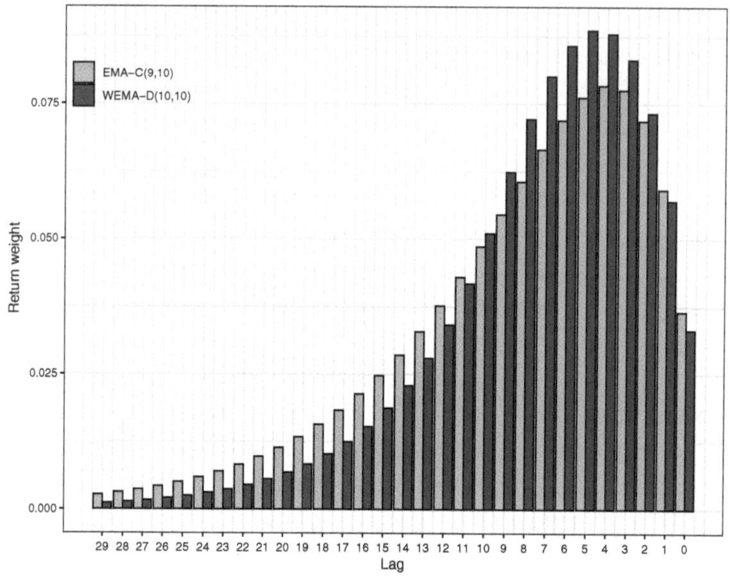

Fig. 8.17 Return weights of the WEMA-D(10,10) rule and the EMA-C(9,10) rule

The second example of compound smoothing is the Hull-EMA, introduced in Hansun et al. (2022). Unlike the WEMA, where the first moving average is the LMA, the Hull-EMA starts with the Hull Moving Average (HMA), as its name suggests. First, the data are smoothed using the HMA, and then the HMA is smoothed by the EMA. The Hull-EMA is expressed as:

$$\text{Hull-EMA}_t(m, n, P) = EMA_t(m, HMA(n, P)),$$

where n represents the window size for the HMA, and m is the parameter used to determine the decay constant in the EMA.

Figure 8.18 displays the weights of the HMA(20), along with the weights of the EMA(10,HMA(20)) and EMA(20,HMA(20)). The HMA, in theory, is a very smooth moving average, where the weight distribution resembles a one-cycle damped sine wave. In this pattern, the first half of the cycle consists of large positive weights, while the second half contains smaller negative weights.

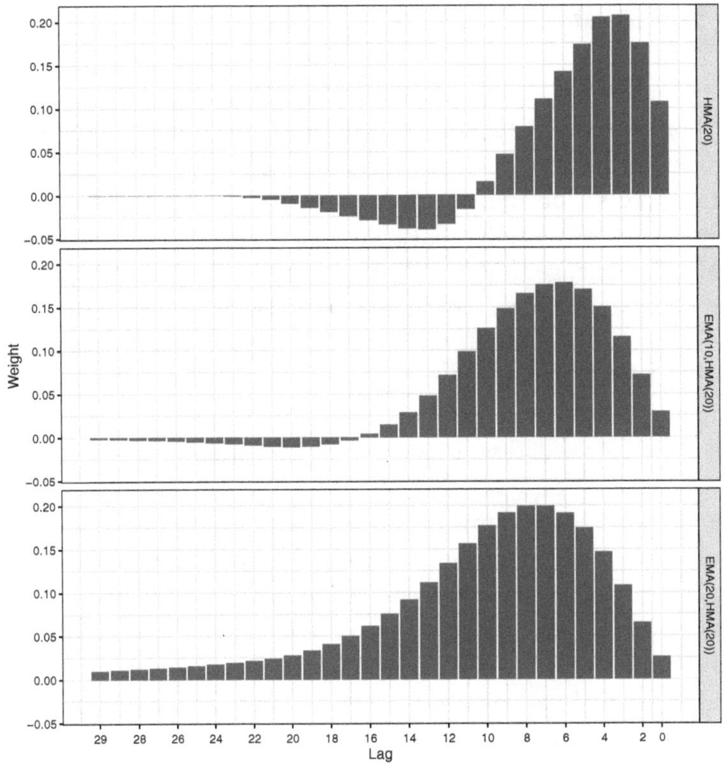

Fig. 8.18 Weights of the HMA(20), EMA(10,HMA(20)), and EMA(20,HMA(20))

When the HMA is smoothed by the EMA, the outcome depends on the chosen decay constant in the EMA, which is calculated as $\lambda = (m-1)/(m+1)$. In the case of the EMA(10, HMA(20)), the decay constant is relatively small, resulting in compound smoothing that retains negative weights. In contrast, with the EMA(20, HMA(20)), the decay constant is relatively large, leading to a loss of negative weights after smoothing. In both scenarios, the shape of the weights after compound smoothing primarily resembles a smooth hump. This shape is similar to the weights found in the double EMA crossover rule or trading strategies based on multiple-smoothed EMAs. Thus, we can conclude that the weight distribution in the Hull-EMA is neither unique nor original.

8.8 Summary

The goal of a moving average is to smooth out price fluctuations and highlight the direction of trends. Therefore, at first glance, the primary requirement for a moving average is to provide effective smoothing properties. Over time, traders have introduced various types of moving averages, claiming they offer better smoothing than conventional ones like the Simple Moving Average (SMA), Linear Moving Average (LMA), and Exponential Moving Average (EMA).

The problem is that, until now, traders have lacked a quantitative method to objectively measure the smoothness of a moving average. Progress in this area has largely relied on ad hoc ideas and intuition. As a result, claims of superior smoothing for certain moving averages have been based on anecdotal evidence and lack objective validation. Moreover, traders often overlook that a moving average must be not only smooth but also responsive and accurate. Overemphasizing smoothness can undermine both responsiveness and accuracy.

In this book, we introduced three novel quantitative measures to assess the accuracy, responsiveness, and smoothness of trend-following rules. These metrics enabled, for the first time, an objective evaluation of various moving averages commonly regarded as highly smooth. This chapter examines whether replacing traditional moving averages with these alternatives can enhance the efficiency of trend-following rules.

First, we argued that a moving average with high smoothness should be used in the Moving Average Direction (MA-D) rule rather than in the price and moving average crossover (P-MA) rule or the double moving average crossover (MA-C) rule. The reason is that, in the P-MA rule, the return weights decrease with the return lag, regardless of the moving average used. In the MA-C rule, the return weights follow a hump-shaped pattern, which is also independent of the moving average type. Only in the MA-D rule do the return weights mirror the shape of the price weights in the moving average. As a result, the MA-D rule is the only one that preserves the high smoothness of the moving average.

The Sine Weighted Moving Average (SWMA) and the Gaussian Moving Average (GMA) are the two moving averages with the highest smoothness. However, they fall short in terms of responsiveness and accuracy. In principle, these moving averages offer a good balance between smoothness and responsiveness. However, the MA-C rule, which uses a conventional moving average, provides the same balance between smoothness and responsiveness while achieving a better tradeoff between accuracy and responsiveness than the MA-D rule that relies on either the SWMA or GMA.

We examined multiple-smoothed moving averages based on the SMA, LMA, and EMA. From our analysis, we reached two main conclusions. First, the double-smoothed moving average demonstrates better properties than triple-smoothed or higher-order moving averages. In other words, multiple smoothing iterations beyond two are not effective. Second, even double-smoothed moving averages do not enhance the efficiency of trend-following. Typically, the MA-D rule that employs a double moving average does not perform better than the MA-C rule using a conventional moving average.

Our analysis suggests that the double-smoothed LMA and the Arnaud Legoux Moving Average (ALMA) are the most effective options among all considered moving averages with enhanced smoothness. Specifically, when used in the MA-D rule, their performance is comparable to that of the MA-C rule utilizing a conventional moving average. However, their effectiveness does not exceed that of the MA-C rule with a traditional moving average. We also found that the recommended parameters for the ALMA are not optimal and proposed new parameters that enhance its properties.

Finally, we investigated whether compound smoothing, where one moving average is smoothed by another of a different type, yields a highly original and unique distribution of weights. Our results indicate that the weight distribution resulting from compound smoothing exhibits a smooth, hump-shaped form, characteristic of all MA-C rules. Therefore, the properties of trading rules that use moving averages with compound smoothing can be matched by those based on conventional moving averages.

References

Hansun, S. (2013-8). A New Approach of Moving Average Method in Time Series Analysis. In *2013 Conference on New Media Studies (CoNMedia)* (pp. 1–4). IEEE.

Hansun, S., Charles, V., Gherman, T., & Varadarajan, V. (2022). Hull-WEMA: A Novel Zero-Lag Approach in the Moving Average Family, with an Application to Covid-19. *International Journal of Management and Decision Making, 21*(1), 92–112.

Hutson, J. K. (1984). TRIX: Triple Exponential Smoothing Oscillator. *Technical Analysis of Stocks and Commodities, 2*(3), 91–93.

Lafferty, P. E. (1999). How Smooth Is Your Data Smoother. *Technical Analysis of Stocks and Commodities, 17*(6), 251–256.

Legoux, A., & Kouzis-Loukas, D. (2009). In Search for the Perfect Moving Average. https://www.forexfactory.com/attachment.php?attachmentid=1123528&d=1359078631 [Online; Retrieved 7 October, 2024]

Zakamulin, V., & Giner, J. (2023). Optimal Trend-Following With Transaction Costs. *International Review of Financial Analysis, 90*, Article 102928.

9

Moving Averages with Reduced Lag Time

9.1 Introduction

The moving average is a valuable tool for traders as it helps to reduce the impact of short-term price fluctuations, enabling them to better identify price trends. By calculating an average value from price data, the trajectory of the price becomes more stable and easier to analyze. However, the downside is that moving averages rely on past price data, causing them to lag behind current market conditions. This lagging feature complicates the use of moving averages as trading signals. Delayed signals generated by moving averages could lead traders to miss advantageous trading opportunities or suffer financial losses.

Traders have long sought to develop zero-lag moving averages that respond immediately to market changes, allowing for prompt trading decisions. This has led to the development of several versions of "zero-lag" moving averages.[1] Advocates of these moving averages claim that they not only have minimal lag but are also smoother than traditional moving averages. However, these claims are based primarily on anecdotal evidence and visual examples, with no objective data to support them.

Traditionally, traders calculate the average lag time of a moving average using a formula similar to the one used for determining the center of mass in physics. As a result, the average lag time corresponds to the center of gravity of the price weights. Traders can adjust these price weights in the moving average, enabling them to control the lag time. By assigning negative price weights, the lag time

[1] Note that the term "zero-lag" moving average is always written in quotation marks because the trading rules based on these moving averages in reality do not have zero lag times.

V. Zakamulin and J. Giner, *The Ultimate Moving Average Handbook*,
https://doi.org/10.1007/978-3-031-90907-8_9

can be reduced to zero or even become negative, causing the moving average to lead the price instead of lagging behind it.

When these "zero-lag" moving averages are applied to price data, a visual comparison between the price curve and the smoothed price curve might suggest that the moving average is lag-free. However, relying only on visual comparisons can be misleading, especially if you are not aware of which aspects of the price dynamics to focus on when assessing the lagging behavior of the moving average.

There are several issues with the traditional method of measuring the average lag time of a moving average. The primary problem is that this measure is accurate only when prices are consistently rising. In such cases, it correctly reflects the average delay of the moving average. However, when prices are consistently falling, the same measure, intended to calculate the average lag time, actually ends up calculating the lead time instead.

Traders misunderstand the concept of lag time when discussing moving averages. They mistakenly calculate the lag time during trending markets. However, what they actually need to know is the time lag between a change in the trend and the corresponding change in the trading signal. In the correct definition, the trading signal always lags behind a trend's turning point, whether the trend is shifting from an uptrend to a downtrend or from a downtrend to an uptrend.

Moreover, it is important to note that trading signals are rarely based solely on the moving average. Typically, these signals are generated by crossover rules, such as a price crossing the moving average or two moving averages crossing each other. Therefore, the focus should shift from measuring the lag time of the moving average itself to measuring the lag time of the trading rule that uses moving averages.

Most of the time, prices are either trending upward or downward, so a "zero-lag" moving average tends to closely follow the price trajectory. However, a close inspection of the moving average around a trend's turning point reveals that after the trend changes direction, the "zero-lag" moving average continues to move in the original direction for a while before eventually reversing course. This effect, known as "overshooting," is often considered by traders to be a minor issue that can be ignored. However, overshooting actually highlights the inherent lag in what is termed a "zero-lag" moving average. In other words, overshooting is a manifestation of the lagging nature of any "zero-lag" moving average.

In this book, we introduce a new quantitative measure called the average lag time of a trading rule. This measure consistently assesses the average delay between a trend's turning point and the change in the trading signal, regardless of the trading rule used. Additionally, we propose two other novel measures: one to evaluate the smoothness of the trading signal and another to assess the accuracy of the trend-following rule in identifying the trend's direction.

With these measures, we can now comprehensively and objectively analyze the characteristics of "zero-lag" moving averages for the first time. This analysis will help determine whether these moving averages truly exhibit zero lag time and high smoothness simultaneously and whether they are indeed superior to traditional moving averages.

We start this chapter by describing how to reduce the lag time of moving averages and outlining the typical approach to creating a "zero-lag" moving average. We also explain why the average lag time of a moving average can be easily manipulated. Next, we review the most popular variants of "zero-lag" moving averages. We then discuss practical trading rules based on "zero-lag" moving averages. Finally, we compare the characteristics of trading rules based on various moving averages to determine which "zero-lag" moving average is the most effective and assess whether these trading rules are truly superior to those based on traditional moving averages.

9.2 How to Reduce the Lag Time of the Moving Average

There are a few ways to reduce the lag time of a moving average. One approach is to decrease the size of the averaging window. By using a smaller number of periods for calculating the moving average, it becomes more responsive to current price changes. For instance, switching from a 50-day Simple Moving Average (SMA) to a 25-day SMA cuts the lag time in half. Another way to reduce lag is by assigning larger weights to more recent prices and smaller weights to older prices when computing the moving average. For example, instead of the SMA that assigns equal weights to all prices, you can opt for the Linear Moving Average (LMA). The LMA gives more weight to recent prices, making the moving average more sensitive to recent price movements and reducing the lag time.

Regrettably, decreasing the size of the averaging window also reduces the smoothness of the moving average. A shorter averaging window tends to retain more noise, hence leading to less smoothed data. Additionally, overweighting more recent prices also negatively impacts the smoothness. However, the size of the averaging window remains constant in this case, so the loss of smoothness is not as significant when compared to reducing the size of the averaging window.

To improve the smoothness of a moving average, it is important to reduce its lag time by increasing the size of the averaging window, rather than decreasing it. At first, it might seem impossible to reduce the lag time while simultaneously increasing the window size. However, it is achievable, and we will explain how. Unfortunately, this method has a drawback: it reduces the accuracy of the moving average.

The approach often employed in the creation of "zero-lag" moving averages is to incorporate the difference between the current price and the moving average of past prices into the calculation of the moving average. This adjustment brings the moving average value nearer to the current price, creating the impression that the new moving average is much faster than the original, without compromising the smoothness of the trend line. The idea behind this approach is demonstrated in Fig. 9.1.

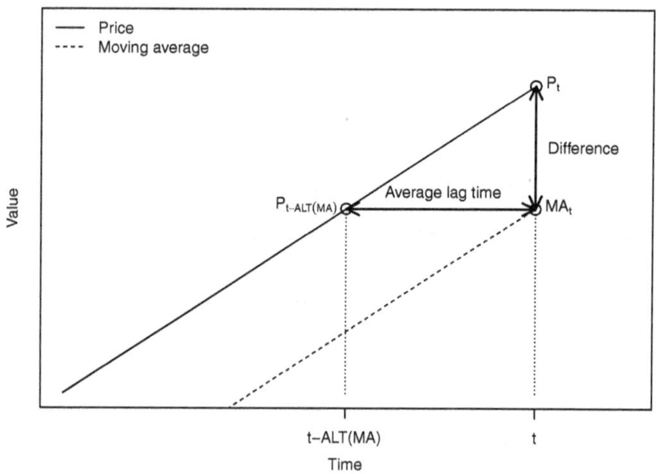

Fig. 9.1 Illustration of the average lag time of the moving average and the difference between the current price and the value of the moving average

Specifically, Fig. 9.1 plots the price and the value of the moving average. Since we focus on measuring the average lag time, we disregard the noise in the data and assume that the price steadily increases. As the price increases, the value of the moving average also increases. However, the current value of the moving average, represented by MA_t, is below the current price, represented by P_t. The lag time of the moving average is defined as the time difference between MA_t and the most recent past price that matches the value of MA_t. This past price is denoted as $P_{t-\text{ALT(MA)}}$, where ALT(MA) stands for the average lag time of the moving average. By definition, $P_{t-\text{ALT(MA)}} = MA_t$.

The difference between the current price and the moving average value is expressed as $P_t - MA_t$. The straightforward idea to adjust the moving average involves adding this difference to the existing moving average value, which yields $MA_t + (P_t - MA_t)$. However, this adjustment does not produce the desired outcome as it only outputs the current price P_t.

John Tukey (1977) proposed a method for adjusting the moving average of past data toward the current data point. To apply Tukey's method to price data, the following steps are taken:

1. Smooth the time series of prices P using a moving average to obtain $MA(P)$.
2. Calculate the difference between the price and the moving average: $P - MA(P)$.
3. Smooth the difference obtained in step 2 using the same moving average.
4. Add the smoothed difference from step 3 to the smoothed price series from step 1.

This smoothing method was termed "twicing" by John Tukey. The name "twicing" originates from the fact that the same moving average is used twice in the calculation: first, when computing the difference between the price and moving average, and second, when smoothing the price adjusted by the difference.

The mathematical computation of the adjusted moving average can be written as:

$$AMA_t(n, P) = MA_t(n, P) + MA_t(n, P - MA(P)),$$

where n represents the size of the averaging window and $AMA_t(n, P)$ represents the adjusted value of the moving average.

An alternative way to compute the adjusted value of the moving average is by utilizing the fact that the moving average is a linear operator. This alternative calculation can be expressed as:

$$AMA_t(n, P) = 2\,MA_t(n, P) - MA_t(n, MA(n, P)). \qquad (9.1)$$

In this approach, the adjusted moving average is calculated as twice the moving average of prices minus the double moving average of prices.

The "twicing" method reduces the ALT(MA) measure to exactly zero, regardless of the moving average type. This result follows directly from the properties of the ALT(MA) measure discussed in Chapter 2.

First, ALT(MA) satisfies a linearity property, which states that the average lag time of a linear combination of moving averages equals the corresponding linear combination of their average lag times. Mathematically,

$$\text{ALT}(a \cdot MA_1 + b \cdot MA_2) = a \cdot \text{ALT}(MA_1) + b \cdot \text{ALT}(MA_2),$$

where a and b are scalars satisfying the condition $a + b = 1$, and MA_1 and MA_2 are two moving averages.

Second, the average lag time of a k-smoothed moving average scales linearly with k, meaning

$$\text{ALT}(MA^{*k}) = k \cdot \text{ALT}(MA),$$

where MA^{*k} denotes the repeated application of the moving average k times.

The "twicing" method constructs the adjusted moving average (AMA) as a linear combination of two moving averages with weights 2 and -1, so that the sum of the weights is $2 - 1 = 1$. Therefore, the average lag time of the AMA constructed using the "twicing" method is:

$$\begin{aligned}\text{ALT}(AMA) &= \text{ALT}(2 \cdot MA - 1 \cdot MA(MA)) = 2 \cdot \text{ALT}(MA) - 1 \cdot \text{ALT}(MA(MA)) \\ &= 2 \cdot \text{ALT}(MA) - 1 \cdot (2 \cdot \text{ALT}(MA)) = 0.\end{aligned}$$

Notably, while the "twicing" method eliminates the average lag time, it also increases the effective averaging window. If the original moving average $MA(n, P)$ has a window size of n, the adjusted moving average uses the double-smoothed moving average $MA(n, MA(n, P))$, which has an expanded window size of $2n - 1$.

Numerous additional methods have been proposed to reduce the lag time associated with a moving average. Some methods aim to adjust the value of the moving average based on the difference between the moving average and the current price, while others utilize more complex techniques, like Digital Signal Processing (DSP). The averaging window size in a "zero-lag" moving average is usually large, enhancing the smoothness of the resulting average.

All methods for reducing the lag in moving averages may seem very sophisticated. Traders who propose these methods might appear to be rocket scientists because their techniques seem cutting-edge. However, there is a simple and straightforward technical explanation for why the average lag time in a moving average can be easily manipulated.

Consider again the computation of the average lag time of the moving average:

$$\text{ALT}(MA) = \frac{\sum_{i=0}^{n-1} w_i \times i}{\sum_{i=0}^{n-1} w_i}, \tag{9.2}$$

where w_i represents the weight assigned to price P_{t-i} in the computation of the moving average. This formula for calculating the lag time of a moving average follows the same principle as the formula for computing the center of mass in physics. Each price weight w_i is multiplied by its corresponding lag number $i \in [0, n-1]$. The resulting products are then summed up and divided by the sum of the price weights.

It is important to note that as long as all price weights are non-negative, the average lag time is positive. However, if we permit negative price weights, the average lag time can reach zero or even become negative. This would indicate that the moving average is no longer a lagging indicator but rather a leading indicator of the price action. It is worth noting that traders typically avoid suggesting moving averages with negative lag time as it raises an apparent paradox: how can you use past price data to develop a leading indicator of price action? This paradox is much less apparent when traders devise moving averages with a zero lag time.

A thorough examination of the price weights used in all "zero-lag" moving averages reveals that distant prices are assigned negative weights. Although these negative weights are relatively small in absolute value compared to the weights given to more recent prices, Eq. (9.2) demonstrates that the impact of these distant price weights on the calculation of lag time grows larger as the price lag becomes more distant. Consequently, the inclusion of even small distant price weights significantly affects the computation of the lag time of the moving average.

To summarize, the ALT(MA) measure can be easily manipulated. All methods for reducing the lag in a moving average ultimately assign negative weights to past prices, no matter how advanced they seem. Visual demonstrations using "zero-lag" moving averages may appear convincing because they align the moving average more closely with the price. Unfortunately, traders often overlook that ALT(MA) is a highly misleading measure that is generally unrelated to the time delay between a trend change and the corresponding adjustment in the trading signal.

9.3 A Survey of Moving Average Variants

9.3.1 Double and Triple Exponential Moving Averages

It is a common misconception that the Double Exponential Moving Average (DEMA) and the Triple Exponential Moving Average (TEMA) were introduced by Patrick Mulloy in his two articles published in 1994. In reality, these moving averages were proposed much earlier by Robert G. Brown in his book

Smoothing, Forecasting and Prediction of Discrete Time Series (1963). When presenting these moving averages, Mulloy follows the same motivation and derivation outlined in Brown's work. Although he includes Brown's book in the reference sections of his articles, he neglects to explicitly acknowledge it in the text or credit Brown as the original creator of these moving averages.

As the name suggests, the DEMA is computed using a combination of Exponential Moving Averages (EMAs). The formula for calculating the DEMA is as follows:

$$DEMA_t(n, P) = 2\,EMA_t(n, P) - EMA_t(n, EMA(n, P)), \tag{9.3}$$

where $EMA_t(n, P)$ denotes the EMA computed using the decay constant $\lambda = (n-1)/(n+1)$.

The comparison between Eqs. (9.1) and (9.3) highlights the similarity between the DEMA and Tukey's "twicing" smoothing method proposed in 1977. The DEMA eliminates the lag inherent in the EMA by incorporating the difference between the current price and the EMA into its calculation. This adjustment is evident in an alternative representation of the DEMA:

$$DEMA_t(n, P) = EMA_t\big(n, P + (P - EMA(n, P))\big).$$

The TEMA value is calculated using the formula:

$$\begin{aligned} TEMA(n, P) =& 3\,EMA_t(n, P) - 3\,EMA_t(n, EMA(n, P)) \\ &+ EMA_t(EMA(n, EMA(n, P))). \end{aligned} \tag{9.4}$$

By utilizing the linearity property of moving averages, we can rewrite the TEMA formula as:

$$TEMA(n, P) = EMA_t\big(n, P + 2(P - EMA(n, P)) - EMA(n, P - EMA(n, P))\big).$$

In other words, to eliminate the lag time and improve the smoothing, the TEMA method adds the double discrepancy $P_t - EMA_t(n, P)$ to the last closing price, subtracts the smoothed value of this discrepancy, and then applies exponential smoothing to the resulting time series.

It is noteworthy that both DEMA and TEMA have an average lag time of exactly zero:

$$ALT(DEMA) = 0, \quad ALT(TEMA) = 0.$$

The DEMA is a specific variant of the adjusted moving average constructed via the "twicing" method, which directly results in $ALT(DEMA) = 0$. In contrast, the TEMA is formed as a linear combination of three moving averages with weights 3, −3, and 1, respectively, so that the sum of the weights is $3 - 3 + 1 = 1$.

The zero lag property of the TEMA follows from the linearity of the ALT(MA) operator and the additive nature of lag in repeated smoothing. In particular, since:

$$\mathrm{ALT}(EMA(EMA)) = 2\,\mathrm{ALT}(EMA)$$

and

$$\mathrm{ALT}(EMA(EMA(EMA))) = 3\,\mathrm{ALT}(EMA),$$

we have:

$$\begin{aligned}\mathrm{ALT}(TEMA) &= \mathrm{ALT}\Big(3\,EMA - 3\,EMA(EMA) + EMA(EMA(EMA))\Big)\\ &= 3\,\mathrm{ALT}(EMA) - 3\,(2\,\mathrm{ALT}(EMA)) + 1\,(3\,\mathrm{ALT}(EMA))\\ &= 3\,\mathrm{ALT}(EMA) - 6\,\mathrm{ALT}(EMA) + 3\,\mathrm{ALT}(EMA) = 0.\end{aligned}$$

Thus, both DEMA and TEMA are designed to have an average lag time of zero.

Figure 9.2 displays the price weights of the DEMA(11) and TEMA(11). While any EMA is formally calculated using an infinite averaging window size, the price weights decay rapidly with the lag number, rendering distant weights insignificant. Similarly, both DEMA(11) and TEMA(11) are computed using infinitely large window sizes. The figure illustrates the price weights up to the lag of 24, as weights beyond this range become too small to be noticeable.

From Fig. 9.2, it is evident that both the DEMA(11) and TEMA(11) have negative weights for distant prices. Specifically, the DEMA(11) assigns negative weights to prices starting from lag 11, whereas the TEMA(11) has negative weights starting from lag 8. The TEMA(11) method exhibits better smoothness than the DEMA(11) because the shape of its price weights is closer to the shape of a damped sine wave[2] compared to the shape of the price weights of the DEMA.

Lastly, it is crucial to point out that the terms "Double EMA" and "Triple EMA," as suggested by Patrick Mulloy, are misleading and may cause confusion about the actual computation and interpretation of these moving averages. Typically, a "double EMA" would be understood as the EMA applied to another EMA, written as $EMA_t(n, EMA(n, P))$. However, the DEMA is not cal-

[2] In the previous chapters of this book, we showed that the smoothest weighting functions are built by summing sine waves of increasing frequency. Visually, these functions resemble a single damped sine wave.

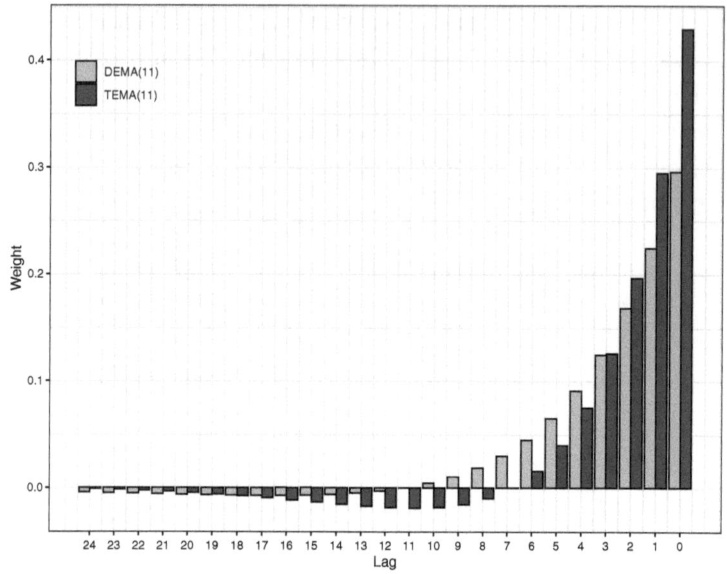

Fig. 9.2 Price weights of the DEMA(11) and TEMA(11). The weights are cut off at lag 24

culated this way. Instead, it is derived from the difference between twice the EMA and the double EMA.

For instance, in Brown's (1963) book, when price dynamics are modeled as a linear trend with added noise, the optimal forecasting of future prices involves both a single EMA, $EMA_t(n, P)$, and a double EMA, $EMA_t(n, EMA(n, P))$. The optimal forecast uses the difference $2\,EMA_t(n, P) - EMA_t(n, EMA(n, P))$. However, Brown does not refer to this difference as a "double EMA."

9.3.2 Zero Lag Exponential Moving Average

This type of a moving average with a reduced lag time was proposed by Ehlers and Way (2010), and is known as the Zero Lag Exponential Moving Average (ZLEMA). As the name suggests, it is based on the EMA. The idea behind the ZLEMA is similar to that of the DEMA, in that both adjust the value of the EMA, using the difference between the current price and the moving average value. However, the significant distinction is that the ZLEMA defines the difference as $P_t - P_{t-\mathrm{ALT(EMA)}}$, where ALT(EMA) represents the average lag time of the $EMA(n)$. In other words, the difference is calculated between the current price and the lagged price,[3] where the lag corresponds to the average lag time of the EMA (for a visual illustration, see Fig. 9.1).

The average lag time of the $EMA(n)$ is computed as:

$$ALT(EMA) = \frac{n-1}{2}.$$

Therefore, the difference can be represented as:

$$P_t - P_{t-\frac{n-1}{2}}.$$

Furthermore, we introduce the notation:

$$P_{t-\frac{n-1}{2}} = Lag_{\frac{n-1}{2}}\left(P_t\right),$$

where Lag_k is the lag operator that can be defined as follows:

$$Lag_k(P_t) = P_{t-k}.$$

Simply put, $Lag_k(P_t)$ refers to the value of the price time series at time $t - k$.

The approach proposed by Ehlers and Way (2010) involves smoothing both the price and the estimated discrepancy. Therefore, the formula for ZLEMA is given by:

$$ZLEMA(n, P) = EMA\Big(n, P + \big(P - Lag_{\frac{n-1}{2}}\left(P\right)\big)\Big). \tag{9.5}$$

By utilizing the linearity property, the ZLEMA formula can be expressed as:

$$ZLEMA(n, P) = 2\,EMA(n, P) - EMA\Big(n, Lag_{\frac{n-1}{2}}\left(P\right)\Big).$$

Consequently, the ZLEMA can be seen as the difference between two instances of the EMA calculated using the price, and one instance of EMA computed using the price lagged by $(n - 1)/2$ observations.

In contrast to the DEMA, the ZLEMA uses different price weights, despite seemingly using a similar method of finding the difference between the price and the moving average of prices. Figure 9.3 illustrates the price weights of ZLEMA(15). It is noteworthy that the most recent price weights in the

---

[3] Note that, in principle, $P_{t-\mathrm{ALT(EMA)}} = EMA_t(n, P)$, but using $P_{t-\mathrm{ALT(EMA)}}$ yields a different result compared to using $EMA_t(n, P)$.

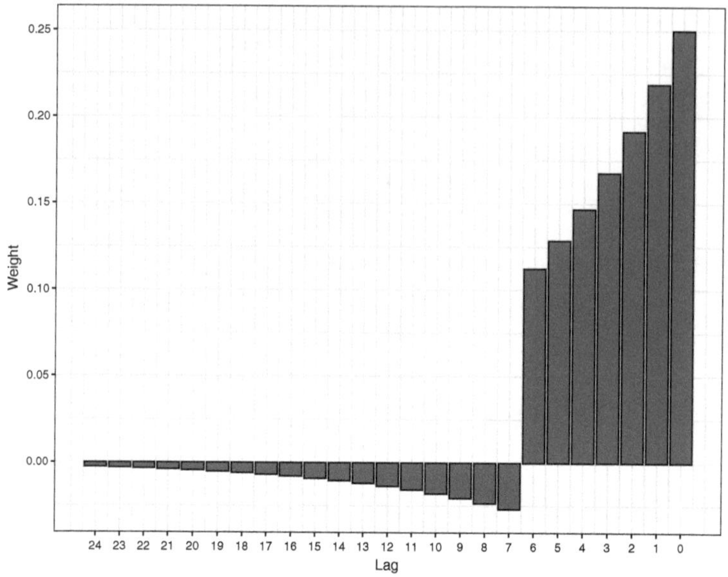

Fig. 9.3 Price weights of the ZLEMA(15). The weights are cut off at lag 24

ZLEMA(15) closely resemble the pattern observed in the EMA(15). Specifically, these price weights decrease exponentially with the price lag. However, from lag 7 onwards, the price weights abruptly become negative. As the lag number increases, these negative weights gradually approach zero.

9.3.3 Hull Moving Average

In 2005, Alan Hull suggested a technique to reduce the average lag time by combining three Linear Moving Averages (LMAs) with varying window sizes. This technique results in a Hull Moving Average (HMA) that is computed using the following formula:

$$HMA(n, P) = LMA\left(\sqrt{n}, 2\,LMA(n/2, P) - LMA(n, P)\right). \quad (9.6)$$

Essentially, this formula involves first calculating the LMA with a window size of $n/2$, multiplying it by 2, and then subtracting from it the LMA with a window size of n. Finally, the resultant difference is further smoothed using the LMA with a window size of $\sqrt{n}$.

According to Alan Hull, the HMA "almost eliminates lag altogether and manages to improve smoothing simultaneously." Although the lag time of the HMA is not zero, it is significantly lower than that of the original LMA.

Moreover, the HMA does offer a higher level of smoothness, making it an improvement in both responsiveness and stability.

To understand how the HMA lessens lag time, let us examine the difference between the two instances of $LMA(n/2)$ and one instance of $LMA(n)$. We can express this difference as:

$$2\,LMA(n/2,P) - LMA(n,P) = LMA(n/2,P) + \underbrace{LMA(n/2,P) - LMA(n,P)}_{\text{Compensation term}}.$$

In this equation, the first term is the $LMA(n/2)$, which tends to lag behind the current price during upward trends. To mitigate this lagging effect and bring the moving average closer to the current price, a compensation term, which is represented by the second part of the equation, is added. The compensation term, $LMA(n/2) - LMA(n)$, serves to reduce the lag in the moving average. Ultimately, this leads to an adjusted moving average with significantly reduced lag time.

Figure 9.4 illustrates the price weights of the adjusted moving average, which is calculated as $2\,LMA(15) - LMA(30)$. Initially, the price weights decline in a linear fashion to a point below zero. However, the weights subsequently rise linearly back to zero. This approach reduces the average delay time as this adjusted moving average assigns negative weights to distant prices.

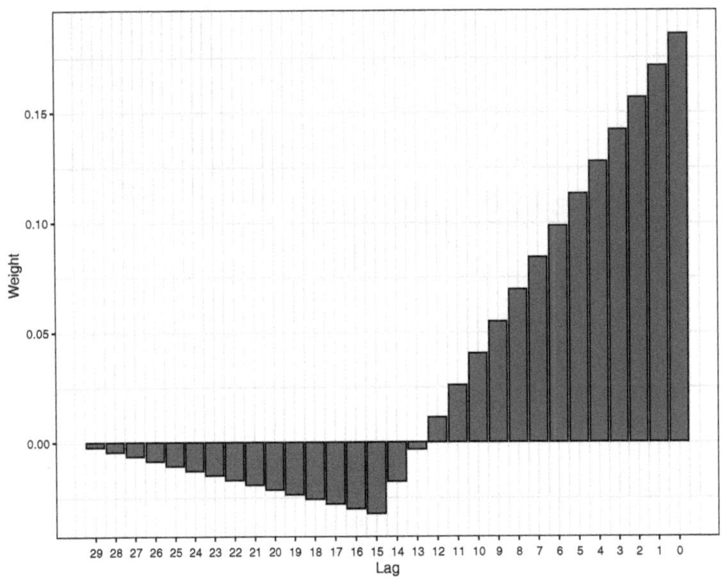

Fig. 9.4 Price weights of the moving average computed as $2\,LMA(15) - LMA(30)$

Although the adjusted moving average reduces the lag time, it lacks smoothness because of the discontinuous nature of the price-weighting function. Specifically, the function jumps from zero to a significant positive weight at the start. It then follows with a decreasing linear segment, followed by an increasing linear segment, with a sharp break between these two phases. To mitigate this issue and enhance smoothness, the adjusted moving average is further smoothed using the LMA with a window size of $\sqrt{30}$.

Figure 9.5 displays the price weights of the HMA(30), which represent a smoother version of the price weights resulting from $2\,LMA(15) - LMA(30)$. The price weights of the HMA(30) exhibit a damped sine wave shape, gradually transitioning from zero to positive, subsequently to negative values, before returning back to zero. This particular shape is known for its high level of smoothness, which has been widely discussed in previous chapters of this book.

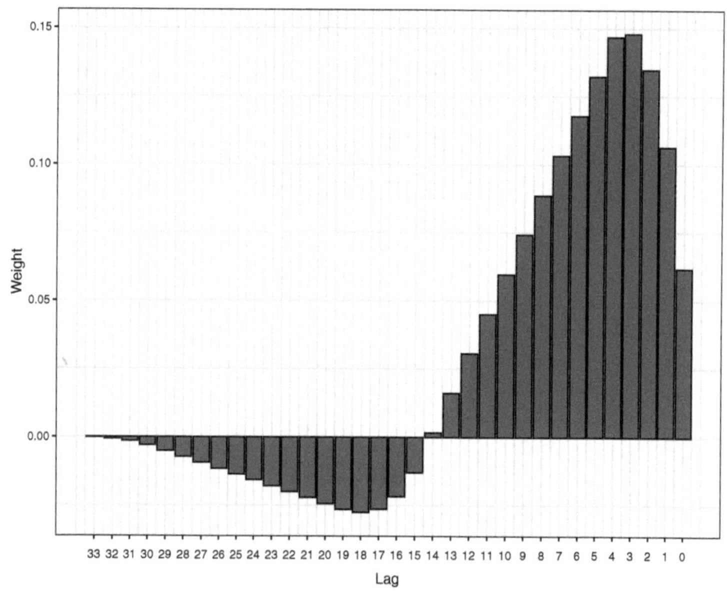

Fig. 9.5 Price weights of the HMA(30)

Compared to LMA(n), HMA(n) not only has a significantly smaller lag time but also offers improved smoothness. This enhanced smoothness arises from two factors: first, the return weight distribution in HMA(n) is inherently smoother, and second, its effective averaging window size is $n + \sqrt{n} - 1$, which is longer than the simple n-length window used in LMA(n).

9.3.4 Tillson T3 Moving Average

Developed by Tim Tillson in (1998), the Tillson T3 moving average is promoted as superior to traditional moving averages due to its enhanced responsiveness and smoothness. Moreover, the creator of the T3 moving average claims that it solves the problem of overshooting inherent in all "zero-lag" moving averages.

The T3 moving average is an improvement over the DEMA popularized by Patrick Mulloy. Tim Tillson introduces a Generalized DEMA (GD) as the foundation for the T3 moving average. The GD is calculated using the following formula:

$$GD_t(n, v, P) = (1 + v)EMA_t(n, P) - v\, EMA_t(n, EMA(n, P)).$$

In this equation, n represents the size of the averaging window, which is used to determine the decay constant in the EMA. The volume factor, denoted as v and ranging from 0 to 1, controls the responsiveness of the GD. When v is set to 0, the GD simplifies to the EMA. Conversely, when v is set to 1, the GD becomes equivalent to the DEMA. The author recommends using $v = 0.7$ for optimal results.

To address the lack of smoothness in both the DEMA and the GD, Tim Tillson proposes applying the GD three times to the price data. This results in the computation of the T3 moving average according to:

$$T3_t(n, P) = GD_t(n, GD(n, GD(n, P))). \tag{9.7}$$

For simplicity, we omit the dependence on v in this notation.

To illustrate how the triple application of the GD improves the responsiveness and smoothing of the moving average, Fig. 9.6 plots the return weights of the GD(8), GD(8,GD(8)), and GD(8,GD(8,GD(8))). That is, this figure shows the return weights of the single GD, double GD, and triple GD.

The single GD suffers from a lack of smoothness because of an initial jump from zero to a significant positive weight, followed by a steep exponential decline. On the other hand, the triple application of the GD produces a price-weighting function that resembles the shape of a damped sine wave. Notably, the negative price weights in the T3 moving average are larger in absolute value than those in the GD for the corresponding negative price weights. This means that the T3 moving average is not only smoother but also more responsive than its predecessor, the GD.

Now we turn to discussing the effect of the volume parameter v. For illustration, Fig. 9.7 plots the price weights of T3($v = 1.0$) versus the price weights

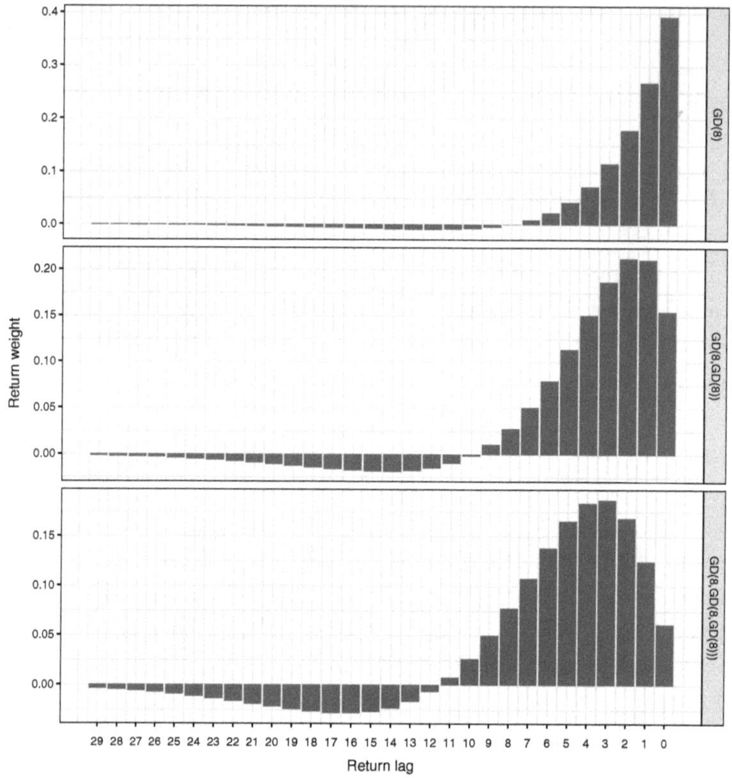

Fig. 9.6 Price weights of the GD(8), GD(8,GD(8)), and GD(8,GD(8,GD(8)))

of T3($v = 0.7$). The weights of the former moving average equal those of the triple DEMA, while the weights of the latter moving average are computed using the recommended value of the volume parameter.

Reducing the volume parameter from 1.0 to 0.7 decreases the absolute values of distant negative price weights. Consequently, a smaller volume parameter makes the T3 moving average less responsive. Yet, the shape of the price weights retains their smoothness. Therefore, the T3($v = 0.7$) moving average is less responsive than T3($v = 1.0$), while the smoothness of both these moving averages is quite high.

Finally, in this section, we want to verify whether the T3 moving average effectively eliminates the issue of overshooting commonly associated with all "zero-lag" moving averages. When the price steadily trends upward or downward, there is no overshooting and a zero-lag moving average closely tracks the movement of the price. Overshooting occurs when a "zero-lag" moving average temporarily continues to move in the wrong direction after a turning point in the trend. This results in a delay in recognizing the trend reversal.

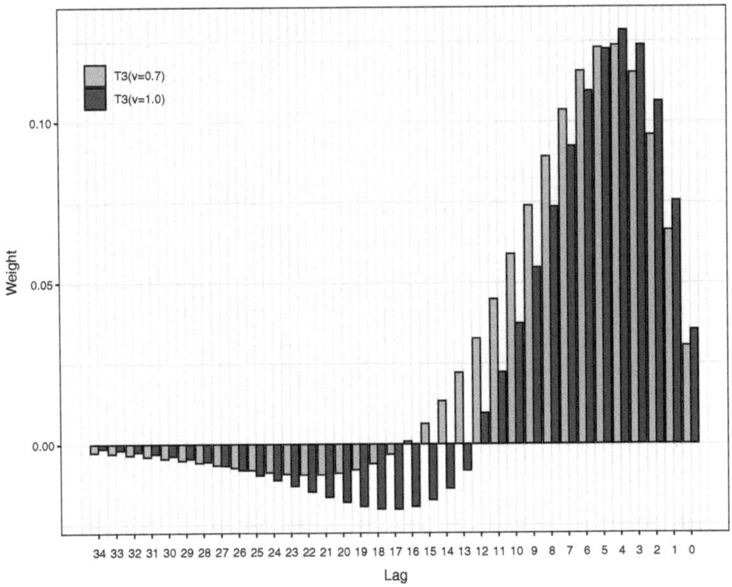

Fig. 9.7 Price weights of T3($v = 1.0$) versus the price weights of T3($v = 0.7$). The weights are cut off at lag 34

The overshooting effect can also be seen in the non-monotone trajectory of the value of the technical indicator after a change in the trend. For illustration, we assume that the trend-following strategy employs the direction of the T3 moving average rule. In particular, this rule generates a Buy trading signal when the T3 moving average increases and a Sell trading signal when the T3 moving average decreases. In our notation, this is the T3-D rule.

To provide a better understanding, Fig. 9.8 displays the mean returns and reactions of T3-D($v = 1.0$) and T3-D($v = 0.7$) technical indicators to changes in mean return values. Initially, the mean return is assumed to be $\mu = 0.2$ until time $t_0 = 0$, followed by a shift to $\mu = -0.2$ from time t_0 onwards. The peak of the price trend corresponds to t_0 on the dotted line in the figure. The other lines depict the responses of the T3-D($v = 1.0$) and T3-D($v = 0.7$) technical indicators to the change in the price trend.

It is important to note that the mean returns switch from μ to $-\mu$ instantaneously, whereas there is a delay in the trading signal's response. This delay can be determined by calculating the time difference between the point of trend change and when the technical indicator's value reaches zero.

When using a conventional moving average such as SMA, LMA, or EMA in a trading rule, the value of the technical indicator decreases gradually and monotonically from μ to $-\mu$, without any overshooting. However, when

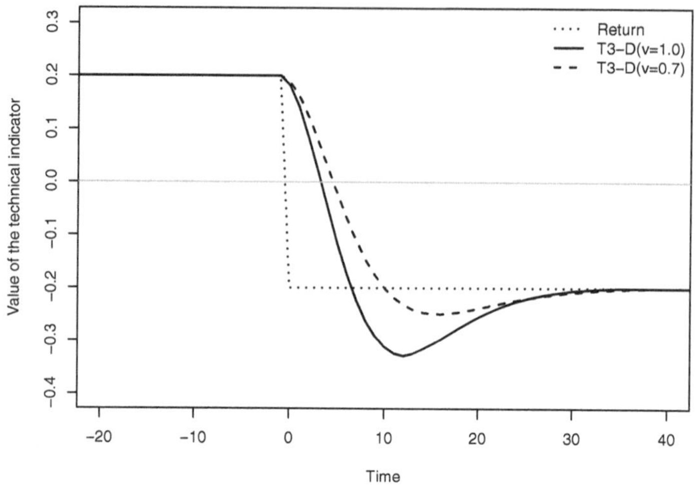

Fig. 9.8 Change in the mean returns and the values of the T3-D(v=1.0) and T3-D(v=0.7) technical indicators

using a T3-D technical indicator, there is a gradual decrease following a trend change, but it is non-monotonic. Specifically, the T3-D indicator initially decreases below $-\mu$ and then rebounds to settle at $-\mu$. This phenomenon is another indication of the overshooting effect. The presence of negative weights associated with distant return values is the sole cause of this effect.

The curves in Fig. 9.8 indicate that the T3-D($v = 0.7$) technical indicator has a longer delay time and smaller overshooting compared to the T3-D($v = 1.0$) technical indicator. However, it is evident that even with the recommended value of $v = 0.7$, the overshooting is not completely eliminated, contrary to Tim Tillson's claim. The crucial conclusion drawn from this analysis is that as long as there are negative weights in the moving average, the overshooting effect will persist. The only way to avoid overshooting is by prohibiting negative weights.

9.3.5 End Point Moving Average

The End Point Moving Average (EPMA), developed by Patrick Lafferty in (1995), is a moving average that fits a straight line to the n most recent prices using ordinary least squares technique. The EPMA is calculated by taking the last point on the fitted line. This methodology is also known as the Least Squares Moving Average or the Moving Linear Regression, due to its use of linear regression.

While the EPMA uses linear regression to calculate its value, it can still be classified as a type of moving average. This is because the EPMA formula, derived in the Appendix of this chapter, follows the general structure of a weighted moving average computation. Specifically, the EPMA formula can be written as:

$$EPMA_t(n, P) = \frac{\sum_{i=0}^{n-1}(2n - 3i - 1)P_{t-i}}{\sum_{i=0}^{n-1}(2n - 3i - 1)}.$$

In this equation, the weight given to each price P_{t-i} is determined by the following formula:

$$w_i = 2n - 3i - 1.$$

Thus, the EPMA can be interpreted as a linear moving average of the past n prices, with both positive and negative coefficients.

Similarly to the DEMA and TEMA, the EPMA has an average lag time of precisely zero:

$$ALT(EPMA) = 0.$$

A detailed proof of this formula can be found in the Appendix of this chapter.

As previously discussed, achieving a zero lag time necessitates the utilization of negative price weights. Figure 9.9 showcases the price weights of the EPMA(20), illustrating that the weights progressively decrease from a positive value to a negative value. This further validates the EPMA's status as a moving average with a reduced lag time.

However, the average lag time of a trading rule based on the EPMA will not be zero. Additionally, the shape of the price weights of the EPMA lacks smoothness. Therefore, it is doubtful that the EPMA achieves a good balance between responsiveness and smoothness.

9.4 Trading with Reduced-Lag Moving Averages

In the previous section, we explored various types of "zero-lag" moving averages. While the DEMA(n), TEMA(n), and EPMA(n) have indeed a true zero lag time according to the definition of the average lag time of the moving average, ALT(MA), the HMA(n), and ZLEMA(n) come close to achieving zero lag. The T3(n) moving average, on the other hand, has some lag time although it is still significantly reduced compared to traditional moving averages computed using the same parameter n.

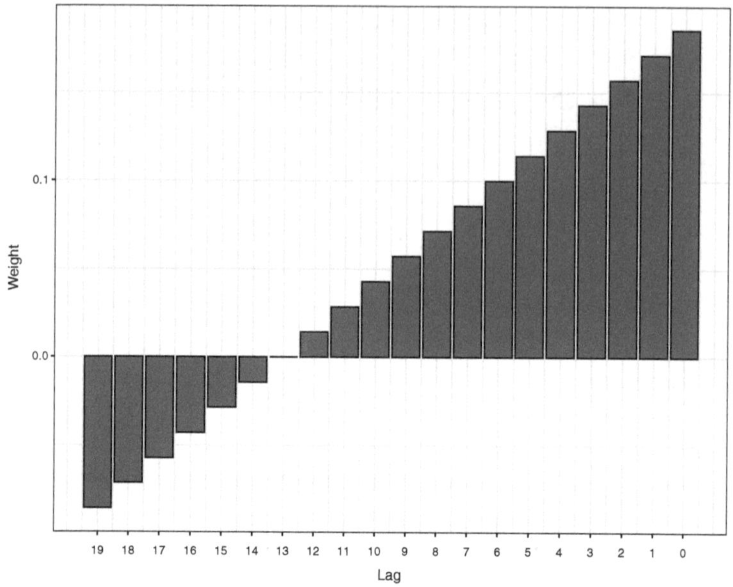

Fig. 9.9 Price weights of the EPMA(20)

The objective of this section is to explore the optimal utilization of "zero-lag" moving averages in trend-following strategies. This analysis is invaluable for traders as these moving averages differ substantially from conventional ones such as SMA, LMA, and EMA. Therefore, it is crucial for traders to comprehend all the intricacies of these "zero-lag" moving averages and beware of the potential pitfalls when using them in traditional trading strategies.

The most commonly used trend-following rules are the crossover rules, which include the price and moving average crossover (P-MA) and the double moving average crossover (MA-C). These rules take advantage of the delayed nature of a moving average. Essentially, when prices trend upward, the moving average falls behind the price, while in a downward trend, the moving average precedes the price. This difference between the price and the moving average is what generates the trading signal. As a result, when a "zero-lag" moving average is used in the P-MA rule, the trading signal fails to accurately determine the trend direction in a trending market. This means that the signal is not reliable when it comes to identifying whether the trend is upward or downward.

Hence, the most rational trading strategy that utilizes a "zero-lag" moving average is the moving average direction (MA-D) rule. This rule follows a straightforward principle: when prices are on an upward trend, the moving average value of prices tends to increase, and conversely, in downtrends, the moving average typically decreases. Thus, when the moving average value has risen over the last period, a Buy signal is generated, and a Sell signal is triggered when it has decreased.

Formally, the technical indicator for the MA-D rule is computed as follows:

$$I_t^{\text{MA-D}}(n) = MA_t(n) - MA_{t-1}(n).$$

In this equation, $I_t^{\text{MA-D}}(n)$ represents the technical indicator for the moving average direction rule. $MA_t(n)$ refers to the current value of the moving average, and $MA_{t-1}(n)$ represents the previous value of the moving average.

The technical indicator for any trend-following rule based on moving averages of prices can alternatively be represented as a single moving average of past returns:

$$I_t(n) = \sum_{i=0}^{n-1} \theta_i r_{t-i},$$

where r_{t-i} denotes the return at time $t - i$ and θ_i represents the weight of r_{t-i} in the computation of the moving average.

It is worth noting that in the MA-D rule, the return weights θ_i are derived by scaling the price weights w_i by a positive constant c. This means that $\theta_i = c \times w_i$. As a result, the shape of the return weights corresponds to that of the price weights. Hence, the figures provided above enable traders to identify the shape of the return weights in the MA-D rules that employ "zero-lag" moving averages.

The rest of this section is devoted to demonstration of the drawbacks of using "zero-lag" moving averages in the crossover rules. We start with the price and End Point Moving Average crossover rule, P-EPMA(n), where the trading signal is triggered based on the difference between the current price and the EPMA of n prices. Figure 9.10 plots the return weights of the technical indicator of the P-EPMA(20) crossover rule.

It is important to note that the sum of all the return weights in the P-EPMA rule is zero, which results in the Noise Suppression Factor (NSF) being zero as well. The NSF measures the accuracy of the rule in identifying the trend direction when it continues in its current path. As a result, the accuracy of the rule in identifying the trend direction in trending markets is zero.[4]

Traders may be tempted to substitute the price with a "zero-lag" moving average in the price and moving average crossover rule. At first glance, this combination appears to offer an advantage over the standard price and moving

---

[4] Note that the shape of the return weights in the P-EPMA rule resembles that of the Moving Average Convergence/Divergence (MACD) rule. As a result, like MACD, the P-EPMA rule can only detect trend changes, not trend direction.

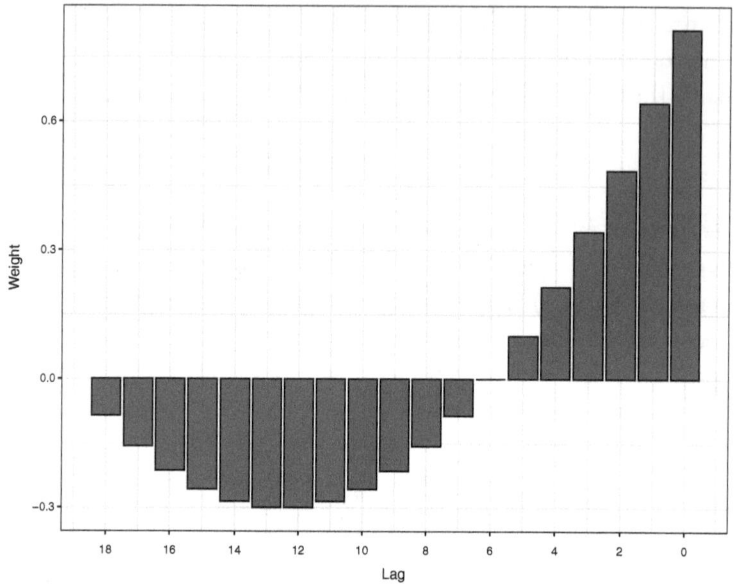

Fig. 9.10 Return weights of the technical indicator of the P-EPMA(20) crossover rule

average crossover rule, as the "zero-lag" moving average is noticeably smoother than the price.

Figure 9.11 illustrates the impact of replacing the price with a "zero-lag" moving average, showcasing the return weights of the DEMA(5) and EMA(20) crossover rule. The return weights in this trading rule have a hump-shaped form that can be generated using a standard double EMA crossover rule, such as the 3- and 20-period EMA crossover rule. Therefore, this trading rule does not provide any benefits over the standard double crossover rule.

Lastly, we examine trading with the T3 moving average. Unlike other "zero-lag" moving averages, this moving average is relatively slower when the volume factor v is notably less than one. As it has a clear lag time, it can be used in standard crossover rules in theory. However, we need to determine whether incorporating it in the standard crossover rule makes sense.

Figure 9.12 displays the return weights of the technical indicator of the price and T3(10) crossover (P-T3(10)) rule, where the T3 moving average is computed using a volume factor of $v = 0.7$. The return weights in the T3-D rule are shown in Fig. 9.7. To discern the qualitative differences between the T3-D and P-T3 rules, we can compare their return weights. A visual examination indicates that the return weights in the P-T3 rule are not as smooth as those in the T3-D rule. This is due to the return weights in the T3-D rule more closely resembling a damped sine wave than those in the P-T3 rule. Furthermore,

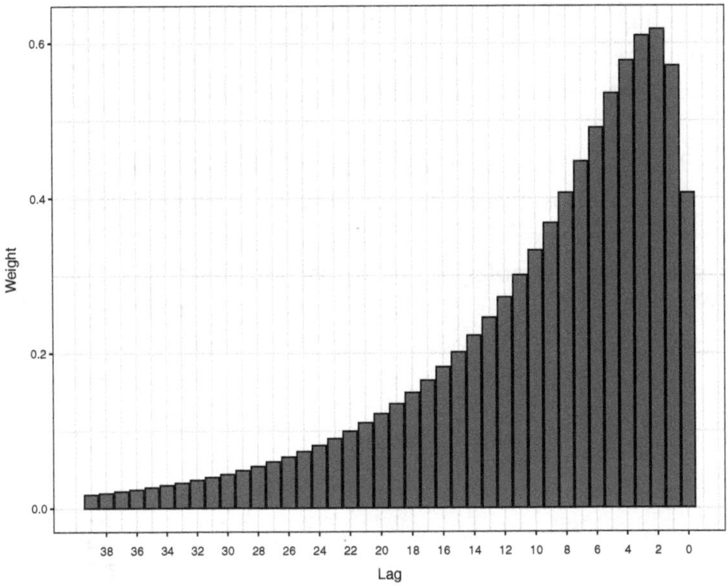

Fig. 9.11 Return weights of the technical indicator of the DEMA(5) and EMA(20) crossover rule

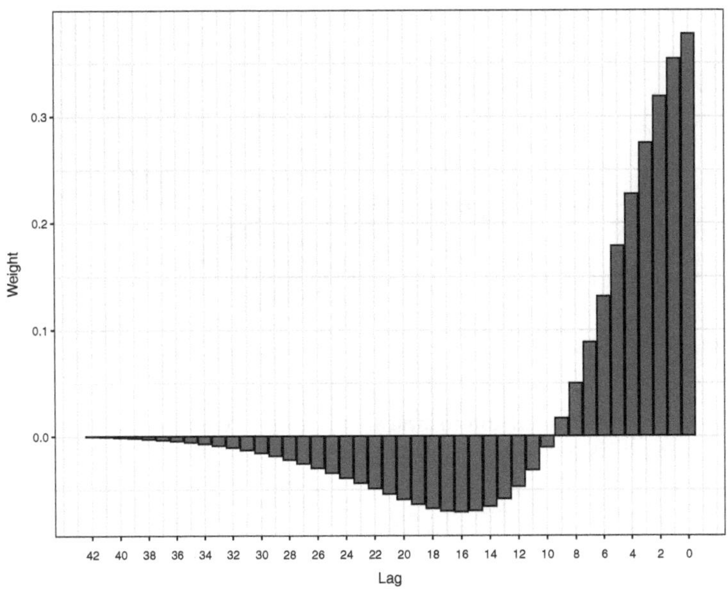

Fig. 9.12 Return weights of the technical indicator of the P-T3(10) rule, where the T3 moving average is computed using a volume factor of $v = 0.7$

the negative tail of the return weights in the P-T3 rule is more substantial compared to the T3-D rule. Based on this, the P-T3 rule has lower accuracy in identifying trend direction and exhibits greater overshooting than the T3-D rule.

Figure 9.13 illustrates the return weights of the technical indicator of the 5- and 10-period T3 crossover rule, where the T3 moving average is computed using a volume factor of $v = 0.7$. The return weights in this rule exhibit a smooth shape that resembles the return weights in the MACD rule, where the sum of positive weights equals the sum of negative weights. However, as discussed previously, the MACD rule is not suitable for use in trending markets. Consequently, the T3-C rule presents challenges when applied in trending market conditions.

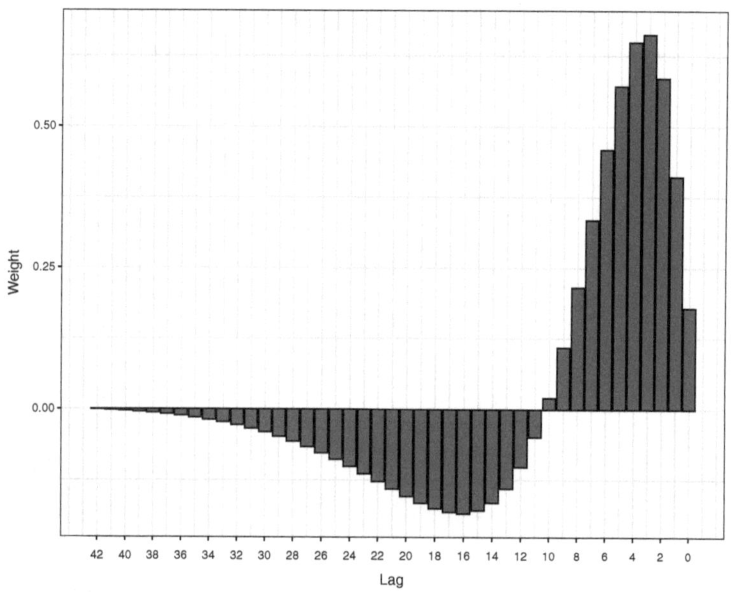

Fig. 9.13 Return weights of the technical indicator of the T3-C(5,10) rule, where the T3 moving average is computed using a volume factor of $v = 0.7$

9.5 Comparing Reduced-Lag Moving Averages

Traders have proposed various types of "zero-lag" moving averages, and in this chapter, we have reviewed the most popular variants. Each of these moving averages is claimed to possess unique characteristics and be superior to its predecessors. However, there is currently no answer as to which of these moving averages is the best.

Advocates of these “zero-lag” moving averages argue that they outperform conventional moving averages that lag behind upward trending prices. These proponents claim that these moving averages not only have little to no lag time, but they also provide a smoother representation of the data compared to traditional moving averages. Unfortunately, there is currently no objective evidence to support these claims. The support for these assertions is based solely on anecdotal evidence and visual illustrations.

This section has two goals. First, we aim to objectively compare the characteristics of the trading rules based on “zero-lag” moving averages in order to determine the most effective one. Second, we examine whether trading rules based on “zero-lag” moving averages are indeed superior to those based on traditional moving averages.

Throughout this book, we argue that there is no sense to evaluate the characteristics of moving averages in isolation. Instead, the focus should be on evaluating the characteristics of trading rules that are based on moving averages. This is because a trading signal in a trend-following rule is triggered by the relationship between the price and a moving average, the relationship between multiple moving averages, or the change in the value of a moving average.

Our objective comparison is based on applying three novel quantitative measures to evaluate the characteristics of trading rules based on both “zero-lag” and traditional moving averages. The first measure is the Noise Suppression Factor (NSF), which assesses the accuracy of a trading rule in identifying the trend direction. The second measure is the Average Lag Time (ALT), which evaluates the average delay between a turning point in the trend and the change in the trading signal. The third measure is the Smoothness Index (SMI), which evaluates the persistence of the trading signal. These measures are calculated using only the return weights in a technical indicator. Therefore, the performance of a trading rule is entirely determined by the shape of return weights in its technical indicator or return weighting function.

All of the reviewed “zero-lag” moving averages are determined by a single parameter, denoted as n. For the HMA and EPMA, this parameter sets the size of the averaging window, while for the DEMA, TEMA, ZLEMA, and T3 moving averages, it is used to compute the decay constant in the calculation of the exponential moving average.

As argued in the previous section, the most practical trading strategy employing a “zero-lag” moving average is the MA-D rule. This rule suggests that the direction of the moving average can act as a reliable indicator of the market trend. Specifically, an upward-moving average signals a bullish trend, while a downward-moving average suggests a bearish trend.

The use of a single parameter greatly facilitates the comparison of trading strategies based on "zero-lag" moving averages. It is important to note that changing this parameter affects all quantitative measures of the trading rule, including accuracy, responsiveness, and smoothness.

When comparing trading rules based on "zero-lag" moving averages, it is essential to consider multiple measures simultaneously, rather than relying on a single metric. For example, one cannot conclude that the DEMA-D(n) rule is superior to the P-SMA(n) rule solely based on its shorter lag time. This is because the lag time of the P-SMA rule can be reduced by decreasing the size of the averaging window, allowing it to match the lag time of the DEMA-D(n) rule at a specific window size m.

It is also impossible to employ all three quantitative measures simultaneously when comparing trading rules. Our previous analysis in this book has shown that no trading rule can be considered ideal based on all three measures. Hence, it is advisable to use a two-measure comparison approach instead. We advocate comparing trading rules using the ALT and SMI measures, and the ALT and NSF measures, as it is the most straightforward and logical method.

The idea behind our comparison is as follows. Let us consider the ALT and SMI measures. These measures are probably the most relevant because the proponents of "zero-lag" moving averages claim that they not only have a shorter lag time compared to traditional moving averages but also offer better smoothness. The main concept behind our comparison is to find a trading rule that effectively combines both responsiveness and smoothness. In other words, we are searching for the trading rule that provides the highest smoothness for a given level of responsiveness or the trading rule that offers the best responsiveness for a given level of smoothness.

To ensure that the parameter n does not influence the choice of the best trading rule, we have adopted a standardized approach to compare competing rules. We start by varying the value of n and calculating the ALT and SMI for each rule. Based on this evaluation, we then plot a curve in the ALT-SMI space for each trading rule. These curves help visualize the relationship between responsiveness and smoothness for each rule in the set of examined rules. If a curve consistently lies above another curve, the trading rule associated with that curve is considered more efficient. We also use a similar method to compare the efficiencies of the rules in the ALT-NSF space.

Among the considered "zero-lag" moving averages, the HMA and T3 moving averages have similar price weight shapes as shown in Figs. 9.4 and 9.7. On the other hand, the other moving averages show different price weight shapes.

Based on this observation, we can assume that the HMA-D and T3-D trading rules should have similar characteristics. To test this assumption, the left panel in Fig. 9.14 displays the combinations of the ALT and SMI for the HMA-D and T3-D rules. The right panel of the same figure shows the combinations of the ALT and NSF.

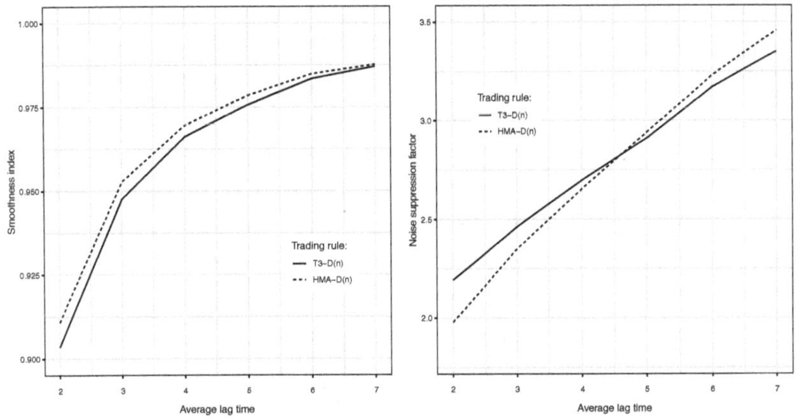

Fig. 9.14 Comparison of the effectiveness of the HMA-D and T3-D rules . The left panel plots the set of combinations of the ALT and SMI for the HMA-D and T3-D rules. The right panel plots the set of combinations of the ALT and NSF for the same rules

The curves presented in Fig. 9.14 validate our assumption. Upon observation, we notice that the curve related to the HMA-D rule lies marginally above the curve representing the T3-D rule in the ALT-SMI space. Thus, the HMA-D rule demonstrates a slightly better smoothness than the T3-D rule with the same average lag time. However, the improvement in smoothness is minimal. Additionally, both rules show similar curves in the ALT-NSF space, indicating they share the same features. Consequently, we can conclude that the HMA-D and T3-D rules possess similar characteristics.

For the next comparison, we examine the HMA-D(n), EPMA-D(n), ZLEMA-D(n), TEMA-D(n), and DEMA-D(n) rules. Each of these rules possesses unique price weight shapes. The T3-D(n) rule is not included as it is fundamentally the same as the HMA-D(n) rule. Furthermore, we also use the SMA-C($n/4, n$) rule, which is a double SMA crossover rule where the shorter window's size is a fourth of the longer window's size. The SMA-C($n/4, n$) rule is a popular trend-following rule that has a reputation for its smoothness. We use this rule to test whether the trading rules based on "zero-lag" moving averages are superior compared to trading rules based on traditional moving averages.

In Fig. 9.15, the top panel displays the combinations of the ALT and SMI for the selected set of rules. The bottom panel shows the combinations of the ALT and NSF for the same rules. Each rule is represented by a curve that depicts a tradeoff between the ALT and either the SMI or NSF. Every curve slopes upward, indicating that as the ALT increases, both the SMI and NSF increase as well. It is important to note that the higher the curve associated with a trading rule, the more efficient that rule is.

Upon evaluating the efficiency of the rules in the ALT-SMI space, it is found that the most efficient rule is the HMA-D rule. This rule provides the highest smoothness for a given lag time or the shortest lag time for a given smoothness. Surprisingly, the second most efficient rule is the SMA-C rule. This means that the SMA-C rule offers a shorter lag time for the same level of smoothness compared to the EPMA-D, ZLEMA-D, TEMA-D, and DEMA-D rules. Alternatively, the SMA-C rule provides higher smoothness for the same lag time compared to the same set of rules. This finding is unexpected as it contradicts the common belief that trading rules based on "zero-lag" moving averages deliver a better tradeoff between responsiveness and smoothness than the trading rules based on traditional moving averages.

In the ALT-NSF space, the efficiency of the rules, from best to worst, are: DEMA-D, TEMA-D, SMA-C, ZLEMA-D, EPMA-D, and HMA-D. Typically, improving the efficiency of a rule in the ALT-SMI space results in a reduction of efficiency in the ALT-NSF space. Hence, the HMA-D rule that has the best tradeoff between responsiveness and smoothness demonstrates the worst tradeoff between responsiveness and accuracy.

The SMA-C rule does not adhere to the typical pattern as it provides the second-best tradeoff between responsiveness and smoothness, which should typically result in the second-worst tradeoff between responsiveness and accuracy. However, this rule surprisingly provides the third-best tradeoff between responsiveness and accuracy. Based on our results, it appears that the SMA-C rule is more effective than the ZLEMA-D and EPMA-D rules in both the ALT-SMI and ALT-NSF spaces. That is, for the same level of responsiveness, the SMA-C rule has better smoothness and accuracy than the ZLEMA-D and EPMA-D rules.

The DEMA-D and TEMA-D rules provide a worse tradeoff between responsiveness and smoothness than the SMA-C rule, but they offer a better tradeoff between responsiveness and accuracy. However, the SMA-C rule is not the best rule regarding the tradeoff between responsiveness and accuracy. The most responsive and accurate rules are the price and moving average crossover (P-MA) rules. Therefore, to verify if the rules based on "zero-lag" moving averages

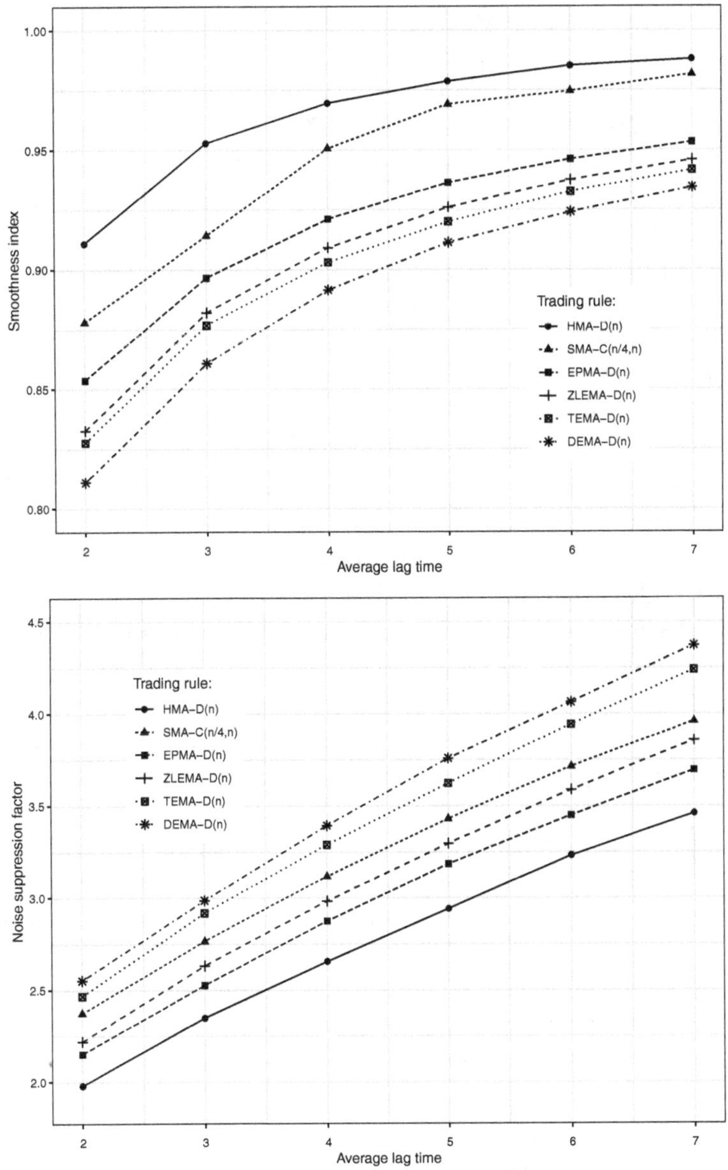

Fig. 9.15 Comparison of the effectiveness of the trading rules based on "zero-lag" moving averages and the SMA-C rule. The top panel plots the set of combinations of the ALT and SMI for the selected set of rules. The bottom panel plots the set of combinations of the ALT and NSF for the same rules

are more efficient than those based on traditional moving averages, we include the P-SMA rule in our comparison.

In the last comparison round, we analyze the efficiency of five different trading rules: P-SMA(n), EPMA-D(n), ZLEMA-D(n), TEMA-D(n), and DEMA-D(n). The top panel of Fig. 9.16 displays the combinations of the ALT and SMI for these rules, while the bottom panel shows the combinations of the ALT and NSF. From the curves on the bottom panel, it is clear that the P-SMA rule strikes the best balance between responsiveness and accuracy. The DEMA-D rule is almost as efficient as the P-SMA rule in the ALT-NSF space, while the P-SMA rule is more efficient than the DEMA-D rule in the ALT-SMI space. Furthermore, the P-SMA rule is as efficient as the TEMA-D rule. These findings lead us to conclude that neither the DEMA-D nor the TEMA-D rules surpass the efficiency of the P-SMA rule.

In summary, our analysis focused on the efficiency of trend-following rules using six different "zero-lag" moving averages. Contrary to common belief, we found that four out of the six trend-following rules we analyzed were not superior to rules based on traditional moving averages. Only the rules based on the HMA and T3 moving averages showed an improvement in the tradeoff between responsiveness and smoothness compared to the traditional moving averages. However, this improvement comes at the expense of worsening the tradeoff between responsiveness and accuracy. Therefore, traders should carefully consider in which markets these rules can enhance the profitability of the trend-following strategy.

The HMA and T3 moving averages exhibit similar characteristics and provide a good balance between responsiveness and smoothness. In concluding this section, we aim to explore how close these rules come to the most efficient rule in terms of responsiveness and smoothness.

To address this question, we investigate the potential for enhancing the efficiency of the HMA-D(40) rule and evaluate the extent to which this can be achieved. We adopt the following approach. First, we measure the accuracy, responsiveness, and smoothness of the HMA-D(40) rule. Then, using a numerical method, we aim to find the return weights in a technical indicator that exhibits the same accuracy and responsiveness as the HMA-D(40) rule but with better smoothness. Formally, we solve the following optimization problem:

$$\max_{\boldsymbol{\theta}} SMI(\boldsymbol{\theta}) \text{ subject to } \boldsymbol{\theta}'\mathbf{1} = 1,\ ALT(\boldsymbol{\theta}) = k,\ \text{and } NSF(\boldsymbol{\theta}) = m,$$

where $\boldsymbol{\theta}$ is the vector of return weights in the technical indicator that has the same number of lags as the technical indicator of the HMA-D(40) rule. The

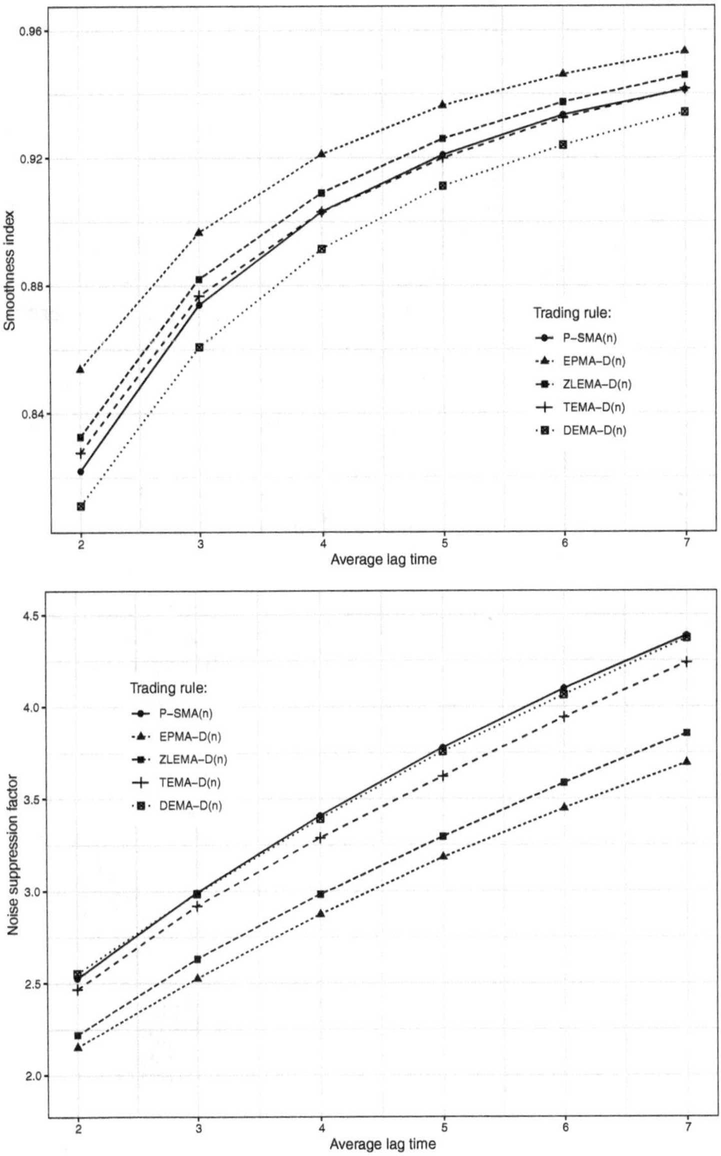

Fig. 9.16 Comparison of the effectiveness of the trading rules based on "zero-lag" moving averages and the P-MA rule. The top panel plots the set of combinations of the ALT and SMI for the selected set of rules. The bottom panel plots the set of combinations of the ALT and NSF for the same rules

objective is to maximize the SMI while satisfying three equality constraints. The first constraint $\boldsymbol{\theta}'\mathbf{1} = 1$ ensures that the sum of weights equals 1. The second constraint $ALT(\boldsymbol{\theta}) = k$ sets the value of ALT to the corresponding value of the HMA-D(40) rule, and the third constraint $NSF(\boldsymbol{\theta}) = m$ sets the value of NSF to the corresponding value of the HMA-D(40) rule.

The smoothness of a trading rule is strongly related to its ability to minimize whipsaw trades, which can be assessed by the one-period probability of a position reversal. For the HMA-D(40) rule, this probability is estimated at 6.4%. Through numerical optimization, we have found an alternative rule with the same level of responsiveness and accuracy, but with a slightly lower probability of reversal at 6.3%, representing an improvement of 1.5%. This suggests that the HMA and T3 moving averages are nearly optimal in terms of both responsiveness and smoothness.

To provide a visual representation, Fig. 9.17 displays the price weights of two moving averages: the HMA(40) and an improved version with slightly better smoothness. This improved version is obtained using the numerical optimization method outlined above. Both moving averages have positive and negative parts, but their negative parts differ noticeably. The negative parts of both resemble a hump-shaped form. However, while the hump in the HMA is located toward the most recent lags, the improved HMA's hump is located

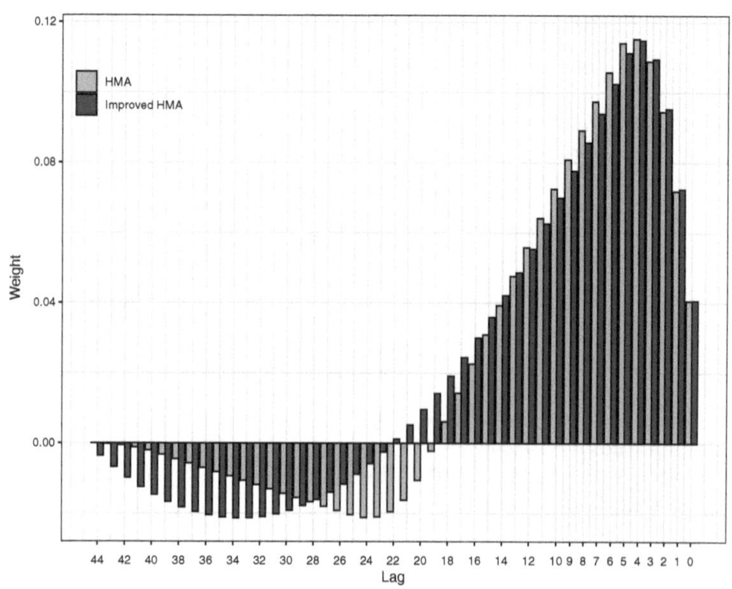

Fig. 9.17 Price weights of the HMA(40) and the price weights of the improved version with slightly better smoothness

in the middle of negative weights. The positive parts of both largely overlap. Essentially, the weights of the improved HMA represent a slightly smoothed version of the HMA's weights.

9.6 Summary

Traders have long aimed to create zero-lag moving averages that react instantly to market changes, enabling quicker trading decisions. This pursuit has resulted in multiple versions of "zero-lag" moving averages. Proponents of these moving averages argue that they offer minimal lag and greater smoothness compared to traditional ones. However, these claims are mostly supported by anecdotal evidence and visual examples, lacking objective data for validation.

In this book, we introduce three new quantitative measures to evaluate the key characteristics of trend-following rules based on moving averages: accuracy, responsiveness, and smoothness. By applying these measures, we provide a thorough and objective analysis of "zero-lag" moving averages. The goal is to determine whether these moving averages genuinely achieve both zero lag time and high smoothness, and whether they outperform traditional moving averages.

The set of analyzed "zero-lag" moving averages includes the most popular variants: the Double and Triple Exponential Moving Averages (DEMA and TEMA), the Zero-Lag Exponential Moving Average (ZLEMA), the Hull Moving Average (HMA), the End Point Moving Average (EPMA), and the Tillson T3 Moving Average. Among these moving averages, the DEMA, TEMA, and EPMA have exactly zero average lag time based on the traditional definition of lag time for moving averages.

We propose that the most practical trading rule for these "zero-lag" moving averages is the moving average direction rule, which triggers a Buy signal when the moving average rises and a Sell signal when it falls. For comparison, we also include the most common trading rules based on traditional moving averages: the price and Simple Moving Average (SMA) crossover rule and the double SMA crossover rule.

Our analysis shows that trading rules based on DEMA, TEMA, ZLEMA, and EPMA are less efficient than traditional trading rules. Specifically, the double SMA crossover rule offers better accuracy and smoothness for the same lag time compared to the ZLEMA and EPMA-based rules. Similarly, the price and SMA crossover rule outperform the DEMA and TEMA-based rules in efficiency.

On the other hand, trading rules based on the HMA and T3 moving averages outperform traditional rules when considering the tradeoff between responsiveness and smoothness. Specifically, these rules provide greater smoothness for the same level of responsiveness. However, this improvement comes at the cost of reducing accuracy. In other words, while you can design a trading rule that is both fast and smooth, it requires sacrificing some level of accuracy.

We conclude that the idea of a truly zero-lag moving average remains elusive. By "truly" zero-lag, we refer to a moving average that enables a trading rule to react instantly to trend changes. However, such a trading rule must also accurately identify the trend's direction and produce consistent signals to minimize whipsaw trades. Achieving all these criteria simultaneously is not possible.

As demonstrated earlier in this book, it is possible for a trading rule to have minimal lag time while being highly smooth. However, achieving this combination requires a complete sacrifice in the rule's accuracy. While such a rule responds immediately to trend changes, the response is short-lived. In a trending market, this rule has zero accuracy in identifying the trend direction. Therefore, strictly speaking, it does not qualify as a truly trend-following rule.

Appendix 9.A Useful Formulas

Consider a finite arithmetic sequence $\{1, 2, 3, \ldots, n\}$ of consecutive integers from 1 to n. The sum of all terms in the sequence and the sum of squares are given by:

$$\sum_{i=1}^{n} i = \frac{n(n+1)}{2}, \quad \sum_{i=1}^{n} i^2 = \frac{n(n+1)(2n+1)}{6}.$$

If the sequence contains integers from 0 to $n-1$, then the sums become:

$$\sum_{i=0}^{n-1} i = \frac{n(n-1)}{2}, \quad \sum_{i=0}^{n-1} i^2 = \frac{(n-1)n(2n-1)}{6}.$$

Appendix 9.B Price Weights in the End Point Moving Average

Consider a vector $\mathbf{P} = [P_1, P_2, \ldots, P_n]$ representing the most recent prices indexed by the vector $\mathbf{x} = [1, 2, \ldots, n]$. P_n represents the most recent price, while P_1 represents the most distant price.

To compute the EPMA, we employ a linear regression to fit a straight line to a set of data points (x_i, P_i). This line is represented by the equation:

$$y_i = a + b\,x_i,$$

where a is the intercept and b is the slope. Our goal is to find the values of a and b that provide the best fit for the given data points.

The least squares method is used to determine the best-fit values for a and b. In this method, the aim is to minimize the sum of squared residuals by adjusting a and b. The squared residuals are the differences between the predicted values (y_i) and the actual values (P_i), squared and summed up. Mathematically, the problem can be expressed as:

$$\min_{a,b} \sum_{i=1}^{n} (y_i - P_i)^2.$$

The values of a and b that minimize this expression are considered the optimal parameter values for the linear regression model.

The analytical solution to the optimization problem above is well-known. The values of a and b that minimize the sum of squared residuals can be calculated using the following formulas:

$$a = \frac{\sum_{i=1}^{n} P_i - b \sum_{i=1}^{n} x_i}{n}, \qquad b = \frac{n \sum_{i=1}^{n} x_i P_i - \sum_{i=1}^{n} x_i \sum_{i=1}^{n} P_i}{n \sum_{i=1}^{n} x_i^2 - \left(\sum_{i=1}^{n} x_i\right)^2}.$$

Using the formulas for the sum of an arithmetic sequence and the sum of the squares of an arithmetic sequence, we get:

$$\sum_{i=1}^{n} x_i = \frac{n(n+1)}{2}, \qquad \sum_{i=1}^{n} x_i^2 = \frac{n(n+1)(2n+1)}{6}.$$

Therefore, after simplifying, the expressions for a and b can be written as:

$$a = \frac{\sum_{i=1}^{n} P_i}{n} - \left(\frac{n+1}{2}\right) b, \quad b = \frac{12 \sum_{i=1}^{n} i P_i - 6(n+1) \sum_{i=1}^{n} P_i}{n(n+1)(n-1)}.$$

The value of the EPMA is represented by the value of the last fitted point. This means that EPMA(n) satisfies the condition:

$$EPMA(n) = a + bn = \frac{\sum_{i=1}^{n} P_i}{n} + \left(\frac{n-1}{2}\right) b.$$

Substituting b into the equation above yields:

$$EPMA(n) = \frac{\sum_{i=1}^{n} P_i}{n} + \frac{6 \sum_{i=1}^{n} i P_i - 3(n+1) \sum_{i=1}^{n} P_i}{n+1} = \frac{6}{n(n+1)} \sum_{i=1}^{n} i P_i - \frac{2}{n} \sum_{i=1}^{n} P_i.$$

Further simplification results in the expression:

$$EPMA(n) = \sum_{i=1}^{n} \frac{2(3i - n - 1)}{n(n+1)} P_i = \sum_{i=1}^{n} w_i P_i.$$

That is, the EPMA(n) represents a moving average of the past n prices where the weight of price P_i is given by the formula:

$$w_i = \frac{2(3i - n - 1)}{n(n+1)}.$$

This weight equation ensures that the sum of all weights is equal to one, making it a normalized weight. The factor $\frac{2}{n(n+1)}$ acts as a normalization factor in this case. The non-normalized price weights are given by:

$$w_i = 3i - n - 1.$$

Finally, it is important to clarify that our standard convention considers the most recent price as P_t, not P_n, and the furthest price as P_{t-n+1}, not P_1. Therefore, to calculate the time-t value of the EPMA using our convention, the following formula must be used:

$$EPMA_t(n, P) = \frac{\sum_{i=0}^{n-1} (2n - 3i - 1) P_{t-i}}{\sum_{i=0}^{n-1} (2n - 3i - 1)}.$$

Moreover, note that the price weights of the EPMA in our standard convention are given by:

$$w_i = 2n - 3i - 1.$$

Appendix 9.C Average Lag Time of the End Point Moving Average

Our objective is to demonstrate that the EPMA has an average lag time of zero. It is essential to recall that we calculate the average lag time of a moving average using the formula below:

$$\mathrm{ALT}(MA) = \frac{\sum_{i=0}^{n-1} i \times w_i}{\sum_{i=0}^{n-1} w_i}.$$

To prove that the ALT(EPMA) is zero, we need to show that $\sum_{i=0}^{n-1} i \times w_i = 0$. The calculations are as follows:

$$\sum_{i=0}^{n-1} i(2n - 3i - 1) = (2n - 1)\sum_{i=0}^{n-1} i - 3\sum_{i=0}^{n-1} i^2 = \frac{n(n-1)(2n-1)}{2} - \frac{3(n-1)n(2n-1)}{6} = 0.$$

Therefore, we have shown that ALT(EPMA) equals zero.

References

Brown, R. G. (1963). *Smoothing, Forecasting and Prediction of Discrete Time Series.* Prentice-Hall.

Ehlers, J. F., & Way, R. (2010). Zero Lag (Well, Almost). *Technical Analysis of Stocks and Commodities, 28*(12), 30–35.

Hull, A. (2005). How to Reduce Lag in a Moving Average. http://www.alanhull.com/hull-moving-average

Lafferty, P. E. (1995). The End Point Moving Average. *Technical Analysis of Stocks and Commodities, 13*(10), 413–417.

Mulloy, P. G. (1994). Smoothing Data With Faster Moving Averages. *Technical Analysis of Stocks and Commodities, 12*(1), 11–19.

Mulloy, P. G. (1994). Smoothing Data With Less Lag. *Technical Analysis of Stocks and Commodities, 12*(2), 72–80.

Tillson, J. (1998). Smoothing Techniques For More Accurate Signals. *Technical Analysis of Stocks and Commodities, 16*(1), 33–37.

Tukey, J. (1977). Exploratory Data Analysis. Pearson.

10

A Digital Signal Processing Approach to Moving Averages

10.1 Introduction

Moving averages are foundational tools for trend-following in financial markets, prized for their ability to smooth data and reveal underlying trends. In the pursuit of a superior balance between smoothness and responsiveness, traders and analysts have introduced numerous variants of moving averages over time. Many of these innovations are directly inspired by techniques from Digital Signal Processing (DSP), a field that provides a rigorous framework for understanding and designing filters tailored to specific purposes.

DSP uses algorithms to analyze, transform, and enhance signals, extracting valuable information or improving their quality. One of its core applications is filtering, where certain frequency components of a signal are either amplified or suppressed. Filters are tailored to allow or block specific frequency ranges, with common types including low-pass, high-pass, and band-pass filters.

In DSP terms, a moving average functions as a low-pass filter. It allows low-frequency components, representing the underlying price trend, to pass through while reducing the influence of high-frequency components typically associated with random price fluctuations or "noise."

DSP is particularly well suited for analyzing cyclic behavior because of the way filters transform input frequencies. The key characteristics of a DSP filter—the amplitude response and phase delay—determine how each frequency in a signal is affected.

When a signal passes through a DSP filter, each input frequency is retained, meaning it remains at the same frequency. However, both its amplitude and phase may be altered based on the filter's characteristics. The amplitude response defines how the magnitude of each frequency is either amplified or

V. Zakamulin and J. Giner, *The Ultimate Moving Average Handbook*,
https://doi.org/10.1007/978-3-031-90907-8_10

attenuated, enabling filters to emphasize or suppress specific frequency components. Additionally, the phase of each frequency is shifted, and this shift can be quantified as a phase delay, which represents the time delay introduced by the filter.

DSP provides a powerful framework for studying periodic phenomena in financial markets. While stock prices do not exhibit consistent cyclical behavior with fixed frequencies, numerous theories suggest that market dynamics can often be described in terms of cycles. Increasing empirical evidence supports this view, indicating that market movements can be analyzed as a series of irregular cycles.

These cycles do not have a single fixed frequency but instead exhibit a degree of randomness, with their frequencies varying over time. However, the distribution of these frequencies tends to cluster around an average value. This characteristic makes DSP particularly well suited for analyzing market dynamics, as it enables the design of filters that optimally extract trends from noisy price data. By isolating and emphasizing the dominant cyclical components, DSP techniques can help reveal underlying market trends, providing valuable insights for financial analysis and strategy development.

Numerous theories about stock price cycles have been proposed by various economists, traders, and analysts, each highlighting unique aspects of market behavior. Among the earliest and most influential is Dow Theory, which laid the foundation for trend-following strategies. This theory suggests that markets move in three types of trends: primary trends (long-term), secondary trends (medium-term), and minor trends (short-term), offering a framework for understanding market movements over different time horizons.

Another prominent theory is the Elliott Wave Theory, developed by Ralph Nelson Elliott. Elliott proposed that market movements follow a repetitive wave pattern driven by investor psychology and natural cycles. These patterns consist of five waves in the direction of the main trend and three corrective waves against it, forming a complete cycle. Furthermore, each wave can be subdivided into smaller waves, creating a fractal structure. This fractal nature reflects the self-similar and scalable dynamics of market behavior.

Hurst's Cycle Theory, introduced by J.M. Hurst in the 1970s, also deserves mention. Hurst theorized that price movements are influenced by multiple overlapping cycles of varying lengths, ranging from short term (intraday) to long term (spanning years or decades). These cycles are often harmonically related, meaning their lengths are proportional to one another, with larger cycles being multiples of smaller ones. Hurst emphasized that when cycles of different lengths align, reaching their troughs simultaneously, they produce significant turning points in the market. By analyzing these alignments, traders can identify potential market reversals.

Both Elliott Wave Theory and Hurst's Cycle Theory suggest that stock cycles are not perfectly regular like sine waves, though they share some conceptual similarities. Cyclical market behavior reflects human psychology and collective sentiment, resulting in rhythmic but irregular patterns. These cycles are subject to noise, external shocks, and nonlinear dynamics, which differentiate them from smooth, symmetrical oscillations.

Despite this irregularity, frequency-domain analysis can still provide valuable insights. By analyzing the periodicities and dominant frequencies in price data, traders can uncover hidden cycles and gain a deeper understanding of market dynamics. Such analysis is particularly useful for identifying recurring patterns, timing strategies, and improving decision-making in the inherently noisy and complex environment of financial markets.

The ultimate objective of this chapter is to evaluate several popular DSP-inspired moving averages and compare their performance with traditional and exotic moving averages. Proponents of DSP-inspired moving averages argue that these techniques provide superior performance, offering improved smoothness, responsiveness, and noise reduction. By employing three key metrics—accuracy, responsiveness, and smoothness—this chapter aims to assess these claims and determine whether DSP-inspired moving averages truly outperform traditional variants.

Before addressing this main goal, the chapter begins with an introduction to DSP concepts as they relate to trend-following. This material explains how to analyze filters in the frequency domain rather than the time domain, emphasizing the importance of understanding the relationship between these two domains and how signals can be transformed between them. It also details how filtering alters an input signal: the amplitude of each frequency component changes, and the phase is shifted. For example, high-frequency components, typically linked to noise, are attenuated, while low-frequency components, representing trends, experience a phase shift that corresponds to a measurable time delay.

Building on this foundation, the chapter examines the characteristics of conventional moving averages and the trend-following rules derived from them, using DSP principles. By analyzing their behavior in the frequency domain, this approach provides deeper insights into their strengths and limitations, setting the stage for a rigorous comparison with DSP-inspired moving averages.

10.2 Digital Filters in the Time Domain

From a DSP perspective, moving averages function as digital filters. These filters are fundamental tools for signal manipulation, allowing specific frequencies to be amplified while others are attenuated. Figure 10.1 illustrates the general structure of a digital filter, which produces the output signal $y[n]$ in response to the input signal $x[n]$. Both $x[n]$ and $y[n]$ are discrete-time signals, where n represents discrete time points.[1]

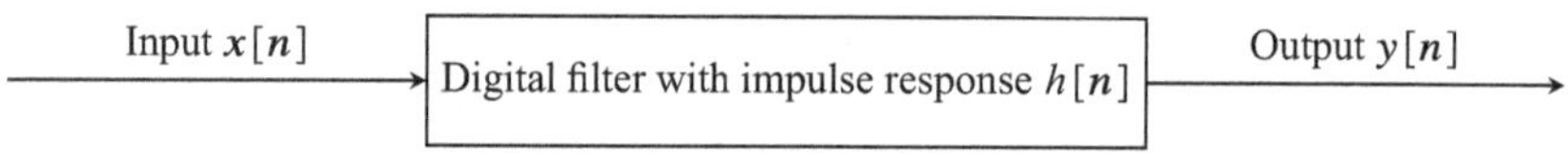

Fig. 10.1 General structure of a digital filter, which produces the output signal $y[n]$ in response to the input signal $x[n]$. A filter is fully characterized by the impulse response function $h[n]$

Every input signal can be decomposed into a series of fundamental components called impulses. An *impulse* is a unique discrete-time signal that consists entirely of zeros, except for a single non-zero value at a specific point. This decomposition allows signals to be analyzed and processed one sample at a time.

A fundamental concept in DSP is the delta function $\delta[n]$, also known as the *unit impulse*. The unit impulse is a discrete-time signal that is defined as follows:

$$\delta[n] = \begin{cases} 1 & \text{if } n = 0, \\ 0 & \text{otherwise.} \end{cases}$$

This function serves as the building block for analyzing and processing signals, as it represents a signal that is zero everywhere except at a single point in time, where it takes the value 1.

A digital filter is completely characterized by its *impulse response* $h[n]$. The impulse response represents the filter's output when a unit impulse is applied as the input. In essence, it describes how the system responds to a single impulse and serves as a fundamental representation of its behavior. The impulse response contains all the information required to determine how the system processes any arbitrary input signal.

The output of a discrete-time system can be determined by the *convolution* of the input signal $x[n]$ with the system's impulse response $h[n]$. The convolution

[1] In DSP literature, continuous-time signals are typically denoted as $x(t)$ and $y(t)$, whereas discrete-time signals are represented as $x[n]$ and $y[n]$.

operation is denoted by the symbol $*$, and the resulting output $y[n]$ is expressed as:

$$y[n] = h[n] * x[n].$$

In mathematical terms, the input $x[n]$ is convolved with the impulse response $h[n]$ to yield the output $y[n]$.

For a system with an N-length impulse response $h[n]$, the discrete-time convolution is mathematically defined as:

$$y[n] = \sum_{k=0}^{N-1} h[k]x[n-k].$$

This formula computes the output at time n by summing the weighted contributions of the input signal, where the weights are determined by the impulse response.

The impulse response $h[n]$ is the filter's response to the delta function $\delta[n]$:

$$h[n] = h[n] * \delta[n].$$

This equation also states that the impulse response remains unchanged when convolved with the delta function. This property underscores the delta function's role as the "identity" for convolution in signal processing.

Two fundamental types of filters in DSP are *Finite Impulse Response* (FIR) and *Infinite Impulse Response* (IIR) filters. While both types of filters serve similar purposes in modifying signals, they differ in structure, characteristics, and typical applications.

FIR filters are characterized by having a finite-duration impulse response, meaning the filter's output will eventually settle to zero after a finite number of steps, even when a single impulse is applied. This finite-duration behavior contrasts with IIR filters, where the impulse response continues indefinitely.

An example of an FIR filter is a 3-point Linear Moving Average (LMA), which computes a linearly weighted average of the three most recent observations. For this case, the convolution equation for the output $y[n]$ is:

$$y[n] = \frac{3}{6}x[n] + \frac{2}{6}x[n-1] + \frac{1}{6}x[n-2].$$

To compute the impulse response of the LMA(3), we apply the unit impulse $\delta[n]$ as the input. For $x[n] = \delta[n]$, the convolution steps will be as follows.

For $n = 0$:

$$y[0] = \frac{3}{6} \cdot x[0] + \frac{2}{6} \cdot x[-1] + \frac{1}{6} \cdot x[-2] = \frac{3}{6} \cdot 1 + \frac{2}{6} \cdot 0 + \frac{1}{6} \cdot 0 = \frac{3}{6}.$$

For $n = 1$:

$$y[1] = \frac{3}{6} \cdot x[1] + \frac{2}{6} \cdot x[0] + \frac{1}{6} \cdot x[-1] = \frac{3}{6} \cdot 0 + \frac{2}{6} \cdot 1 + \frac{1}{6} \cdot 0 = \frac{2}{6}.$$

For $n = 2$:

$$y[2] = \frac{3}{6} \cdot x[2] + \frac{2}{6} \cdot x[1] + \frac{1}{6} \cdot x[0] = \frac{3}{6} \cdot 0 + \frac{2}{6} \cdot 0 + \frac{1}{6} \cdot 1 = \frac{1}{6}.$$

For $n \geq 3$, the output is 0 because $x[n] = 0$ for $n \geq 1$. Thus, the impulse response of the LMA(3) is:

$$h[n] = \left\{ \frac{3}{6}, \frac{2}{6}, \frac{1}{6}, 0, 0, 0, \ldots \right\}.$$

An example of an IIR filter is the Exponential Moving Average (EMA), which is a recursive filter. The EMA can be defined recursively as:

$$y[n] = (1 - \lambda)x[n] + \lambda y[n - 1],$$

where λ is the smoothing constant, $0 < \lambda < 1$.

To compute the impulse response, we need to apply $x[n] = \delta[n]$ as the input. At $n = 0$, we have:

$$y[0] = (1 - \lambda) \cdot x[0] + \lambda \cdot y[-1] = (1 - \lambda) \cdot 1 + \lambda \cdot 0 = (1 - \lambda).$$

At $n = 1$, the output is:

$$y[1] = (1 - \lambda) \cdot x[1] + \lambda \cdot y[0] = (1 - \lambda) \cdot 0 + \lambda \cdot (1 - \lambda) = (1 - \lambda)\lambda.$$

At $n = 2$, we have:

$$y[2] = (1 - \lambda) \cdot x[2] + \lambda \cdot y[1] = (1 - \lambda) \cdot 0 + \lambda \cdot (1 - \lambda)\lambda = (1 - \lambda)\lambda^2.$$

Thus, the impulse response $h[n]$ of the EMA filter is:

$$h[n] = (1 - \lambda)\lambda^n, \quad n = 0, 1, 2, 3, \ldots$$

This shows that the impulse response of the EMA filter decays exponentially, and the impulse response continues indefinitely, which is characteristic of an IIR filter.

10.3 Digital Filters in the Frequency Domain

Frequency-domain analysis is a crucial concept in signal processing, offering a powerful alternative to time-domain analysis for understanding and manipulating signals. By examining the frequency content of a signal instead of its time-domain variations, this approach uncovers underlying periodicities, dominant frequencies, and spectral characteristics that may not be immediately evident in the time domain. It enables a deeper understanding of how signals behave in response to various operations and conditions.

The origins of frequency-domain analysis can be traced back to the groundbreaking work of Joseph Fourier, an 18th-century French mathematician and physicist. Fourier introduced the revolutionary idea that any periodic signal could be represented as a sum of sinusoids, each with its own frequency, amplitude, and phase. This concept is now known as the Fourier Series. Later, the development of the Fourier transform extended this idea to handle non-periodic signals, fundamentally transforming how we analyze signals. Fourier's insights provided the foundation for much of modern signal processing, and his work remains indispensable in diverse fields such as engineering, physics, image processing, communications, and audio analysis.

Frequency-domain analysis offers several significant advantages over time-domain analysis:

Clarity of Signal Features: Decomposing complex signals into simpler sinusoidal components allows for a clearer understanding of signal features that might be hidden in the time domain. By examining the frequency components, periodicities, and dominant frequencies of a signal, we can gain insights into its structure that are often obscured by time-domain fluctuations. For instance, periodic signals or patterns within noise can be more easily identified in the frequency domain.

Simplified Mathematical Operations: Many signal processing operations, such as convolution, which are computationally complex in the time domain, become much simpler in the frequency domain. Convolution, for example, transforms into element-wise multiplication when using the Fourier transform, significantly reducing the computational effort and providing more efficient methods for filtering and signal manipulation. This simplification is particularly beneficial when dealing with large datasets or real-time processing tasks.

System Design and Analysis: Frequency-domain analysis is essential for the design and analysis of systems (such as filters) that must behave in specific ways across different frequency ranges. It provides the tools to isolate and manipulate specific frequency components of a signal. For example, in filter design, frequency-domain analysis allows us to design low-pass, high-pass, band-pass, or band-stop filters to target specific frequency ranges. This capability is critical in applications such as noise reduction, signal enhancement, and communication systems, where it is often necessary to eliminate or suppress unwanted frequency components, like noise, while preserving the desired signal.

Insight into Spectral Characteristics: The frequency domain provides valuable insights into the spectral characteristics of signals. For example, signals that are periodic in nature will exhibit distinct spectral peaks, while aperiodic signals may have continuous spectra. Understanding the distribution of energy or power across different frequencies can provide important information about the signal's origin, its underlying processes, and potential applications. In many systems, certain frequencies correspond to known behaviors, such as resonances or harmonics, and frequency-domain analysis can be used to identify and analyze these behaviors.

10.3.1 Frequency and Period

We assume that periodicity exists in many phenomena, meaning that certain patterns or behaviors repeat over time. The frequency of a cyclic signal is calculated as $f = \frac{1}{T}$, where T is the period, the time it takes for the signal to complete one cycle. For example, if a cycle lasts 20 days, the frequency is $f = \frac{1}{20} = 0.05$ cycles per day. In contrast, a cycle lasting 4 days corresponds to a higher frequency of $f = \frac{1}{4} = 0.25$ cycles per day.

In practice, especially in fields like trading, we often deal with sampled data rather than continuous signals. Here, we gather individual data points (samples) at regular intervals, regardless of the underlying time frame. Whether the data is in days, months, years, or seconds is irrelevant; what matters is that we collect the samples at fixed time intervals, or periodicity. In this context, it is common to measure cycles in terms of samples or bars, referencing the frequency of events relative to the sampling rate or the bars in a chart.

For example, instead of saying that a cycle lasts 20 days, we can express it as 20 samples, assuming daily data is being used. In this case, the corresponding frequency would be $f = \frac{1}{20} = 0.05$ cycles per sample.

In digital signal processing, the highest frequency considered is the *Nyquist frequency*, defined as $f = \frac{1}{2} = 0.5$ cycles per sample. This corresponds to the shortest measurable cycle, which consists of 2 samples per cycle. According to the *Nyquist sampling criterion*, at least two samples are required to accurately represent a cycle. For instance, with daily data, the shortest measurable cycle would span 2 days.

Frequency analysis is typically concerned with frequencies ranging from 0 to 0.5 cycles per sample. A frequency of 0 represents signals with an infinite cycle duration, such as a constant signal or the DC component, while a frequency of 0.5 corresponds to the shortest possible cycle, spanning 2 samples.

Furthermore, the *angular frequency*, denoted as w, is related to the frequency by $w = 2\pi f$ radians per sample. Thus, the highest angular frequency considered is π radians per sample.

To summarize, all frequency information is scaled relative to the sampling frequency. Therefore, our primary concern is to limit the frequencies to the range from 0 to a maximum of 0.5 cycles per sample (or π radians per sample). This restriction simplifies the problem and is a key feature in frequency analysis.

In contrast, fields like acoustics and electromagnetism typically work with absolute frequencies, measured in cycles per second (Hz). For example, in acoustics, the sampling rate may be quite high—such as 10,000 samples per second—enabling the analysis of frequencies ranging from 0 Hz up to the Nyquist limit of 5,000 Hz. However, when these frequencies are expressed relative to the sampling frequency, they still fall within the same range of 0 to 0.5 cycles per sample, consistent with the principles of digital signal processing.

10.3.2 Types of Digital Filters

Once the fundamental principles of frequency analysis are understood, our main objective is to apply this knowledge to design digital filters that can remove unwanted frequencies from a signal. For instance, we might want to filter out high-frequency noise that distorts the underlying trends of a signal.

Digital filters are essential tools in signal processing, designed to modify or extract specific components of a signal based on its frequency content. There are three primary types of digital filters, each serving a distinct purpose:

- *Low-Pass Filters* allow frequencies below a specified cutoff frequency to pass through while attenuating higher frequencies. The cutoff frequency is typically defined as the point where the signal's power is reduced to half of its original value. Low-pass filters are commonly used to remove high-frequency noise or to extract slow-varying trends from a signal.

- *High-Pass Filters* operate in the opposite way, allowing frequencies above a specified cutoff to pass while attenuating lower frequencies. These filters are frequently used to remove low-frequency noise, such as baseline drift, or to emphasize rapid changes in a signal.
- *Band-Pass Filters* permit only a specific range of frequencies to pass while attenuating frequencies outside this range. These filters are ideal for isolating signals of interest within a particular frequency band, which is useful in applications like communication systems or audio processing.

Figure 10.2 illustrates the frequency response functions for the three main types of digital filters: low-pass, high-pass, and band-pass.

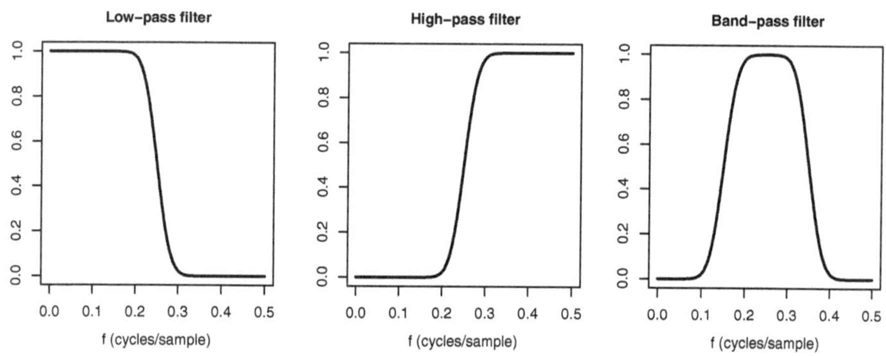

Fig. 10.2 Frequency response functions for the three main types of digital filters: low-pass, high-pass, and band-pass

In the time domain, a filter processes an input signal by convolving it with the filter's impulse response. This means the output at each time point is computed as the weighted sum of the input signal, where the weights are defined by the impulse response. In the frequency domain, the process is more straightforward: the output's frequency spectrum is obtained by multiplying the input's frequency spectrum with the filter's frequency response.

To understand the effect of a moving average filter, with impulse response $h[n]$, on an input signal $x[n]$, the output $y[n] = h[n] * x[n]$ is a convolution. This operation can be more easily interpreted in the frequency domain, where convolution in the time domain becomes simple multiplication.

The filter's frequency response is represented by the function $H(f)$ or $H(w)$, where f is the frequency and w is the angular frequency. The magnitude of this function indicates which frequencies are passed through and which are attenuated. By selectively enhancing or suppressing specific frequency components, these filters provide precise control over signal characteristics, enabling applications such as noise reduction, feature extraction, and signal analysis.

The output signal in the frequency domain, $Y(w)$, can be directly calculated by multiplying the frequency response of the filter, $H(w)$, with the frequency spectrum of the input signal, $X(w)$. This fundamental property of frequency-domain analysis will be explored in more detail in the following sections.

10.3.3 An Example

To illustrate these concepts, let us consider an example with three sine waves of different frequencies: 5 Hz, 15 Hz, and 30 Hz, sampled at a rate of 1,000 samples per second. For completeness, the corresponding relative frequencies are 0.005, 0.015, and 0.030 cycles per sample. However, for clarity, we will continue using the frequencies in Hz. The combination of these three waves is given by:

$$x[n] = x_1[n] + x_2[n] + x_3[n] = \sin(2\pi 5n) + \sin(2\pi 15n) + \sin(2\pi 30n).$$

The left panel of Fig. 10.3 shows each sine wave $x_i[n]$ and their sum $x[n]$ in the time domain, considering $n \in [0, 1000]$ samples, which corresponds to $t \in [0, 1]$ second. The right panel of Fig. 10.3 presents the frequency components of the individual and combined signals. The spikes at 5 Hz, 15 Hz, and 30 Hz are evident.

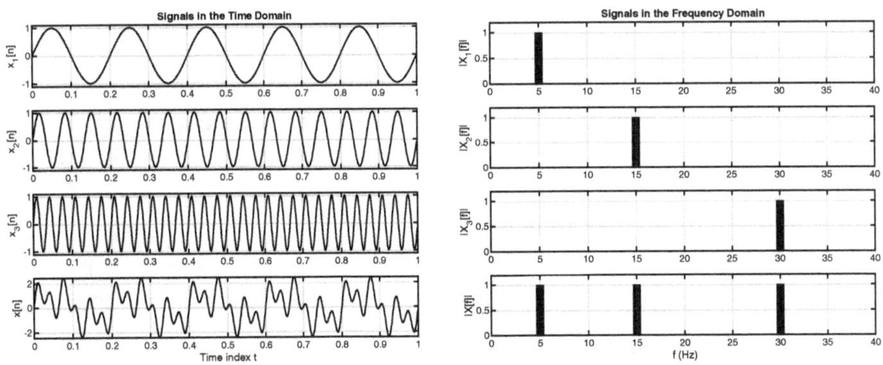

Fig. 10.3 Three sinusoidal signals and their sum: time domain (left) and frequency domain (right)

Next, suppose we apply a low-pass filter with a cutoff frequency of 6 Hz to the combined signal $x[n]$. The cutoff frequency is the point where the amplitude drops by approximately 70% (or $1/\sqrt{2}$) of its original value. The filter's frequency response is shown at the top of Fig. 10.4. Frequencies above 6 Hz are attenuated, while frequencies below 6 Hz remain nearly unaffected. The middle panel of Fig. 10.4 shows the output signal with the 15 Hz and 30 Hz components removed, leaving only the 5 Hz signal. The bottom panel shows the filtered time series, which effectively contains only $x_1[n]$.

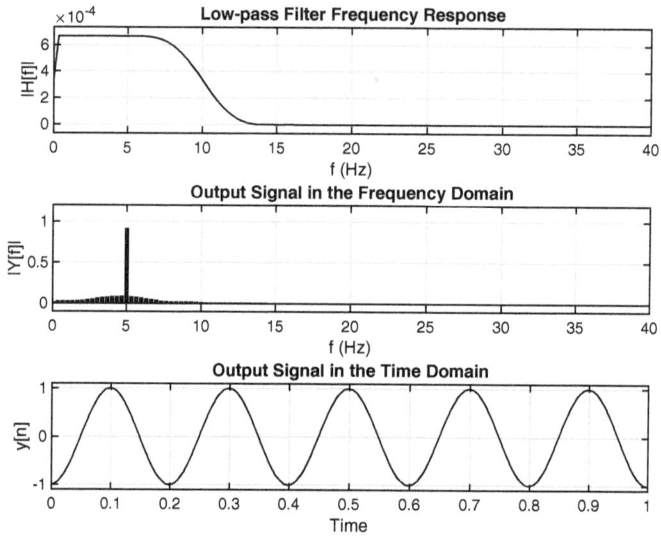

Fig. 10.4 Low-pass filter

Now, suppose we apply a high-pass filter with a cutoff frequency of 29 Hz. This filter attenuates frequencies below 29 Hz. Figure 10.5 shows the effect of this filter on $x[n]$, where the 5 Hz and 15 Hz components are removed, leaving only the 30 Hz component. The bottom panel shows the resulting time series, which contains only $x_3[n]$.

Finally, suppose we apply a band-pass filter with a passband between 10 Hz and 20 Hz. Figure 10.6 demonstrates that the 5 Hz and 30 Hz components are removed, leaving only the 15 Hz component. The bottom panel shows the output time series, which contains only $x_2[n]$.

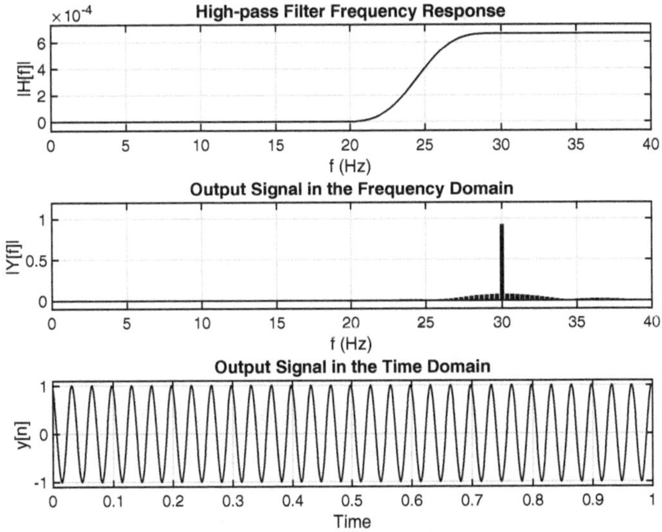

Fig. 10.5 High-pass filter

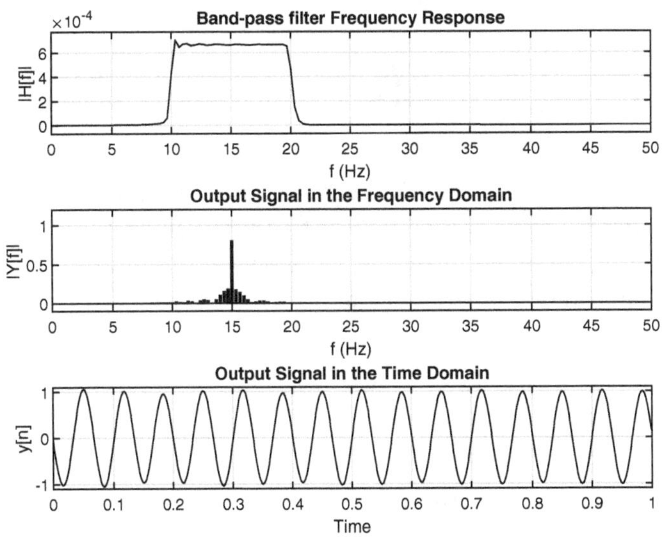

Fig. 10.6 Band-pass filter

10.4 Conversion Between Time and Frequency Domains

10.4.1 The Idea

To analyze the intensity of a signal as a function of its constituent frequencies, the goal is to decompose the signal into a sum of sine and cosine waves at different frequencies. For a signal of length N, denoted as $x[n]$, the longest cycle that can be represented by the data has a period $T = N$. The corresponding frequency, $f = \frac{1}{N}$, is the lowest possible frequency and is referred to as the *fundamental frequency*.

From this fundamental frequency, we define the *harmonic frequencies*, which are integer multiples of the fundamental frequency. These frequencies are expressed as $f_k = \frac{k}{N}$, where $k = 0, 1, \ldots, \frac{N}{2}$. The upper limit, $\frac{N}{2}$, ensures that we avoid frequencies higher than the Nyquist frequency, beyond which aliasing would occur. The period of each harmonic frequency is given by $T_k = \frac{N}{k}$.

The signal $x[n]$ can then be expressed as a sum of sinusoidal components:

$$x[n] = \sum_{k=0}^{N/2} \left[A_k \cos\left(2\pi \frac{k}{N} n\right) + B_k \sin\left(2\pi \frac{k}{N} n\right) \right].$$

Here, the coefficients A_k and B_k determine the amplitude of the cosine and sine components corresponding to each frequency f_k.

Using the trigonometric identity $A\cos(x) + B\sin(x) = C\cos(x + \theta)$, the expression can be rewritten in a more compact form:

$$x[n] = \sum_{k=0}^{N/2} C_k \cos\left(2\pi \frac{k}{N} n + \theta_k\right),$$

where C_k represents the amplitude of each frequency component, and θ_k is the phase angle.

By applying Euler's formula, $e^{jx} = \cos(x) + j\sin(x)$, the sinusoidal components can be expressed in terms of complex numbers.[2]

Using complex coefficients X_k, which encapsulate both amplitude and phase information, the notation becomes more concise. A complex number X_k can be expressed in either rectangular form $X_k = \mathrm{Re}(X_k) + j\mathrm{Im}(X_k)$ or polar form

[2] In DSP and electrical engineering, j is used as the imaginary unit ($j^2 = -1$) instead of i, which is commonly reserved for representing electrical current.

$X_k = |X_k|e^{j\theta_k}$. Substituting this into the signal representation, we obtain:

$$C_k \cos\left(2\pi \frac{k}{N} n + \theta_k\right) = \mathrm{Re}\left[X_k e^{j2\pi \frac{k}{N} n}\right] = \mathrm{Re}\left[|X_k| e^{j(2\pi \frac{k}{N} n + \theta_k)}\right].$$

Thus, the signal $x[n]$ can be written as:

$$x[n] = \mathrm{Re}\left[\sum_{k=0}^{N/2} X_k e^{j2\pi \frac{k}{N} n}\right].$$

10.4.2 Inverse Discrete Fourier Transform

The equation above represents the real-valued form of the *Inverse Discrete Fourier Transform* (IDFT), which reconstructs a signal from its frequency components. By removing the real part operator, generalizing to complex-valued signals, and extending the summation to account for both positive and negative frequencies, we obtain the standard IDFT formula:

$$x[n] = \frac{1}{N} \sum_{k=0}^{N-1} X_k e^{j w_k n},$$

where $n = 0, \ldots, N-1$, and the angular frequencies are given by $w_k = 2\pi \frac{k}{N}$.

In this formulation, the frequency index k is implicitly extended to include both positive and negative frequencies by using modular indexing. Specifically, while the summation index runs from $k = 0$ to $N-1$, the corresponding frequency components are interpreted as spanning $k = -N/2+1, \ldots, N/2$, ensuring a complete representation of the frequency spectrum. This symmetry allows the IDFT to fully reconstruct the original signal from its discrete frequency components.

The factor $\frac{1}{N}$ ensures proper normalization, though it can alternatively be incorporated into the definition of X_k.

This compact complex notation is widely used because it simplifies mathematical operations and provides an elegant framework for frequency-domain analysis.

10.4.3 Discrete Fourier Transform

To compute the frequency components X_k from a given time-domain signal $x[n]$, we use the *Discrete Fourier Transform* (DFT). Leveraging the orthogonality properties of complex exponentials, as described in Oppenheim and Schafer (2010), the DFT is defined as:

$$X_k = \sum_{n=0}^{N-1} x[n]e^{-jw_k n},$$

where $k = 0, \ldots, N-1$ and $w_k = 2\pi \frac{k}{N}$. The DFT provides a discrete representation of the frequency content of a signal, making it ideal for numerical computations.

10.4.4 The z-Transform

The z-transform is a powerful mathematical tool in DSP that extends the idea of the DFT to a broader and more general framework. While the DFT maps discrete-time signals to the frequency domain using complex exponentials, the z-transform introduces a complex variable z that provides a more comprehensive view of the signal in both the time and frequency domains.

Given a discrete sequence $x[n]$, the z-transform $X(z)$ is defined as:

$$X(z) = \sum_{n=-\infty}^{\infty} x[n]z^{-n},$$

where z is a complex number, often expressed in polar form as $z = re^{jw}$, with r representing the magnitude and w the angular frequency. This formulation allows the z-transform to analyze both the magnitude and phase characteristics of a signal across the complex plane.

The z-transform extends the concept of frequency analysis by generalizing the Discrete-Time Fourier Transform (DTFT) to the entire complex plane. When the magnitude of z is set to $r = 1$, the z-transform reduces to the DTFT, which provides a continuous frequency representation of the signal. This occurs because, for $r = 1$, the complex variable z lies on the unit circle in the complex plane, where $z = e^{jw}$. In contrast, the Discrete Fourier Transform (DFT) samples the DTFT at a finite set of discrete frequencies, making it a specific case of the DTFT used for practical computations.

One of the key advantages of the z-transform is its ability to handle more general discrete-time systems, including systems that have both feedforward and feedback components. This is particularly useful when designing and analyzing digital filters, where the system behavior is characterized by a transfer function.

Convolution is a fundamental operation in signal processing that combines two signals to produce a third. In the time domain, convolution involves multiplying and summing sequence elements, which can be computationally expensive. However, in the z-domain, convolution simplifies to multiplication. Specifically, if $x_1[n]$ and $x_2[n]$ are two signals, their convolution in the time domain is given by $x_1[n] * x_2[n]$. The z-transforms of these signals are denoted as $X_1(z)$ and $X_2(z)$, respectively. In the z-domain, the convolution operation becomes the simple multiplication of these two z-transforms:

$$Z\left(x_1[n] * x_2[n]\right) = X_1(z)X_2(z).$$

This simplification makes signal processing more efficient, as it reduces the complex time-domain operation to a straightforward multiplication in the z-domain.

The z-transform is also fundamental in analyzing the behavior of discrete-time systems. A system's behavior is often described by its impulse response, $h[n]$, which is the system's output when the input is a unit impulse $\delta[n]$. The z-transform of $h[n]$ is called the transfer function $H(z)$, and it fully characterizes the system's response in the frequency domain:

$$H(z) = \sum_{n=0}^{\infty} h[n]z^{-n}.$$

In the equation above, the summation starts from $n = 0$ because we assume a causal system, meaning $h[n] = 0$ for $n < 0$.

The transfer function relates the input and output signals of the system. If $x[n]$ is the input and $y[n]$ is the output, the output can be found by convolution of $x[n]$ and $h[n]$ in the time domain:

$$y[n] = h[n] * x[n],$$

which in the z-domain becomes:

$$Y(z) = H(z)X(z).$$

Thus, the z-transform transforms convolution into simple multiplication, making it a powerful tool for system analysis and design.

A common application of the z-transform is in the analysis and design of digital filters, especially IIR filters. The general difference equation for an IIR filter is:

$$y[n] = \sum_{k=0}^{m} b_k x[n-k] - \sum_{k=1}^{q} a_k y[n-k],$$

where $x[n]$ is the input and $y[n]$ is the output. Applying the z-transform to this difference equation, we obtain the transfer function $H(z)$:

$$H(z) = \frac{Y(z)}{X(z)} = \frac{\sum_{k=0}^{m} b_k z^{-k}}{1 + \sum_{k=1}^{q} a_k z^{-k}}.$$

This transfer function describes the system as the ratio of two polynomials in z^{-1}, and it can be used to study the system's behavior in both the time and frequency domains.

To analyze the frequency response of a system, we substitute $z = e^{jw}$ into the transfer function. This gives the frequency response $H(w)$, which is a complex function of the angular frequency w. The magnitude $|H(w)|$ and phase $\theta(w)$ of the frequency response are of particular interest, as they describe how the system affects the amplitude and phase of the input signal across different frequencies:

$$H(w) = |H(w)|e^{j\theta(w)}.$$

This frequency response is crucial for understanding the filtering properties of digital systems.

In summary, the z-transform is a powerful and versatile tool in digital signal processing. It provides a general framework for analyzing discrete-time signals and systems in both the time and frequency domains. By extending the concept of the DFT, the z-transform simplifies operations like convolution and system analysis, making it essential for filter design and stability analysis. When z lies on the unit circle ($r = 1$), the z-transform reduces to the DTFT, connecting the two methods and enabling a deeper understanding of discrete-time systems.

10.5 Quantifying Phase and Signal Delays

10.5.1 Phase Delay

When a signal of a single frequency passes through a filter, the output retains the same frequency but undergoes changes in amplitude and phase, determined by the filter's frequency response and phase behavior at that frequency. For moving average filters, which are linear and time-invariant, this means that a sinusoidal input with frequency w produces an output sinusoid of the same frequency, but with a modified amplitude and a phase shift $\theta(w)$. This phase shift, typically negative, indicates a time lag between the input and output signals.

Mathematically, if the input signal is a sinusoidal function of the form:

$$x[t] = A\cos(wt),$$

where A is the amplitude and w is the angular frequency,[3] then the output signal after passing through the filter can be described as:

$$y[t] = A \cdot |H(w)| \cos(wt + \theta(w)),$$

where $|H(w)|$ is the filter's magnitude response, affecting the amplitude, and $\theta(w)$ represents the phase shift introduced by the filter.

The phase shift can be transformed to the phase delay. The phase delay $\tau_{\text{phase}}(w)$ is the time delay corresponding to this phase shift, and it is given by:

$$\tau_{\text{phase}}(w) = -\frac{\theta(w)}{w}. \tag{10.1}$$

The negative sign indicates that a negative phase shift corresponds to a positive time delay (i.e., the output is delayed compared to the input). Thus, the phase delay quantifies the time shift for each frequency component of the input signal as it passes through the filter, helping us understand how the filter affects the timing of different frequencies in the signal.

A useful way to better understand the concept of phase delay is as follows: the cosine input signal $x[t]$ reaches its first maximum at $t = 0$. However, due to the filter, the output $y[t]$ will reach its maximum at a different time. Specifically, the maximum occurs when the total phase of the cosine function

---

[3] In DSP literature, a discrete signal x is typically represented as $x[n]$, where n denotes the time index. However, in our convention, n refers to the size of the averaging window in a moving average. To avoid confusion, we use $x[t]$ to represent the signal in this section.

is zero, which gives the condition:

$$w\tau_{\text{phase}}(w) + \theta(w) = 0.$$

Solving this yields the expression for phase delay, as shown in Eq. (10.1).

Figure 10.7 illustrates the concept of phase delay with an example. The price dynamics are represented by a cosine wave with a period of $T = 125$ samples. The 50-period Simple Moving Average (SMA) of the prices is computed. The resulting SMA(50) is also a cosine wave but with a reduced amplitude and a phase shift. While the price reaches its maximum at time $t = 0$ (marked by point A), the SMA(50) reaches its maximum $\frac{n-1}{2} = \frac{50-1}{2} = 24.5$ samples later (marked by point B). This delay illustrates the effect of the SMA filter on the phase of the input signal.

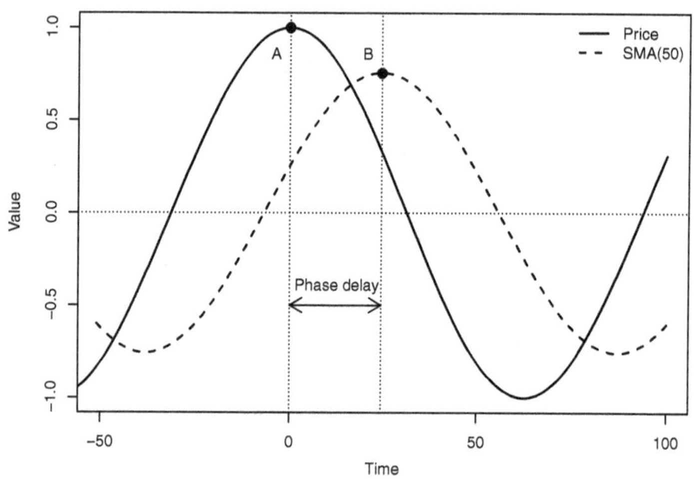

Fig. 10.7 Phase delay illustration

Note that the phase delay of the SMA(n) can be determined using the concept of the Average Lag Time of a Moving Average (ALT(MA)), as introduced by Brown (1963). This measure represents the average "age" of the data contributing to the moving average. The ALT(MA) is calculated using the following formula:

$$\text{ALT}(MA) = \frac{\sum_{i=0}^{n-1} h_i \times i}{\sum_{i=0}^{n-1} h_i}, \tag{10.2}$$

where n is the window size of the moving average, and h_i is the weight assigned to the price P_{t-i}.[4]

An additional key property of the SMA(n) is that it introduces a uniform phase delay across all input frequencies, classifying it as a linear-phase filter. This behavior, however, is not unique to the SMA. All moving averages with symmetric weights around their center exhibit the same characteristics: the phase delay time is given by $(n-1)/2$, and this delay remains consistent for all input frequencies. These features emphasize the uniform phase response of symmetric moving averages.

For non-symmetric moving averages like the LMA or the EMA, the ALT(MA) method cannot be used to compute the phase delay. This is illustrated in the left panel of Fig. 10.8, where the price dynamics resemble those in Fig. 10.7: the price process is modeled as a cosine wave with a period of $T = 125$ samples. According to Brown (1963), the average lag time, calculated using Eq. (10.2), should be identical for both the EMA(50) and SMA(50). However, the plot shows that the phase delay of the EMA(50) is 17 samples, while that of the SMA(50) for the same frequency is 24.5 samples.

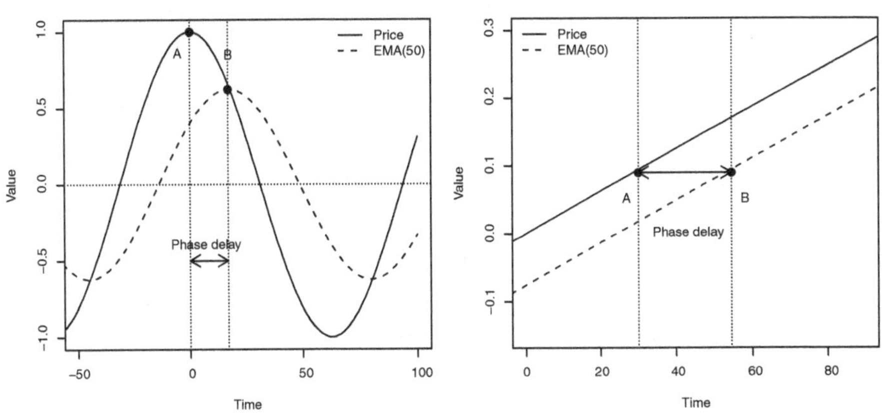

Fig. 10.8 Phase delay of the EMA(50). In the left panel, the cosine wave has a period of $T = 125$ samples, while in the right panel, the sine wave has a period of $T = 2000$ samples

To summarize, the ALT(MA) measure is applicable only when a moving average has symmetric weights around the middle, ensuring a consistent phase delay across all frequencies. For non-symmetric moving averages, the phase

[4] In the context of moving averages, the price weights are typically denoted by w_i. However, in DSP literature, w_i is commonly used to represent angular frequency, while the price weights are instead referred to as the filter impulse response coefficients, h_i.

delay varies with signal frequency and is therefore not constant. However, the ALT(MA) measure remains valid for extremely low-frequency signals. The following proposition formalizes this concept:

Proposition 10.1 *In the limit as w approaches zero, the phase delay of a moving average filter approaches the ALT(MA). Formally:*

$$\lim_{w \to 0} \tau_{phase}(w) = ALT(MA).$$

The proof is provided in the Appendix.

It is important to note that at zero frequency, the phase delay is undefined because zero frequency corresponds to a signal that does not change over time. In simple terms, it represents a constant or average value of the signal. Since a constant signal has no variation, there is no phase delay at zero frequency. However, as the frequency approaches zero, a sinusoidal signal $\sin(wt)$ can be approximated as a straight line with a positive slope for $t > 0$. This can be shown using the Taylor series approximation $\sin(x) \approx x$ for very small x.

To illustrate, the right panel of Fig. 10.8 shows a price process modeled as a sine wave with a period of $T = 2000$ samples. Both the price and the EMA(50) appear as two lines with the same positive slope. The horizontal distance between these two lines converges to $\text{ALT}(\text{EMA}(50)) = \frac{50-1}{2} = 24.5$ as T approaches infinity.

As discussed earlier in this book, the ALT(MA) measure is only meaningful when the price trend remains constant, which, in most cases, is not of interest because it implies no changes in the trend. However, there is an exception: the ALT(MA) measure can still be used to evaluate the average lag time of a moving average when the price weights are symmetric around the center. In this case, the phase delay remains constant across all frequencies.

10.5.2 Signal Delay

There are four primary trend-following rules based on moving averages of prices: the Momentum (MOM) rule, the Price and Moving Average crossover (P-MA) rule, the double Moving Average Crossover (MA-C) rule, and the Moving Average Direction (MA-D) rule. The technical indicators for these rules are defined as follows:

$$
\begin{aligned}
I_t^{\text{MOM}(n)} &= P_t - P_{t-n+1}, \\
I_t^{\text{P-MA}}(n) &= P_t - MA_t(n, P), \\
I_t^{\text{MA-C}}(s, l) &= MA_t(s, P) - MA_t(l, P), \\
I_t^{\text{MA-D}}(n) &= MA_t(n, P) - MA_{t-1}(n, P),
\end{aligned}
$$

where P_{t-i} is the price at time $t - i$ and $MA_t(n, P)$ is the moving average of prices with a window size of n. The trading signal for each rule is generated as:

$$
\text{Signal} = \begin{cases} \text{Buy} & \text{if } I_t^{\text{TR}} > 0, \\ \text{Sell} & \text{if } I_t^{\text{TR}} \leq 0, \end{cases}
$$

where I_t^{TR} denotes the technical indicator of rule TR.

The MA-D rule generates a Buy signal when the moving average increases and a Sell signal when it decreases. Consequently, the signal delay time of this rule corresponds to the phase delay of the moving average it uses. The MOM(n) rule is equivalent to the SMA-D$(n - 1)$ rule, meaning the signal delay of the MOM(n) rule matches the phase delay of the SMA$(n - 1)$. Alternatively, the MOM(n) rule can be interpreted as a P-MA(n) rule that employs a specialized moving average, where all price weights are zero except for the weight assigned to the most distant price.

Any P-MA(l) rule can be regarded as a special case of the MA-C(s, l) rule when $s = 1$. Thus, the MA-C(s, l) rule acts as a general trading strategy encompassing both the P-MA and MA-C rules. Our objective now is to evaluate the signal delay of the MA-C rule.

We assume the price is represented by a sinusoidal function of the form $P_t = A\cos(wt)$, where A is the amplitude and w is the angular frequency. The shorter moving average $MA_t(s, P)$ and the longer moving average $MA_t(l, P)$ are two signals that, after passing through their respective filters, can be expressed as:

$$
MA_t(s, P) = AH_s\cos(wt + \theta_s), \quad MA_t(l, P) = AH_l\cos(wt + \theta_l),
$$

where H_s and θ_s are the magnitude response and phase shift introduced by the shorter moving average, and H_l and θ_l are the magnitude response and phase shift introduced by the longer moving average. For brevity, we omit the explicit dependence of the magnitude response and phase shift on the angular frequency w.

The technical indicator for the MA-C rule is then the difference between the two signals:

$$I_t^{\text{MA-C}}(s,l) = AH_s\cos(wt+\theta_s) - AH_l\cos(wt+\theta_l) = AH_i\cos(wt+\theta_i),$$

where H_i and θ_i represent the magnitude response and phase shift of the resulting signal from the technical indicator. These are given by:

$$H_i = \sqrt{H_s^2 + H_l^2 - 2H_sH_l\cos(\theta_s - \theta_l)},$$

$$\theta_i = \arctan\left(\frac{H_s\sin(\theta_s) - H_l\sin(\theta_l)}{H_s\cos(\theta_s) - H_l\cos(\theta_l)}\right). \tag{10.3}$$

It is important to note that the signal delay of the MA-D rule coincides with the phase delay of the moving average used in this rule. For example, a Sell signal is triggered when the cosine wave reaches its maximum and begins to decrease. In stark contrast, the signal in the MA-C rule is triggered when the technical indicator crosses zero. Consequently, the signal delay in the MA-C rule can be obtained by solving the following equation:

$$\cos(w\tau_{\text{signal}} + \theta_i) = 0,$$

where τ_{signal} represents the signal delay and θ_i is given by Eq. (10.3). The cosine function $\cos(x)$ equals zero when:

$$x = \frac{\pi}{2} + m\pi, \quad m \in \mathbb{Z},$$

where $\mathbb{Z}$ refers to the set of all integer numbers, both positive and negative, including zero. Therefore, the general solution to the equation is:

$$w\tau_{\text{signal}} + \theta_i = \frac{\pi}{2} + m\pi.$$

Solving for τ_{signal}, we get:

$$\tau_{\text{signal}} = \frac{\frac{\pi}{2} + m\pi - \theta_i}{w}.$$

To find the first solution after time $t = 0$, we choose the smallest m such that $\tau_{\text{signal}} > 0$.

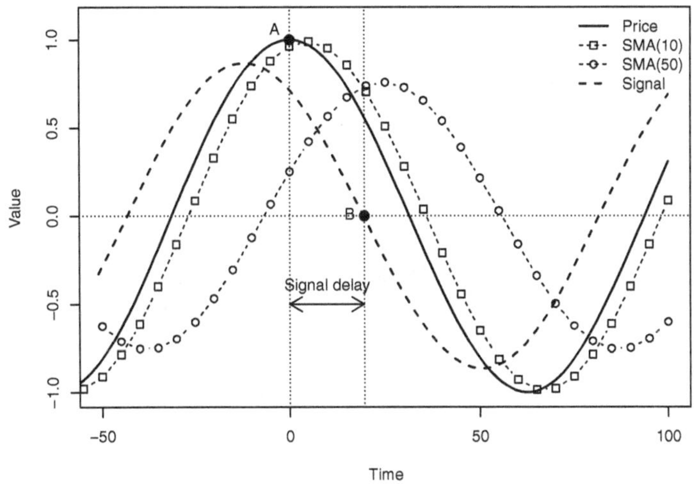

Fig. 10.9 Illustration of the signal delay in the SMA-C(10,50) rule

Figure 10.9 illustrates the signal delay in the SMA-C(10,50) rule. The price dynamics are modeled as a cosine wave with a period of $T = 125$ samples. The 10-period and 50-period SMAs represent the shorter and longer moving averages, respectively. The trading signal is derived from the difference between the shorter and longer SMAs.

At time $t = 0$, the price reaches its maximum (marked by point A). However, the trading signal reaches its maximum earlier. This behavior indicates a positive phase shift for the trading signal, i.e., $\theta_i > 0$. The trading signal undergoes a change when it crosses zero, which occurs after time 0 (marked by point B). Assuming $0 < \theta_i < \frac{\pi}{2}$, the first zero crossing occurs when $m = 0$. Consequently, the signal delay is given by:

$$\tau_{\text{signal}} = \frac{\frac{\pi}{2} - \theta_i}{w}. \tag{10.4}$$

10.6 Frequency-Domain Analysis of Conventional Moving Averages

This section examines conventional moving averages from the DSP perspective. These moving averages include the SMA, LMA, and EMA. Each of these moving averages functions as a low-pass filter. However, their frequency-domain characteristics differ due to the distinct weighting functions they employ.

When analyzing the frequency response of a filter, expressed as $H(w) = |H(w)|e^{j\theta(w)}$, two components provide valuable insights: the magnitude response $|H(w)|$ and the phase shift $\theta(w)$. The magnitude response indicates how the filter attenuates or amplifies sinusoidal components across different frequencies, revealing which frequencies are passed through and which are suppressed. The phase shift $\theta(w)$ represents the angular delay introduced between the input and output signals, showing how the filter affects the timing of different frequency components. Rather than directly reporting $\theta(w)$, we focus on the phase delay, as it offers a clearer understanding of how quickly a moving average filter reacts to changes in trend direction.

10.6.1 Simple Moving Average

Using the z-transform notation, the transfer function of SMA(n) filter is:

$$H(z) = \frac{1}{n} + \frac{1}{n}z^{-1} + \frac{1}{n}z^{-2} + \ldots + \frac{1}{n}z^{-(n-1)},$$

where z^{-1} denotes one bar of lag as a multiplicative operator.

The left panel of Fig. 10.10 illustrates the magnitude response of the SMA(4) and SMA(12) filters. In both cases, the SMA(n) acts as a low-pass filter. A constant component (zero frequency) in the input signal passes through the filter without attenuation, while higher frequencies are progressively attenuated.

Notably, certain higher frequencies, specifically $\frac{i}{n}$ where $i \in [1, 2, \ldots, \frac{n}{2}]$, are completely suppressed by the filter. These frequencies correspond to the harmonics of the n-bar cycle. For example, consider the SMA(10). The average value of a 10-bar sinusoidal wave over its 10-bar cycle is zero. Similarly, the average value of a 5-bar sinusoidal wave (the first harmonic of the 10-bar cycle) over a 10-bar period is also zero, and so on for higher harmonics. This suppression of specific harmonics is a direct consequence of the uniform weighting function used in SMA filters, which creates destructive interference for these frequencies.

The right panel of Fig. 10.10 displays the phase delay of the SMA(4) and SMA(12) filters. For SMA filters, the phase delay is constant and equals $\tau_{\text{phase}} = \frac{n-1}{2}$, where n is the window size. This result aligns with the ALT(SMA(n)). Specifically, for SMA(4), the phase delay is $\tau_{\text{phase}} = 1.5$ periods, while for SMA(12), the phase delay is $\tau_{\text{phase}} = 5.5$ periods. As shown in the figure, the phase delay of SMA filters is represented by horizontal lines, indicating that the delay is uniform across all frequencies.

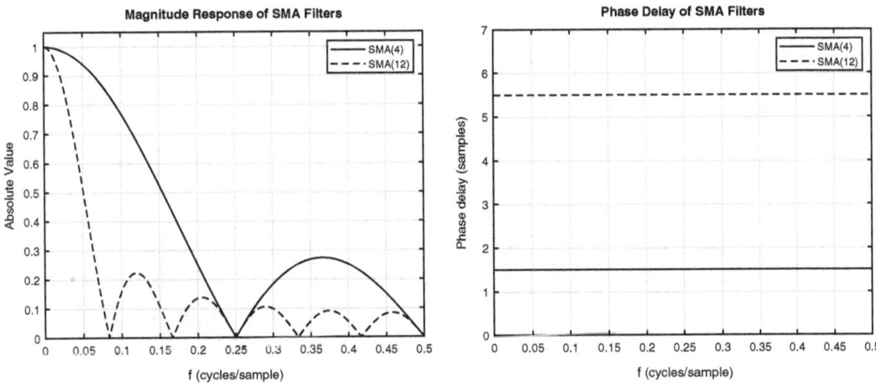

Fig. 10.10 Magnitude response (left) and phase delay (right) of SMA filters

The constant phase delay of SMA filters is often desirable in many signal processing applications, such as audio, where maintaining consistent timing across all frequency components minimizes distortion and preserves the signal's integrity. However, in trend-following applications, this consistency may not be as critical. Instead, a smaller delay might be preferable, especially when prices change quickly, as it allows the filter to respond more rapidly to shifts in the market trend.

However, the SMA filter's tendency to completely suppress specific harmonics of the n-bar cycle is a significant drawback. This suppression can lead to an over-simplified representation of the signal, as valuable frequency components may be lost. Consequently, while the SMA is effective for basic smoothing tasks, its frequency-domain limitations suggest that alternative moving averages with more refined frequency responses may be preferable in many cases.

10.6.2 Linear Moving Average

The transfer function of the LMA(n) filter is given by:

$$
\begin{aligned}
H(z) = \frac{n}{N} + \frac{n-1}{N}z^{-1} + \frac{n-2}{N}z^{-2} \\
+ \ldots + \frac{1}{N}z^{-(n-1)},
\end{aligned}
$$

where $N = \frac{n(n+1)}{2}$ is the normalization constant, equal to the sum of all integers from 1 to n.

The LMA(n) filter can be interpreted as a weighted superposition of n SMA(k) filters, with k decreasing from n to 1. For example, LMA(4) can be represented as:

$$LMA(4) = \frac{1}{10}\big[4 \cdot SMA(4) + 3 \cdot SMA(3) + 2 \cdot SMA(2) + 1 \cdot SMA(1)\big].$$

Here, the largest weight is assigned to SMA(4), which dominates the behavior of the filter. Consequently, the frequency response of LMA(4) is quite similar to that of SMA(4), although the cancellation of certain frequencies in SMA(4) is smoothed in LMA(4) due to the contributions of the other terms in the summation.

The left panel of Fig. 10.11 displays the magnitude responses of LMA(4) and LMA(12). The magnitude response exhibits a non-monotonic decrease, as the frequencies $\frac{1}{n}, \frac{2}{n}, \ldots, \frac{1}{2}$ are attenuated more significantly than their neighboring frequencies. This characteristic stems from the filter's design. Compared to their SMA counterparts, these filters exhibit a more uniform attenuation across frequencies.

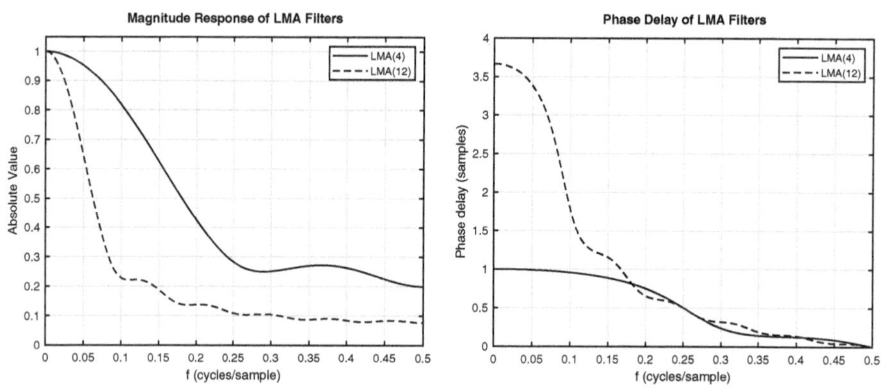

Fig. 10.11 Magnitude response (left) and phase delay (right) of LMA filters

The right panel of Fig. 10.11 illustrates the phase delay of LMA(4) and LMA(12). As the frequency approaches zero, the phase delays converge to 1 and 3.67 periods, respectively. This behavior aligns with the ALT(LMA(n))$= \frac{n-1}{3}$. In general, the phase delay decreases as the signal frequency increases, indicating that higher-frequency components experience less delay.

In many contexts, such as audio signal processing, frequency-dependent lag times are considered highly undesirable because they cause distortion between the input and output signals. For example, varying delays across frequencies in audio signals lead to phase distortion, which degrades sound quality.

However, in trend-following applications, this property can sometimes be beneficial. Frequency-dependent phase delay allows the filter to react more promptly to rapid price changes, improving responsiveness to sudden market shifts. Nevertheless, whether this characteristic is truly advantageous in trading strategies requires further investigation. A more comprehensive analysis is needed to assess its potential impact on trading rules and their effectiveness.

10.6.3 Exponential Moving Average

The recursive representation of an EMA(n) filter is given by the following equation:

$$y[n] = (1 - \lambda)x[n] + \lambda y[n - 1].$$

In the frequency domain, using the z-transform, this recursive relation becomes:

$$Y(z) = (1 - \lambda)X(z) + \lambda Y(z)z^{-1}.$$

By factoring and solving for the transfer function, we obtain the EMA filter's transfer function as:

$$H(z) = \frac{Y(z)}{X(z)} = \frac{1 - \lambda}{1 - \lambda z^{-1}}.$$

EMA filters belong to the class of IIR filters, similar to other well-known filters such as Butterworth, Chebyshev, and Elliptic filters. In contrast to FIR filters, IIR filters are characterized by transfer functions that are ratios of polynomials. The poles of the transfer function, which correspond to the zeros of the denominator, are especially important in determining the filter's behavior.

The left panel of Fig. 10.12 illustrates the magnitude responses of EMA(4) and EMA(12). Given that $\lambda = \frac{n-1}{n+1}$, we have $\lambda = 0.6$ for EMA(4) and $\lambda = 0.846$ for EMA(12). As n increases, λ increases, meaning that the filter places less weight on the current input value and more weight on past output values, leading to a smoother response.

The right panel of Fig. 10.12 shows the phase delay of the EMA filters, measured in terms of the number of samples. As the signal frequency approaches zero, the phase delay is 1.5 periods for EMA(4) and 5.5 periods for EMA(12), consistent with the formula $\text{ALT}(\text{EMA}(n)) = \frac{n-1}{2}$. As the signal frequency increases, the phase delay decreases rapidly toward zero.

Notably, the phase delay of the EMA(n) at zero frequency coincides with that of the SMA(n). This is because, in the original design of the EMA, Brown (1963) suggested it as an alternative to the SMA and designed the EMA such

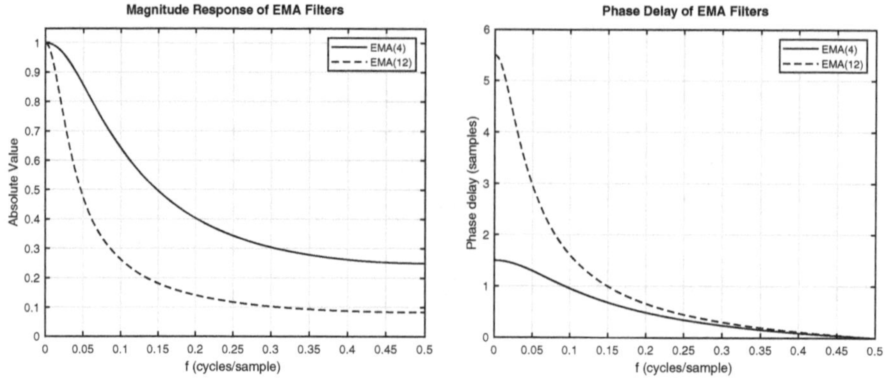

Fig. 10.12 Magnitude response (left) and phase delay (right) of EMA filters

that its lag time would match the lag time of the SMA. Specifically, Brown proposed choosing the parameter n such that the lag times of both EMA(n) and SMA(n) would be the same. However, in practice, the lag times of the two filters are equal only at zero frequency. For non-zero frequencies, the lag times differ, with the EMA exhibiting a smaller phase delay.

10.7 Spectral Analysis of Moving Average-Based Trading Rules

The value of a moving average alone cannot generate the trading signal for a trend-following rule. Instead, the trading signal is triggered by specific relationships: between consecutive values of the moving average (as in the MA-D rule), between the price and the moving average (as in the P-MA rule), or between two moving averages computed with different window sizes (as in the MA-C rule).

As a result, understanding the magnitude response and phase delay of a moving average does not directly reveal the magnitude response and phase delay of the signal produced by a trading rule. In this section, we focus on exploring the magnitude response of various P-MA and MA-C rules derived from conventional moving averages. The consideration of signal delay is excluded from this analysis. In principle, the signal delay time can be calculated using Eq. (10.4), assuming specific constraints on the variable θ_i, which represents the phase shift of the trading signal in either the P-MA or MA-C rule. However, further investigation is required to ensure accurate results, so this topic will not be addressed here.

We do not consider the MA-D rules because each MA-D rule typically corresponds to a specific P-MA rule. For instance, the LMA-D rule aligns with the P-SMA rule, while the EMA-D rule is equivalent to the P-EMA rule. Additionally, the MOM rule can be interpreted as either a special case of the P-MA rule or equivalent to the SMA-D rule.

10.7.1 Price and Moving Average Crossover Rules

The technical indicator of a P-MA rule represents the difference between the price and the moving average of prices. Its impulse response function, $h_{\text{P-MA}}[n]$, is given by:

$$h_{\text{P-MA}}[n] = 1 - h_{\text{MA}}[n],$$

where $h_{\text{MA}}[n]$ is the impulse response of the moving average. Assuming the moving average operates as a FIR filter, which applies to both the SMA and LMA, the transfer function of the P-MA rule is expressed as:

$$H_{\text{P-MA}}(z) = 1 - H_{\text{MA}}(z) = (1 - h_0) - h_1 z^{-1} - h_2 z^{-2} - \ldots - h_{n-1} z^{-(n-1)},$$

where $H_{\text{MA}}(z)$ represents the transfer function of the moving average. This equation indicates that the impulse response of a P-MA rule consists of a large positive first coefficient, followed by a sequence of smaller negative coefficients.

The transfer function of the P-EMA rule is given by:

$$H_{\text{P-EMA}}(z) = 1 - H_{\text{EMA}}(z) = 1 - \frac{1-\lambda}{1-\lambda z^{-1}} = \lambda \frac{1-z^{-1}}{1-\lambda z^{-1}},$$

while the transfer function of the MOM rule is:

$$H_{\text{MOM}}(z) = 1 - z^{-(n-1)}.$$

Figures 10.13 and 10.14 display the magnitude response of the P-SMA, P-LMA, P-EMA, and MOM filters. A key observation from visually inspecting the magnitude responses is that all these filters behave as high-pass filters, attenuating low frequencies while allowing high frequencies to pass through. The MOM filters, in particular, exhibit an unusual high-pass behavior, completely suppressing frequencies of the form $\frac{i}{n}$, where $i \in \{0, 1, \ldots, \frac{n-1}{2}\}$.

The key takeaway from the fact that the P-MA rule functions as a high-pass filter is that the properties of the moving average, which acts as a low-pass filter, have little to no impact on the characteristics of the P-MA rule itself.

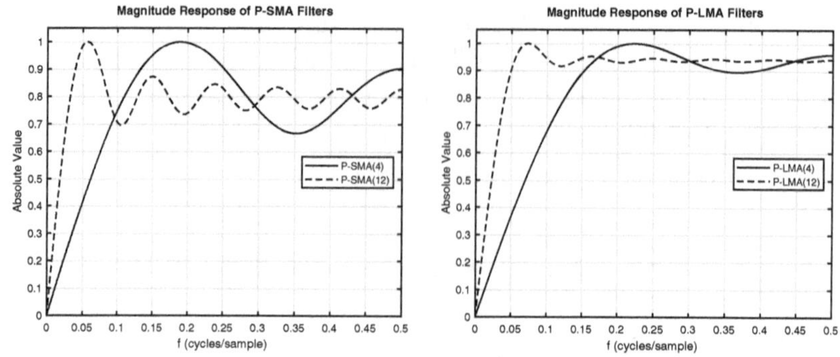

Fig. 10.13 Magnitude response of the P-SMA (left) and P-LMA filters (right)

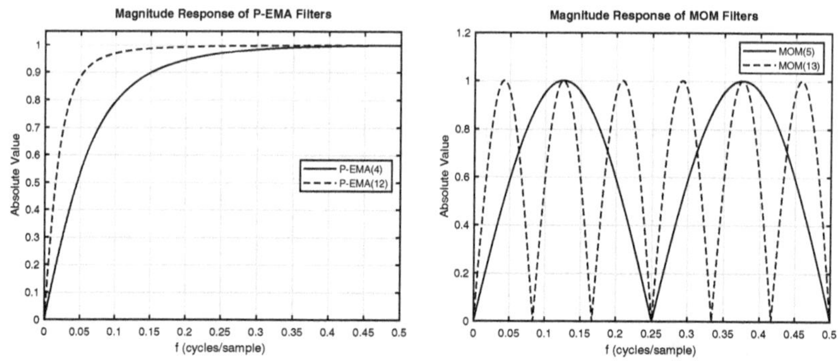

Fig. 10.14 Magnitude response of the P-EMA (left) and MOM filters (right)

Specifically, even if we know the responsiveness and smoothness of the moving average, these attributes do not carry over to the P-MA rule. For instance, the smoothness of the moving average provides no meaningful insight into the smoothness of the P-MA rule that is based on it.

The use of a high-pass filter in trading is puzzling, especially since the trading signal is typically of low frequency, while high frequencies are usually associated with noise. The resolution of this paradox lies in understanding that the P-MA rule functions as a high-pass filter only in terms of DSP. In practice, however, the trading signal of the P-MA rule remains low frequency. The issue is that the signal is heavily attenuated compared to the input. Figure 10.15 illustrates this problem.

Specifically, Fig. 10.15 shows the price with noise, the SMA, and the signal from the P-SMA rule. The price process is represented as a sinusoidal wave with a period of $T = 125$ samples, while additive noise is a much higher-frequency sinusoidal wave with a period of $T = 5$ samples. The SMA effectively suppresses this noise in the price. However, when the smooth SMA is subtracted

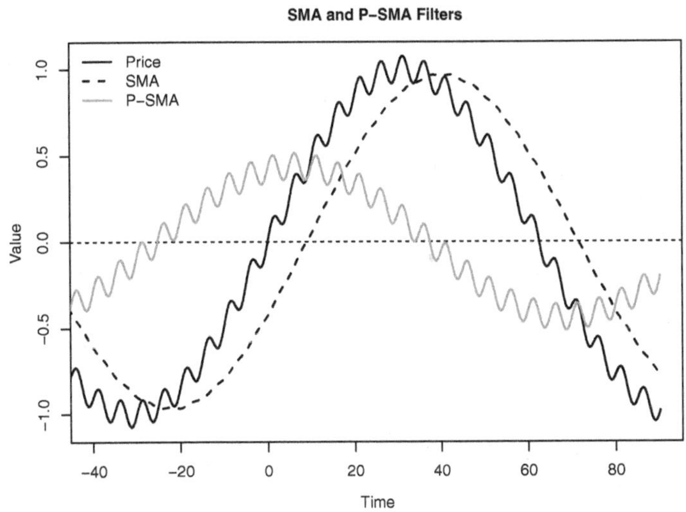

Fig. 10.15 Price with the noise, the SMA, and the signal of the P-SMA rule

from the noisy price, the resulting signal retains the noise without any attenuation. At the same time, the amplitude of the low-frequency signal (with a period of $T = 125$ samples) is significantly reduced compared to the amplitude of the original price.

In essence, the P-MA rule attenuates the signal while allowing the noise to pass through. From a DSP standpoint, this makes the P-MA rule a high-pass filter. However, this behavior is undesirable because the noise generates false signals (whipsaws) whenever the signal crosses zero.

10.7.2 Double Moving Average Crossover Rules

Double moving average crossover rules, functioning as band-pass filters, offer a significant advantage over traditional price and moving average crossovers. This advantage arises from the band-pass filter's ability to capture signals within a specific frequency range, effectively filtering out both long-term (or secular) trends and high-frequency noise.

In traditional price and moving average crossover rules, market noise can trigger false signals (whipsaws), leading to poor decision-making. The double moving average crossover addresses this issue by smoothing out high-frequency fluctuations. By using two moving averages with different window sizes, this approach reduces noise while still capturing relevant trends, resulting in more reliable trading signals.

Furthermore, traditional crossover rules react to all price movements, including short-term fluctuations that may be insignificant. In contrast, the double moving average crossover focuses on mid-range frequencies, filtering out those irrelevant short-term movements. This allows the strategy to capture only the most meaningful market trends, those with sufficient duration and significance, improving the quality of the signals generated.

The key strength of the double moving average crossover lies in its ability to balance responsiveness and stability. The short-term moving average reacts quickly to market changes, while the long-term moving average provides stability, helping to prevent false signals. This dual approach ensures that the trading strategy remains adaptive to genuine market trends, without being overly sensitive to transient, short-term price movements.

Figure 10.16 highlights the advantage of the SMA-C rule over the corresponding P-SMA rule. As in Fig. 10.15, the price process is modeled as a sinusoidal wave with a period of $T = 125$ samples, while additive noise is represented by a much higher-frequency sinusoidal wave with a period of $T = 5$ samples. The long SMA in Fig. 10.16 is identical to the SMA in Fig. 10.15, while the new time series corresponds to a short SMA.

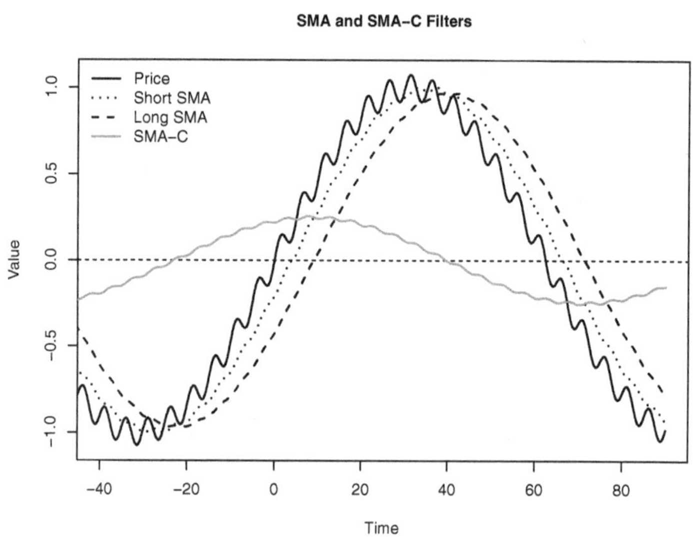

Fig. 10.16 Price with the noise, the short and long SMAs, and the signal of the SMA-C rule

The difference between the two rules lies in their respective signals: the P-SMA rule generates its signal by subtracting the SMA from the price, whereas the SMA-C rule derives its signal from the difference between the short and long SMAs. Both SMAs suppress noise, albeit to varying degrees. However, the signal produced by the SMA-C rule contains significantly less noise compared to the P-SMA rule.

The transfer function of the MA-C filter is expressed as:

$$H_{\text{MA-C}}(z) = H_{\text{MA-s}}(z) - H_{\text{MA-l}}(z),$$

where $H_{\text{MA-s}}(z)$ and $H_{\text{MA-l}}(z)$ represent the transfer functions of the short and long moving averages, respectively. Since both short and long moving averages are low-pass filters with different cutoff frequencies, their subtraction results in a band-pass filter.

The transfer functions of the SMA-C and LMA-C rules are straightforward to compute because both SMA and LMA are FIR filters. Therefore, the focus here is on the EMA-C rule, where each filter is an IIR filter. For the EMA-C rule, the difference in the impulse responses of the short and long EMAs forms the new impulse response, and the difference in their transfer functions yields the new transfer function:

$$H_{\text{EMA-C}}(z) = \frac{1-\lambda_s}{1-\lambda_s z^{-1}} - \frac{1-\lambda_l}{1-\lambda_l z^{-1}} = \frac{(\lambda_l - \lambda_s)(1-z^{-1})}{(1-\lambda_s z^{-1})(1-\lambda_l z^{-1})},$$

or equivalently,

$$H_{\text{EMA-C}}(z) = \frac{(\lambda_l - \lambda_s)(1-z^{-1})}{1-(\lambda_s+\lambda_l)z^{-1} + \lambda_s\lambda_l z^{-2}},$$

where λ_s and λ_l are the smoothing constants of the short and long EMAs, respectively.

The left panel of Fig. 10.17 displays the magnitude response of the SMA-C filters, while the right panel shows the magnitude response of the LMA-C filters. Fig. 10.18 illustrates the magnitude response of the EMA-C filters. All MA-C filters exhibit band-pass behavior, effectively suppressing both very low frequencies and high frequencies. However, notable differences emerge in the smoothness of their magnitude responses and the strength of their attenuation at high frequencies:

The SMA-C filters exhibit a less smooth magnitude response compared to other filters, characterized by noticeable fluctuations across the frequency range. These irregularities reflect uneven sensitivity to specific frequencies. However, SMA-C filters offer strong attenuation at high frequencies, which makes them effective for noise suppression.

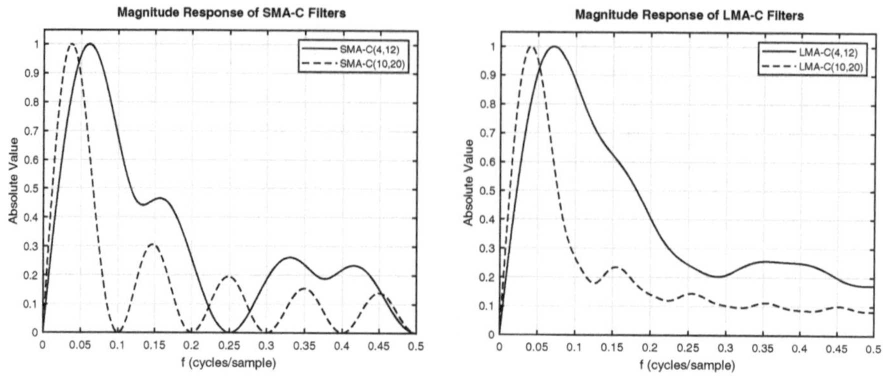

Fig. 10.17 Magnitude response of the SMA-C (left) and LMA-C filters (right)

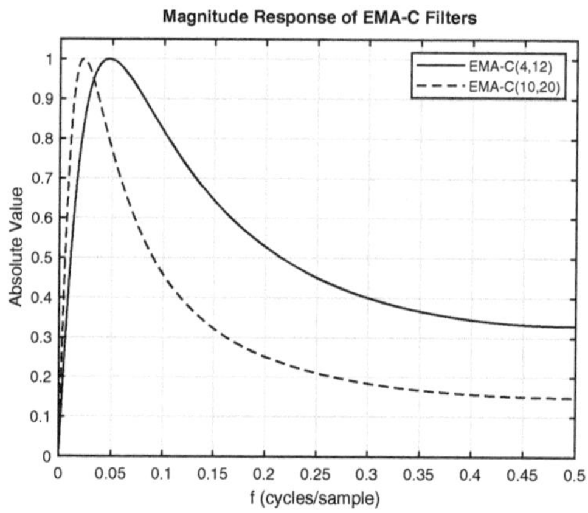

Fig. 10.18 Magnitude response of the EMA-C filters

Similar to the SMA-C filters, LMA-C filters attenuate high frequencies effectively. Additionally, their magnitude response is notably smoother than that of the SMA-C filters, indicating better consistency in frequency handling. The LMA-C filters strike a balance between noise suppression and band-pass performance.

The EMA-C filters stand out for their exceptionally smooth magnitude response, with minimal fluctuations in the passband. This smoothness ensures a more stable and predictable filtering effect across the band. However, the EMA-C filters do not attenuate high frequencies as strongly as SMA-C or LMA-C filters, potentially allowing more noise to pass through.

10.8 DSP-Motivated Moving Averages

This section reviews several examples of moving averages motivated by DSP techniques. All these moving averages can be understood within a unified framework. Specifically, each of these DSP-based moving averages can be seen as a particular realization of a general second-order filter, whose transfer function is expressed as:

$$H(z) = \frac{Y(z)}{X(z)} = \frac{b_0 + b_1 z^{-1} + b_2 z^{-2}}{1 + a_1 z^{-1} + a_2 z^{-2}}.$$

This second-order filter is highly flexible and can be configured as a low-pass, high-pass, or band-pass filter depending on the values of the coefficients a_1, a_2, b_0, b_1, and b_2. The nature of the filter's frequency response is determined by these coefficients, allowing for a variety of applications in smoothing, signal enhancement, or noise reduction.

In the time domain, the corresponding difference equation, which represents the second-order filter, is given by:

$$y[n] = b_0 x[n] + b_1 x[n-1] + b_2 x[n-2] - a_1 y[n-1] - a_2 y[n-2].$$

This equation defines the relationship between the input signal $x[n]$ and the output signal $y[n]$ at any discrete time index n. The coefficients b_0, b_1, and b_2 determine the weights applied to the current and past input values, while a_1 and a_2 control the feedback, affecting the output based on previous values of $y[n]$.

When the coefficients $a_1 = a_2 = 0$, the filter becomes a FIR filter, meaning it has no feedback and its output depends solely on the current and past input values. In contrast, if either $a_1 \neq 0$ or $a_2 \neq 0$ (or both), the filter becomes an IIR filter, which involves feedback and can lead to a more complex dynamic response with potential for resonance or oscillation.

These properties of second-order filters make them an essential building block in many DSP applications, including moving averages, where they provide a means to adaptively smooth signals while maintaining flexibility in frequency response characteristics.

10.8.1 Butterworth Filters

In designing a low-pass filter, one approach is to achieve a sharp frequency cutoff, making the filter as close as possible to an ideal low-pass filter. Filters like Chebyshev and Elliptic are designed for this purpose, offering a steeper roll-off than other types. However, these filters come with a tradeoff: they introduce ripples in the passband, which can lead to signal distortion or overshoot near the cutoff frequency.

Another strategy is to design a filter with a flat frequency response in the passband, ensuring no distortion in the desired frequency range. Butterworth filters are known for this characteristic, offering a maximally flat passband. However, they sacrifice sharpness in the cutoff, resulting in a slower roll-off and a broader transition region between the passband and stopband.

Moving averages based on Butterworth filters are often employed in trend-following strategies. Many traders consider them superior to traditional or exotic moving averages due to their solid foundation in DSP techniques.

The transfer response of Butterworth filters is governed by a single parameter: the cutoff frequency. This frequency is defined as the point where the filter attenuates the input signal by a factor of $1/\sqrt{2}$. Frequencies below the cutoff are passed with minimal attenuation, while frequencies above the cutoff are increasingly rejected, with the filter designed to minimize their impact as much as possible.

For a second-order Butterworth filter, the transfer function is expressed in terms of the digital cutoff frequency f_d and the sampling frequency f_s. The transfer function in z-domain is given by:

$$H(z) = \frac{\frac{C^2}{D}(1 + 2z^{-1} + z^{-2})}{1 + \frac{2(C^2-1)}{D}z^{-1} + \frac{1-\sqrt{2}C+C^2}{D}z^{-2}},$$

where $D = 1 + \sqrt{2}C + C^2$ and $C = \tan\left(w_d \frac{T_s}{2}\right)$, or equivalently, $C = \tan\left(\pi \frac{f_d}{f_s}\right)$. Here, $f_s = 1/T_s$ is the sampling frequency (which is 1 in our case), and f_d represents the desired digital cutoff frequency.

Figure 10.19 illustrates the impulse response (price weights) of a second-order low-pass Butterworth filter designed to eliminate cycles with periods shorter than $T = 20$, corresponding to a digital cutoff frequency $f_d = 0.05$. The impulse response function exhibits a damped sine wave, a characteristic behavior of many so-called "zero-lag" moving averages, which are known for minimizing lag time while retaining the smoothing effect.

The left panel of Fig. 10.20 displays the magnitude response of second-order Butterworth filters with cutoff frequencies of 0.05 ($T = 20$ cycles) and 0.1 ($T = 10$ cycles). The magnitude response shows a smooth decay, characteristic of Butterworth filters. The right panel of Fig. 10.20 illustrates the phase delay of these filters. At zero frequency, the phase delay is approximately 2.2 and 4.5

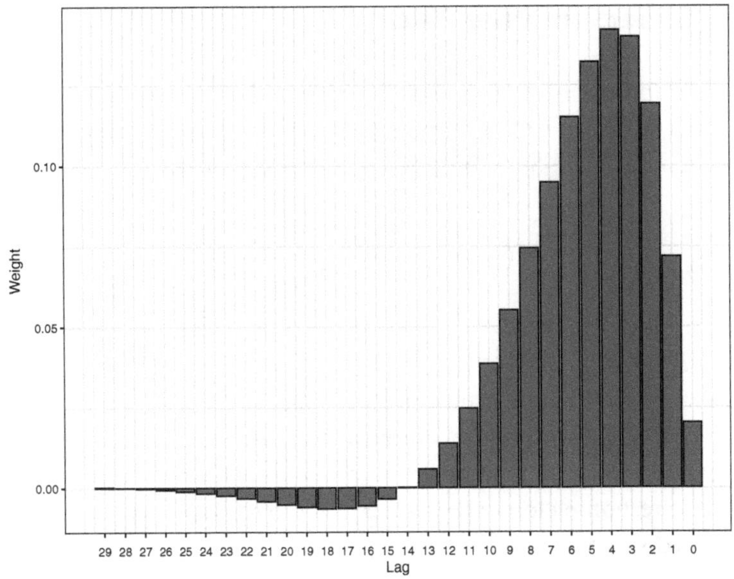

Fig. 10.19 Impulse response of a second-order Butterworth filter with a cutoff frequency of $f_d = 0.05$

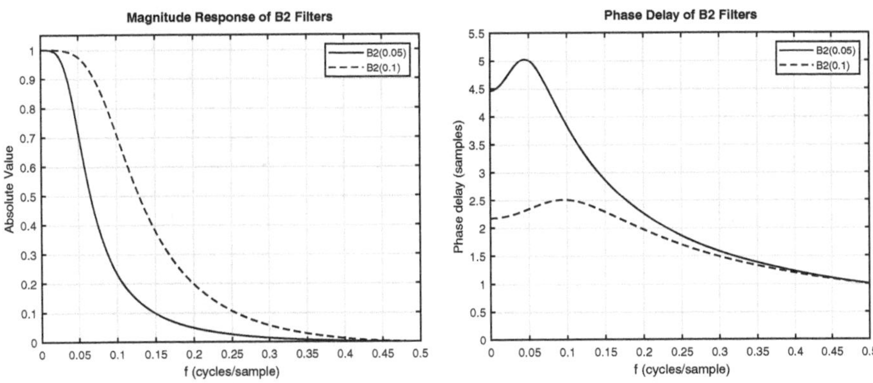

Fig. 10.20 Magnitude response (left) and phase delay (right) of second-order Butterworth filters with different cutoff frequencies ($f_d = 0.05$ and $f_d = 0.1$)

periods, indicating relatively low delay. Additionally, it is important to note that a lower cutoff frequency results in a smoother response and consequently a larger phase delay, similar to how a larger window size n leads to increased lag time.

10.8.2 SuperSmoother Filter

The SuperSmoother filter, proposed by Ehlers (2013), simplifies the low-pass Butterworth filter while maintaining its essential characteristics. The z-transfer function of a two-pole SuperSmoother filter is given by:

$$H(z) = \frac{c_0(1 + z^{-1})}{1 + c_1 z^{-1} + c_2 z^{-2}},$$

where $c_1 = -2e^{-\frac{\sqrt{2}\pi}{T}} \cos\left(\frac{\sqrt{2}\pi}{T}\right)$, $c_2 = e^{-2\frac{\sqrt{2}\pi}{T}}$, and $c_0 = \frac{1}{2}(1 + c_1 + c_2)$. The parameter T represents the cutoff period.

Figure 10.21 illustrates the impulse response of a second-order SuperSmoother filter designed to eliminate cycles with periods shorter than $T = 20$. The impulse response closely resembles that of the Butterworth filter, displaying a damped sine wave.

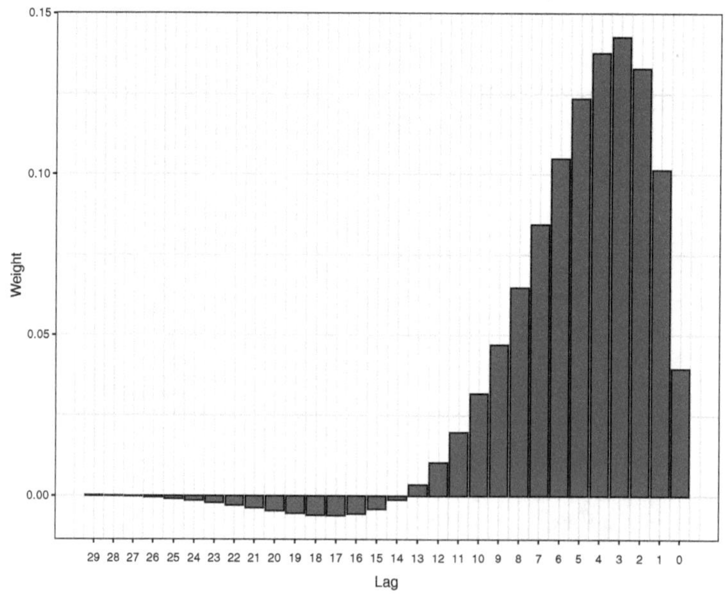

Fig. 10.21 Impulse response of a second-order SuperSmoother filter with a cutoff period of $T = 20$

The left panel of Fig. 10.22 shows the magnitude response of second-order SuperSmoother filters with cutoff periods of $T = 20$ and $T = 10$. The right panel of Fig. 10.22 presents the phase delay of these filters. Both the magnitude response and phase delay indicate that the SuperSmoother filter closely resembles the Butterworth filter, exhibiting similar characteristics in terms of smooth attenuation and phase behavior.

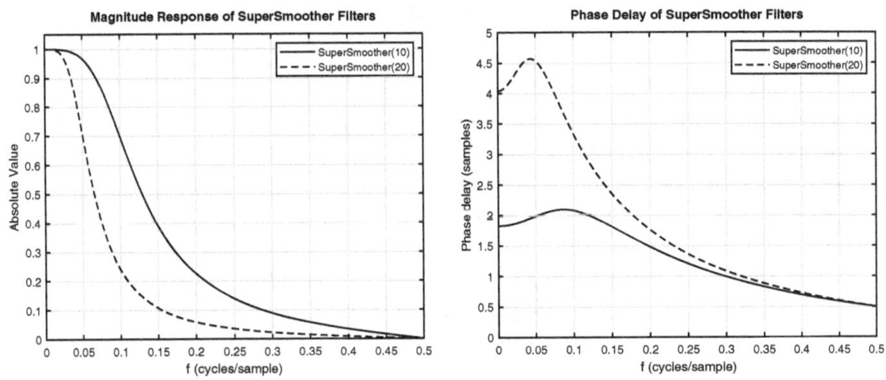

Fig. 10.22 Magnitude response (left) and phase delay (right) of second-order SuperSmoother filters with different cutoff periods $T = 10$ and $T = 20$

10.8.3 Regularized Filter

A Regularized filter was introduced by Chris Satchwell in (2003), designed to enhance the standard EMA. This Regularized filter incorporates a smoothing mechanism based on the least squares method, which allows it to more effectively reduce noise while retaining key trend information. The result is a moving average that offers improved smoothness and reduced lag time compared to the traditional EMA, making it more responsive to market changes.

The EMA is computed as:

$$y[n] = \alpha x[n] + (1 - \alpha) y[n - 1],$$

where $x[n]$ is the input price at time n, $y[n]$ is the output of the EMA, and $\alpha = 1 - \lambda$ is the smoothing factor.

To enhance the EMA and achieve a better tradeoff between smoothness and responsiveness, the Regularized filter minimizes the following objective function:

$$(y[n] - \alpha x[n] - (1 - \alpha) y[n - 1])^2 + \beta \left(y[n] - 2y[n - 1] + y[n - 2]\right)^2,$$

where

- The first term, $(y[n] - \alpha x[n] - (1-\alpha)y[n-1])^2$, enforces adherence to the standard EMA computation, ensuring the filter remains close to the input data.
- The second term, $\beta\,(y[n] - 2y[n-1] + y[n-2])^2$, penalizes large changes in the second derivative of $y[n]$, promoting smoothness in the output.
- β is the regularization parameter that controls the tradeoff between data fidelity and smoothness:
  - A higher β enforces greater smoothness, reducing sensitivity to noise.
  - A lower β prioritizes responsiveness, allowing the filter to adapt more quickly to changes in the input.

This formulation allows the Regularized filter to retain the simplicity of the EMA while introducing a more sophisticated balance between trend adherence and noise reduction. By optimizing the objective function, the Regularized filter provides smoother and more reliable trend estimates without significantly increasing lag.

The z-transfer function of a Regularized filter is given by:

$$H(z) = \frac{\frac{\alpha}{1+\beta}}{1 - \frac{1-\alpha+2\beta}{1+\beta}z^{-1} + \frac{\beta}{1+\beta}z^{-2}},$$

where $\alpha = 1 - \lambda$, and $0 < \lambda < 1$ is the smoothing constant in the EMA. The optimal selection of the parameter β in the Regularized filter is not explicitly defined and may depend on the specific application and data characteristics. However, Ehlers (2004) provides a practical guideline, recommending the value $\beta = e^{\frac{0.16}{\alpha}}$. For instance, when $\alpha = 0.33$, the corresponding value of β is approximately 1.624.

Figure 10.23 shows the impulse response of a Regularized filter with $\alpha = 0.2$ and the recommended value of β. The response closely resembles those of the Butterworth and SuperSmoother filters, featuring a damped sine wave pattern.

The left panel of Fig. 10.24 shows the magnitude response of Regularized filters with parameter sets $\{\alpha = 0.33, \beta = 1.624\}$ and $\{\alpha = 0.33, \beta = 5\}$. The right panel illustrates their phase delay. Increasing β beyond the recommended value enhances the smoothness of the filter's impulse response but also amplifies negative weights at distant return lags. This adjustment reduces the cutoff frequency and introduces significant irregularities in both the magni-

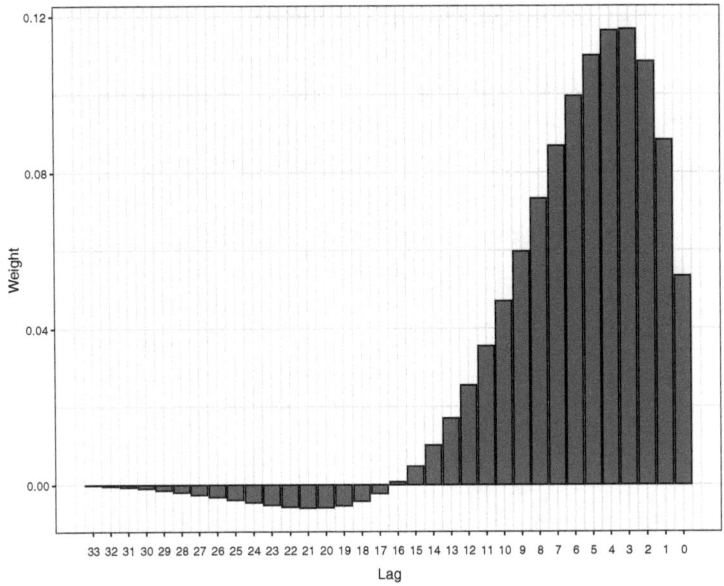

Fig. 10.23 Impulse response of a Regularized filter with $\alpha = 0.2$

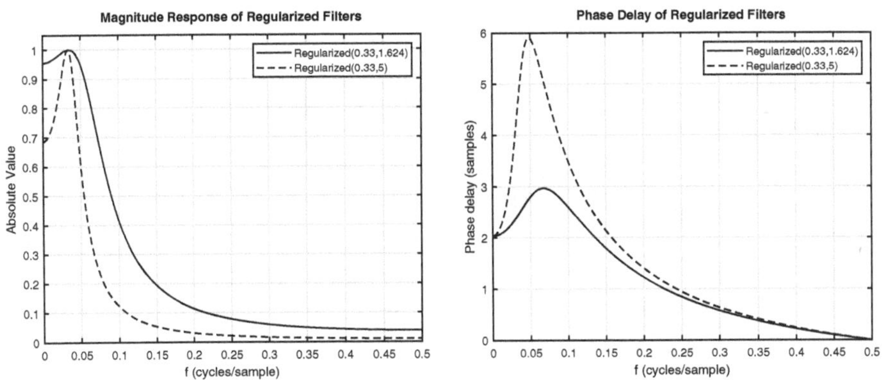

Fig. 10.24 Magnitude response (left) and phase delay (right) of second-order Regularized filters with $\{\alpha = 0.33, \beta = 1.624\}$ and $\{\alpha = 0.33, \beta = 5\}$

tude response and phase delay, resulting in highly uneven curves across signal frequencies. An interesting observation is that the value of β does not influence the filter's phase delay at zero frequency, indicating that the delay remains constant at the low-frequency limit regardless of β.

10.8.4 Instantaneous Trendline Filter

The Instantaneous Trendline filter was developed by John Ehlers in 2004. The procedure for constructing a filter of this type is as follows: let the transfer function of a moving average filter be denoted as $H(z)$. This filter functions as a low-pass filter. To derive the corresponding high-pass filter, the complement of the unity is taken, yielding $HP(z) = 1 - H(z)$.

Next, the high-pass filter is applied twice in succession, effectively increasing its attenuation of low frequencies. Since the repeated application of a high-pass filter still results in a high-pass effect, the transfer function of the Instantaneous Trendline filter is then obtained by complementing the unity once more:

$$IT(z) = 1 - HP^2(z).$$

The transfer function of the Instantaneous Trendline filter can also be expressed as follows:

$$\begin{aligned} IT(z) &= 1 - HP^2(z) = 1 - (1 - H(z))^2 \\ &= 2H(z) - H^2(z) = H(z)(2 - H(z)). \end{aligned}$$

This transfer function can be expressed in the time domain through the following operations:

$$IT_t = MA_t(2P - MA(P)) = MA_t(P + (P - MA(P))), \qquad (10.5)$$

where IT_t represents the Instantaneous Trendline filter at time t, P denotes the time series of prices, and $MA(P)$ is the moving average used as the basis for constructing the filter.

The method for constructing the Instantaneous Trendline filter, as proposed by John Ehlers and expressed in the time domain by Eq. (10.5), was well known long before his work. Specifically, Eq. (10.5) describes the "twicing" method introduced by John Tukey in (1977). This technique involves first computing a moving average of the price series, then adjusting the sequence by adding the difference between the original price and the first moving average. Finally, a second moving average is applied to this modified sequence. The "twicing" method was specifically designed to produce a zero-lag moving average from any given moving average.

It is important to note, however, that the "zero-lag" moving average created using the "twicing" method achieves zero delay time only according to the definition of the average lag time suggested by Robert Brown in (1963). This definition calculates the average "age" of the data used in the moving average. In the frequency domain, we have shown that zero lag is achieved only at zero signal frequency.

When the underlying moving average in the Instantaneous Trendline filter is the EMA, the Instantaneous Trendline filter simplifies to the Double EMA (DEMA), which was already introduced by Robert Brown in (1963) and subsequently popularized by Patrick Mulloy in his article published in 1994.

However, in the Instantaneous Trendline filter, John Ehlers used not the standard EMA but its modified version defined as:

$$y[n] = \frac{\alpha}{2}(x[n] + x[n-1]) + (1-\alpha)y[n-1].$$

This modified EMA achieves slightly better smoothness than the standard EMA because it incorporates two consecutive prices ($x[n]$ and $x[n-1]$) rather than relying solely on the current price ($x[n]$).

The z-transfer function of the Instantaneous Trendline filter is given by:

$$IT(z) = \frac{(\alpha - \frac{\alpha^2}{4}) - \frac{\alpha^2}{2}z^{-1} - (\alpha - \frac{3}{4}\alpha^2)z^{-2}}{1 - 2(1-\alpha)z^{-1} + (1-\alpha)^2 z^{-2}}. \tag{10.6}$$

Here, the only parameter is $\alpha = \frac{2}{n+1}$, where n represents the size of the averaging window in the modified EMA used to compute α.

Figure 10.25 illustrates the impulse response of the Instantaneous Trendline filter for $\alpha = 0.2$. The impulse response of this filter differs from those of the Butterworth, SuperSmoother, and Regularized filters. Since the Instantaneous Trendline filter is derived from a modified EMA, which closely resembles the conventional EMA, its impulse response is similar to that of the DEMA. The key distinction lies in the weight distribution: while the DEMA assigns the largest weight at lag zero, the Instantaneous Trendline filter places the maximum weight at lag one.

The left panel of Fig. 10.26 presents the magnitude response of the Instantaneous Trendline filters for $\alpha = 0.1$ and $\alpha = 0.05$, while the right panel shows their phase delay. The magnitude response curves confirm that the filter functions as a low-pass filter. At zero input frequency, the phase delay is zero. For low frequencies that pass through the filter, however, the phase delay becomes significantly large. As the input frequency increases, the phase delay gradually decreases. However, these high frequencies are strongly attenuated by this filter.

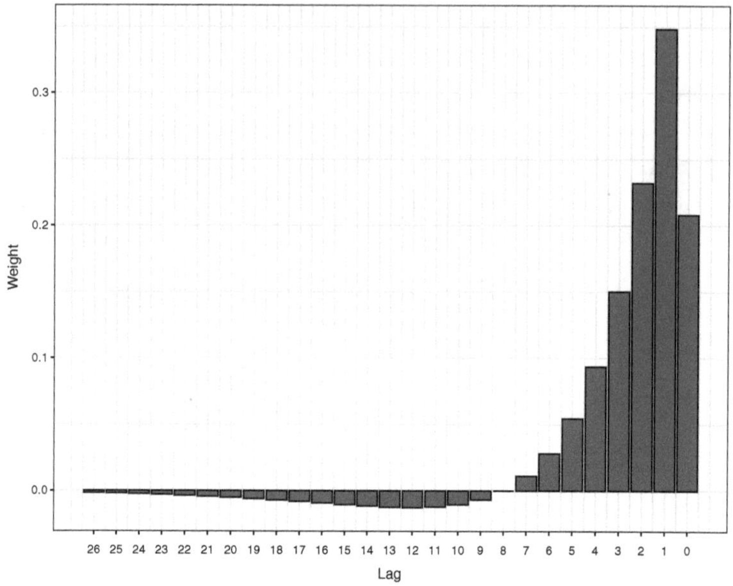

Fig. 10.25 Impulse response of the Instantaneous Trendline filter with $\alpha = 0.2$

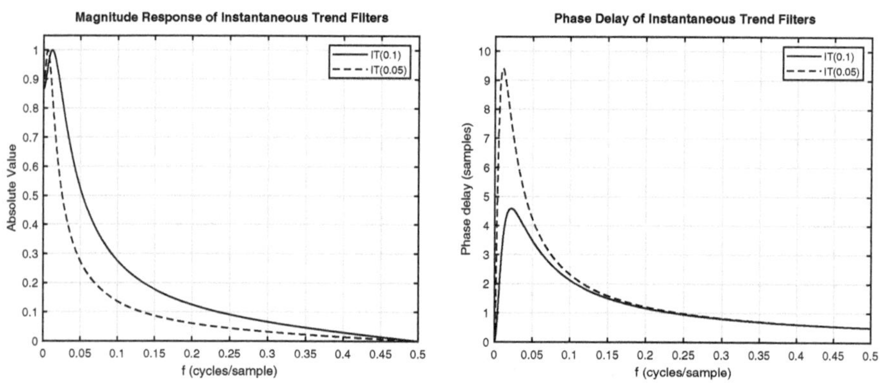

Fig. 10.26 Magnitude response (left) and phase delay (right) of Instantaneous Trendline filters with $\alpha = 0.1$ and $\alpha = 0.05$

10.8.5 Comparing DSP-Motivated Moving Averages

Many variants of moving averages for trend-following in financial markets have been inspired by techniques from DSP. In this chapter, we reviewed the most popular types. Each of these moving averages is often promoted as having unique features and being superior to both conventional moving averages and other exotic alternatives.

To someone unfamiliar with frequency-domain analysis or the mathematically advanced concept of Fourier transforms, these DSP-inspired methods might appear to involve complex, almost "rocket science" techniques for designing moving averages. However, our analysis of the price weighting functions of these popular DSP-inspired moving averages reveals that their structures are neither original nor unique. Instead, they closely resemble the "zero-lag" moving averages discussed in the previous chapter. For instance, the weighting functions of the Butterworth, SuperSmoother, and Regularized filters are remarkably similar to those of the Hull Moving Average (HMA) and the Tillson T3 moving average. Similarly, the weighting function of the Instantaneous Trendline filter is nearly identical to that of the DEMA.

The discussion above suggests that the properties of trading rules based on DSP-motivated moving averages should be similar to those based on "zero-lag" moving averages. However, it may be premature to draw definitive conclusions. The objective of this section is to conduct an unbiased comparison of trading rules based on DSP-inspired moving averages to evaluate whether they offer advantages over those based on conventional and "zero-lag" moving averages.

DSP-motivated moving averages derive their characteristics from the specific shape of their weighting functions. To preserve these original shapes, the most appropriate trading rule for DSP-inspired moving averages is the MA-D rule. In contrast, the P-MA and MA-C rules significantly distort the weighting functions of any moving average. Specifically, P-MA rules heavily overweight the most recent return lags, while MA-C rules produce hump-shaped weighting functions for returns, regardless of the moving average used.

As in the previous two chapters, we use three innovative quantitative measures to objectively evaluate the characteristics of trading rules. The first measure, the Noise Suppression Factor (NSF), evaluates how effectively a trading rule identifies the trend direction. The second measure, the Average Lag Time (ALT), quantifies the average delay between a trend turning point and the corresponding change in the trading signal. The third measure, the Smoothness Index (SMI), assesses the consistency and stability of the trading signal. These measures are derived solely from the return weights within a technical indicator. Consequently, the performance of a trading rule is entirely determined by the shape of its return weighting function.

Our analysis in the previous chapters demonstrates that it is not feasible to use all three quantitative measures simultaneously when comparing trading rules. Specifically, no trading rule can be deemed optimal across all three measures. Therefore, a two-measure comparison approach is recommended. We suggest focusing on comparisons using the ALT and SMI measures or the ALT and NSF measures, as this approach is both straightforward and logical.

The idea behind our comparison is as follows. Let us consider the ALT and SMI measures as an example. The main concept behind our comparison is to find a trading rule that effectively combines both responsiveness and smoothness. In other words, we are searching for the trading rule that provides the highest smoothness for a given level of responsiveness or the trading rule that offers the best responsiveness for a given level of smoothness.

In our comparison, alongside trading rules based on DSP-motivated moving averages, we include the HMA-D(n) trading rule and the SMA-C($n/4$, n) trading rule. The HMA, being one of the best "zero-lag" moving averages, closely resembles DSP-motivated moving averages, making it a natural benchmark for comparison. Additionally, the SMA-C rule, where the shorter moving average is one-fourth the size of the longer moving average, represents a standard trend-following approach. This allows us to assess whether trading rules based on DSP-motivated moving averages offer any advantages over this widely used trend-following strategy.

In all the trading rules considered, the weighting function is determined by a single parameter.[5] To ensure that the comparison of trading rules is not biased by parameter selection, we have adopted a standardized evaluation approach. Specifically, we vary the parameter value for each rule and compute the corresponding ALT and SMI metrics. Using these metrics, we plot a curve for each trading rule in the ALT-SMI space. These curves illustrate the tradeoff between responsiveness and smoothness for the examined rules. A trading rule is considered more efficient if its curve consistently lies above another rule's curve. A similar method is applied to compare the efficiencies of trading rules in the ALT-NSF space.

Figure 10.27 presents the performance of the selected trading rules in two panels. The top panel illustrates the combinations of ALT and SMI, while the bottom panel depicts the combinations of ALT and NSF for the same set of rules. Each trading rule is represented by a curve, highlighting the tradeoff between ALT and either SMI or NSF. The upward slope of all curves indicates that as ALT increases, both SMI and NSF also increase. Notably, the higher the curve corresponding to a trading rule, the more efficient that rule is considered.

An evaluation of the efficiency of the trading rules in the ALT-SMI space reveals that the HMA-D rule is the most efficient. This rule achieves the highest smoothness for a given lag time or the shortest lag time for a given smoothness. The second most efficient rule is based on the Regularized moving average. In contrast, the least efficient rule is based on the Instantaneous Trendline

---

[5] The Regularized moving average has two parameters, α and β, but we follow the recommended choice of $\beta = e^{\frac{0.16}{\alpha}}$.

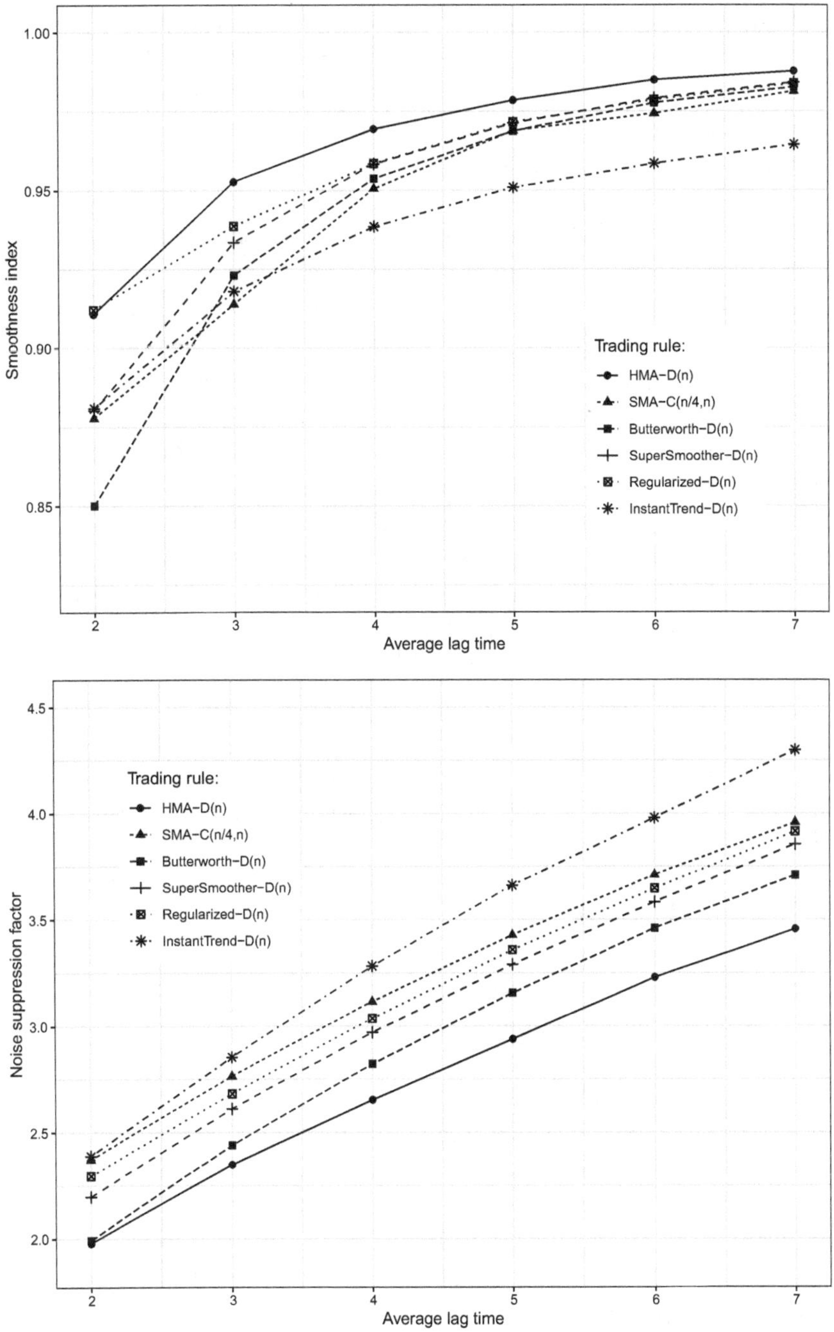

Fig. 10.27 Comparison of the effectiveness of trading rules based on DSP-inspired moving averages, the HMA-D rule, and the SMA-C rule. The top panel plots the set of combinations of the ALT and SMI for the selected set of rules. The bottom panel plots the set of combinations of the ALT and NSF for the same rules

moving average, which is unsurprising given that its weighting function is the least smooth. The SMA-C rule ranks as the second least efficient. However, as ALT increases, all trading rules, except the one based on the Instantaneous Trendline moving average, demonstrate a relatively similar tradeoff between responsiveness and smoothness.

In the ALT-NSF space, the ranking of the trading rules is entirely reversed compared to the ALT-SMI space. Specifically, the best-performing rule is based on the Instantaneous Trendline moving average, while the worst-performing rule is based on the HMA. Consequently, the HMA-D rule, which offers the best tradeoff between responsiveness and smoothness, exhibits the poorest tradeoff between responsiveness and accuracy. Notably, the SMA-C rule ranks as the second-best rule in the ALT-NSF space.

In summary, DSP-motivated moving averages do not outperform the HMA moving average in terms of the tradeoff between responsiveness and smoothness. Compared to the SMA-C rule, the trading rules based on DSP-motivated moving averages show some improvement, but only when a very short lag time is required. As the lag time increases, the advantage of DSP-motivated rules diminishes. Furthermore, the SMA-C rule outperforms most of the DSP-motivated rules in terms of the tradeoff between responsiveness and accuracy. Therefore, we conclude that trading rules based on DSP-motivated moving averages are not superior to conventional trading rules. Traders must exercise caution when deciding whether DSP-motivated moving averages are more suitable than conventional moving averages for specific applications.

10.9 Conclusions

In their quest to develop the "ideal" moving average for trend-following, traders and analysts have proposed numerous variants of so-called exotic moving averages. However, the majority of these exotic moving averages are ad hoc in nature, and their design has not been grounded in a rigorous theoretical framework. This lack of theoretical underpinning often limits their effectiveness and consistency in various market conditions. In stark contrast, many of the more refined variants of exotic moving averages are inspired by DSP techniques. These DSP-based approaches are built on a solid theoretical foundation, offering a structured and systematic method for designing filters that are optimized for processing input signals.

In DSP, filters are typically analyzed in the frequency domain, as opposed to the traditional time-domain analysis commonly applied to moving averages. This frequency-domain perspective introduces two significant challenges in designing trend-following rules and comparing the characteristics of DSP-inspired moving averages with conventional and exotic moving averages.

First and foremost, DSP offers a robust framework for capturing periodic phenomena in financial markets. While some theories suggest that stock prices exhibit consistent cyclical behavior with fixed frequencies, the majority of academics strongly disagree with this idea, as financial markets are influenced by a wide range of unpredictable factors. This disagreement complicates the application of DSP techniques, which are designed for periodic signals, to financial data, where trends often do not follow consistent cycles.

Secondly, when analyzing moving averages using DSP techniques, the focus is placed on the magnitude response of the filter and its phase shift. The magnitude response indicates how the filter attenuates or passes through input frequencies, while the phase shift illustrates how the timing of input frequencies is altered. Most moving averages function as low-pass filters, but determining which frequency response shape is "better" for accuracy and smoothness remains unclear. Furthermore, although phase shift is often reported, it offers limited utility for decision-making in trading strategies. A more practical approach is to convert the phase shift into phase delay time, as this directly correlates with the responsiveness of the filter and is more relevant for assessing how quickly a moving average reacts to changes in the market.

Although stock market dynamics may not be inherently cyclical, DSP analysis can still provide valuable insights into the properties of moving averages and the trend-following rules derived from them. For instance, some trading rules exhibit smooth and monotonic magnitude responses, while others do not. Traders who prioritize these characteristics can select rules with smooth and monotonic magnitude responses if they believe it is beneficial. Additionally, frequency-domain analysis reveals that filter delay time is typically not constant; it varies depending on the frequency of the input signal.

While every moving average acts as a low-pass filter, attenuating the high frequencies in the input signal that are typically associated with noise, DSP analysis suggests that trend-following rules based on moving averages function as either high-pass or band-pass filters. This creates an apparent paradox: how can a trading rule, designed to capture the low frequencies associated with trends, simultaneously act as a high-pass filter that suppresses those low frequencies while allowing noise to pass through? Typically, this paradox is not addressed directly in DSP analysis.

We may be the first to address this apparent paradox. In our interpretation, a trading rule that behaves like a high-pass filter does so unintentionally. The signal generated by the rule remains predominantly low frequency. However, when this signal passes through a high-pass filter, it is attenuated, whereas noise, which is inherently high frequency, remains largely unaffected. As a result, the low-frequency signal can become significantly contaminated by high-frequency noise.

This highlights an inherent issue with trend-following rules—one that is not readily apparent when the rules are analyzed in the time domain. To mitigate the impact of high-frequency noise, it is preferable to use a trading rule that functions as a band-pass filter. Such a rule attenuates both the low-frequency components associated with the signal and the high-frequency components linked to noise.

In this chapter, we analyzed several popular variants of DSP-inspired moving averages and assessed their potential to enhance the characteristics of trend-following rules. Our analysis shows that the price weights used in these DSP-inspired moving averages are very similar to those found in many "zero-lag" moving averages. As a result, DSP-motivated moving averages are neither original nor unique. These moving averages offer a poorer balance between responsiveness and smoothness compared to the best "zero-lag" moving averages, but a better tradeoff between responsiveness and accuracy. Moreover, while DSP-inspired moving averages outperform the traditional double moving average crossover rule in terms of responsiveness and smoothness, they perform worse in terms of the tradeoff between responsiveness and accuracy. Therefore, we conclude that DSP-inspired moving averages do not offer a clear advantage over either other exotic moving averages or conventional moving averages.

Appendix 10.A Proof of Proposition 10.1

Consider an n-order FIR filter with impulse response coefficients $\{h_0, h_1, h_2, \dots, h_{n-1}\}$, where these coefficients correspond to the price weights in a moving average. Without loss of generality, we can extend this to include IIR filters by letting $n \to \infty$. The transfer function of this filter is given by:

$$H(z) = \sum_{k=0}^{n-1} h_k z^{-k}.$$

The frequency response is obtained by substituting $z^{-1} = e^{-jw}$, where w is the angular frequency. This gives the complex frequency response:

$$H(w) = \sum_{k=0}^{n-1} h_k e^{-jkw}.$$

Using Euler's formula, $e^{-jkw} = \cos(kw) - j\sin(kw)$, we can rewrite $H(w)$ as:

$$H(w) = \sum_{k=0}^{n-1} h_k e^{-jkw} = \sum_{k=0}^{n-1} h_k \cos(kw) - j \sum_{k=0}^{n-1} h_k \sin(kw).$$

We can now express $H(w)$ in polar form as:

$$H(w) = |H(w)| e^{j\theta(w)},$$

where $\theta(w)$ is the phase function. From trigonometry, the phase angle is given by:

$$\theta(w) = \arctan\left(\frac{\operatorname{Im}(H(w))}{\operatorname{Re}(H(w))}\right) = \arctan\left(\frac{-\sum_{k=0}^{n-1} h_k \sin(kw)}{\sum_{k=0}^{n-1} h_k \cos(kw)}\right).$$

At zero frequency, $w = 0$, the sine terms in the numerator vanish, so we have:

$$\theta(0) = \arctan\left(\frac{\operatorname{Im}(H(0))}{\operatorname{Re}(H(0))}\right) = \arctan\left(\frac{0}{\sum_{k=0}^{n-1} h_k}\right) = 0.$$

The phase delay is defined as:

$$\tau_{\text{phase}}(w) = -\frac{\theta(w)}{w}.$$

Using the expression for $\theta(w)$, we obtain:

$$\tau_{\text{phase}}(w) = -\frac{1}{w} \arctan\left(\frac{-\sum_{k=0}^{n-1} h_k \sin(kw)}{\sum_{k=0}^{n-1} h_k \cos(kw)}\right).$$

At $w = 0$, $\tau_{\text{phase}}(w)$ is undefined due to division by zero. However, we can define $\tau_{\text{phase}}(0)$ as the limit of $\tau_{\text{phase}}(w)$ as w approaches zero:

$$\tau_{\text{phase}}(0) = \lim_{w \to 0} -\frac{\theta(w)}{w}.$$

This represents an indeterminate form $\frac{0}{0}$, so we apply L'Hôpital's rule to evaluate the limit by differentiating the numerator and denominator.

The derivative of $-\theta(w)$ is given by:

$$-\theta'(w) = \frac{1}{1+\left(\frac{\operatorname{Im}(H(w))}{\operatorname{Re}(H(w))}\right)^2} \cdot \frac{\sum_{k=0}^{n-1} h_k k \cos(kw) \sum_{k=0}^{n-1} h_k \cos(kw)}{\left(\sum_{k=0}^{n-1} h_k \cos(kw)\right)^2}$$
$$+ \frac{1}{1+\left(\frac{\operatorname{Im}(H(w))}{\operatorname{Re}(H(w))}\right)^2} \cdot \frac{\sum_{k=0}^{n-1} h_k k \sin(kw) \sum_{k=0}^{n-1} h_k \sin(kw)}{\left(\sum_{k=0}^{n-1} h_k \cos(kw)\right)^2}.$$

By setting $w = 0$ into the expression for the derivative, we get:

$$\tau_{\text{phase}}(0) = -\theta'(w)\big|_{w=0} = \frac{\sum_{k=0}^{n-1} h_k k}{\sum_{k=0}^{n-1} h_k}.$$

This is the desired result, confirming that the phase delay at zero frequency, $\tau_{\text{phase}}(0)$, corresponds to the average lag time of the moving average, ALT(MA), and can be written as:

$$\tau_{\text{phase}}(0) = \frac{h_0 \cdot 0 + h_1 \cdot 1 + h_2 \cdot 2 + \cdots + h_{n-1} \cdot (n-1)}{\sum_{k=0}^{n-1} h_k}.$$

Thus, we have proven that $\tau_{\text{phase}}(w)$ approaches ALT(MA) as w approaches zero.

References

Brown, R. G. (1963). *Smoothing, Forecasting and Prediction of Discrete Time Series.* Prentice-Hall.

Ehlers, J. F. (2004). *Cybernetic Analysis for Stocks and Futures: Cutting-Edge DSP Technology to Improve Your Trading.* Wiley.

Ehlers, J. F. (2013). *Cycle Analytics for Traders. Advanced Technical Trading Concepts.* Wiley.

Hurst, J. M. (1970). *Profit Magic of Stock Transaction Timing.* Prentice-Hall.

Mulloy, P. G. (1994). Smoothing Data With Faster Moving Averages. *Technical Analysis of Stocks and Commodities, 12*(1), 11–19.

Oppenheim, A. V., & Schafer R. W. (2010). *Discrete-Time Signal Processing* (3rd Edn.). Pearson.

Satchwell, C. (2003). Regularization. *Technical Analysis of Stocks and Commodities, 21*(7), 38–41.

Tukey, J. (1977). *Exploratory Data Analysis.* Pearson.

Part IV

Advanced Topics

11

Optimal Trend-Following Under a General Persistent Return Process

11.1 Introduction

In the earlier parts of this book, we introduced a framework for analyzing the characteristics of technical indicators used in trend-following strategies. This framework enables us to measure the accuracy, responsiveness, and smoothness of any technical indicator. These measurements help us compare different technical indicators and identify those that balance accuracy, responsiveness, and smoothness effectively.

Unfortunately, our analysis reveals that no single technical indicator excels in all quantitative measures simultaneously. Some indicators offer a good balance between accuracy and responsiveness, while others show a better balance between smoothness and responsiveness. As a result, our measures do not identify a single superior technical indicator across all metrics.

Each technical indicator is calculated as a moving average of returns over a window of n observations. It is rather obvious that there is an optimal value of n that maximizes the performance of a trend-following strategy. However, our framework is not able to determine this optimal n. The optimal value depends on the return dynamics of a specific financial market, including the persistence of the return process and the average trend duration.

This discussion highlights that it is impossible to determine the best technical indicator for following market trends without knowing the parameters of the return process. Therefore, in this chapter, we assume complete knowledge of the return process model. Armed with this knowledge, we aim to identify the optimal technical indicator for trend-following.

This chapter is divided into two main sections. The first section presents a general model of a persistent return process. In the second section, we deter-

V. Zakamulin and J. Giner, *The Ultimate Moving Average Handbook*,
https://doi.org/10.1007/978-3-031-90907-8_11

mine the optimal technical indicator for following trends based on this return process. Since transaction costs significantly impact the performance of trend-following strategies, we also take these costs into account.

When modeling the return process, it is crucial to ensure its persistence. Persistence refers to the tendency of returns to follow a consistent pattern over time. Specifically, if the return in the last period was positive, the next period's return is likely to be positive as well, and similarly, if the last period's return was negative, the next period's return is likely to be negative. This characteristic of persistence leads to the formation of price trends, manifesting as either upward or downward movements in asset prices.

In practical terms, this means that positive returns tend to cluster together, creating upward trends, while negative returns cluster together, resulting in downward trends. Understanding and modeling this persistence is essential for accurately predicting future returns and making informed investment decisions. This behavior can be observed in various financial instruments and markets, reflecting the underlying economic conditions and investor sentiment.

There are two primary models used to represent a return process with persistence: the AutoRegressive Moving Average (ARMA) process and the Markov chain model. The ARMA model combines two components: autoregression (AR) and moving average (MA). The autoregressive component specifies that the current value of the series is partially based on its previous values, capturing the persistence in returns. The moving average component accounts for the dependency between an observation and a residual error from a moving average model applied to lagged observations. By combining these two components, the ARMA model effectively captures both the past values and the residual errors, providing a robust framework for modeling persistent return processes.

In the Markov chain model, the return process is characterized by random shifts between multiple regimes or states. Each regime represents a different set of return characteristics, such as different levels of volatility or different mean returns. The transitions between these regimes are governed by a Markov process, meaning that the probability of moving to a particular state depends only on the current state and not on the sequence of events that preceded it.

At first glance, an ARMA model and a Markov chain model may appear very different. However, there is a one-to-one correspondence between the return processes in these models. A careful analysis reveals that the return process in a Markov chain model is indistinguishable from the return process in a specific ARMA model. This equivalence arises because both models can capture the persistent nature of returns, albeit through different mechanisms.

Additionally, each ARMA model can be transformed into an AR model with an infinite number of lags. However, the influence of these lags diminishes as they become more distant, so including an infinite number of lags is not problematic for our analysis. We can safely disregard the influence of the distant lags and assume that the number of lags is finite. Consequently, our primary focus for analysis is an AR process with p return lags. In this process, the current return is a linear function of a constant and past returns. This process is fully specified by a constant and p autoregressive coefficients.

In the second section of this chapter, we determine the optimal technical indicator for following trends when the return process is modeled by a persistent AR process. The optimal technical indicator is defined as the one that maximizes the performance of a trend-following strategy. To achieve this, we build a theoretical model where we derive the expression for the strategy's performance, explicitly incorporating transaction costs. By considering these costs, we ensure that our model reflects real-world trading conditions more accurately. We then identify the return weights within the technical indicator that maximize the performance of the trend-following strategy.

Based on our theoretical analysis, we arrive to the following conclusions. First, we find that the optimal number of return lags in a technical indicator is equal to the number of autoregressive coefficients in the AR process for returns ($n = p$). Second, without any transaction costs, the optimal return weights closely resemble the pattern of the autoregressive coefficients in the return process, with the weights reflecting a positive linear scaling transformation of these coefficients. Third, when transaction costs are present, the optimal return-weighting function becomes a smoothed version of the autoregressive coefficients. Finally, the degree of smoothing applied to the coefficients is influenced by the level of transaction costs, with higher transaction costs resulting in higher degrees of smoothing.

11.2 Return Process

11.2.1 Stationarity Assumption

Stationarity is a fundamental concept in time series analysis, and it refers to the feature of a statistical process whose properties do not depend on the time at which it is observed. In other words, when a time series is said to be stationary, it means that its statistical characteristics are stable over time.

There are several important reasons why stationarity is crucial in time series analysis. First, stationarity allows us to estimate the parameters of the time series process accurately. If a time series is non-stationary, the estimated parameters will depend on the chosen time period for estimation. This makes the results highly sensitive and unreliable. By ensuring stationarity, we can obtain consistent and meaningful parameter estimates.

Second, stationarity is essential for accurate forecasting of future values in a time series. If the statistical properties of a series are changing over time, it becomes challenging to make accurate predictions. Stationary time series exhibit stable patterns and behaviors over time, making it easier to understand and forecast future values.

Furthermore, stationarity simplifies the analysis and interpretation of time series data. Stationary series have constant statistical properties, such as mean and variance, which facilitate the application of various analytical techniques. Non-stationary series, on the other hand, can have complex patterns and trends that make it difficult to interpret the data and draw meaningful conclusions.

In summary, stationarity is critical in time series analysis because it allows for accurate parameter estimation, reliable forecasting, and simpler data analysis and interpretation. By ensuring stationarity, we can obtain more robust and meaningful insights from time series data.

The time series stationarity exists in two forms: strong and weak. The strong form of stationarity, also known as strict sense stationarity or strong stationarity, requires a time series to have an identical probability distribution for any finite time interval. This means that the statistical properties of the time series should not change over time, and the probability distribution of the series should be the same at any point in time.

Denote the return observation at time t by r_t. The strong form of stationarity of returns requires that the probabilistic behavior of the collection of return observations

$$\{r_t, r_{t+1}, \ldots, r_{t+k}\}$$

be identical to the time-shifted collection

$$\{r_{t+s}, r_{t+1+s}, \ldots, r_{t+k+s}\}$$

for all $k \in 1, 2, \ldots$ and all $s \in \pm 1, \pm 2, \ldots$. In other words, if a time series is strictly stationary, the joint distribution of any set of observations in the series is invariant under shifts in time.

The weak form of stationarity, also known as weak stationarity or second-order stationarity, refers to the condition where only the first two moments of a time series are time invariant. In other words, a time series is weakly stationary if:

1. The mean of the time series remains constant over time.
2. The autocovariance, or the covariance between any two observations at different time points, only depends on the time lag between them and not on the specific time points.

Mathematically, for a weakly stationary time series, this can be expressed as follows. Denote by $\mu_t = E[r_t]$ the mean value of the returns at time t. The weak form of stationarity requires that:

$$\mu_t = \mu,$$

where μ is a constant.

Denote the autocovariance function by $Cov(r_t, r_{t+k})$, which is the covariance between the returns at times t and $t + k$. The weak form of stationarity requires that for any time shift s:

$$Cov(r_t, r_{t+k}) = Cov(r_{t+s}, r_{t+k+s}),$$

for all $k \in 1, 2, \ldots$ and all $s \in \pm 1, \pm 2, \ldots$.

Note that by definition:

$$Cov(r_t, r_t) = Var(r_t) = \sigma^2,$$

where $Var(r_t)$ denotes the variance of r_t and σ denotes the standard deviation of r_t. Therefore, if the returns are weakly stationary, the variance of returns remains constant over time.

It is worth noting that in finance, returns, not prices, are the primary time series for modeling. If the return observations are denoted by $r_1, r_2, \ldots, r_t$, then the price observations at times 1 and t can be expressed as:

$$P_1 = P_0(1 + r_1), \quad P_t = P_0 \prod_{i=1}^{t} (1 + r_i),$$

where P_0 is the price at time 0. These expressions motivate that the probability distribution of P_t is very different from that of P_1. Specifically, while the probability distribution of P_1 depends only on the return r_1, the probability distribution of P_t depends on the product of all returns from r_1 to r_t. Therefore, the price series is not stationary. For example, as time goes on, the mean price and its variance tend to increase.

11.2.2 Autoregressive Process

The autoregressive (AR) process is a type of time series model that describes the relationship between an observation and a linear combination of the past p observations. It is denoted as $AR(p)$, where p represents the order of the autoregressive model.

Specifically, if the returns follow an $AR(p)$ process, the time t return observation is modeled as a linear combination of p previous observations, plus a random noise term. Mathematically, it can be represented as:

$$r_t = \eta + \phi_1 r_{t-1} + \phi_2 r_{t-2} + \ldots + \phi_p r_{t-p} + \varepsilon_t = \eta + \sum_{i=1}^{p} \phi_i r_{t-i} + \varepsilon_t, \tag{11.1}$$

where p is the number of autoregressive terms, η is a constant term, $\{\phi_1, \phi_2, \ldots, \phi_p\}$ are the autoregressive coefficients, r_{t-i} is the return observed at time $t-i$, and ε_t is the noise term which is i.i.d. random process with zero mean and variance of σ_ε^2. That is, $\varepsilon_t \sim iid(0, \sigma_\varepsilon^2)$.

The autoregressive coefficients represent the strength and direction of the relationship between the current observation and the past observations. The random noise term represents the error or residual component in the model.

The mean and variance of r_t are calculated using the formulas below (see Box et al., 2016, Chapter 3):

$$\mu = E[r_t] = \frac{\eta}{1 - \sum_{i=1}^{p} \phi_i}, \qquad \sigma^2 = Var(r_t) = \frac{\sigma_\varepsilon^2}{1 - \sum_{i=1}^{p} \phi_i \rho_i}, \tag{11.2}$$

where $\rho_i = Cor(r_t, r_{t-i})$ represents the autocorrelation between r_t and r_{t-i}.

The required autocorrelations ρ_i can be determined from the autoregressive coefficients ϕ_i by solving the Yule-Walker equations. To do this, we multiply Eq. (11.1) by r_{t-k}, take the expectation, and divide the result by the variance of r_t. This gives us the recursive relationship for the autocorrelation coefficients of the $AR(p)$ process:

$$\rho_k = \phi_1 \rho_{k-1} + \phi_2 \rho_{k-2} + \ldots + \phi_p \rho_{k-p}. \tag{11.3}$$

Setting $k = 1, 2, \ldots, p$ in Eq. (11.3) and using $\rho_0 = 1$ and $\rho_{-i} = \rho_i$, we derive the Yule-Walker equations:

$$\mathbf{R}\boldsymbol{\phi} = \boldsymbol{\rho}, \tag{11.4}$$

where $\boldsymbol{\phi}' = [\phi_1, \phi_2, \ldots, \phi_p]$ is the $p \times 1$ vector[1] that contains the autoregressive coefficients, $\boldsymbol{\rho}' = [\rho_1, \rho_2, \ldots, \rho_p]$ is the $p \times 1$ vector of the autocorrelation coefficients, and $\mathbf{R}$ is the $p \times p$ matrix given by:

$$\boldsymbol{R} = \begin{bmatrix} 1 & \rho_1 & \rho_2 & \cdots & \rho_{p-1} \\ \rho_1 & 1 & \rho_1 & \cdots & \rho_{p-2} \\ \rho_2 & \rho_1 & 1 & \cdots & \rho_{p-3} \\ \vdots & \vdots & \vdots & \ddots & \vdots \\ \rho_{p-1} & \rho_{p-2} & \rho_{p-3} & \cdots & 1 \end{bmatrix}. \tag{11.5}$$

The matrix $\mathbf{R}$ is a Toeplitz matrix, meaning that each descending diagonal from left to right is constant. The Yule-Walker equations can be solved using methods for linear equations, such as the Levinson-Durbin recursion, which is computationally efficient for Toeplitz matrices. Given numerical values for $\{\phi_1, \phi_2, \ldots, \phi_p\}$, the Yule-Walker equations yield numerical values for $\{\rho_1, \rho_2, \ldots, \rho_p\}$. Equation (11.3) can then be recursively used to obtain numerical values for ρ_k for any $k > p$.

On the other hand, if we know the $p \times 1$ vector $\boldsymbol{\rho}' = [\rho_1, \rho_2, \ldots, \rho_p]$ of the autocorrelation coefficients, we can use the Yule-Walker equations to calculate the autoregressive coefficients of the return process. The solution is given by:

$$\boldsymbol{\phi} = \boldsymbol{R}^{-1}\boldsymbol{\rho}, \tag{11.6}$$

where $\boldsymbol{R}^{-1}$ is the inverse of matrix $\mathbf{R}$.

The AR(0) process is, in fact, the process where the returns are independent and identically distributed:

$$r_t = \eta + \varepsilon_t. \tag{11.7}$$

Here, the independence of returns means that all autocorrelations are zero, $\rho_k = 0$ for any $k \neq 0$. When returns are independent, past returns do not influence future returns, meaning that past returns cannot be used to predict future returns.

The simplest example of an autoregressive process is the AR(1) process:

$$r_t = \eta + \phi_1 r_{t-1} + \varepsilon_t. \tag{11.8}$$

[1] In linear algebra, a vector has an orientation: it is either a row vector or a column vector. By default, a vector is considered a column vector. The notation $\mathbf{x}'$ represents the transpose of vector $\mathbf{x}$. If $\mathbf{x}$ is a row vector, then $\mathbf{x}'$ transforms it into a column vector and vice versa.

In the AR(1) model, the return process exhibits time series dependence. When return observations are dependent, past returns can be used to predict future returns. In this model, the value of r_t is determined by η plus ϕ_1 times the value of r_{t-1} plus some random noise. This simple model is often used to represent time series data with short memory, meaning that the influence of past values diminishes quickly.

The autocorrelation function of the AR(1) process at lag k is given by:

$$\rho_k = \phi_1^k. \tag{11.9}$$

This shows that the correlation between r_t and r_{t-k} decreases exponentially with k.

The AR(2) process, or second-order autoregressive process, is expressed as:

$$r_t = \eta + \phi_1 r_{t-1} + \phi_2 r_{t-2} + \varepsilon_t. \tag{11.10}$$

The AR(2) model captures the idea that the current value of the series is a linear function of its two most recent values plus some random noise. This allows the model to represent more complex time series data. The autocorrelation function of the AR(2) process depends on ϕ_1 and ϕ_2 and exhibits more complex behavior than in the AR(1) process, potentially involving oscillations or exponential decay. Therefore, besides the time series data with short memory, the AR(2) model is able to produce series with cyclic or oscillatory behavior.

If the return process is persistent, the prices exhibit short-term momentum or trends. This means that positive returns are likely to be followed by positive returns, and negative returns are likely to be followed by negative returns. Such behavior is typically characterized by positive autocorrelation in the returns. In financial markets, this can lead to the identification of momentum trading strategies, where traders buy assets that have performed well in the past and sell assets that have performed poorly.

Since our goal is to model price trends using the $AR(p)$ process, we often need to select numerical values for $\{\phi_1, \phi_2, \ldots, \phi_p\}$ that ensure positive autocorrelation coefficients for the $AR(p)$ process. This guarantees the presence of short-term momentum in prices. The simplest approach is to use only positive autoregressive coefficients. Specifically, Zakamulin and Giner (2020) prove that if all coefficients $\{\phi_1, \phi_2, \ldots, \phi_p\}$ of the $AR(p)$ process are positive, then all autocorrelation coefficients ρ_k will also be positive.

Every $AR(p)$ process is mean-reverting, meaning that over time, the value of the process returns to its long-run mean. Specifically, even if the $AR(p)$ process is persistent, if its value is above the mean, it will likely decrease toward it. Conversely, if it is below the mean, it will likely increase toward it.

The speed at which the process reverts to the mean is inversely proportional to the sum of the autoregressive coefficients, $\kappa = \sum_{i=1}^{p} \phi_i$. A smaller value of κ indicates faster mean reversion. Thus, κ serves as a measure of the persistence of the $AR(p)$ process. This measure was proposed by Andrews and Chen (1994) and later by Marques (2005).

If all the coefficients $\{\phi_1, \phi_2, \dots, \phi_p\}$ of the $AR(p)$ process are non-negative, increasing the value of any ϕ_i or the order p increases the persistence of the process. Therefore, the choices for p and ϕ_i affect the persistence and duration of the price trend. Generally, increasing the number of autoregressive terms or the values of the coefficients results in a stronger and longer-lasting price trend.

11.2.3 Moving Average Process

The $MA(q)$ process, or moving average process of order q, is a time series model where the current value of the series, r_t, is expressed as a linear combination of past white noise error terms. Unlike the AR process, the MA process does not depend on past values of the series itself but on past errors. The $MA(q)$ model is defined as:

$$r_t = \eta + \varepsilon_t - \vartheta_1 \varepsilon_{t-1} - \dots - \vartheta_q \varepsilon_{t-q} = \eta + \varepsilon_t - \sum_{i=1}^{q} \vartheta_i \varepsilon_{t-i}, \quad (11.11)$$

where q is the number of moving average terms, η is a constant term, $\{\vartheta_1, \vartheta_2, \dots, \vartheta_q\}$ are the moving average coefficients, and ε_{t-i} is the noise term at time $t-i$, $i \in [0, 1, \dots, q]$.

The mean and variance of r_t are given by:

$$\mu = E[r_t] = \eta, \qquad \sigma^2 = Var(r_t) = (1 + \vartheta_1^2 + \dots + \vartheta_q^2)\sigma_\varepsilon^2. \quad (11.12)$$

The autocorrelation function of r_t at lag k is calculated using the formula below (see Box et al., 2016), Chapter 3):

$$\rho_k = \begin{cases} \frac{\vartheta_1 + \vartheta_1 \vartheta_{k+1} + \dots + \vartheta_{q-k} \vartheta_q}{1 + \vartheta_1^2 + \dots + \vartheta_q^2} & k = 1, 2, \dots, q, \\ 0 & k > q. \end{cases} \quad (11.13)$$

The $MA(q)$ model captures the idea that the current value of the series is influenced by a finite number of past shocks (error terms). This makes it useful for modeling time series data where past shocks have a short-term effect on the current value.

As an example, the MA(2) process can be written as:

$$r_t = \eta + \varepsilon_t - \vartheta_1 \varepsilon_{t-1} - \vartheta_2 \varepsilon_{t-2}. \tag{11.14}$$

In this example, the current value r_t depends on the current white noise term ε_t and the two most recent past white noise terms ε_{t-1} and ε_{t-2}, weighted by the coefficients ϑ_1 and ϑ_2, respectively. This model is useful for capturing short-term dependencies in the data.

11.2.4 Autoregressive Moving Average Process

The $ARMA(p, q)$ process, or autoregressive moving average process of order p and q, is a time series model that combines both autoregressive (AR) and moving average (MA) components. Specifically, p denotes the number of autoregressive terms, while q signifies the number of moving average terms. This model is widely used in time series analysis to describe and predict future values based on past values and past errors.

The $ARMA(p, q)$ process is defined by the following equation:

$$r_t = \eta + \sum_{i=1}^{p} \phi_i r_{t-i} + \varepsilon_t - \sum_{i=1}^{q} \vartheta_i \varepsilon_{t-i}. \tag{11.15}$$

When $q = 0$, the $ARMA(p, q)$ process simplifies to the $AR(p)$ process, while when $p = 0$, the $ARMA(p, q)$ process simplifies to the $MA(q)$ process. When both $p = 0$ and $q = 0$, the $ARMA(p, q)$ process reduces to a purely white noise process, indicating independent returns with no autocorrelation.

Consider an ARMA(1,1) process where $p = 1$ and $q = 1$. The model can be written as:

$$r_t = \eta + \phi_1 r_{t-1} + \varepsilon_t - \vartheta_1 \varepsilon_{t-1}. \tag{11.16}$$

In this example, the current value of r_t depends on the mean η, the previous value r_{t-1} weighted by the coefficient ϕ_1, the current white noise term ε_t, and the previous white noise term ε_{t-1} weighted by the coefficient ϑ_1. This ARMA(1,1) model can capture both the persistence in the time series due to r_{t-1} and the short-term shocks due to ε_{t-1}.

The mean and variance of the ARMA(1,1) process are given by Box et al. (2016), Chapter 3:

$$\mu = E[r_t] = \frac{\eta}{1-\phi_1}, \qquad \sigma^2 = Var(r_t) = \frac{1-2\phi_1\vartheta_1+\vartheta_1^2}{1-\phi_1^2}\sigma_\varepsilon^2. \tag{11.17}$$

The lag-1 autocorrelation of the ARMA(1,1) process is also provided by Box et al. (2016), Chapter 3:

$$\rho_1 = \frac{(\phi_1-\vartheta_1)(1-\phi_1\vartheta_1)}{1-2\phi_1\vartheta_1+\vartheta_1^2}. \tag{11.18}$$

Then for any lag $k > 1$, the autocorrelation ρ_k is given by:

$$\rho_k = \rho_1\phi_1^{k-1}. \tag{11.19}$$

A stationary $ARMA(p,q)$ process can be expressed either as an $AR(\infty)$ (autoregressive process of infinite order) or as an $MA(\infty)$ (moving average process of infinite order). This transformation is useful because it allows one to represent the ARMA process using only either the AR component with an infinite number of lags or the MA component with an infinite number of lags, simplifying some theoretical analyses.

The ARMA(1,1) process can be transformed to the $AR(\infty)$ process using the following sequence of steps. First, we solve the ARMA(1,1) equation for:

$$\varepsilon_t = r_t - \eta - \phi_1 r_{t-1} + \vartheta_1\varepsilon_{t-1}.$$

From the equation above, we deduce the equation for ε_{t-1}:

$$\varepsilon_{t-1} = r_{t-1} - \eta - \phi_1 r_{t-2} + \vartheta_1\varepsilon_{t-2}.$$

Substituting this expression for ε_{t-1} back into the original ARMA(1,1) equation, we get:

$$r_t = \eta(1+\vartheta_1) + (\phi_1-\vartheta_1)r_{t-1} + \phi_1\vartheta_1 r_{t-2} + \varepsilon_t - \vartheta_1^2\varepsilon_{t-2}.$$

By repeating this process iteratively, we arrive at the final expression:

$$r_t = \frac{\eta}{1-\vartheta_1} + \sum_{i=1}^{\infty}(\phi_1-\vartheta_1)\vartheta_1^{i-1}r_{t-i} + \varepsilon_t. \tag{11.20}$$

This equation represents the $AR(\infty)$ process derived from the ARMA(1,1) process. It shows that the current value r_t depends on an infinite sum of past values r_{t-i} and a constant term, which contributes to the overall level of the series.

11.2.5 Regime-Shifting Process

The $ARMA(p, q)$ model states that the current value of the return process depends explicitly on its past values and past shocks. Under certain conditions, such as positive autoregressive coefficients, the return process exhibits persistence. Therefore, this model supports the use of trend-following investing strategies.

A regime-shifting process is another alternative model where the return process exhibits persistence. In this model, returns follow a stochastic process that randomly switches between two or more states. However, because the probability of transitioning from one state to another in a given period is low, the process tends to remain in the same state for extended periods. This state persistence carries over to the return process, creating trends in prices.

We remind the reader that our quantitative measures of accuracy, responsiveness, and smoothness of a technical indicator of a trend-following rule are loosely motivated by a two-state regime-shifting model. In particular, we assume that the return r_t is a discrete-time stochastic process that randomly switches between bull and bear states. The return distribution depends on the state as follows:

$$r_t = \begin{cases} \mu_0 + \sigma_0 z_t & \text{in the bear state,} \\ \mu_1 + \sigma_1 z_t & \text{in the bull state.} \end{cases} \tag{11.21}$$

Here, μ_0 and σ_0 are the mean and standard deviation of returns in the bear state, while μ_1 and σ_1 are the mean and standard deviation of returns in the bull state. The variable z_t is a random variable that is identically and independently distributed over time, with zero mean and unit variance. It is crucial to note that we assume independence of returns within each state, meaning that all covariances $Cov(z_i, z_j)$ are zero when $i \neq j$.

However, a full description of a regime-shifting model requires specifying not only the probability distribution of returns in each state but also the transition probabilities between the states. In this chapter, we focus on the Markov chain model, where the state transition probabilities are constant.

The state transition probabilities form a square matrix $\mathbf{P}$, where each element is defined as:

$$p_{ij} = Prob(S_{t+1} = j | S_t = i),$$

where $S_t = i$ signifies that the state of the process at time t is i, and the state at the next time $t + 1$ is j. Thus, the probability p_{ij} represents the one-period probability of transitioning from state i to state j. The probability p_{ii}, called the self-transition probability of state i, quantifies the likelihood that the state of the process remains the same over one period.

In a 2-state Markov chain model for returns, the one-period transition probability matrix is given by:

$$\mathbf{P} = \begin{pmatrix} p_{00} & p_{01} \\ p_{10} & p_{11} \end{pmatrix}. \tag{11.22}$$

For instance, if the process is in state 0, then over a single period, the process transits to state 1 with probability p_{01} or remains in state 0 with probability $p_{00} = 1 - p_{01}$. The left panel in Fig. 11.1 illustrates a Markov chain model specified by the transition probability matrix in (11.22).

It is crucial to emphasize that a 2-state Markov chain model for returns is defined by two key components. Specifically, Eq. (11.21) describes the return process in each state, while Eq. (11.22) outlines the transition probabilities between the states.

In principle, a financial market does not need to have only two states. We can alternatively assume that a financial market has three states: bull market, bear market, and a sideways market. The return distribution in this model depends on the state as follows:

$$r_t = \begin{cases} \mu_0 + \sigma_0 z_t & \text{in the bear state,} \\ \mu_1 + \sigma_1 z_t & \text{in the bull state,} \\ \mu_2 + \sigma_2 z_t & \text{in the sideways state.} \end{cases} \tag{11.23}$$

As before, states 0 and 1 are the bear and bull markets, respectively. The new state, 2, is the sideways market, where, for example, the mean return μ_2 is zero. In this 3-state model for returns, the one-period transition probability matrix is given by:

$$\mathbf{P} = \begin{pmatrix} p_{00} & p_{01} & p_{02} \\ p_{10} & p_{11} & p_{12} \\ p_{20} & p_{21} & p_{22} \end{pmatrix}. \tag{11.24}$$

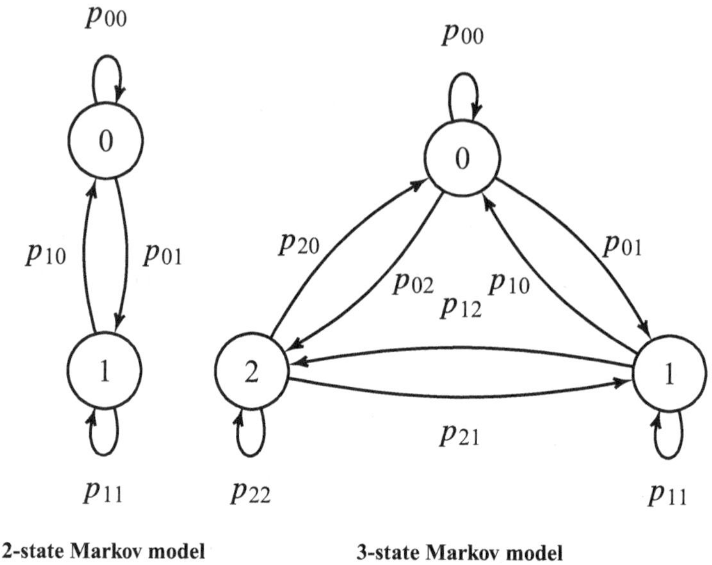

Fig. 11.1 Different Markov chain topologies. The left panel exhibits a 2-state Markov model, with the states identified by the numbers 0 and 1. The right panel presents a 3-state Markov model in which the states are identified by the numbers 0, 1, and 2

In this case, if the process is in state 0, then over a single period, it transitions to state 1 with probability p_{01}, to state 2 with probability p_{02}, or remains in state 0 with probability $p_{00} = 1 - p_{01} - p_{02}$. The right panel in Fig. 11.1 illustrates a Markov chain model specified by the transition probability matrix in (11.24).

Although a Markov chain model for returns and an ARMA model for returns appear to be distinct, Poskitt and Chung (1996) established a one-to-one correspondence between the two models. In particular, they demonstrated that a k-state Markov chain model can be represented by an $ARMA(k-1, k-1)$ model with a zero-mean white noise process. For instance, the returns generated by a 2-state Markov chain model are indistinguishable from the returns generated by an ARMA(1,1) model. Hence, the return process given by Eqs. (11.21) and (11.22) can be represented as an ARMA(1,1) process, which is shown in Eq. (11.16).

It should be pointed out that the return process in a Markov chain model is not strictly stationary due to the differences in return distributions between the bull and bear states of the market. Nonetheless, the return process can be considered stationary in the weak sense. This means that the process has a constant unconditional mean and variance over time, and the covariance between any two observations at different time points only depends on their time lag rather than their specific time points.

11.2.6 Optimal Forecasting of Return Process

In the preceding sections, we examined the return process in the ARMA model and the Markov chain model. In the case of the Markov model, the return process is statistically indistinguishable from the returns generated by a specific ARMA model. Furthermore, it is possible to view each ARMA process as an AR process with an infinite number of return lags. As a result, the AR process for return can be regarded as a fundamental process. In this section, we consider the optimal forecasting of an AR process.

Specifically, we assume that the market returns follow an autoregressive process of order p, $AR(p)$, where p can be any positive integer. This process is defined in Eq. (11.1). It is well known that if the returns follow this process, the best predictor of future returns has the same functional form as the $AR(p)$ process being predicted (see Box et al., 2016, Chapter 5). Specifically, the best predictor of future returns is given by:

$$\hat{r}_{t+1} = \eta + \sum_{i=0}^{p-1} \phi_{i+1} r_{t-i}, \tag{11.25}$$

where $\hat{r}_{t+1}$ is the predicted value at time $t + 1$.

Interestingly, if $\eta = 0$, then the best predictor is given by:

$$\hat{r}_{t+1} = \sum_{i=0}^{p-1} \phi_{i+1} r_{t-i}. \tag{11.26}$$

The equation above specifies the best predictor for the future value of returns. However, for trend-following investing purposes, traders are not interested in the specific numerical value of future returns. Instead, they are only interested in whether the future return will be positive or negative. In other words, trend-following investing recommends buying the risky asset when the predicted return is positive and selling the risky asset when the predicted return is negative.

The best predictor of the sign of future returns, when $\eta = 0$, can be expressed as:

$$v_{t+1} = \sum_{i=0}^{p-1} a \times \phi_{i+1} r_{t-i},$$

$$\widehat{\text{sign}(r_{t+1})} = \begin{cases} 1, & \text{if } v_{t+1} > 0, \\ -1, & \text{if } v_{t+1} \leq 0. \end{cases}$$

where a is a positive constant, $\text{sign}(x)$ is the mathematical sign function, and v_{t+1} serves as a predictor for the sign of the future return r_{t+1}. The notation $\widehat{\text{sign}(r_{t+1})}$ represents the predicted sign of the return at time $t + 1$.

That is, the optimal return weights for the best predictor of the sign of future returns correspond to a positive scaling of the autoregressive coefficients of the return process.

Interestingly, the best predictor of the sign of future returns has the same functional form as a technical indicator used in trend-following investing. This indicator is given by:

$$I_t(p) = \sum_{i=0}^{p-1} \theta_i r_{t-i}, \tag{11.27}$$

where $\theta_i = a \times \phi_{i+1}$. When $\eta \neq 0$ but is still rather small, the optimal technical indicator still has a similar functional form:

$$I_t(p) \approx \sum_{i=0}^{p-1} \theta_i r_{t-i}. \tag{11.28}$$

Upon initial examination, the question of finding the optimal predictor of future returns and the optimal technical indicator may seem straightforward: the weighting function for returns should resemble the autoregressive coefficients of the return process. However, the objective of a technical indicator is not solely to predict the value or sign of future returns, but rather to generate Buy and Sell signals for trading. These signals must maximize the performance of the trend-following strategy while considering transaction costs. As a result, the optimal return weights in a technical indicator may differ significantly from the shape of the autoregressive coefficients of the return process.

11.3 Optimal Trend-Following

11.3.1 Preliminaries

In this section, we aim to address the following question. Assuming the returns follow an $AR(p)$ process with known autoregressive coefficients represented by the $p \times 1$ vector $\boldsymbol{\phi}' = [\phi_1, \phi_2, \ldots, \phi_p]$, what is the $p \times 1$ vector $\boldsymbol{\theta}' = [\theta_0, \theta_1, \ldots, \theta_{p-1}]$ of return weights in the optimal technical indicator?

We assume that the optimal technical indicator uses the same number of return lags as the autoregressive (AR) process for returns, meaning $n = p$. While, in theory, the optimal indicator could use a different number of lags ($n \neq p$), it is highly unlikely that $n < p$, since return lags beyond n still influence the current return. If $n > p$, then all return weights from lag $p + 1$ to lag n will be zero.

The optimal technical indicator of a trading rule maximizes the performance of the trend-following strategy. This means selecting the return weights $\boldsymbol{\theta}$ that ensure the best performance of the strategy. The most popular performance measure in finance is the Sharpe ratio, developed by Nobel laureate William F. Sharpe. The Sharpe ratio evaluates an investment's performance by adjusting for its risk. It compares the return of an investment to its risk, helping to understand how much excess return is earned for the extra volatility endured by holding a riskier asset.

To compute the Sharpe ratio, we need the mean excess return and the standard deviation of the trend-following strategy. Let R_t represent the random return of the trend-following strategy and r_f the risk-free rate of return, which is assumed to be constant over time. The Sharpe ratio is computed using the following formula:

$$SR(R_t) = \frac{E[R_t] - r_f}{\sqrt{Var[R_t]}}, \tag{11.29}$$

where $E[R_t]$ is the expected return of the trend-following strategy and $Var[R_t]$ is the variance of the returns.

The Sharpe ratio is a fraction where the numerator is the mean excess return, which is the mean return minus the risk-free rate. The denominator is the standard deviation of the returns, which measures risk. Thus, the Sharpe ratio is typically interpreted as the risk-adjusted return or the reward-to-risk ratio.

In the subsequent sections of this chapter, our goal is to derive the analytical solution for the Sharpe ratio of the trend-following strategy, assuming that the technical indicator uses the return weights given by the arbitrary vector $\boldsymbol{\theta}$. For clarity, we will first consider the case without transaction costs and then address the more complex case with transaction costs.

Next, we aim to find the return weights $\boldsymbol{\theta}$ that maximize the Sharpe ratio of the trend-following strategy. While this problem is not analytically tractable, having the analytical solution for the Sharpe ratio allows us to solve it numerically using standard numerical optimization methods.

11.3.2 Strategy Performance in the Absence of Transaction Costs

We formulate the analytical model similarly to the one proposed by Zakamulin and Giner (2022) and used subsequently in the paper by Zakamulin and Giner (2023). Specifically, we assume that the returns follow the $AR(p)$ process specified by Eq. (11.1). The trend following rule is defined by Eq. (11.27).

We consider a long-only trend-following strategy designed to generate profits and limit losses by investing in the risky asset only when prices are trending upwards. The return at time t for this strategy is given by:

$$R_t = \begin{cases} r_t & \text{if } I_{t-1}(p) > 0, \\ r_f & \text{otherwise,} \end{cases} \tag{11.30}$$

where r_t represents the risky return at time t, and r_f is the constant risk-free rate of return. This strategy prescribes investing in the risky asset when the trading signal is Buy. When the trading signal is Sell, the strategy involves selling the risky asset and investing in the risk-free instrument. Note that the return at time t is determined by the value of the trading indicator at time $t-1$.

For simplicity of the model, we assume that the innovations in the $AR(p)$ process for returns, denoted as ε_t, follow a normal distribution. Consequently, the joint distribution of financial asset returns r_t and the technical indicator $I_{t-1}(p)$ follows a bivariate normal distribution:

$$\begin{bmatrix} r_t \\ I_{t-1}(p) \end{bmatrix} = \mathcal{N}\left(\begin{bmatrix} \mu \\ m \end{bmatrix}, \begin{bmatrix} \sigma^2 & \varrho\sigma v \\ \varrho\sigma v & v^2 \end{bmatrix}\right). \tag{11.31}$$

Here, $\mathcal{N}(\cdot, \cdot)$ denotes the bivariate normal probability distribution, with μ and σ^2 representing the mean and variance of r_t, and m and v^2 representing the mean and variance of $I_{t-1}(p)$. The correlation coefficient between r_t and $I_{t-1}(p)$ is denoted as ϱ.

The mean and variance of r_t are specified by Eq. (11.2). The mean and variance of $I_{t-1}(p)$ are defined as follows (refer to Zakamulin and Giner (2022)):

$$m = \mathbf{1}'\boldsymbol{\theta}\mu, \qquad v^2 = \boldsymbol{\theta}'\boldsymbol{R}\boldsymbol{\theta}\sigma^2, \tag{11.32}$$

where $\mathbf{1}$ is the $p \times 1$ vector of ones and $\boldsymbol{R}$ is the $p \times p$ matrix defined by Eq. (11.5). The correlation coefficient ϱ between r_t and $I_{t-1}(p)$ is computed as follows (see Zakamulin and Giner (2020)):

$$\varrho = \frac{\boldsymbol{\theta}'\boldsymbol{R}\,\boldsymbol{\phi}}{\sqrt{\boldsymbol{\theta}'\boldsymbol{R}\boldsymbol{\theta}}}. \tag{11.33}$$

Zakamulin and Giner (2022) derive the analytical solutions for both the expected return and the variance of returns of the trend-following strategy specified by Eq. (11.30). These solutions are expressed as follows:

$$E[R_t] = (\mu - r_f)\Phi(-d) + r_f + g, \tag{11.34}$$

$$Var[R_t] = (\mu^2 + \sigma^2)\Phi(-d) + g(2\mu + \sigma\varrho d) + r_f^2\Phi(d) - E[R_t]^2, \tag{11.35}$$

where

$$d = -\frac{m}{v}, \quad g = \sigma\varrho\,\varphi(d),$$

and $\varphi(.)$ and $\Phi(.)$ denote the probability density function and the cumulative distribution function of the standard normal random variable:

$$\varphi(z) = \frac{1}{\sqrt{2\pi}}e^{-\frac{z^2}{2}}, \quad \Phi(d) = \int_{-\infty}^{d} \varphi(z)dz.$$

With these expressions for the expected return and variance of returns of the trend-following strategy, we are equipped to calculate the strategy's Sharpe ratio.

11.3.3 Strategy Performance in the Presence of Transaction Costs

We remind the reader that it is commonly assumed that transaction costs are proportional to the amount traded. Under this assumption, when the trader buys or sells a risky asset, the transaction costs represent a fixed percentage, τ, which is subtracted from the return of the trend-following strategy. Here,

τ denotes the one-way transaction costs. Additionally, it is standard practice to consider trading in the risk-free asset as free from any associated costs. Therefore, the return to the trend-following strategy at time t in the presence of transaction costs is expressed as follows:

$$R_t|TC = \begin{cases} r_t & \text{if } I_{t-1}(p) > 0, I_{t-2}(p) > 0, \\ r_t - \tau & \text{if } I_{t-1}(p) > 0, I_{t-2}(p) < 0, \\ r_f & \text{if } I_{t-1}(p) < 0, I_{t-2}(p) < 0, \\ r_f - \tau & \text{if } I_{t-1}(p) < 0, I_{t-2}(p) > 0, \end{cases} \tag{11.36}$$

where $R_t|TC$ denotes the return to the trend-following strategy conditional on transaction costs.

Note that transaction costs are deducted from the returns of the trend-following strategy whenever there is a trade in the risky asset. For instance, a Buy signal indicates that the trader should hold the risky asset. If the condition $I_{t-1}(p) > 0$ and $I_{t-2}(p) > 0$ is met, it means both the previous and current signals are Buy signals. In this case, the trader already holds the asset and continues to do so, resulting in no transaction costs.

However, if a Buy signal follows a Sell signal, represented by the condition $I_{t-1}(p) > 0$ and $I_{t-2}(p) < 0$, the trader needs to buy the risky asset, incurring transaction costs. Similarly, transaction costs are incurred when a Sell signal follows a Buy signal, indicated by the condition $I_{t-1}(p) < 0$ and $I_{t-2}(p) > 0$.

The following equality is self-evident:

$$R_t|TC = R_t - TC_t,$$

where R_t represents the return to the trend-following strategy at time t without transaction costs, as specified by Eq. (11.30), and TC_t denotes the transaction costs at time t, given by:

$$TC_t = \begin{cases} \tau & \text{if } I_{t-1}(p) > 0, I_{t-2}(p) < 0 \text{ or } I_{t-1}(p) < 0, I_{t-2}(p) > 0, \\ 0 & \text{if } I_{t-1}(p) > 0, I_{t-2}(p) > 0 \text{ or } I_{t-1}(p) < 0, I_{t-2}(p) < 0. \end{cases} \tag{11.37}$$

The expected transaction costs over one period are given by:

$$E[TC_t] = \tau \, Prob(\text{Rev}),$$

where $Prob(\text{Rev})$ represents the probability of a position reversal, which is essentially the likelihood of executing a trade. A position reversal occurs when a Buy signal at time $t-2$ is reversed to a Sell signal at time $t-1$, or vice versa. The probability of a position reversal is determined by:

$$Prob(\text{Rev}) = Prob(I_{t-1}(n) > 0, I_{t-2}(n) < 0) + Prob(I_{t-1}(n) < 0, I_{t-2}(n) > 0).$$

In the chapter on quantitative measures of a technical indicator, we derived the expression for this probability. Specifically, this probability is given by:

$$Prob(\text{Rev}) = \frac{1}{2} - \frac{1}{\pi}\arcsin(\text{SMI}(I(p))), \tag{11.38}$$

where $\arcsin(\cdot)$ represents the inverse trigonometric sine function, and $\text{SMI}(I(p))$ denotes the Smoothness Index (SMI) of the technical indicator $I(p)$. The smoothness of a technical indicator is calculated using the following formula:

$$\text{SMI}(I(p)) = \frac{\sum_{i=0}^{p-2} \theta_i \theta_{i+1}}{\sum_{i=0}^{p-1} \theta_i^2}.$$

The transaction costs at time t follow a two-point distribution. Specifically, these costs can be described as a random variable taking the value τ with a probability of $Prob(\text{Rev})$, and assuming the value 0 with a probability of $1 - Prob(\text{Rev})$. The mean and variance of the transaction costs are determined as follows:

$$E[TC_t] = \tau\, Prob(\text{Rev}), \quad Var[TC_t] = \tau^2 Prob(\text{Rev})(1 - Prob(\text{Rev})), \tag{11.39}$$

where $Prob(\text{Rev})$ is specified by Eq. (11.38).

The expected return of the trend-following strategy, considering transaction costs, is given by:

$$E[R_t|TC] = E[R_t - TC_t] = E[R_t] - E[TC_t], \tag{11.40}$$

where $E[R_t]$ s the expected return of the trend-following strategy without transaction costs, as specified by Eq. (11.34). The variance of returns for the trend-following strategy, including transaction costs, can be calculated using the following equation:

$$Var[R_t|TC] = Var[R_t] - 2Cov(R_t, TC_t) + Var[TC_t], \tag{11.41}$$

where $Var[R_t]$ refers to the variance of returns for the trend-following strategy without transaction costs, as given in Eq. (11.35), and $Cov(R_t, TC_t)$ represents the covariance between R_t and TC_t.

Zakamulin and Giner (2023) show that $Cov(R_t, TC_t) \approx 0$. As a result, the solution for the Sharpe ratio of the trend-following strategy in the presence of transaction costs can be expressed as:

$$SR(R_t|TC) = \frac{E[R_t] - E[TC_t] - r_f}{\sqrt{Var[R_t] + Var[TC_t]}}. \tag{11.42}$$

11.3.4 Results of Numerical Optimization

In the preceding section, we derived analytical solutions for the Sharpe ratio of the trend-following strategy incorporating transaction costs. This solution allows us to assess the performance of the trend-following strategy using return weights defined by the vector $\boldsymbol{\theta}' = [\theta_0, \theta_1, \ldots, \theta_{p-1}]$, assuming that the financial asset returns follow an $AR(p)$ process with autoregressive coefficients specified by the vector $\boldsymbol{\phi}' = [\phi_1, \phi_2, \ldots, \phi_p]$.

This section focuses on determining the optimal return weights that maximize the Sharpe ratio. To achieve this objective, we need to solve the following optimization problem:

$$\max_{\boldsymbol{\theta}} \quad SR(R_t|TC) \text{ subject to } \boldsymbol{\theta}'\mathbf{1} = 1. \tag{11.43}$$

It is important to note that positive scaling of the return weights $\boldsymbol{\theta}$ within a technical indicator results in an equivalent technical indicator, since the trading signal depends on the sign of the indicator's value. As a result, there are infinitely many solutions for the optimal return weights without imposing an additional constraint. To establish a unique solution, we assume that the sum of all return weights equals one.

Regrettably, the optimization problem specified by Eq. (11.43) does not have an analytical solution. However, it can be effectively solved using numerical methods for nonlinear optimization.

Since the autoregressive parameters in the real-life return process are largely unknown, we explore two alternative assumptions. The first assumption posits that the autoregressive coefficients decrease linearly with the lag of returns:

$$\phi_i = a(p - i + 1), \tag{11.44}$$

where $i \in [1, p]$ is the return lag and $a > 0$ is a scaling factor. The second assumption assumes constant autoregressive coefficients:

$$\phi_i = b, \tag{11.45}$$

where $b > 0$.

In both cases, we suppose that the trend persistence, κ, which is determined by the sum of the autoregressive coefficients, is fixed at $\kappa = 0.30$. This value aligns with empirical estimates found in the studies by Zakamulin and Giner (2022) and Zakamulin and Giner (2023). For the scenario where the autoregressive coefficients decrease linearly with the return lag, the parameter a is calculated using the formula:

$$a = \frac{2\kappa}{p(p+1)}. \tag{11.46}$$

Alternatively, in the case where the autoregressive coefficients remain constant, the parameter b is determined by:

$$b = \frac{\kappa}{p}. \tag{11.47}$$

The motivation behind our two alternative assumptions is as follows: when implementing the trend-following strategy on a monthly basis, two popular trading rules are the P-SMA rule and the MOM rule. In the P-SMA rule, return weights in the technical indicator decrease linearly with the return lag. Conversely, in the MOM rule, return weights remain constant. The popularity of each rule often correlates with its empirical profitability. The rationale is straightforward: if a rule outperforms others, its technical indicator likely employs optimal return weights. However, a puzzle arises because these two rules use distinctly different return weights. Consequently, both cannot be simultaneously optimal. We will delve into resolving this puzzle later in this book. For now, we proceed by assuming two different forms of autoregressive coefficients.

We address the optimization problem (11.43) using realistic parameters. Specifically, we assume a mean annual risky return of $\mu = 10\%$ and a standard deviation of $\sigma = 20\%$. The annual risk-free rate is $r_f = 3\%$. The trend-following strategy is executed on a bi-weekly basis. The bi-weekly returns of a financial asset are modeled using an AR(25) process with coefficients that are either constant or linearly decreasing.

Figure 11.2 shows the optimal return weights for technical indicators at various levels of proportional transaction costs. Specifically, the left column, labeled "Constant," displays the optimal return weights when the autoregressive coefficients are constant. The right column, labeled "Linearly decreasing," shows the optimal return weights when the autoregressive coefficients decrease linearly with the return lag. The proportional transaction costs are set to values of $\tau \in \{0\%, 0.25\%, 1\%\}$.

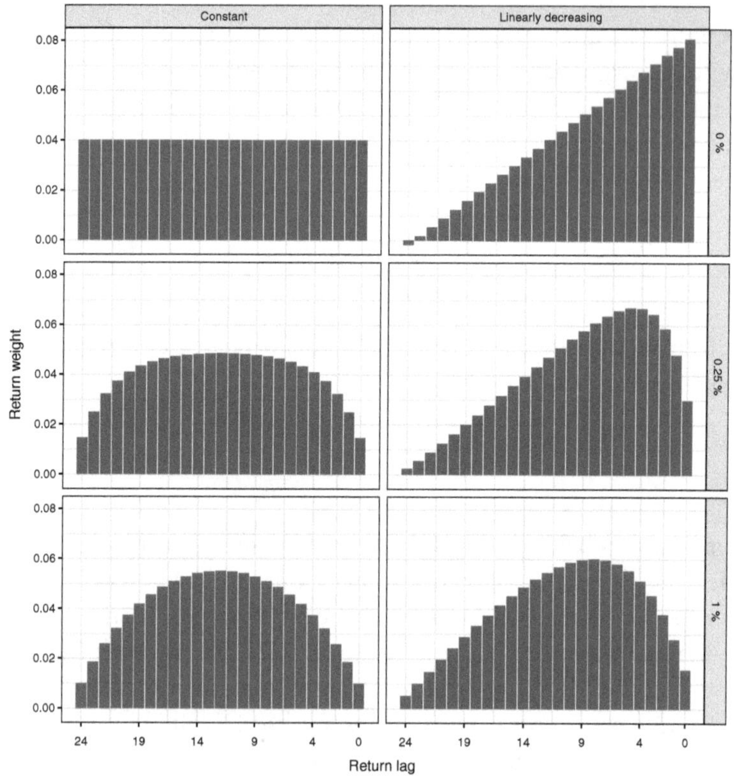

Fig. 11.2 Optimal return weights for technical indicators at various levels of proportional transaction costs. The left column, labeled "Constant," displays the optimal return weights when the autoregressive coefficients are constant. The right column, labeled "Linearly decreasing," shows the optimal return weights when the autoregressive coefficients decrease linearly with the return lag. The proportional transaction costs are set to values of $\tau \in \{0\%, 0.25\%, 1\%\}$

The plots in Fig. 11.2 suggest several important observations. First, in the absence of transaction costs, the shape of the optimal return weights closely mirrors the pattern of the autoregressive coefficients in the return process. Specifically, when the autoregressive coefficients are constant, the optimal return weights in the technical indicator are also constant. Similarly, when the autoregressive coefficients decrease linearly with the return lag, the optimal return weights decrease linearly with the lag number as well.

Our second observation highlights that, in the presence of transaction costs, the optimal return-weighting function becomes a smoothed version of the autoregressive coefficients. When the autoregressive coefficients of the return process are constant, it is optimal to follow the trend by reducing the values of the most recent and most distant return weights. In the case where the autoregressive coefficients decrease linearly, the optimal return-weighting function forms a hump-like shape under transaction costs. Specifically, reducing the weights of the most recent return lags appears to be optimal with transaction costs. In this scenario, the optimal return weights initially increase, reach a peak, and then progressively decline as the lag number increases.

Our third observation underscores that the level of transaction costs influences the degree of smoothing applied to the autoregressive coefficients. When the autoregressive coefficients are constant, increasing the level of proportional transaction costs causes the shape of the optimal return weights in the technical indicator to converge to a sine-weighted moving average of returns. For a fixed number of return lags, this shape minimizes the expected transaction costs of a trading strategy. When the autoregressive coefficients decrease linearly, the level of transaction costs affects the position of the maximum return weight. Specifically, as transaction costs increase, the maximum return weight shifts to higher lag numbers.

In the subsequent chapter, theoretical considerations suggest that the scenario where the autoregressive coefficients of the return process decrease linearly with the lag number is much more likely than the scenario where the autoregressive coefficients are constant. Consequently, theory indicates that, in the absence of transaction costs, the optimal strategy is to follow the trend using the price and SMA crossover (P-SMA) rule. However, when transaction costs are present, the optimal strategy is closer to the double LMA crossover (LMA-C) rule, which can be closely approximated by the double SMA crossover (SMA-C) rule. Therefore, our theoretical model explains the popularity of the double SMA crossover rule. This rule is favored because it is optimal and its optimality is demonstrated by its superior empirical performance.

11.4 Summary

Earlier in this book, we introduced measures to quantify the accuracy, responsiveness, and smoothness of technical indicators for trend-following rules. These measures are of genuine importance for traders and investment professionals, as they greatly assist in comparing and contrasting the characteristics of various technical indicators.

One of the main advantages of these measures is that they are virtually model independent and rely solely on the return weights in the technical indicator of a trend-following rule, which is derived from moving averages of prices. However, this model-free advantage comes with a significant drawback. Specifically, these measures do not allow us to identify the return weights of the most optimal technical indicator for a particular financial market. While they can help identify a technical indicator that balances accuracy, responsiveness, and smoothness, they do not provide insight into specific details, such as the optimal number of return lags, n, in the technical indicator.

Finding the optimal technical indicator is impossible without fully understanding the return process. This chapter aims to achieve two main objectives. First, it introduces the popular model of the return process with persistence, focusing on the autoregressive (AR) process. In this model, the current return is a linear function of a constant and p return lags. Using this process, we identify the optimal technical indicator that maximizes the performance of a trend-following strategy, accounting for transaction costs. The results of this investigation lead us to the following conclusions.

First, based on general considerations, we deduced that the optimal number of return lags in a technical indicator should match the number of autoregressive coefficients in the AR process for returns ($n = p$). Second, without transaction costs, the optimal return weights closely follow the pattern of the autoregressive coefficients, reflecting a positive linear scaling transformation of these coefficients. Third, when transaction costs are introduced, the optimal return-weighting function becomes a smoothed version of the autoregressive coefficients. Finally, the degree of smoothing applied to the coefficients is influenced by the level of transaction costs, with higher transaction costs resulting in greater smoothing.

The economic intuition behind the results of the theoretical modeling in this chapter closely aligns with those obtained through quantitative measures. Our analysis reveals that, in the absence of transaction costs, the smoothness of a technical indicator is less important than the optimal tradeoff between accuracy and responsiveness. In this context, the price and moving average (P-MA) rules offer a good balance between accurately identifying trend directions and being responsive to trend reversals. However, when transaction costs are introduced, the double moving average crossover (MA-C) rules outperform the P-MA rules. The MA-C rules strike a better balance between smoothness and responsiveness, significantly reducing the number of whipsaw trades.

Furthermore, the theoretical modeling results presented in this chapter are confirmed using real-world data. Specifically, Zakamulin and Giner (2023) validate the theoretical model's predictions and demonstrate the benefits of the optimal trend-following strategy with transaction costs using data from several real-world financial markets. This study shows that the empirical results align well with the theoretical predictions, supporting the reliability of the proposed framework. Additionally, by drawing on data from various financial markets, the authors provide compelling evidence of the superiority of our optimal trend-following strategy, particularly when transaction costs are considered.

References

Andrews, D., & Chen, H. Y. (1994). Approximately Median-Unbiased Estimation of Autoregressive Models. *Journal of Business & Economic Statistics, 12*, 187–204.

Box, G. E. P., Jenkins, G. M., Reinsel, G. C., & Ljung, G. M. (2016). *Time Series Analysis: Forecasting and Control* (5th edn.). Wiley.

Marques, C. R. (2005). Inflation Persistence: Facts or Artifacts? *Banco de Portugal Economic bulletin, 11*(2), 69–79.

Poskitt, D. S., & Chung, S.-H. (1996). Markov Chain Models, Time Series Analysis and Extreme Value Theory. *Advances in Applied Probability, 28*(2), 405–425.

Zakamulin, V., & Giner, J. (2020). Trend Following with Momentum Versus Moving Average: A Tale of Differences. *Quantitative Finance, 20*(6), 985–1007.

Zakamulin, V., & Giner, J. (2022). Time Series Momentum in the US Stock Market: Empirical Evidence and Theoretical Analysis. *International Review of Financial Analysis, 82*, Article 102173.

Zakamulin, V., & Giner, J. (2023). Optimal Trend-Following With Transaction Costs. *International Review of Financial Analysis, 90*, Article 102928.

12

Optimal Trend-Following Rules in Two-State Regime-Switching Models

12.1 Introduction

A great deal of trend-following rules is employed to determine the direction of financial markets. These rules typically rely on past prices and use various types of moving averages. The Simple Moving Average (SMA) is the most widely used moving average, but there are also less common types such as the Linear Moving Average (LMA) and Exponential Moving Average (EMA). Each moving average is calculated based on a specific window size for averaging. Additionally, trend-following rules can be based on a single moving average or a combination of moving averages. For instance, a price and moving average crossover (P-MA) rule generates trading signals by comparing the price to a moving average of prices. There are different variations of price and moving average crossovers, including P-SMA, P-LMA, and P-EMA.

Another common trend-following strategy is the double moving average crossover (MA-C) rule, which uses two moving averages of different window sizes. Some examples of double crossovers include SMA-C, LMA-C, and EMA-C. The Moving Average Convergence/Divergence (MACD) rule is a popular alternative strategy that uses three EMAs. Additionally, the Momentum (MOM) rule can also be viewed as a type of moving average rule. Finally, there are various exotic moving averages that claim to offer better responsiveness and smoothness than traditional approaches.

Given the wide range of trend-following rules, moving averages, and window sizes available, investment professionals may find themselves with an overwhelming number of choices. However, it is important to note that, from an academic standpoint, these trend-following rules are considered ad hoc, lacking theoretical justification for their optimality. The introduction of these rules

V. Zakamulin and J. Giner, *The Ultimate Moving Average Handbook*,
https://doi.org/10.1007/978-3-031-90907-8_12

is usually based on superficial reasoning and supported only by anecdotal evidence of their alleged superior performance. As a result, caution should be exercised when selecting and relying on these rules for investment decision-making.

A modern scientific approach to selecting a trend-following rule involves backtesting existing rules using historical data and choosing the rule with the best observed performance. However, it is important to note that since these rules are ad hoc and backtest results can be influenced by noise, there is no guarantee that the rule with the best backtest performance is truly the most optimal. It is also possible that a more profitable rule exists but has not yet been discovered or tested.

One way to express the technical indicator for a trend-following rule is by using a moving average of prices, either single or multiple. However, an alternative approach is to represent the same indicator as a single moving average of past returns. This means that instead of considering the actual price values, the indicator focuses on the returns derived from those prices. The different trend-following rules mainly differ in the weighting function applied to the returns. These trading rules apply different weights to past returns over the averaging window. Therefore, determining the optimal trend-following rule boils down to finding the optimal return weights for the technical indicator.

The preceding chapter of this book presents a demonstration that establishes how the optimal technical indicator's return weights can be determined using only the autoregressive coefficients of the return process. If transaction costs are not an issue, the optimal return weights correspond to the autoregressive coefficients themselves. If transaction costs are present, the optimal return weights become a more refined version of the autoregressive coefficients, incorporating additional smoothing to reduce these costs. The level of smoothing increases as transaction costs rise.

In view of the aforesaid, the question of determining the optimal return weights in a trading indicator appears straightforward from a theoretical perspective. One could estimate the autoregressive coefficients of a real-life return process through linear regression. Unfortunately, this approach proves inadequate since the autoregressive coefficients of a real-life return process are rather small and escape detection. In particular, Zakamulin and Giner (2022) demonstrate that accurately estimating these coefficients is a challenging task, and even using all the historical data available spanning around 150 years is not enough. They suggest that obtaining reliable estimates would require analyzing data for approximately 650 years at the monthly frequency. Therefore, empirical estimation of autoregressive coefficients is not a viable option.

The only remaining avenue to gain insights into the return weights for the optimal trend-following rule is through theoretical analysis. In this chapter, we aim to choose a sensible model for the return process and utilize it to identify the return weights for the optimal technical indicator that follows trends.

While it is true that no model can perfectly represent reality, we firmly believe that models are still highly valuable in providing insights into the optimal trend-following indicator. As the noted academic George Box once said, "All models are wrong, but some are useful." This means that while models are simplifications of complex systems, they can still be beneficial despite not capturing every detail of the real world. Models allow us to understand, make informed decisions, and make predictions. They enable us to identify patterns and relationships, offering guidance in situations where having no model would leave us uncertain and uninformed.

To accurately model the return process, it is crucial to ensure that the process is realistic. In order for a return process model to be considered realistic, it should be able to replicate certain stylized facts observed in financial asset returns. These stylized facts, extensively documented in the econometric literature, include fat tails, negative skewness, volatility clustering, short-term momentum, and medium-term mean reversion. One widely accepted model that can reproduce these stylized facts is the two-state regime-switching model for stock returns. This model, as examined in the works of Timmermann (2000), Frühwirth-Schnatter (2006), and Giner and Zakamulin (2023), incorporates a random switching mechanism between bull and bear states. A model of this nature, which successfully captures the stylized facts associated with financial asset returns, is likely to be able to accurately replicate autoregressive coefficients as well.

It is worth mentioning that our quantitative metrics for accuracy, responsiveness, and smoothness of a trend-following technical indicator are based on a two-state regime-switching model. However, unlike the regime-switching model, our metrics do not require any parametric assumptions. Instead, we calculate them solely based on the return weights within the technical indicator, without considering mean state returns, state volatilities, transition probabilities between states, or probability distributions of state duration times. By eliminating the dependence on complex parametric assumptions, our metrics focus exclusively on the specific qualities of a technical indicator. As a result, our measures are both highly generalized and broadly applicable. On the downside, our measures do not allow traders to determine the optimal technical indicator to follow the trends in a specific financial market.

This chapter provides a comprehensive specification of a two-state regime-switching model and identifies the optimal trend-following technical indicator.

We explore two kinds of regime-switching models, namely Markov and semi-Markov models. Although Markov models are relatively straightforward, they fail to capture the medium-term mean reversion observed in real-life financial asset returns. On the other hand, semi-Markov models are more intricate but have the ability to replicate the mean reversion.

Our findings indicate that the price and EMA crossover is the best trend-following strategy in the absence of transaction costs, when the returns are modeled using a Markov process. We can determine the optimal EMA window size by using an analytical solution that factors in the parameters of the Markov return process. Our comparative statics analysis reveals that the optimal window size predominantly depends on the signal-to-noise ratio of returns and the state transition probabilities. As the signal-to-noise ratio or the state transition probability increases, the optimal window size decreases. However, in the presence of transaction costs, the double EMA crossover is the most effective trend-following strategy, and the size of the shorter window is dependent on the level of proportional transaction costs.

In a semi-Markov model with transaction costs, the optimal trend-following strategy shares similarities with the MACD rule. When the return process follows a Markov model, the returns show short-term momentum, meaning that the autoregressive coefficients are strictly positive and decrease exponentially with the return lag. However, in a semi-Markov model, the return process exhibits both short-term momentum and medium-term mean reversion. This is reflected in positive autocorrelation at short lags for short-term momentum and negative autocorrelation at longer lags for medium-term mean reversion. When transaction costs are considered, the optimal return weights in a semi-Markov model represent a smoothed version of the autoregressive coefficients. This results in a damped waveform shape for the optimal return weights. One example of such a shape is a heavily damped sine wave.

12.2 Optimal Trend-Following Under Autoregressive Return Process

In this section, we reiterate our methodology for selecting the most suitable technical indicator for trend-following strategies when returns follow an autoregressive process. We chose the autoregressive process because of its ease of use, versatility, and the direct relationship between returns in a regime-switching model and those modeled using an autoregressive approach. Autoregressive modeling is widely recognized and quite popular for modeling persistent returns of financial assets. Therefore, it is a practical and commonly used tool in finance.

The technical indicator of a trend-following strategy can be calculated using returns instead of prices. In this case, the value of the technical indicator at time t, denoted as $I_t(n)$, is computed using a moving average of the previous n returns. The formula for calculating the indicator is as follows:

$$I_t(n) = \sum_{i=0}^{n-1} \theta_i r_{t-i}, \tag{12.1}$$

where r_{t-i} represents the return at lag i, with θ_i denoting the weight of the return r_{t-i} in the moving average computation.

In the context where returns follow an autoregressive process of order p, denoted as $AR(p)$, the return observation at time t can be expressed as a linear combination of p previous observations, along with a random noise term. This mathematical representation is as follows:

$$r_t = \eta + \sum_{i=1}^{p} \phi_i r_{t-i} + \varepsilon_t. \tag{12.2}$$

Here, p refers to the number of autoregressive terms in the model, η represents a constant term, $\{\phi_1, \phi_2, \ldots, \phi_p\}$ denotes the autoregressive coefficients, r_{t-i} signifies the return observed at time $t - i$, and ε_t is the noise term, which follows an independently and identically distributed (i.i.d.) random process with a mean of zero and a variance of σ_ε^2.

Our analysis focuses on the long-only trend-following strategy, which involves selling the risky asset and investing in the risk-free asset when a Sell signal is generated. There is another type of trend-following strategy, known as the long-short strategy, where the trader shorts the risky asset when a Sell signal is triggered. However, we exclude the long-short strategy from our analysis as empirical evidence suggests its performance is significantly poorer than the long-only strategy, as noted in the findings of Zakamulin and Giner (2022).

In the previous chapter, we demonstrated that in the absence of transaction costs, the optimal return weights in a technical indicator bear close resemblance to the autoregressive coefficients and represent a positive linear scaling transformation of these coefficients. Specifically, the optimal technical indicator, assuming no transaction costs, can be expressed as follows:

$$I_t(p) \approx \sum_{i=0}^{p-1} (a \times \phi_{i+1}) r_{t-i}. \tag{12.3}$$

Here, a can represent any positive real number. The optimal technical indicator comprises the same number of return lags as the number of autoregressive coefficients present in the return process, that is, $n = p$, and the optimal weight assigned to the return observed at lag i is equal to $\theta_i = a \times \phi_{i+1}$.

In the presence of transaction costs, the weights assigned to the optimal technical indicator are those that optimize the performance of the trend-following strategy, with performance measured in terms of the Sharpe ratio. The problem of maximizing the Sharpe ratio subject to proportional transaction costs is framed as follows:

$$\max_{\boldsymbol{\theta}} \quad SR(R_t|TC) \text{ subject to } \boldsymbol{\theta}'\mathbf{1} = 1. \tag{12.4}$$

Here, $SR(\cdot)$ refers to the Sharpe ratio, $R_t|TC$ denotes the returns of the long-only strategy in the presence of transaction costs,[1] $\boldsymbol{\theta}' = [\theta_0, \theta_1, \ldots, \theta_{p-1}]$ represents a $p \times 1$ vector comprising the return weights, and $\mathbf{1}$ is a $p \times 1$ vector with all elements being ones. $\boldsymbol{\theta}'\mathbf{1} = 1$ imposes the constraint that the sum of all return weights equates to unity, necessary for determining a unique solution to the optimal return weights.

The equation for the Sharpe ratio of the trend-following strategy when considering transaction costs is as follows:

$$SR(R_t|TC) = \frac{E[R_t] - E[TC_t] - r_f}{\sqrt{Var[R_t] + Var[TC_t]}}. \tag{12.5}$$

In this equation, $E[R_t]$ represents the mean returns of the trend-following strategy in the absence of transaction costs, while $E[TC_t]$ represents the mean transaction costs. The variable r_f is the risk-free rate of return. Additionally, $Var[R_t]$ and $Var[TC_t]$ represent the variances of returns and transaction costs, respectively. Note that $Var[R_t]$ signifies the variance in the absence of transaction costs.

The expressions for the mean and variance of returns to the trend-following strategy are given by:

$$E[R_t] = (\mu - r_f)\Phi(-d) + r_f + g, \tag{12.6}$$

$$Var[R_t] = (\mu^2 + \sigma^2)\Phi(-d) + g(2\mu + \sigma\varrho d) + r_f^2\Phi(d) - E[R_t]^2. \tag{12.7}$$

[1] Specifically, R_t represents the returns generated by the long-only trend-following strategy, while TC represents the transaction costs incurred during the trading period. The notation $R_t|TC$ is used to indicate that the returns to the trend-following strategy are computed after taking into account the impact of trading costs.

In these equations, μ represents the mean of the autoregressive process for returns, while σ^2 represents the variance. These can be calculated using the following formulas:

$$\mu = E[r_t] = \frac{\eta}{1 - \sum_{i=1}^{p} \phi_i}, \qquad \sigma^2 = Var(r_t) = \frac{\sigma_\varepsilon^2}{1 - \sum_{i=1}^{p} \phi_i \rho_i}, \tag{12.8}$$

where ρ_i represents the lag i autocorrelation of the autoregressive process for returns. The variable d is defined as $-\frac{m}{v}$, and the variable g is calculated as $\sigma \varrho \varphi(d)$, where $\varphi(.)$ and $\Phi(.)$ represent the probability density function and cumulative distribution function of the standard normal random variable, respectively:

$$\varphi(z) = \frac{1}{\sqrt{2\pi}} e^{-\frac{z^2}{2}}, \quad \Phi(d) = \int_{-\infty}^{d} \varphi(z) dz.$$

The variables m and v^2 denote the mean and variance of the technical indicator. They are specified by:

$$m = E[I_t(n)] = \mathbf{1}'\boldsymbol{\theta}\mu, \qquad v^2 = Var[I_t(n)] = \boldsymbol{\theta}'\boldsymbol{R}\boldsymbol{\theta}\sigma^2, \tag{12.9}$$

where $\boldsymbol{R}$ is a matrix with dimensions $p \times p$ defined as:

$$\boldsymbol{R} = \begin{bmatrix} 1 & \rho_1 & \rho_2 & \cdots \rho_{p-1} \\ \rho_1 & 1 & \rho_1 & \cdots \rho_{p-2} \\ \rho_2 & \rho_1 & 1 & \cdots \rho_{p-3} \\ \vdots & \vdots & \vdots & \ddots \quad \vdots \\ \rho_{p-1} & \rho_{p-2} & \rho_{p-3} & \cdots \quad 1 \end{bmatrix}. \tag{12.10}$$

The variable ϱ represents the correlation coefficient between the current value of the technical indicator and the next period return. It is calculated using the formula:

$$\varrho = \frac{\boldsymbol{\theta}'\boldsymbol{R}\boldsymbol{\phi}}{\sqrt{\boldsymbol{\theta}'\boldsymbol{R}\boldsymbol{\theta}}}. \tag{12.11}$$

where $\boldsymbol{\phi}' = [\phi_1, \phi_2, \ldots, \phi_p]$ is the $p \times 1$ vector of autoregressive coefficients, and $\boldsymbol{\rho}' = [\rho_1, \rho_2, \ldots, \rho_p]$ is the $p \times 1$ vector of autocorrelation coefficients.

The autocorrelation coefficients ρ_i can be determined from the autoregressive coefficients ϕ_i by solving the Yule-Walker equations:

$$\mathbf{R}\boldsymbol{\phi} = \boldsymbol{\rho}. \tag{12.12}$$

Finally, the mean and variance of transaction costs are given by:

$$E[TC_t] = \tau \, Prob(\text{Rev}), \quad Var[TC_t] = \tau^2 Prob(\text{Rev})(1 - Prob(\text{Rev})). \tag{12.13}$$

Here, τ represents the level of proportional transaction costs and $Prob(\text{Rev})$ is the probability of trade reversal specified by the following equation:

$$Prob(\text{Rev}) = \frac{1}{2} - \frac{1}{\pi} \arcsin(\text{SMI}(I(p))), \tag{12.14}$$

where $\arcsin(\cdot)$ represents the inverse trigonometric sine function and $\text{SMI}(I(p))$ denotes the Smoothness Index (SMI) of the technical indicator $I(p)$. The smoothness of a technical indicator is calculated using the following formula:

$$\text{SMI}(I(p)) = \frac{\sum_{i=0}^{p-2} \theta_i \theta_{i+1}}{\sum_{i=0}^{p-1} \theta_i^2}.$$

The computation of the Sharpe ratio using Eq. (12.5) may seem complicated, but it is manageable. The process involves specifying the autoregressive process for returns, selecting the level of transaction costs, and choosing an arbitrary set of return weights in a trading indicator. The maximization problem (12.4) does not have an analytical solution, so numerical optimization methods must be used to solve it. Fortunately, standard numerical methods are available in many software packages and can be used to solve the problem efficiently.

12.3 Autoregressive Coefficients in a Two-State Regime-Switching Model

We begin by specifying the return process in a two-state regime-switching model. This return process can alternatively be expressed as an autoregressive process. By determining the autoregressive coefficients of this process, we can derive the weights of the technical indicator for optimal trend-following.

The objective of this section is to present the solution for the autoregressive coefficients of the return process defined by a two-state regime-switching model. This solution is highly general and can be applied to any regime-shifting model, regardless of the transition probability distribution. Specifically, it is applicable to both conventional Markov models and more complex semi-Markov models.

The return process in a two-state model, denoted as r_t, is a discrete-time stochastic process that undergoes random switches between two distinct regimes or states: A and B. State A represents a bullish market state, while state B represents a bearish market state. The state space of the process is defined as $S_t \in \{A, B\}$.

The distribution of returns is dependent on the current state, S_t, and can be expressed as follows:

$$r_t = \begin{cases} \mu_A + \sigma_A z_t & \text{if } S_t = A, \\ \mu_B + \sigma_B z_t & \text{if } S_t = B. \end{cases} \tag{12.15}$$

In the above equation, μ_A and σ_A represent the mean and standard deviation of returns in state A, respectively. Similarly, μ_B and σ_B represent the mean and standard deviation of returns in state B, respectively. The term z_t represents a random variable that is independently and identically distributed over time, with a mean of zero and a variance of one.

The probability of transition from state I to state J over a period of k time steps is represented by the conditional probability $p_{IJ}(k)$. These multi-period transition probabilities play a crucial role in predicting the future state of the process. Specifically, $p_{IJ}(k)$ denotes the probability of the process transitioning from state I to state J over k time steps.

To represent the k-period transition probability distribution of the two-state regime-switching process, we use a 2×2 transition probability matrix $\mathbf{P}(k)$, which is defined as follows:

$$\mathbf{P}(k) = \begin{pmatrix} p_{AA}(k) & p_{AB}(k) \\ p_{BA}(k) & p_{BB}(k) \end{pmatrix}.$$

In the above equation, $p_{AA}(k)$ denotes the probability of the process remaining in state A over k time steps, while $p_{AB}(k)$ denotes the probability of the process transitioning from state A to state B over k time steps. Similarly, $p_{BA}(k)$ denotes the probability of the process transitioning from state B to state A over k time steps, and $p_{BB}(k)$ denotes the probability of the process remaining in state B over k time steps.

The steady-state or stationary probabilities of the two-state regime-switching model are denoted by π_A and π_B and are defined as follows:

$$\pi_A = Prob(S_t = A), \quad \pi_B = Prob(S_t = B).$$

The steady-state or stationary probabilities represent the long-term probabilities of being in each state of the regime-switching model. These probabilities indicate the equilibrium distribution of the process, where the probabilities of being in each state no longer change over time.

Specifically, π_A represents the probability of the process being in state A in the long run, while π_B represents the probability of the process being in state B in the long run. These probabilities can be interpreted as the proportion of time the process spends in each state when it reaches a steady state.

The return autocorrelation function, denoted as ρ_k, measures the correlation between returns at different time lags, or periods. The expression for ρ_k, as derived by Giner and Zakamulin (2023), is given by:

$$\rho_k = \frac{\pi_A \pi_B (\mu_A - \mu_B)^2 - (\mu_A - \mu_B)(\pi_A \, p_{AB}(k) \, \mu_A - \pi_B \, p_{BA}(k) \, \mu_B)}{\sigma^2}, \tag{12.16}$$

where σ^2 represents the variance of the return process and is defined as:

$$\sigma^2 = \pi_A \sigma_A^2 + \pi_B \sigma_B^2 + \pi_A \pi_B (\mu_A - \mu_B)^2.$$

It is important to note that the autocorrelation function ρ_k only depends on the k-period transition probabilities $p_{AB}(k)$ and $p_{BA}(k)$. The calculation of these probabilities is influenced by whether the regime-switching model is Markov or semi-Markov, and will be discussed in detail in the following sections.

Once we have obtained the $p \times 1$ vector $\boldsymbol{\rho}' = [\rho_1, \rho_2, \ldots, \rho_p]$ of autocorrelation coefficients, we can determine the autoregressive coefficients of the return process $\boldsymbol{\phi}' = [\phi_1, \phi_2, \ldots, \phi_p]$ by solving the Yule-Walker equations (12.12). The solution is given by:

$$\boldsymbol{\phi} = \boldsymbol{R}^{-1} \boldsymbol{\rho}, \tag{12.17}$$

where $\boldsymbol{R}^{-1}$ denotes the inverse of the matrix $\mathbf{R}$.

12.4 Optimal Trend-Following in a Conventional Markov Model

12.4.1 Optimal Trend-Following in the Absence of Transaction Costs

Analytical Solution

Figure 12.1 illustrates the topology of a conventional two-state Markov model where the process can occupy either state A or state B. The one-period transition probability matrix for this model is given by:

$$\mathbf{P} = \begin{pmatrix} p_{AA} & p_{AB} \\ p_{BA} & p_{BB} \end{pmatrix} = \begin{pmatrix} 1-\alpha & \alpha \\ \beta & 1-\beta \end{pmatrix}. \qquad (12.18)$$

The one-period transition probability matrix provides information about the immediate dynamics of a two-state regime-switching process by representing the instantaneous probabilities of transitioning from one state to another. For instance, if the process is in state A, it will transit to state B with probability p_{AB} or remain in state A with probability $p_{AA} = 1 - p_{AB}$. Similarly, when the process is in state B, it will transit to state A with probability p_{BA} or remain in state B with probability $p_{BB} = 1 - p_{BA}$. To simplify the notation, we denote the probability p_{AB} as α and the probability p_{BA} as β.

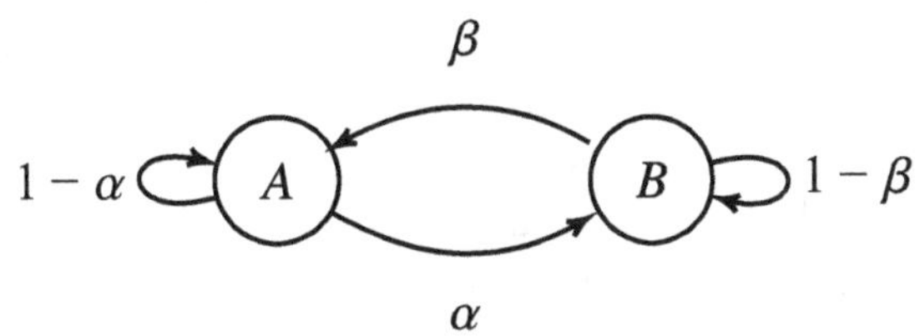

Fig. 12.1 Topology of a conventional Markov model. State A is a bull state of the market, while state B is a bear state of the market

The elements of the k-period transition probability matrix $\mathbf{P}(k)$ are obtained by raising the one-period transition probability matrix $\mathbf{P}$ to the power of k, that is, $\mathbf{P}(k) = \mathbf{P}^k$. The resulting matrix gives the probabilities of the system being in each state after k periods (see, for example, Hamilton (1994), Chapter 22):

$$\mathbf{P}(k) = \begin{pmatrix} p_{AA}(k) & p_{AB}(k) \\ p_{BA}(k) & p_{BB}(k) \end{pmatrix} = \begin{pmatrix} \pi_A + \pi_B\delta^k & \pi_B - \pi_B\delta^k \\ \pi_A - \pi_A\delta^k & \pi_B + \pi_A\delta^k \end{pmatrix}, \qquad (12.19)$$

where

$$\delta = 1 - \alpha - \beta, \tag{12.20}$$

and the steady-state probabilities are given by:

$$\pi_A = \frac{\beta}{\alpha + \beta}, \quad \pi_B = \frac{\alpha}{\alpha + \beta}. \tag{12.21}$$

To calculate the lag-k autocorrelation, we can use the solutions for $p_{AB}(k)$ and $p_{BA}(k)$, the probabilities of transitioning from state A to state B and from state B to state A after k periods, respectively. By substituting these solutions into Eq. (12.16), we obtain the expression for the lag-k autocorrelation:

$$\rho_k = c\,\delta^k, \tag{12.22}$$

where c is a constant given by:

$$c = \frac{\pi_A \pi_B (\mu_A - \mu_B)^2}{\sigma^2}. \tag{12.23}$$

Since the real-life state transition probabilities are quite low, the value of δ is positive. As a result, the return process defined by the Markov model exhibits persistence. For instance, when the market is in a bull state, it tends to stay in that state. The autocorrelation of returns decreases exponentially toward zero as the lag k increases, indicating that the relationship between returns weakens over time.

The solution for the autoregressive coefficients of a return process following a two-state conventional Markov model is given by Eq. (12.22). According to Poskitt and Chung (1996), an h-state Markov model can be represented as an $ARMA(h-1, h-1)$ model with a homogeneous zero-mean white noise process. Therefore, the observations of the return process in a two-state Markov model are identical to those of an ARMA(1,1) model. This means that the return process in a two-state Markov model can also be expressed as:

$$r_t = \omega + \varphi r_{t-1} + \varepsilon_t - \vartheta \varepsilon_{t-1}, \tag{12.24}$$

where ω, φ, and ϑ are constants and ε_t is a homogeneous zero-mean white noise process.

Any invertible $ARMA(p, q)$ process can be represented as an $AR(\infty)$ process. In the previous chapter of this book, we have shown that the $AR(\infty)$ representation of the process defined by Eq. (12.24) is given by:

$$r_t = \gamma + \sum_{i=1}^{\infty} (\varphi - \vartheta)\vartheta^{i-1} r_{t-i} + \varepsilon_t. \tag{12.25}$$

Equation (12.25) can be viewed as Eq. (12.2) where the autoregressive terms are specified by:

$$\phi_i = (\varphi - \vartheta)\vartheta^{i-1}. \tag{12.26}$$

Based on this result, we can conclude that the optimal technical indicator for returns following a two-state Markov model and without transaction costs is expressed by:

$$I_t(n) = \sum_{i=0}^{\infty} a(\varphi - \vartheta)\vartheta^i r_{t-i}, \tag{12.27}$$

where $a > 0$ is any real constant. Apparently, this technical indicator corresponds to the technical indicator of the price and EMA crossover (P-EMA) rule when $a = (\varphi - \vartheta)^{-1}$. The technical indicator of the P-EMA rule is specified by:

$$I_t(n) = \sum_{i=0}^{\infty} \lambda^i r_{t-i}, \tag{12.28}$$

where the decay constant $\lambda = \vartheta$ and the value of n is given by $n = \frac{1+\vartheta}{1-\vartheta}$.

Our objective now is to derive the analytical expressions for φ and ϑ. According to Box et al. (2016), Chapter 3, the lag-1 autocorrelation of the ARMA(1,1) process can be expressed as:

$$\rho_1 = \frac{(\varphi - \vartheta)(1 - \varphi\vartheta)}{1 - 2\varphi\vartheta + \vartheta^2}. \tag{12.29}$$

Furthermore, for any ρ_k where $k > 1$, we have:

$$\rho_k = \rho_1 \varphi^{k-1}. \tag{12.30}$$

The expression for the lag-k return autocorrelation in Eq. (12.30) is similar to the lag-k return autocorrelation in Eq. (12.22). This similarity directly stems from the duality between a two-state Markov process and an ARMA(1,1) process. By comparing Eqs. (12.30) and (12.22), we can infer that:

$$\varphi = \delta = 1 - \alpha - \beta. \tag{12.31}$$

This expression is intuitive because φ captures the persistence of the ARMA(1,1) process. As the values of α and β decrease, φ increases, indicating greater persistence. A higher φ means the process is more likely to remain in its current state rather than transition to another.

We can compute the analytic formula for ϑ by equating Eqs. (12.29) and (12.22) when $k = 1$. This leads to the following equation:

$$\frac{(\varphi - \vartheta)(1 - \varphi\vartheta)}{1 - 2\varphi\vartheta + \vartheta^2} = c\,\varphi. \tag{12.32}$$

This equation is quadratic in ϑ, and thus, we can solve for ϑ using the quadratic formula. Doing so gives us two roots:

$$\vartheta_1 = d - \sqrt{d^2 - 1}, \quad \vartheta_2 = d + \sqrt{d^2 - 1},$$

where d is given by:

$$d = \frac{1 + \varphi^2(1 - 2c)}{2\varphi(1 - c)}. \tag{12.33}$$

Since $d > 1$ (otherwise, both roots are complex numbers), we can conclude that $\vartheta_2 > 1$. Consequently, in this case, the ARMA(1,1) process is non-stationary, and the only valid solution to Eq. (12.32) is given by ϑ_1. Therefore, we have the analytical formula for ϑ as follows:

$$\vartheta = d - \sqrt{d^2 - 1}. \tag{12.34}$$

Comparative Statics Analysis

In the absence of transaction costs, we are able to obtain the analytical solution for the autoregressive coefficients of the return process and, consequently, the return weights in the optimal technical indicator for trend-following. This analytical solution allows us to conduct a comparative statics analysis, providing valuable insights into the dependence of the optimal decay constant, λ, on the model parameters.

In particular, under the conventional Markov chain assumption, the autoregressive coefficients of the return process are specified by Eq. (12.25). As a result, the technical indicator of the P-EMA(n) trading rule uses the decay constant $\lambda = \vartheta$. Equation (12.34) provides the solution for ϑ. By applying this equation to empirical data (as discussed in a specific section below in this chapter), we estimate the optimal decay constant to be $\lambda = 0.803$. Consequently, the optimal n in the P-EMA rule is approximately 9.

While we are able to estimate the optimal size of the averaging window in the P-EMA rule, there remains a lack of fundamental understanding regarding how the optimal window size depends on model parameters. To address this gap, a comparative statics analysis is necessary. There are six parameters in the Markov process for returns: $\alpha, \beta, \mu_A, \mu_B, \sigma_A$, and σ_B. However, empirical data suggests that market states differ mainly in the mean returns rather than the standard deviation. Therefore, for simplicity, we assume that $\mu_A = -\mu_B = \mu$ and $\sigma_A = \sigma_B = \sigma$. Additionally, the transition probability β is roughly twice as large as the transition probability α. Thus, for simplicity, we assume that $\beta = 2\alpha$. These assumptions allow us to investigate how the optimal n in the P-EMA(n) rule depends on three key parameters: μ, σ, and α.

To begin our comparative statics analysis, we fix $\alpha = 0.05$ and set σ to values of 20% and 30%, and calculate the optimal n for various values of μ ranging from 10% to 40%. These results are displayed in Panel A of Fig. 12.2. Next, we fix $\alpha = 0.05$ and set μ to values of 20% and 30%, and calculate the optimal n for various values of σ ranging from 10% to 40%. These results are displayed in Panel B of Fig. 12.2.

The conclusion that can be drawn from these figures is that the optimal window size of the P-EMA rule increases when the state volatility increases or the mean state return decreases. The fraction $\frac{|\mu_A - \mu_B|}{\sigma}$ can be interpreted as the *signal-to-noise ratio* of the market returns, where a higher ratio corresponds to a smaller optimal n and a lower ratio corresponds to a larger optimal n.

Finally, we investigate the dependence of the optimal n on the transition probability α. For this purpose, we fix $\frac{|\mu_A - \mu_B|}{\sigma} \in \{2, 3\}$ (in annual terms) and vary $\alpha \in [0.02, 0.20]$. Panel C of Fig. 12.2 plots the results. We conclude that the optimal n decreases as the state transition probability increases.

An economic interpretation of the results of our comparative statics analysis is as follows: any trend-following indicator must simultaneously achieve two goals: accurately determining the trend direction and identifying turning points in the trend as early as possible. First, it is important to note that any trend-following indicator identifies turning points in the trend with some delay. Second, as the averaging window size increases, both the accuracy in forecasting the trend direction and the lag time in determining trend change increase.

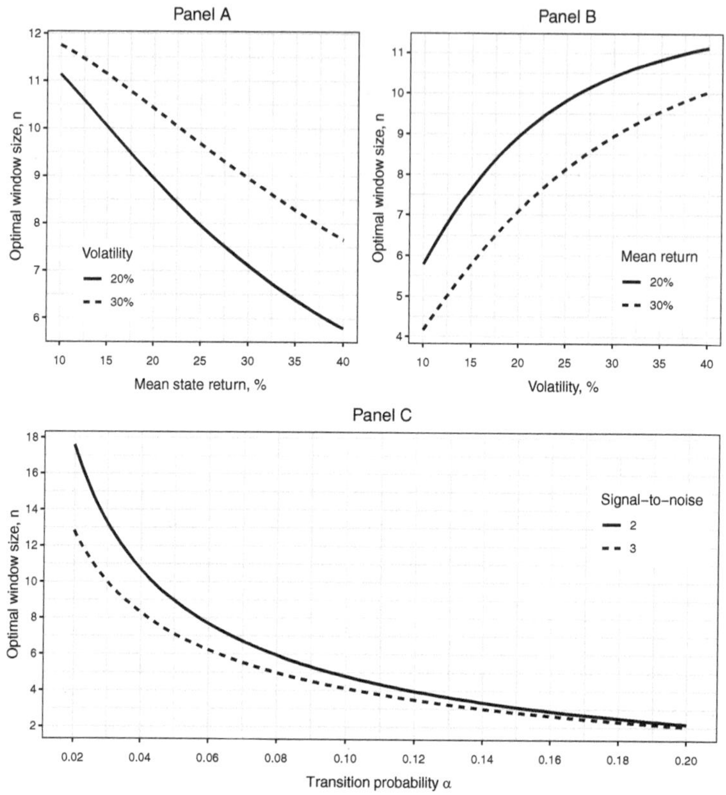

Fig. 12.2 Comparative statics of the optimal window size in the P-EMA rule as a function of the Markov model parameters

Therefore, it is not possible to achieve both goals simultaneously; instead, one must find the optimal tradeoff between accuracy and lag time.

The higher the signal-to-noise ratio of returns, the easier it is to identify the trend direction. Therefore, a high signal-to-noise ratio allows for a decrease in lag time without a significant sacrifice in accuracy by decreasing the averaging window size. This explains why the optimal window size decreases when either the state mean return increases or the state volatility decreases. The negative relationship between the state transition probability and the optimal window size can be explained similarly. The larger the state transition probability, the shorter the time the market stays in the same state. Consequently, if the market state changes frequently, an indicator with a shorter delay time is necessary. This shorter delay time can be achieved by decreasing the averaging window size.

To conclude this section, we note that the results of the comparative statics analysis of our theoretical model support and expand on the hypothesis proposed by Kaufman (1995). In particular, Kaufman proposed the use of an EMA, where the size of the averaging window is directly proportional to the market volatility. The Kaufman Adaptive Moving Average decreases (increases) the averaging window size when the return volatility is low (high). Our analysis confirms his hypothesis that the optimal window size is affected by market volatility and adds that the optimal window size is also influenced by the mean market return and state transition probabilities.

12.4.2 Optimal Trend-Following in the Presence of Transaction Costs and Empirical Application

Section 12.2 of this chapter outlines a procedure to determine the return weights of the optimal technical indicator, taking transaction costs into account. The procedure begins by identifying the autoregressive coefficients of the return process under a two-state Markov model. Then, an appropriate transaction cost level is selected and numerical optimization is performed. The result of the numerical optimization is the vector of return weights for the technical indicators that ensure the best performance of the trend-following strategy.

In the absence of transaction costs, the return weights of the optimal technical indicator decrease exponentially with the return lag. However, when transaction costs are present, these return weights become a smoothed version of those without transaction costs. Consequently, the qualitative shape of the return weights with transaction costs can be anticipated. Specifically, the return weights form a hump shape, where the weights for both the most recent and the most distant return lags are smaller than those in the middle of the averaging window.

To provide a concrete example, we estimate the optimal return weights to follow trends in the US stock market under various levels of transaction costs. This is achieved through an empirical application using real-world data, specifically monthly returns from the S&P 500 stock market index spanning January 1926 to December 2020. The S&P 500 index serves as a benchmark for the US stock market. We sourced the data from the Center for Research in Security Prices (CRSP) database. To identify bull and bear markets, we reconstructed the stock index values from the returns and applied the method proposed by Pagan and Sossounov (2003), which is widely recognized in the literature for this purpose.

Table 12.1 provides a summary of the descriptive statistics of the bull and bear states in the US stock market. These statistics closely match those reported in the study by Pagan and Sossounov (2003).

Table 12.1 Summary statistics of the bull and bear market states. Duration is measured in months. Mean returns and standard deviations are annualized and reported in percentages. Transition probability is the probability to transit to another state over a month

Statistic	Bull markets	Bear markets
Number of states	26	25
Average duration	28.54	13.48
Stationary probability, %	67.92	32.08
Transition probability, %	3.50	7.42
Mean return, %	23.79	–28.69
Standard deviation, %	16.19	19.70

From 1926 to 2020, there were 26 bull and 25 bear markets. The average duration of a bull market was approximately 28.5 months, while the average duration of a bear market was around 13.5 months. This suggests that, on average, bull markets tend to last approximately twice as long as bear markets.

The stationary state probabilities also support this observation. The probability of the US stock market being in a bull state was approximately 67.9%, while the probability of being in a bear state was about 32.1%. Similarly, the transition probability from a bear to a bull state, β, is about twice as large as the transition probability from a bull to a bear state, α. This supports the observation that bull markets tend to last longer than bear markets.

In terms of returns, the mean return during a bull market was 23.8%, while during a bear market, it was -28.7%. Additionally, the standard deviation of returns was 16.2% during a bull market and 19.7% during a bear market. These statistics highlight the differences in return characteristics between bull and bear markets.

The optimal decay constant for the P-EMA rule in our analysis is estimated to be $\lambda = 0.803$, yielding an optimal n of nearly 9. Thus, the optimal technical indicator is specified using a 9-month "averaging window." This aligns with common trading practices and is supported by empirical evidence.

For instance, the 10-month P-SMA rule is a popular trend-following strategy among traders (Faber, 2007). Additionally, the paper by Zakamulin and Giner (2020) provides evidence of strong similarities among various technical indicators based on moving averages. Specifically, the correlation between the trading signals of the 9-month P-EMA rule and the 10-month P-SMA rule is close to 100%, indicating that both trading signals are almost identical. These results lend further support to the choice of a 9-month averaging window for the technical indicator.

Figure 12.3 illustrates the optimal return weights for technical indicators at three different levels of proportional transaction costs: $\tau \in \{0.0\%, 0.5\%, 1.0\%\}$. The upper panel displays the optimal return weights in the absence of transaction costs, corresponding to the P-EMA(9) trading rule. The middle panel presents the optimal return weights with transaction costs set at 0.5%, while the bottom panel shows the optimal return weights with transaction costs are 1.0%.

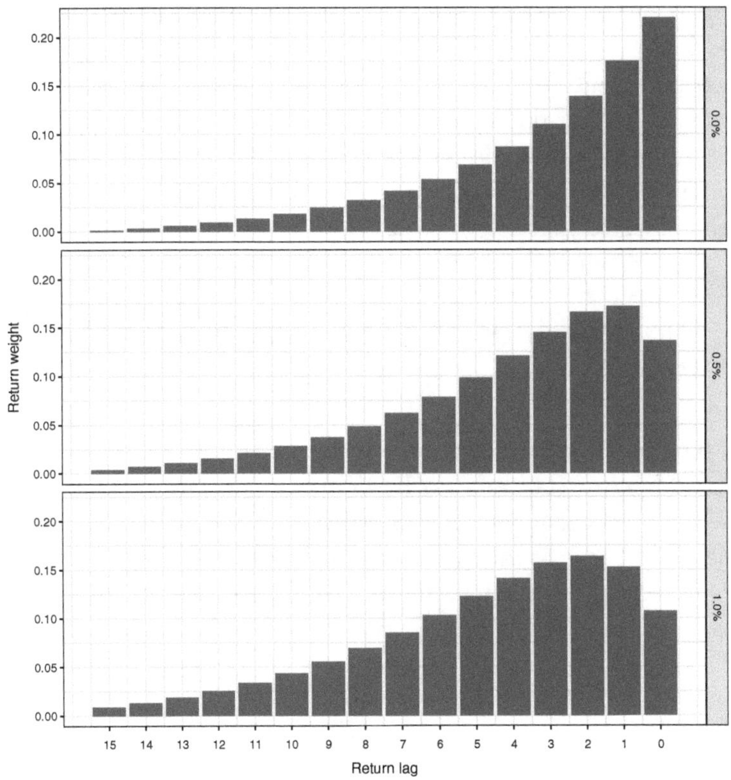

Fig. 12.3 Optimal return weights for technical indicators at various levels of proportional transaction costs. The return process is modeled using a conventional Markov model, with parameters estimated from empirical S&P 500 index data. The proportional transaction costs are set to $\tau \in \{0.0\%, 0.5\%, 1.0\%\}$

When the return process is modeled as a conventional Markov chain and transaction costs are present, the return weights of the optimal technical indicator can be approximated by the return weights in the double EMA crossover (EMA-C) rule. Specifically, when transaction costs are 0.5%, the optimal technical indicator closely resembles the EMA-C(2.5,9) rule. When transaction costs are 1.0%, the optimal technical indicator is similar to the EMA-C(4.5,9) rule. In both scenarios, the longer averaging window is set to 9. In the former case, the shorter averaging window is 2.5, and in the latter, it is 4.5.[2]

In conclusion, when the return process is modeled by a Markov chain, the optimal trend-following rule closely approximates the EMA-C(s, l) rule. The size of the longer averaging window, l, is determined by the parameters of the return process. In contrast, the size of the shorter averaging window, s, is related to the level of transaction costs. In the absence of transaction costs, $s = 0$. When the level of transaction costs increases, the value of s also increases.

The economic intuition behind this relationship is as follows: the larger the value of s, the greater the reduction in the weights of the most recent return lags. Therefore, increasing the size of s enhances the smoothness of the EMA-C rule. Better smoothness reduces the number of whipsaw trades, which in turn lowers the expected transaction costs.

12.5 Shortcomings of the Conventional Markov Model

The Markov property, often referred to in the context of Markov processes, states that the future state of a stochastic process depends only on the current state and not on the sequence of events that preceded it. In other words, given the present, the future is independent of the past.

Mathematically, for a stochastic process S_t, the Markov property can be expressed as:

$$Prob(S_{t+1}|S_t, \dots, S_0) = Prob(S_{t+1}|S_t). \qquad (12.35)$$

On the left-hand side of this equation, $Prob(S_{t+1}|S_t, \dots, S_0)$ signifies the probability of transitioning to state S_{t+1} conditioned on the process's states up to the current time (that is, $S_t, S_{t-1}, S_{t-2}, \dots, S_0$). On the right-hand side of this equation, $Prob(S_{t+1}|S_t)$ denotes the probability of transitioning to state S_{t+1}, conditioned only on the current state S_t.

In simpler terms, the Markov property states that the state of the process at a future time $t + 1$ depends solely on the present state S_t and does not depend on

[2] In principle, the sizes of both the shorter and longer averaging windows are specified as integer numbers. However, in cases where the moving average is exponential, the size of the averaging window does not correspond to the number of prices used to compute the average. When using the EMA, the size of the averaging window is used to compute the decay constant, allowing it to be a real number rather than strictly an integer.

the sequence of states that preceded it $(S_{t-1}, S_{t-2}, \ldots)$. This property implies that once the current state S_t is known, the history of the process before time t becomes irrelevant for predicting future states.

Memorylessness, as an intuitive consequence of the Markov property, describes the property of a stochastic process where the future evolution of the process does not "remember" its past states beyond its current state. In other words, the past history of the process does not influence how the process will behave in the future beyond its current state.

The absence of duration dependence is related to memorylessness but specifically refers to the idea that the probability of a future event occurring does not depend on how much time has passed since the last event occurred. In other words, the probability distribution governing the process remains the same regardless of the time elapsed since the last occurrence of the event.

In the context of market states, the absence of duration dependence implies that the probability of transitioning from one state (such as bull market) to another (like bear market) remains constant over time and does not depend on how long the current state has persisted. This concept suggests that the likelihood of a market transition is the same regardless of whether the market has been in a bull phase for a short period or an extended duration.

For instance, if the probability of a market transitioning from a bull to a bear state within a given time frame is p, this probability remains the same irrespective of whether the bull market has lasted for a few months or several years. This property is often observed in stochastic processes like Markov processes, where the transition probabilities between states are stationary and independent of the process's past history or duration in its current state.

However, while the Markov property is quite useful in modeling various real-world phenomena, it does not adequately capture the transitioning between bull and bear market states. Extensive empirical research, including studies by Cochran and Defina (1995), Maheu and McCurdy (2000), Lunde and Timmermann (2004), Ohn et al. (2004), Harman and Zuehlke (2007), and Zakamulin (2022), consistently documents that stock market cycles exhibit duration dependence. Specifically, these studies find positive duration dependence in both bull and bear market states.

Positive duration dependence implies that the longer a market state persists (whether bull or bear), the greater the likelihood that it will end. This contrasts with the Markov property, which assumes that the probability of transitioning to a new state remains constant over time and is independent of how long the current state has persisted. In stock market cycles, however, the probability of a bull market ending increases as the bull market continues, and similarly for bear markets. This phenomenon suggests a nuanced approach to modeling market dynamics that goes beyond the strict assumptions of the Markov process.

Positive duration dependence in stock market states produces mean-reverting behavior in stock market returns. Mean reversion often refers to the tendency of a market's returns to gravitate back toward its historical average or mean over time. According to this interpretation, after experiencing periods of unusually high or low returns, stocks or markets are expected to return to their long-term average performance.

However, there exists another perspective on mean reversion. In this alternative view, mean reversion implies more than just returning to the mean. It suggests that market movements can exhibit significant swings. This type of mean reversion theory posits that when stocks or markets move excessively in one direction, they are not merely correcting to the mean but are likely to overshoot in the opposite direction. For example, a period of above-average returns often precedes a subsequent period of below-average returns, and vice versa. This pattern reflects a more dynamic fluctuation around the mean rather than a simple regression to it.

The alternative view on mean reversion in stock returns is fully in agreement with a regime-switching behavior in market returns. A bull market is a period of above-average market returns. A bull market inevitably transits to a bear market which is a period of below-average returns. When market states exhibit positive duration dependence, there is some regularity in stock market cycles.

While return persistence is characterized by positive autocorrelation at short lags, mean reversion is characterized by negative autocorrelation at longer lags. Empirical research extensively documents the presence of mean reversion in stock market returns. Key studies include Fama and French (1988), Jegadeesh (1991), Balvers et al. (2000), and more recently, Giner and Zakamulin (2023).

The conventional two-state Markov model is widely used in modeling stock returns and successfully replicates several stylized facts of financial asset returns, such as fat tails, negative skewness, volatility clustering, and short-term momentum. However, it falls short in capturing medium-term mean reversion. A key limitation of the Markov model is that the probability of transitioning between states remains constant and does not depend on how long a state has persisted.

Because of this, the dynamics of returns in a Markov model do not fully mirror real-world behaviors. As a result, technical indicators optimized for tracking trends within a Markov framework may not perform optimally in actual financial markets.

To address these shortcomings, there is a pressing need to develop regime-switching models that incorporate positive duration dependence and mean reversion. These models would more accurately reflect the complex dynamics observed in financial markets. Investigating optimal trend-following strategies within such models is crucial for improving market analysis and forecasting.

This topic will be further explored in the remainder of this chapter, with a focus on advancing our understanding and modeling capabilities in financial market dynamics. Specifically, the exploration will delve into developing models that incorporate positive duration dependence and mean reversion, aiming to create a more realistic representation of market behavior. Additionally, the chapter will investigate optimal trend-following strategies within these enhanced models, addressing the limitations of conventional Markov frameworks and seeking to improve performance in real market environments.

12.6 Optimal Trend-Following in a Semi-Markov Model

12.6.1 Topology Design

A significant limitation of conventional Markov models is their memorylessness, meaning that the probability of a state change does not depend on the time elapsed since entering the state. In other words, Markov models lack duration dependence. To address this, one can replace a Markov switching model with a semi-Markov switching model, which incorporates duration dependence.

However, while semi-Markov models offer great flexibility and can more accurately model a broader range of real-world processes, they do so at the cost of increased mathematical, computational, and interpretative complexity. Specifically, semi-Markov models are not analytically tractable, requiring solutions to be obtained through numerical methods. These methods are often highly complex, involving difficult recursive numerical algorithms. Consequently, practical applications of semi-Markov models are relatively rare.

One simple method for constructing a semi-Markov model is by using an expanded-state Markov model. In an expanded-state Markov model, each individual state of the process is represented by several sub-states within a conventional Markov model. Although this approach offers less flexibility compared to an authentic semi-Markov model, it has a significant advantage: it allows the application of all well-established methods available for Markov models. For instance, instead of implementing complex recursive numerical algorithms, one can compute the multi-period transition probability matrix using straightforward matrix multiplication.

Giner and Zakamulin (2023) proposed an expanded-state Markov model with a specific state transition structure for the return process. They demonstrated that this return process exhibits short-term persistence and medium-term mean reversion. Through empirical application, they calibrated this model to real-world data and showed that the fit is reasonably good. Subsequently, Zakamulin and Giner (2024) investigated optimal trend-following within their expanded-state Markov model, albeit in the absence of transaction costs.

The goal of this section is to explain the construction of the expanded-state Markov model suggested by Giner and Zakamulin and detail its properties. Furthermore, this section examines optimal trend-following in this model, in both the absence and presence of transaction costs.

Figure 12.4 illustrates the topology of the expanded-state Markov model proposed by Giner and Zakamulin. This model comprises two macro (semi-Markovian) states, A and B. As before, state A represents a bullish market state, while state B represents a bearish market state. Macro-state A is divided into q sub-states (denoted by $A_1, A_2, \ldots, A_q$), and macro-state B is divided into s sub-states (denoted by $B_1, B_2, \ldots, B_s$). When both $q = 1$ and $s = 1$, this expanded-state Markov model simplifies to the conventional Markov model depicted in Fig. 12.1.

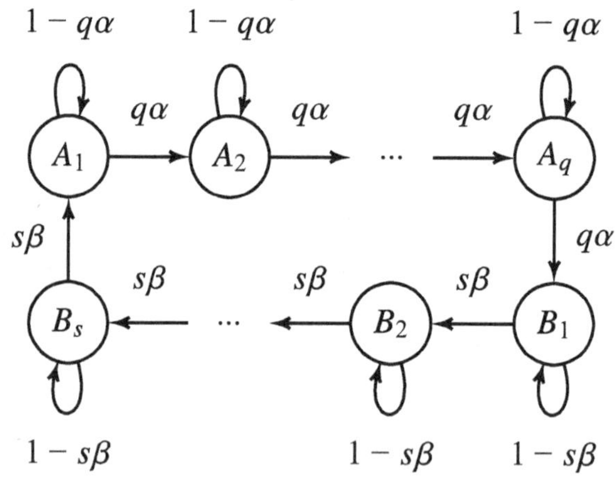

Fig. 12.4 Topology of the expanded-state Markov model. Macro-state (semi-Markovian state) A is a bull state of the market and is represented by q sub-states (Markovian states) denoted as $A_1, A_2, \ldots, A_q$. Macro-state B is a bear state of the market and consists of s sub-states denoted as $B_1, B_2, \ldots, B_s$

As long as the return process occupies state A_i, $i \in [1, q]$, the market is in the bull state. Each of the q sub-states of macro-state A is with self-transition, and the transition to the next macro-state is possible only from the last qth sub-state. The transition probability from state A_i to the next state A_{i+1} or

B_1 is $q\alpha$, while the self-transition probability is $1 - q\alpha$. Similarly, as long as the return process occupies state B_i, $i \in [1, s]$, the market is in the bear state. In this case, the transition and self-transition probabilities are $s\beta$ and $1 - s\beta$, respectively.

Note that we assume that the transition probability $q\alpha$ is the same for each sub-state $1, 2, \ldots, q$ of state A. Under this assumption, macro-state A duration time, d_A, follows a negative binomial distribution $d_A \sim NB(q)$. The probability mass function of this distribution is specified by:

$$f(n, q, p_{ii}) = Prob(d_A = n) = \binom{n-1}{n-q}(1 - q\alpha)^q (q\alpha)^{n-q}, \quad n \geq q. \tag{12.36}$$

The geometric distribution is a special case of the negative binomial distribution when $q = 1$. That is, the state duration times in the conventional Markov model follows the geometric distribution.

The mean duration times for macro-states A and B are given by:

$$E[d_A] = \frac{q}{1 - q\alpha}, \quad E[d_B] = \frac{s}{1 - s\alpha},$$

where $E[d_A]$ denotes the mean duration time of macro-state A, and $E[d_B]$ denotes the mean duration time of macro-state B.

A very useful tool for duration analysis is the hazard function, defined as the probability that an event will occur in the next instant, given that it has not occurred yet. The hazard function is defined as:

$$h(n) = \frac{f(n)}{1 - F(n)},$$

where $f(n)$ is the probability mass function of the state durations and $F(n)$ is the corresponding cumulative distribution function.

Essentially, the hazard function gives a conditional failure rate, which enables analysts to measure the likelihood of an event ending given that it has lasted up to a particular point in time. For instance, while analyzing the duration of a market state, the hazard function gives the probability that the market state ends at time n, given that it has lasted till that time.

The hazard function can also help identify duration dependence, which refers to whether the probability of an event occurring at a particular time depends on how long it has lasted. If the hazard function is constant, there is no duration dependence, meaning that the likelihood of an event ending remains the same regardless of how long it has already lasted. In contrast, if the hazard function is an increasing function of time, there is positive duration dependence, suggesting that the longer an event lasts, the more likely it is to end.

The left panel of Fig. 12.5 illustrates various shapes of the negative binomial distribution $NB(q)$ for $q \in 1, 2, 4$, while the right panel shows the shapes of the corresponding hazard functions. For consistent comparison, the mean state duration time is always 20, regardless of the value of q. That is, regardless of the shape of the probability distribution that describes the transition between macro-states A and B, the mean duration time of macro-state A is the same.

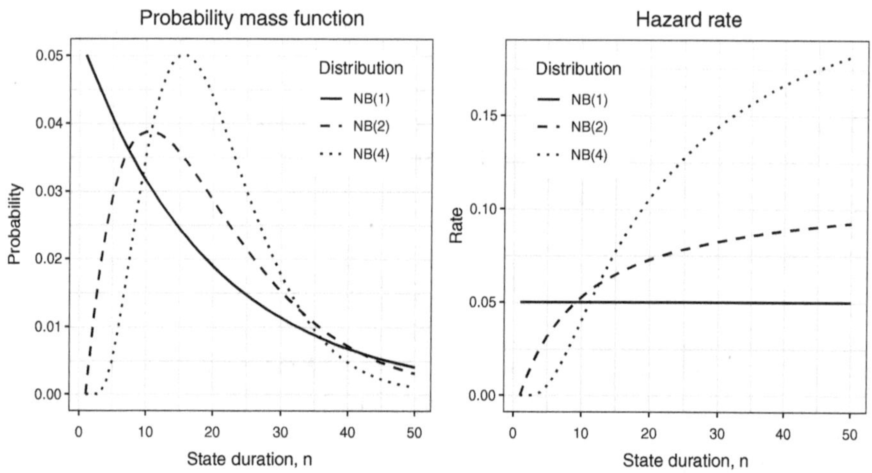

Fig. 12.5 Probability mass functions and hazard rates of state durations in the expanded-state Markov model. The left panel presents the probability mass function of the negative binomial distribution $NB(q)$ for $q \in \{1, 2, 4\}$. The right panel displays the corresponding hazard rates. In all cases, the mean state duration remains 20

Note that in the conventional Markov model where $q = 1$, the probability mass function follows an exponential decrease, while the hazard function remains constant. A constant hazard function indicates that the probability of a state ending is independent of how long the process has been in that state. This means that for $q = 1$, the distribution of state duration is memoryless.

When $q > 1$, we observe positive duration dependence in the state duration distribution. This can be attributed to the hazard function, which has an increasing slope with the state duration (age) n. As q increases, the hazard function slope becomes steeper. This leads to a higher probability of state termination and a stronger positive duration dependence.

Increasing the value of q leads to a more concentrated shape of the probability mass function around the mean duration time. When $q = 1$ and there is no duration dependence, the probability of state termination is high for short durations and remains relatively high for long durations compared to cases where $q > 1$. This means that in a memoryless distribution, the state duration time can vary greatly, ranging from very short to very long. However, with $q > 1$, the probability of state termination is low for both small and large durations. As a result, in the presence of positive duration dependence, the state duration time tends to cluster around the mean duration time. This clustering effect gives rise to periodicity in state changes and induces mean-reverting behavior.

12.6.2 Computation of Transition Probabilities and Autoregressive Coefficients

To understand the expanded-state Markov model more clearly, consider a straightforward example where each macro-state is composed of only two sub-states, $q = s = 2$. Specifically, state A is divided into sub-states A_1 and A_2, while state B is divided into sub-states B_1 and B_2. In this scenario, the one-period transition probability matrix is as follows:

$$\mathbf{P} = \begin{bmatrix} p_{A_1A_1} & p_{A_1A_2} & p_{A_1B_1} & p_{A_1B_2} \\ p_{A_2A_1} & p_{A_2A_2} & p_{A_2B_1} & p_{A_2B_2} \\ p_{B_1A_1} & p_{B_1A_2} & p_{B_1B_1} & p_{B_1B_2} \\ p_{B_2A_1} & p_{B_2A_2} & p_{B_2B_1} & p_{B_2B_2} \end{bmatrix} = \begin{bmatrix} 1-2\alpha & 2\alpha & 0 & 0 \\ 0 & 1-2\alpha & 2\alpha & 0 \\ 0 & 0 & 1-2\beta & 2\beta \\ 2\beta & 0 & 0 & 1-2\beta \end{bmatrix}. \tag{12.37}$$

To illustrate, if the process is currently in sub-state A_1, it has two possibilities during a single period. Specifically, it can transition to sub-state A_2 with a probability of $p_{A_1A_2} = 2\alpha$, or it can remain in sub-state A_1 with a probability of $p_{A_1A_1} = 1 - 2\alpha$. In the case the process is in sub-state A_2, it has two potential outcomes over one period. In particular, it may transition to sub-state B_1 with a probability of $p_{A_2B_1} = 2\alpha$, or it may persist in sub-state A_2 with a probability of $p_{A_2A_2} = 1 - 2\alpha$. Similarly, if the process occupies state B_1, it can either transition to sub-state B_2 with a probability of $p_{B_1B_2} = 2\beta$, or it can stay in sub-state B_1 with a probability of $p_{B_1B_1} = 1 - 2\beta$ during a single period. Finally, if the process is in sub-state B_2, it may either transition to sub-state A_1 with a probability of $p_{B_2A_1} = 2\beta$, or it may remain in sub-state B_2 with a probability of $p_{B_2B_2} = 1 - 2\beta$ over a single period.

It is worth noting that the probabilities of remaining in the same sub-state for A_1 and A_2 (B_1 and B_2) are equal, denoted as $p_{A_1A_1} = p_{A_2A_2}$ ($p_{B_1B_1} = p_{B_2B_2}$). This implies that the probabilities of transitioning from one sub-state of macro-state A (B) to another sub-state or to a different macro-state are also equal to each other, symbolized as $p_{A_1A_2} = p_{A_2B_1}$ ($p_{B_1B_2} = p_{B_2A_1}$).

In the extended-state Markov model described by the transition probability matrix in (12.37), the self-transition probability of macro-state A can be calculated as follows. Given that the process is in macro-state A, it is equally probable to be in either sub-state A_1 or A_2. If the process is currently in sub-state A_1, then the probability of remaining in macro-state A is the sum of $p_{A_1A_1}$ and $p_{A_1A_2}$. Similarly, if the process is in sub-state A_2, the probability of remaining in macro-state A is the sum of $p_{A_2A_1}$ and $p_{A_2A_2}$. Hence, the probability p_{AA} can be computed as the average of $p_{A_1A_1} + p_{A_1A_2}$ and $p_{A_2A_1} + p_{A_2A_2}$.

All other transition probabilities can be calculated in a similar fashion:

$$\begin{aligned}
p_{AA} &= (p_{A_1A_1} + p_{A_1A_2} + p_{A_2A_1} + p_{A_2A_2})/2,\\
p_{AB} &= (p_{A_1B_1} + p_{A_1B_2} + p_{A_2B_1} + p_{A_2B_2})/2,\\
p_{BA} &= (p_{B_1A_1} + p_{B_1A_2} + p_{B_2A_1} + p_{B_2A_2})/2,\\
p_{BB} &= (p_{B_1B_1} + p_{B_1B_2} + p_{B_2B_1} + p_{B_2B_2})/2.
\end{aligned} \tag{12.38}$$

The k-period transition probability matrix in the extended-state Markov model can be represented as:

$$\mathbf{P}(k) = \mathbf{P}^k = \begin{bmatrix} p_{A_1A_1}(k) & p_{A_1A_2}(k) & p_{A_1B_1}(k) & p_{A_1B_2}(k) \\ p_{A_2A_1}(k) & p_{A_2A_2}(k) & p_{A_2B_1}(k) & p_{A_2B_2}(k) \\ p_{B_1A_1}(k) & p_{B_1A_2}(k) & p_{B_1B_1}(k) & p_{B_1B_2}(k) \\ p_{B_2A_1}(k) & p_{B_2A_2}(k) & p_{B_2B_1}(k) & p_{B_2B_2}(k) \end{bmatrix}. \tag{12.39}$$

It is important to note that the k-period transition probability matrix is obtained by raising the one-period transition probability matrix $\mathbf{P}$ to the power of k.

The k-period transition probabilities of macro-states A and B are computed similarly to how we calculated the one-period transition probabilities. For example, the k-period self-transition probability of macro-state A is computed as $p_{AA}(k) = (p_{A_1A_1}(k) + p_{A_1A_2}(k) + p_{A_2A_1}(k) + p_{A_2A_2}(k))/2$. This probability represents the likelihood of the process, starting in macro-state A, of remaining in macro-state A after k periods. Similarly, we can compute the k-period transition probabilities for macro-state B.

In the expanded-state Markov model, the one-period transition probabilities are chosen to be consistent with the one-period transition probabilities of macro-states in the conventional Markov model. For instance, if $p_{AA} = 1 - \alpha$ represents the probability of staying in macro-state A in the conventional model, then in the expanded-state model, we select $(p_{A_1A_1} +$

$p_{A_1A_2} + p_{A_2A_1} + p_{A_2A_2})/2 = 1 - \alpha$, where α is the probability of transitioning from macro-state A to macro-state B in the conventional model. This alignment ensures that both models have the same average duration time in each macro-state.

Moreover, the expanded-state Markov model shares the same macro-state stationary probabilities (π_A and π_B) with the conventional Markov model. This means that over the long run, the proportion of time spent in each macro-state will be the same in both models. This provides a convenient basis for comparing and contrasting the behavior of the process under different modeling approaches.

By maintaining these consistent features between the expanded-state and conventional Markov models, we facilitate a straightforward comparison and comprehension of the results obtained from each model. This comparability allows us to leverage the insights and analyses from the conventional Markov model in the context of the expanded-state Markov model.

Now, let us consider a general scenario where macro-states A and B are composed of q and s sub-states, respectively. In this case, the one-period transition probability matrix, $\mathbf{P}$, is a $(q+s) \times (q+s)$ matrix that can be partitioned as follows:

$$\mathbf{P} = \left[\begin{array}{c|c} \mathbf{P}_{AA} & \mathbf{P}_{AB} \\ \hline \mathbf{P}_{BA} & \mathbf{P}_{BB} \end{array}\right],$$

where $\mathbf{P}_{AA}$ is the $q \times q$ sub-matrix, $\mathbf{P}_{AB}$ is the $q \times s$ sub-matrix, $\mathbf{P}_{BA}$ is the $s \times q$ sub-matrix, and $\mathbf{P}_{BB}$ is the $s \times s$ sub-matrix.

In the general scenario, the one-period transition probabilities between sub-states follow the relation $p_{A_iA_{i+1}} = q\alpha$ and $p_{B_iB_{i+1}} = s\beta$. For example, for each of the q sub-states in macro-state A, the transition probability is q times the corresponding transition probability in a standard Markov model. This relationship guarantees that both the semi-Markov and Markov models have the same one-period self-transition probabilities and transition probabilities between states A and B.

To calculate the self-transition probability (p_{AA} or p_{BB}) of macro-states A or B, we sum all elements in the corresponding sub-matrix ($\mathbf{P}_{AA}$ or $\mathbf{P}_{BB}$) and divide the result by q or s. We can then obtain the complementary probability (p_{AB} or p_{BA}) by subtracting the self-transition probability from 1. For any number of sub-states in each macro-state, we can compute the k-period transition probability matrix using $\mathbf{P}(k) = \mathbf{P}^k$.

Giner and Zakamulin (2023) demonstrate that the expanded-state Markov model with two sub-states for each macro-state can be analyzed analytically. Specifically, they derive analytical solutions for the k-period transition probabilities $p_{AB}(k)$ and $p_{BA}(k)$, which are necessary to calculate the lag-k return autocorrelation. As a result, in the absence of transaction costs, an analytical solution for the return weights in the optimal trend-following strategy can be computed when the bull and bear state duration times follow the $NB(2)$ distribution. Regardless of the number of sub-states in each macro-state, the k-period transition probabilities can be computed using matrix multiplication techniques available in commonly used mathematical software programs, provided that the one-period transition probability matrix in the expanded-state Markov model is defined.

Figure 12.6 plots the monthly autoregressive coefficients in the expanded-state Markov model with q sub-states for each macro-state, with $q \in \{1, 2, 4\}$. These autoregressive coefficients are computed numerically using the following model parameters: the annualized mean returns for state A and state B are $\mu_A = 25\%$ and $\mu_B = -25\%$. Both states have annualized standard deviations of returns at $\sigma_A = \sigma_B = 18\%$. The average duration of state A is 28 months, while the average duration of state B is 14 months.

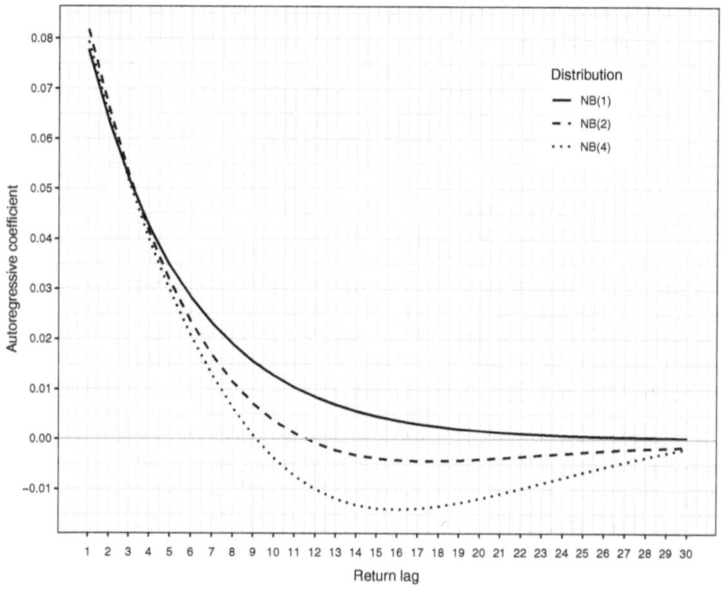

Fig. 12.6 Monthly autoregressive coefficients in the expanded-state Markov model with q sub-states for each macro-state, with $q \in \{1, 2, 4\}$. The annualized mean state returns are $\mu_A = 25\%$ and $\mu_B = -25\%$. Both states have annualized standard deviations of returns at $\sigma_A = \sigma_B = 18\%$. The average duration of state A is 28 months, while the average duration of state B is 14 months. Autoregressive coefficients are considered up to lag 30

The curves in Fig. 12.6 suggest the following observations. In the conventional Markov model, state duration times follow a memoryless NB(1) distribution. In this scenario, the autoregressive coefficients are always positive and decrease exponentially toward zero as the lag length increases, resulting in the return process exhibiting only short-term momentum.

In contrast, the expanded-state Markov model with $q > 1$ shows autoregressive coefficients that exhibit a damped oscillating behavior around zero, periodically switching from positive to negative. Due to the rapid decay of these oscillations, we primarily observe positive autocorrelations at short lags and negative autocorrelations at longer lags.

To summarize, when state duration times exhibit positive duration dependence, the return process shows a pattern of short-term momentum followed by mean reversion. This pattern is characterized by positive return autocorrelation at shorter lags, indicating short-term momentum, and negative autocorrelation at longer lags, indicating medium-term mean reversion. Interestingly, Fig. 12.6 illustrates that as the degree of positive duration dependence q increases, the mean-reverting behavior becomes more pronounced. In other words, a stronger positive duration dependence leads to a more significant mean-reverting behavior.

12.6.3 Empirical Application

In our empirical application, we utilized the same dataset as discussed in Sect. 12.4.2. By utilizing the durations of the identified bull and bear states, we fitted the $NB(q)$ distribution to the state duration data to determine the optimal value of q. The maximum likelihood estimation method was used for this purpose. Through our analysis, we discovered that the negative binomial distribution with $q = 4$ generated the highest log-likelihood function for both bull and bear market states. In line with Zakamulin and Giner (2024), we can safely conclude that the durations of both bull and bear states are best captured by the $NB(4)$ distribution.

When transaction costs are not a factor, the return weights in the optimal technical indicator align with the autoregressive coefficients. However, in the presence of transaction costs, the calculation of the optimal return weights requires a numerical approach outlined in Sect. 12.2. It is important to note that this procedure aims to identify the return weights that optimize the performance of the trend-following strategy while considering the impact of transaction costs. The results of this numerical procedure are illustrated in Fig. 12.7, which shows the optimal return weights for technical indicators at varying levels of proportional transaction costs $\tau \in \{0.0\%, 0.5\%, 1.0\%\}$.

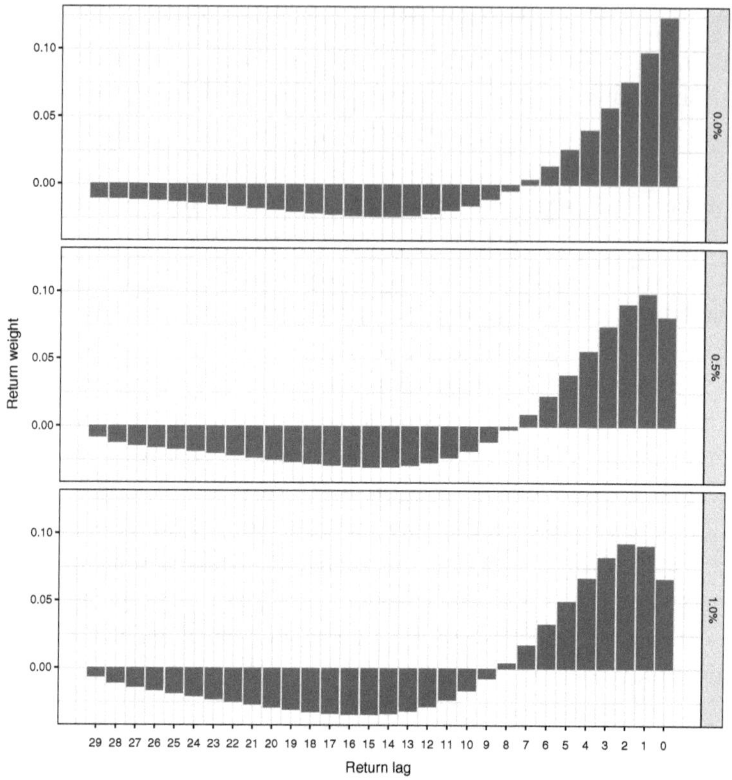

Fig. 12.7 Optimal return weights for technical indicators at various levels of proportional transaction costs. The return process is modeled using the expanded-state Markov model with four sub-states for each state, with parameters estimated from empirical S&P 500 index data. The proportional transaction costs are set to $\tau \in \{0.0\%, 0.5\%, 1.0\%\}$. The optimal return weights are considered up to lag 30

When transaction costs are not a consideration, $\tau = 0.0\%$, the pattern of the optimal return weights closely resembles the autoregressive coefficients of the return process governed by the NB(4) distribution for the state duration times. In this scenario, the autoregressive coefficients and the optimal return weights are positive and steadily decrease up until lag 8. If we focus only on the lags with positive weights and disregard the lags with negative weights, we can observe that the optimal return weights closely follow the return weights of the price and 10-month SMA crossover (P-SMA(10)) rule.

To illustrate this point, Fig. 12.8 shows a comparison between the optimal return weights in the absence of transaction costs and those in the P-SMA(10) rule. The figure confirms a strong similarity between the positive weights obtained from the optimal trading rule and those produced by the P-SMA(10) rule. This illustration advocates that, according to our theoretical model, the P-SMA(10) rule accurately captures the optimal positive weights and the duration of short-term momentum, which tends to last for around 9 months before experiencing a reversal.

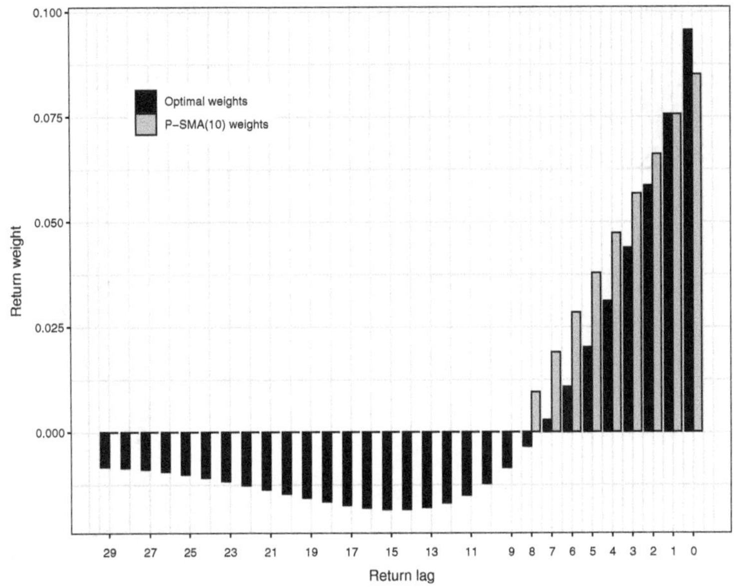

Fig. 12.8 Optimal return weights in the absence of transaction costs and the return weights in the P-SMA(10) rule. The optimal return weights are considered up to lag 30

However, our model suggests that the P-SMA(10) rule is not quite optimal for trading. This rule only considers short-term momentum and does not take into account information about medium-term mean reversion. We have found that the negative autoregressive coefficients are mainly located between lags 9 and 30, forming a U-shaped pattern. Although each negative weight is relatively small, there are more negative return weights than positive return weights. Consequently, the total sum of all return weights in the optimal technical indicator is almost zero.

In the presence of transaction costs, the optimal return weights exhibit notable similarity to those observed in the Moving Average Convergence/Divergence (MACD) rule. The MACD rule employs three EMAs to generate trading signals, and its return weights are determined by three parameters, namely s, l, and n. Here, s and l refer to the short and long moving averages, respectively, while n specifies the size of the moving average for the final smoothing. Thus, the notation MACD(s, l, n) represents the MACD rule with a specific set of values for s, l, and n.

To identify the MACD(s, l, n) rule that closely resembles the return weights in the optimal trading rule, a selection process can be employed. By comparing the shape of the return weights in the optimal trading rule with those of various MACD(s, l, n) rules, we can determine the closest correspondence. After conducting this analysis, we find that when transaction costs are at $\tau = 0.5\%$, the MACD(3,17,12) rule exhibits the highest similarity with the optimal trading rule. On the other hand, when the level of transaction costs is $\tau = 1.0\%$, the MACD(10,12,7) rule demonstrates the best resemblance to the optimal trading rule.

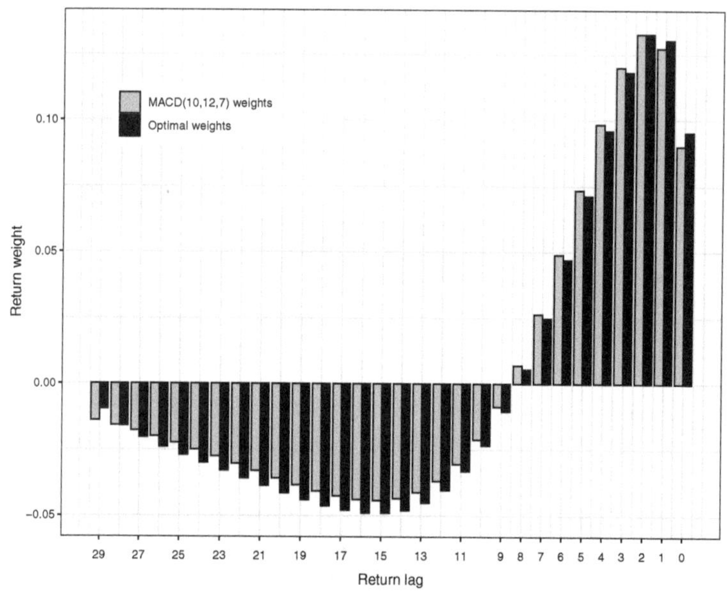

Fig. 12.9 Optimal return weights for $\tau = 1.0\%$ and the return weights in the MACD(10,12,7) rule. In both rules, the return weights are considered up to lag 30

For clarity, Fig. 12.9 displays the return weights in the optimal trading rule when $\tau = 1.0\%$, along with those in the MACD(10,12,7) rule. As depicted in the figure, the resemblance between the two sets of return weights is quite strong. Specifically, not only do the positive return weights in the optimal and MACD rules exhibit considerable similarity, but the negative return weights also closely resemble each other.

As we have previously discussed in this book, using the MACD rule can be challenging in trending markets with no mean reversion. Although the MACD rule boasts excellent responsiveness and smoothness, its trading signals are accurate only over a relatively short period following a trend reversal. Nevertheless, our theoretical model suggests that the MACD rule is nearly optimal in markets with strong mean reversion tendencies and when transaction costs are significant. In such scenarios, the MACD rule combines short-term momentum and medium-term mean reversion signals, delivering smooth trading signals that substantially reduce the frequency of whipsaw trades.

It is important to note that while the return weights in the MACD rule closely resemble those in the optimal trading rule, using the MACD rule for trend-following carries certain risks. In practice, selecting the optimal MACD parameters typically requires backtesting. However, the MACD rule is over-parameterized, with three parameters to optimize, increasing the risk of over-fitting. Overfitting occurs when a trading strategy is excessively tailored to historical data, resulting in poor performance on new or unseen data.

To mitigate the risk of overfitting and ensure the robustness of a trading strategy in live trading conditions, it is important to exercise caution when implementing the MACD rule. Instead, using the P-SMA(10) rule for trend-following can be a safer approach. Empirical studies such as Zakamulin and Giner (2024) indicate that while the optimal trading rule outperforms the P-SMA(10) rule, the difference in profitability between the two is not substantial. In other words, the profitability of a trend-following strategy is mainly derived from utilizing the short-term momentum of the market. Although using medium-term mean reversion can enhance the profitability of the strategy to some extent, it may require advanced knowledge of market dynamics to capitalize fully. Without such knowledge, trading may lead to significant losses and financial harm. Therefore, a cautious and informed approach should be undertaken when implementing trading strategies aimed at profiting from mean reversion.

12.7 Summary

Various trend-following rules are used to identify market direction by relying on past prices and incorporating different types of moving averages. These moving averages require selecting appropriate window sizes for averaging. The wide variety of rules, moving averages, and window sizes can make it challenging for investment professionals to choose the most suitable strategy.

One alternative approach to represent a technical indicator for a trend-following rule is to use a single moving average of past returns instead of moving averages of prices. This method simplifies the differences between various trading rules to the variations in the weighting function for past returns.

In essence, there are four main shapes of the weighting function for returns. The first shape involves equal return weights, as seen in the MOM rule. The second shape has return weights that decrease with the return lag, which is characteristic of all P-MA rules. The third shape exhibits a hump-shaped form where the weights of both the most recent and most distant returns are reduced compared to the weights in the middle. This hump shape is observed in all MA-C rules and certain MA-D rules that utilize moving averages with enhanced smoothness. Lastly, the weighting function for returns can take the damped waveform shape, where the weights of the most recent return lags are positive and the weights of distant return lags are negative. This shape is commonly used in trading rules that employ moving averages with reduced lag time and in the MACD rule.

Regrettably, from an academic perspective, these trend-following rules are deemed ad hoc, as they lack theoretical justification for their optimality. The introduction of these rules is usually based on superficial reasoning and supported only by anecdotal evidence of their purported superior performance. Consequently, caution should be exercised when selecting and relying on these rules for investment decision-making. Moreover, there is an urgent need for a theoretical investigation of optimal trend-following.

This book proposes quantitative measures of accuracy, responsiveness, and smoothness, which can be computed using only the weighting function for returns in a trend-following rule. These measures enable traders to compare the properties of different trend-following rules. Unfortunately, these measures do not answer the question of which trading rule is optimal for a particular market. This question has two sub-questions. The first sub-question is what shape of the return weights is optimal. The second sub-question is what is the optimal number of return lags in the moving averages. For instance, suppose we determine that the P-SMA(n) is optimal for following trends in a specific financial market. The question remains, what value of n is optimal?

Determining the optimal trading rule in a specific financial market is inherently complex and cannot be answered without a thorough understanding of the market's return process. This is because the optimal return weights in a technical indicator of a trend-following rule are derived from the autoregressive coefficients of the return process. Empirically estimating these coefficients is challenging, as they are small and often undetectable. The only remaining option is a theoretical analysis of the autoregressive coefficients within a realistic return process.

Therefore, to determine the optimal rule, we must begin by selecting a realistic return process that accurately replicates the key characteristics of financial asset returns. In this context, a two-state regime-switching model for stock returns is often employed. This model assumes that the market fluctuates between bull and bear states, reflecting different market conditions.

In our study, we employ both Markov and semi-Markov regime-switching models to examine optimal trend-following strategies. We begin by exploring the Markov model, which is a simple and tractable model that captures short-term momentum in returns, leading to the formation of price trends. However, one serious limitation of the Markov model is its inability to incorporate mean reversion, a phenomenon extensively observed in empirical studies. To address this drawback, we then delve into a semi-Markov model, which is more complex but offers the advantage of replicating not only short-term momentum but also mean reversion in returns. By considering both types of models, we gain a comprehensive understanding of optimal trend-following strategies in different market conditions.

Our findings are summarized in Fig. 12.10. The top row of the figure presents the optimal return weights in a technical indicator for trend-following in a Markov model without and with transaction costs. The bottom row of the same figure shows the optimal return weights for trend-following in a semi-Markov model. We fit both types of models to historical returns data of the S&P 500 index to derive these results. These optimal return weights represent the most effective weighting functions for capturing the trends in a given market environment.

Our analysis reveals that in a Markov model without transaction costs, the optimal trend-following rule is the P-EMA(n) rule. The return weights in this rule decline exponentially as the return lag increases. The optimal size n used to calculate the decay constant depends on the signal-to-noise ratio of returns and state transition probabilities, which determine the mean duration of each state. We find that the optimal size n decreases as the mean state returns increase, state volatilities decrease, and the mean duration of each state decreases. These factors affect the speed at which the trend-following rule adapts to changes in market conditions and therefore play a crucial role in determining the optimal strategy for trend-following.

In a Markov model that accounts for transaction costs, the optimal return weights exhibit a smoothed version of the optimal return weights in the absence of transaction costs. The optimal return weighting function takes a hump shape and can be implemented using the EMA-C(s, l) rule. The size of the longer window, l, is determined similarly to the size n in the P-EMA(n) rule. The size of the shorter window, s, is dependent on the level of transaction costs. Specifically, increasing transaction costs lead to a larger value of s, resulting in a technical indicator that is smoother and better able to mitigate the impact of whipsaw trades on trading performance. Thus, the optimal strategy in the

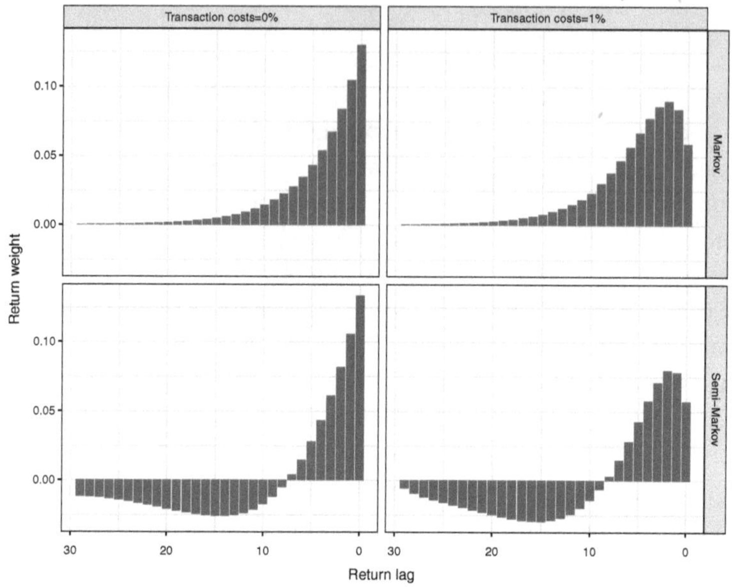

Fig. 12.10 Optimal return weights for trend-following in a Markov model and a semi-Markov model. Both types of models are fitted to historical returns data of the S&P 500 index. The left column plots the optimal return weights in the absence of transaction costs, while the right column shows the optimal return weights in the presence of transaction costs

presence of transaction costs involves balancing trend-following signals against trading costs to enhance overall performance.

In a semi-Markov model that does not account for transaction costs, the optimal return weights exhibit a distinct pattern. Initially, they decrease almost linearly to zero, followed by a small further decrease into negative territory, before gradually increasing back toward zero. The return weights consist of two parts, the first being a short, positive section that bears similarities to the return weights in the P-SMA rule. The second is a long, U-shaped negative tail that enables the trader to profit from medium-term mean reversion. While the positive part captures short-term momentum in returns, the negative part allows for additional gains from the mean reversion effect.

When transaction costs are considered in a semi-Markov model, the optimal return weights undergo some adjustments. They represent a smoothed version of the return weights in the absence of transaction costs. The first positive part of the return weights takes on a hump-shaped pattern that exhibits a high degree of smoothness. On the other hand, the second negative part of the return weights remains relatively unchanged, as this type of shape tends to be inherently smooth. Both positive and negative parts contribute to the total weighting function for returns, resulting in a damped waveform shape. This shape of the weighting function for returns resembles the shape of the return weights used in the MACD rule.

After conducting our theoretical analysis, we have discovered three primary shapes for optimal return weights: weights that decrease with the return lag, weights that exhibit a hump-shaped curve, and weights that follow a damped waveform. Each of these shapes is considered optimal under specific conditions, such as particular return processes and transaction costs. It is important to note that these optimal shapes can be achieved by using EMAs with different window sizes (decay constants). The choice of optimal window sizes is dependent on the parameters of the return process. The mean duration of the shortest state, particularly the bear state, appears to be the most critical parameter. For example, in the case of the P-EMA rule, the optimal window size is significantly shorter than the average duration of the bear state. Finally, our analysis does not support equally weighted return weights as an optimal shape.

References

Andrews, D., & Chen, H. Y. (1994). Approximately Median-Unbiased Estimation of Autoregressive Models. *Journal of Business & Economic Statistics, 12*, 187–204.

Balvers, R., Wu, Y., & Gilliland, E. (2000). Mean Reversion across National Stock Markets and Parametric Contrarian Investment Strategies. *Journal of Finance, 55*(2), 745–772.

Box, G. E. P., Jenkins, G. M., Reinsel, G. C., & Ljung, G. M. (2016). *Time Series Analysis: Forecasting and Control* (5th Edn.). Wiley.

Cochran, S. J., & Defina, R. H. (1995). Duration Dependence in the US Stock Market Cycle: A Parametric Approach. *Applied Financial Economics, 5*(5), 309–318.

Cont, R. (2001). Empirical Properties of Asset Returns: Stylized Facts and Statistical Issues. *Quantitative Finance, 1*(2), 223–236.

Faber, M. T. (2007). A Quantitative Approach to Tactical Asset Allocation. *Journal of Wealth Management, 9*(4), 69–79.

Fama, E. F., & French, K. R. (1988). Permanent and Temporary Components of Stock Prices. *Journal of Political Economy, 96*(2), 246–273.

Frühwirth-Schnatter, S. (2006). *Finite Mixture and Markov Switching Models.* Springer.

Giner, J., & Zakamulin, V. (2023). A Regime-Switching Model of Stock Returns with Momentum and Mean Reversion. *Economic Modelling, 122*, Article 106237.

Hamilton, J. D. (1994). *Time Series Analysis.* Princeton.

Harman, Y. S., & Zuehlke, T. W. (2007). Nonlinear Duration Dependence in Stock Market Cycles. *Review of Financial Economics, 16*(4), 350–362.

Jegadeesh, N. (1991). Seasonality in Stock Price Mean Reversion: Evidence from the U.S. and the U.K. *Journal of Finance, 46*(4), 1427–1444.

Kaufman, P. (1995). *Smarter Trading: Improving Performance in Changing Markets.* McGraw-Hill, Inc.

Lunde, A., & Timmermann, A. (2004). Duration Dependence in Stock Prices: An Analysis of Bull and Bear Markets. *Journal of Business and Economic Statistics, 22*(3), 253–273.

Maheu, J. M., & McCurdy, T. H. (2000). Identifying Bull and Bear Markets in Stock Returns. *Journal of Business and Economic Statistics, 18*(1), 100–112.

Ohn, J., Taylor, L. W., & Pagan, A. (2004). Testing for Duration Dependence in Economic Cycles. *Econometrics Journal, 7*(2), 528–549.

Pagan, A. R., & Sossounov, K. A. (2003). A Simple Framework for Analysing Bull and Bear Markets. *Journal of Applied Econometrics, 18*(1), 23–46.

Poskitt, D. S., & Chung, S.-H. (1996). Markov Chain Models, Time Series Analysis and Extreme Value Theory. *Advances in Applied Probability, 28*(2), 405–425.

Timmermann, A. (2000). Moments of Markov Switching Models. *Journal of Econometrics, 96*(1), 75–111.

Zakamulin, V. (2017). *Market Timing with Moving Averages: The Anatomy and Performance of Trading Rules.* Palgrave Macmillan

Zakamulin, V. (2022). Revisiting the Duration Dependence in the US Stock Market Cycles. *Applied Economics, 55*(4), 357–368.

Zakamulin, V., & Giner, J. (2020). Trend Following with Momentum Versus Moving Average: A Tale of Differences. *Quantitative Finance, 20*(6), 985–1007.

Zakamulin, V., & Giner, J. (2022). Time Series Momentum in the US Stock Market: Empirical Evidence and Theoretical Analysis. *International Review of Financial Analysis, 82,* Article 102173.

Zakamulin, V., & Giner, J. (2023). Optimal Trend-Following With Transaction Costs. *International Review of Financial Analysis, 90,* Article 102928.

Zakamulin, V., & Giner, J. (2024). Optimal Trend-Following Rules in Two-State Regime-Switching Models. *Journal of Asset Management, 25,* 327–348.

13

Profitability of Suboptimal Trend-Following Rules

13.1 Introduction

After the trader decides to implement a trend-following strategy, the next critical decision is to select the most suitable trend-following trading rule. There are various trend-following rules available, many of which are based on calculating moving averages of past prices. These moving averages can be conventional, such as simple or exponential moving averages, or more exotic. To calculate each moving average, the trader must determine the window size, which adds to the complexity of choosing a rule.

When faced with numerous potential trend-following rules, moving averages, and window sizes, the trader needs to carefully consider and select a single rule, determine the type of moving averages to use, and specify the appropriate window sizes. This can be a daunting task, but it seems to be essential for successful trading. Therefore, traders need to devise a methodology that allows them to select the most suitable trading rule.

The primary objective is to find a trading rule that is optimal for identifying and capitalizing on trends in a specific financial market. Determining the optimal trading rule involves selecting a rule that ensures the best possible performance for the trend-following strategy.

The first step in selecting the best trading rule is to obtain historical data for the desired financial market. The historical data sample must be sufficiently long to cover different market conditions, including several interchanging bull and bear markets, as well as periods of turbulence and calm. Having a comprehensive dataset ensures that the selected trading rule can be tested under various scenarios, providing a more accurate assessment of its performance.

V. Zakamulin and J. Giner, *The Ultimate Moving Average Handbook*,
https://doi.org/10.1007/978-3-031-90907-8_13

The second step in selecting the best trading rule is to choose an appropriate performance measure. Among the various performance measures available, the Sharpe ratio stands out as the most widely used and supported by financial theory. The Sharpe ratio helps traders assess the risk-adjusted return of a trading strategy, allowing them to compare the performance of different strategies on a level playing field.

Once the data is gathered and the performance measure is selected, the third step is to implement a procedure to find the best trend-following rule based on historical performance. The underlying idea is that the rule that performed the best in the past will likely continue to perform well in the future. There are two main variants of the procedure to identify the best trend-following rule: estimating the autoregressive coefficients of the return process and backtesting all potential trend-following rules.

Specifically, instead of computing one or several moving averages of past prices, the technical indicator of a trend-following rule can alternatively be computed as a single moving average of past returns. This moving average is calculated by multiplying each return by an appropriate weight and then summing all the products.

In earlier chapters of this book, we demonstrated that the return weights in the optimal technical indicator should align with the autoregressive coefficients of the return process. This alignment ensures the highest attainable Sharpe ratio for the trend-following strategy. Therefore, determining the optimal technical indicator involves identifying the order of the autoregressive process and estimating its coefficients. Traders can estimate these autoregressive coefficients using a standard Ordinary Least Squares (OLS) regression model.

The second approach to determining the optimal trading rule is based on backtesting. This method involves evaluating every possible combination of trading rules, moving averages, and window sizes to identify the most effective one. The evaluation procedure involves simulating the returns for each combination within the defined parameter space using historical data. Subsequently, the trader calculates the chosen performance measure (e.g., Sharpe ratio) for each combination. The best trend-following rule is the combination with the highest performance measure.

Traders typically rely on the backtesting method to identify the best trading rule. This method is widely regarded as thorough and effective in ensuring that the optimal rule is found. Traders also believe that the primary disadvantage of this method is its computational intensity and time-consuming nature, especially when handling large datasets and numerous parameter combinations.

We begin this chapter by evaluating the precision of each approach in accurately identifying the best trend-following rule. To assess the precision of the first approach, we use a historical sample of returns spanning 150 years. We estimate the autoregressive coefficients of the return process using an OLS regression model and analyze the statistical confidence intervals for these coefficients. Our findings reveal that the precision of estimating the autoregressive coefficients is alarmingly poor, severely hindering traders' ability to identify the optimal trading rule with any substantial degree of certainty.

The precision of the backtesting approach to finding the best trading rule is evaluated using simulated artificial historical return data. In this simulated sample, the best trading rule is known because it is determined by the shape of the autoregressive coefficients and the order of the autoregressive process. We test a set of trading rules, including the optimal one, using the backtesting procedure. Our results reveal that the precision and reliability of the backtesting methodology in accurately identifying the optimal trading rule are profoundly inadequate. Even with relatively long sample sizes, the probability of correctly pinpointing the best trading rule remains low.

Consequently, we conclude that none of the existing methods for identifying the best trading rule are both precise and reliable. This lack of precision has significant consequences for traders and their strategies. Most importantly, if the optimal trading rule cannot be identified accurately, traders are left using suboptimal rules. These suboptimal rules can result in missed opportunities for profit and increased risk, leading to overall poorer performance in trend-following strategies.

We continue this chapter with a study that investigates the performance of suboptimal trading rules. The primary objectives are to address two crucial questions. The first question is: what is the magnitude of the loss in profitability associated with using a non-optimal trend-following rule? Understanding this will help quantify the impact of relying on suboptimal strategies and provide insight into the potential financial setbacks traders might face.

The second question is: can a non-optimal trend-following strategy outperform a passive buy-and-hold strategy? This comparison will evaluate whether even imperfect trend-following rules offer a performance advantage over a passive investment approach, and if so, to what extent. By examining these questions, we aim to shed light on the practical implications of using non-optimal trading rules and offer guidance on their relative effectiveness compared to optimal investment strategies.

When traders realize that their trading rule is not optimal, the preconceived belief is that a suboptimal rule will significantly underperform compared to the optimal rule and may even perform worse than a buy-and-hold strategy. However, our findings demonstrate that these expectations are typically incorrect. Needless to say, the loss in profitability associated with using a suboptimal trend-following rule depends on the degree of dissimilarity between the optimal and suboptimal rules. Yet, our results suggest that, more often than not, the loss in profitability is not substantial, and a suboptimal rule can still outperform the passive buy-and-hold strategy.

The unexpected results can be clarified by the fact that even though two trend-following rules may appear to be notably different, they often have a significant level of performance similarity. This similarity is due to the strong correlation between the trading signals generated by various trend-following rules. The high correlation means that different rules tend to produce similar signals, ultimately leading to comparable performance. Consequently, even a suboptimal trend-following rule can effectively identify and exploit price trends, resulting in profitable outcomes.

13.2 Empirical Hurdles in Determining the Optimal Trend-Following Rule

13.2.1 Autoregressive Return Process

The purpose of this section is to provide a brief overview of the p-order autoregressive process, also known as $AR(p)$. This process is a simple and manageable return process in which the current return value is influenced by previous return values.

As a reminder, the baseline model used in this book to analyze trend-following rules is a two-state regime-shifting model for returns. In this model, there are two states, namely the bull and bear market states. However, despite the regime-shifting nature, the return process in this model can also be represented as an infinite-order autoregressive process. Due to the fact that the autoregressive coefficients in this process decline relatively quickly, an infinite-order autoregressive process can be approximated by a finite-order autoregressive process.

In an $AR(p)$ process, the return at time t is modeled as a combination of p previous returns and a random noise term. This is represented mathematically as:

$$r_t = \eta + \phi_1 r_{t-1} + \phi_2 r_{t-2} + \ldots + \phi_p r_{t-p} + \varepsilon_t = \eta + \sum_{i=1}^{p} \phi_i r_{t-i} + \varepsilon_t, \tag{13.1}$$

where p is the number of autoregressive terms, η is a constant term, $\{\phi_1, \phi_2, \ldots, \phi_p\}$ are the autoregressive coefficients, r_{t-i} is the return observed at time $t - i$, and ε_t is the noise term which is i.i.d. random process with zero mean and variance of σ_ε^2.

To calculate the mean and variance of r_t, the following formulas are used:

$$\mu = E[r_t] = \frac{\eta}{1 - \sum_{i=1}^{p} \phi_i}, \quad \sigma^2 = Var(r_t) = \frac{\sigma_\varepsilon^2}{1 - \sum_{i=1}^{p} \phi_i \rho_i}. \quad (13.2)$$

Here, μ represents the mean value of r_t and σ^2 represents its variance. The autocorrelation between r_t and r_{t-i} is denoted as ρ_i. These autocorrelations can be obtained by solving the Yule-Walker equations, which depend on the autoregressive coefficients ϕ_i.

If the return process exhibits persistence, positive returns tend to be followed by positive returns, and negative returns by negative returns. This creates short-term momentum or trends in prices. Such behavior is typically characterized by positive autocorrelation in returns, where past returns tend to reinforce future returns in the same direction. As a consequence, traders may use trend-following rules or strategies that capitalize on this momentum.

The measure of persistence in an $AR(p)$ process is given by the sum of its autoregressive coefficients, denoted as $\kappa = \sum_{i=1}^{p} \phi_i$. A smaller value of κ indicates weak persistence, while a larger value of κ indicates strong persistence.

13.2.2 Optimal Trend-Following

A technical indicator for a trend-following rule can be calculated as a moving average of n past returns. Mathematically, this can be represented as:

$$I_t(n) = \sum_{i=0}^{n-1} \theta_i r_{t-i}, \quad (13.3)$$

where θ_i represents the weight of return r_{t-i} in the calculation of the moving average.

The objective of a technical indicator is to generate trading signals for buying and selling. The value of the technical indicator determines the trading signal according to the following rule:

$$\text{Signal}_{t+1} = \begin{cases} \text{Buy} & \text{if } I_t(n) > 0, \\ \text{Sell} & \text{if } I_t(n) \leq 0. \end{cases} \quad (13.4)$$

According to this rule, a Buy signal is generated if the value of the technical indicator is positive, and a Sell signal is generated otherwise.

The optimal technical indicator is one that guarantees the highest level of performance or profitability for the trend-following rule. When the returns follow an $AR(p)$ process and there are no transaction costs, the optimal technical indicator can be represented as:

$$I_t(p) = \sum_{i=0}^{p-1} (a \times \phi_{i+1}) r_{t-i}, \tag{13.5}$$

where a is an arbitrary positive real constant. Specifically, the optimal number of return lags in the technical indicator equals the order of the autoregressive process, $n = p$, and the return weights represent a positive scaling transformation of the autoregressive coefficients, $\theta_i = a \times \phi_{i+1}$, implying that the shape of the return weights resembles the shape of the autoregressive coefficients.

Consequently, determining the optimal technical indicator essentially involves identifying the autoregressive process order and estimating its coefficients. To achieve this, traders must gather relevant historical data for a specific financial market. Afterward, they can carry out the $AR(p)$ model identification procedure using this data.

13.2.3 Empirical Estimation of Autoregressive Coefficients

The identification procedure for the $AR(p)$ model is typically done by regressing the current return on the returns from the past p periods. In our illustrative study, we utilize monthly data from Robert Shiller's reconstructed S&P Composite Index from January 1870 to December 2020. This dataset, compiled by Nobel laureate Robert Shiller, extends the historical returns of the S&P 500 back to 1870, providing a rich dataset with over 150 years of market history for analysis.

Determining the appropriate order, denoted by p, for the autoregressive process can be challenging, and there is often a high degree of uncertainty involved. In our analysis of monthly data, we observe that trend-following rules typically use a window size that never exceeds 12 observations. Therefore, in order to align with this common practice, we restrict the number of autoregressive terms, p, to 12.

To estimate the autoregressive coefficients, we employ an OLS regression model. However, standard OLS regression assumes that error terms are both

Table 13.1 Estimated autoregressive coefficients ϕ_i of the $AR(p)$ process for the returns of the S&P Composite index. The reported standard errors are Newey-West heteroskedasticity and autocorrelation consistent standard errors computed using 12 lags. Bold values indicate statistical significance at the 5% level

Parameter	Estimate	Std. error
ϕ_1	0.075	0.044
ϕ_2	0.004	0.038
ϕ_3	−0.080	0.043
ϕ_4	0.031	0.031
ϕ_5	**0.091**	0.024
ϕ_6	−0.058	0.039
ϕ_7	0.033	0.032
ϕ_8	0.058	0.034
ϕ_9	0.016	0.041
ϕ_{10}	0.006	0.034
ϕ_{11}	0.013	0.037
ϕ_{12}	−0.005	0.033

normally distributed and independent, which is typically not the case in financial data. As a result, the standard errors produced by this method can be unreliable. To address this issue, we use Newey-West heteroskedasticity and autocorrelation consistent (HAC) standard errors computed using 12 lags. This method enables us to obtain correct standard errors of estimation for the autoregressive coefficients.

Table 13.1 presents the estimated autoregressive coefficients ϕ_i of the $AR(p)$ process for the returns of the S&P Composite index. The table includes the estimated autoregressive coefficients and their corresponding standard errors of estimation.

It is essential to note that the estimated value of an autoregressive coefficient is a random variable with a well-defined probability distribution. As such, the estimated coefficient does not necessarily equal its true value. According to statistical theory, in 95% of cases, the true value of an estimated coefficient will fall between a lower and an upper boundary. The lower boundary is computed as the estimated value minus two times the standard error of estimation, while the upper boundary is the estimated value plus two times of the standard error of estimation. This provides a measure of the uncertainty surrounding the estimated values of the autoregressive coefficients.

Based on the data in Table 13.1, we conclude with 95% confidence that only the autoregressive coefficient at lag 5, ϕ_5, is positive. However, there is considerable uncertainty around its true value, which has a 95% probability of falling within the range of 0.043 to 0.139. For the remaining autoregressive coefficients, the possibility that their true values are zero cannot be ruled out.

It is worth noting that in statistics, a high level of certainty is required to make a statement about the existence of empirical evidence. Hence, significance levels such as 99%, 95%, and 90% are commonly used to establish confidence intervals. Among them, the 95% confidence level is the most commonly used.

Thus, while many autoregressive coefficients may be positive, we may not have sufficient statistical evidence to assert that they are. For instance, consider the autoregressive coefficient at the first lag, ϕ_1. There is a 95% likelihood that the true value of ϕ_1 falls within the range of -0.013 to 0.163. Although the upper boundary is significantly positive, the lower boundary is just below zero. However, since the value of zero lies within the 95% confidence interval, we cannot reject the hypothesis that its true value is zero. This illustrates the importance of considering both the estimated values and the uncertainty surrounding them when interpreting statistical results.

To obtain more precise estimates of the autoregressive coefficients, it is necessary to have a longer historical sample. Statistical theory suggests that in order to double the precision of estimation and reduce the standard errors by a factor of two, the sample length needs to be quadrupled. In our specific case, this would require a sample length of at least 600 years. However, the reality is that the longest available historical sample of stock market returns is only 220 years. Furthermore, even within this limited range, the reliability of returns over the first 70 years is highly questionable due to the calculation being based on data from only a few existing stocks at that time.

The challenge we face is that the strength of the empirical trend is too weak. This lack of strength makes it difficult to precisely estimate the autoregressive coefficients, as well as to determine the correct order of the $AR(p)$ process.

In a study conducted by Zakamulin and Giner (2022), they empirically estimated the trend strength represented by the variable κ, which is defined as the sum of the autoregressive coefficients, expressed mathematically as $\kappa = \sum_{i=1}^{p} \phi_i$. Their method involved analyzing returns that were aggregated over multiple periods, leading them to estimate κ to be approximately 0.3. Unfortunately, their method does not allow for the estimation of individual autoregressive coefficients or the determination of the process order. Instead, it only provides an estimate of the sum of the autoregressive coefficients.

To illustrate the challenges in estimating autoregressive coefficients, consider an example where the order of the $AR(p)$ process is $p = 10$ and all autoregressive coefficients are the same, $\phi_i = 0.03$. This value is obtained by dividing the estimated trend strength κ by the number of autoregressive coefficients p. Note that the value of 0.03 is approximately equal to the standard error of the coefficient estimation, as shown in Table 13.1. In order for all the estimated autoregressive coefficients to be statistically significant and differ from zero, the standard errors of estimation would need to be reduced by at least a factor of two. However, even in this scenario, the 95% confidence interval for each coefficient would range from zero to 0.06. This implies that it is highly unlikely for all estimated coefficients to be equal.

To summarize, estimating the autoregressive coefficients of the return process to determine the optimal return weights in a trend-following rule is not feasible due to the high level of uncertainty surrounding the estimated values. Real-life autoregressive coefficients tend to be small and difficult to detect with precision, making it challenging to accurately estimate the parameters for use in technical indicators.

13.2.4 Finding the Best Trading Rule by Backtesting

The most popular method for finding the best trend-following rule is through backtesting existing rules using relevant historical data. The idea is that each rule utilizes a unique shape of the return-weighting function, and a broad range of existing rules can potentially cover all possible shapes. This allows traders to explore different shapes and window sizes in the technical indicators of trend-following rules by varying the number of observations in the moving averages of returns. By conducting a backtest, traders can determine the rule that provides the best performance, which is thought to correspond to the optimal return weights. These weights should align with the autoregressive coefficients of the return process, providing the most reliable and profitable trend-following strategy.

The primary objective of this section is to examine whether a backtest has the ability to recover the optimal trend-following rule. To conduct this investigation, we employ a simulation method. This method entails generating a simulated sample of returns that follow a predetermined autoregressive process. Subsequently, this simulated sample is utilized to backtest a set of rules. Finally, we compare the return weights employed by the best-performing rule in the backtest with the autoregressive coefficients of the simulated return process.

By using this simulation-based approach, we can assess the ability of a backtest to accurately capture the relationship between the autoregressive coefficients and the return weights. If the best rule identified through the backtest indeed yields return weights that align closely with the known autoregressive coefficients, it provides evidence that the backtest has successfully recovered the optimal trend-following rule. On the other hand, if the return weights deviate significantly from the autoregressive coefficients, it suggests that the backtest may not effectively recover the optimal rule.

This simulation-based analysis helps to validate the reliability of backtesting as a means to uncover the optimal trend-following rule. By comparing the return weights from the backtest to the known autoregressive coefficients, we can gain insights into how well the backtest captures the underlying dynamics of the return process and assess its ability to generate profitable trading strategies in the future.

During our simulations, we utilize two different shapes for the autoregressive coefficients. In the first scenario, all autoregressive coefficients are identical. Under this condition, the optimal trading rule is the Momentum (MOM) rule. The technical indicator of the MOM rule employs equal return weights. In other words, this rule allocates the same weight to each observation when calculating the trend.

In the second scenario, the autoregressive coefficients decrease linearly with the return lag. Under this condition, the Price and Simple Moving Average crossover (P-SMA) rule is the optimal trading rule. The technical indicator of the P-SMA rule employs linearly decreasing weights. In this case, the rule weighs recent observations more heavily than past observations.

By simulating these two different shapes for the autoregressive coefficients, we can evaluate how well the backtesting method recovers the optimal rule. It is important to note that our analysis involves only two alternative trading rules, each specified by a single parameter—the size of the averaging window. Thus, we exclusively employ the MOM(n) and P-SMA(n) rules. Our study aims to demonstrate that even in this simplistic setting, pinpointing the optimal rule is a challenging task.

In our simulations, we maintain a constant trend strength of $\kappa = 0.3$. It is worth noting that this trend strength is chosen to match the empirically estimated trend strength observed in the S&P Composite stock market index. In our simulations, we ensure that the mean and variance of the simulated returns match the respective parameters of the returns observed in the S&P Composite index. This matching is done to ensure that the simulated data closely replicates the statistical properties of the real market returns.

We start our investigation with the scenario where the trader has knowledge of the optimal trading rule but is uncertain about the optimal number of return lags (window size) to employ. First, we assume that the returns follow an $AR(9)$ process in which all autoregressive coefficients are alike. Therefore, the true optimal trading rule is the MOM(9) rule. However, the trader is unaware of the optimal number of return lags and must determine this through a backtest.

More specifically, the trader selects the size of the averaging window n and simulates the returns of the MOM(n) strategy over a given sample period $\left(R_{1,n}, R_{2,n}, \ldots, R_{T,n}\right)$, where $R_{t,n}$ denotes the strategy's return in period t, and n denotes the window size in the MOM rule. We consider a long-only trend-following strategy, where the time-t return is given by:

$$R_{t,n} = \begin{cases} r_t & \text{if } MOM_{t-1}(n) > 0, \\ r_f & \text{otherwise,} \end{cases} \tag{13.6}$$

where r_t represents the market return, r_f denotes the risk-free rate of return, and $MOM_{t-1}(n)$ is the value of the technical indicator for the MOM(n) rule at time $t-1$. In this strategy, the trader invests in the risky asset when the trading signal is Buy, which occurs when $MOM_{t-1}(n) > 0$. Conversely, when the trading signal is Sell, the strategy involves selling the risky asset and investing in the risk-free instrument.

The trader adjusts the window size n within the selected range, generating a set of simulated returns for n trend-following strategies. The next step is determining the optimal window size, n^*, that yields the best performance. To do this, the trader calculates the Sharpe ratio for each strategy based on the simulated returns, using it to measure its risk-adjusted performance.

The optimal number of lags, n^*, is determined by selecting the value of n that maximizes the Sharpe ratio of the trend-following strategy. Formally, this is expressed as:

$$n^* = \arg \max_{n \in [n_{\min}, n_{\max}]} SR\left(R_{1,n}, R_{2,n}, \ldots, R_{T,n}\right),$$

where $n_{\min}$ and $n_{\max}$ represent the minimum and maximum values of n that are considered in the optimization.

Although the backtesting procedure could correctly identify the optimal value of $n^* = 9$ with a sufficiently large sample size, in practice, the precision of estimation is impacted by the length of the sample and the random variation in the returns. Therefore, our goal is to evaluate the accuracy of the estimation of the optimal number of lags in the MOM rule in relation to the length of the sample.

To accomplish this, we fix the horizon length of the sample at $Y \in [10, 30, 50, 100]$ years and simulate returns following an $AR(9)$ process. Then, by varying the value of n in the MOM(n) strategy over the range $n \in [1, 24]$, we generate the returns for a set of MOM(n) strategies and select the value of n^* that maximizes the Sharpe ratio. To assess the precision of the estimation of the optimal number of lags in the trading rule, we compute the

Table 13.2 Results of the simulation study where the returns follow an $AR(9)$ process with equal autoregressive coefficients. The optimal trading rule is the MOM rule with $n = 9$ return lags. The value of n^* denotes the optimal number of lags in the MOM rule found using the backtesting methodology. For each horizon, the table reports the probability of n^* being 9, 9 ± 1, 9 ± 2, 9 ± 3, and 9 ± 4

Horizon, years	Probability of n^* **being**				
	9	9 ± 1	9 ± 2	9 ± 3	9 ± 4
10	0.06	0.17	0.27	0.37	0.47
30	0.09	0.23	0.35	0.46	0.56
50	0.11	0.27	0.41	0.52	0.62
100	0.15	0.35	0.51	0.63	0.72

probability of n^* being 9, within a range of values that vary by ± 1, ± 2, ± 3, and ± 4. For each horizon of Y years, we perform 100,000 simulations.

Table 13.2 reports the results of this simulations study. The results reveal that the precision of the backtesting method is extremely poor in terms of accurately identifying the optimal number of lags in the MOM rule. Even for a sample length of 100 years, there is only a 15% chance of correctly identifying that $n^* = 9$. Moreover, there is still a 28% probability that the estimated value of n^* falls outside the range 9 ± 4. For a sample length of 10 years, the probability of accurately identifying n is only 6%, and the probability that the estimated value of n^* falls outside the range 9 ± 4 reaches 53%.

To further illustrate the precision of the estimation of the optimal number of lags in the MOM trading rule, Fig. 13.1 presents the empirical probability distribution of the estimated number of optimal return lags n^* obtained using the backtesting methodology. The simulated sample length considered here is 50 years.

In the empirical probability distribution function, we observe a sharp peak at $n = 9$, indicating that 9 is the most frequently identified value for n in the simulations. Moreover, the median value of the empirical distribution is also $n = 9$. This means that there is an equal probability of the identified value of n being below or above 9. Although the distribution has substantial variation around the peak, the central tendency of the estimated values aligns with the true optimal value of $n = 9$.

In our second experiment, we consider a different setting where the returns follow an $AR(9)$ process with linearly decreasing autoregressive coefficients. In this setting, the true optimal trading rule is the P-SMA(9) rule. We assume that the trader is aware of the optimal trading rule being the P-SMA rule but is not aware of the optimal number of return lags and must determine this through a backtesting methodology.

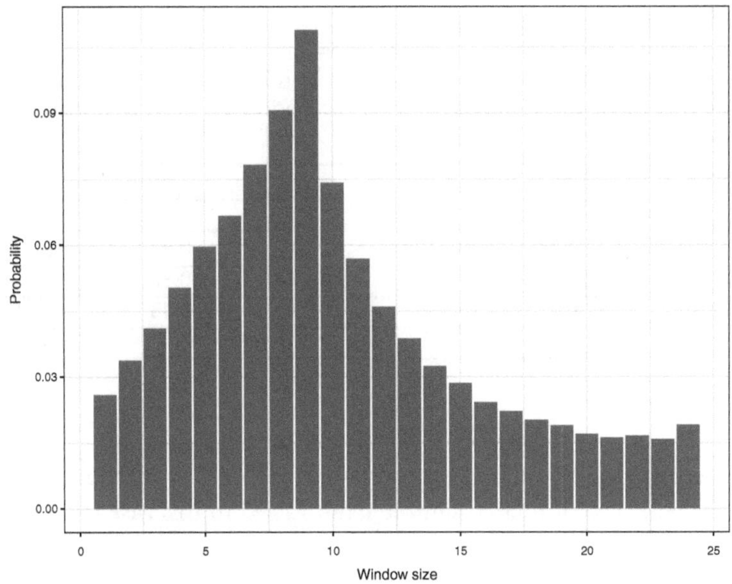

Fig. 13.1 Empirical probability distribution of the optimal return lags n^* obtained through the backtesting methodology when the simulated sample length is 50 years. The returns follow an $AR(9)$ process with equal autoregressive coefficients. The optimal number of lags in the MOM rule equals $n^* = 9$

The backtesting methodology used to determine the optimal number of return lags in the P-SMA rule follows the same simulation procedure as described earlier for the MOM rule. In Table 13.3, we present the results obtained from this simulation study.

These results indicate that the precision of identifying the optimal number of return lags for the P-SMA rule is slightly lower compared to that of the MOM rule. For instance, when the sample length is 100 years, there is only an 8% probability of correctly identifying that $n^* = 9$. This suggests that the estimated value of the optimal number of lags n^* may deviate more frequently from the true optimal value in the P-SMA rule compared to the MOM rule.

Additionally, for the same horizon length of 100 years, the simulation results reveal that there is a considerable probability (37%) that the estimated value of n^* falls outside the range of 9 ± 4. This suggests that the estimation for the P-SMA rule is subject to more uncertainty and variability, as evidenced by a larger proportion of estimated values significantly deviating from the true optimal value.

To enhance the understanding of the precision of estimating the optimal number of lags in the P-SMA trading rule, we present Fig. 13.2. This figure showcases the empirical probability distribution of the estimated number of

Table 13.3 Results of the simulation study where the returns follow an $AR(9)$ process with linearly decreasing autoregressive coefficients. The optimal trading rule is the P-SMA rule with $n = 9$ return lags. The value of n^* denotes the optimal number of lags in the P-SMA rule found using the backtesting methodology. For each horizon, the table reports the probability of n^* being 9, 9 ± 1, 9 ± 2, 9 ± 3, and 9 ± 4

Horizon, years	Probability of n^* **being**				
	9	9 ± 1	9 ± 2	9 ± 3	9 ± 4
10	0.04	0.13	0.22	0.32	0.41
30	0.06	0.17	0.27	0.38	0.48
50	0.06	0.19	0.31	0.43	0.54
100	0.08	0.23	0.38	0.51	0.63

optimal return lags n^* obtained through the backtesting methodology. As for the MOM rule, the simulated sample length used in this case is 50 years.

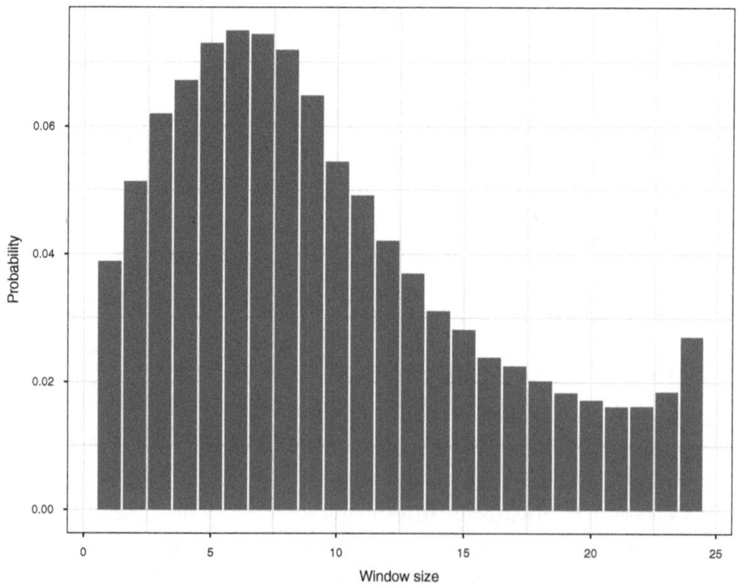

Fig. 13.2 Empirical probability distribution of the optimal return lags n^* obtained through the backtesting methodology when the simulated sample length is 50 years. The returns follow an $AR(9)$ process with linearly decreasing autoregressive coefficients. The optimal number of lags in the P-SMA rule equals $n^* = 9$

The empirical probability distribution function in Fig. 13.2 indicates a relatively smooth peak around $n = 6$, highlighting that 6 is the most frequently identified value for n in the simulations. Furthermore, the median value of the empirical distribution is $n = 8$, indicating that there is an equal probability of the estimated value of n^* being below or above 8. This finding implies that there is a tendency for the estimated value of n^* to be smaller than the true optimal value of $n = 9$. This outcome is not surprising, as when the autoregressive coefficients decrease linearly, the distant autoregressive coefficients become too small compared to the noise in the data.

Overall, the empirical probability distribution in Fig. 13.2 shows that the estimation process for the optimal number of return lags in the P-SMA rule is subject to more significant uncertainty and variability than that of the MOM rule. Our results suggest that the backtesting methodology tends to underestimate the optimal number of return lags in the P-SMA rule.

In our initial analysis, we considered a scenario where the trader knew the optimal trading rule but was uncertain about the appropriate number of return lags to use. In the final experiment, we reverse this situation: the trader now knows the optimal number of return lags but is unsure about which trading rule to apply.

In this investigation, we aim to evaluate the precision of the backtesting methodology in correctly identifying the optimal trading rule. Specifically, we simulate returns that follow the $AR(9)$ process with equal autoregressive coefficients, where the MOM(9) rule is the optimal trading rule. However, the trader in this setting is unaware of the optimal trading rule and must use the backtesting methodology to assess two rules: the MOM(9) rule and the P-SMA(9) rule.

As before, we perform 100,000 simulations for each horizon of Y years, with the optimal rule being the rule with the highest Sharpe ratio in a backtest. Due to substantial noise in the data, the optimal rule identified by the backtest can be either the MOM(9) rule or the P-SMA(9) rule. The primary objective of this experiment is to calculate the probability of accurately recognizing the optimal trading rule to be the MOM(9) rule using the backtesting methodology.

In the subsequent phase of our experiment, we simulate returns that adhere to the $AR(9)$ process with autoregressive coefficients that decrease linearly. In this case, the optimal trading rule is the P-SMA(9) rule. The trader, who is unaware of the optimal trading rule, employs the backtesting methodology to assess two rules: the MOM(9) rule and the P-SMA(9) rule. The goal of this particular experiment is to determine the probability of correctly identifying the optimal trading rule to be the P-SMA(9) rule using the backtesting methodology.

The results of our simulation study are reported in Table 13.4. These outcomes emphasize that even in a situation where the trader is aware of the optimal number of return lags and only two possible variations of a trend-

Table 13.4 Probability of correct identification of the optimal trading rule. In the simulated sample of returns, either the MOM(9) or P-SMA(9) rule is optimal. Both rules are tested using a backtest. The reported probability is the percentages of times the optimal trading rule is identified correctly

Horizon, years	Probability of correct identification	
	MOM	P-SMA
10	0.54	0.56
30	0.57	0.60
50	0.59	0.62
100	0.62	0.67

following rule exist, the accuracy in identifying the optimal trading rule is far from perfect. For instance, even with a sample length of 100 years, the probability of correctly recognizing that the optimal trading rule is the MOM(9) rule is only 62%. For the P-SMA(9) rule, the precision is slightly higher. Specifically, with the same sample length of 100 years, the probability of correctly identifying that the optimal trading rule is the P-SMA(9) rule is 67%.

Over a span of 10 years, the accuracy in identifying the optimal trading rule is only barely above 50%. This implies that in this instance, the precision of the backtest is only slightly superior to chance—tossing a coin to choose between two trading rules.

Another surprising finding is that the accuracy in identifying the optimal trading rule increases at a slow pace as the length of the horizon expands. For instance, the percentage of correctly identifying the MOM(9) rule only drops slightly from 62% to 54% when the sample length is reduced to 10 years instead of 100 years. As for the P-SMA(9) rule, the corresponding percentages are slightly higher, with 67% accuracy for the longer sample and 56% for the shorter one. This suggests that the backtesting methodology maintains low precision even when the historical sample encompasses an extensive long-term period.

In conclusion, our simulation study has illuminated the limitations and challenges associated with the backtesting methodology in identifying the optimal trading rule and estimating the optimal number of return lags.

First and foremost, our findings indicate that the precision and reliability of the backtesting methodology in accurately identifying the optimal trading rule are remarkably poor. Even with relatively long sample sizes, the probability of correctly identifying the best trading rule remains small. Furthermore, not only is the trading rule typically wrongly identified, but the number of return lags in the technical indicator is also typically incorrect.

Hence, it is crucial to recognize that the task of identifying the optimal trend-following rule using the backtesting methodology is extremely challenging. The conclusions we have derived stem from a simplified scenario where there are only two variants of a trend-following rule, each possessing just one parameter that can assume values from a relatively limited range. However, in real life, traders encounter numerous alternative trading rules, each of which may comprise multiple parameters that can take on a wide range of possible values.

An additional significant simplification we have made in our analysis is assuming that the parameters of the return process remain constant over time, irrespective of sample length. In reality, market dynamics are frequently much more complicated, with structural breaks being a common occurrence. During these breaks, both the autoregressive coefficients and the order of the $AR(p)$ process may change over time. Taking into account the possibility of structural breaks and the evolving nature of market dynamics only intensifies the difficulties involved in identifying the optimal trading rule.

13.3 Evaluating the Performance of Suboptimal Trend-Following Rules

The results obtained in the previous section highlight the difficulty of finding the optimal trend-following rule through empirical search. It can be likened to searching for a needle in a haystack, with virtually zero chances of success. Both the OLS regression method and the backtesting method fail to accurately identify the optimal trend-following rule.

These findings lead us to conclude that traders typically employ suboptimal rules when it comes to following trends in financial markets. This raises important questions: what is the extent of the loss in profitability when using a non-optimal trend-following rule? Can a non-optimal trend-following strategy outperform the passive buy-and-hold strategy? This section aims to address these questions and provide insights into the performance of non-optimal trend-following strategies.

13.3.1 Theoretical Foundations for Evaluating Performance

We measure the performance of the trend-following strategy by using the Sharpe ratio. The Sharpe ratio is the most widely used measure of risk-adjusted returns in investment analysis. It helps an investor to assess whether the excess return earned by a portfolio is due to good investment decisions or merely a result of the extra risk taken on by the investor.

The Sharpe ratio is calculated by dividing the portfolio's excess return over the risk-free rate by the portfolio's standard deviation. It measures the excess return per unit of risk taken. The higher the Sharpe ratio, the better the risk-adjusted performance of the portfolio.

To determine the Sharpe ratio, two key values are needed: the mean excess return and the standard deviation of the trend-following strategy. The trend-following strategy's random returns are represented by the variable R_t, while the risk-free rate of return, which remains constant over time, is denoted by r_f. The formula for computing the Sharpe ratio is as follows:

$$SR(R_t) = \frac{E[R_t] - r_f}{\sqrt{Var[R_t]}}, \tag{13.7}$$

where $E[R_t]$ denotes the mean return of the trend-following strategy and $Var[R_t]$ is the variance of the returns.

We examine a long-only approach to trend-following that seeks to generate profits and minimize losses by investing in the risky asset when prices are trending upward. When prices decline, funds are invested in the risk-free asset. The strategy's return at time t is given by:

$$R_t = \begin{cases} r_t & \text{if } I_{t-1}(n) > 0, \\ r_f & \text{otherwise,} \end{cases} \tag{13.8}$$

where r_t refers to the market return at time t, r_f refers to the risk-free rate of return, and $I_{t-1}(n)$ represents the time $t-1$ value of the technical indicator of the trend-following rule. This strategy specifies investment in the risky asset whenever the trading signal is Buy. Conversely, when the trading signal is Sell, the strategy involves selling the risky asset and committing to the risk-free instrument. Of note, the strategy's return at time t is determined by the value of the trading indicator at time $t-1$.

To simplify the model, we assume that the unexpected changes in the $AR(p)$ return process, represented by ε_t, conform to a normal distribution. This implies that the joint distribution of financial asset returns r_t and the technical indicator $I_{t-1}(n)$ also conforms to a bivariate normal distribution:

$$\begin{bmatrix} r_t \\ I_{t-1}(n) \end{bmatrix} = \mathcal{N}\left(\begin{bmatrix} \mu \\ m \end{bmatrix}, \begin{bmatrix} \sigma^2 & \varrho\sigma v \\ \varrho\sigma v & v^2 \end{bmatrix} \right). \tag{13.9}$$

In this context, $\mathcal{N}(\cdot, \cdot)$ represents the bivariate normal probability distribution, where μ and σ^2 denote the mean and variance of r_t, and m and v^2 represent the mean and variance of $I_{t-1}(n)$. The correlation coefficient between r_t and $I_{t-1}(n)$ is denoted by ϱ.

We have previously introduced this theoretical model in earlier chapters of the book. The analytical solution for the mean return, variance of returns, and consequently the Sharpe ratio of the trend-following strategy has been presented in the paper by Zakamulin and Giner (2022).

Specifically, the mean and variance of r_t are specified by Eq. (13.2). The mean and variance of $I_{t-1}(n)$ are defined as follows:

$$m = \mathbf{1}'\boldsymbol{\theta}\mu, \qquad v^2 = \boldsymbol{\theta}'\boldsymbol{R}_{n,n}\boldsymbol{\theta}\sigma^2, \tag{13.10}$$

where $\mathbf{1}$ is the $n \times 1$ vector of ones, $\boldsymbol{\theta}' = [\theta_1, \theta_2, \ldots, \theta_n]$ is the $n \times 1$ vector of return weights, and $\boldsymbol{R}_{n,n}$ is the $n \times n$ matrix defined by equation:

$$\boldsymbol{R}_{n,n} = \begin{bmatrix} 1 & \rho_1 & \rho_2 & \cdots & \rho_{n-1} \\ \rho_1 & 1 & \rho_1 & \cdots & \rho_{n-2} \\ \rho_2 & \rho_1 & 1 & \cdots & \rho_{n-3} \\ \vdots & \vdots & \vdots & \ddots & \vdots \\ \rho_{n-1} & \rho_{n-2} & \rho_{n-3} & \cdots & 1 \end{bmatrix}, \tag{13.11}$$

where ρ_i represents the market return autocorrelation at lag i.

The correlation coefficient ϱ between r_t and $I_{t-1}(n)$ is computed as follows (see Zakamulin and Giner, 2020):

$$\varrho = \frac{\boldsymbol{\theta}'\boldsymbol{R}\,\boldsymbol{\phi}}{\sqrt{\boldsymbol{\theta}'\boldsymbol{R}\boldsymbol{\theta}}}. \tag{13.12}$$

where $\boldsymbol{\phi}' = [\phi_1, \phi_2, \ldots, \phi_p]$ is the $p \times 1$ vector of autoregressive coefficients of r_t and $\boldsymbol{R}_{n,p}$ is the $n \times p$ matrix given by:

$$\boldsymbol{R}_{n,p} = \begin{bmatrix} 1 & \rho_1 & \rho_2 & \cdots & \rho_{p-1} \\ \rho_1 & 1 & \rho_1 & \cdots & \rho_{p-2} \\ \rho_2 & \rho_1 & 1 & \cdots & \rho_{p-3} \\ \vdots & \vdots & \vdots & \ddots & \vdots \\ \rho_{n-1} & \rho_{n-2} & \rho_{n-3} & \cdots & \rho_{|p-n|} \end{bmatrix}.$$

The analytical solutions for both the expected return and the variance of returns of the trend-following strategy are expressed as follows:

$$E[R_t] = (\mu - r_f)\Phi(-d) + r_f + g, \tag{13.13}$$

$$Var[R_t] = (\mu^2 + \sigma^2)\Phi(-d) + g(2\mu + \sigma\varrho\, d) + r_f^2\Phi(d) - E[R_t]^2, \tag{13.14}$$

where

$$d = -\frac{m}{v}, \quad g = \sigma\varrho\,\varphi(d),$$

and $\varphi(.)$ and $\Phi(.)$ denote the probability density function and the cumulative distribution function of the standard normal random variable:

$$\varphi(z) = \frac{1}{\sqrt{2\pi}}e^{-\frac{z^2}{2}}, \quad \Phi(d) = \int_{-\infty}^{d}\varphi(z)dz.$$

Using these formulas for the expected return and variance of returns of the trend-following strategy, we have the necessary tools to calculate the Sharpe ratio of the strategy.

The Sharpe ratio of the passive buy-and-hold strategy is computed as:

$$SR(r_t) = \frac{\mu - r_f}{\sigma}. \tag{13.15}$$

If the returns of the market are independent, the past returns cannot offer an insight into future returns. This implies that the correlation coefficient ϱ between r_t and $I_{t-1}(n)$ is zero. In such cases, the Sharpe ratio of the trend-following strategy is inferior to that of the buy-and-hold strategy. However, as the correlation coefficient ϱ increases, so does the Sharpe ratio of the trend-following strategy.

Zakamulin and Giner (2020) show that the correlation coefficient ϱ reaches its maximum value when the vector of return weights $\boldsymbol{\theta}$ is a positive scaling transformation of the vector of autoregressive coefficients $\boldsymbol{\phi}$, i.e., $\boldsymbol{\theta} = a \times \boldsymbol{\phi}$, where a is any positive number. This means that when the return weights are a scaled version of the autoregressive coefficients, the Sharpe ratio of the trend-following strategy is maximized.

If the return weights of a trend-following indicator do not fulfill the condition $\boldsymbol{\theta} = a \times \boldsymbol{\phi}$, then the Sharpe ratio of the trend-following strategy is suboptimal. In such cases, the greater the difference between the weights of the trend-following indicator and the optimal trend-following indicator, the less profitable the trend-following strategy becomes.[1]

In the upcoming sections of this chapter, we aim to explore the degree of profitability loss that occurs when a trader employs a non-optimal vector of return weights in the technical indicator. Additionally, we will investigate whether a suboptimal trend-following strategy can outperform the passive buy-and-hold strategy. To accomplish this, we will rely on the theoretical model outlined in the previous sections to guide our investigation.

13.3.2 Analysis of Suboptimal Trend-Following Rules

Stationary Autoregressive Process

In this section, we consider the scenario where the autoregressive return process is stationary, meaning that its parameters remain stable over time. The key parameters that determine the optimal trend-following strategy are the order of the autoregressive process and the shape of the autoregressive coefficients.

In our analysis, we focus on two distinct cases. In both cases, the returns follow an autoregressive process of order 9, denoted as $AR(9)$. The mean and variance of these returns are set to match the corresponding parameters of the returns of the S&P Composite index. Additionally, the trend strength is set to the estimated trend strength observed in the S&P Composite index, which is represented by the parameter $\kappa = 0.3$.

In the first case, all the autoregressive coefficients are the same, while in the second case, the coefficients decrease linearly with the lag of the returns. As a result, the optimal trend-following rule in the first case is represented by the MOM(9) rule. On the other hand, in the second case, the P-SMA(9) rule represents the optimal strategy.

The trader, being unaware of the optimal trend-following rule, decides to follow the trends using either the MOM(n) rule or the P-SMA(n) rule. We assume that the value of n can vary from 1 to 18. For each selected value of n, we calculate the performance of both the MOM(n) and P-SMA(n) rules.

[1] It is important to note that the formula for the Sharpe ratio of the trend-following strategy defines its true value, or the expected value. However, when the Sharpe ratio is calculated using historical data, statistical theory states that its estimate is a realization of a random variable. The actual Sharpe ratio lies within the range specified by the estimated Sharpe ratio plus or minus two times the standard error of the estimation of the Sharpe ratio. This means that the Sharpe ratio calculated using empirical data is its true value plus some amount of noise. The noise in the estimation of the Sharpe ratio becomes more significant when the data sample is shorter. When the sample size is small, there is a higher probability of encountering random variations in the data, leading to a larger discrepancy between the true value of the Sharpe ratio and its estimated value.

Figure 13.3 shows the performance (Sharpe ratio) of various MOM(n) and P-SMA(n) rules when the optimal trading rule is the MOM(9) rule. For comparison, the Sharpe ratio of the passive buy-and-hold strategy is also shown in this figure.

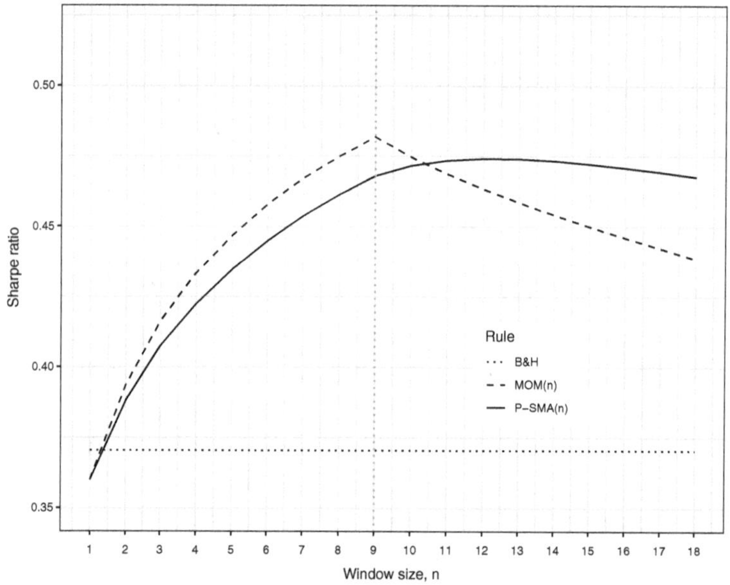

Fig. 13.3 Sharpe ratio of various MOM(n) and P-SMA(n) rules when the optimal trading rule is the MOM(9) rule. For comparison, the Sharpe ratio of the passive buy-and-hold (B&H) strategy is also shown

It is known beforehand that the performance of the MOM(n) rule for $n \neq 9$ will be lower than the optimal MOM(9) rule. However, the critical question is how significant the loss in performance is when n is not optimal. The results depicted in Fig. 13.3 suggest that the difference in performance is relatively small when n does not deviate substantially from 9.

More specifically, we observe that the Sharpe ratio of the optimal MOM(9) rule is 30% higher than that of the buy-and-hold strategy. Furthermore, the performance of the MOM(n) rule for $n = 9 \pm 3$ is at most 5% lower than the performance of the MOM(9) rule. When $n = 9 \pm 5$ in the MOM(n) rule, the maximum loss in performance is approximately 7%. As indicated by the curves in Fig. 13.3, only the performance of the MOM(1) rule is inferior to that of the buy-and-hold strategy. For all values of n greater than 1 within the selected range, the MOM(n) rule outperforms the buy-and-hold strategy.

The P-SMA(n) rule is suboptimal when the autoregressive coefficients of the return process are alike. Nevertheless, the curves in Fig. 13.3 suggest that, as for the MOM rule, for all values of n greater than 1 within the selected range, the P-SMA(n) rule outperforms the buy-and-hold strategy.

The difference in the performances of the MOM(n) and P-SMA(n) rules are relatively small. For example, the performance of the P-SMA(12) rule is only 1.5% lower than the performance of the optimal MOM(9) rule. When $n < 11$, the MOM(n) rule exhibits marginally superior performance to the corresponding P-SMA(n) rule. However, for $n \geq 11$, the performance relationship is reversed, with the P-SMA(n) rule displaying slightly better performance than the MOM(n) rule.

In Fig. 13.4, we can observe the performance of different MOM(n) and P-SMA(n) rules when the optimal trading rule is the P-SMA(9) rule. In this case, the Sharpe ratio of the P-SMA(9) rule is 37.5% higher than the Sharpe ratio of the buy-and-hold strategy. Moreover, for all values of n within the selected range, both the MOM(n) and P-SMA(n) strategies outperform the buy-and-hold strategy.[2]

We also observe that the performance of the MOM(6) rule is only 1.4% lower than the performance of the optimal P-SMA(9) rule. Moreover, for $n \leq 7$, the performance of the MOM(n) rule is nearly identical to the performance of the corresponding P-SMA(n) rule. However, as n exceeds 7 and continues to increase, the performance of the MOM(n) rule starts to decline compared to the performance of the corresponding P-SMA(n) rule.

Our analysis primarily concentrates on the comparative performances of the MOM and P-SMA rules due to their distinct return-weighting functions. Notably, the MOM rule assigns equal weights to all returns, while the P-SMA rule employs linearly decreasing return weights. We have opted not to investigate the other P-MA rules in our analysis since they all feature decreasing return weights. For instance, in the Price and Linear Moving Average crossover (P-LMA) rule, the return weights decrease almost quadratically. In contrast, the Price and Exponential Moving Average crossover (P-EMA) rule utilizes exponentially decreasing return weights. Although the decrease is nonlinear, the shape of the return weights in these rules closely resembles that of the P-SMA rule. Given this similarity in the shape of return weights, it is expected that the differences in performance between the P-SMA, P-LMA, and P-EMA rules should be relatively small.

---

[2] Throughout our analysis, the trend strength, measured by the sum of the autoregressive coefficients κ, remains constant. However, it is important to note that the Sharpe ratio of the trend-following strategy depends not only on the value of κ, but also on the shape of the autoregressive coefficients. Specifically, the more heavily weighted the most recent autoregressive coefficients are, the higher the Sharpe ratio of the trend-following strategy. Therefore, the Sharpe ratios of various trend-following strategies are higher when the autoregressive coefficients decrease with the return lag compared to the case of equal autoregressive coefficients.

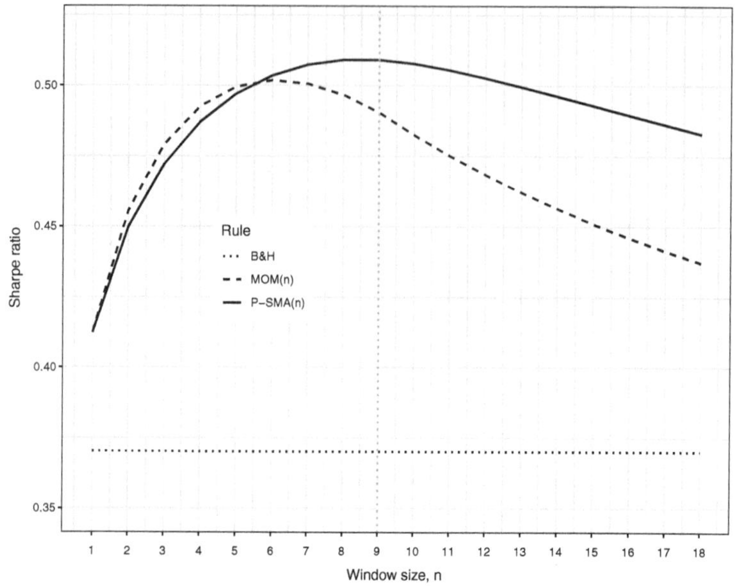

Fig. 13.4 Sharpe ratio of various MOM(n) and P-SMA(n) rules when the optimal trading rule is the P-SMA(9) rule. For comparison, the Sharpe ratio of the passive buy-and-hold (B&H) strategy is also shown

To demonstrate that the performances of various P-MA rules are quite similar, Fig. 13.5 depicts the Sharpe ratio of different P-SMA(n), P-LMA(n), and P-EMA(n) rules where the optimal trading rule is the P-SMA(9) rule. The curves in this figure reveal that when $n = 9 \pm 3$, the maximum performance differential between these rules is approximately 4%. Over the entire range of selected n values, the maximum difference is less than 9%. These results confirm the substantial similarity between the rules with similar return-weighting function shapes.

Upon initial examination, the observed results in this section may challenge preconceived expectations. Traditionally, a suboptimal rule is expected to have significantly lower performance than the optimal rule. Similarly, it is intuitive to believe that a trend-following rule with a different shape and a variable number of return weights would result in significantly inferior performance compared to the optimal rule. However, our findings demonstrate that these expectations are incorrect. We observe that although these rules differ in their shape and weighting, their performances are not substantially different from each other.

The counterintuitive results can be explained by the fact that two different trend-following rules exhibit a relatively high degree of performance similar-

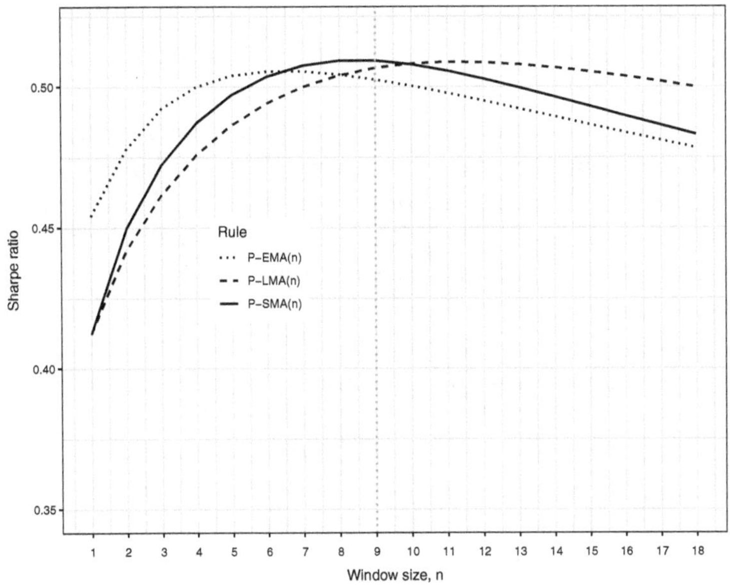

Fig. 13.5 Sharpe ratio of various P-SMA(n), P-LMA(n), and P-EMA(n) rules when the optimal trading rule is the P-SMA(9) rule

ity, despite using different return-weighting functions. The study conducted by Zakamulin and Giner (2020) provides a comprehensive examination of this particular concept. Specifically, this study examines the correlation between trading signals of various trend-following rules. Surprisingly, this correlation is found to be relatively high, even in cases where the return-weighting functions appear to be different. This high correlation implies that different trend-following rules tend to generate similar signals, leading to comparable performance. As a result, even a non-optimal trend-following rule can effectively identify and capitalize on price trends, leading to profitable outcomes.

Random Autoregressive Process

Identifying the optimal trading rule is exceptionally complicated, even when the autoregressive return process is stationary. Still, in this scenario, there exists a non-zero probability that the best trading rule in a backtest coincides with the true optimal trading rule. However, it is highly likely for the parameters of the autoregressive process to change randomly over time. There are no reasonable arguments to suggest that the parameters of the autoregressive process for returns remain constant over a long period. In such situations, where the parameters are changing, it becomes completely impossible to estimate the optimal trading rule. This section aims to investigate the performance of trend-following rules when the trader employs an arbitrary trading rule and market trends are random.

First, we examine two scenarios where the shape of the autoregressive coefficients and the strength of the trend remain the same, but the order of the autoregressive process varies randomly over time. In the first scenario, all autoregressive coefficients in the $AR(p)$ process are identical, while the order p follows a uniform distribution between 1 and 18. In the second scenario, the autoregressive coefficients decrease linearly, but as in the first scenario, p remains uniformly distributed over the same range. In both cases, the sum of the autoregressive coefficients is held constant, regardless of the process order p.

The trader is unaware of the optimal trading rule and chooses to follow trends using either the MOM(n) rule or the P-SMA(n) rule with an arbitrary number of return weights $n \in [1, 18]$. The trend-following rule's performance for a given n is computed as the average performance of the rule over all possible values of p.

Figure 13.6 displays the average Sharpe ratios of various MOM(n) and P-SMA(n) rules used to follow trends. In this analysis, the trend is modeled by an $AR(p)$ process with equal autoregressive coefficients, where p follows a uniform distribution from 1 to 18. The figure also includes the Sharpe ratio of the passive buy-and-hold strategy for comparison. By visually inspecting the curves in the figure, we can draw the following observations. First, for any selected value of n, both the MOM(n) and P-SMA(n) rules consistently outperform the buy-and-hold strategy. Second, when $n < 6$, the MOM(n) and P-SMA(n) rules exhibit virtually similar performance. However, for $n \geq 6$, the P-SMA(n) rule consistently outperforms the MOM(n) rule, and this performance gap increases as n becomes larger.

In Fig. 13.7, we can see the average Sharpe ratios of different MOM(n) and P-SMA(n) rules when the trend is modeled by an $AR(p)$ process with linearly decreasing autoregressive coefficients. As before, the value of p follows a uniform distribution from 1 to 18. Similar to the previous case, both the MOM(n) and P-SMA(n) rules consistently outperform the buy-and-hold strategy for any selected value of n. However, unlike the previous case, the P-SMA(n) rule outperforms the MOM(n) rule consistently for $n > 2$, and the performance gap between these two rules is larger.

Finally, we consider a scenario where the order and shape of the autoregressive coefficients in the $AR(p)$ process change randomly over time. As with the previous scenarios, the value of p follows a uniform distribution from 1 to 18. Moreover, each time the value of p changes, the shape of the autoregressive

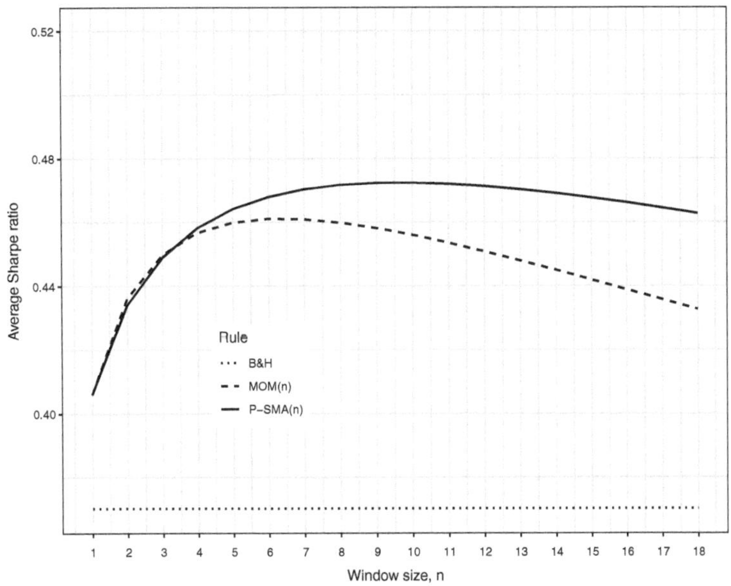

Fig. 13.6 Average Sharpe ratio of various MOM(n) and P-SMA(n) rules when the trend is modeled by an $AR(p)$ with equal autoregressive coefficients and where p is uniformly distributed on 1 to 18. For comparison, the Sharpe ratio of the passive buy-and-hold (**B&H**) strategy is also shown

coefficients changes too. We assume that the probability of the autoregressive coefficients being either constant or linearly decreasing is equal. Regardless of the order of the process and the shape of the autoregressive coefficients, the trend strength remains constant at $\kappa = 0.3$.

Similarly to the previous scenarios, the trader does not have knowledge of the optimal trading rule at each given time and chooses to follow the trends using either the MOM(n) or P-SMA(n) rule with an arbitrary value of n. The performance of the trend-following rule for a specific n is calculated as the average performance of the rule over all possible values of p and different shapes of the autoregressive coefficients.

Figure 13.8 reports the computed average Sharpe ratios of various MOM(n) and P-SMA(n) rules. The curves in this figure show a remarkable similarity to the respective curves in Figs. 13.6 and 13.7. Similarly to the previous scenarios, we observe that all trend-following rules outperform the passive buy-and-hold strategy for any value of n. Moreover, the P-SMA(n) rule is typically more profitable than the corresponding MOM(n) rule, consistent with the previous findings.

Following our analysis, we can draw two critical conclusions. First, it is not necessary for trend-following rules to be optimal or close to optimal to

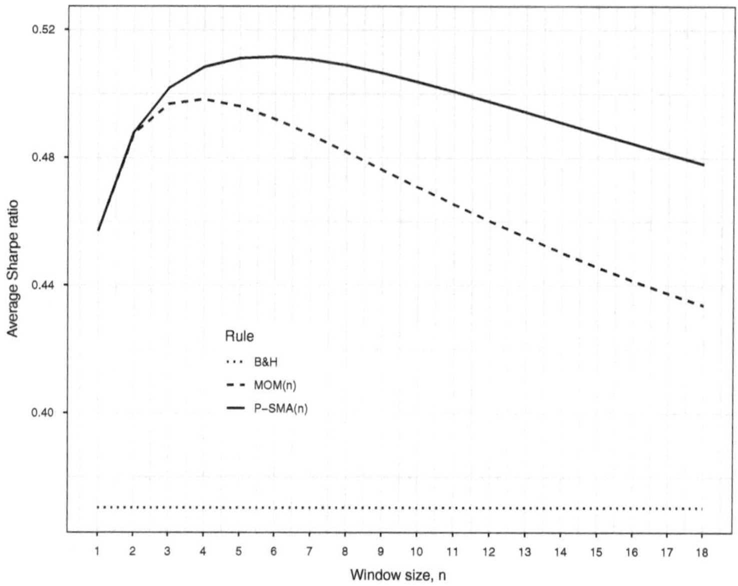

Fig. 13.7 Average Sharpe ratio of various MOM(n) and P-SMA(n) rules when the trend is modeled by an $AR(p)$ with linearly decreasing autoregressive coefficients and where p is uniformly distributed on 1 to 18. For comparison, the Sharpe ratio of the passive buy-and-hold (**B&H**) strategy is also shown

make a profit from price trends. Our research indicates that trend direction can be identified using a moving average of recent return observations, and regardless of the type of moving average used, if past returns were positive, the moving average will remain positive as well. Hence, trend-following strategies are robust to the nature of the autoregressive process for returns. The only requirement for profiting from trends is that the trend strength must not be too weak.

Second, the P-MA rules, where return weights decrease with the return lag, are more profitable than the MOM rule where all return weights are the same. In other words, the P-MA rules are more robust than the MOM rule to the underlying trend processes. This is due to the idea that when the true order of the autoregressive process is unknown, the most recent returns are more relevant and safe to use than the most distant returns. This is because, regardless of whether the order of the process is short or long, the most recent returns are always used in computing the trading signal. Distant returns are only necessary when the order of the process is long.

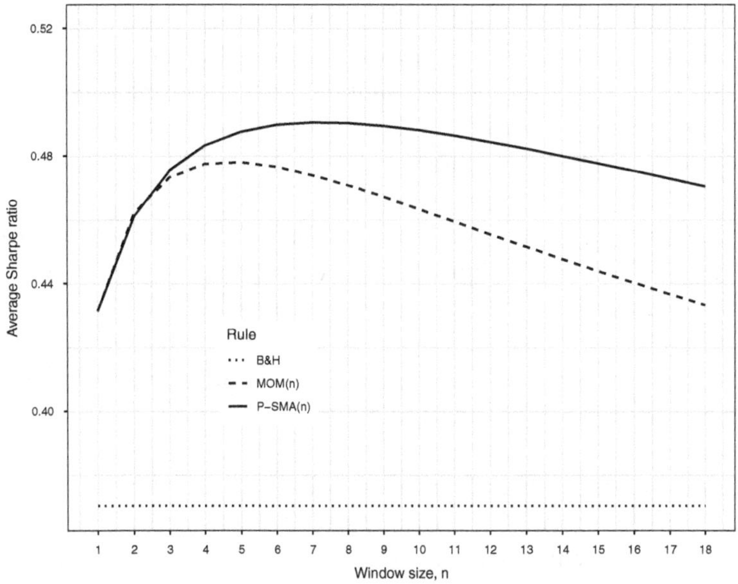

Fig. 13.8 Average Sharpe ratio of various MOM(n) and P-SMA(n) rules when the trend is modeled by an $AR(p)$ where p is uniformly distributed on 1 to 18 and where there is equal probability of the autoregressive coefficients being either constant or linearly decreasing. For comparison, the Sharpe ratio of the passive buy-and-hold (B&H) strategy is also shown

13.4 Summary

Traders commonly have faith in the effectiveness of trend-following strategies, backed by substantial empirical evidence. When implementing such a strategy, the most crucial decision for a trader is to select an appropriate trading rule that will successfully capture trends in a specific financial market.

The most popular approach to determining the optimal trading rule is based on backtesting. This method involves an exhaustive search for the best trading rule among a wide range of potential alternatives. It entails testing numerous combinations of trading rules, moving averages, and their parameters to identify the rule that has delivered the highest performance over a relevant historical period.

The backtesting method is highly favored and widely used due to two fundamental beliefs. First, the backtesting method is widely regarded as thorough and effective in ensuring that the optimal rule is found. Second, it is believed that the trading rule that has produced the best results in the past is likely to continue to perform well in the future. In this chapter, we validated the accuracy of these two beliefs.

The results of our investigation bring both bad and good news for traders. The bad news is that the backtesting methodology has revealed to have a very low degree of accuracy and dependability. Even when using a lengthy sample for analysis, there is a small probability of identifying the optimal trading rule correctly. This implies that traders typically use suboptimal rules to follow market trends.

On the other hand, the good news is that trend-following strategies have shown to be resilient to variations in trading rules. This may come as a surprise, but it can be explained by the fact that seemingly different trend-following rules generate highly correlated trading signals resulting in a significant degree of performance similarity. Consequently, even a suboptimal trend-following rule can still be useful in recognizing and capitalizing on price trends, resulting in profitable results.

Additionally, we conducted an analysis of the scenario where trend dynamics exhibit random changes over time. In such cases, it becomes impossible to identify the currently optimal trend-following rule as it keeps changing. However, our findings suggest that despite this uncertainty, trend-following strategies still display robust performance and are capable to beat the buy-and-hold strategy.

References

Zakamulin, V., & Giner, J. (2020). Trend Following with Momentum Versus Moving Average: A Tale of Differences. *Quantitative Finance, 20*(6), 985–1007.

Zakamulin, V., & Giner, J. (2022). Time Series Momentum in the US Stock Market: Empirical Evidence and Theoretical Analysis. *International Review of Financial Analysis, 82,* Article 102173.

14

Optimal Trading Frequency for Trend-Following Strategies

14.1 Introduction

In this chapter, we explore the decision of determining the optimal trading frequency[1] for a trend-following strategy. Many traders intuitively believe that daily trading is better than, for instance, monthly trading. The basic idea behind this hunch is that when you check trading signals daily, you can react more quickly to what is happening in the market. But there is a catch—this quick response might lead to getting tricked by false signals, often called "whipsaws."

The issue with these false signals is that they can mess up the effectiveness of the daily-based trend-following strategy. Whipsaws happen when price movements seem to indicate that a trend is reversing. This can make traders jump into action, only to find out later that the original trend continues. When you look at daily data, the ups and downs in prices can make these false signals worse, possibly causing you to make wrong decisions and end up with losses.

Surprisingly, only a few academic studies have investigated whether daily trading offers advantages over trading at lower frequencies. Typically, such studies incorporate a comparison between daily and monthly trading. One such study, conducted by Clare et al. (2013), examined this question by analyzing the S&P 500 index data from 1988 to 2011. They employed the back-testing methodology and considered the Price and Simple Moving Average crossover (P-SMA) rule and double SMA crossover (SMA-C) rule. The findings from their study indicate that there is no significant advantage in daily trading

[1] It is worth noting that when we speak of a "trading frequency," we do not mean that the trader changes the positions at the end of each period. Rather, it means that the trading signals are generated at the end of each period, but the positions are changed when the trading signal is changed.

V. Zakamulin and J. Giner, *The Ultimate Moving Average Handbook*,
https://doi.org/10.1007/978-3-031-90907-8_14

compared to trading on a monthly basis. In essence, the performance of trading rules remains quite consistent regardless of the data frequency.

Another study, conducted by Zakamulin (2017, Chapters 9 and 10), explored the same question using daily and monthly data from different US stock market indices spanning from 1944 to 2015. This study used various price and moving average crossover (P-MA) rules and double moving average crossover (MA-C) rules, evaluating both back-testing and forward-testing approaches. The outcomes of this study suggest that, during back-tests, following trends on a daily basis yields slightly better performance than monthly-based trend-following. However, in forward-tests, the daily-based trend-following exhibits slightly worse performance than its monthly counterpart. Overall, both studies advocate that the choice of trading frequency does not significantly impact trading outcomes.

The studies discussed in the previous paragraphs aimed to address the question of the most effective data frequency empirically. In this chapter, we take a pioneering step by approaching the same query analytically. This marks the first instance where we delve into this question through an analytical lens. We investigate the optimal trading frequency using two alternative approaches.

The first approach involves the quantitative assessment of the parameters of trend-following rules implemented at different trading frequencies. These parameters include the Noise Suppression Factor (NSF), Average Lag Time (ALT), and Expected Number of Whipsaws (ENW). The advantage of this approach lies in its virtually non-parametric nature, assuming only that market dynamics consist of two regimes: bull and bear. This method allows for an effective evaluation of trading rule properties without heavily relying on specific market assumptions.

Unfortunately, as we have often observed in the previous chapters of this book, using three quantitative metrics simultaneously seldom allows us to identify the most superior trading rule among various alternatives. The superiority of a trading rule is closely tied to its profitability. Therefore, to accurately select the optimal trading frequency, we must examine the profitability of a trend-following rule at different frequencies and choose the one where profitability is maximized.

In the second approach, we make specific parametric assumptions about the market return process and then investigate the performance of trend-following rules at various trading frequencies. The conclusions drawn from this approach are heavily dependent on these parametric assumptions. To ensure accuracy, we base our assumptions on realistic market dynamics and calibrate the parameters to those of the S&P 500 stock market index.

The results of both our theoretical approaches suggest that the choice of trading frequency is largely irrelevant. Specifically, the parameters and profitabilities of optimal trend-following strategies implemented at various trading frequencies are nearly identical. Therefore, our theoretical findings are in close agreement with the empirical results reported in the literature.

14.2 Selecting the Optimal Trading Frequency Using Quantitative Measures

14.2.1 Preliminaries

This section focuses on determining the optimal trading frequency by utilizing three quantitative measures suggested in this book, namely the NSF, ALT, and ENW. To streamline the discussion, we compare and contrast the quantitative measures of various trend-following rules at the daily and monthly frequencies. By drawing conclusions from this analysis, we can subsequently apply them to other trading frequencies.

The NSF serves as a gauge for the precision of a trading rule, offering insights into its capacity to sift through market noise and provide dependable signals. Conversely, the ALT quantifies the responsiveness of the trading rule, allowing us to grasp how swiftly it adjusts to evolving market conditions. The ENW is a function of the Smoothness Index (SMI). We opt for the ENW over the SMI because while we can recalibrate and measure the NSF and ALT of daily and monthly rules using a uniform scale, the same feasibility is not present for the SMI. Nonetheless, considering the intrinsic connection between the SMI and the ENW, we choose to evaluate the trading rules using the ENW in place of the SMI. Unlike the SMI, the ENW of both daily and monthly rules can be recalibrated and measured using a uniform scale.

For a consistent comparison, we will evaluate the parameters of both daily and monthly rules using identical measurement units. Irrespective of the trading frequency, we will compute the NSF on a daily basis. In contrast, we will calculate the ALT as a fraction of a year. Similarly, for any trading frequency, we will estimate the ENW per year. Now, let us determine the number of trading days in a year. The standard trading hours for US stock exchanges span from Monday through Friday, starting at 9:30 a.m. and closing at 4:00 p.m. On average, a year encompasses 252 trading days. Given that there are 12 months in a year, the average count of trading days per month is 21 ($252/12 = 21$). Consequently, a year is comprised of 12 months, with each month encompassing an average of 21 trading days.

As a final comment, in this chapter, we consider only the Momentum (MOM), price and moving average crossover (P-MA), and double moving average crossover (MA-C) rules based on the standard moving averages: Simple Moving Average (SMA), Linear Moving Average (LMA), and Exponential Moving Average (EMA). There are three key reasons driving this decision. First, these moving averages and associated rules are the most widely recognized and commonly used among traders. Second, we possess analytical solutions for the NSF, ALT, and ENW to these rules. Third, we are confident that the insights gleaned from the analysis of these rules and moving averages can be extrapolated to encompass all other trading rules and exotic moving averages.

14.2.2 Noise Suppression Factors for Monthly and Daily Rules

In this section, our objective is to compare the accuracy of trading rules implemented on a daily and monthly basis. Accuracy here refers to the percentage of correct trading signals, known as the Hit Ratio (HR), generated by a rule when the trend continues in the same direction. Assuming that financial asset returns follow a normal distribution, we calculate the hit ratio of the technical indicator $I(n)$ as follows:

$$\mathrm{HR}(I(n)) = \Phi\left(SNR(I(n))\right), \tag{14.1}$$

where $SNR(I(n))$ represents the signal-to-noise ratio of the technical indicator $I(n)$, and $\Phi(.)$ is the cumulative distribution function of a standard normal random variable. Given that $\Phi(x)$ is an increasing function of x, it follows that the hit ratio of a trading rule rises alongside an increase in the SNR of the rule. As a result, the trading rule exhibiting the highest SNR stands as the most accurate rule.

The SNR of the technical indicator is determined by the product of the NSF of the technical indicator and the SNR of the returns, r:

$$SNR(I(n)) = NSF(I(n)) \times SNR(r). \tag{14.2}$$

We suppose that the trading rule implemented on a daily basis uses n_d (daily) return observations, while the trading rule implemented on a monthly basis uses n_m (monthly) return observations. The SNR of the trading rule implemented on a daily basis is given by:

$$SNR(I(n_d)) = NSF(I(n_d)) \times SNR(r_d),$$

Table 14.1 Trading rules and their noise suppression factors

Trading rule	Noise suppression factor
MOM(n)	$\sqrt{n}$
P-SMA(n)	$0.87\sqrt{n}$
P-LMA(n)	$0.75\sqrt{n}$
P-EMA(n)	$\sqrt{n}$
SMA-C(s, l)	$0.87\sqrt{l}$
LMA-C(s, l)	$\frac{\sqrt{5l}}{3\sqrt{l-\frac{s}{3}}}$
EMA-C(s, l)	$\sqrt{l+s}$

where $NSF(I(n_d))$ represents the NSF of $I(n_d)$ and $SNR(r_d)$ signifies the SNR of daily returns. In a similar fashion, the SNR for the monthly trading rule is expressed as:

$$SNR(I(n_m)) = NSF(I(n_m)) \times SNR(r_m),$$

where $NSF(I(n_m))$ is the NSF of $I(n_m)$ and $SNR(r_m)$ denotes the SNR of monthly returns.

Table 14.1 lists the trading rules and analytical solutions to their NSFs. Many of these analytical solutions are approximations derived from simplified assumptions. It is essential to highlight that the analytical solution for nearly all rules can be expressed as $NSF = a\sqrt{p}$, where a represents a positive constant, and p indicates the total number of return lags within a trading rule ($p = n$ for the MOM(n) and P-MA(n) rules, $p = l$ for the SMA-C(s, l) rule, and $p = s + l$ for the EMA-C(s, l) rule).

Let us suppose that the market is in a bull state where the process for daily returns is given by:

$$r_{d,t} = \mu + \sigma z_t,$$

where $\mu > 0$ is the mean daily return, σ is the standard deviation of daily returns, and z_t is a standard normal random variable, $z_t \sim \mathcal{N}(0, 1)$. The SNR of daily returns is given by:

$$SNR(r_d) = \frac{\mu}{\sigma}.$$

What is the SNR of monthly returns? If the daily returns are in the form of logarithmic returns, then the computation of monthly returns involves summing up the daily returns as follows:

$$r_{m,t} = \sum_{s=1}^{21} r_{d,s}.$$

For non-logarithmic returns, this equation holds approximately true. In essence, the monthly return can be approximated by adding up the daily returns. The next step is to re-write the equation above as:

$$r_{m,t} = \sum_{s=1}^{21} (\mu + \sigma z_s) = 21\mu + \sigma \sum_{s=1}^{21} z_s = 21\mu + \sigma Z_t.$$

The term $Z_t = \sum_{s=1}^{21} z_s$ represents a random variable that results from the summation of 21 standard normal random variables. As the normal distribution falls under the category of stable distributions, Z_t emerges as a random variable following a normal distribution. The mean value of Z_t is calculated as:

$$E[Z_t] = E\left[\sum_{s=1}^{21} z_s\right] = \sum_{s=1}^{21} E[z_s] = 0.$$

We make the assumption that the daily returns are independent. Thus, the variance of Z_t equals the sum of the variances of 21 random variables z_s:

$$Var[Z_t] = Var\left[\sum_{s=1}^{21} z_s\right] = \sum_{s=1}^{21} Var[z_s] = 21.$$

Consequently, we deduce that $Z_t \sim \mathcal{N}(0, 21)$. In simpler terms, Z_t follows a normal distribution with a mean of 0 and a variance of 21 (equivalent to a standard deviation of $\sqrt{21}$). Therefore, Z_t can be represented in the following manner:

$$Z_t = \sqrt{21} z_t,$$

where z_t symbolizes a standard normal random variable.

In summary, the process governing monthly returns can be expressed as follows:

$$r_{m,t} = 21\mu + \sqrt{21}\sigma z_t.$$

It is worth noting that the average monthly return amounts to 21 times the average daily return, while the standard deviation for monthly returns is $\sqrt{21}$ times the daily standard deviation. The SNR of monthly returns is given by:

$$SNR(r_m) = \frac{21\mu}{\sqrt{21}\sigma} = \sqrt{21} \times SNR(r_d).$$

This indicates that the SNR of monthly returns is $\sqrt{21}$ times that of daily returns. This finding holds valuable insights, revealing that monthly returns exhibit superior signal quality compared to daily returns. The aggregation of daily returns into monthly returns amplifies both the signal's power and the noise's power. However, the signal power increase outpaces the noise power rise, leading to this favorable outcome.

The relationship expressed by the equation above motivates that one can compare the NSFs of trading rules executed on both monthly and daily bases. However, for a precise and equitable comparison of the two NSFs, it is imperative to adjust the NSF of the monthly trading rule by a factor of $\sqrt{21}$. In essence, the comparison can be made between:

$$NSF(I(n_m)) \times \sqrt{21} \text{ compared to } NSF(I(n_d)).$$

That is, to ensure an equitable and unbiased comparison of the NSFs for trading rules implemented on both monthly and daily bases, it is essential to multiply the NSF of the monthly rule by a factor of $\sqrt{21}$. This adjustment accounts for the higher SNR of the monthly returns compared to the SNR of the corresponding daily returns.

Now, we are equipped to compare the signal-to-noise ratios of technical indicators calculated using both daily and monthly returns. We make the assumption that each technical indicator is computed using the same size of an averaging window. Specifically, if n_d denotes the averaging window's size for the technical indicator computed using daily returns, then the size of the averaging window for the technical indicator computed using monthly returns is $n_m = \frac{n_d}{21}$.

For any P-MA(n) rule and the MOM(n) rule, the NSF for the technical indicator utilizing daily returns can be expressed as:

$$NSF(I(n_d)) = a\sqrt{n_d}.$$

The NSF for the corresponding technical indicator utilizing monthly returns is given by:

$$NSF(I(n_m)) = a\sqrt{n_m}\sqrt{21} = a\sqrt{\frac{n_d}{21}}\sqrt{21} = a\sqrt{n_d} = NSF(I(n_d)).$$

In simpler terms, the NSF for the technical indicator computed using monthly returns equals the NSF for the technical indicator computed using daily returns, provided that $n_m = \frac{n_d}{21}$. For instance, the NSF of the P-SMA rule calculated using 210 daily returns is equal to the NSF of the P-SMA rule computed using 10 monthly returns. This conclusion extends to the technical indicators of the MA-C rules as well. In essence, when it comes to detecting trend direction accurately, there is no inherent advantage in trading using daily data as opposed to monthly data, as long as $n_m = \frac{n_d}{21}$—meaning that the count of monthly returns corresponds to the count of daily returns divided by the number of trading days in a month.

14.2.3 Average Lag Times for Monthly and Daily Rules

In this section, we compare the average lag times of trading rules implemented on a daily and monthly basis. It is important to keep in mind that any trading rule based on moving averages of past data is inherently a lagging technical indicator. The ALT of the trading rule $I(n)$ is the average time it takes for a trend-following rule to change the trading signal when the trend direction changes.

Table 14.2 lists the main trading rules and analytical solutions to their average lag times. Again, it is worth emphasizing that most of these analytical solutions are approximations derived from simplified assumptions. Note that for the MOM(n) and all P-MA(n) rules, the analytical solution is given by $ALT = a \times n$, whereas, for all MA-C(s, l) rules, the analytical solution is given by $ALT = a \times l + b \times s$, where a and b are positive constants. It is essential to observe that the average lag time is a linear function of the number of return observations used in a trading rule.

As in the preceding section, we suppose that the trading rule implemented on a daily basis uses n_d (daily) return observations, while the trading rule implemented on a monthly basis uses n_m (monthly) return observations. When comparing the average lag times of these rules, it is crucial to standardize the

Table 14.2 Trading rules and their average lag times. In all MA-C(s, l) rules, k_s and k_l denote the average lag time of the corresponding P-MA(s) and P-MA(l) rules. As an example, for the SMA-C(s, l) rule, $k_s = 0.293s$ and $k_l = 0.293l$

Trading rule	Average lag time
MOM(n)	$0.5n$
P-SMA(n)	$0.293n$
P-LMA(n)	$0.206n$
P-EMA(n)	$0.347n$
SMA-C(s, l)	$k_l + 1.414k_s$
LMA-C(s, l)	$k_l + 1.442k_s$
EMA-C(s, l)	$k_l + 1.443k_s$

measurement to a common scale of a year. This ensures accurate comparison. Thus, the average lag time of a P-MA(n_d) rule implemented daily is calculated as follows:

$$ALT(I(n_d)) = \frac{a \times n_d}{252},$$

whereas the average lag time of an P-MA(n_m) rule implemented monthly is given by:

$$ALT(I(n_m)) = \frac{a \times n_m}{12}.$$

When $n_m = \frac{n_d}{21}$, the expression for the ALT of the monthly trading rule reduces to:

$$ALT(I(n_m)) = \frac{a\frac{n_d}{21}}{12} = \frac{a \times n_d}{252} = ALT(I(n_d)).$$

In simpler terms, if n_m is set to $\frac{n_d}{21}$, the average lag time for a P-MA rule computed using monthly returns becomes identical to the average lag time for the corresponding P-MA rule computed using daily returns.

This similarity also extends to all MA-C rules and can be illustrated as follows. Let us consider an MA-C rule implemented on a daily basis using s_d and l_d daily return observations for the shorter and longer moving averages, respectively. The corresponding MA-C rule implemented on a monthly basis employs $s_m = \frac{s_d}{21}$ and $l_m = \frac{l_d}{21}$ monthly return observations for the same moving averages. Under these assumptions:

$$\begin{aligned} ALT(I(s_m, l_m)) &= \frac{a \times l_m + b \times s_m}{12} = \frac{a \times \frac{l_d}{21} + b \times \frac{s_d}{21}}{12} \\ &= \frac{a \times l_d + b \times s_d}{252} = ALT(I(s_d, l_d)). \end{aligned}$$

To put it simply, the average lag time of an MA-C rule computed using monthly returns matches the average lag time of the corresponding MA-C rule computed using daily returns if $s_m = \frac{s_d}{21}$ and $l_m = \frac{l_d}{21}$.

The calculations provided above might mistakenly suggest that there is no difference in delay time between trading with daily or monthly data. However, it is important to acknowledge a significant distinction. When implementing a trading rule on a monthly basis, the monthly returns are not aggregated over the preceding 21 days, but rather they are calendar-month returns calculated using month-end prices. This has an important implication. In the monthly trading scenario, a new trading signal can only be generated at the end of each month—at the end of January, the end of February, and so on. Conversely, with daily trading, a new trading signal can be generated at the end of each trading day. This distinction underscores that monthly trading involves a more extended interval between potential trading signal updates due to the reliance on calendar months.

To repeat, if the monthly returns were calculated using returns aggregated over the preceding 21 trading days, then the average lag time for a trading rule executed on a monthly basis would indeed match that of the corresponding trading rule implemented on a daily basis. However, given that the monthly returns reflect calendar-month returns, a trading rule executed daily is capable of identifying trend reversals earlier than its monthly counterpart.

This difference in timing translates into a range of potential lead times for trend turning points: from 1 day earlier to up to 20 days earlier, compared to monthly trading. On average, a trading rule implemented on a monthly basis identifies a trend turning point 10 days later than the equivalent rule implemented on a daily basis. Consequently, for a justifiable comparison of delay times, it becomes essential to compute the average lag time for a trading rule utilizing month-end data as follows:

$$ALT(I(n_m)) = \frac{ALT(I(n_m))}{12} + \frac{10}{252},$$

where $\frac{ALT(I(n_m))}{12}$ represents the average lag time (in years) for the trading rule employing n_m monthly returns, and $\frac{10}{252}$ accounts for the additional delay from using month-end data. The term $\frac{10}{252}$, referred to as the "month-end delay correction," accounts for the additional lag introduced by using month-end data, ensuring a fair comparison between the average lag times of daily and monthly trading frequencies.

To provide a clear example of how a fair comparison should be conducted, let us examine the average lag time of the P-SMA rule utilizing 210 daily returns and the corresponding P-SMA rule using 10 monthly returns (the equivalence follows from 210/21=10). Table 14.2 reports that the ALT of the P-SMA(n) rule equals $0.293n$. Therefore, for the 210-day P-SMA rule, the average lag time is given by:

$$ALT(\text{210-day P-SMA}) = \frac{0.293 \times 210}{252} = 0.244 \text{ years.}$$

For the corresponding 10-month P-SMA rule, the average lag time is computed as follows:

$$ALT(\text{10-month P-SMA}) = \frac{0.293 \times 10}{12} + \frac{10}{252} = 0.284 \text{ years.}$$

This example demonstrates that in comparison with daily trading, monthly trading involves identifying a trend turning point with an average delay of 0.04 years, which equates to 10 trading days.

14.2.4 Expected Number of Whipsaws for Monthly and Daily Rules

In this section, our focus shifts toward comparing the expected number of whipsaw trades that result from trading rules executed daily and monthly. As with the previous discussions, we continue to assume that the trading rule implemented daily relies on n_d (daily) return observations, while its monthly counterpart employs n_m (monthly) return observations.

To ensure a correct comparison of trading rules operating at distinct data frequencies, it is essential to adopt a uniform metric. A natural metric is the expected annual number of whipsaw trades. We remind the reader that over a single trading period, the probability of a position reversal is given by:

$$Prob(\text{Reversal}) = \frac{1}{2} - \frac{1}{\pi} \arcsin(SMI(I(n))),$$

where $\arcsin(\cdot)$ is the inverse trigonometric sine function and $SMI(I(n))$ represents the Smoothness Index of the technical indicator $I(n)$. The SMI is, in fact, the first-order autocorrelation function of the technical indicator.

Consequently, the expected number of whipsaws a year is computed as follows:

$$ENW(I(n)) = N\left(\frac{1}{2} - \frac{1}{\pi} \arcsin(SMI(I(n)))\right),$$

where N corresponds to the number of trading periods within a year. Therefore, for an $I(n_d)$ rule implemented on a daily basis, the expected annual number of whipsaws is given by:

$$ENW(I(n_d)) = 252\left(\frac{1}{2} - \frac{1}{\pi}\arcsin(SMI(I(n_d)))\right).$$

Similarly, for an $I(n_m)$ rule executed on a monthly basis, the expected annual number of whipsaws can be computed as:

$$ENW(I(n_m)) = 12\left(\frac{1}{2} - \frac{1}{\pi}\arcsin(SMI(I(n_m)))\right).$$

As mentioned earlier, we continue to assume that n_m corresponds to $\frac{n_d}{21}$. However, a challenge emerges due to the intricate nature of the analytical expressions governing the smoothness index for various trading strategies. The function $\arcsin(\cdot)$ behaves in a markedly nonlinear manner when $SMI(I(n))$ is in proximity to 1. This intricate behavior impedes a straightforward analytical comparison of the expected number of whipsaw trades between trading rules executed daily and those executed monthly. To facilitate a meaningful comparison, it becomes necessary to carry out a numerical calculation of the expected number of whipsaws. Despite this numerical approach, we can still make a reasoned or informed estimation regarding the trading frequency likely to yield the highest expected number of whipsaws.

It is worth noting that the $SMI(I(n))$ tends to increase as n becomes larger. Consequently, in the context of daily trading, $SMI(I(n_d))$ holds a higher value compared to $SMI(I(n_m))$ associated with monthly trading. This difference leads to the conclusion that the probability of a position reversal over a day is lower than the probability of a position reversal over a month. However, there is a substantial disparity between the number of trading days and the number of months within a year. This intriguing insight allows us to hypothesize that the expected number of whipsaw trades per year is lower with monthly trading compared to daily trading.

14.2.5 Examples of Comparison

The preceding discussion leads us to several key conclusions. First, the accuracy in detecting trend direction remains comparable between daily and monthly trading. Second, when engaging in daily trading, the time delay in recognizing trend turning points averages 10 days less than with monthly trading. Third, this slight advantage of daily trading is, unfortunately, offset by a notable drawback. Specifically, daily trading is associated with a substantial increase in the expected number of whipsaw trades, as compared to monthly trading. The extent of this increase remains uncertain. To clarify this, numerical computations are necessary. It is important to remember, however, that all these conclusions are made under the assumption that the number of monthly observations is the result of dividing the number of daily observations by 21 (i.e., $n_m = \frac{n_d}{21}$). The issue arises from the fact that n_m must be an integer number, but there is no guarantee that the division $\frac{n_d}{21}$ will always yield an integer. As an illustration, consider the popular 50- and 200-day SMA crossover trading strategy. Neither $\frac{50}{21}$ nor $\frac{200}{21}$ results in an integer. Consequently, comparing the trading rules implemented on both a daily and monthly basis using quantitative measures is not straightforward. In this section, we demonstrate how to conduct this comparison.

Before providing specific examples for comparison, it is important to recall our established convention. In the context of a P-SMA(n) rule, the variable n represents the number of return observations used in calculating a moving average. It is worth noting that "SMA" pertains to the weighting function applied to prices, not returns. However, in practical applications, n signifies the number of price observations utilized in computing a moving average. For instance, when the term "10-month SMA rule" is mentioned, it indicates that a simple (equally-weighted) moving average of the most recent 10 prices is computed. A Buy (Sell) trading signal is generated when the latest price is above (below) the simple moving average of the past 10 prices. Notably, the count of return observations corresponds to the count of price observations minus 1. Therefore, employing the concept of "trading with a 10-month SMA" within our framework implies utilizing the P-SMA(9) rule. Within our interpretation, the P-SMA(9) rule signifies that a Buy (Sell) trading signal emerges when the linear moving average of the last 9 returns is positive (negative).

Our convention is grounded in the observation that any trading rule employing single or multiple moving averages of prices can be equivalently expressed as a trading rule reliant on a single moving average of returns. It is worth noting that our convention deviates from the standard approach. To facilitate more comprehensible and relatable comparisons, we will transition to the standard convention for the remainder of this section, wherein the number of price observations is employed instead of the number of return observations.

It is essential to highlight that most of our analytical findings showcased in Tables 14.1 and 14.2 rest on simplifications and approximations. To ensure a dependable comparison of trading rules, we carry out exact numerical computations of the NSF, ALT, and ENW in this section.

Table 14.3 Comparison of trading with 50- and 200-day SMA crossover and trading with 10-month SMA. Average lag time is measured as a fraction of a year. The expected number of whipsaws is per year

	50- & 200-day SMA	10-month SMA
Noise suppression factor	12.25	12.22
Average lag time	0.31	0.27
Expected number of whipsaws	1.60	2.18

Let us consider our initial example for comparison, which draws from the fact that the widely embraced trading rule in daily trading is the 50- and 200-day SMA crossover. Conversely, in monthly trading, the prevailing trading strategy appears to be the 10-month SMA (see, among others, Faber, 2007 and Clare et al., 2013). Table 14.3 reports the outcomes of comparing the parameters of these two prominent trading rules. Our first observation is that both rules exhibit a comparable level of accuracy in identifying trend direction. While the 10-month SMA rule boasts a slightly shorter average lag time, the 50- and 200-day SMA crossover exhibits a slightly lower expected number of whipsaw trades. Essentially, each rule has a minor edge and a minor drawback over the other. A reasonable assumption is that the real-world performances of these two rules are quite similar.

The issue with the initial example of comparison is that an SMA-C rule was compared to a P-SMA rule. A fair comparison requires that both rules belong to the same type. Therefore, in our second example, we compare the parameters of the 200-day SMA rule and the 10-month SMA rule. The parameters of these rules are reported in Table 14.4. First, note that both rules have identical accuracy in detecting trend direction. Second, the 200-day SMA rule showcases a marginally shorter average lag time compared to the 10-month SMA rule. Third and most important, the 200-day SMA rule has a substantially higher expected number of whipsaw trades than the 10-month SMA rule. That is, a slight advantage comes with a significant disadvantage. Therefore, we firmly believe that the performance of the 10-month SMA rule is better than the performance of the 200-day SMA rule.

Our third comparison example is related to the first one and is motivated by the findings documented in Zakamulin (2017, Chapter 9). In particular, Zakamulin examines the performance of various P-MA and MA-C rules using the long-run historical data on the S&P 500 index. When monthly data are used, he finds that the best performing rule is the 2- and 10-month SMA crossover rule. Table 14.5 compares the parameters of the 50- and 200-day SMA crossover rule and the 2- and 10-month SMA crossover rule. The evident

Table 14.4 Comparison of trading with 200-day SMA and trading with 10-month SMA. Average lag time is measured as a fraction of a year. The expected number of whipsaw trades is per year

	200-day SMA	**10-month SMA**
Noise suppression factor	12.23	12.22
Average lag time	0.23	0.27
Expected number of whipsaws	9.84	2.18

Table 14.5 Comparison of trading with 50- and 200-day SMA crossover and trading with 2- and 10-month SMA crossover. Average lag time is measured as a fraction of a year. The expected number of whipsaw trades is per year

	50- & 200-day SMA	2- & 10-month SMA
Noise suppression factor	12.25	12.36
Average lag time	0.31	0.30
Expected number of whipsaws	1.60	1.64

and unequivocal conclusion drawn from the values presented in this table is that both rules exhibit nearly indistinguishable parameters. A reasonable inference would be that the real-world performance of these two rules should be essentially identical.

The challenge with the preceding example arises from the dissimilar sizes of the shorter and longer moving averages in the two alternative rules. Specifically, in the 50- and 200-day SMA crossover rule, the shorter (longer) moving average is computed using 49 (199) daily return observations. In contrast, within the 2- and 10-month SMA crossover rule, the shorter (longer) moving average is calculated using 21 (189) daily return observations, which are then aggregated into monthly observations. In our fourth example, we will contrast the 43- and 190-day SMA crossover rule with the 3- and 10-month SMA crossover rule. By doing so, both rules will share the same sizes for their shorter and longer moving averages. In essence, this example establishes a direct one-to-one correspondence between the daily and monthly rules. The parameters of these rules are detailed in Table 14.6.

The discussion in Sect. 14.2.2 implies an equivalent accuracy between both rules in detecting trend direction. However, the findings illustrated in Table 14.6 unveil variations in the NSFs. This inconsistency arises from the reliance on approximate expressions for the NSFs of different trading rules in Sect. 14.2.2, whereas the values detailed in Table 14.6 originate from precise numerical computations. Compared to the 43- and 190-day SMA crossover rule, the

Table 14.6 Comparison of trading with 43- and 190-day SMA crossover and trading with 3- and 10-month SMA crossover. Average lag time is measured as a fraction of a year. The expected number of whipsaw trades is per year

	43- & 190-day SMA	3- & 10-month SMA
Noise suppression factor	11.94	12.40
Average lag time	0.28	0.34
Expected number of whipsaws	1.75	1.44

3- and 10-month SMA crossover rule demonstrates a slightly greater NSF and a somewhat reduced ENW. Simultaneously, the 3- and 10-month SMA crossover rule entails a slightly longer ALT when compared to the 43- and 190-day SMA crossover rule. However, these parameter distinctions remain relatively minor.

Our fifth and concluding example is influenced by the preference of certain traders to employ the Momentum rule (MOM(n)) instead of rules grounded in SMA. For instance, Antonacci (2014) endorses using the 12-month MOM rule. This rule's performance is also explored in Gwilym et al. (2010). It is important to recall that the trading signal in this rule hinges on the disparity between the latest price and the price from n months (or days) ago. A variant of this rule, known as the Time-Series Momentum rule (TSMOM(n)), was introduced by Moskowitz et al. (2012). Fundamentally, this rule equates to the MOM(n) rule. The sole distinction is that in the MOM(n) rule, n designates the number of price observations, while in the TSMOM(n) rule, n signifies the count of return observations. Consequently, the relationship between the two rules can be expressed as follows: $TSMOM(n) \equiv MOM(n+1)$. Moskowitz et al. (2012) advocate for employing the 12-month TSMOM rule. In the realm of daily trading, the 12-month TSMOM rule is analogous to trading using the 252-day MOM rule.

Table 14.7 reports the parameters of the 252-day MOM rule, 12-month TSMOM rule, and 12-month MOM rule. As expected, compared to the 12-month TSMOM, the 12-month MOM (equivalent to the 11-month TSMOM

Table 14.7 Comparison of trading with 252-day MOM, trading with 12-month TSMOM, and trading with 12-month MOM. Average lag time is measured as a fraction of a year. The expected number of whipsaw trades is per year

	252-day MOM	12-month TSMOM	12-month MOM
Noise suppression factor	15.84	15.87	15.20
Average lag time	0.50	0.54	0.50
Expected number of whipsaws	7.16	1.57	1.64

rule) has a slightly shorter average lag time, a marginally lower NSF, and a marginally larger expected number of whipsaw trades. Yet, the parameters do not differ much; hence, it is reasonable to assume that the performance of these two rules is quite similar. Compared to the 252-day MOM rule, the 12-month TSMOM rule has virtually the same NSF, a slightly longer average lag time, and a substantially reduced expected number of whipsaw trades. Consequently, our conclusion leans toward favoring trading with the 12-month TSMOM rule over the 252-day MOM rule.

14.3 Parametric Approach to Selecting the Optimal Trading Frequency

14.3.1 Motivation

In this section, we adopt a parametric approach following the methodology used in the preceding chapters of this book. Specifically, we assume that the returns follow an autoregressive process of order p, denoted by $AR(p)$. This type of process is persistent and thus lends itself well to trend-following strategies. The objective of the trader is to identify the most effective technical indicator for tracking trends in the financial market. The optimal technical indicator is the one that yields the highest risk-adjusted performance for the trading strategy, which is measured by the Sharpe ratio.

To streamline the analysis, we assume that the trader possesses knowledge of the parameters of the $AR(p)$ process. These parameters encompass the process' order and the values of the autoregressive coefficients. As demonstrated in previous chapters of this book, in the absence of transaction costs, the return weights in the optimal technical indicator mirror the shape of the autoregressive coefficients.

However, we acknowledge that trading in financial assets incurs transaction costs which may significantly diminish the effectiveness of the trend-following strategy. Therefore, the objective of the trader is to select return weights in the optimal technical indicator that maximize the Sharpe ratio of the trend-following strategy while accounting for transaction costs. In this scenario, it is no longer optimal to employ the return weights with the same shape as the autoregressive coefficients. With transaction costs in play, the optimal return weights represent a smoothed version of the autoregressive coefficients' shape.

It is essential to note that the total transaction costs incurred by a trend-following strategy can be altered not only by modifying the shape of the return-weighting function but also by adjusting the trading frequency. Intuitively, adopting a lower trading frequency is expected to result in lower expected trading costs.

The objective of this section is to examine the impact of trading frequency on the effectiveness of the trend-following strategy. Specifically, we are interested in finding the optimal trading frequency for trend-following trading. It is crucial to emphasize that for each trading frequency, we calculate the return weights in the optimal technical indicator. Therefore, the optimization process occurs in two dimensions: the first dimension involves determining the optimal vector of return weights for each trading frequency, and the second dimension involves selecting the optimal trading frequency.

14.3.2 Model Formulation

The theoretical model, which has been discussed in previous chapters, is summarized below for clarity and self-contentedness. We assume that the returns adhere to the $AR(p)$ model. The objective for investors is to determine the optimal return weights for the technical indicator, with the aim of maximizing the Sharpe ratio of the trend-following strategy while taking into account transaction costs.

Specifically, the $AR(p)$ process for returns is defined by the following equation:

$$r_t = c + \sum_{i=1}^{p} \phi_i r_{t-i} + \varepsilon_t, \tag{14.3}$$

where r_{t-i} is the return observed at time $t - i$, c is a constant, $\{\phi_1, \phi_2, \ldots, \phi_p\}$ are the autoregressive coefficients, and ε_t are i.i.d. random variables with zero mean and variance of σ_ε^2.

The mean and variance of r_t are given by:

$$\mu = E[r_t] = \frac{c}{1 - \sum_{i=1}^{p} \phi_i}, \qquad \sigma^2 = Var(r_t) = \frac{\sigma_\varepsilon^2}{1 - \sum_{i=1}^{p} \phi_i \rho_i}, \tag{14.4}$$

where ρ_i denotes the autocorrelation between r_t and r_{t-i}. The required autocorrelations can be found by solving the Yule-Walker linear equations.

The technical indicator for a trend-following rule at time t is computed as a moving average of past p return observations. The equation for the technical indicator is as follows:

$$I_t(p) = \sum_{i=0}^{p-1} \theta_i r_{t-i}, \tag{14.5}$$

where p is the size of the averaging window, and θ_i is the weight assigned to return r_{t-i}. It should be noted that the number of return lags utilized in the technical indicator equals the order of the autoregressive process for returns.

The trend-following strategy involves investing in the risky asset when the trading signal is Buy. Conversely, when the trading signal is Sell, the strategy involves selling the risky asset and investing in the risk-free instrument. There are transaction costs associated with buying and selling the risky asset, with a fixed percentage of τ subtracted from the return of the trend-following strategy. Trading in the risk-free asset incurs no transaction costs. The return of the trend-following strategy at time t is denoted as R_t and is defined as follows:[2]

$$R_t = \begin{cases} r_t & \text{if } I_{t-1}(p) > 0,\, I_{t-2}(p) > 0, \\ r_t - \tau & \text{if } I_{t-1}(p) > 0,\, I_{t-2}(p) < 0, \\ r_f & \text{if } I_{t-1}(p) < 0,\, I_{t-2}(p) < 0, \\ r_f - \tau & \text{if } I_{t-1}(p) < 0,\, I_{t-2}(p) > 0, \end{cases} \tag{14.6}$$

where r_f denotes the constant risk-free rate of return.

The performance of the trend-following strategy is evaluated using the Sharpe ratio, which is computed using the formula:

$$SR(R_t) = \frac{E[R_t] - r_f}{\sqrt{Var[R_t]}}, \tag{14.7}$$

where $E[R_t]$ represents the expected return of the trend-following strategy and $Var[R_t]$ denotes the variance of the returns.

The expected return of the trend-following strategy and the variance of the returns are computed as:

$$E[R_t] = (\mu - r_f)\Phi(-d) + r_f + g - \tau\, Prob(\text{Rev}), \tag{14.8}$$

$$\begin{aligned} Var[R_t] &= (\mu^2 + \sigma^2)\Phi(-d) + g(2\mu + \sigma\varrho d) + r_f^2\Phi(d) \\ &\quad - \big((\mu - r_f)\Phi(-d) + r_f + g\big)^2 + \tau^2 Prob(\text{Rev})(1 - Prob(\text{Rev})), \end{aligned} \tag{14.9}$$

where

$$d = -\frac{m}{v}, \quad g = \sigma\varrho\,\varphi(d),$$

[2] In previous chapters, we used the notation $R_t|TC$ to indicate that returns include transaction costs. For brevity, this chapter simplifies the notation to R_t.

and $\varphi(.)$ and $\Phi(.)$ denote the probability density function and the cumulative distribution function of the standard normal random variable:

$$\varphi(z) = \frac{1}{\sqrt{2\pi}} e^{-\frac{z^2}{2}}, \quad \Phi(d) = \int_{-\infty}^{d} \varphi(z) dz.$$

The variables m and v represent the mean value and variance of the technical indicator, respectively. The equations for m and v are as follows:

$$m = \mathbf{1}'\boldsymbol{\theta}\mu, \qquad v^2 = \boldsymbol{\theta}'\boldsymbol{R}_{p,p}\boldsymbol{\theta}\sigma^2, \tag{14.10}$$

where $\mathbf{1}$ is the $p \times 1$ vector of ones, $\boldsymbol{\theta}$ is the $p \times 1$ vector of the return weights in the technical indicator, and $\boldsymbol{R}_{p,p}$ is the $p \times p$ matrix defined by:

$$\boldsymbol{R}_{p,p} = \begin{bmatrix} 1 & \rho_1 & \rho_2 & \cdots & \rho_{p-1} \\ \rho_1 & 1 & \rho_1 & \cdots & \rho_{p-2} \\ \rho_2 & \rho_1 & 1 & \cdots & \rho_{p-3} \\ \vdots & \vdots & \vdots & \ddots & \vdots \\ \rho_{p-1} & \rho_{p-2} & \rho_{p-3} & \cdots & 1 \end{bmatrix}. \tag{14.11}$$

The variable ϱ denotes the correlation coefficient between r_t and $I_{t-1}(p)$ and is computed as follows:

$$\varrho = \frac{\boldsymbol{\theta}'\boldsymbol{R}_{p,p}\boldsymbol{\phi}}{\sqrt{\boldsymbol{\theta}'\boldsymbol{R}_{p,p}\boldsymbol{\theta}}}, \tag{14.12}$$

where $\boldsymbol{\phi}$ is the $p \times 1$ vector of the autoregressive coefficients.

Finally, $Prob(\text{Rev})$ denotes the probability of position reversal over one period. This probability is computed as:

$$Prob(\text{Rev}) = \frac{1}{2} - \frac{1}{\pi} \arcsin(\text{SMI}(I(p))), \tag{14.13}$$

where $\arcsin(\cdot)$ represents the inverse trigonometric sine function, and $\text{SMI}(I(p))$ denotes the Smoothness Index (SMI) of the technical indicator $I(p)$. The smoothness of a technical indicator is calculated using the following formula:

$$\text{SMI}(I(p)) = \frac{\sum_{i=0}^{p-2} \theta_i \theta_{i+1}}{\sum_{i=0}^{p-1} \theta_i^2}.$$

The trader's goal is to determine the optimal return weights in the technical indicator to maximize the Sharpe ratio of the trend-following strategy. Formally, the trader solves the following optimization problem:

$$\max_{\boldsymbol{\theta}} \quad SR(R_t) \text{ subject to } \boldsymbol{\theta}'\mathbf{1} = 1, \tag{14.14}$$

where the condition $\boldsymbol{\theta}'\mathbf{1} = 1$ ensures that the sum of return weights is equal to one, providing a unique solution.

Unfortunately, the optimization problem defined by Eq. (14.14) does not have an analytical solution. Nonetheless, it can be solved using standard numerical methods for nonlinear optimization. These methods involve iteratively searching for the optimal return weights that maximize the Sharpe ratio of the trend-following strategy.

14.3.3 Temporally Aggregated Autoregressive Process

Our analysis assumes that the market return, as described in Eq. (14.3), pertains to daily returns. However, the trader observes the market returns over time periods of $d \geq 1$ days. Despite the frequency of observation, it is apparent that the market returns follow the $AR(h)$ process where $h = p/d$. For instance, if the original order of the autoregressive process for daily returns is $p = 200$, then over weekly periods that span 5 working days, the process' order becomes $200/5 = 40$.

For ease of analysis, we assume that the trend-following strategy is implemented using log returns. We also suppose that the time period from $t - 1$ to t encompasses d days, and we denote the market returns for this period as r_t^d:

$$r_t^d = \sum_{i=1}^{d} r_{t-1,i},$$

where $r_{t-1,i}$ represents the return for day i over the period from $t - 1$ to t. Note that r_t^d is a time series of the market returns aggregated over d-day periods. These aggregated market returns follow an $AR(h)$ process, similar to that defined in Eq. (14.3):

$$r_t^d = c^d + \sum_{i=1}^{h} \phi_i^d r_{t-i}^d + \varepsilon_t^d, \tag{14.15}$$

where $\boldsymbol{\phi}_h^d = [\phi_1^d, \phi_2^d, \ldots, \phi_h^d]'$ is the $h \times 1$ vector of the autoregressive coefficients to be determined.

Denote by ρ_k^d the autocorrelation of order k of the $AR(h)$ process for the aggregated market returns. When we know the elements of the vector that contains the first h autocorrelations, $\boldsymbol{\rho}_h^d = [\rho_1^d, \rho_2^d, \ldots, \rho_h^d]'$, the autoregressive coefficients can be found by solving the Yule-Walker equations:

$$\begin{bmatrix} 1 & \rho_1^d & \rho_2^d & \cdots & \rho_{h-1}^d \\ \rho_1^d & 1 & \rho_1^d & \cdots & \rho_{h-2}^d \\ \rho_2^d & \rho_1^d & 1 & \cdots & \rho_{h-3}^d \\ \vdots & \vdots & \vdots & \ddots & \vdots \\ \rho_{h-1}^d & \rho_{h-2}^d & \rho_{h-3}^d & \cdots & 1 \end{bmatrix} \begin{bmatrix} \phi_1^d \\ \phi_2^d \\ \phi_3^d \\ \vdots \\ \phi_h^d \end{bmatrix} = \begin{bmatrix} \rho_1^d \\ \rho_2^d \\ \rho_3^d \\ \vdots \\ \rho_h^d \end{bmatrix}, \tag{14.16}$$

or more concisely:

$$\boldsymbol{R}_{h,h}^d \boldsymbol{\phi}_h^d = \boldsymbol{\rho}_h^d, \tag{14.17}$$

where $\boldsymbol{R}_{h,h}^d$ represents the $h \times h$ matrix defined similarly to Eq. (14.11).

A stock exchange operates from Monday to Friday and remains closed during weekends and public holidays. The number of trading days in a year can vary, but on average, there are typically around 252 trading days per year.

To calculate the number of trading periods in a year, we use the formula $250/d$ or $252/d$, depending on whether we are considering a week or a month as the aggregated period. Assuming there are 5 trading days in a week and 250 trading days in a year, we find that the number of weekly return observations in a year is 50.

When implementing a trend-following strategy on a monthly basis, we assume there are 21 trading days in a month and 252 trading days in a year. Consequently, the number of monthly returns observed in a year is 12.

The autocorrelation ρ_k^d is computed as:

$$\rho_k^d = \frac{Cov\left(\sum_{i=0}^{d-1} r_{t-i}, \sum_{j=0}^{d-1} r_{t-kd-j}\right)}{\sqrt{Var(\sum_{i=0}^{d-1} r_{t-i})Var(\sum_{j=0}^{d-1} r_{t-kd-j})}}.$$

Because the return process must be stationary, the following condition must be satisfied: $Var(\sum_{j=0}^{d-1} r_{t-kd-j}) = Var(\sum_{i=0}^{d-1} r_{t-i})$. The latter variance is computed as:

$$Var\left(\sum_{i=0}^{d-1} r_{t-i}\right) = \sum_{i=0}^{d-1}\sum_{j=0}^{d-1} Cov(r_{t-i}, r_{t-j}) = \sum_{i=0}^{d-1}\sum_{j=0}^{d-1} \rho_{|j-i|}\sigma^2 = \mathbf{1}_d' \boldsymbol{R}_{d,d}\mathbf{1}_d\sigma^2, \tag{14.18}$$

where $\mathbf{1}_d$ is the $d \times 1$ vector of ones and $\boldsymbol{R}_{d,d}$ is a $d \times d$ matrix that is similar to the one defined by the Eq. (14.11).

The covariance in the expression for ρ_k^d is computed as:

$$\begin{aligned} Cov\left(\sum_{i=0}^{d-1} r_{t-i}, \sum_{j=0}^{d-1} r_{t-kd-j}\right) &= \sum_{i=0}^{d-1}\sum_{j=0}^{d-1} Cov(r_{t-i}, r_{t-kd-j}) \\ &= \sum_{i=0}^{d-1}\sum_{j=0}^{d-1} \rho_{|kd+j-i|}\sigma^2 \\ &= \mathbf{1}_d' \boldsymbol{Q}_{d,d}^k \mathbf{1}_d\sigma^2, \end{aligned} \tag{14.19}$$

where $\boldsymbol{Q}_{d,d}^k$ is the $d \times d$ matrix given by:

$$\boldsymbol{Q}_{d,d}^k = \begin{bmatrix} \rho_{kd} & \rho_{kd+1} & \rho_{kd+2} & \cdots & \rho_{kd+d-1} \\ \rho_{kd-1} & \rho_{kd} & \rho_{kd+1} & \cdots & \rho_{kd+d-2} \\ \rho_{kd-2} & \rho_{kd-1} & \rho_{kd} & \cdots & \rho_{kd+d-3} \\ \vdots & \vdots & \vdots & \ddots & \vdots \\ \rho_{kd-d+1} & \rho_{kd-d+2} & \rho_{kd-d+3} & \cdots & \rho_{kd} \end{bmatrix}. \tag{14.20}$$

Consequently, the autocorrelation ρ_k^d is given by:

$$\rho_k^d = \frac{\mathbf{1}_d' \boldsymbol{Q}_{d,d}^k \mathbf{1}_d}{\mathbf{1}_d' \boldsymbol{R}_{d,d}\mathbf{1}_d}. \tag{14.21}$$

14.3.4 Solution Algorithm and Computational Results

We establish a problem framework that is both coherent and realistic. In this framework, we consider market returns at a daily frequency, with either 250 or 252 trading days in a year. When implementing a trend-following strategy on a daily or weekly basis, we assume 250 trading days in a year. However, if a trend-following strategy is implemented on a monthly basis, we suppose that there are 252 trading days in a year.

We assume that the daily returns follow an AR(200) process with coefficients that decrease linearly with the return lag. There are two main reasons behind this assumption. The first reason is theoretical, as a linearly decreasing shape of the autoregressive coefficients provides a good approximation to the exponentially decreasing shape found in a theoretical two-state Markov switching model for returns. This model was developed by Zakamulin and Giner (2024). The second reason for our assumption relates to the well-known 10-month (200-day) price and SMA crossover (P-SMA) rule, which has gained popularity among traders. We believe that the rule's popularity is a reflection of its profitability, which in turn is connected to its optimality.

Additionally, we assume that the trend strength, which is measured by the sum of all autoregressive coefficients, is equal to $\kappa = \sum_{i=1}^{p} \phi_i = 0.30$. This value was estimated by Zakamulin and Giner (2022), using long-term data for the S&P 500 stock market index.

The trader has the option to implement a trend-following strategy on a daily, weekly, or monthly basis. We assume that the observation frequency aligns with the trading frequency. For example, if the trading is done on a weekly basis, the trader observes weekly returns that aggregate daily returns over five days. The value of the trading indicator is also calculated using weekly returns.

Regardless of the observation frequency, we assume that market returns follow an $AR(h = p/d)$ process where p represents the number of autoregressive terms in daily returns and d denotes the aggregation period in days. We also assume that the trader knows the parameters of this process.

In the absence of transaction costs, the shape of the return weights in a technical indicator mirrors the shape of the autoregressive coefficients. Consequently, provided there are no trading costs, the optimal technical indicator is the price and h-period SMA crossover (P-SMA(h)) rule. The size of the averaging window, h, in this rule corresponds to the order of the autoregressive process for the aggregated returns.

In the presence of transaction costs, the s- and h-period double SMA crossover (SMA-C(s, h)) rule approximates the optimal trend-following rule. This approximation is supported by the findings reported by Zakamulin and Giner (2023). The size of the shorter window s is selected to maximize the Sharpe ratio of the trading strategy. It is important to note that the specific size of s is dependent on the level of transaction costs and the trading frequency.

Since there is a significant amount of uncertainty surrounding the appropriate level of transaction costs, we explore the impact of varying proportional transaction costs from 0% to 1%.

Our objective is to compare the maximum Sharpe ratios for each trading frequency and each level of transaction costs. We seek to determine the optimal trading frequency for a given level of transaction costs, which is the frequency at which the Sharpe ratio achieves its highest value.

The preceding sections have presented analytical results that enable us to determine the parameters of the aggregated $AR(h)$ process for market returns. Additionally, we can calculate the Sharpe ratio of the trading strategy that employs the s- and p-period double SMA crossover rule. By adjusting s within the range of 0 to $h/2$, we can identify the optimal value that maximizes the Sharpe ratio. Using this approach, we can calculate the highest Sharpe ratios for the daily, weekly, and monthly strategies at various levels of transaction costs.

In order to ensure fair comparisons, it is important to use a common time scale in performance measurements. Typically, the square-root-of-time rule is utilized to adjust the Sharpe ratio to a common frequency when the returns are independent. However, since there is time-series dependence in all return series in our case, the square-root-of-time rule cannot be applied. Thus, we turn to the Monte Carlo simulation method to address this limitation and resolve the issue.

To provide accurate results, we have developed an algorithm that follows several steps. First, we simulate the daily AR(200) process for market returns. If the trading strategy is implemented on a lower observation frequency, we aggregate the daily returns to the required frequency. Next, we determine the optimal return weights of the technical indicator using analytical results and simple numerical optimization. Subsequently, we simulate the optimal trend-following strategy and aggregate the returns to the annual frequency to compute the annual Sharpe ratio.

In order to replicate real-world scenarios, we select the daily parameters of the market returns to align with those of the S&P 500 stock market index. This includes a mean annual market return of 10% and a standard deviation of 20%. Additionally, we set the annual risk-free rate of return at 3%. We ensure that the length of the simulated time series is adequate to limit the standard error of estimation of the annual Sharpe ratio to less than 1%.

To appreciate the significance of optimal trend-following in the presence of transaction costs, we examine a simplified scenario prior to presenting the results of the full-scale optimization problem. In this scenario, we assume that the trader consistently follows trends using the P-SMA(h) rule, regardless of the level of trading costs. However, it should be noted that this rule is only optimal in the absence of transaction costs. The computational results for this scenario are illustrated in Fig. 14.1.

Specifically, Fig. 14.1 presents the Sharpe ratio of the trend-following strategy versus the level of transaction costs for each trading frequency considered.

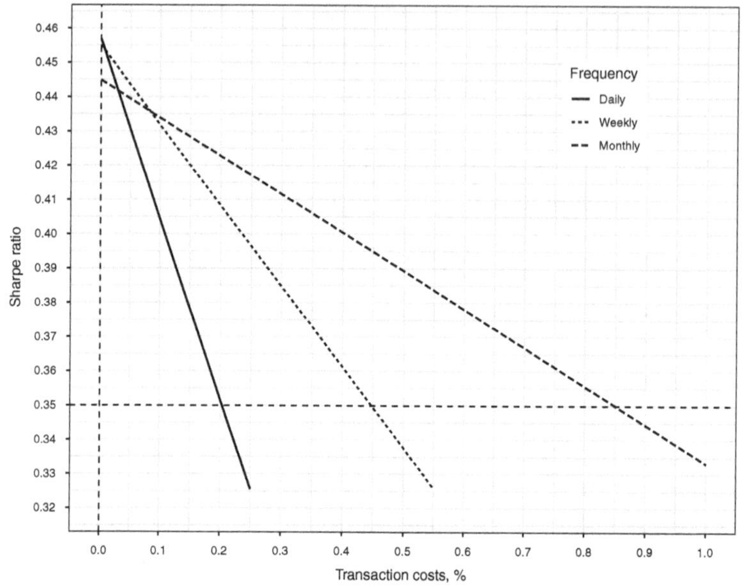

Fig. 14.1 Sharpe ratio of the non-optimized trend-following strategy versus the level of transaction costs. The trend-following strategy is implemented on a daily, weekly, or monthly basis. At each trading frequency, the return-weighting function in a trading indicator has the same functional form as the autoregressive coefficients for the market returns. For the sake of comparison, the dashed horizontal line shows the Sharpe ratio of the passive buy-and-hold strategy. All Sharpe ratios are annualized

The trend-following strategy is implemented on a daily, weekly, or monthly basis, and the dashed horizontal line shows the Sharpe ratio of the passive buy-and-hold strategy (0.35) for comparison purposes. The following observations can be made from the results. First, in the absence of transaction costs, higher-frequency trading provides a benefit, but the advantage of daily data over monthly data is negligible. The Sharpe ratio for daily and monthly trading frequencies is 0.444 and 0.439, respectively, with only about a 1% difference. Second, lower-frequency trading incurs less transaction costs, with break-even transaction costs[3] of 0.2%, 0.45%, and 0.87% for daily, weekly, and monthly trading frequencies, respectively. Finally, monthly trading yields the best performance when transaction costs exceed 0.15%. Since real-world trading costs are typically higher, this suggests that the 10-month P-SMA rule is preferable to the 200-day P-SMA rule in practical market conditions.

[3] Break-even transaction costs refer to the level of transaction costs at which the Sharpe ratio of the trend-following strategy is equal to that of the buy-and-hold strategy.

We now present the results of the full-scale optimization problem, where the return weights of the trading indicator are optimized to deliver the highest Sharpe ratio of the trend-following strategy. Figure 14.2 displays the full-scale optimization results, which vastly differ from those presented in Fig. 14.1. The most obvious conclusion is that selecting optimal return weights in the technical indicator can significantly improve the performance of the trend-following strategy in the presence of transaction costs, with the performance improvement being more significant at higher trading frequency. For instance, the break-even transaction costs of trading at a daily frequency increase from 0.2% to more than 1.0% following the weights optimization. The second notable observation is that the differences in trading at various frequencies are marginal with the Sharpe ratios of the trading strategies implemented at various frequencies typically being within 1% of each other.

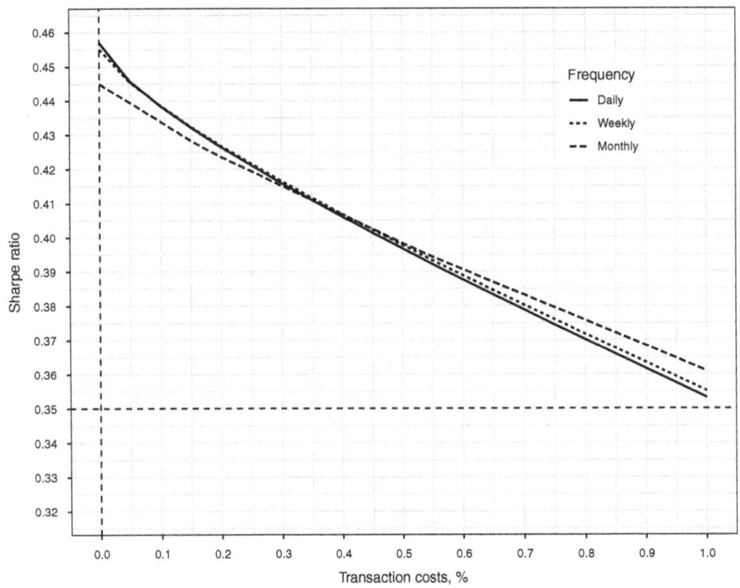

Fig. 14.2 Sharpe ratio of the optimized trend-following strategy versus the level of transaction costs. The trend-following strategy is implemented on a daily, weekly, or monthly basis. At each trading frequency, the return-weighting function in a trading indicator maximizes the Sharpe ratio of the trend-following strategy. For the sake of comparison, the dashed horizontal line shows the Sharpe ratio of the passive buy-and-hold strategy. All Sharpe ratios are annualized

In summary, the theoretical results presented in this section align closely with the empirical results reported in the literature and our own theoretical results obtained through the quantitative measures of accuracy, responsiveness, and smoothness of a technical indicator. Despite the conventional wisdom that the choice of trading frequency significantly impacts the performance of a trend-following strategy, both empirical and theoretical results indicate that the choice of trading frequency has limited impact on the performance of the trend-following strategy, both with and without transaction costs. It is worth emphasizing, however, that the irrelevance of trading frequency in the presence of transaction costs is dependent on the technical indicator employing the optimal return weights.

14.4 Summary

Numerous traders exhibit a preference for implementing trend-following rules on a daily basis as opposed to a monthly one. This inclination is grounded on an intuitive notion that utilizing daily data provides better responsiveness to market dynamics. Several academic studies have explored empirically whether an advantage exists in trading with daily data versus monthly data. Contrary to conventional belief, the outcomes from these studies propose that monthly data perform on par with daily data. In this chapter, potentially for the first time, we delve into the same inquiry analytically. We investigate the question of optimal trading frequency using two alternative approaches.

The central idea in the first approach is to compare and contrast the parameters of trading rules executed on both a daily and monthly basis. These parameters encompass the Noise Suppression Factor (a measure of trend direction accuracy), the Average Lag Time, and the Expected Number of Whipsaw trades.

Initially, we undertake the comparison employing approximate solutions for the Noise Suppression Factors and Average Lag Times across various trading rules. Assuming that the number of monthly return observations equates to the number of daily return observations divided by the days in a month, our findings indicate that the accuracy in identifying trend direction remains consistent between daily and monthly trading. Nevertheless, daily trading demonstrates an average lag time of approximately 10 days shorter in pinpointing trend reversal points compared to monthly trading. Analytically evaluating the expected number of whipsaws in daily and monthly trading appears challenging. However, a plausible inference is that monthly trading generally yields fewer expected whipsaw trades than daily trading.

Subsequently, we offer several concrete examples that compare the parameters of trading rules executed on both daily and monthly bases. These examples yield two primary conclusions. First, in the realm of daily trading, it is advisable to avoid using trend-following rules grounded in a single moving average (such as the MOM and P-MA rules). These rules tend to exhibit an excessively high expected number of whipsaw trades. Hence, when engaging in daily trading, it is recommended to exclusively utilize double moving average crossover rules. Second, our findings align with the findings reported in empirical studies. Particularly, our analytical results propose that there is no discernible advantage in trading with daily data over monthly data. For instance, we ascertain that trading with the commonly employed 50- and 200-day SMA crossover rule is analogous to trading with the 2- and 10-month SMA crossover rule. Specifically, both rules share identical parameters, thereby indicating similar empirical performance. Compared to the 2- and 10-month SMA crossover rule, the prevalent 10-month SMA rule displays a slightly shorter average lag time and a slightly elevated expected number of whipsaw trades. A reasonable inference is that the performance of the 10-month SMA rule should be consistent with that of the 2- and 10-month SMA crossover rule.

The second approach aims to compare the performance of a trend-following strategy at different trading frequencies and select the frequency that provides the maximum performance. The approach involves making specific parametric assumptions about the daily return process of the market, aggregating daily returns over different horizons (weekly and monthly), and selecting the optimal double SMA crossover rule that maximizes the Sharpe ratio of the trend-following strategy in the presence of transaction costs. To ensure the reliability of this approach, realistic market dynamics and parameters similar to those of the S&P 500 stock market index are used.

The results of the second approach correlate well with the results of the first approach. The study shows that the profitability of optimal trend-following strategies at different trading frequencies is almost the same. Therefore, the choice of trading frequency is not very significant. However, it should be noted that the irrelevance of trading frequency in the presence of transaction costs depends on the technical indicator utilizing the optimal return weights. The optimal return weights vary based on both the trading frequency and the level of transaction costs.

References

Antonacci, G. (2014). *Dual Momentum Investing: An Innovative Strategy for Higher Returns with Lower Risk.* McGraw-Hill.

Clare, A., Seaton, J., Smith, P. N., & Thomas, S. (2013). Breaking Into the Blackbox: Trend Following, Stop losses and the Frequency of Trading - The Case of the S&P500. *Journal of Asset Management, 14*(3), 182–194.

Faber, M. T. (2007). A Quantitative Approach to Tactical Asset Allocation. *Journal of Wealth Management, 9*(4), 69–79.

Gwilym, O., Clare, A., Seaton, J., & Thomas, S. (2010). Price and Momentum as Robust Tactical Approaches to Global Equity Investing. *Journal of Investing, 19*(3), 80–91.

Moskowitz, T. J., Ooi, Y. H., & Pedersen, L. H. (2012). Time Series Momentum. *Journal of Financial Economics, 104*(2), 228–250.

Zakamulin, V. (2017). *Market Timing with Moving Averages: The Anatomy and Performance of Trading Rules.* Springer.

Zakamulin, V., & Giner, J. (2022). Time Series Momentum in the US Stock Market: Empirical Evidence and Theoretical Analysis. *International Review of Financial Analysis, 82,* Article 102173.

Zakamulin, V., & Giner, J. (2023). Optimal Trend-Following With Transaction Costs. *International Review of Financial Analysis, 90,* Article 102928.

Zakamulin, V., & Giner, J. (2024). Optimal Trend-Following Rules in Two-State Regime-Switching Models. *Journal of Asset Management, 25*(4), 327–348.

Part V

End of Part IV

15

Summary and Conclusions

15.1 Revisiting the Book's Purpose

For nearly a century, moving averages have been employed to smooth price movements and emphasize the direction of trends. Their rapid evolution began in the 1990s, driven by the widespread availability of personal computers and the accessibility of stock price data via the Internet. Since then, traders, engineers, and scientists have continued to innovate, proposing new types of moving averages. Each new variant is typically claimed to offer advantages over existing ones.

Moving averages serve as the foundation for various trend-following rules designed to capitalize on persistent market trends. These rules generate trading signals based on the relationship between the current price and a moving average, the change in the value of a moving average, the interaction between two different moving averages, or even more complex combinations of multiple moving averages.

Although moving averages are widely used and play a crucial role in trend-following strategies, the existing literature surprisingly lacks systematic and comprehensive coverage of the topic. No single book serves as a definitive reference on the various types of moving averages and the trend-following rules derived from them. This book addresses that gap by providing a detailed and practical guide for traders, researchers, and practitioners to better understand and effectively utilize these fundamental tools.

Yet, this book's purpose goes beyond merely providing a comprehensive reference on moving averages and the trend-following rules that utilize them. The primary challenge in trend-following lies in the overwhelming variety of moving averages and trading rules available, which can leave traders, especially

V. Zakamulin and J. Giner, *The Ultimate Moving Average Handbook*,
https://doi.org/10.1007/978-3-031-90907-8_15

beginners, confused and uncertain. Many struggle to determine which trading rule to adopt and which type of moving average to use for effectively following trends in a specific financial market. Additionally, each moving average requires at least one parameter, such as the averaging window size, yet there is little guidance on how to select these parameters.

Therefore, trend-following with moving averages remains an art. Traders must navigate a vast and intricate array of choices, relying not only on technical expertise but also on intuition and experience, often refined through trial and error. The diversity of market conditions and asset characteristics adds further complexity, demanding a deep and nuanced understanding of how different moving averages respond in various scenarios. Consequently, the application of moving averages is largely shaped by individual judgment and subjective interpretation.

The field of trend-following with moving averages faces significant challenges due to the lack of quantitative measures for evaluating the characteristics of moving averages and the rules built upon them. Traders generally agree that a moving average should be both smooth and responsive. However, despite nearly a century of use, no established metric exists to quantify smoothness. More perplexing is the absence of a shared understanding of what "smoothness" truly means in this context. When it comes to responsiveness, traders continue to rely on an ad hoc metric introduced long ago. Despite its widespread use, the suitability and relevance of this measure for assessing the lag time of a moving average have never been critically examined.

Another apparent issue is the excessive focus on developing new moving averages, each claiming to offer superior properties compared to existing ones. Traders often overlook the fact that trading signals are not generated solely based on the value of a moving average. Instead, signal generation varies across trend-following rules and, in many cases, depends on complex interactions between multiple moving averages. Ultimately, traders should prioritize understanding the properties of the trend-following rules themselves rather than solely concentrating on the characteristics of the individual moving averages employed within these rules.

The ultimate goal of this book is to bring scientific rigor to the art of trend-following. Specifically, it aims to provide a quantitatively grounded framework for evaluating moving averages and the trading rules they support. The book begins by identifying the key properties of trend-following rules based on moving averages and then offers methods for quantifying these properties. These methods are grounded in rigorous mathematical formulations and substantiated by empirical evidence, establishing their firm foundation in scientific principles.

By introducing quantitative measures, this book enables objective analysis of the characteristics of trend-following rules and explores whether certain moving averages can enhance their effectiveness. Furthermore, these measures open the door to creating new rules that optimize the tradeoff between various performance metrics.

The introduction of quantitative metrics that objectively evaluate the characteristics of trading rules represents a significant breakthrough in the field of trend-following with moving averages. However, these metrics alone do not provide a means of selecting the most efficient rule for following trends in a specific financial market. To address this gap, this book goes beyond quantitative measures, offering a comprehensive theoretical analysis of optimal trend-following. It explores how the parameters of optimal rules depend on the dynamics of a particular financial market and existing market frictions. Lastly, the book also discusses the optimal implementation of trend-following rules, providing practical insights for effective application.

15.2 Moving Averages and Anatomy of Trend-Following Rules

Typically, the average value in a dataset is computed by summing all elements and dividing the total by the number of elements. In trend-following strategies, a moving average is calculated as the weighted average of prices within a specified window. To compute a general weighted moving average at time t, the calculation incorporates the most recent closing price P_t along with $n-1$ previous prices P_{t-i}, where i ranges from 1 to $n-1$. Each price is assigned a specific weight. Formally, the general weighted moving average of a price series P at time t is defined as:

$$
\begin{aligned}
MA_t(n, P) &= \frac{w_0 P_t + w_1 P_{t-1} + w_2 P_{t-2} + \ldots + w_{n-1} P_{t-n+1}}{w_0 + w_1 + w_2 + \ldots + w_{n-1}} \\
&= \frac{\sum_{i=0}^{n-1} w_i P_{t-i}}{\sum_{i=0}^{n-1} w_i},
\end{aligned}
\tag{15.1}
$$

where w_i denotes the weight assigned to price P_{t-i} in the computation.

Despite the vast variety of moving averages, each one adheres to the structure of Eq. (15.1). The primary distinction among them lies in the price weights $w_0, w_1, \ldots, w_{n-1}$, which are typically functions of the window size n.

Conventional types of moving averages include the Simple Moving Average (SMA), the Linear Moving Average (LMA), and the Exponential Moving

Average (EMA). These moving averages are defined by the size of the averaging window n:

Simple Moving Average (SMA): All price weights are equal, with $w_i = 1$ for all $i \in \{0, 1, \ldots, n-1\}$.

Linear Moving Average (LMA): Price weights decrease linearly with lag, such that $w_i = n - i$.

Exponential Moving Average (EMA): This moving average uses an effectively infinite window size, but is also parameterized by n. In the EMA, price weights decrease geometrically with lag, following $w_i = \lambda^i$, $i \in [0, \infty)$, where λ is the decay constant computed as $\lambda = (n-1)/(n+1)$.

There are four fundamental trend-following rules based on moving averages of prices:

Price and Moving Average Crossover (P-MA): This rule generates a Buy signal when the moving average is below the current price and a Sell signal otherwise.

Double Moving Average Crossover (MA-C): This rule uses two moving averages: one with a shorter window size and another with a longer window size. A Buy signal is generated when the shorter moving average is above the longer moving average, while a Sell signal is triggered in the opposite scenario.

Moving Average Direction (MA-D): This straightforward rule issues a Buy signal when the moving average value is increasing and a Sell signal when it is decreasing.

Momentum (MOM): This rule generates a Buy signal when the current price exceeds the price from a specified number of periods ago. Although this rule does not explicitly rely on a moving average, the earlier price can be viewed as a specialized moving average where all weights are zero except for the weight on the most distant price in the window.

Each rule, except the MOM rule, can employ different types of moving averages. In the MA-C rule, it is common to use two moving averages of the same type. However, it is also possible to mix different types of moving averages within this rule, offering greater flexibility in capturing trends.

A technical indicator in a trend-following rule represents the formal mathematical calculation of the trading signal. For all such rules, the technical indicator is derived as a weighted sum of prices within the averaging window, with the condition that the sum of all price weights equals zero. The general computation of the technical trading indicator for each rule is expressed as:

$$I_t(n) = \sum_{i=0}^{m} \upsilon_i P_{t-i}, \tag{15.2}$$

where $I_t(n)$ represents the value of the technical indicator computed using parameter n, υ_i denotes the weight assigned to price P_{t-i}, and $m = n$ for the MA-D rule, while $m = n - 1$ for all other rules. The zero-sum condition for the weights is given by:

$$\sum_{i=0}^{m} \upsilon_i = 0.$$

When the value of the technical indicator is positive, the trading signal is a Buy; otherwise, it is a Sell. In essence, the trading signal is determined by the sign of the computed weighted sum:

$$\text{Trading signal} = \begin{cases} \text{Buy} & \text{if } I_t(n) > 0, \\ \text{Sell} & \text{if } I_t(n) \leq 0. \end{cases}$$

Alternatively, the technical indicator can be expressed as a moving average of price changes or returns:

$$I_t(n) = \sum_{i=0}^{n-2} \theta_i r_{t-i}, \tag{15.3}$$

where θ_i represents the weight assigned to return $r_{t-i} = (P_{t-i} - P_{t-i-1})/P_{t-i-1}$ in the moving average calculation. The return weights θ_i are derived from the price weights w_i. The sum of these weights is positive, ensuring that $\sum_{i=0}^{n-2} \theta_i > 0$. Since the trading signal depends only on the sign of the moving average, the weights θ_i can be freely rescaled so that their sum equals one $\sum_{i=0}^{n-2} \theta_i = 1$.

We argue that the alternative form of computing the trading indicator, as a moving average of returns, is preferable for several reasons.

First, prices within a window are inherently strongly interrelated. For instance, two consecutive prices differ only slightly, with $\Delta P_{t-i} = P_{t-i} - P_{t-i-1}$. This means that the price P_{t-i} consists of the previous price P_{t-i-1} plus a small price change ΔP_{t-i}, which reflects new information revealed during the interval from $t - i - 1$ to $t - i$. Consequently, calculating a weighted sum of these highly correlated prices does not clearly show how each piece of new information contributes to the trading signal.

In contrast, consecutive price changes or returns are largely independent. When prices trend upward, price changes or returns tend to be positive on average. Conversely, when prices trend downward, they tend to be negative on average. This weak dependence makes it more logical to analyze the average price change or return within a moving window to determine whether prices are trending upward or downward. The weights assigned to price changes or returns must be tailored to effectively follow trends specific to a given financial market, while accounting for existing market frictions.

Second, and equally important, it is a long-standing tradition in finance to present models based on returns and analyze optimal decision-making under various return processes. The return-based formulation of the trading indicator aligns with this tradition and provides a framework for investigating optimal trend-following strategies. By modeling returns, researchers can explore the dynamics of price movements and assess the performance of trading rules under specific return processes. Additionally, one can incorporate market frictions, such as transaction costs, into the analysis. These frictions are critical in real-world applications, as they can significantly impact the profitability of trading strategies. By accounting for such factors, the return-based formulation allows for the design of strategies that are not only theoretically optimal but also practically viable.

The analysis of return weights in various trend-following rules that use conventional moving averages reveals that, despite the wide range of possible combinations, only three basic return-weighting functions emerge. These functions are illustrated in Fig. 15.1.

The first shape features equal return weights across all lags, characteristic of the MOM rule. The second shape involves return weights that decrease with the return lag, as seen in all P-MA rules. While the specific form of the decreasing function varies depending on the type of moving average, the common feature is that the weights gradually decrease to zero as the lag increases.

The third type of weighting function, observed in all MA-C rules, is hump-shaped, with the peak located near the most recent lag. In this case, the weights first increase, reach a maximum, and then decrease. The specific form of the increasing and decreasing function depends on the type of moving average used.

The analysis of the technical indicator for the MA-D rule shows that it typically corresponds to a specific P-MA rule or the MOM rule. For instance, the SMA-D rule is equivalent to the MOM rule, while the LMA-D rule corresponds to the P-SMA rule.

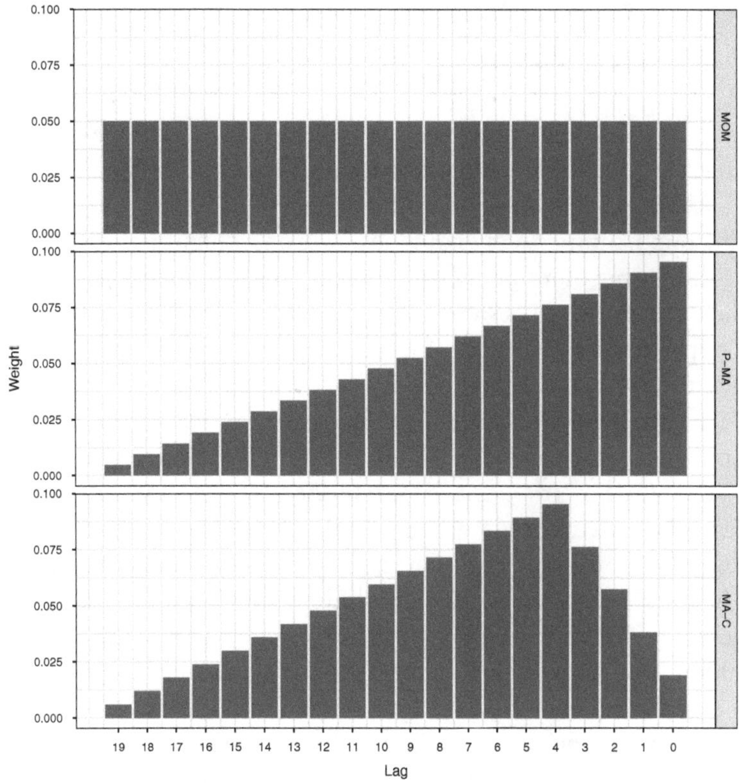

Fig. 15.1 Illustrations of the three basic shapes of the return weights in the MOM, P-MA, and MA-C rules

The knowledge of the return weights in the technical indicators of various trend-following rules enables traders to clearly identify the similarities and differences between different combinations of trading rules with moving averages. For example, if the return weight patterns are more or less similar between two rules, the conclusion is that these rules are likely to have comparable effectiveness in following trends. Conversely, if the return weights differ significantly, it suggests that the rules differ inherently in their ability to follow trends effectively.

Since the only difference between trading rules based on moving averages lies in the shape of the return weights, it follows that the properties of these rules are entirely determined by their return-weighting functions. Therefore, the quantitative evaluation of the various characteristics of trading rules must be based on the return weights.

15.3 Key Properties of Trading Rules and Their Measurement

Responsiveness is undeniably one of the most critical properties of trend-following rules. These rules inherently identify trend turning points with some degree of delay, which can significantly impact their effectiveness in capturing profitable opportunities or avoiding losses. Consequently, the ability to measure the delay time of a trading rule becomes not just useful but essential. All other factors being equal, a shorter delay is preferable, as it enables the trading rule to respond more swiftly to emerging trends, reducing the risk of lagging behind critical market movements.

Traders often highlight smoothness, alongside responsiveness, as a key property of moving averages. The challenge lies in the fact that, to date, no systematically developed metric has been established to quantify smoothness. This lack of a standardized measure arises from the absence of consensus on a precise definition of smoothness. The debate is shaped by two competing perspectives.

The first perspective associates smoothness with the moving average's ability to reduce noise. In this view, a smoother moving average is better at filtering out the "randomness" in price movements, offering a more accurate and reliable trading signal. The second perspective defines smoothness in terms of signal stability. From this angle, a smoother moving average generates signals that are less sensitive to minor price fluctuations, thereby reducing the occurrence of false signals and promoting greater stability in trading decisions.

These differing definitions underscore the inherent complexity of the concept of smoothness. For some, smoothness centers on the technical ability to filter out noise, while for others, it focuses on the practical implications for trading outcomes. This divergence in perspectives makes the development of a universally accepted smoothness metric particularly challenging.

Recognizing the importance of these two competing perspectives, we propose two distinct metrics to address them individually. The first is a noise reduction metric, which quantifies the extent to which a moving average filters out frequent random price variations, thereby enhancing the accuracy of trading signals. The second is a signal stability metric, which measures the consistency of trading signals, thereby reducing the occurrence of false trades. The noise reduction property is intrinsically linked to the accuracy of a trend-following rule, as it directly impacts the reliability of trend signals. In contrast, the stability of trading signals is closely associated with the smoothness property, reflecting the rule's ability to provide consistent signals by minimizing reactions to minor price fluctuations.

In summary, we propose that a trend-following rule's technical indicator should exhibit three essential properties: accuracy, responsiveness, and smoothness. To evaluate these properties, we introduce the following three metrics:

Noise Suppression Factor (NSF): The NSF metric measures the technical indicator's ability to filter out noise, ensuring that the signals provided are accurate and reliable for trading decisions.

Average Lag Time (ALT): The ALT metric assesses how quickly the technical indicator reacts to trend changes, reflecting its responsiveness and the timeliness of its trading signals.

Smoothness Index (SMI): The SMI metric quantifies the smoothness of the technical indicator, highlighting the stability and consistency of the trading signals over time.

The rationale behind the proposed measures is rooted in a well-established regime-switching model for returns. In this model, returns follow a stochastic process that randomly shifts between bull and bear states. Notably, these market states are identifiable and exhibit persistence, providing a strong justification for the use of trend-following investment strategies. Although our metrics are inspired by a regime-switching model, they are independent of the model's parameters. Instead, the proposed measures are computed solely using the return weights in the technical indicator.

The NSF and SMI measures are computed using the following formulas:

$$NSF = \frac{\sum_{i=0}^{n-1} \theta_i}{\sqrt{\sum_{i=0}^{n-1} \theta_i^2}}, \qquad SMI = \frac{\sum_{i=0}^{n-2} \theta_i \theta_{i+1}}{\sum_{i=0}^{n-1} \theta_i^2},$$

where n denotes the number of return lags in a technical indicator. The ALT is determined by solving the equation:

$$\sum_{i=0}^{ALT-1} \theta_i = \frac{1}{2} \sum_{i=0}^{n-1} \theta_i.$$

We derive the analytical solutions for the accuracy, responsiveness, and smoothness measures applied to trend-following rules that use conventional moving averages. Our analysis of these results reveals an interesting pattern across various technical indicators. In particular, as the value of n increases, the NSF, ALT, and SMI measures also rise. This suggests that higher values of n result in more accurate and smoother signals, albeit at the expense of reduced responsiveness in trading rules. These findings underscore an important consideration in trading rule design: improving one aspect, such as accuracy or smoothness, often comes with a tradeoff in another, like responsiveness. Achieving optimal performance across all quantitative measures simultaneously remains a challenging goal.

Our quantitative metrics offer an objective framework for comparing the effectiveness of various trend-following rules. Our analysis reveals that the P-MA rules achieve an excellent balance between responsiveness and accuracy, making them ideal for traders who require both timely and reliable signals. In contrast, the MA-C rules provide an optimal tradeoff between responsiveness and smoothness, excelling in environments where signal stability is critical while still maintaining sensitivity to market trends. Meanwhile, the MOM rule excels in accuracy but sacrifices responsiveness, making it less effective in quickly changing market conditions.

15.4 Uncovering the Optimal Trend-Following Rule

Our quantitative measures enable traders to uncover the return weights in the optimal trading rules. The optimal rules for a single measure represent the simplest scenario, where the trader selects the size of the averaging window n and determines the return weights that optimize one specific metric: accuracy, responsiveness, or smoothness. Figure 15.2 illustrates the weighting functions that optimize each of these individual metrics.

Starting with the top panel, Fig. 15.2 illustrates the weighting function of the technical indicator with the highest accuracy. This weighting function corresponds to the MOM technical indicator, where all returns are given equal weight. In the bottom panel, we observe the weighting function of the indicator with the largest smoothness, known as the Sine-Weighted Moving Average (SWMA), which represents the first half of a sine wave cycle. Notably, the weighting functions of both the most accurate and the smoothest technical indicators are symmetrical around the center. As a result, these indicators exhibit poor responsiveness, with their ALTs equal to $n/2$.

In the middle panel of Fig. 15.2, we can see the weighting function of the technical indicator with the smallest ALT. This particular weighting function assigns zero weight to all return lags except the most recent one. Consequently, the ALT of this technical indicator is equal to 1. It is worth noting that while this technical indicator is the most responsive, it comes at the cost of being the least accurate and smooth.

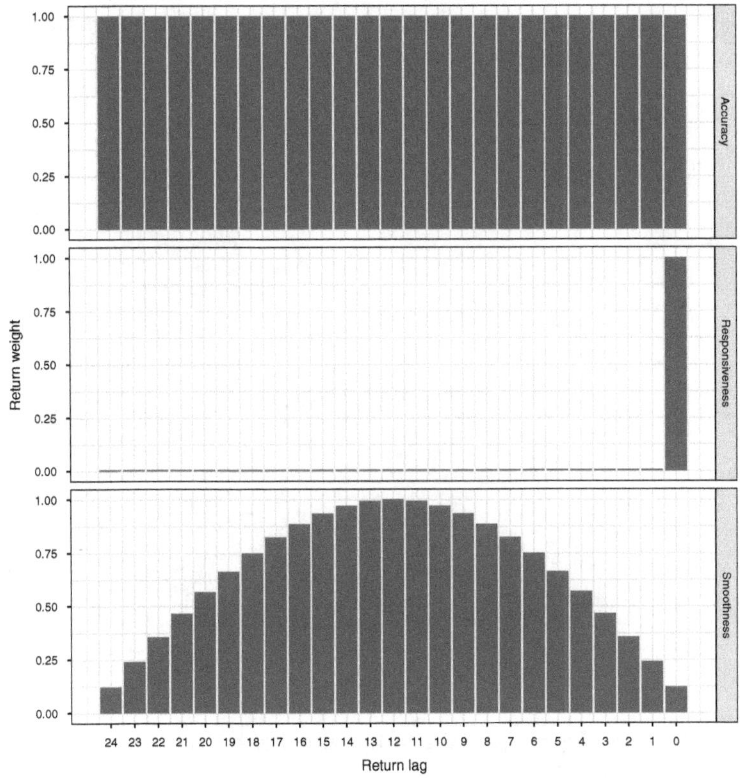

Fig. 15.2 Weighting functions of the technical indicators that maximize (1) accuracy, (2) responsiveness, and (3) smoothness for the averaging window of size $n = 25$ return observations

Uncovering the return weights of the technical indicator that represents the optimal tradeoff between responsiveness and either accuracy or smoothness is relatively straightforward. The process begins by defining the window size n and specifying the desired level of ALT. Then, using either analytical or numerical methods, one determines the return weights of the trading rule that maximizes either accuracy or smoothness, given the specified ALT.

Figure 15.3 shows the weighting function of the technical indicator with $n = 24$ that maximizes the NSF when the ALT is 8. Intuition offers a clear explanation for this shape. Specifically, the return weights in the trading rule that achieves an efficient tradeoff between accuracy and responsiveness exhibit a composite pattern. This pattern can be seen as a blend of the weighting shapes that maximize accuracy and those that maximize responsiveness. In this case, the return weights follow a distinct structure where the weights for the most recent lags are equal and large, while the weights for all other lags are also equal but comparatively smaller.

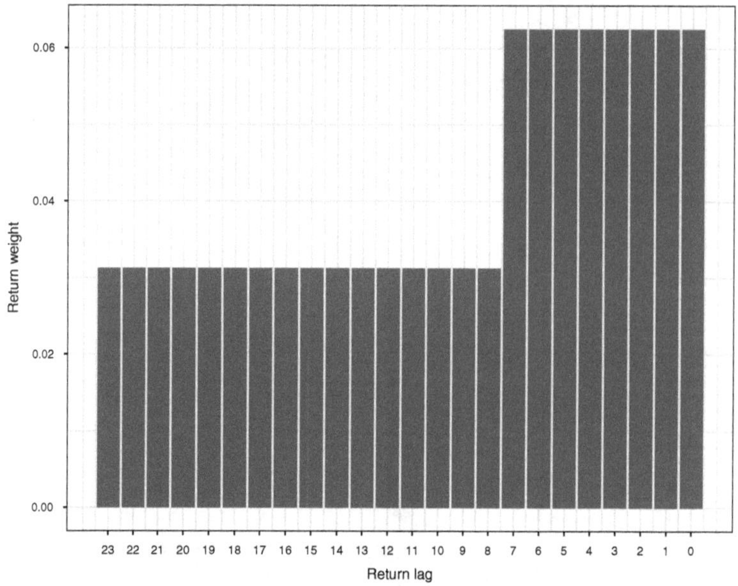

Fig. 15.3 Weighting functions of the technical indicator with $n = 24$ that maximizes the NSF when the ALT is 8

Figure 15.4 shows the weighting functions of the technical indicator with $n = 24$ that maximizes the SMI when the ALT is either 9 or 5. When negative return weights are allowed, two distinct patterns emerge. In the first scenario, with an ALT of 9, the optimal weighting function takes the form of a smooth hump leaning to the right, with more weight assigned to the most recent return lags. This shape can be interpreted as a combination of the patterns that maximize smoothness and responsiveness. To achieve smoothness, the return weights must form a symmetrical hump, akin to the first half of a sine wave. In contrast, maximizing responsiveness concentrates the weights on the most recent return observation. The resulting shape, a smooth hump leaning rightward, reflects the superposition of these two influences.

When the ALT is 9, all return weights are positive, but as the ALT decreases to 5, the distant return weights become negative. In this case, the shape of the weighting function resembles a damped sine wave. As the ALT decreases, the number of distant negative weights increases, and their amplitude becomes larger. In theory, the ALT can be reduced to a single period while maintaining a relatively high level of smoothness. However, it is crucial to note that achieving high smoothness alongside high responsiveness comes at the cost of accuracy.

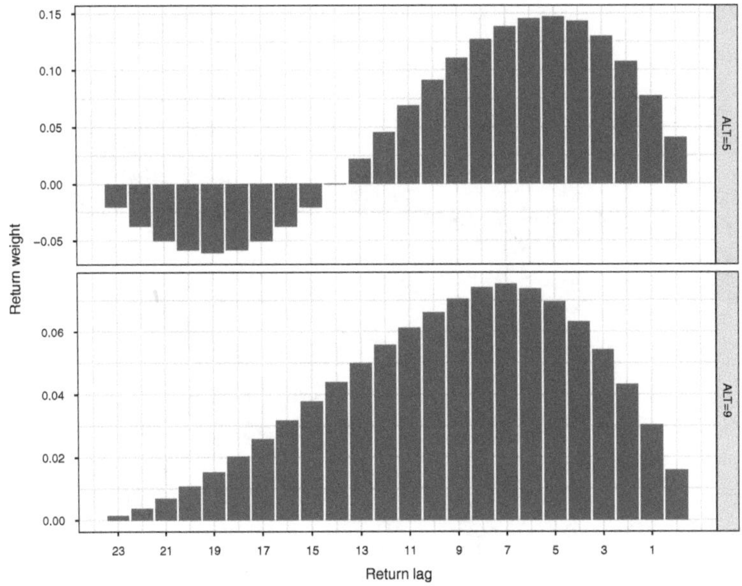

Fig. 15.4 Weighting functions of the technical indicator with $n = 24$ that has the maximum smoothness when the ALT equals either 5 or 9

In other words, a trading rule can be both highly responsive and smooth, but this combination often comes at the cost of significantly reduced accuracy. This reinforces the idea that optimizing one or two properties typically leads to the deterioration of others.

The most challenging task is finding the optimal shape of the return weights in a trading rule that achieves the best balance among all three properties. This problem can be approached by the following method: first, specific levels for responsiveness and accuracy are defined. Then, using a numerical method, the shape that maximizes smoothness is determined, subject to the constraints on responsiveness and accuracy. However, a limitation of this approach is that the optimization results are influenced by the arbitrary selection of parameter levels for responsiveness and accuracy.

Illustrative examples are shown in Fig. 15.5, which plots the shapes of the return weights for the efficient trading rule that strikes an optimal balance among the three properties. These shapes can be understood as a blend of two distinct forms: the shape that optimizes accuracy and responsiveness, and the shape that optimizes smoothness and responsiveness. Specifically, the shape in the upper (lower) panel of Fig. 15.5 combines elements from the upper (lower) panel of Fig. 15.4 and the shape from Fig. 15.3.

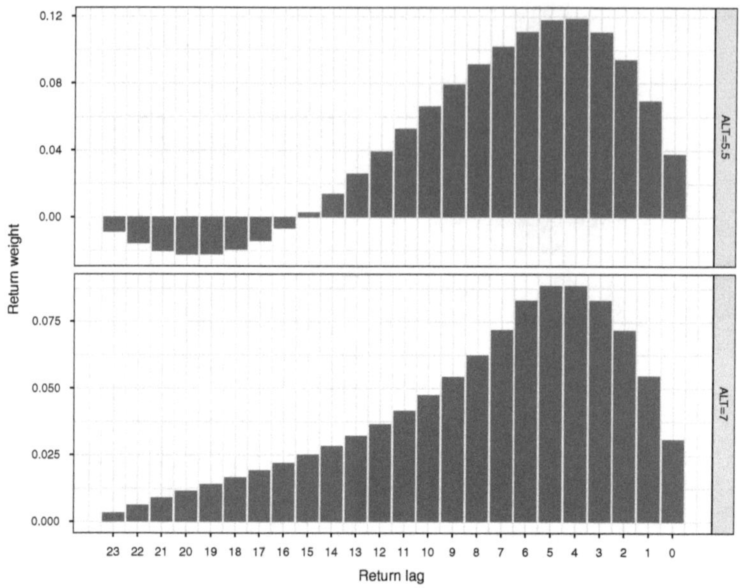

Fig. 15.5 Weighting functions of the efficient trading rule with $n = 24$ that strikes the optimal balance between three properties

As a final note, the shape of the return weights that achieves an optimal balance among all three properties, as depicted in the lower panel of Fig. 15.5, closely resembles the typical shape found in the MA-C rule using a conventional moving average. The use of the LMA in the MA-C rule results in the greatest similarity between the optimal shape and the one produced by the LMA-C rule. Specifically, the shape shown in Fig. 15.5, lower panel, closely mirrors the shape in the LMA-C(5,24) rule.

To summarize, our results indicate that the MA-C rule is a trading rule that effectively balances all key properties of a trend-following rule. Specifically, it offers high accuracy and smoothness while maintaining responsiveness. By switching from the MA-C rule to the P-MA rule, one can improve the tradeoff between responsiveness and accuracy, though at the cost of reduced smoothness. Conversely, transitioning from the MA-C rule to a rule where the return weights take the shape of a damped sine wave improves the tradeoff between responsiveness and smoothness, but at the expense of reduced accuracy.

15.5 Quantitative Analysis of Exotic Moving Averages

Conventional moving averages include the SMA, LMA, and EMA, while all other types are generally classified as exotic moving averages. The category of exotic moving averages is vast and often poorly understood. These can be grouped into three main types: those designed for enhanced smoothness, those aimed at reducing lag time, and those inspired by Digital Signal Processing (DSP) techniques. Exotic moving averages are frequently surrounded by myths and anecdotal claims.

This book goes beyond simply describing popular exotic moving averages. Its primary focus is to quantitatively evaluate the various claims associated with them. Specifically, it seeks to determine whether exotic moving averages genuinely improve the effectiveness of trend-following strategies compared to conventional moving averages.

When employing exotic moving averages, a crucial question arises: in which types of trend-following rules can these moving averages be utilized most effectively? We propose that the MA-D rule is the most logical choice. This is because exotic moving averages derive their unique properties from the specific shape of their price weights, and in the MA-D rule, the return weights mirror this shape.

In contrast, all P-MA rules impose a structure where return weights consistently decrease with the return lag, irrespective of the moving average used. Similarly, in all MA-C rules, the return weights follow a hump-shaped distribution, again independent of the type of moving average. These inherent differences highlight the distinct advantages of the MA-D rule when leveraging the unique characteristics of exotic moving averages.

15.5.1 Moving Averages with Enhanced Smoothness

At first glance, since the purpose of a moving average is to smooth out price fluctuations and reveal trend directions, effective smoothing seems to be its most important requirement. Guided by this notion, traders have developed various moving averages over time, often claiming they offer superior smoothing compared to traditional ones.

However, the challenge lies in the absence of a quantitative method to objectively assess the smoothness of a moving average. Progress in this field has largely relied on subjective judgments and intuition. Consequently, claims of improved smoothing have always been anecdotal and lack rigorous validation. Furthermore, traders often neglect the fact that a moving average must balance smoothness with responsiveness. Focusing too heavily on smoothness can significantly compromise responsiveness.

There are two main approaches to enhancing the smoothness of a moving average while keeping the parameter n, which defines the averaging window size, fixed.

The first approach involves applying a conventional moving average multiple times. Each successive application further reduces the fluctuations left by the previous iteration, effectively minimizing noise and enhancing the clarity of the underlying trend. The key considerations for this method are selecting the type of moving average to use and determining the optimal number of iterations required to achieve the optimal level of smoothing.

The second approach involves optimizing the price weights within the moving average to achieve the highest possible smoothness for a given window size. However, due to the lack of a well-defined quantitative measure for evaluating smoothness, this method has historically relied on ad hoc ideas and intuition rather than systematic analysis.

We evaluated the first approach and arrived at two key conclusions. First, a double-smoothed moving average exhibits better properties than triple-smoothed or higher-order moving averages, meaning additional smoothing iterations beyond two are generally ineffective. Second, even double-smoothed moving averages fail to improve the efficiency of trend-following. In most cases, the MA-D rule utilizing a double moving average does not outperform the MA-C rule that employs a conventional moving average of the same type.

Traders have observed that repeated smoothing causes the price weights in a multi-smoothed moving average to form a bell-shaped curve, symmetric around its mean. The low efficiency of multi-smoothed moving averages stems from the fact that each additional smoothing step significantly expands the effective averaging window. Specifically, for a moving average with a window size of n, the window size in a k-smoothed moving average increases to $k(n-1)+1$. The issue is that most of the weight becomes concentrated near the center, while the weights at the edges diminish to near zero, reducing the influence of recent and past prices alike.

The logical approach was to retain the bell-shaped distribution of price weights in a moving average while spreading them across an entire window of relatively shorter size. This concept led to the development of the Sine-Weighted Moving Average (SWMA), the Gaussian Moving Average (GMA), and the Arnaud Legoux Moving Average (ALMA).

The availability of a quantitative metric to measure the smoothness of trading signals from a technical indicator enabled us to determine the optimal shape of the return weights for maximizing smoothness. We have shown that the SWMA offers the highest smoothness for a given window size. However, while the SWMA-D rule is the smoothest, it is also one of the least responsive trading rules. This issue arises because the weight distribution in the SWMA is symmetric around the center, leading to an average lag time of $n/2$. The same problem occurs with the GMA, where the weights are similarly symmetric around the middle.

In the ALMA, the weight distribution follows a Gaussian shape as well. However, unlike the GMA, where the distribution is centered in the middle of the window, the ALMA shifts the mean of the Gaussian distribution closer to the beginning of the averaging window. This adjustment assigns more weight to recent prices. As a result, the ALMA retains the smoothness of the Gaussian distribution while improving responsiveness compared to the GMA.

The ALMA requires the specification of two additional parameters, besides the size of the averaging window. These parameters control the standard deviation of the Gaussian distribution and the position of its mean within the window. Until now, the selection of these parameters has been largely arbitrary. However, our quantitative metrics enable traders to determine the optimal values for these parameters, ensuring improved performance.

In summary, our analysis found that the double-smoothed LMA and the ALMA, when optimized with the best parameters, are the most effective moving averages with enhanced smoothness among those considered. The return weights of these moving averages closely resemble those shown in the lower panel of Fig. 15.5, indicating their ability to balance accuracy, responsiveness, and smoothness effectively. However, when used in the MA-D rule, their performance is on par with that of the MA-C rule using a conventional moving average. This leads to the key conclusion: trend-following rules based on the best moving averages with enhanced smoothness do not outperform the MA-C rule using traditional moving averages.

15.5.2 Moving Averages with Reduced Lag Time

The moving average is a useful tool for traders, as it helps smooth out short-term price fluctuations and makes it easier to identify underlying trends. However, its main limitation is that it lags behind current market conditions. This delay can result in missed opportunities or financial losses for traders.

To address this, traders have sought to develop zero-lag moving averages that respond immediately to market changes, allowing for faster decision-making. This effort has led to the creation of several "zero-lag" moving averages. Creators of these moving averages claim that they offer not only minimal or zero lag but also superior smoothness compared to traditional moving averages. However, these claims are primarily based on anecdotal evidence and visual examples, lacking robust, objective data for validation.

To be fair, several versions of these "zero-lag" moving averages do indeed exhibit zero lag time, as measured by an ad hoc metric introduced nearly 60 years ago. However, we demonstrate the limitations of this measure and argue that it is highly misleading. This metric evaluates the average time gap between the current price and the moving average in scenarios where the price either consistently increases or decreases. In other words, it applies to situations where the price trend remains unchanged, and thus, the trading signal stays constant. In contrast, a more meaningful measure of lag time should be linked to the time difference between a change in the price trend and the subsequent shift in the trading signal.

This book presents three innovative quantitative measures to assess the key characteristics of trend-following rules based on moving averages: accuracy, responsiveness, and smoothness. By applying these measures, we offer a comprehensive and objective analysis of "zero-lag" moving averages. The aim of this analysis is to evaluate whether these moving averages truly achieve zero lag time and enhanced smoothness, and whether they outperform traditional moving averages.

Our previous numerical analysis demonstrated that it is possible to reduce lag time while maintaining high smoothness by assigning negative weights to more distant return lags. However, it is important to note that using negative return weights allows a moving average to strike a better balance between responsiveness and smoothness, but at the expense of reduced accuracy.

Our analysis of various moving averages with reduced lag time revealed that they use negative weights for distant lags to shorten the delay. However, the shape of the return weights in most of these "zero-lag" moving averages deviates significantly from the optimal distribution. Among the moving averages we examined, only two employ weighting schemes that closely resemble the optimal distribution of weights. These are the Hull Moving Average (HMA) and the Tillson T3 Moving Average (T3). The return weights of these moving averages closely resemble those shown in the upper panel of Fig. 15.5.

Our analysis of moving averages with reduced lag time shows that MA-D rules based on the best of these averages (HMA and T3) achieve a better tradeoff between responsiveness and smoothness than MA-C rules using conventional moving averages. However, this improvement comes at the expense of reduced accuracy. Therefore, traders must carefully evaluate when and under what conditions HMA and T3 are advantageous.

15.5.3 DSP-Inspired Moving Averages

Many exotic moving averages are inspired by DSP techniques. DSP involves using algorithms to process signals, analyze their components, and apply transformations that enhance the signal or extract valuable information. One of the primary applications of DSP is filtering, where specific frequencies in a signal are either amplified or attenuated. This is achieved using filters that are designed to allow or block particular frequency ranges. Common types of filters include low-pass filters, high-pass filters, and band-pass filters.

From the perspective of DSP, each moving average can be viewed as a low-pass filter. In this context, the moving average works by allowing low-frequency components, which correspond to the underlying price trend, to pass through while attenuating high-frequency components, which are often associated with random price fluctuations or "noise."

Using DSP techniques, traders can design a low-pass filter with a specific cut-off frequency to control the amount of high-frequency noise that is suppressed. By adjusting the filter's order, they can fine-tune the sharpness of the cutoff and the degree of smoothing applied to the price data. A higher-order filter creates a steeper cutoff, more effectively attenuating high-frequency noise, but it may also introduce greater lag. This flexibility makes DSP a potentially powerful tool for trend-following strategies, enabling traders to achieve smoother price signals while maintaining a controlled balance between noise reduction and responsiveness to market changes.

Traders have proposed several variants of low-pass filters, commonly used in DSP, as alternatives to conventional moving averages. Advocates of these DSP-inspired moving averages argue that they offer enhanced performance compared to traditional moving averages, claiming superior smoothness, responsiveness, and noise reduction.

Our analysis of several popular DSP-inspired moving averages revealed that they share similarities with most moving averages designed to reduce lag time. Specifically, we found that the weight distribution in these variants closely resembles the distribution shown in the upper panel of Fig. 15.5. As a result, our conclusions align with those drawn from the analysis of zero-lag moving averages. In particular, while DSP-inspired moving averages can improve the balance between responsiveness and smoothness, they do so at the cost of a worsened balance between responsiveness and accuracy.

15.6 Trend-Following When Market Switches Between Bull and Bear States

The availability of quantitative metrics enables traders to compare different trend-following strategies and identify those that effectively balance accuracy, responsiveness, and smoothness. The introduction of these objective metrics marks a significant advancement in evaluating trend-following techniques using moving averages. However, while these metrics provide valuable insights, they do not fully address all challenges associated with optimal trend-following.

Two key issues remain unresolved:

No universal solution: Our analysis demonstrates that no single technical indicator performs optimally across all quantitative metrics. Some indicators strike a good balance between accuracy and responsiveness, while others achieve better harmony between smoothness and responsiveness. Consequently, our metrics do not identify a universally superior indicator.

Parameter optimization: Even if traders identify a trading rule that offers the best possible balance among the three key properties, they must still determine the optimal parameters for the moving averages used in that rule. These parameters must be tailored to the unique characteristics of each market to effectively capture trends and maximize profitability.

Addressing these key unresolved issues requires moving beyond the three quantitative metrics. Two potential approaches can help tackle these challenges:

Data-driven backtesting: The first approach involves leveraging historical data to perform extensive backtests of all feasible trading rules, aiming to identify the best-performing rule. This method will be discussed in detail in the subsequent section of this chapter.

Theoretical analysis: The second approach focuses on conducting a comprehensive theoretical analysis of optimal trend-following. This is where we begin, delving into the underlying principles to build a robust foundation for understanding and improving trend-following strategies.

A theoretical analysis of optimal trend-following starts with defining a realistic return process that effectively captures the key characteristics of financial asset returns. A commonly used framework for this purpose is the two-state regime-switching model for stock returns. This model assumes that the market alternates between bull and bear states, representing distinct market conditions.

The return process in any multi-state regime-switching model is a specific instance of an autoregressive (AR) process. The AR process is a time series model that describes the relationship between a current return and a linear combination of the previous p returns. It is denoted as $AR(p)$, where p represents the order of the autoregressive model. A full specification of an $AR(p)$ model requires determining the autoregressive coefficients for all p return lags.

The AR process is a well-established and general framework for modeling persistent return behavior and is often analytically tractable. Consequently, we begin our analysis by examining optimal trend-following strategies under the $AR(p)$ process. Our findings indicate that the optimal technical indicator, $I(n)$, uses a number of return lags equal to the order of the process, $n = p$.

Without transaction costs, the return weights in the optimal technical indicator directly align with the autoregressive coefficients. However, when transaction costs are introduced, the return weights are modified to form a smoothed version of the autoregressive coefficients. The degree of smoothing increases with the level of transaction costs.

We extend our analysis by investigating optimal trend-following strategies within a two-state regime-switching framework. Specifically, we utilize both Markov and semi-Markov regime-switching models to explore these strategies.

We begin with the Markov model, a straightforward and analytically tractable framework that captures short-term momentum in returns, which contributes to the formation of price trends. However, a significant limitation of the Markov model is its inability to account for mean reversion, a widely observed phenomenon in empirical studies. To overcome this limitation, we introduce the semi-Markov model, a more complex approach that not only captures short-term momentum but also incorporates mean reversion in returns. By analyzing both models, we achieve a comprehensive understanding of optimal trend-following strategies under varying market dynamics.

Our findings are summarized in Fig. 15.6. The top row illustrates the optimal return weights for a trend-following technical indicator under the Markov model, both without and with transaction costs. The bottom row displays the corresponding optimal return weights for the semi-Markov model. These results are derived by fitting both models to historical returns data from the S&P 500 index. The optimal return weights represent the most effective weighting functions for capturing market trends within their respective frameworks.

Our analysis shows that in a Markov model without transaction costs, the optimal trend-following rule is the P-EMA rule. In this rule, the return weights decline exponentially with increasing return lags. When transaction costs are included, the optimal return weights become a smoothed version of those in the

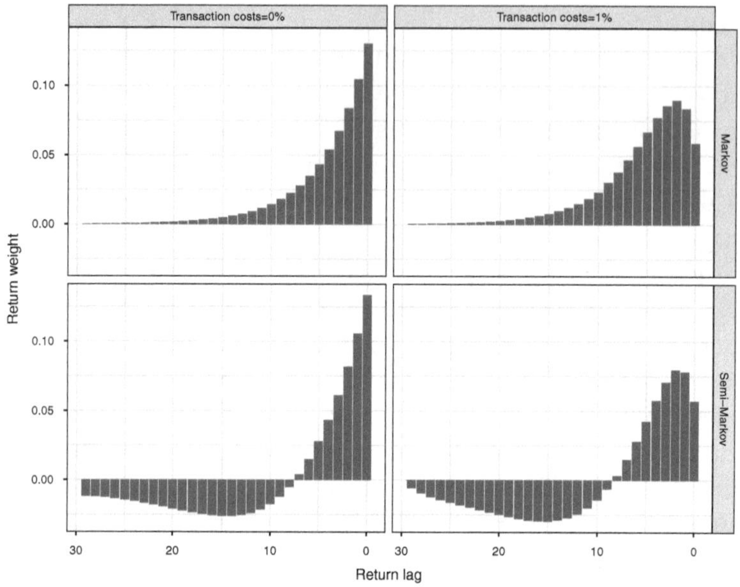

Fig. 15.6 Optimal return weights for trend-following in a Markov model and a semi-Markov model. Both types of models are fitted to historical returns data of the S&P 500 index. The left column plots the optimal return weights in the absence of transaction costs, while the right column shows the optimal return weights in the presence of transaction costs

cost-free case. This smoothing results in a hump-shaped weighting function, which can be implemented using the EMA-C rule.

In a semi-Markov model without transaction costs, the optimal return weights display a unique pattern. Initially, they decrease almost linearly to zero and then dip slightly into negative territory before gradually rising back toward zero. These weights consist of two distinct parts: a short, positive section that gradually decreases to zero, capturing short-term momentum in returns, and a long, U-shaped negative tail that allows the trader to capitalize on medium-term mean reversion.

When transaction costs are considered in a semi-Markov model, the optimal return weights are adjusted to form a smoothed version of the cost-free weights. In this case, the weights resemble a damped waveform, reflecting the tradeoff between effectively capturing trends and minimizing trading costs.

Our findings show that the optimal parameters for moving averages are influenced by three key factors: (1) the signal-to-noise ratio of returns, (2) the state transition probabilities, and (3) the level of transaction costs. For example, the P-EMA(n) rule is optimal when returns follow a Markov model and there are no transaction costs. However, the window size n must be tailored to the characteristics of the return process. Specifically, the optimal window size decreases as the mean state returns increase, state volatilities decrease, or the mean duration of each state shortens. Moreover, when transaction costs are present, the extent of smoothing applied to the return weights is directly influenced by the level of these costs.

In summary, our findings illustrate how frameworks such as the AR process, Markov, and semi-Markov models provide nuanced insights into optimal trend-following strategies, also when transaction costs represent a significant constraint. The analysis highlights the importance of tailoring strategies to specific market conditions and uncovers a diverse range of potential shapes for the return weights in the optimal technical indicator. These shapes are shown to depend on the parametric assumptions of the underlying return process and the magnitude of transaction costs, offering a deeper understanding of how to fine-tune trend-following rules.

15.7 Backtest Precision and the Profitability of Suboptimal Trend-Following

Among traders, backtesting is the most popular approach for determining the optimal trading rule. This method involves systematically evaluating a wide range of potential trading rules by testing numerous combinations of moving averages and their parameters. The goal is to identify the rule that has delivered the best performance over a relevant historical period.

Backtesting is widely regarded as thorough and effective, which has contributed to its popularity. Traders often assume that this approach reliably identifies the optimal rule, as it evaluates performance across a broad set of alternatives. However, despite its widespread use, the precision of the backtesting methodology in accurately identifying the optimal trading rule has not been rigorously examined.

To evaluate the precision of backtesting, we use simulated artificial historical return data. In these simulations, the optimal trading rule is predefined based on the shape of the autoregressive coefficients and the order of the autoregressive process. This setup enables us to assess whether the rule identified through backtesting matches the true optimal rule. We apply the backtesting procedure to a diverse set of trading rules, including the optimal one.

Our findings reveal significant shortcomings in the precision and reliability of the backtesting methodology. Even with relatively large sample sizes, the probability of correctly identifying the optimal trading rule is surprisingly low. This result challenges the prevailing assumption that backtesting is a foolproof method for finding the best trading rule and underscores the need for a more robust and theoretically grounded approach to rule selection.

These findings suggest that traders who rely on backtesting typically end up adopting suboptimal rules. Such rules can lead to missed profit opportunities and heightened risk exposure, ultimately resulting in weaker performance for trend-following strategies. The importance of quantifying the impact of using such suboptimal strategies becomes clear, as it helps highlight the potential financial drawbacks traders may face when they fail to identify the optimal trading rule.

Unexpectedly, our study also reveals that trend-following strategies exhibit a surprising level of resilience to variations in trend dynamics. This result can be attributed to the fact that seemingly distinct trend-following rules often generate highly correlated trading signals, leading to a significant degree of performance similarity. As a result, even suboptimal rules can remain effective at recognizing and capitalizing on price trends, yielding profitable outcomes despite not being the most optimal choices.

Furthermore, we explored scenarios where trend dynamics change randomly over time, making it impossible to identify the optimal trend-following rule in real time, as it constantly shifts. Despite this inherent uncertainty, our analysis suggests that trend-following strategies maintain robust performance and continue to outperform a simple buy-and-hold approach. This highlights the adaptive nature of trend-following strategies, even when confronted with unpredictable and fluctuating market conditions.

15.8 Optimal Trading Frequency

Many traders intuitively believe that daily trading is superior to, for example, weekly or monthly trading. The reasoning behind this belief is that by monitoring trading signals daily, traders can react more swiftly to market movements. However, there is a downside: this quick response can often lead to being misled by false signals, commonly referred to as "whipsaws."

Surprisingly, few academic studies have examined whether daily trading truly offers advantages over trading at lower frequencies. The findings of these studies suggest that the choice of trading frequency has little to no significant effect on trading outcomes. However, these studies are largely empirical, meaning their conclusions may not be applicable to all financial markets.

In this book, we take a groundbreaking approach by addressing this question analytically for the first time. We explore the optimal trading frequency using two distinct approaches.

The first approach centers on comparing the characteristics of trading rules executed on a daily versus a monthly basis. These characteristics include key parameters such as accuracy, responsiveness, and smoothness. Our analysis reveals that the accuracy of the trading rule is virtually unaffected by the choice of trading frequency. However, daily trading offers better responsiveness but lower smoothness compared to monthly trading. Based on these findings, we conclude that daily trading does not have an inherent advantage over monthly trading.

The second approach focuses on comparing the performance of a trend-following strategy across different trading frequencies in order to identify the frequency that maximizes performance. This method involves making specific parametric assumptions about the market's daily return process, aggregating daily returns over different time horizons (such as weekly and monthly), and selecting the optimal trading rule that maximizes the performance of the trend-following strategy in the presence of transaction costs.

The findings from the second approach are consistent with those of the first. The analysis shows that the profitability of optimal trend-following strategies at various trading frequencies is nearly identical. As a result, the choice of trading frequency does not have a significant impact on performance. However, it is important to note that the irrelevance of trading frequency is contingent upon the technical indicator that uses the optimal return weights. These optimal return weights can vary depending on both the trading frequency and the level of transaction costs.

Glossary

Even though trend-following with moving averages has been around for nearly a century, the field still lacks consistent and universally accepted terminology. Our glossary is not a collection of established terms but rather an effort to bring clarity and standardization to the subject. It also clarifies the terminology used in this book.

Accuracy Accuracy is a key property of a trading rule, referring to how effectively it identifies the correct trend direction. It is measured by the Noise Suppression Factor (NSF), which gauges the rule's ability to filter out market noise and avoid false signals.

Average lag time of moving average This term refers to the outdated and ad hoc definition of average lag time, which measures the average age of the data used to compute the moving average. Throughout this book, we demonstrate that this measure only reflects the average lag time in a very specific scenario—when prices are steadily increasing. This situation is of limited practical value because there are no trend changes to identify, which makes it irrelevant for evaluating the responsiveness of a trading rule. In this book, this term is referred to as the ALT(MA) for brevity.

Average lag time of trading rule We introduce this term as a more meaningful alternative to the average lag time of the moving average. The average lag time of a trading rule measures the average delay between a change in the trend and the corresponding shift in the trading signal generated by a trend-following rule. In this book, we refer to this as ALT for brevity.

V. Zakamulin and J. Giner, *The Ultimate Moving Average Handbook*,
https://doi.org/10.1007/978-3-031-90907-8

In some instances, we use ALT(TR) to distinguish it from ALT(MA), the average lag time associated with moving averages.

Conventional (traditional) moving average We refer to the Simple Moving Average (SMA), Linear Moving Average (LMA), and Exponential Moving Average (EMA) as conventional moving averages. All other types of moving averages are classified as "exotic" moving averages. The term "conventional" reflects the fact that these moving averages are the oldest and most widely recognized. In contrast, numerous exotic moving averages emerged much later than the conventional ones.

Double moving average crossover rule This rule generalizes the price and moving average crossover strategy by using two moving averages: a shorter (fast) and a longer (slow) one. A Buy signal is triggered when the shorter moving average crosses above the longer one, while a Sell signal is generated when it falls below. The rationale behind this rule lies in the fact that a moving average's lag increases with its window size: the longer moving average reacts more slowly to price changes than the shorter one. As a result, in an uptrend, the shorter moving average remains above the longer one, while in a downtrend, it stays below. Compared to the price and moving average crossover rule, the double moving average crossover rule is less responsive but provides more stable trading signals, reducing the risk of whipsaws in choppy markets. For brevity, this book refers to this rule as the MA-C rule.

Equivalent trading rules At first glance, two trend-following rules may appear very different. However, a closer analysis of their technical indicators can reveal that they sometimes use the same weighting scheme when computing the indicator. As a result, they generate identical trading signals. We refer to such rules as equivalent trading rules.

Exotic moving average Any moving average that is not a Simple Moving Average (SMA), Linear Moving Average (LMA), or Exponential Moving Average (EMA) is classified as an exotic moving average. We categorize these exotic moving averages into three main types: those with enhanced smoothness, those with reduced lag time, and those inspired by Digital Signal Processing (DSP) techniques.

Long-only strategy A long-only trend-following strategy is a trading approach that involves buying (going long) assets when their prices are rising. During a downtrend, instead of taking short positions, the strategy allocates funds to a risk-free asset, such as cash or Treasury bills, in order to avoid losses. This strategy benefits only from upward price movements and aims to protect capital during downturns by shifting to risk-free assets.

Long-short strategy A long-short trend-following strategy is a trading approach that involves both buying (going long) assets that are in an uptrend and selling (going short) assets that are in a downtrend. This strategy allows the trader to potentially profit from both rising and falling markets by taking long positions in assets that are trending upward and short positions in those that are trending downward.

Momentum rule Momentum is a trend-following rule that generates a Buy signal when the current price exceeds its level from a specified number of periods ago and a Sell signal otherwise. The rationale is that assets with upward momentum are likely to continue rising, while those in decline are expected to keep falling. For brevity, this book refers to it as the MOM rule.

Moving average A moving average is a smoothing technique that calculates the average of past data points over a specified window. Moving averages are widely used in trading to detect trends and generate signals based on price movements relative to the average. Different types of moving averages, such as simple, linear, and exponential, vary in how they assign importance to recent versus older data points.

Moving average direction rule This rule follows a straightforward principle: when prices are in an uptrend, their moving average generally rises, and in a downtrend, it tends to fall. Based on this, a Buy signal is generated when the moving average increases from the previous period, while a Sell signal is triggered when it declines. In this book, this rule is referred to as the MA-D rule for brevity.

Optimal trading rule In this book, we argue that a trading rule should possess three key properties: accuracy, responsiveness, and smoothness. The concept of an optimal trading rule can refer to optimality with respect to one, two, or all three of these properties. When optimizing for multiple properties, the goal is to achieve the best possible balance between them. For example, an optimal tradeoff between accuracy and responsiveness means that the rule attains the highest possible accuracy for a given level of responsiveness or the highest responsiveness for a given level of accuracy. The concept of an optimal trading rule can also refer to optimality with respect to the assumed type of a return process and the level of trading costs. The autoregressive (AR) process serves as the fundamental return model, as both Markov and semi-Markov return models can be reformulated as AR processes.

Price and moving average crossover rule This rule generates a Buy signal when the price is above the moving average and a Sell signal otherwise. Its rationale is based on the lagging nature of moving averages. In an uptrend, the moving average lags behind the price, meaning that its trajectory remains below the price path. Conversely, in a downtrend, the moving average moves ahead of the price, positioning its trajectory above the price path. In this book, this rule is referred to as the P-MA rule for brevity.

Price weighting function A moving average is typically calculated as a weighted sum of prices over a given window. Different moving averages vary in both the distribution of price weights and the size of the averaging window. The price weighting function refers to the specific set of weights assigned to prices in a given moving average.

Price-change weighting function A moving average can be expressed as the last price minus a weighted sum of past price changes over a given window. The price-change weighting function defines the specific set of weights assigned to these price changes in a given moving average.

Regime-shifting return process We assume that any financial market operates within two distinct regimes: bull and bear. The market transitions between these regimes in a stochastic manner. This type of regime-shifting behavior can be modeled using either a Markov or a semi-Markov process. A Markov process is a well-established and widely used approach due to its simplicity and tractability. However, it assumes that the probability of transitioning from one regime to another depends only on the current state, without accounting for the time already spent in that state. In contrast, a semi-Markov process, while more complex, provides a more realistic framework by incorporating the duration of each regime. This added flexibility allows for a better representation of real-world market dynamics, where regime durations are often not memoryless but influenced by underlying economic and financial conditions.

Responsiveness Responsiveness is a key property of a trading rule, referring to how quickly it reacts to changes in the price trend of an asset. It is measured by the Average Lag Time (ALT) of the trading rule, which quantifies the delay in the rule's response to a trend shift.

Return weighting function In a trend-following rule, the value of a technical trading indicator can be calculated using a moving average of price changes over a given window or, alternatively, by averaging returns over the same period. In this book, we prefer returns over price changes. The return weighting function defines how these returns are weighted within a given technical trading indicator. Different trading rules vary in their return weighting functions, and this variation fundamentally shapes their key properties—accuracy, responsiveness, and smoothness. For this reason, we systematically illustrate the return weighting functions of all analyzed trading rules throughout this book.

Smoothness Smoothness is a key property of a trading rule, referring to the stability and consistency of its trading signals over time. It is measured by the Smoothness Index (SMI), which assesses the persistence of the signals, indicating how steady the rule's responses are in the face of price fluctuations.

Technical trading indicator A technical trading indicator is a specific mathematical calculation that translates a verbal trading rule into a numerical form. For example, in the price and moving average crossover rule, the indicator is calculated as the difference between the current price and the moving average. This computed value determines the trading signal: a Buy signal is triggered when the indicator is positive, and a Sell signal when it is negative. In our exposition, all technical trading indicators follow this convention.

Technical indicator A technical indicator is simply a shortened term for *technical trading indicator.*

Trading indicator A trading indicator is another abbreviated term for a *technical trading indicator.*

Trading rule A trading rule is a formal verbal description of how a trading signal is generated. For example: "*Buy the stock if the current price exceeds its moving average. Sell if the price falls below the moving average.*" Here, the term *moving average* refers to any type of moving average. A specific implementation of this rule defines the exact type, such as the 200-day Simple Moving Average.

Trend-following strategy A trend-following strategy is a trading approach that seeks to capitalize on sustained price movements by identifying and following trends. It generates Buy signals when an upward trend is detected and Sell signals when a downward trend is identified.

Whipsaws In trading, whipsaws refer to situations where a price moves in one direction, triggering a trade signal, but then quickly reverses in the opposite direction, leading to a loss. The impact of whipsaws is worsened when trading costs are considered, as frequent trades driven by false signals can significantly erode returns.

Zero-lag moving average A zero-lag moving average is a type of moving average that is claimed to have little to no delay in responding to price changes. However, as we repeatedly demonstrate throughout this book, such moving averages achieve zero or near-zero lag only when evaluated using an outdated and ad hoc definition—one that calculates lag as the average age of the data used in the moving average. We argue that this measure is of limited relevance. The most natural and meaningful definition of lag time is the delay between a trend change and the corresponding shift in the trading signal. Under this definition, true zero-lag moving averages do not exist—all moving averages, regardless of their design, introduce some degree of delay in detecting trend reversals.

Index

V. Zakamulin and J. Giner, *The Ultimate Moving Average Handbook*,
https://doi.org/10.1007/978-3-031-90907-8

FSC
www.fsc.org
MIX
Papier | Fördert gute Waldnutzung
FSC® C083411

Kolibri 360 GmbH
Ferdinand-Jühlke-Straße 7
99095 Erfurt, Deutschland
produktsicherheit@kolibri360.de